JOE KISSELL

50 FAST MAC OS® X TECHNIQUES

Wiley Publishing, Inc.

50 Fast Mac OS® X Techniques

Published by
Wiley Publishing, Inc.
909 Third Avenue
New York, NY 10022

www.wiley.com

ISBN: 0-7645-3911-6

Manufactured in the United States of America

10 9 8 7 6 5 4 3 2 1

1V/RQ/QU/QT/IN

Published by Wiley Publishing, Inc., Indianapolis, Indiana
Published simultaneously in Canada

For general information on our other products and services or to obtain technical support, please contact our Customer Care Department within the U.S. at 800-762-2974, outside the U.S. at 317-572-3993 or fax 317-572-4002.

Wiley also publishes its books in a variety of electronic formats. Some content that appears in print may not be available in electronic books.

Library of Congress Control Number: 2003101788

FOREWORD

For reasons I've never entirely understood, the number three occupies a special place in the world. In fairy tales, the hero must always perform three tasks, Microsoft never gets anything right until the 3.0 release, and, well, lists flow better when they include exactly three items.

Within these covers, you're witnessing Joe Kissell's third authoring effort. Joe's first book was about Nisus Writer, an extremely powerful Macintosh word processor adored by those who like to write in non-Roman alphabets and people like me who get off on creating text macros that incorporate fancy search-and-replaces. Unfortunately for Joe, the entire audience for his Nisus Writer book probably would have fit in a medium-sized football stadium at the time, and Nisus Writer's fortunes have waned even further since then. Although it's an exaggeration, it sometimes feels as though we Nisus Writer users could all gather in a Starbucks for decaf hazelnut lattes without disturbing the regulars.

Though Joe's Nisus Writer book had little chance at the best-seller lists, it was a hot property compared to his second book, which was about Apple's Cyberdog program. Remember Cyberdog? I didn't think so. Cyberdog was a suite of Internet utilities (a Web browser, an e-mail program, and so on) that Apple created using OpenDoc. Remember OpenDoc? I didn't think so. OpenDoc was Apple's foray into component software, such that instead of huge monolithic applications like Microsoft Word and Adobe Photoshop, we'd have small applications to which you could add just the features you wanted merely by installing an OpenDoc component. Unfortunately for Joe, writing a book about a technology that Apple almost immediately "put into maintenance mode" (read: "took out back and shot") isn't nearly as good timing as writing a biography of a popular revolutionary receiving the same treatment at the hands of the ruling junta.

So this book is Joe's third swing at the piñata, his 3.0, and having read the book, I can say it's an exciting triple down the right field line (which lets me both stick to my numerology and avoid the clichéd metaphor of the home run). I particularly like the way Joe doesn't attempt to cover every little feature of Mac OS X because, let's face it, no one gives a hoot about every last feature. With apologies to the vegetarians reading this, we just want the meat, and that's what Joe's techniques provide. They're not merely simple tips; each one, like #19, "Boosting Your Keyboard Efficiency," offers multiple ways you can improve your usage of Mac OS X. I've put a few of Joe's ideas into practice already, and I'm sure you'll find some of the techniques will change the way you work with your Mac for the better. For Joe, the third time's definitely the charm.

If you're reading this while standing in a bookstore, trying to decide if you should buy the book, the answer is yes, so Joe earns his buck in royalties. And if you're reading this in the comfort of your chair after purchasing it, you have my personal thanks. After all, computer book authors have to eat too, and you've just helped keep Joe in Top Ramen noodles for another day.

Adam Engst
Publisher, TidBITS

PREFACE

Welcome to *50 Fast Mac OS X Techniques*. If you want to know how to enhance, extend, and customize your Mac without hiring (or becoming) a computer geek, this is the book for you. Whether you want to customize your Dock, save money on software, make better DVDs, or run your own e-mail server, you'll find what you need here. Each brief, heavily illustrated technique guides you through a particular task step by step.

As a Mac developer, I've watched the evolution of Mac OS X since long before the first public beta was released. Each new version has gotten better and better, and I've been greatly impressed by the wealth of powerful features that are now available to ordinary users. At the same time, I've found that a lot of the cool things I'd like to do with my Mac are not entirely straightforward. After spending hours searching the Web, reading books, consulting documentation, and performing trial-and-error experiments, I've often said to myself, "Wow, that wasn't so hard once I figured it out. But I wish someone had written a book to save me all that effort!" This is that book. I've done all the hard work of figuring out the easiest way to accomplish these tasks while avoiding common pitfalls. Now you can jump straight to a solution without all the tedious research.

HOW THIS BOOK IS DIFFERENT

This book is a bit different from other books on Mac OS X. On the one hand, it is not intended to be an all-purpose instruction manual or reference guide; plenty of features in Mac OS X exist that I don't even mention here. On the other hand, it's not simply a book of tips or quick fixes. As the title suggests, this is a book of *fast techniques*. Each technique teaches you how to accomplish a specific task without having to learn a lot of background or do tedious experimentation on your own.

You can accomplish a particular task in many ways. In general, I don't list every alternative or explain the pros and cons of different approaches in great detail. My goal is to show you the fastest, easiest, most direct way to get the job done, rather than provide an exhaustive discussion of commands, options, and theory. If you need more information than this book can provide, you can find other resources on the book's Web site at `www.wiley.com/compbooks/kissell`.

In selecting techniques, I've tried to strike a balance between *useful* and *cool*. Nearly every technique in this book can help you to save time, energy, or money, but they're also a lot of fun. I like to be able to say to my friends, "Hey! Check out this groovy thing I just got my Mac to do." If that sounds like you, I'm sure you'll enjoy what you find here.

WHO THIS BOOK IS FOR

You do not need to be a Mac expert to follow these techniques — this book was written for users at all levels of experience. Although some of the techniques are certainly more advanced than others, my goal was to make all the techniques here easy enough for a beginner, but interesting enough for an expert. If you're just starting out with Mac OS X, you should find plenty of simple ways to customize your system, work smarter, and enjoy your Mac more. If you're already an expert, you'll learn faster and easier ways of performing some fairly complex tasks.

WHAT YOU WILL NEED TO USE THIS BOOK

The basic requirement to use this book is a computer capable of running Mac OS X. In most cases, the hardware that came with your computer (display, keyboard, and pointing device) will be sufficient. A few techniques make use of additional accessories you may own, such as a multi-button scroll mouse, a Bluetooth cell phone, or an inkjet printer. You will also want to have an Internet connection — and if at all possible I suggest using a broadband connection such as DSL or a cable modem rather than a dial-up account. The extra speed and convenience you'll get from such a high-speed connection is well worth the small additional cost.

The techniques in this book assume that you're using Mac OS X version 10.2 (also known as "Jaguar") or higher. Some techniques won't work at all on older versions of Mac OS X, and others would work only with significant modifications. Because Jaguar was a paid upgrade from the previous version of Mac OS X, a number of users have postponed upgrading. If you're one of them, this is a good opportunity to take the plunge. You'll find not only an enhanced user interface and improved speed, but also numerous behind-the-scenes additions. Without these infrastructure changes, many of the techniques here would not be possible — things like PostScript printing to inkjet printers, easy networking with Windows computers, automating the Finder with Folder Actions, Inkwell handwriting recognition, Mail rules, and many more.

WHAT ABOUT CLASSIC?

Astute readers will notice that not a single technique here involves the Classic environment. If those Classic fans out there will forgive me, my reason is simple: This book is about cool techniques, and there's nothing cool about Classic. The Classic environment, apart from being behind the times visually, is slow, uses an inordinate amount of RAM and CPU time, and is prone to crashing. It does not make use of many of the most exciting features of Mac OS X, and is limited in the way it interacts with native (Cocoa, Carbon, or Java) applications. For all of these reasons, I use Classic as rarely as I possibly can — typically once a month or so to run the odd application that hasn't yet been Carbonized. If your work involves spending more time in Classic, I hope the other techniques presented here can in some small way make up for that inconvenience!

HOW TO USE THIS BOOK

Most of the techniques in this book stand on their own — you can flip directly to any technique that interests you and jump right in. A few techniques make use of skills or modifications learned in others. For example, your personal Web server (Technique 42) will be much more secure if you also use a firewall (Technique 25), and the X windows software you set up to use open-source office programs (Technique 31) will also come in handy when you install a UNIX image-editing application (Technique 33). But I'll point things out where appropriate, and there's no particular reason to read the techniques in order.

But before you start flipping through the book, I strongly suggest reading through the three techniques in the first chapter, called "Read Us First." These techniques explore the UNIX foundation of Mac OS X and the command-line tools you can use to work with it. Because UNIX will come up over and over again in the book, you'll find the other techniques much easier to understand and perform if you have *just a little* experience with the command line first.

I realize, of course, that some die-hard Mac fans resist the command line as being old-fashioned, un-Mac-like, or simply obtuse. I don't dispute any of that — it is not a user-friendly interface, and I wouldn't pretend otherwise. All things being equal, I'd much rather click a translucent blue button than type in an obscure command. However, some extremely cool features in Mac OS X can only be unlocked by using the command line, and others — I hate to say it — are actually easier to do by typing than by clicking and dragging. So I encourage you to have a relaxed attitude about the command line. It's neither good nor evil; it's just a tool. In this book, I'll always try to steer you to the right tool for a particular job, and if that happens to be Terminal, it's no big deal.

CONVENTIONS USED IN THIS BOOK

Most of the instructions in this book are self-explanatory. There are just a few conventions you'll want to know about.

Mac OS X has thousands of folders and many of them have the same names as folders in other locations. To help you get your bearings, I'll use a slash (/) when referring to any file or folder at the top level of your hard drive (or what you see if you double-click the hard drive icon on your desktop). For example, to indicate your main Library folder, I'll say /Library. To show you the location of folders within other folders, I'll again use slashes. So /System/Library/Extensions means the Extensions folder that's inside the Library folder in the System folder that's at the top level of your hard drive.

Your home directory is the one that appears when you click the **Home** button on a Finder toolbar. It's actually located in /Users/*yourusername*. As a shorthand way of referring to your home directory, I'll use a tilde (~). So ~/Library would refer to the Library folder inside the folder bearing your user name, which in turn is inside the Users folder at the top level of the hard drive.

I'm a fan of keyboard shortcuts, and I often mention commands you perform by pressing a combination of keys. I frequently refer to the ⌘ (or "Command") key, which is located next to the spacebar and also has a hollow Apple icon on it. Keyboard shortcuts are performed by holding down one or more modifier keys and then pressing an alphanumeric key. So when I say "press **⌘+Option+I**," I mean hold down the ⌘ and Option keys, then press I, then release all three keys. Some shortcuts also involve the mouse: "**Control+click**" means hold down the Control key while clicking the mouse button.

Throughout the book, I refer to graphics that appear nearby (as in "see **Figure 30.2**"). You'll also see a few cases where figure numbers have an extra designation after them, like (CP.12). The CP stands for "color plate" — see the insert in the middle of the book for a full-color version of this graphic.

Finally, there are a number of places where text appears on a line by itself in a monospaced font like this:

```
cp file1 /usr/local/share/
```

This normally indicates something you need to type into a Terminal window (followed by the Return key). Because this book's columns are narrower than some of the lines of instructions you need to type, sometimes long lines had to be broken to fit. Unless otherwise noted in the text, type Terminal commands on a single line with no spaces where the lines of text break in the book.

ABOUT THE BOOK'S WEB SITE

As a companion to this book, I've created a Web site at `www.wiley.com/compbooks/kissell`. I encourage you to visit the site as you explore these techniques. You'll find lots of useful (and cool!) resources, such as:

- Links to all the software and Web sites mentioned in the book
- Sample files you can download to try out some of the techniques
- Information on updates to Mac OS X (or other software) that require changes in the techniques

- A list of errata (because even the best of us make mistakes)
- A forum in which you can ask questions, post corrections, complain, make suggestions for future editions of this book, or share your own techniques
- Information on other Mac OS X books, Web sites, and mailing lists you may find helpful

HOW TO CONTACT ME

If you have difficulties with any of the techniques in this book, need additional information, or have a burning desire to share your chocolate chip cookie recipes, my e-mailbox is always open. You can contact me at **jwk@mac.com**. If you want to call special attention to your message (and make sure it's not deleted by Mail's spam filter), include the text *50 Fast* somewhere in the subject.

ACKNOWLEDGMENTS

First and foremost, I would like to acknowledge the wonderful contribution of my wife, Morgen Jahnke. She supported and encouraged me every step of the way, and graciously sacrificed time together so that I could write. Not only did she supply inspiration and late-night snacks, she even let me experiment with her iBook and Handspring Treo!

I deeply appreciate the efforts of everyone at Wiley who was involved in the production of this book, particularly Mike Roney (acquisitions editor), Melba Hopper (project editor), Paula Lowell (copy editor), Pieter Paulson (technical editor), Rev Mengle (editorial manager), Carmen Krikorian (permissions editor), and Dale White (project coordinator). They all helped to guide and shape this book, providing suggestions, feedback, constructive criticism, and assistance. Their help has made this a much better book.

My sincere thanks go to my agent, Laura Lewin, along with Jessica Richards and the rest of the staff of Studio B. Laura worked with me on my first Mac book, and her faith in me from the very beginning has been a great blessing.

I'd also like to thank all my colleagues at Kensington for their support and forbearance during this project, which took place during the final months of my time there. It was a great pleasure working with such intelligent and talented people and being part of a legendary Mac company. Special thanks go to Rob Humphrey, Don Varga, Oren Blonstein, Ian Lombard, Cris Fraenkel, Don Angel, Veerappa Ramalingam, Barry Pidgeon, and all the members of Toasted Pop-Tarts.

Much of what I learned to write this book was pieced together from the tips, techniques, and insights posted on numerous Web sites. In particular, I'd like to recognize Mike Bombich and Marc Linyage, who have generously contributed their knowledge and skills to the Mac community. Among the many other sources of information I consulted regularly, sites like tidbits.com, macintouch.com, macosxhints.com, and osxfaq.com proved invaluable in learning how to perform these cool techniques. I thank all those who maintain and contribute to these sites for their tireless efforts.

As I looked back at Acknowledgments I had written for my earlier books, I noticed that I always thanked people for helping me to keep my sanity during what was "an unusually chaotic time." Somehow writing projects tend to appear just when my life is most hectic, and this time was no exception. Having once again finished with most of my brain cells intact, I owe a great debt to the numerous people who contributed indirectly to this book's creation by helping me to stay focused, relaxed, and healthy. I deeply appreciate the encouragement and care I received from the members of First Mennonite Church of San Francisco and the staff of the Inner Research Institute, where I study T'ai Chi Ch'uan. My faithful iFriends, including Johanna Newell ("J"), Jackie Chappell (also "J"), Tom Zähner, Mike Lehmann, and Paola Aliverti, provided laughter, perspective, and support. And as always, I appreciate Adam Engst's gracious assistance and good humor.

Finally, no book on Mac OS X would be complete without giving credit to Apple for its amazing hardware and software. The level of care and detail Apple puts into its products constantly impresses me. Mac OS X is the operating system I've been wanting for years, and my PowerBook and iMac truly make computing a joy.

CONTENTS

CHAPTER 1

READ US FIRST

Ah, the beautiful rounded corners, transparent drop shadows, and antialiased text of . . . the command line? Perhaps, like me, you used DOS many years ago, only to escape into the warm, welcoming arms of the Mac OS and its graphical interface. The command line was a distant memory, and now the most advanced Mac OS brings it back? What could Apple be thinking?

Some die-hard Mac users recoil in horror at the thought of a command-line interface, which seems to contradict everything the Mac has always stood for. In fact, I was one of those people at first. But after I began to see how many cool things I could do with a few keystrokes in the Terminal application, my attitude changed. Because Mac OS X is based on UNIX, the power of thousands of UNIX programs is available, and you can accomplish a great many cool things with just a bit of command-line fiddling. But I still prefer to spend most of my time in the Aqua applications of the graphical interface, I've also come to appreciate the wealth of functionality hidden under the hood. If that requires learning a bit of UNIX, bring it on!

With that in mind, in this chapter, I cover some foundational skills that will help you perform many of the later techniques in the book. This chapter's techniques, by themselves, will not accomplish very much. But after you've mastered them, you'll sail through installing UNIX software, editing hidden preferences, and all the other cool things covered in future chapters.

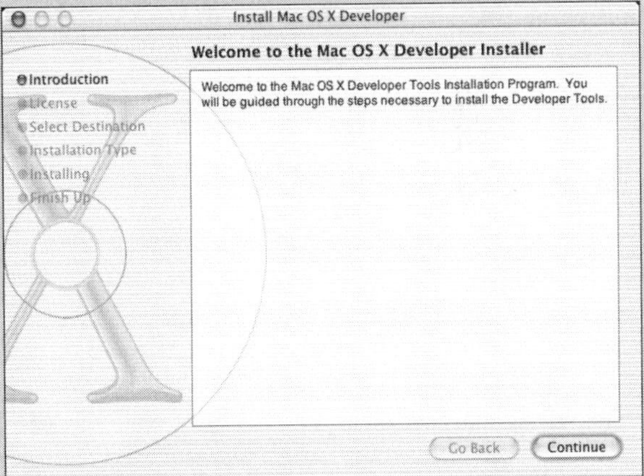

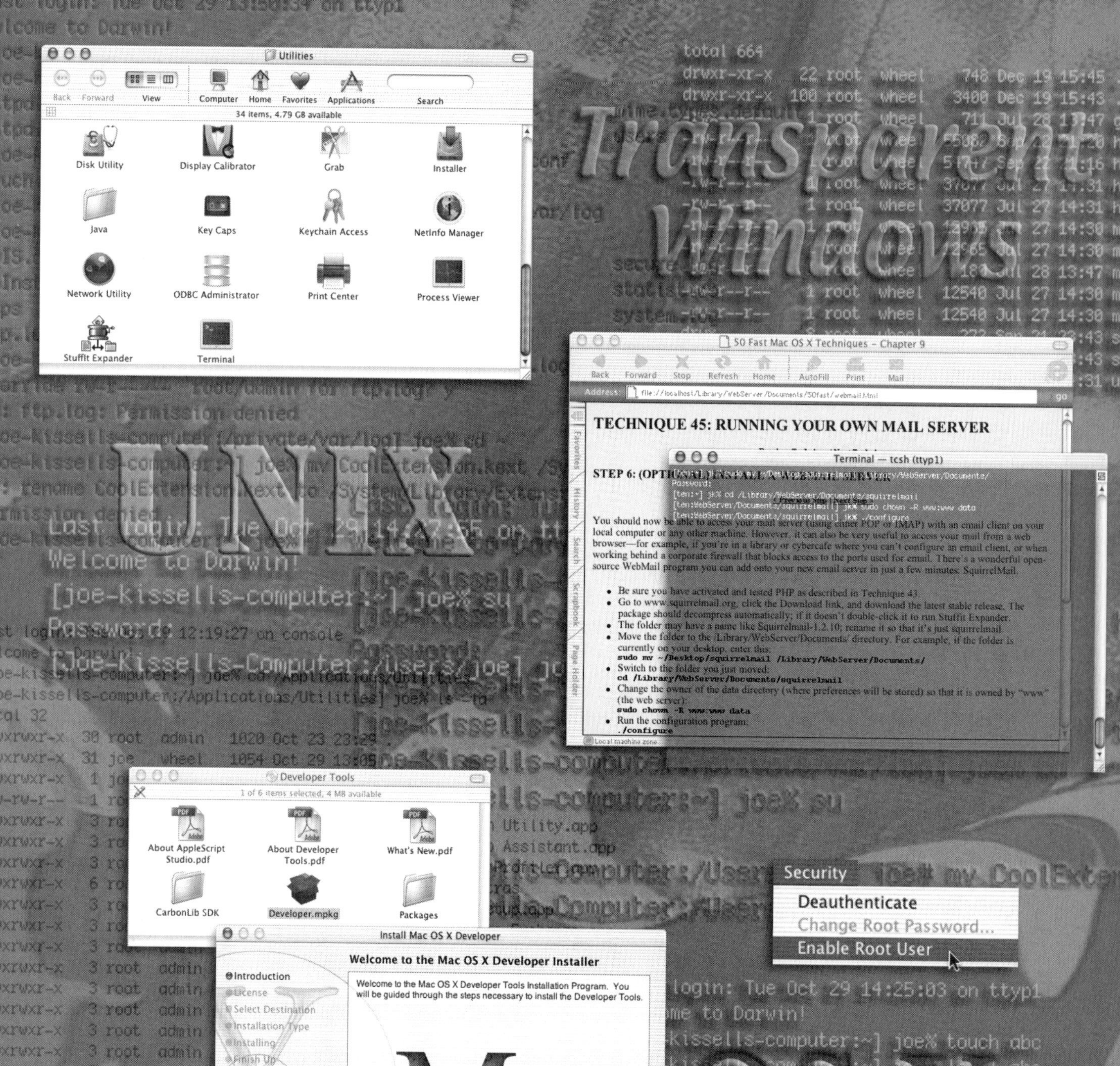

Transparent Windows
UNIX
Mac OS X
Utilities
Disk Utility
Display Calibrator
Grab
Installer
Java
Key Caps
Keychain Access
NetInfo Manager
Network Utility
ODBC Administrator
Print Center
Process Viewer
StuffIt Expander
Terminal
50 Fast Mac OS X Techniques - Chapter 9
TECHNIQUE 45: RUNNING YOUR OWN MAIL SERVER
Terminal — tcsh (ttyp1)
Developer Tools
About AppleScript Studio.pdf
About Developer Tools.pdf
What's New.pdf
CarbonLib SDK
Developer.mpkg
Packages
Install Mac OS X Developer
Welcome to the Mac OS X Developer Installer
Welcome to the Mac OS X Developer Tools Installation Program. You will be guided through the steps necessary to install the Developer Tools.
Introduction
License
Select Destination
Installation Type
Installing
Finish Up
Go Back
Continue
Security
Deauthenticate
Change Root Password...
Enable Root User
#1) Respect the privacy of others.
#2) Think before you type.
Password:

LEARNING JUST ENOUGH UNIX TO BE DANGEROUS

1.1

Terminal — tcsh (ttyp1)

```
Last login: Tue Oct 29 12:19:27 on console
Welcome to Darwin!
[joe-kissells-computer:~] joe% cd /Applications/Utilities
[joe-kissells-computer:/Applications/Utilities] joe% ls -la
total 32
drwxrwxr-x  30 root  admin   1020 Oct 23 23:29 .
drwxrwxr-x  31 joe   wheel   1054 Oct 29 13:05 ..
-rwxrwxr-x   1 joe   admin  12292 Oct 23 23:29 .DS_Store
-rw-rw-r--   1 root  admin      0 Jul 14 04:33 .localized
drwxrwxr-x   3 root  admin    102 Oct 23 16:48 AirPort Admin Utility.app
drwxrwxr-x   3 root  admin    102 Oct 23 16:48 AirPort Setup Assistant.app
drwxrwxr-x   3 root  admin    102 Jul 29 01:04 Apple System Profiler.app
drwxrwxr-x   6 root  admin    204 Jul 29 01:26 Asia Text Extras
drwxrwxr-x   3 root  admin    102 Jul 29 01:04 Audio MIDI Setup.app
drwxrwxr-x   3 root  admin    102 Jul 29 01:09 Bluetooth File Exchange.app
drwxrwxr-x   3 root  admin    102 Jul 29 01:04 CPU Monitor.app
drwxrwxr-x   3 root  admin    102 Jul 29 01:21 ColorSync Utility.app
drwxrwxr-x   3 root  admin    102 Jul 29 01:02 Console.app
drwxrwxr-x   3 root  admin    102 Jul 29 01:17 DigitalColor Meter.app
drwxrwxr-x   3 root  admin    102 Jun 13 18:35 Directory Access.app
drwxrwxr-x   3 root  admin    102 Jul 29 01:01 Disk Copy.app
drwxrwxr-x   3 root  admin    102 Jul 29 01:14 Disk Utility.app
drwxrwxr-x   3 root  admin    102 Jul 29 01:21 Display Calibrator.app
drwxrwxr-x   3 root  admin    102 Jul 29 01:03 Grab.app
drwxrwxr-x   3 root  admin    102 Sep 10 09:05 Installer.app
drwxrwxr-x   5 root  admin    170 Jul 27 20:40 Java
drwxrwxr-x   3 root  admin    102 Jul 29 01:13 Key Caps.app
drwxrwxr-x   3 root  admin    102 Jul 29 01:21 Keychain Access.app
drwxrwxr-x   3 root  admin    102 Jul 29 01:17 NetInfo Manager.app
drwxrwxr-x   3 root  admin    102 Jul 29 01:17 Network Utility.app
drwxrwxr-x   3 root  admin    102 Jul 29 01:03 ODBC Administrator.app
drwxrwxr-x   3 root  admin    102 Jul 29 01:16 Print Center.app
drwxrwxr-x   3 root  admin    102 Jul 29 01:13 Process Viewer.app
drwxrwxr-x   3 root  admin    102 Oct 23 16:49 StuffIt Expander.app
drwxrwxr-x   3 root  admin    102 Oct 23 16:49 Terminal.app
[joe-kissells-computer:/Applications/Utilities] joe%
```

1.2

ABOUT THE FEATURE

Love it or hate it, a type of UNIX forms the core of Mac OS X. What it lacks in friendliness of interface, it makes up for in power, reliability, and flexibility.

Mac OS X is, as you know, built on a type of UNIX. For the most part, the UNIX part of the operating system never shows. You can launch applications, create files, and do all the other things you've always done in the Mac OS without even being aware that UNIX is under the hood. However, some subtle signs — like multiple folders in different places named Library, or the fact that you are asked to log in to your own computer — show that there is more to Mac OS X than meets the eye.

The UNIX layer of Mac OS X can seem quite complex to a typical user, and for that reason Apple has wisely kept it hidden. You can use Mac OS X for years and never see a command-line interface. However, because you're exploring cool techniques here, you need to learn just a bit about UNIX, which means becoming comfortable with the command line and the application used to access it — Terminal.

Many books have been written about UNIX, and a complete listing of commands could run for thousands of pages. In this technique, you learn just the most important basics — the things you'll need to use in other techniques in this book. Appendix B lists a number of other important commands that I can't cover in this technique.

STEP 1: GET COMFORTABLE WITH TERMINAL

Terminal is the name of the application used to display the command-line interface and interact with the UNIX files that are normally hidden. You'll be using it often in this book.

- Open the Terminal application. It's located in the Utilities folder inside your Applications folder. A simple window, like the one shown in **Figure 1.3,** appears.

When you open a Terminal window, you're actually running a program called a *shell,* which interprets what you type and executes commands. Mac OS X includes several shells, with such names as csh, bash, zsh, and tcsh. Each one has a slightly different set of commands and conventions. To keep things simple, I assume here that you're always using the default shell, which is called tcsh (pronounced "tea seashell") and has all the capabilities you need. Although it's technically imprecise, I'll use the term *Terminal* throughout this book to mean a command-line shell program running in a window in the Terminal application.

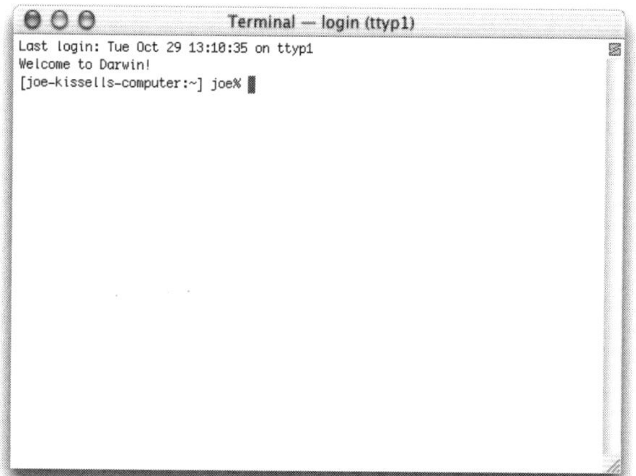

1.3

The first thing you see in a Terminal window is a string of characters, shown in **Figure 1.4,** with a box (that will blink onscreen) at the end. This string of characters is called the *command prompt,* which is another way of saying, "Enter commands here." The first part of the command prompt (in brackets) is what your computer thinks its name is. (This name can be nearly anything, but it makes no difference to the way Terminal works.)

The computer name is followed by a colon (:) and the current directory. If you're in your home directory (/Users/*yourusername*), which you will be upon first opening Terminal, the tilde (~) character is used as shorthand for "home."

Following the brackets is your short user name (`joe`, in this example), followed by a % sign. Because Mac OS X is a multiuser system, the user name reminds you of which user is currently logged in. The % sign indicates the end of the command prompt.

When you type something after the % sign, nothing happens until you press Return. Pressing Return means "try to execute what I just typed as a command." In this book, whenever you see a command-line statement appear on a line by itself, like this

```
cd /Applications/Utilities
```

you should type everything on that line and press **Return**.

Try typing a few easy commands and noticing what happens, just to get a feel for it. For a few suggestions, see **Figure 1.5**.

- Type `date` to display the current date.
- Type `cal` to display a mini calendar of the current month.

```
[joe-kissells-computer:~] joe%
```

1.4

- Type pwd ("print working directory") to display your current location in the file system.
- Type ls ("list") to display a list of the visible files in the current directory.

If you type a command that the system does not recognize, it responds with `Command not found.`

STEP 2: NAVIGATE THE FILE SYSTEM

The first thing you'll need to know is how to move around within the file system. It's really very easy after you get the hang of it. Here are the basics:

- If you haven't already tried entering pwd to display your current location, do so now. Something like /Users/joe (where *joe* is replaced with your current user name) appears. This is your home directory, and it is the same as what you would see if you opened the /Users folder in the Finder and then opened the folder with your user name (the one that looks like a house). The slash (/) at the beginning of the pathname means "the root (topmost) level of the hard drive," whereas a slash anywhere else means "directory." So in this example, you're in the directory named joe, which is inside the directory named Users, which is at the top level of the hard drive.
- To display a list of files and folders in your current location, type ls and press **Return**. A list similar to the first example in **Figure 1.6** appears. One problem with this list is that you can't tell which items are files and which are folders. To solve this problem, type ls -l to display a list of items with attributes, as the second example in **Figure 1.6** shows. Any item with a d as the first attribute is a directory (folder). Don't worry about the rest of that information for now; if you're curious, consult Appendix B. Another problem with this list is that it does not include invisible system files (those whose names begin with a period). To show all files, including invisible ones, type ls -a.

NOTE

Although Mac OS X uses the term *folder*, I use the equivalent UNIX term *directory* when discussing file locations as displayed in Terminal.

Now that you have your bearings, try moving around. The command cd (for "change directory") is

```
Terminal — ttyp1
Last login: Tue Oct 29 13:15:36 on ttyp1
Welcome to Darwin!
[joe-kissells-computer:~] joe% date
Tue Oct 29 13:15:47 PST 2002
[joe-kissells-computer:~] joe% cal
    October 2002
 S  M Tu  W Th  F  S
       1  2  3  4  5
 6  7  8  9 10 11 12
13 14 15 16 17 18 19
20 21 22 23 24 25 26
27 28 29 30 31

[joe-kissells-computer:~] joe% pwd
/Users/joe
[joe-kissells-computer:~] joe% ls
Desktop    Documents Library  Movies    Music     Pictures Public    Sites
[joe-kissells-computer:~] joe%
```

1.5

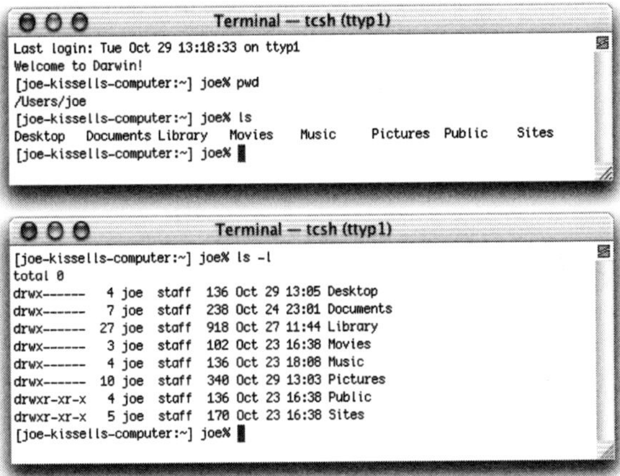

1.6

what you'll use to do so. Here are some examples of how to use this command:

- To move into a directory at the current level, type `cd` followed by a space and the directory name (for example, `cd Desktop`). (If you are entering a directory name that has spaces in it, put the entire directory name in quotes.) If you do this and then type `ls`, a list of the files on your desktop appears.
- To move up a level (into the next higher directory), type `cd ..` and press **Return**. The two periods simply mean "the enclosing directory." If you enter this command and then type `pwd`, you are back in the /Users/*yourusername* directory. Entering `cd..` a second time puts you in the /Users directory.
- To move to a directory within a directory, simply add directions onto one of these commands. For example, if you're at your home directory (~) and type `cd Library/Preferences` (with no slash at the beginning), you move into your personal Preferences directory. If you type `cd ../..`, you move up two levels.
- If you know exactly where on your hard drive a directory is located, you can move directly to that location by typing `cd` followed by the complete pathname. For example, typing `cd /Library/Preferences/Explorer` switches to the Explorer directory, inside the Preferences directory, inside the Library directory at the top level of your hard drive — regardless of where you're starting.

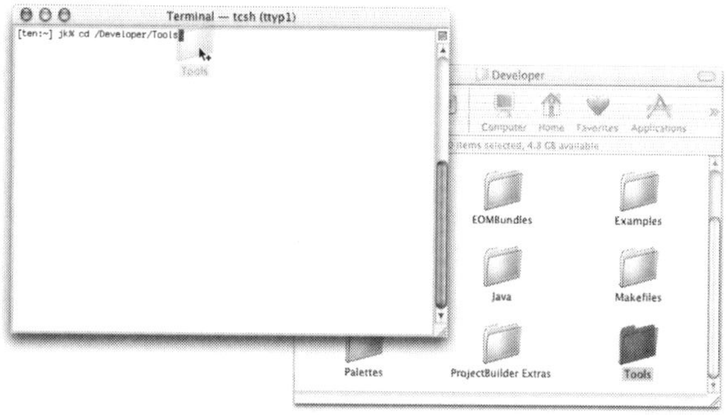

1.7

TIP

The most useful Terminal tip of all time is that you can enter the complete pathname of a file or folder in the Finder simply by dragging and dropping it into a Terminal window (as shown in Figure 1.7). If you want to delete a file you don't own, or quickly switch to a directory that's hard to find, this is a wonderful timesaver. After typing the command to use on the file or folder (like `cd` or `rm`), be sure to type a space before dragging in the file or folder, or the pathname will be copied onto the end of the command and the system won't understand it.

- If you ever get lost and need to find your way home, type `cd ~` to return to your home directory.

STEP 3: EDIT TEXT FILES

One of the most common activities you'll perform in Terminal is editing text files. I should emphasize that using a command-line text editor is, for many Mac users, a very counterintuitive process. Some GUI (graphical user interface) applications, such as BBEdit, allow you to edit the hidden files you work with in this technique, but when working in Terminal, a command-line editor can be a much more efficient way to make quick edits. It pays to know the basics of command-line text editing for many of the techniques that follow.

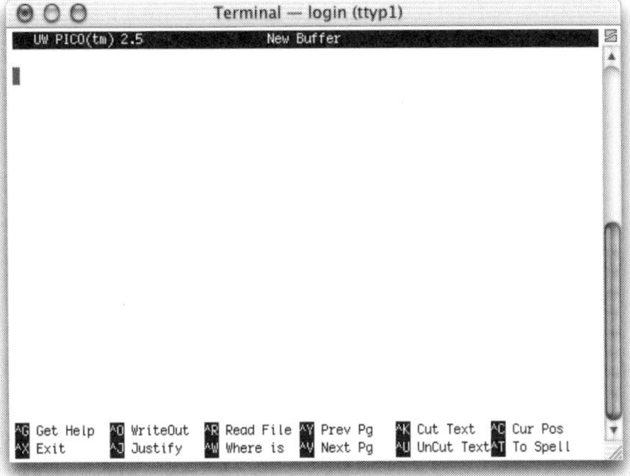

1.8

Although Mac OS X includes several command-line text editors (such as vi and emacs) and many others are available, my recommendation is a built-in program called pico. The SimpleText of the UNIX world, pico is easy to use, and while not particularly powerful, it is more than adequate for all the techniques covered in this book. To edit a text file, follow these steps:

- Type `pico` and press **Return**. Your display changes to the main pico window, as shown in **Figure 1.8**. The pico title bar at the top shows the name of the file if you're editing an existing file; if you're editing a new file, as in this example, it will say New Buffer. The bottom two lines display reminders about some of the common commands available, as also described in **Table 1-1**. The rest of the window is for the text you enter.
- Type any text you like. Because this exercise is for you to learn how the program works, you don't need to save the file. You use pico quite often in the steps that follow.

  The important thing to remember when working in pico is that you are in a virtual window within the Terminal window. So you navigate, select, and edit with the keyboard rather than the mouse. To delete a word, for example, use the Delete key on your keyboard. If you want to move up or down in your pico document, you can't use the Terminal scroll bar; you must use the arrow keys or Control+V/Control+Y for Next/Previous page.
- To quit pico, press **Control+X** and answer `n` if asked whether you want to save the buffer.

TABLE 1-1

PICO COMMANDS

ACTION	COMMAND TO TYPE	PICO TERM
Edit an existing file (or create a new one with this name)	pico *filename*	N/A
Save	Control+O	WriteOut
Quit	Control+X	Exit
Find	Control+W	Where is
Page Down	Control+V	Next Pg
Page Up	Control+Y	Prev Pg
Delete current line	Control+K	Cut Text
Help	Control+G	Get Help

STEP 4: RENAME AND MOVE FILES

UNIX uses a single command to move or rename files: `mv`. It's really not as confusing as it sounds. Here's how to use it:

- Move to your home directory (`cd ~`) and create an empty sample file to experiment with by typing `touch xyz`.
- To rename your file from **xyz** to **abc**, enter

```
mv xyz abc
```

The first string (or *argument*) you type after `mv` is the name of the file you want to rename; the second is the new name. Be sure to put a space after `mv` and between the two arguments.

- After you've done this, type `ls` to list the files in the current directory. **xyz** is gone and **abc** has taken its place, as shown in **Figure 1.9**.

Moving files is similar, except that instead of supplying a new name as the second argument, you supply a new location.

- To move a file to a new location *relative* to your current location (such as your Documents directory), enter

```
mv abc Documents/
```

- To move a file to a specific place on your hard drive that's not within your current directory, you need to enter an *absolute* pathname (the full path from the top, beginning with a slash). For example, to move it to the share/ directory in the local/ directory in the usr/ directory at the top level of your hard drive, enter

```
mv abc /usr/local/share/
```

STEP 5: COPY FILES

Copying files (using the `cp` command for "copy") is very much like moving or renaming them.

- As before, move to your home directory (`cd ~`) and create an empty sample file to experiment with by entering `touch file1`.
- To make a copy of **file1** in the same location named **file2**, enter

```
cp file1 file2
```

The first argument you type after `cp` is the name of the file you want to copy; the second is the name you want the copy to have. Be sure to put a space after `cp` and between the two arguments.

- Now type `ls` to list the files in the current directory. You can see that it contains both **file1** and **file2**.

Copying files to another location follows the same pattern as moving them.

- To copy a file to a new location relative to your current location (such as your Documents directory), enter

```
cp file1 Documents/
```

Figure 1.10 shows the results.

> **NOTE**
>
> **UNIX commands assume that file and directory names do *not* have spaces in them; the space character normally means "end of one command and beginning of the next." To use names with spaces in them, put the entire name in quotes. For example, if you want to rename the file *xyz* to *alphabet soup*, you type `mv xyz "alphabet soup"` and press Return.**

- To copy a file to a specific place on your hard drive that's not within your current directory, you need to enter an absolute pathname. For example, to copy it to the share/ directory in the local/ directory in the usr/ directory at the top level of your hard drive, enter

```
cp file1 /usr/local/share/
```

More details and variations on the `cp` command are in Appendix B.

STEP 6: DELETE FILES

The command to delete files is `rm` (as in "remove"). Use this command with extreme caution, because unlike dragging files to the Trash, when you delete a file with `rm`, you cannot recover it. (See Technique 3 for a way to replace `rm` with a safer command called `trash` that actually moves files to the Trash.)

- Again, create a sample empty file to experiment on by entering `touch xyz`.
- To delete the file, just type `rm xyz` and press **Return**.

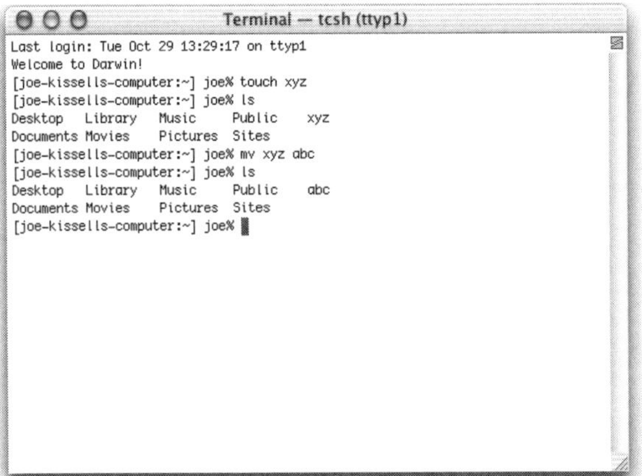

1.9

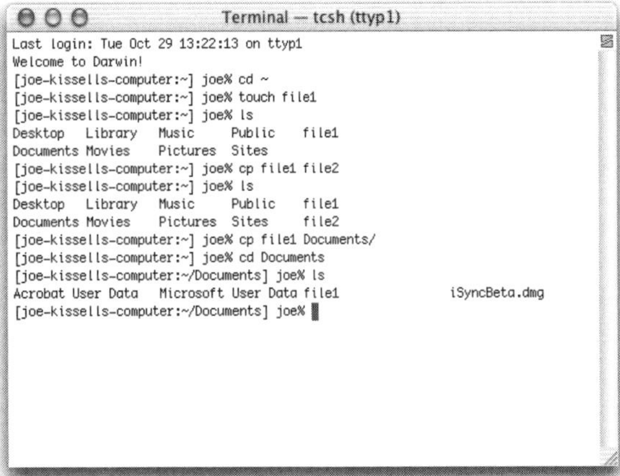

1.10

■ If you try to remove a directory with `rm`, you get an error message. That's because directories need a special version of the `rm` command. To test this, make a sample directory by typing `mkdir mydirectory` and pressing **Return**. Now type `rm mydirectory`, and the following appears:

```
rm: mydirectory: is a directory
```

To get past this error, type `rm -r mydirectory` and press **Return**. The directory disappears without any further complaints.

STEP 7: EXIT THE SHELL

When you're finished working in Terminal, you need to perform an extra step before quitting the application.

■ Type `exit` and press **Return** to end your session. Then you're free to close the window (if necessary) and quit Terminal. Although you could quit Terminal without exiting the shell, wrapping up your sessions cleanly and giving the shell a chance to display any important errors or warnings is always a good idea. Quitting Terminal without exiting the shell is much like unplugging your Mac without choosing Shut Down from the Apple menu: possible but not recommended.

WARNING

When you use `rm -r`, Terminal will perform a *recursive delete*, which means it will delete not only the directory you entered but also all of its enclosed directories and files. A safer way to remove a directory is to use the `rmdir` command in place of `rm -r`, but if the directory is not empty, you will need to delete its contents manually before the directory can be deleted.

TECHNIQUE

2

BECOMING ALL-POWERFUL AS THE ROOT USER

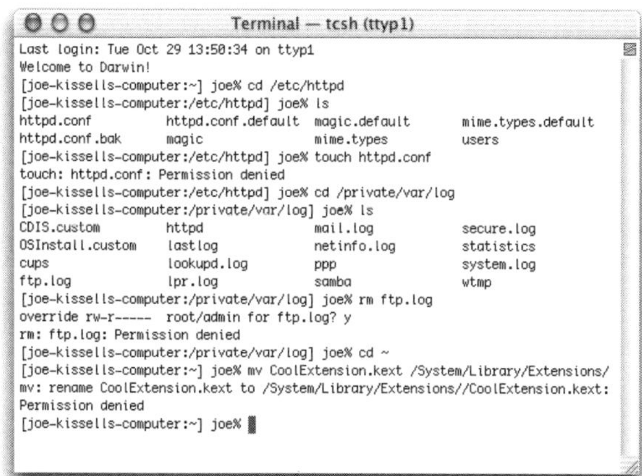

```
Terminal — tcsh (ttyp1)
Last login: Tue Oct 29 13:50:34 on ttyp1
Welcome to Darwin!
[joe-kissells-computer:~] joe% cd /etc/httpd
[joe-kissells-computer:/etc/httpd] joe% ls
httpd.conf          httpd.conf.default  magic.default       mime.types.default
httpd.conf.bak      magic               mime.types          users
[joe-kissells-computer:/etc/httpd] joe% touch httpd.conf
touch: httpd.conf: Permission denied
[joe-kissells-computer:/etc/httpd] joe% cd /private/var/log
[joe-kissells-computer:/private/var/log] joe% ls
CDIS.custom         httpd               mail.log            secure.log
OSInstall.custom    lastlog             netinfo.log         statistics
cups                lookupd.log         ppp                 system.log
ftp.log             lpr.log             samba               wtmp
[joe-kissells-computer:/private/var/log] joe% rm ftp.log
override rw-r----- root/admin for ftp.log? y
rm: ftp.log: Permission denied
[joe-kissells-computer:/private/var/log] joe% cd ~
[joe-kissells-computer:~] joe% mv CoolExtension.kext /System/Library/Extensions/
mv: rename CoolExtension.kext to /System/Library/Extensions//CoolExtension.kext:
Permission denied
[joe-kissells-computer:~] joe%
```

2.1

```
Terminal — tcsh (ttyp1)
Last login: Tue Oct 29 14:11:15 on console
Welcome to Darwin!
[joe-kissells-computer:~] joe% cd /etc/httpd
[joe-kissells-computer:/etc/httpd] joe% sudo touch httpd.conf
Password:
[joe-kissells-computer:/etc/httpd] joe% cd /private/var/log
[joe-kissells-computer:/private/var/log] joe% sudo rm ftp.log
[joe-kissells-computer:/private/var/log] joe% cd ~
[joe-kissells-computer:~] joe% su
Password:
[Joe-Kissells-Computer:/Users/joe] joe# mv CoolExtension.kext /System/Library/Extensions/
[Joe-Kissells-Computer:/Users/joe] joe#
```

2.2

ABOUT THE FEATURE

A mysterious concept to some, the root user is a special type of user account with unlimited access to modify the system. Judicious use of this power can unlock important capabilities in Mac OS X.

Back in the days of Mac OS 9, Macs were inherently single-user machines, and because of that, the user of the machine was, by definition, all-powerful. If you wanted to move, rename, or delete important System files (risky as that might be), nothing prevented you from doing so. Under Mac OS X, however, the rules have changed. Owing to its UNIX underpinnings, Mac OS X is a true multiuser operating system. Each and every file on your computer is marked to indicate what sorts of activities can be done with it and by whom. Even if you're the only user of your particular machine, you'll be asked repeatedly for passwords (for example, when installing software) to confirm that you have the necessary authority.

In order to maintain security in a multiuser environment and prevent you from making changes that could destabilize your system, Apple has hidden a great deal of the complexity of the operating system — and tens of thousands of files — from casual view. And even if you can find the files, you may be greeted with a friendly error message if you try to modify or delete them.

Sometimes, however, even ordinary users need to bypass this security to make certain kinds of modifications to their systems — the very sorts of modifications this book is all about. The only way to do that is to understand, and use, a special kind of user account known as *root*. The root user is much more powerful than a mere Administrator — as root user, you can access or modify absolutely any file on the system, even if you are not the file's owner.

A stern warning is in order here. When you assume the root user identity, you do truly become an all-powerful user of your computer. As such, you can easily damage your system. Use root access only when absolutely necessary, and with great care. You can greatly minimize your risks by diligently backing up your system. See Technique 48, "Backing Up (and Restoring) Data Painlessly."

STEP 1: USE THE SUDO COMMAND

The easiest (and safest) way to perform actions as the root user is to use the `sudo` command. Sudo stands for "superuser do" — the root user is also known as the superuser. As long as you have logged in as an Administrator, you can perform nearly any individual action that requires root access by typing `sudo` before the command. Follow these steps to see how `sudo` works.

- Open the Terminal application (located in /Applications/Utilities).

WARNING

Exercise caution when using root access. If you mistype a command, you could make your system unusable or erase important files in such a way that you cannot recover them.

- At the command prompt, enter

```
touch abc
```

This command simply creates an empty file named **abc**. Now enter

```
ls -l abc
```

The file appears with its owner and permission attributes, as shown in **Figure 2.3**. Notice that the owner is set to your username (in this case, `joe`).

- Now, for comparison, do the same thing as root. All you need to do is put `sudo` (and a space) before the command. At the command prompt, enter

```
sudo touch xyz
```

The very first time you use the `sudo` command, you see the warning in **Figure 2.4**. Thereafter, Mac OS X assumes you remember to act carefully. Enter your password when prompted. You have just created yet another empty file, only this time

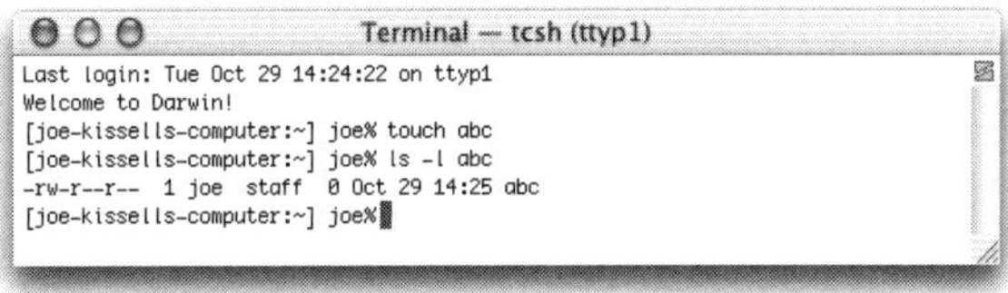

2.3

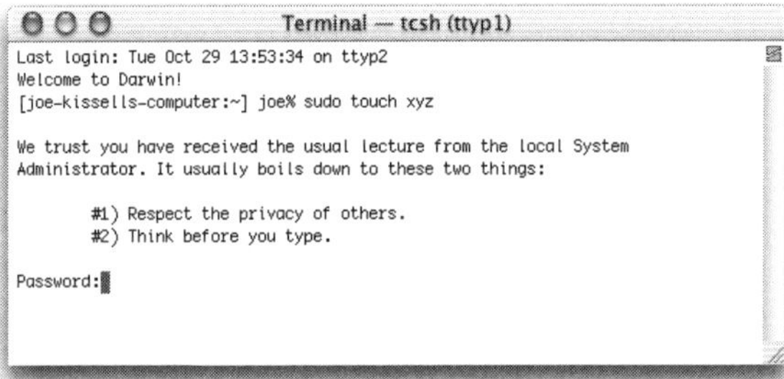

2.4

the file is owned by root. To verify ownership, enter

```
ls -l xyz
```

The new file xyz is owned by root, as shown in **Figure 2.5.**

■ Now delete the two empty files you just created. First, enter

```
rm abc
```

to delete the one you own. Then type

```
rm xyz
```

A warning appears, as shown in **Figure 2.6**, asking whether you want to override root ownership of the file. The root user owns it, so ordinarily, only the root user could delete it. Because you created this file as a superuser, you could simply answer y

NOTE

After you've entered your password for the `sudo` **command, you can continue using** `sudo` **for up to five minutes without having to reenter your password each time.**

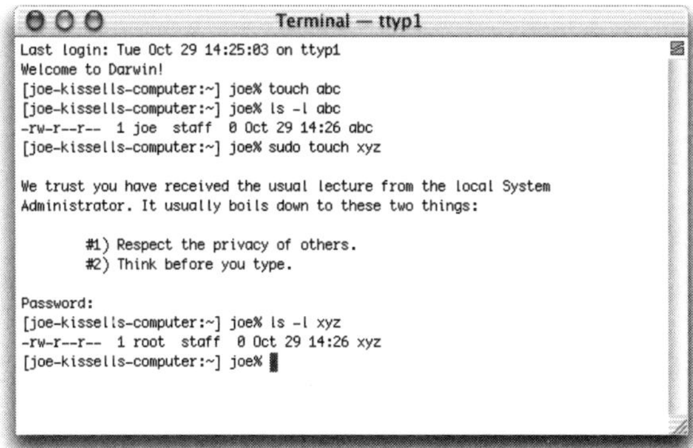

2.5

and the file would disappear. But as this is a `sudo` lesson, I suggest doing it a different way. Type `n` (for "don't override root ownership") and press **Return**. Now enter

```
sudo rm xyz
```

The file will be deleted without any further warnings.

■ You've just used `sudo` with two commands (`touch` and `rm`), but you can use `sudo` with any command that requires root access. For example, to edit a root-owned file using the pico text editor, you enter

```
sudo pico filename
```

To open an application as the root user, you enter

```
sudo open filename
```

and so on. As a general rule, if you attempt to perform a command and get a warning that you don't have permission to do so, the same command preceded by `sudo` will do the trick. On occasion, even `sudo` won't work, and you'll need to log in to the root user's shell account using `su`. (See the upcoming Step 3.)

STEP 2: ENABLE THE ROOT USER

There may be times when you will want to perform a number of commands as root without having to type `sudo` before each one. There may also be occasions

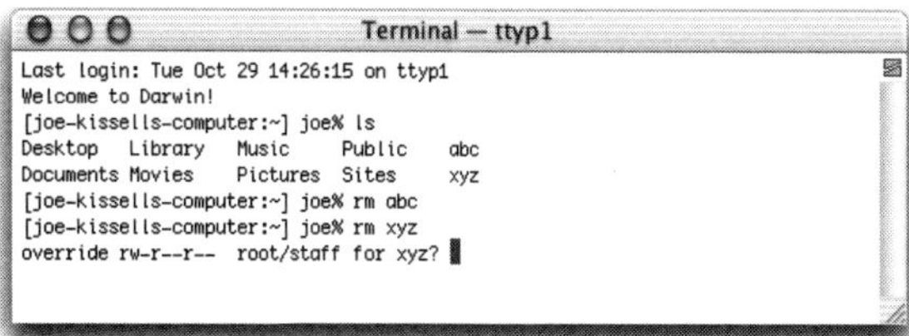

2.6

when you will want to perform activities in the Finder (or other Aqua applications) as root. For these purposes, you'll need to go beyond `sudo` by logging in as the root user.

By default, Apple has disabled the root user account. Before you can assume the authority of the root user, you must turn on this account.

- Open NetInfo Manager, located in the **Utilities** folder in your **Applications** folder.
- Click the lock icon in the lower-left corner of the window. In the dialog that appears, enter the name and password of an Administrator. (Hint: You can use the user name and password you specified when you first installed Mac OS X.) This unlocks NetInfo Manager so that you can make additional changes.
- Choose **Enable Root User** from the **Security** menu, as shown in **Figure 2.7**. An alert appears telling you that the root user password is currently blank. Click **OK** to dismiss this alert.
- Enter a password for the root user, and retype it for verification. If you are the only user of the machine, you may find it convenient to use the same password you specified for your regular user account, because it will be easier to remember. Keep in mind, however, that this password can give anyone (even someone connecting remotely) unfettered access to your computer, so choose a password that is hard to guess — preferably one that includes both letters and numbers. After entering and retyping your new password, click **OK**.
- Another alert appears indicating that you must re-authenticate to make additional changes. Click **OK** to dismiss this alert and then quit NetInfo Manager.

2.7

STEP 3: LOG IN TO THE ROOT USER'S SHELL ACCOUNT

Now that you've enabled the root user account, how do you use it? If you need to perform activities in Terminal as root, you can simply log in to the root user's shell account.

- Open the Terminal application.
- At the command prompt, type `su` and press **Return**. Type your password when prompted and

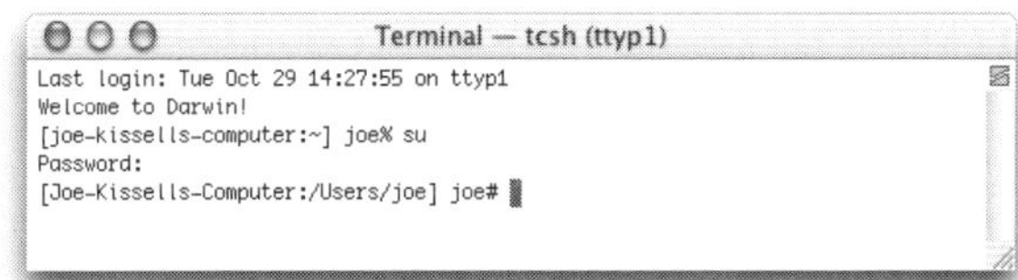

2.8

press **Return** again. Notice that the prompt has changed to a # symbol. This indicates that you are logged in as root. The su command, in this context, means "superuser." (It can also mean "substitute user" if followed by a user name.) Because the superuser is another way of saying root user, you're now logged in as the root user. **Figure 2.8** shows a root login.

- Any files you create now will be owned by root, and you can modify or delete any file on the system. Although I've said it several times already, it bears repeating: *Be very careful.* Root access should only be used when you know you need it, and should be disabled as soon as you're done performing activities that require it.
- To log out as root user, type `exit` and press **Return** to go back to your normal command prompt.
- Exactly when should you use `su`? I use it when I know I'll need to perform more than two or three successive `sudo` commands, because it saves me a lot of typing and I have enough experience to use it safely (as well as good backups in case I make a mistake). In the techniques that appear later in this book, I include `sudo` with each command requiring root access. If you see several such commands and feel comfortable doing so, you can begin your session with `su` and then omit the `sudo` part of the commands that follow.

STEP 4: LOG IN TO YOUR SYSTEM AS ROOT

After you've enabled the root user, you can also log in to Mac OS X's graphical interface as root. Why would you want to do this? The most likely reason would be to edit, delete, or change ownership/permissions of files (see Appendix B) as root using the Finder and desktop applications rather than Terminal. Follow these steps to log in as root:

- Choose **Log Out...** from the Apple menu to log out.
- When the Log In window appears, click the **Other** icon at the bottom of the **Users** list, then enter `root` for the user name and your root password, and click **Log In**.

  Your Finder appears, with the Dock, windows, and all other options set to their defaults. (Remember, the root user is just another user account.)
- When you're finished with the activities that require root access, be sure to log out again, and log back in under your usual user name.

> **NOTE**
>
> **One of the other important reasons for assuming root authority in Terminal is to change file ownership and permissions. The details of how to do so require more space than is available here, and most of the time you can accomplish the same tasks using the Finder's Get Info windows (as you find out in Technique 6, "Getting Info and What to Do with It"). If you really want the lowdown, consult Appendix B.**

3

TECHNIQUE

CUSTOMIZING TERMINAL FOR COMMAND-LINE POWER

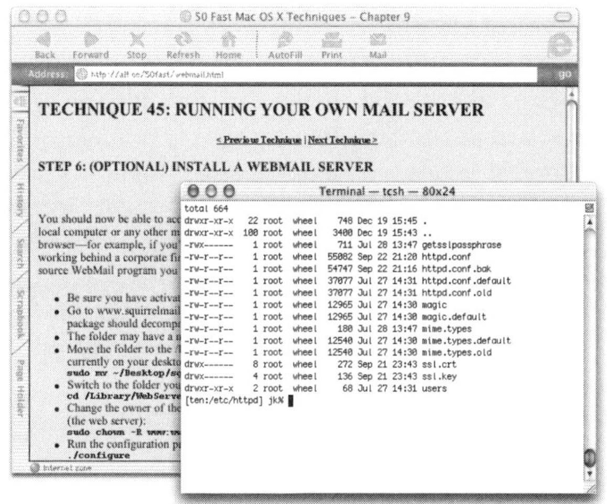

3.1

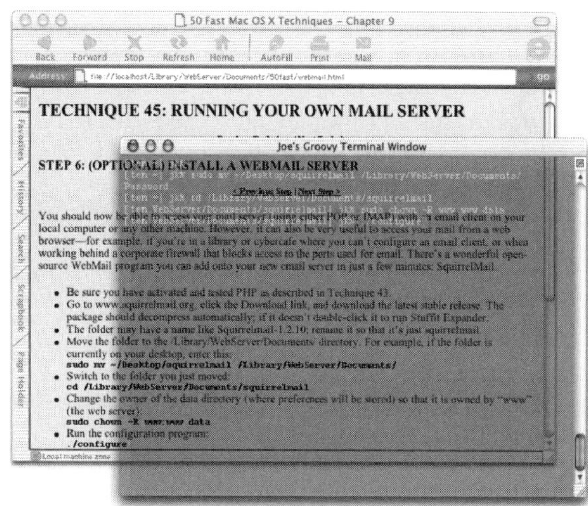

3.2

ABOUT THE FEATURE

The Terminal application is the gateway into the UNIX layer of Mac OS X. The command-line interface it offers lacks the elegance of Aqua, but with some clever customization, it can become painless — and perhaps even fun to use.

I'm going to assume that you don't really *want* to spend a lot of time in the Terminal application. As with a bus or train terminal, it's a useful place to visit from time to time, but not somewhere you want to live. If you're like most people, you'll want to use Terminal only when it's necessary to do a particular task. For that reason, I won't worry too much about showing you the bells and whistles. Although Terminal can be extensively customized — far beyond what is shown here — this technique covers changes that actually make your Terminal more useful during the brief visits you'll make.

STEP 1: ADJUST THE APPEARANCE OF TERMINAL WINDOWS

By default, Terminal windows are relatively small, with black text on an opaque white background, as shown in **Figure 3.3**. If you use Terminal fairly regularly, you'll benefit from making some improvements to the appearance of the windows.

For example, because the amount of information that needs to be displayed using commands like `ls` or `top` is often quite large, having a larger Terminal window can be useful. To modify the appearance of Terminal windows, follow these steps:

- To change the size, choose **Window Settings** from the **Terminal** menu. The Terminal Inspector appears. From the pop-up menu at the top of the window, choose **Window**. Under Dimensions, type new numbers for width (**Columns**) and height (**Rows**). For example, you might choose 120 columns and 40 rows as shown in **Figure 3.4** to display significantly more information than the default without entirely filling a small screen. While you're here, feel free to choose a different title for your Terminal windows if "Terminal" is too boring, and uncheck any or all of the check-boxes if you don't care to display these additional pieces of information in your title bar.
- The color of Terminal window background and text is a matter of taste, but some people find that reading white text on a black background is easier. (This color change also makes finding your Terminal window(s) easier if you have many windows open.) To adjust these colors, choose **Color** from the pop-up menu in the Terminal Inspector. Click the button next to **Background** to display Apple's standard color picker. After choosing a background color, repeat for **Cursor**, **Normal Text**, **Bold Text**, and **Selection**. When you're finished, close the color picker.
- Choose **Display** from the pop-up menu in the Terminal Inspector to adjust the font and size of the text if 10-point Monaco is not to your liking. For best results, choose a monospace font (Monaco and Courier are the usual examples) and leave the **Antialiased text** checkbox unchecked. On this panel, you can also choose a cursor shape and decide whether you want it to blink.
- One final change will make your Terminal a bit less annoying. Choose **Shell** from the pop-up

3.3

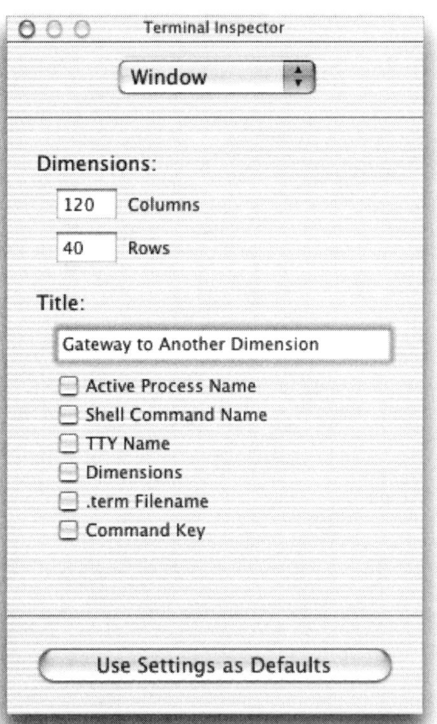

3.4

menu in the Terminal Inspector. Click the radio button next to **Close only if the shell exited cleanly** (as shown in **Figure 3.5**). What this means is that when you end a Terminal session by typing `exit`, the window where that session was running will close automatically (unless there's an error it needs to tell you about). If you leave this setting at its default, you will have to go through an extra step to close windows at the end of each session.

- When you're finished changing settings, click **Use Settings as Defaults**. Otherwise, the changes you make will apply only to your current session.

> **TIP**
>
> **Be sure to choose contrasting colors for background and Normal/Bold Text. If you change the background to black, for example, without changing the default text color, your text will be invisible.**

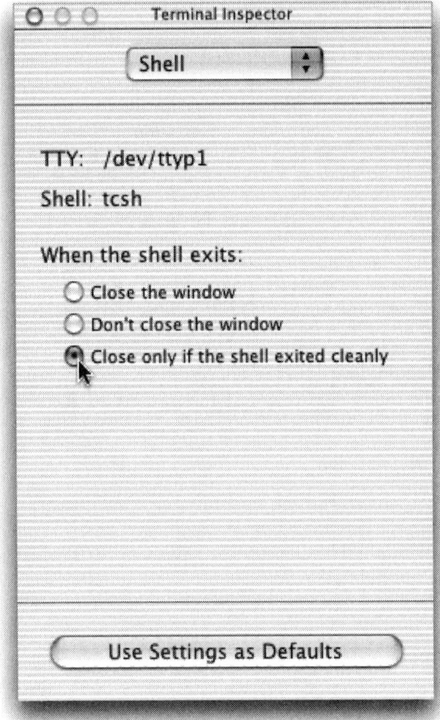

3.5

STEP 2: MAKE YOUR TERMINAL WINDOW TRANSPARENT

Although this is really an appearance-altering step, it's important enough to merit a separate mention. Transparent terminal windows may seem like a frivolous and counterproductive modification, because whatever shows through from behind the window can be distracting. However, there's one extremely good use for transparent Terminal windows besides looking interesting. Suppose you're trying to follow instructions on a Web page (or any other document) that requires typing Terminal commands and you don't have the luxury of a large screen. Ordinarily you would have to switch back and forth between the Web page and your Terminal window, but transparent Terminal windows can eliminate all that switching. Just leave the Web page open in the window behind Terminal, as in **Figure 3.6**, and follow the

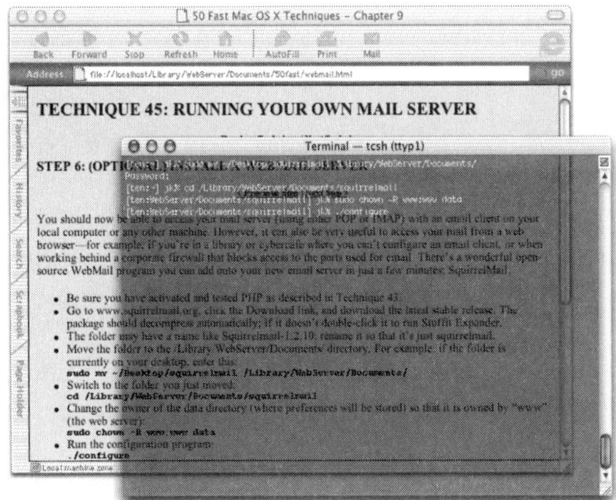

3.6

instructions showing through from behind. To make your Terminal windows transparent:

- Choose **Window Settings** from the **Terminal** menu. The Terminal Inspector appears.
- From the pop-up menu at the top of the window, choose **Color**.
- Move the **Transparency** slider toward the right to increase the transparency. If you use a black background, the fourth or fifth notch from the left will generally give you the best results. With a white background, you may want a lower level of transparency — try the second or third notch.
- To make sure all future Terminal windows you open are transparent as well, click **Use Settings as Defaults**.

STEP 3: SET UP SHELL ALIASES

As you work in Terminal, you'll soon find that you type a number of tedious commands repeatedly. For example, you may find that you always want to display attributes and hidden files when you list files (`ls -la`), or that you frequently switch to the Preferences folder in your user directory (`cd ~/Library/Preferences`). Wouldn't it be nice if you didn't have to type (and remember) all that? You can reduce the likelihood of errors and save keystrokes by setting up shortcuts to commands, which are known as *shell aliases*. (Note that these are an entirely different animal from Finder aliases, which are shortcuts to files or applications.) Typing the alias is equivalent to typing the full command.

Although creating a temporary alias (just for your current session) is possible, creating aliases that will be available every time you use Terminal is much more useful. To do this, you store them in one of the files that loads each time you start a new Terminal session. Several different configuration files can store aliases; the one I discuss here keeps them separate from other startup commands so that they're easier to edit and less likely to break when you update your operating system. If you have multiple users on your machine, this procedure only affects the current user (which can be either an advantage or a disadvantage, depending on your point of view). To set up shell aliases, follow these steps:

- First, add some helpful commands to your shell initialization file (**.tcshrc**), which used to exist in Mac OS X 10.1 but mysteriously vanished in 10.2. One of these commands will point to an external file, which stores aliases.

  Type `pico ~/.tcshrc` to open your initialization file in pico. As shown in **Figure 3.7**, add this line:

```
source /usr/share/tcsh/examples/rc
```

- Press **Control+X** to exit. Answer `y` to the prompt asking whether you want to save the buffer, and press **Return** when asked to confirm the filename. Your **.tcshrc** file has now been updated.
- Next, create the directory in which the new aliases file will live, using the `-p` option to create any intermediate directories that don't already exist:

```
mkdir -p ~/Library/init/tcsh
```

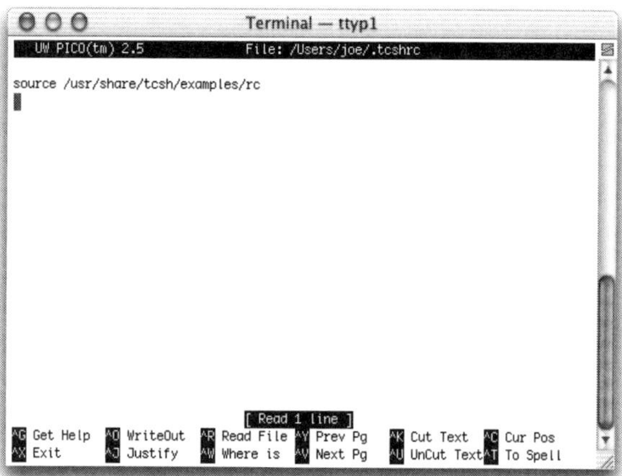

3.7

■ Now create the aliases file itself (named **aliases.mine**):

```
pico ~/Library/init/tcsh/aliases.mine
```

This command opens a new file called aliases.mine in the pico editor.

■ Using the arrow keys, move down to the end of the file, where you add some lines. Each alias looks like

alias *newcommand oldcommand*

where *oldcommand* is what you currently type to perform a command, and *newcommand* is what you want to use from now on. For example, if you want your `ls` command to show attributes and hidden files every time you use it, you type

```
alias ls ls -la
```

Or if you would like an easy command like `docs` to switch you to your Documents directory, you type

```
alias prefs cd ~/Documents
```

You must enter each alias on a separate line. **Table 3-1** lists a few of my favorite alias settings, but feel free to change or omit some of these or add your own. (The last item in Table 3-1 should appear all on one line, with a space between `nouchg` and `~/.Trash`.)

When you're finished, your **aliases.mine** file will look something like **Figure 3.8**.

■ To save your settings, press **Control+X** to exit pico, answer y to the `Save modified buffer?` prompt, and press **Return** at the

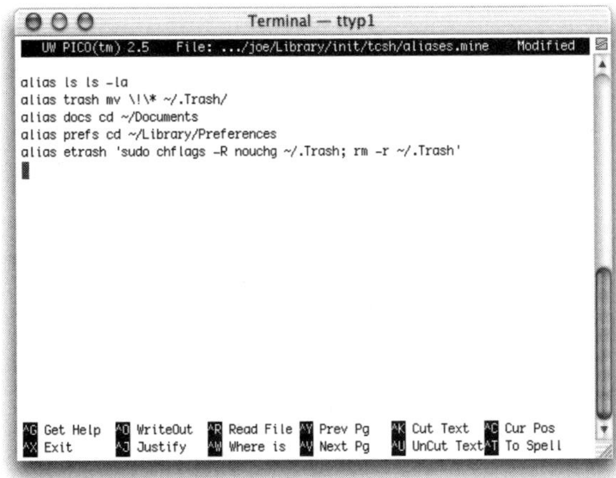

3.8

Table 3-1

Suggested Entries for aliases.mine File

Line in aliases.mine File	Command You Type	Result
`alias ls ls -la`	`ls`	List files, including hidden files, in "long" format (with attributes).
`alias trash mv \!\n ~/.Trash/`	`trash`	Move files to the Finder Trash rather than deleting them immediately (much safer than `rm`).
`alias docs cd ~/Documents`	`docs`	Switch to your Documents directory.
`alias prefs cd ~/Library/Preferences`	`prefs`	Switch to your Preferences directory.
`alias etrash 'sudo chflags -R nouchg ~/.Trash; rm -r ~/.Trash'`	`etrash`	Empty your Trash, even stubborn files that can't ordinarily be deleted. (Requires typing your password.)

prompt `Filename to write : ~/init/tcsh/aliases.mine`.

■ Your alias settings will take effect the next time you open a Terminal window. To test this, choose **New** from the **File** menu to open a new window. (You don't need to quit Terminal, because you can have many windows open at once.) Now type one of your new aliases, such as `prefs`. The command you entered earlier should be executed immediately.

STEP 4: ACTIVATE TERMINAL SHORTCUTS

The aliases you added in Step 3 are highly useful for getting quick access to common commands. You can go even further, though, by turning on some of tcsh's built-in shortcuts that apply to a variety of commands. You do so by going back to the **.tcshrc** file you edited earlier and making some more additions. First add the commands, and then examine what each one does.

■ Type `pico .tcshrc` to open your initialization file in pico. Then use the arrow keys to move to the end of the file and add the following lines, as shown in **Figure 3.9**:

```
set correct = all
set complete = enhance
set autolist
set history = 1000
set savehist = (1000 merge)
```

To save your settings, press **Control+X** to exit pico, answer y to the `Save modified buffer?` prompt and press **Return** when asked to confirm the filename. Your new settings will take effect the next time you open a Terminal window.

■ The first command, `set correct = all`, turns on automatic correction of mistyped commands. (The "`all`" part makes the autocorrection apply to all words on the line, not just the initial command.) If you make a typing error while entering a command, autocorrect will try to guess what you meant to say. For example, if you enter

```
lis /usr/bnn
```

you will see

```
OK? ls /usr/bin?
```

Autocorrect substitutes its best guess for your misspellings. To accept the corrected command, type y; if the guess was wrong, type `n` to cancel.

■ The next two lines, `set complete = enhance` and `set autolist`, together turn on a very nifty autocompletion feature that can save you lots of typing. (The "enhance" part of the command makes autocompletion even more powerful by making it case insensitive.) After typing a few characters of a command (or even just one), press **Tab**. Autocomplete will try to guess the rest of the command you were trying to type. If there's only one possible choice, it simply fills it in for you. If there are several, it lists them on a new line. For example, suppose you entered

```
ls ~/d
```

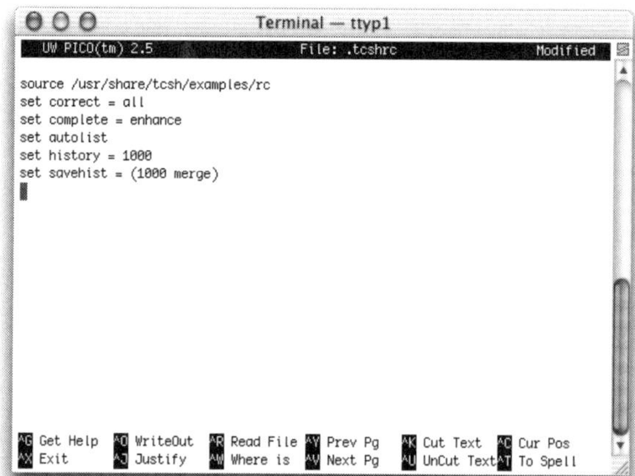

3.9

and then pressed **Tab**. Autocomplete would figure out which items in your home directory started with *D* (remember, you made the command ignore case) and display

```
Desktop/    Documents@@
% ls ~/d
```

Because two items begin with D, it shows them both. Notice that it redisplays what you just typed, so you don't have to repeat it. Now type `o` next to the `D` and press **Tab**. Autocomplete fills in the rest of the line for you, like this:

```
% ls ~/Documents
```

- Finally, the last two lines, `set history = 1000` and `set savehist = (1000 merge)`, have to do with your command history. Everything you type in Terminal is remembered, so repeating an earlier command without retyping it is easy. Just press the up-arrow key to display the last command you typed; keep pressing to cycle through all the commands that came before it. When you get to one you want to use again, press **Return**. The lines you just added increase the number of previous commands your shell remembers from 150 to 1,000 and also preserves that history list even after you've quit Terminal. In addition, the `merge` part ensures that even if you have multiple Terminal windows open, the command histories from all windows will be saved.

STEP 5: INSTALL THE DEVELOPER TOOLS

This last step is only tangentially related to Terminal as such, but because this is the end of the "Read Us First" chapter, I would be doing you a disservice by not mentioning it. Each copy of Mac OS X includes a CD called Developer Tools. The tools on this CD are mainly geared toward people who write software for Mac OS X, and most users who are not developers never bother looking at it. It turns out, however, that some handy items are on this CD that anyone can use — including a few that will make Terminal sessions easier. As long as you have a few hundred megabytes to spare on your hard drive, installing these tools is well worth a few minutes of your time. To install Developer Tools, follow these steps:

- Find the Developer Tools CD that came with your copy of Mac OS X. It's the one at the bottom of the pile, collecting dust.
- Insert the CD and double-click the file **Developer.mpkg**, as shown in **Figure 3.10**. The installer runs; follow the prompts to complete the installation. Installing this software does not require a restart, and you can eject the CD when you're done.

Among other things, this package includes a folder of command-line tools that increase your arsenal of UNIX commands. However, they're a bit awkward to use unless you tell your shell where to find them.

- One last time, edit the **.tcshrc** file. In Terminal, type `pico ~/.tcshrc` to open your shell initialization file in pico.

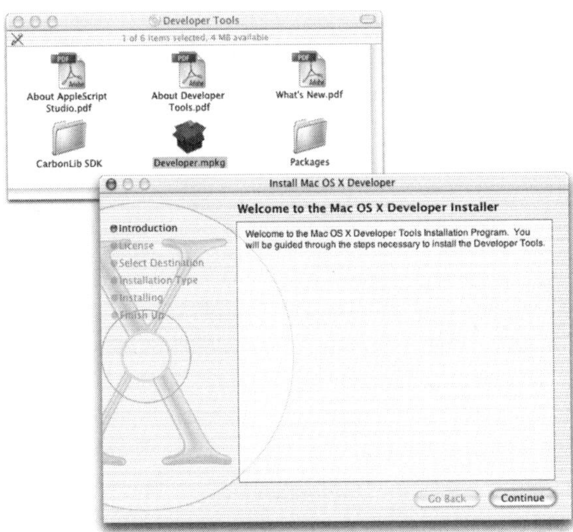

3.10

■ Use the arrow keys to move to the end of the file and type

```
set path = ($path /Developer/Tools)
```

■ As usual, press **Control+X** to quit, answer `y` to the `Save buffer?` prompt, and press **Return** to confirm the filename.

From now on, every new Terminal window you open will inherit the ability to launch about 25 new programs simply by your typing their names — without this step, you would have had to type the exact path to the program, which is not fun. And what are these new programs? I mention a few of them in later techniques, and a few more in Appendix C. But to give you a taste, here are a few examples:

- CpMac, a special version of the `cp` (copy) command that understands resource forks that appear in some Mac files
- MvMac, a resource fork-savvy `mv` (move/rename) tool
- SetFile, which allows you to change file type, creator, and other Finder attributes for a file from the command line

The Developer Tools package you just installed also includes a number of graphical desktop applications you'll be seeing later, such as Property List Editor, Sketch, and WorldText. Feel free to browse through the newly installed Developer folder — and especially the Applications folder inside it — to see all the new goodies.

NOTE

If Mac OS X came preinstalled on your computer, your Developer Tools installer may be located in /Applications/Installers rather than on a separate CD-ROM.

CHAPTER 2

AQUA'S HIDDEN TREASURES

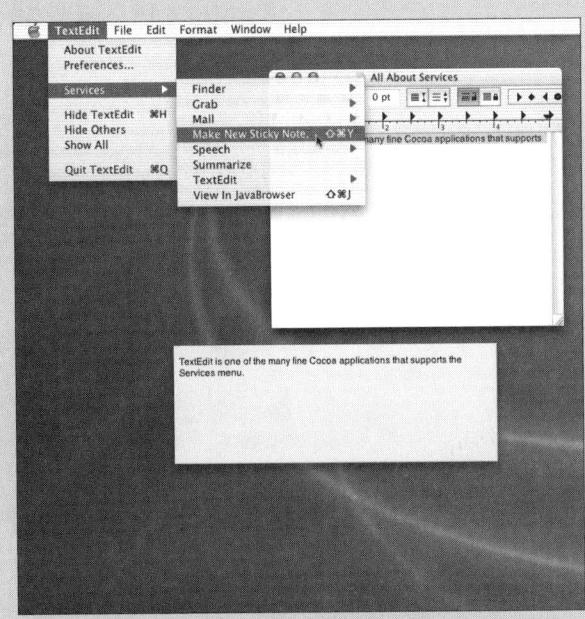

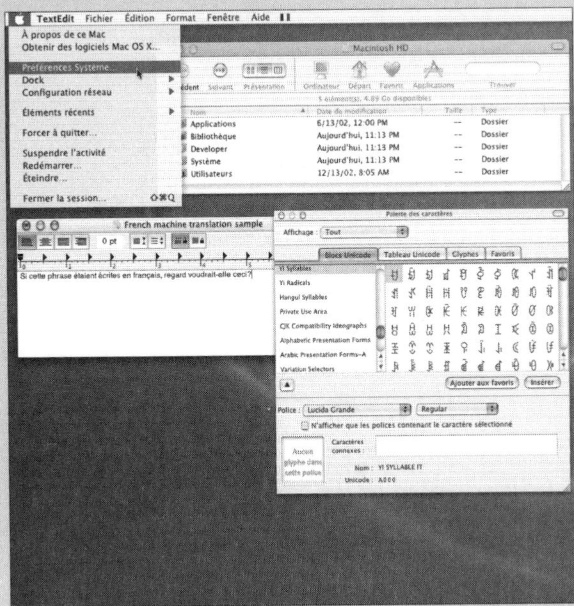

Mac OS X's gorgeous user interface, known as Aqua, is not only pretty to look at, but it is also extremely talented. The array of labor-saving controls, shortcuts, and interface widgets of all sorts can make short work of tasks that would have been awkward, if not impossible, under Mac OS 9.

With all the hoopla over such impressive buzzwords as Apache, UNIX, and preemptive multitasking, a number of Aqua's best features have received very little attention. This chapter explores techniques that exploit some of these easy-to-overlook, but extremely cool capabilities. First you look at the Finder's strange and wonderful Column View. Then you see how a feature called Services can integrate your applications with each other. You move on to techniques for making the most of everyday tasks like changing file attributes and finding files on your hard drive. After a quick look at the ways you can save time and effort with Mac OS X's built-in PDF support, you finish the chapter with some interesting uses of your system's multilingual features.

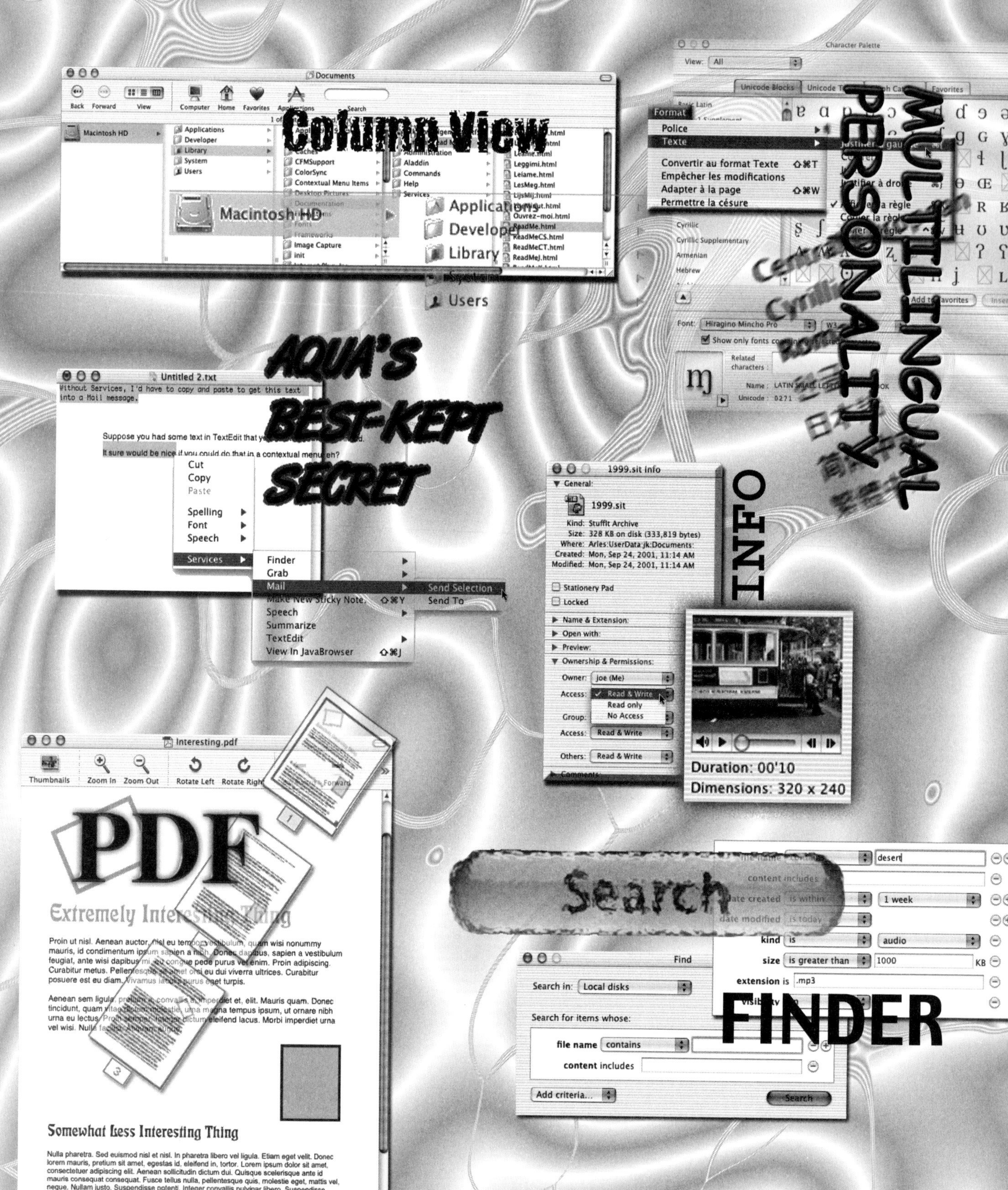
Column View
AQUA'S BEST-KEPT SECRET
MULTILINGUAL PERSONALITY
INFO
PDF
Search
FINDER

PREVENTING WINDOW OVERLOAD WITH COLUMN VIEW

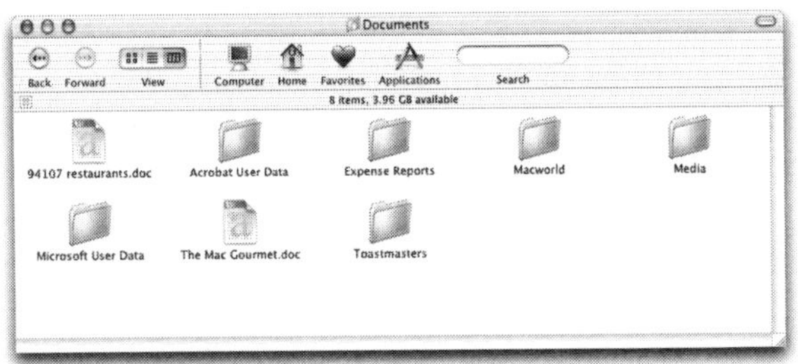

4.1

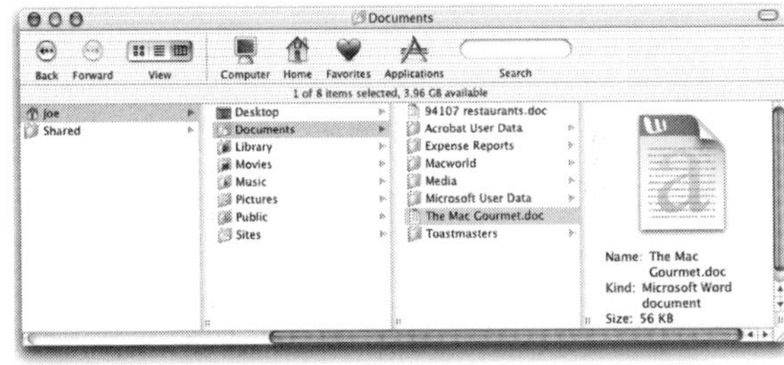

4.2

ABOUT THE FEATURE

Unlike the conventional Icon and List Views, Mac OS X's unique Column View displays the entire path of any file, while providing amazingly fast navigation. It also includes such bonus features as a built-in media player.

Every Finder window offers three different ways of looking at the files and folders inside it: Icon View, List View, and Column View, as shown in **Figure 4.3**. You can easily switch views at any time by using commands on the **View** menu (**As Icons**, **As List**, or **As Columns**), their keyboard equivalents (**⌘+1**, **⌘+2**, and **⌘+3**, respectively), or the **View** buttons on a toolbar (see **Figure 4.4**). While Icon View and List View should be familiar to anyone who has used earlier versions of the Mac OS (or Windows, for that matter), Column View is quite a bit different. It is also, by far, the most powerful and easy-to-use view (after you get used to it) and can save you loads of time and effort.

This technique is about understanding Column View and using it to save time and energy. But the best reason to use Column View is that it's fun, especially when trying to impress a PC user looking over your shoulder.

Before I get into the specifics, though, I must emphasize one key point: A *window* is not the same thing as a *folder*. In Mac OS 9, each folder could have its contents displayed in only one window at a time, so thinking of a window as *belonging to* a particular folder became natural. That wasn't truly the case even then, but under Mac OS X you can have several different windows open at the same time, with different sizes, views, and sorting orders, but all displaying files from a single folder. So when I talk about having a Column View window open, I'm not talking about having any particular folder open. The reason for this distinction should become clear in just a moment.

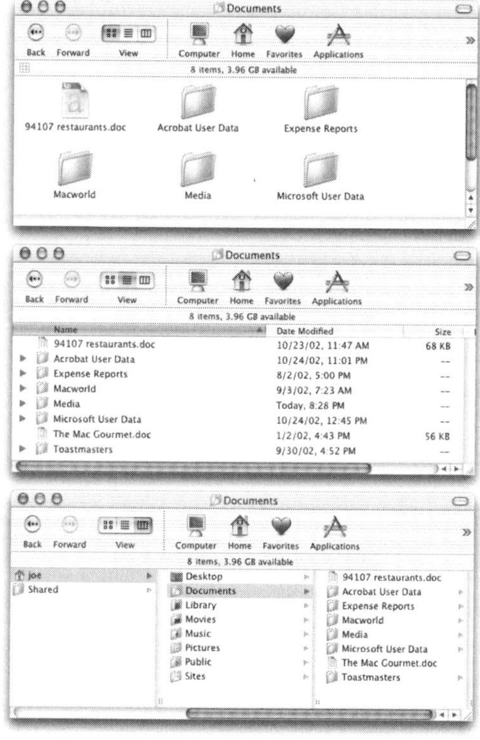

4.3

4.4

STEP 1: LEAVE A COLUMN VIEW WINDOW OPEN

In order to get to know Column View — and to use it most effectively — open a window in Column View and keep it open all the time. This might seem strange and uncomfortable if you're in the habit of closing windows as soon as you're done with them (or if you have a really cool background pattern that you don't want to hide). Far from increasing screen clutter, however, doing this will actually *decrease* the number of windows you need to have open, because in many cases, a single Column View window can do the work of many Icon or List View windows. To use Column View, follow these steps:

- Double-click any folder or volume (or just press **⌘+N**) to open a new window. As I mentioned earlier, which folder you start with doesn't matter at all, because Column View can always display everything on your computer. Resize the window so that it is wide enough to fill up most of your screen. If you haven't already done so, choose **as Columns** from the **View** menu to display this window in Column View. (You can also select

Column View by clicking the Column View button on your toolbar or by pressing ⌘+3.)

- Because you're trying to reduce unnecessary window clutter, you can use Column View to its best advantage by making it your default view, and by reducing the number of new windows created when you open folders. To do this, choose **Preferences** from the **Finder** menu. Make sure the checkbox next to **Always open folders in a new window** is unchecked. Then make sure the checkbox next to **Open new windows in Column View** is checked and close Finder Preferences.
- The toolbar is extremely useful in Column View. If it's not already visible, choose **Show Toolbar** from the **View** menu (or just press **⌘+B**). Your window should now look something like **Figure 4.5**. (To get even more mileage out of Column View, see Technique 10 for ways to enhance your toolbar.)
- Before you start exploring Column View, remember: *Keep this window open.* Resist the temptation to close it — and if you do close it, be sure to open a new window right away. If you need to see what's behind the window, click the yellow **Minimize** button on the left side of the title bar to minimize it to the Dock. Then you can easily click its Dock icon to redisplay it without actually closing the window. (If you use WindowShade X as described in Technique 11, you can also simply "roll up" the title bar.)

STEP 2: NAVIGATE IN COLUMN VIEW

Getting around Column View is extremely simple after you get your bearings. To navigate in Column View, follow these steps:

- At the bottom of the window is a horizontal scroll bar. Slide the blue scroller all the way over to the left to see the top level of your computer — your hard drive(s) and any other volumes you may have mounted such as your iPod, your .mac iDisk, or a network volume. Any icon with an arrow to its right means "this is a container"; in other words, it's a folder or volume. Click the arrow to see what's in it. Its contents display in the column to the right. **Figure 4.6** shows a Column View window expanded several levels deep.
- Column View always shows you the path to get to a particular file — just follow the highlighted folders from left to right. As you go deeper into folders within folders, eventually you'll run out of columns, so Column View will automatically slide

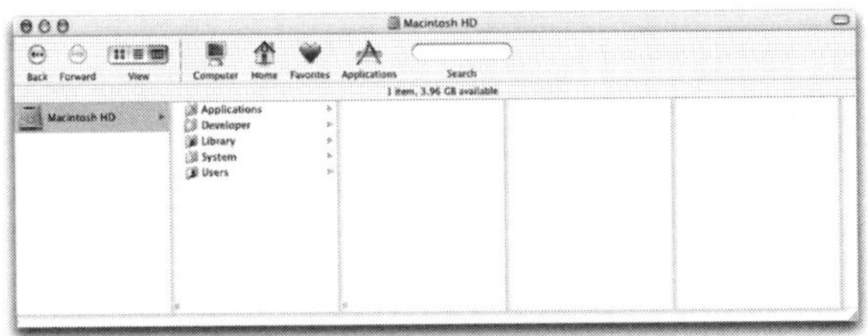

4.5

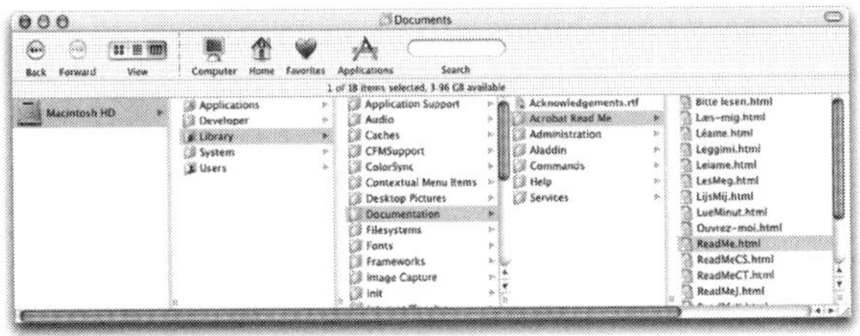

4.6

the entire display to the left. Even if you go 20 levels deep into your hard drive, you can always scroll the display back to the left to see exactly where you came from — or to choose a different path.

- Select a new file or folder in Column View and then use the **Back** button in the toolbar to go back to whatever was visible in the window before your last click. Note that this does not move you "up" in the hierarchy — that's what the horizontal scroll bar is for. Rather, it's a way to return to previous selections quickly. After you've gone back one or more steps, you can also use the **Forward** button to return to later window states.
- The Finder conventions you're already familiar with — Shift+click to select a range of files, ⌘+click to select noncontiguous files, drag-and-drop, spring-loaded folders, and so on — work just as well within Column View. The only peculiarity comes when you use the spring-loaded folder feature to drag a folder or file that's already in the Column View onto another folder in Column View. When you use this feature, the folder opens in a new window with whatever view was last used for it, regardless of your window settings in Finder Preferences. This does not apply if you drag a file from the desktop (or another window) into your Column View window.
- Click a toolbar button that represents a folder or volume to make the selected location jump into view in your current window rather than opening a new window. This works as long as you unchecked **Always open folders in a new window** in Finder Preferences.

> **TIP**
>
> Although there are many great reasons to use Column View, there's also one very good reason not to. Files and folders in Column View are always sorted alphabetically by name. Unlike List View, no options exist for sorting them by date modified, size, or kind, or to reverse the sorting order. If you have a large number of items in a folder that need to be displayed in a particular order, use List View. To force a new window to open even if you have checked Always open folders in a new window in Finder Preferences, press the ⌘ key while double-clicking the folder in Column View.

Because you can see the contents of any folder with just a click or two and move files between folders with drag-and-drop, you may find that for most of your work you never need to open another Finder window. Everything you need to access is already there!

STEP 3: USE PREVIEW

The very best part of Column View, and the main reason it will save you time, is that it includes a built-in all-purpose media player. Without opening any applications or even double-clicking, you can view pictures, play movies and sounds, and even preview PDF documents right in your Column View window. If you're looking for a particular file among many that are similar, this feature can be immensely convenient. To use the Preview feature, follow these steps:

- Make sure Preview is turned on. To do this, make sure your Column View window is active and choose **Show View Options** from the **View** menu. In the **View Options** window that appears (**Figure 4.7**), make sure **Show preview column** is checked.
- Now use Column View to navigate to a folder containing some graphics — perhaps your Pictures folder. Click any graphic, and a thumbnail view of it appears in the column to the right. Along with the thumbnail is useful information such as the file size, dimensions (in pixels), and creation and modification dates.

You can do the same thing with a movie — like the latest trailer you downloaded from Apple's QuickTime Web site. When you select a movie, a mini QuickTime player appears in the Preview column, complete with Play, Rewind, and Forward buttons and a volume control. See **Figure 4.8** for an example.

4.7

NOTE

The Preview column can display any type of media recognized by QuickTime — including JPEG, GIF, PNG, TIFF, and BMP graphics, QuickTime and AVI movies, MP3 and WAV audio files, and even PDFs, among many others.

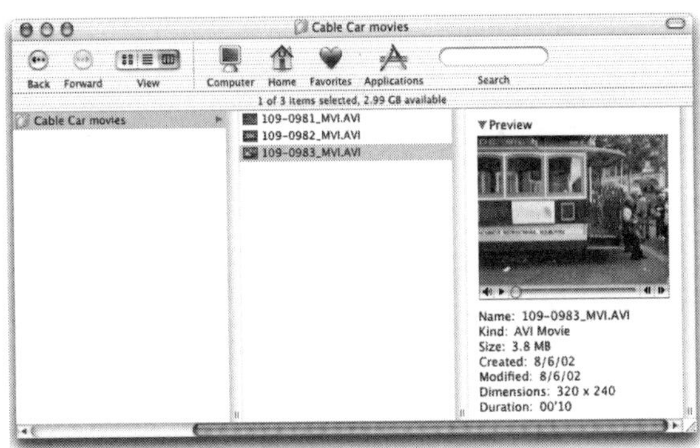

4.8

- Last but not least, try an MP3 file from your iTunes folder. As with movies, you get a complete QuickTime control bar and information about the song, including its size and duration.
- If you ever get annoyed with Preview — or just want another column to display your files and folders — you can always turn it off. Just choose **Show View Options** from the **View** menu and uncheck **Show preview column**.

STEP 4: RESIZE COLUMNS

Column View excels at displaying a lot of information at once. Sometimes, however, the columns can be too narrow to display an entire filename. You may also find that previews of graphics and movies are a bit too small. Luckily, you can easily resize columns, either collectively or individually.

- To resize all columns at once, click and drag the resize widget (the double bar symbol at the bottom of any column divider). As you drag left or right, all of your columns shrink or grow equally. This dragging also, of course, changes how many columns are in view at any time. Keep in mind that Column View is most useful when you have at least three columns visible.
- To resize just one column, hold down the Option key while clicking and dragging the resize widget in the column divider immediately to its right, as shown in **Figure 4.9**.

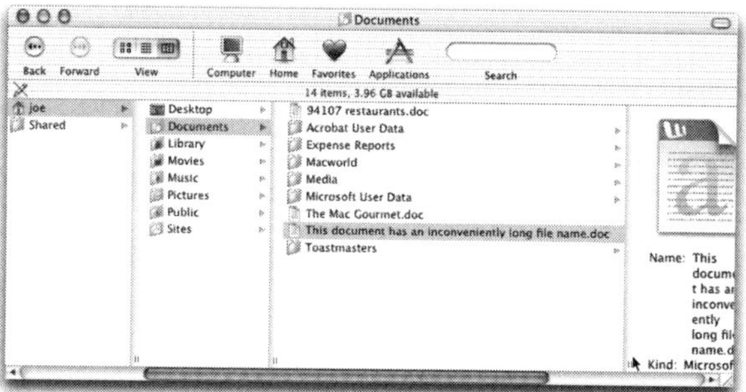

4.9

UNLOCKING AQUA'S BEST-KEPT SECRET: SERVICES

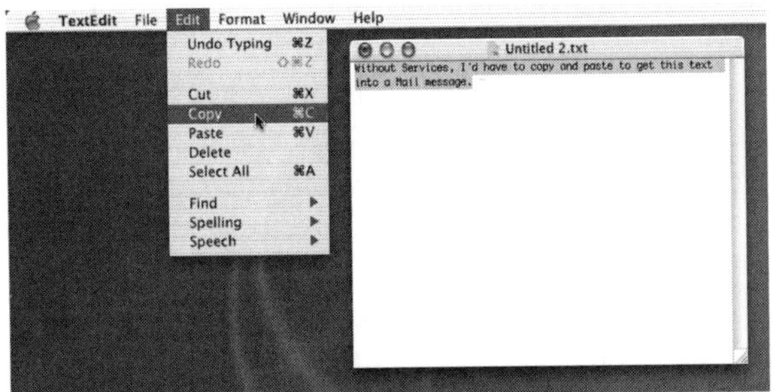

5.1

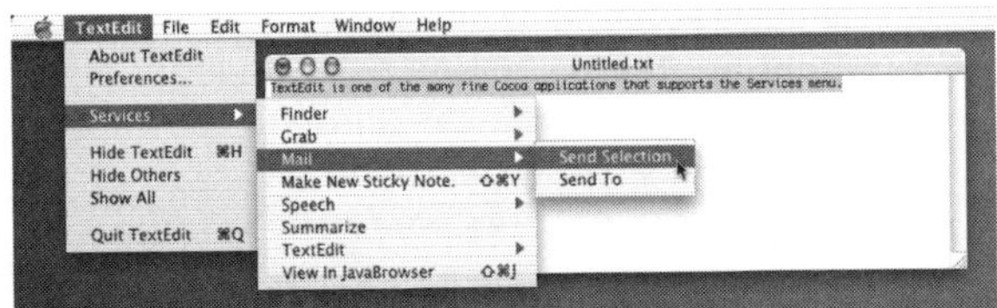

5.2

ABOUT THE FEATURE

The obscure and unassuming Services menu in Mac OS X makes accessing the features of one application while working in another easy.

If you've been using a Mac for a while, you may recall a period in the mid-'90s when Apple was vigorously promoting a technology called OpenDoc. In a nutshell, OpenDoc provided a way for small software programs to share their capabilities and data with each other, making the features of one program available in documents that were created by another program. Apple shipped a set of Internet-related OpenDoc modules (collectively called Cyberdog) with several versions of the Mac OS, and I have the dubious distinction of having coauthored a book about it. I say dubious, because before long, Apple cancelled all work on OpenDoc and Cyberdog and this once-promising technology became a bit of a joke — much like the early Newton PDAs.

And yet, just as some features from the Newton have made their way back into Mac OS X (think of Inkwell handwriting recognition or the "poof" animation when removing items from the Dock), so, too, have some elements of OpenDoc — in spirit, at least. One of the most interesting and underused features in Mac OS X is something called *Services.* Simply put,

Services give you a way to access features from one application in another. Using Services can save you time, reduce application switching, and enable you to work more efficiently.

There's just one problem, and unfortunately it's a significant one: Services only work in *some* applications — and perhaps not your favorite ones. Most applications designed exclusively for Mac OS X using Apple's Cocoa framework support Services. Carbon applications — typically, updated versions of Mac OS 9 applications — seldom support Services (or support them only in a limited fashion). Classic apps don't support Services at all.

Still, in those applications where Services work, they can be tremendously useful. In this technique, you learn how to use Services, which applications make best use of them, and where to find new Services.

STEP 1: EXPLORE THE SERVICES MENU

Like contextual menus, Services can operate on different sorts of objects (files, text selections, URLs, and so on) and appear in a menu. Unlike contextual menus, though, the Services menu is always in the same place, and its content rarely varies. It appears as a submenu of the application menu (that is, the menu just to the right of the Apple menu — the one that takes on the name of the current application). To try Services, follow these steps:

- Start by selecting a file (any file) in the Finder. Go to the **Finder** menu and, with the mouse button still held down, highlight the **Services** menu, as shown in **Figure 5.3**. You can see that it includes several submenus. Choosing a command from the Services menu or any of its submenus performs that command on the selected file. For fun, choose **Speech** and then choose **Start Speaking Text** from the submenu. Assuming your system volume is not muted, Mac OS X speaks the entire pathname of the selected file.
- As another example, with a file still selected in the Finder, choose **Send File** from the **Mail** submenu. Apple's Mail application opens and creates a new blank message with the selected file already enclosed as an attachment. (If you don't actually want to mail the file to anyone, feel free to close that message without sending it.)
- To see how Services work with a text selection, try typing your name in a text-based application like Mail or TextEdit. Select it and choose **Make New Sticky Note** from the Services menu. Stickies opens and creates a new note containing whatever you had selected, as shown in **Figure 5.4**.

This exercise is just a warm-up to acquaint you with the idea of Services, though. Read on for even cooler applications of this feature.

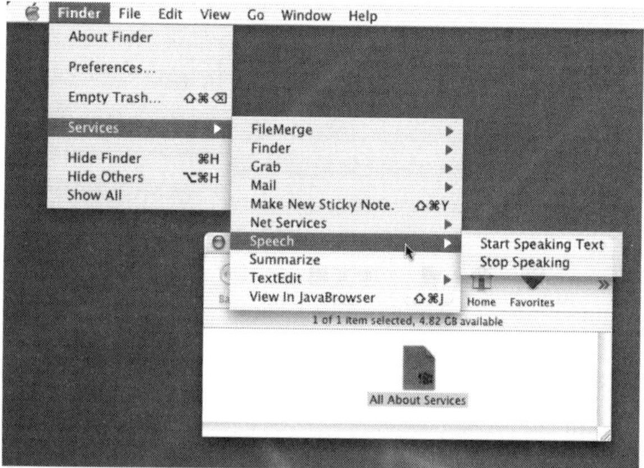

5.3

STEP 2: USE APPLICATIONS THAT SUPPORT SERVICES

First the bad news: Some of the most popular applications on Mac OS X don't support Services at all — at least not in their current versions as of this writing. Here are a few applications with *no* Services support:

- **Microsoft Office:** Word, Excel, Entourage, PowerPoint
- **Many Web browsers:** Internet Explorer, iCab, Netscape, Mozilla, and Opera

- **Graphics applications:** iPhoto, Acrobat, Photoshop, and Preview

Now the good news: You can still use Services in plenty of applications — and that number is growing all the time. Here's a small sampling of Services-aware applications:

Apple software:

- Address Book
- FileMerge (part of Developer Tools)
- Finder
- Grab
- iCal
- iChat
- iTunes
- Mail
- Stickies
- Terminal
- TextEdit

Third-party software:

- BBEdit (the full version only, not BBEdit Lite)
- FileXaminer
- OmniWeb
- Path Finder
- PGP
- QuicKeys
- textSOAP
- URL Manager Pro
- XRay

To make use of Services, you need to use applications that enable the commands on the Services menu.

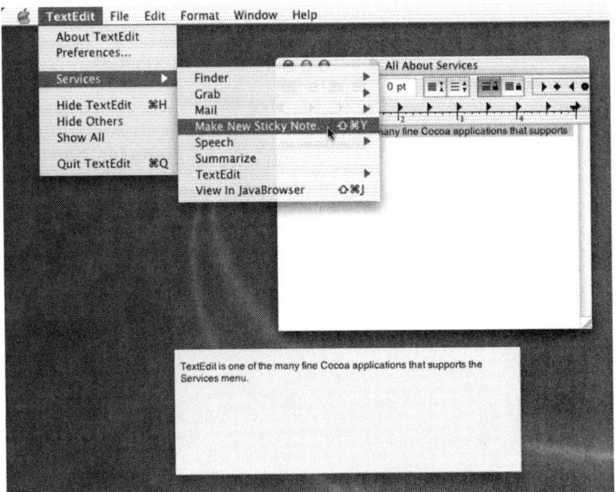

5.4

STEP 3: USE THE BUILT-IN SERVICES

Mac OS X includes a variety of interesting Services you can put to use immediately. Here are some excellent examples:

- If you have an audio file you want to send to a friend, Services can make doing it a snap. Open iTunes and select any song. Now select **Mail** from the **Services** menu (as shown in **Figure 5.5**) and choose **Send File** from the submenu. Mail opens and creates a new message with the song already enclosed. (Obligatory reminder: Don't steal music!)
- Using the excellent (and free) OmniWeb browser, find a news story that interests you. Using your mouse, highlight the text of the article and choose **Summarize** from the **Services** menu. A new window opens, displaying a brief summary of the text you highlighted. By adjusting the slider at the bottom of the window, you can change the length of the summary.
- If you want to capture a picture of your screen (like the many screen shots used in this book), make sure you're in a Services-aware application like TextEdit or Stickies. Choose **Grab** from the

5.5

Services menu and then choose **Screen** from the submenu. When the dialog shown in **Figure 5.6** appears, follow the instructions and click outside the window to capture an image of your entire screen.

Services invite experimentation, so feel free to play with some of the other commands available on the Services menu. If all the commands (other than the submenu names) are dimmed, you're in an application that is not Services-aware. If just certain commands are dimmed, it usually means you do not have the right kind of object selected. (Some Services work only with text and some, only with files, for example.)

STEP 4: ADD NEW SERVICES

Although Apple's built-in Services can be quite useful, you can add dozens of third-party Services. You can add commands to your Services menu in two ways. The first is to install new applications that include Services commands. The second is to install

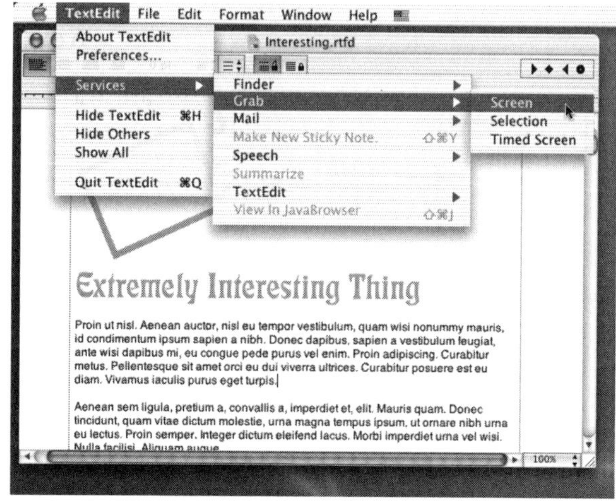

5.6

TABLE 5-1

PRODUCTS SUPPORTING SERVICES

APPLICATION	SOURCE	COMMANDS ADDED TO SERVICES MENU
FileXaminer (File utility)	`www.gideonsoftworks.com/filexaminer.html`	Batch Get Info on Selected, Get Info on Selection (Get Info submenu)
OmniWeb (Web browser)	`www.omnigroup.com`	Open URL in OmniWeb
PGP (Encryption software)	`www.pgp.com`	Decrypt-Verify, Encrypt, Encrypt & Sign, Sign, Wipe (on PGP submenu)
PTHPasteboard (Multiple clipboard utility)	`www.pth.com/PTHPasteboard/`	Paste from PTHPasteboard
QuicKeys X (Macro utility)	`www.cesoft.com`	Create QuicKeys Shortcut
Path Finder (Alternative file browser)	`www.cocoatech.com/`	Show Item (on Path Finder submenu)
textSOAP (Text-cleaning utility)	`www.unmarked.com/`	27 different text-cleaning commands (on textSOAP submenu)
URL Manager Pro (Bookmark manager)	`www.url-manager.com/`	Add Bookmark
XRay (File utility)	`www.brockerhoff.net/xray/`	XRay Path

standalone Services that are not part of any application. **Table 5-1** lists a sampling of Services-aware applications and standalone Services.

If you want to find more Services, visit `www.versiontracker.com`, click the Mac OS X tab, and search for "services." Not every match will be the type of Service discussed here, but many of them will be.

STEP 5: USE SERVICES FROM CONTEXTUAL MENUS

If you're thinking Services are pretty cool but just a bit awkward to use, this last step will make them much more convenient:

- Download Nicholas Riley's free ICeCoffEE (available from `web.sabi.net/nriley/software/`). ICeCoffEE is a tiny program that does two incredibly useful things very well. First, it allows you to ⌘+click a URL in a document window to open it in your Web browser, which is much quicker than copying, switching to your browser, and pasting. But more importantly, it puts a copy of the Services menu right in your contextual menus for text selections, as shown in **Figure 5.7**. This feature makes getting to Services much easier, because you don't have to move your pointer all the way to the Apple menu.

NOTE

Not all Services add commands to the Services menu. The Apple Spell service included with Mac OS X, for example, provides check-while-you-type spell checking capabilities to Mail, TextEdit, and other applications. Its commands are available, if you need them, on a contextual menu. Still other Services provide additional behind-the-scenes functionality without any overt user interface.

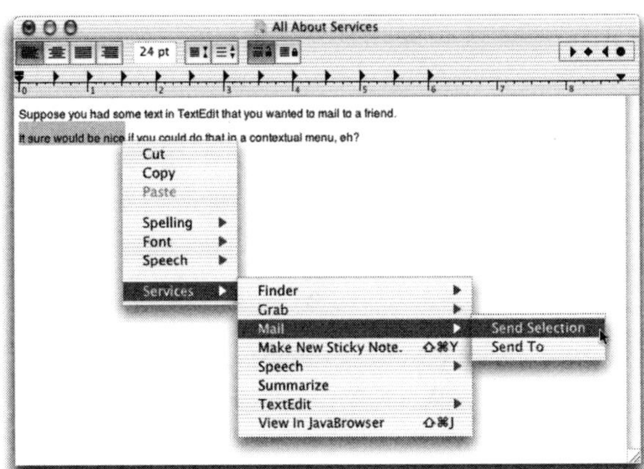

5.7

TECHNIQUE 6

GETTING INFO AND WHAT TO DO WITH IT

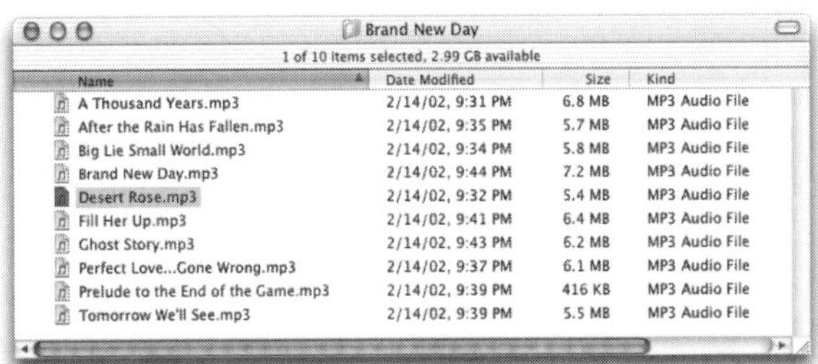

6.1

6.2

ABOUT THE FEATURE

The Mac OS has always had a Get Info command, which lists numerous file and folder properties. In Mac OS X, the Get Info command has become much more useful by giving additional information and more ways of using it.

The lowly Info window that displays information about the selected Finder item is not exactly the flashiest feature in Mac OS X. But with the release of Mac OS X 10.2, you can now get quite a lot of info with Get Info, and more importantly, you can use this window to make important changes to your files that previously would have taken a trip to Terminal (or a third-party utility).

Although some good reasons still exist to use other software to tweak file attributes (as you'll see), you can get surprisingly far with the capabilities built into Mac OS X. In this technique, you learn the ins and outs of the Info window.

STEP 1: GET INFO ON A FILE, FOLDER, OR VOLUME

To display information about a file, folder, or volume, follow these steps:

- First, select a file in the Finder.
- Press ⌘+I (or choose **Get Info** from the Finder's **File** menu or a contextual menu). A window similar to that shown in **Figure 6.3** appears. The top of this window is the **General** section, which contains basic information like the file's kind, size, location, and creation and modification dates.
- Display or hide different portions of the window. Below the **General** section of the window are several other window portions you can display or hide by clicking their disclosure triangles (or *triangles* for short). You can display any or all of these portions, though the window can get quite tall if they're all visible (as shown in **Figure 6.4**). In the following steps you see how each of these categories is used.

Info windows for folders and volumes are similar, but contain slightly different options, as shown in **Figure 6.5**.

Mac OS X actually contains another type of Info window known as the *Inspector*. You can see the two info windows side by side in **Figure 6.6**. As you can see, they display the same information and are nearly identical except for the title bar. What makes the Inspector different is that it's a floating window, which means that it is always visible in front of any other windows you may have open. It's also dynamic, so you can leave it open and select different files or folders, and its content changes to provide information

6.3

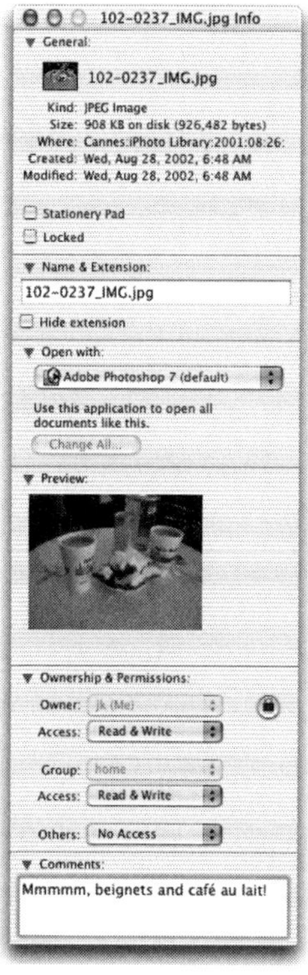

6.4

on whatever you've selected. In most cases, the regular Info window is more convenient to work with.

■ To use the Inspector instead of (or in addition to) the regular Info window, select one or more icons in the Finder and press **⌘+Option+I** (or hold down the **Option** key and choose **Show Inspector** from the **File** menu).

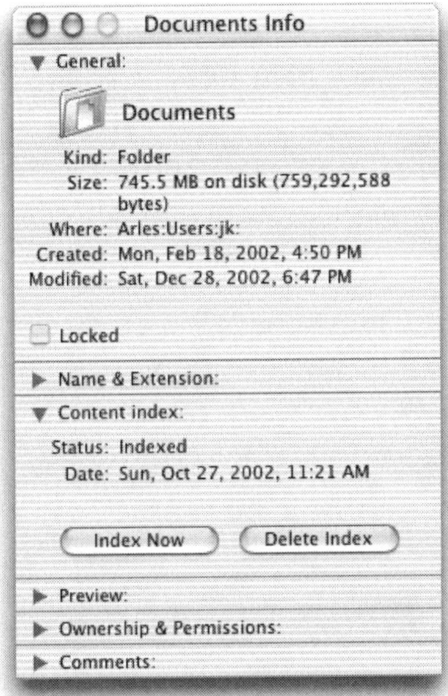

6.5

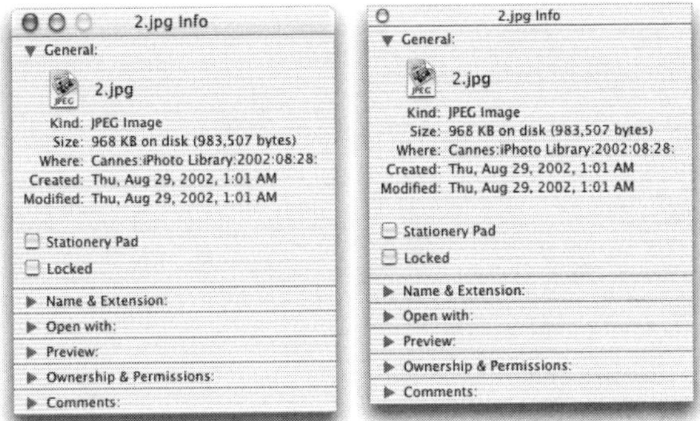

6.6

STEP 2: SET GENERAL INFO OPTIONS

Depending on the type of file you've selected, you may have one or two checkboxes available in the General area. (See **Figure 6.7**.) All files and folders display a **Locked** checkbox, and files (but not folders) also have a **Stationery Pad** checkbox.

■ Check the **Locked** box to prevent the file from being changed or deleted. If you try to empty the Trash with a locked file in it, you'll get an error message. To delete locked files, you can either uncheck the **Locked** checkbox in the Info window, or simply hold down the **Option** key while choosing **Empty Trash**.

■ Check the **Stationery Pad** box to convert your file to a stationery pad. Every time you open the file, a *copy* of the file actually opens, leaving the original intact. As the term stationery implies, this feature is useful for forms, templates, and other documents that are all based on the same basic contents.

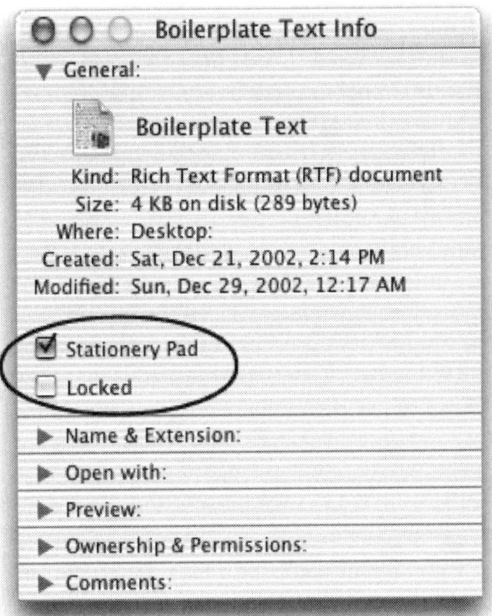

6.7

STEP 3: SET NAME & EXTENSION

Files in Mac OS X use an *extension* — a dot followed by one or more characters at the end of the filename — to designate what type of document it is. Ordinarily these extensions are hidden. However, you can't always tell what file format a document uses by looking at its icon, and on occasion you may want to know (or correct a filename with an incorrect extension).

- Click the triangle next to **Name & Extension** to display that portion of the window. The entire filename, including extension, appears, as shown in **Figure 6.8**.
- To rename the file, just type in a new name.
- To display its extension (in Finder windows, Open and Save dialogs, and so on), uncheck **Hide extension**. Conversely, check the box to hide an extension that's already visible.

STEP 4: CHANGE WHICH APPLICATION OPENS A FILE

Some types of files can be opened by numerous applications. For instance, Word, TextEdit, and AppleWorks can all open text files; Preview and Acrobat Reader can both open PDFs; and Preview, iPhoto, Internet Explorer, and dozens of other programs can open JPEGs. The application designated as the one to open a particular file is known as its *creator* (even if that application didn't actually create the file).

6.8

■ To change a file's creator, click the triangle next to **Open with**. The pop-up menu that appears displays a list of applications that can open this file. (See **Figure 6.9** for an example.) Choose a different application from this list to change the creator. If you're certain that an application can open this type of file but it's not in the list, choose **Other...** and navigate to that application manually.

■ If you want to make all files of the same type as this one open with a particular application, click **Change All...**. Keep in mind that this only affects files already on your hard drive.

STEP 5: PREVIEW A FILE

The Info window can also display a preview of certain kinds of files, just like the Preview pane in Column View.

■ Click the triangle next to **Preview** to display a thumbnail of the file. (This option applies only to file types QuickTime understands, such as pictures, PDFs, and other multimedia files. Other files just display their icon in the Preview area.) If the file is a movie or audio file, as in **Figure 6.10**, you'll see a mini QuickTime player right in the Info window that allows you to play it without opening any other applications — just like you see in Column View.

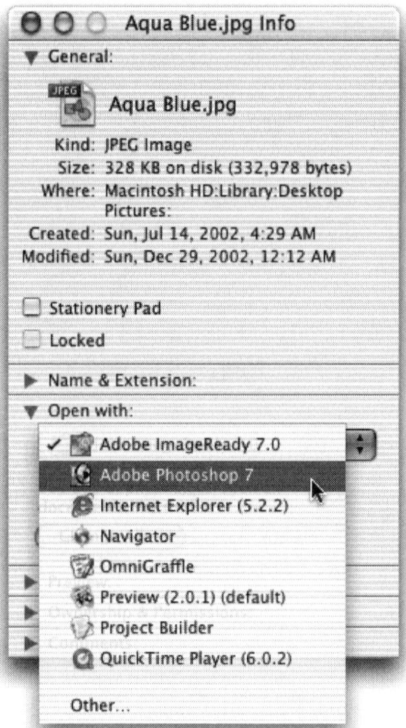

6.9

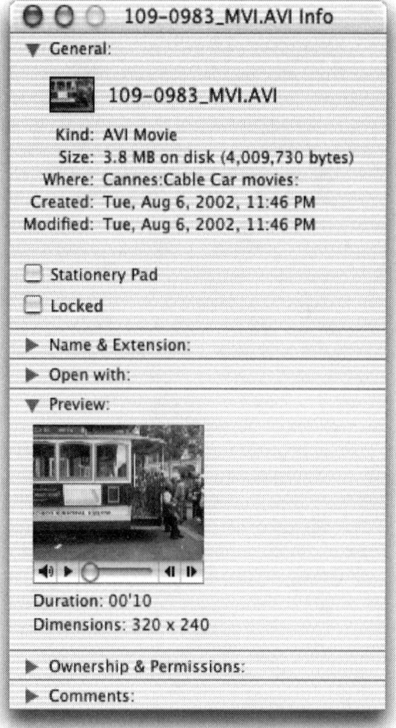

6.10

STEP 6: CHANGE OWNERSHIP & PERMISSIONS

If you're lucky, you'll rarely have to do this — but knowing how it's done is important just in case. Every Mac OS X file has a designated *owner* — one of the computer's users who has the right to modify, move, or delete it. In most cases, that owner will be you. Occasionally, however, for one reason or another a file gets set with an incorrect owner. When this happens, you may not be able to modify it, even if you originally created it. There may also be times you'll want to change a file's owner to be someone else — for example, some files need to be "owned" by a user named www to work properly with a Web server.

- To change a file's owner, click the triangle next to **Ownership & Permissions**, as shown in **Figure 6.11**. The **Owner** and **Group** menus will initially be disabled; click the lock icon to access them. Choose a new owner from the **Owner** pop-up menu.
- Each Mac OS X user is also a member of one or more *groups* — sets of users. For most files you own, the **Group** should be set to **staff (Me)**.

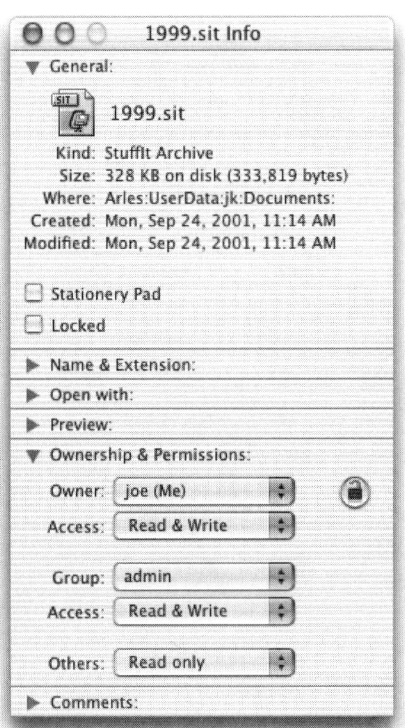

6.11

In addition to owners, each file has a series of attributes called *permissions* that specify what kinds of things different groups of people can do with the file. For example, the **Owner** of a file can usually read or write it. You may want to give a **Group** of users more limited access — such as the ability to read but not write the file. And depending on the file and your computer setup, you may want to limit access even further for those who are not a member of the selected group (known as **Others**).

- To change the permissions for the file's owner — whether you or another user — choose **Read & Write**, **Read only**, or **No Access** from the **Access** pop-up menu below **Owner**. **Figure 6.12** shows an example.
- To change permissions for the selected group of users, choose **Read & Write**, **Read only**, or **No Access** from the Group's **Access** menu.
- To change permissions for all users other than the owner and members of the selected group, choose the appropriate access level from the **Others** menu.

That said, the general rule for changing ownership or permissions is to do it only in response to an error. If you get a warning message about file ownership or permissions while trying to access or delete a file, this is where you can go to fix it. But Mac OS X is very picky about these settings, and changing them unnecessarily can lead to headaches later. For more information on ownership and permissions, see Appendix B.

STEP 7: ADD COMMENTS

The final portion of the Info window allows you to store freeform comments.

- If you want to make a note to yourself about a file without modifying the file's contents, click the triangle next to **Comments** (see **Figure 6.13**) and type your comments here. Ordinarily, you see these comments only in the Info window, but you can display them in List View, too. To do so, open a window in List View and choose **Show View Options** from the **View** menu. Click the checkbox next to **Comments** and resize the window, if necessary, to show the Comments column.

STEP 8: GET MORE INFO WITH THIRD-PARTY UTILITIES

Under Mac OS X 10.2 and later, your options for making changes in the Info window are significantly greater than they were in earlier versions of Mac OS X. Sometimes, however, you'll need to do even more. For example, the Info window doesn't allow you to make a file invisible (or visible), to set whether it can be executed as a UNIX command, or to change the file's creation or modification date. For such tasks, you need to use Terminal or a third-party utility.

Many fine utilities can help you here, including Super Get Info ($20 from BareBones Software, `www.barebones.com`), FileXaminer ($10 from Gideon Softworks, `www.gideonsoftworks.com/filexaminer.html`), or my favorite, XRay ($10 from Rainer Brockerhoff, `www.brockerhoff.net/xray/`), shown in **Figure 6.14**. As you can see, XRay gives you a much finer level of control than the Finder's Info window. It even installs a convenient contextual menu command so you can use XRay to get more info on any file with a single click.

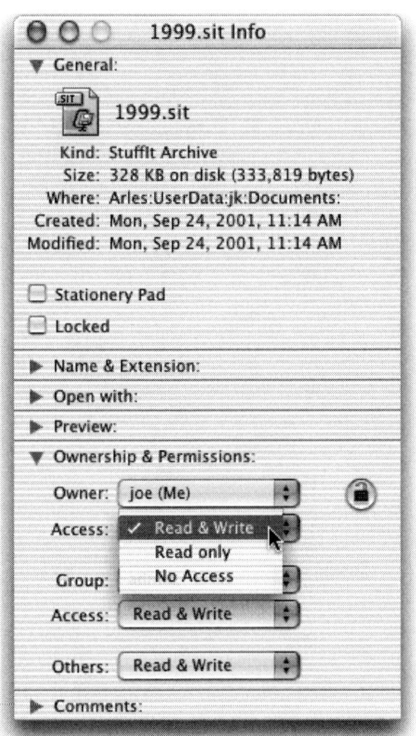

6.12

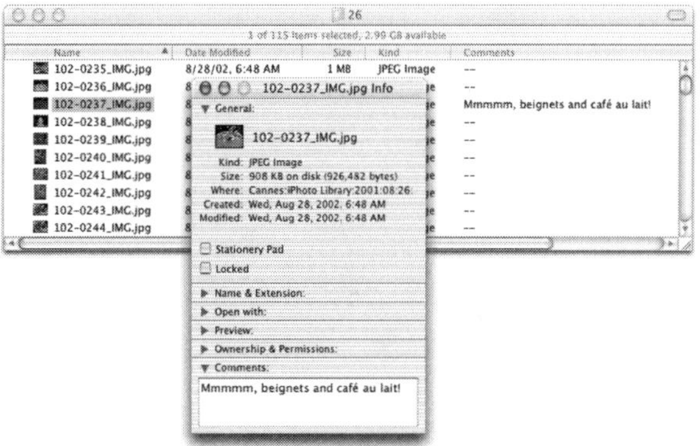

6.13

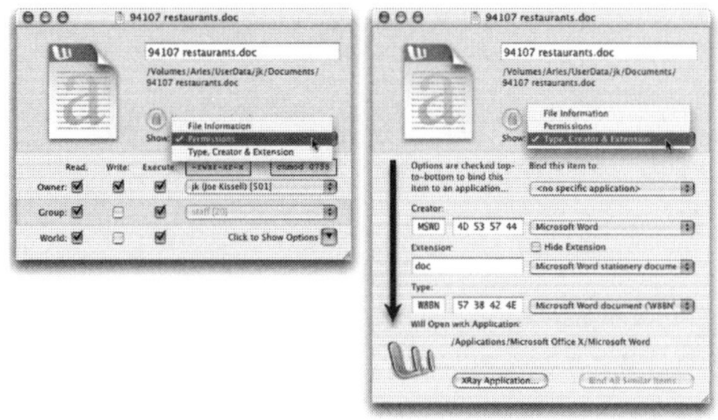

6.14

FINDING FILES WITH THE FINDER

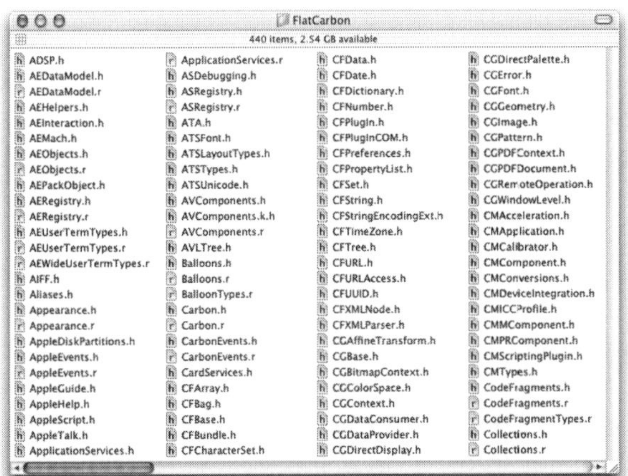

7.1

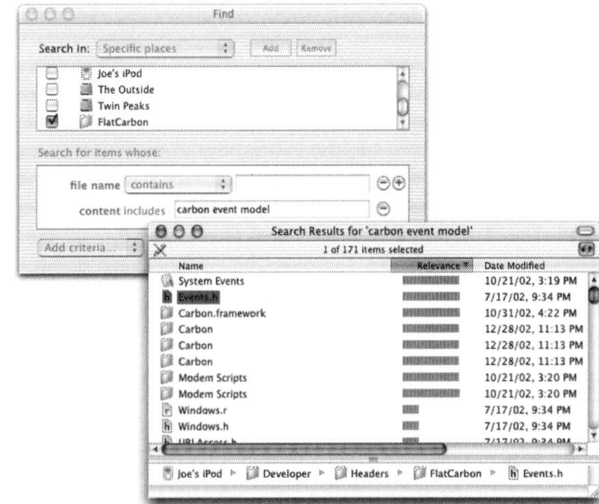

7.2

ABOUT THE FEATURE

The more files you add to your computer, the more difficult locating just the one you're looking for can be. Mac OS X's Finder is truly worthy of its name with a variety of fast and convenient ways to find files.

The Finder is the program that displays your volumes, folders, and files in windows and allows you to select, move, delete, open them, and so on. Given its name, you might think that one of its key features would be, in fact, *finding* files. Ironically, that hasn't been the case for a long time. From Mac OS 8 through Mac OS X 10.1, using the **Find** command in the Finder actually opened a separate application called Sherlock to locate files on your hard drive. Although very powerful, its lack of integration with the Finder made it tedious to use.

With version 10.2, however, "finding" is back in the Finder with a vengeance. The Finder now has not one, but two separate built-in Find tools. In this technique, you learn how easy finding files with either tool is; then you go one step further and find out how to find files that the Finder can't.

STEP 1: FIND FILES WITH THE SEARCH BOX

As if to make up for past transgressions, Apple has put a Search box in the toolbar of Finder windows that makes finding files falling-off-a-log simple. To use the Search box, follow these steps:

- Open any Finder window containing files or folders.
- Make sure the toolbar is visible. If it isn't, click the pill-shaped button on the right edge of the title bar to display it.
- Make sure the Search box is visible, as shown in **Figure 7.3**. If it isn't, there are two possible reasons. First, the window may be too narrow. A chevron (») symbol in the upper-right corner of your toolbar means there are toolbar buttons that can't be shown. Drag the resize box to widen the window. If your window still doesn't show the Search box, you may need to add it to the toolbar. Choose **Customize Toolbar...** from the **View** menu, drag the Search box onto your toolbar, and click **Done**.
- Type a few characters of a filename into the **Search** box and press **Return**. The window title changes to **Search results for '*your search term*' in '*where you're searching*'**, and the window begins to list files whose names include the characters you typed. **Figure 7.4** shows you an example.

A few words of explanation are in order here. First, searches using the Search box start from the volume or folder displayed in the window when you begin the search. (If your window is in Column View, it begins from the rightmost *highlighted* folder or volume.) So if you double-click your hard drive icon and begin the search there, it will search your entire hard drive. On the other hand, if you open the window for a particular folder, the search will only look in that folder (and all of its subfolders). This feature can be very useful for limiting the scope of a search.

Second, you may find that you want to cancel a search before it's finished. To do so, click the square button with the X on it, located on the right side of the status bar. When you click it, the icon changes to a circular double-arrow shape; click again to restart the search.

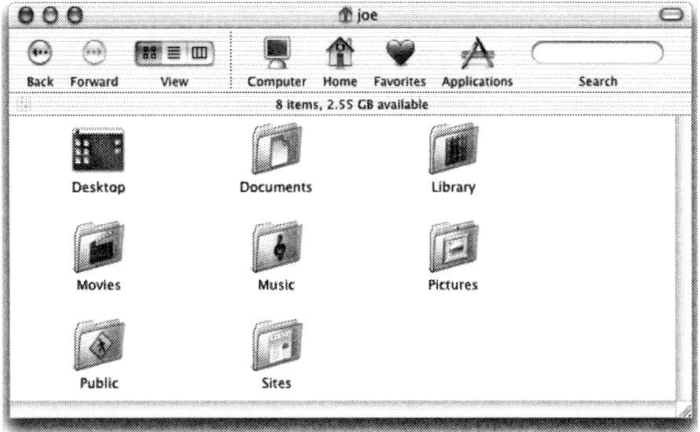

7.3

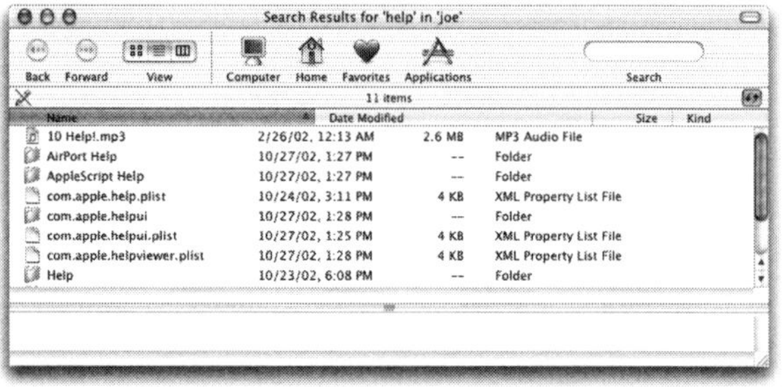

7.4

Third, if you want to clear the contents of the Search box to do another search, click the round X on the right side of the Search box. Some additional searching tips are as follows:

- Click any file in the list of found items, and the bottom portion of the window will display its path, either in a Column View-like arrangement (the top example in **Figure 7.5**) or, if you drag the divider upward a bit (the bottom example), the more conventional outline hierarchy.
- As in any other Finder window, you can click a column heading (Name, Date Modified, Size, or Kind) to sort by that attribute; click a second time to reverse the sort order.
- Now that you've found a file, you can do all the usual things with it, just as though this were any other Finder window — double-click to open the file; drag and drop it to a new location; Get Info on it; and so on. (Be sure to select the file in the main list, not the one in the location window below.)
- To open the folder containing a selected file as a separate window, press **⌘+R**.
- To return your window to whatever was being displayed before the search, click the **Back** button.

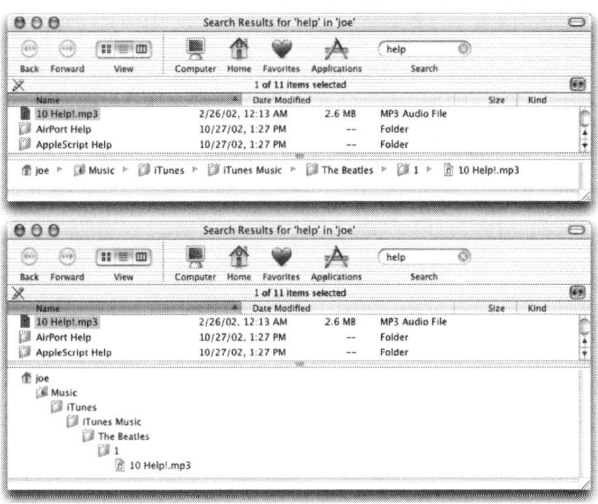

7.5

STEP 2: FIND FILES WITH THE FIND COMMAND

Using the Search box is quite easy, but it's also limited. For one thing, you can only search titles of files, not their contents, sizes, or any other attributes. For another thing, you can't easily choose to search just certain locations on your computer. Mac OS X's outstanding Find command picks up where Search boxes leave off.

Using **Find** you could, if you wanted to, restrict your search to graphics files larger than 100K whose names begin with "cat," or to documents created within the last three days that contain some mention of the word "litter." Best of all, you can do all this instantly in the Finder without having to wait for Sherlock to open, as you did before Mac OS X 10.2.

- To use the Find feature, just press **⌘+F** or choose **Find...** from the Finder's **File** menu. A window like that shown in **Figure 7.6** appears immediately.
- To do a basic search, enter part of a filename in the blank next to **filename contains** and click **Search**. A Search Results window appears, listing matching files. This window is exactly like the list shown when you use the Search box in a toolbar, except that it's a standalone window, which means you can perform multiple searches at the same time and have as many different Search Results windows visible as you like.

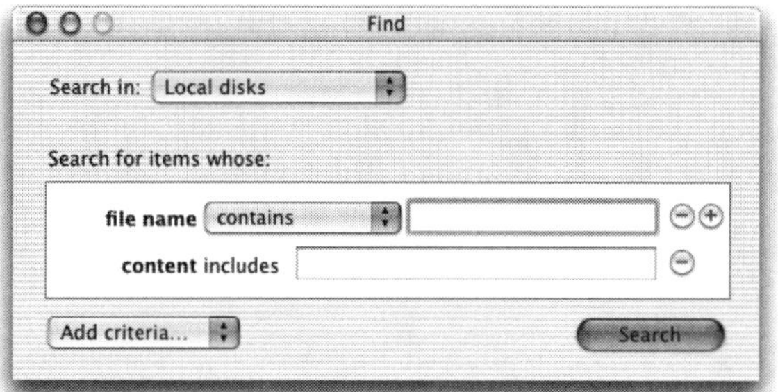

7.6

- To find files based on more than one element of their name, click the + icon next to the filename field. This adds a second (or even a third) filename field. By entering, for example, "peanut" in one and "butter" in the other, you can find all files whose names include both "peanut" and "butter." You can also change **contains** to **starts with**, **ends with**, or **is**, so you could search for, say, all files whose names *begin with* "hello" and *end with* "world." To go back to just one filename element, click the – icon next to the one you don't want.

STEP 3: NARROW YOUR SEARCH BY LOCATION

You can make your search more focused by searching only in certain places.

- To limit your search based on location, use the pop-up **Search in** menu. The default choice is **Local disks**, which means your hard drive and any other volumes physically attached to your computer (such as an iPod or other FireWire drive). To expand your search to include mounted network volumes (including your iDisk if applicable), choose **Everywhere**. If you want to search only documents within your home folder and its subfolders, choose **Home**.
- A fourth choice on the **Search in** menu lets you get more specific still about where you search. If you choose **Specific places**, the view changes, as shown in **Figure 7.7**, to list all your mounted volumes. Use the checkboxes to select or deselect volumes to search in. If you want to limit your search to a particular folder, click **Add** and navigate to that folder (or just drag it into the list if it's visible in the Finder). Be sure to uncheck locations you don't want to search.

STEP 4: SEARCH FOR TEXT INSIDE FILES

If you don't know even part of the name of the file you're looking for, you can also search by a number of criteria. The coolest of these criteria is *content*. While your computer is idle, Mac OS X is busy indexing the files on your hard drive — making a catalog of which files contain which words. When you search by content, you are actually searching this index, which is extremely fast.

7.7

- To search for files containing specific text, type the text into the **content** field and click **Search**. When you perform a search based on content, the Search Results window will include an additional column called **Relevance** (as shown in **Figure 7.8**), which indicates how frequently your search term appeared in each of the files relative to their overall length.

> **TIP**
>
> **Sometimes the index files Mac OS X uses for content-based searches aren't updated as quickly as you might like. If you search for something you know is in a file but don't get the right results, you might need to update your index file. To do this, select the folder or volume containing your file and choose Get Info from the File menu. Click the disclosure triangle next to Content index and click Index Now. After your index has been updated, Find should be able to locate your files.**

STEP 5: ADD MORE SEARCH CRITERIA

In most cases, searching by filename or file contents is sufficient to find what you're looking for. If not, you can add additional criteria to search other file attributes.

- To add a new search criterion, click the pop-up **Add criteria...** menu at the bottom of the Find window. Each time you choose something from this menu, additional controls appear in the window, as shown in **Figure 7.9**. You can add any or all of the following:
  - **date created**
  - **date modified**
  - **kind** (meaning alias, application, folder, document, audio, image, or movie)
  - **size**
  - **extension** (the tag at the end of filenames that indicates what type of file it is — like .gz, .doc, or .jpeg)
  - **visibility** (allowing you to search for files with the "invisible" attribute set, as well as files in the UNIX layer of Mac OS X whose names begin with a period)
- To remove a search criterion from your list, click the – icon next to it.

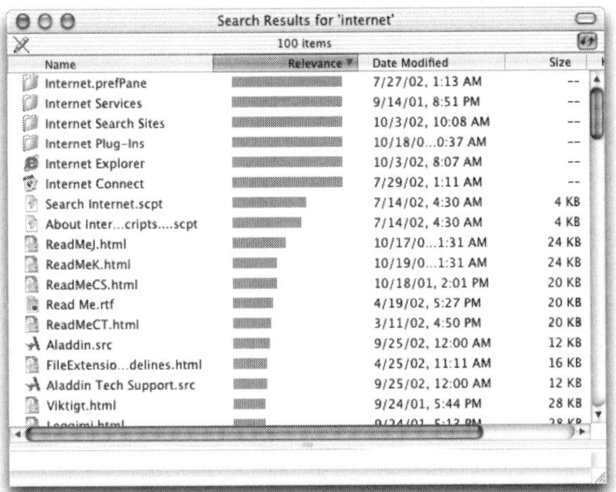

7.8

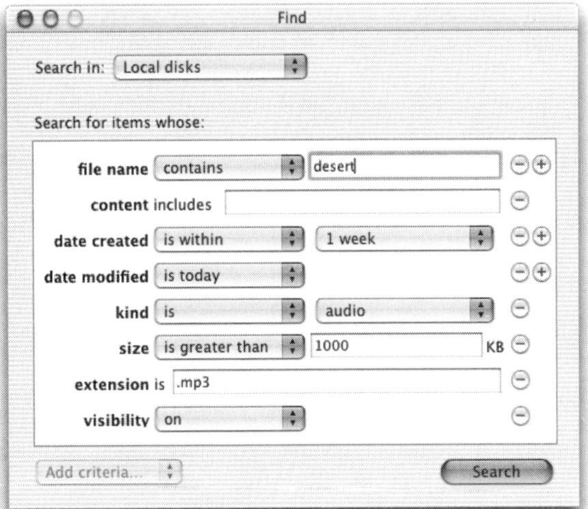

7.9

TECHNIQUE **8**

SOLVING FILE COMPATIBILITY PROBLEMS WITH PDF

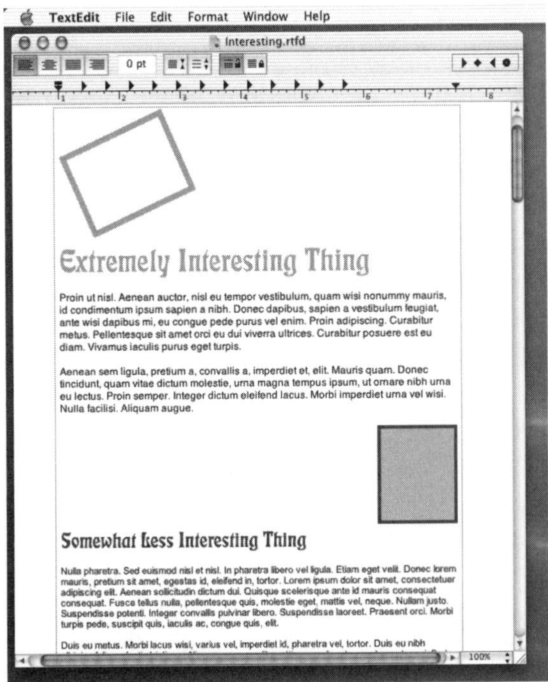

8.1

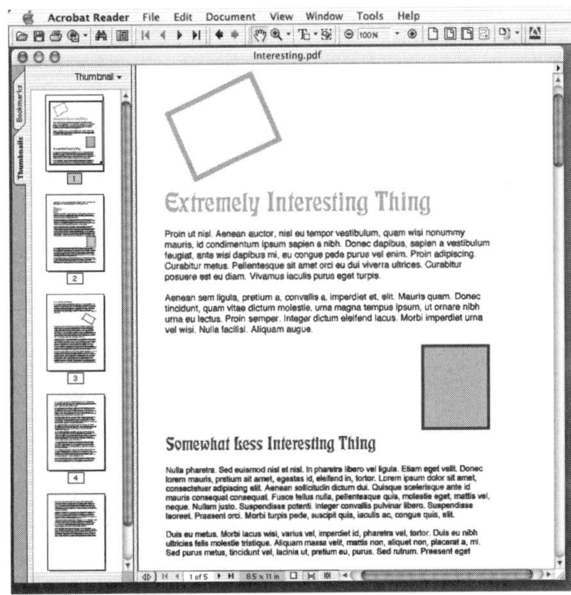

8.2

ABOUT THE FEATURE

Adobe's PDF (Portable Document Format) is a way to exchange files with all their formatting, fonts, and graphics intact — even across platforms and on computers with completely different software. Mac OS X's imaging system is based on PDF, so nearly every application can use PDF files in some way.

Adobe's PDF (Portable Document Format) is a very popular file format that can be viewed on nearly any Mac, Windows, Linux, Palm OS, or PocketPC computer with the appropriate viewer software installed. The remarkable thing about PDF is that it preserves fonts, graphics, layouts, and other attributes of a document, so that it looks almost identical on any machine where it's viewed — even if that machine doesn't have the fonts or other software used to create the original.

One of the most exciting aspects of Mac OS X's Aqua interface is the fact that all the 2D graphics you see onscreen are based on PDF. Why is this exciting? Now, without any additional software, every single Mac OS X application that can print files can also save in PDF format. And many applications — even a few that might surprise you — can also display PDF files that were created in this way. To take this a step further, you can now use PDF files in many places where a graphic format like JPEG, TIFF, or GIF would ordinarily be required.

There are, alas, a couple of limitations to Mac OS X's implementation of PDF that keep it from being the truly universal file format solution. First and most importantly, although any application can *save* files in PDF format and many applications can *read* the PDF files, the only way at present to *edit* existing PDF files is to use Adobe Acrobat, a $249 commercial application. Secondly, the PDF files created in most Mac OS X applications do not adhere completely to the PDF specification (resulting in occasional compatibility problems), are not suitable for high-resolution printing, and lack many of PDF's niftiest features — like bookmarks, digital signatures, hyperlinks, and forms. Again, you need the full version of Acrobat for these features.

All that said, PDF still offers a wealth of possibilities in Mac OS X. This technique offers all you need to know to become comfortable using PDF.

STEP 1: SAVE AS PDF FROM ANY APPLICATION

Any Mac OS X application that can print (excluding, naturally, Classic applications) can also create PDF files.

- From your application's **File** menu, choose **Page Setup**. Adjust paper size, margins, and orientation (portrait or landscape) to suit the use of your PDF. For example, if you expect your PDF to be printed, you'll most likely want to choose Letter-size paper with a portrait orientation. If you want to use your PDF as a graphic, a smaller size and landscape orientation may be more appropriate. Click **OK** when you're done.
- From the **File** menu, choose **Print**. If you want your PDF file to contain just certain pages of your document, enter the desired page range. At the bottom of the Print dialog that appears (**Figure 8.3**) click the **Save as PDF...** button.
- Enter a name for your PDF file, choose its location, and click **Save**. You're done! You've just created a PDF file that can be viewed on nearly any computer in the world.

STEP 2: VIEW, SEARCH, AND PRINT PDF FILES

Mac OS X includes two applications to view PDF files: Preview (from Apple) and Adobe Acrobat Reader. By default, PDF files you create using the Print dialog open automatically in Preview, but you can always choose to open any PDF file in either application.

- To view a PDF file, double-click it. It opens in either Preview (**Figure 8.4**) or Acrobat Reader (**Figure 8.5**), depending on how it was saved. (You can tell which it will be by looking at the icon. If it has a stylized red A and the word Adobe on it, it's an Acrobat PDF. Otherwise, it will open in

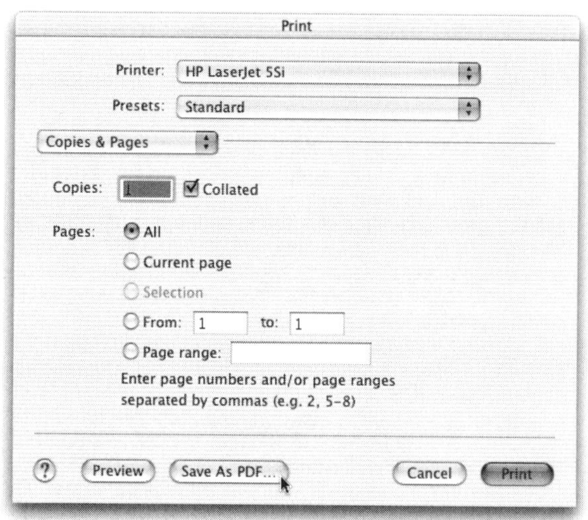

8.3

Preview.) Either program allows you to view and print PDFs.

Each program has unique advantages; which one you choose depends on your needs. Both display your image with optional thumbnails, and you can zoom in or out, and rotate individual pages. Acrobat Reader is by far the more powerful of the two, allowing you to search for text within PDF files, copy text and graphics for pasting into other applications, and use digital signatures for document security. Preview, on the other hand, has one advantage I greatly value: scroll wheel support. If your mouse or trackball has a scroll wheel, you can use it to scroll through the thumbnail list of a long PDF, and if you turn on **Continuous Scrolling** from the **View** menu, you can also use the scroll wheel to scroll through the main view of your document. (The pane that scrolls will be the one under your mouse pointer.)

- To open a PDF in an application other than its default viewer (sometimes referred to as its *creator*), right-click (or Control+click) the file in the Finder. Choose the **Open With** submenu of the contextual menu (see **Figure 8.6**) and then choose the application you want to use to open the file. (Depending on what software you have installed, this menu may contain additional choices besides Preview and Acrobat Reader.)

8.4

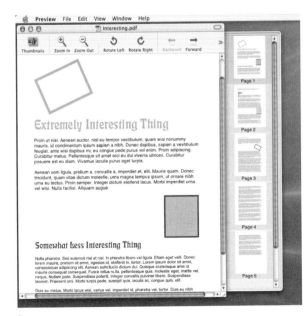

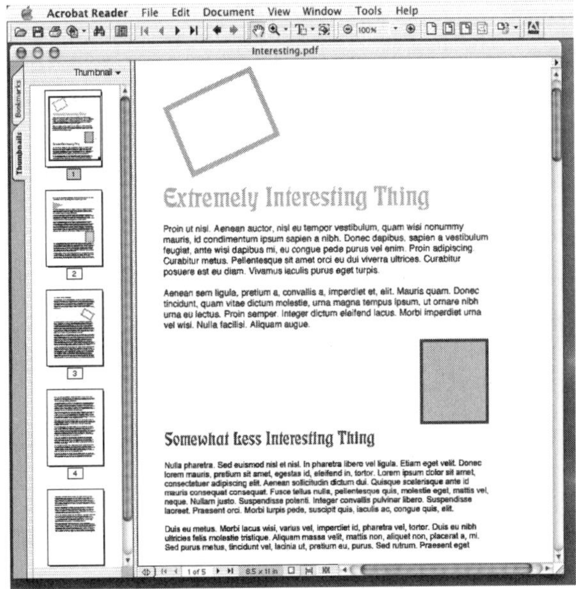

8.5

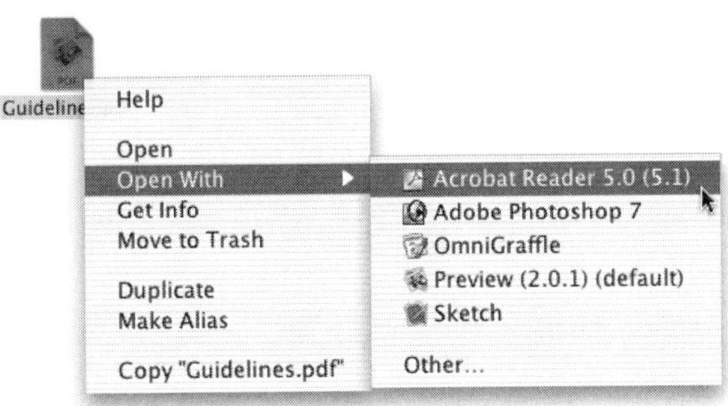

8.6

STEP 3: CHOOSE A DEFAULT APPLICATION TO OPEN PDF FILES

There may be a certain PDF that you *always* want to open in Acrobat Reader, even though it's a Preview file (or vice versa). To avoid having to use the **Open With** contextual menu every time, you can change the file's creator permanently. To do so, follow these steps:

- With the file selected in the Finder, choose **Get Info** from the **File** menu.
- Click the disclosure triangle next to **Open with** and use the pop-up menu to choose which application you want to open the file from now on. (See **Figure 8.7**.) The document's icon changes to reflect your choice.

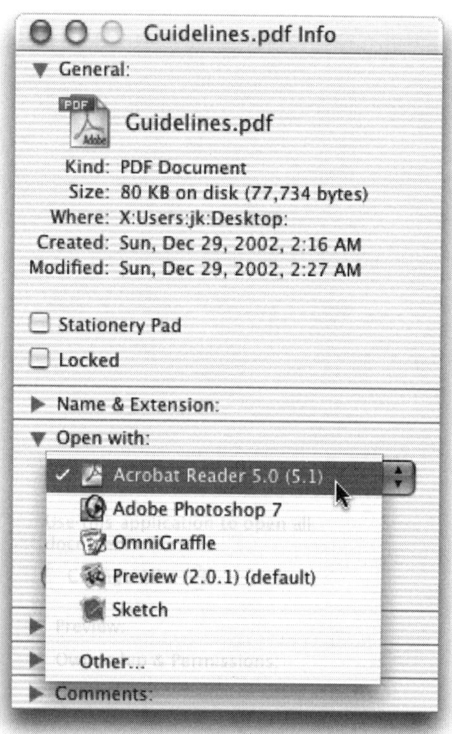

8.7

Over time, you may develop a strong preference for one application over the other and decide you want all your PDF files to open in a particular application.

- To make the change in creator apply to all PDF files, click **Change All...** and answer **Continue** to the confirmation dialog. Be aware, however, that this option affects only PDF files already on your hard drive. New files you create or download may still have a different creator.

STEP 4: USE PDF FILES AS GRAPHICS

Although PDF is great for distributing technical papers, book layouts, marketing brochures, and so on, you can also use it in place of conventional graphics formats like JPEG or TIFF. In general, you can use a PDF anywhere in Mac OS X you might normally use some other graphic. Here are some examples:

- If you have a graphics application like Photoshop or Photoshop Elements, you can open your PDF just like any other graphic and edit it in bitmap mode. If your PDF has multiple pages, you'll be asked when you open the file which page you want to use.
- Numerous other programs can't directly open PDF files, but can use them as graphics within other documents. For example, if you drag a PDF into a Microsoft Word v. X document, it will be inserted on your current page just like any other graphic. The same applies to AppleWorks and numerous other applications.
- If you installed Apple's Developer Tools (see Technique 3 for details), you'll also have a very simple graphics application called Sketch on your computer. It's located in **/Developer/Applications**. Sketch can also use PDF files if you drag and drop them into an existing window.
- Any window that has an *image well* — a small box or area where you're supposed to drag and drop a graphic — can use PDFs as well. You'll find

these boxes in Address Book, iChat, and numerous other applications.

Finally, I would be remiss if I didn't put in a plug for the full, commercial version of Adobe Acrobat. Although it's not cheap at $249, it is the only application that will let you directly edit the contents of PDF files (such as making text changes) rather than simply manipulate them as bitmap images. Acrobat is a very powerful application, yet it's also easy to use — its interface looks almost exactly like that of Acrobat Reader. If your work involves extensive use of PDF files, you'll find the investment worthwhile.

NOTE

Some Cocoa applications actually *embed* entire PDF files rather than display them as graphics. If you drag a PDF into Stickies or TextEdit, for example, you'll see the file icon in your document. These applications have the curious ability to create documents that contain other entire documents. If you were to move the file you just created to another machine (or e-mail it to a friend), you would double-click the icon in the file to open the entire PDF in Acrobat Reader or Preview.

ACCESSING YOUR MAC'S MULTILINGUAL PERSONALITY

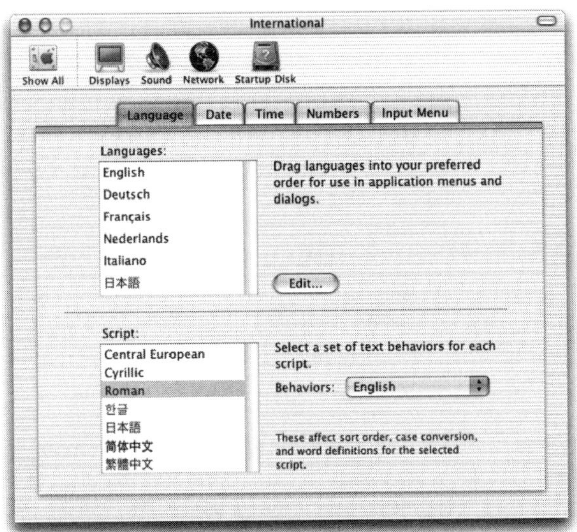

9.1

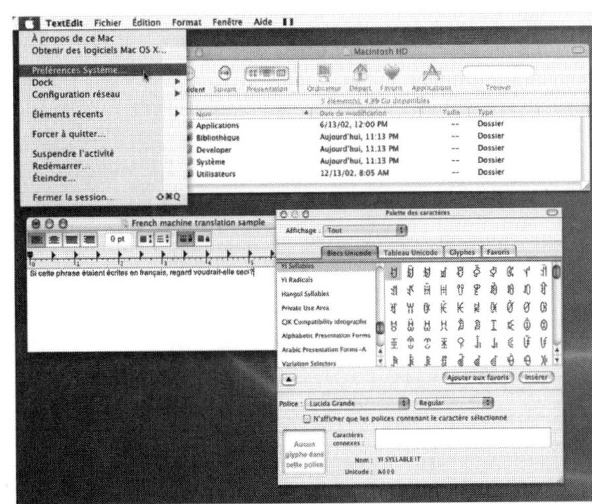

9.2

ABOUT THE FEATURE

Mac OS X includes advanced capabilities for working in a variety of languages. Even for users who work in only one language, the multilingual features offer intriguing possibilities.

Wait! Stop! I can see your eyes drifting away. If you use just a single language — especially if that languge is English — you may be saying to yourself, "Bah! I only speak English. What do I care about multilingual computing? Next chapter!" Not so fast there, Buster. The extensive language capabilities of our favorite operating system offer interesting possibilities for you — yes, *you* — even if you don't know any other languages. Of course, if you do know multiple languages, there are even niftier things to show you.

Two aspects of Mac OS X are of particular interest in this technique. The first is Unicode, a platform-neutral standard that specifies a unique number for each of tens of thousands of characters, covering the majority of the world's 6,800-plus languages. Fonts and applications designed for Unicode can — in theory at least — use any of these characters. A lot of those characters, though by no means all, are already installed on your Mac and can be put to interesting uses.

The other thing that's different about Mac OS X is that applications are designed to be *localized* — translated into other languages — much more easily than before. In fact, Mac OS X has been localized into a number of languages. Instead of having to buy a separate version of the OS if you speak, say, German, all those extra languages are already built into every copy of the OS. This means that with just a few clicks, you can convert the menus, buttons, and other controls in your Finder (and many other applications) into another language.

In this technique, you see how to put Mac OS X's multilingual features to good use. The first few steps are applicable to everyone; the last few are useful primarily if you can read more than one language.

STEP 1: ADD THE INPUT MENU

By default, most of the tools that allow Mac OS X to work with additional languages are hidden. Before you can use them you need to turn them on.

> **NOTE**
>
> **This technique makes use of a number of foreign-language files that are included as part of the default Mac OS X installation. When you installed Mac OS X, if you used all the default ("Easy Install") options, you'll be in good shape. Some people, however, choose to perform a Custom Install and deselect some components of the operating system in order to save hard drive space. If you unchecked the options Fonts for Additional Languages, Additional Asian Fonts, or Localized Files during installation, you may not be able to use all of this technique.**

- Open System Preferences and click the **International** icon; then select the **Input Menu** tab. A screen like that in **Figure 9.3** appears.

This tab lists the keyboard layouts and input methods built into Mac OS X. A *keyboard layout* is simply a map that defines which characters are typed by pressing which keys. An input method specifies how to enter characters when there are more than will fit on your keyboard (as in Japanese), or when characters change their shape depending on their position within a word (as in Arabic).

- Besides keyboard layouts and input methods for many different languages and localities, this menu contains an item called Character Palette. Click the **checkbox** next to **Character Palette** now and quit System Preferences.

Notice that a new icon has appeared on your menu bar. If you selected *only* the Character Palette, that icon will look like a rounded box; if you selected other keyboard layouts as well, it will look like a flag

9.3

representing the nationality of your primary keyboard layout (see **Figure 9.4**). Either way, this icon is called the Input Menu. Any other keyboard layouts or input methods you later choose from the Input Menu tab will be added to this menu.

STEP 2: USE THE CHARACTER PALETTE FOR DINGBATS AND SYMBOLS

I promised you that there would be something cool here even if you don't know a second language. Here it is. You probably know that some fonts on your computer, such as Symbol and Zapf Dingbats, contain special characters — math symbols, bullets, arrows, and so on. What you may not realize is that hundreds of additional symbols are hidden in portions of Unicode fonts that you cannot access just by using the keyboard.

- Open the TextEdit application.
- Go to your newly installed Input Menu and choose **Show Character Palette**. A window similar to the one shown in **Figure 9.5** appears.

This palette gives you access to every single character in every font on your computer — and thanks to Unicode, there are thousands of them. Although the Character Palette isn't as convenient to use as the keyboard, it does provide easy, categorized access to characters you only need occasionally.

- In its initial state, the Character Palette displays a list of symbol categories on the left. Click a category to display its available symbols.
- To insert any symbol into your document, highlight the symbol and click **Insert** (or just double-click the symbol).

If you insert a symbol into your document and then check to see what font it's in, you may be surprised to discover that it comes from a Chinese, Japanese, or other non-Roman font. The beauty of Character Palette is that you don't need to know which font is being used. However, in some cases, several different versions of a character are available in a variety of fonts. You may, for example, want to specify whether the symbol you insert is from a serif or sans serif font.

- Click the triangle icon in the bottom-left corner of the Character Palette to expand the window. Check the box next to **Show only fonts containing**

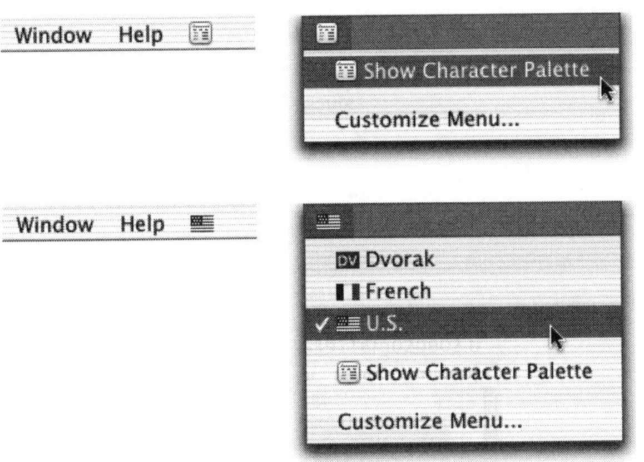

9.4

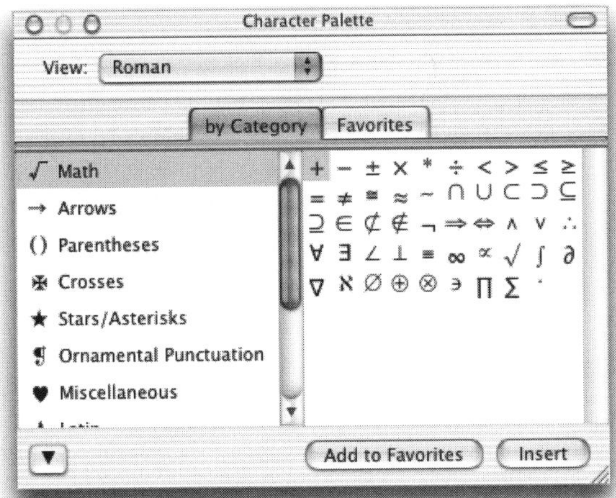

9.5

selected character, as shown in **Figure 9.6**. Now, each time you select a character, the **Font** menu will list all and only the fonts containing that character. A font listed in parentheses means it was the most recently selected font, but it does not contain your selected character.

But wait, there's more! Right now your Character Palette is only displaying symbols that are common in languages that use the Roman alphabet (like English, French, German, Spanish, and Italian).

■ To see the whole kit and caboodle, choose **All** from the pop-up **View** menu at the top of the Character Palette. Your window changes to show several tabs. Resize the window to make it larger — you'll appreciate the extra view. (See **Figure 9.7**.)

■ The left-hand pane now lists dozens of different languages and symbol groups. Scroll through these to explore thousands of additional symbols. (The **Unicode Table** tab and the **Glyph Catalog** tab give you alternative, uncategorized views of the same characters.)

Among the goodies you can find here are additional punctuation symbols, currency symbols, geometric shapes, and Enclosed Alphanumerics (letters and numbers in circles or parentheses). Linguists will also appreciate the presence of numerous IPA (International Phonetic Alphabet) symbols, such as the symbol for a labiodental nasal consonant, highlighted in **Figure 9.8**.

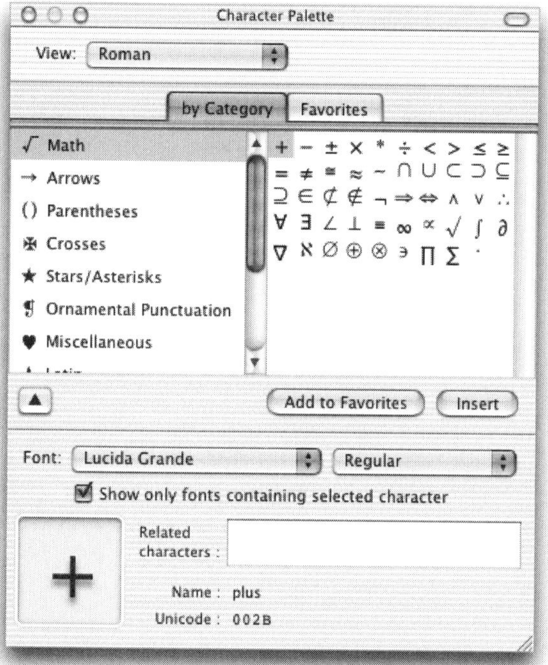

9.6

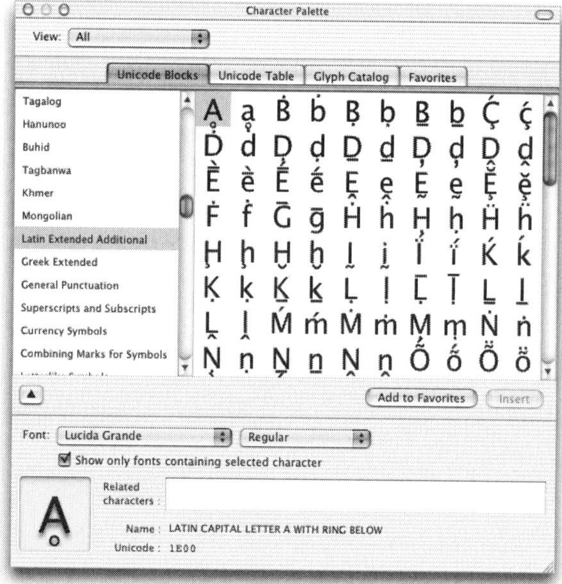

9.7

STEP 3: OBTAIN UNICODE FONTS

As you browse through the vast numbers of characters in Character Palette, you will notice a number of blank spots — and even entirely blank categories. This is because none of the fonts included with Mac OS X include all the Unicode symbols. If you want to fill in some of the blanks, you need to obtain fonts with more of the symbols.

Luckily, a number of Unicode fonts are on the market — including several free ones. Though none of the free fonts contain *all* the Unicode characters, you can certainly get quite a few more than the standard Mac OS X installation. Following are some sources for Unicode fonts:

- The official Unicode Web site has a page of links for all sorts of font and keyboard resources: `www.unicode.org/unicode/onlinedat/resources.html`.
- The Bitstream Cyberbit font contains an astonishing 29,934 different glyphs (characters), and you can download it for free from `ftp://ftp.netscape.com/pub/communicator/extras/fonts/windows/Cyberbit.ZIP`. Don't be put off by the fact that it claims to be a Windows font. It works fine on Mac OS X, too.
- The TITUS Cyberbit font has fewer characters (9,568) but includes some that the Bitstream Cyberbit does not. It's free for noncommercial use from `titus.fkidg1.uni-frankfurt.de/unicode/tituut.asp`.

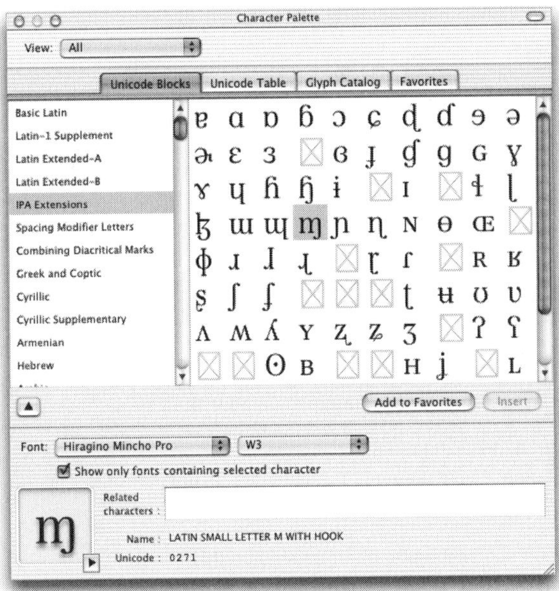

9.8

After you've downloaded or purchased a font, you need to install it by placing it in the main Fonts folder. In Mac OS 9, you could do this by dragging the file onto your closed System Folder. In Mac OS X, you must drag it directly into the proper location.

- To install a font, drag the file (typically ending in .TTF for TrueType font) to **/Library/Fonts**. You may need to quit and reopen running applications to make use of your new fonts.

STEP 4: SWITCH LANGUAGES

If English is your only language, you can skip this step — unless you're just curious (or want to play a prank on your friends). In this final step, you learn how to change the entire Mac OS X user interface — menus, buttons, and all — into another language.

Mac OS X includes all the files necessary to run the operating system, as well as enter and edit text, in more than a dozen languages, and that list is growing.

However, a word of caution: The fact that Mac OS X can run in multiple languages does not mean that all your *applications* can. Each application must be individually localized for every supported language. So you are likely to find that if you switch the language of your operating system, some parts of it will remain in English.

- Open System Preferences and click the **International** icon. Select the **Language** tab, as shown in **Figure 9.9**.

The top list contains all the languages for which the necessary files have been installed on your system. If you chose to deselect Asian languages during installation, for example, they will be missing from this list. Although these languages are the only ones in which Mac OS X is available, individual applications might be available in additional languages. (To add languages to this list — just in case a localized Gaelic or Esperanto version of your favorite utility happens to appear — click **Edit...** and select additional languages from the list that appears. Curiously, Klingon — `www.kli.org` — does not appear in the list.)

- To switch the primary language of your computer, click a language in the list and drag it to the top. If you can read multiple languages, arrange the list in the order of your level of proficiency. For example, if you are fluent in French but can also get by in German, put **Français** first, then **Deutsch**, and then **English**. This way, if a given application has not been localized into your first-choice language but *has* been localized into another on the list, it will be displayed in the first available language listed.
- Choose **Log Out** from the Apple menu to log out. Then log back in, entering your normal user name and password.

Your Mac now features menus and dialogs in your chosen language. **Figure 9.10** shows what some parts of the interface look like in French. Notice that some things are still in English, because not every application has been localized into French.

- You can switch languages back at any point by returning to the **Language** tab and reordering the languages. Remember to log out and log back in for your changes to take effect.

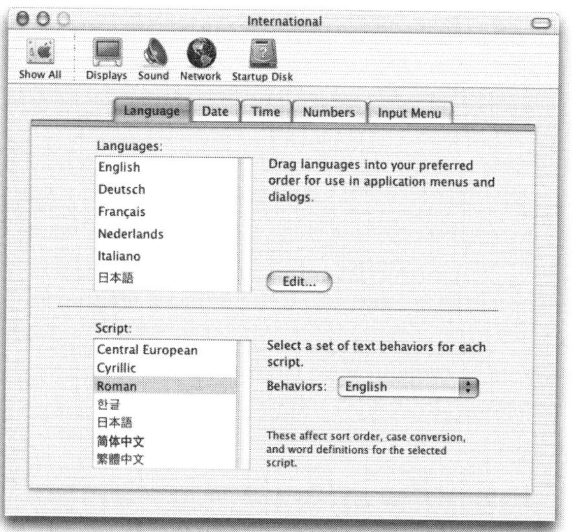

9.9

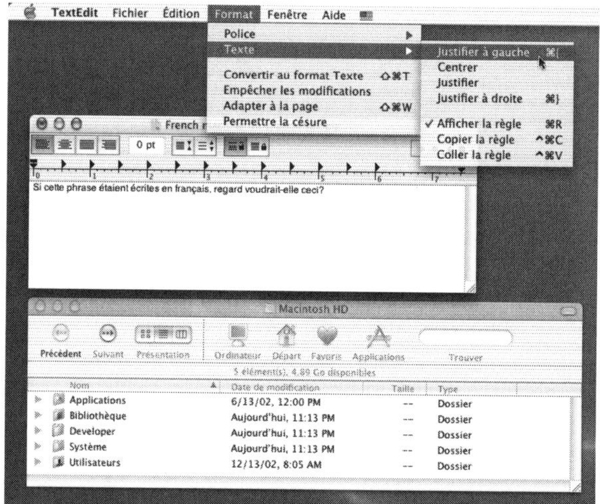

9.10

CUSTOMIZING MAC OS X

Mac users have always been a creative bunch. One way that creativity manifests itself is in the way we like to customize our computers. Nearly every aspect of Mac OS X can be adjusted, enhanced, or otherwise tweaked to suit your personality and your individual style of working. Some modifications are just for fun, while others can boost your productivity, save you time, and make your Mac a genuine partner in your work.

The techniques covered in this chapter all involve some sort of customization. Whether it's sprucing up your toolbars with additional icons, turning your desktop into an animated aquarium, or bringing back your favorite interface features from Mac OS 9, the next several techniques can help you to make your Mac truly personal. Some of the techniques even contradict each other a bit ("Add more icons to your Dock! No, wait — remove them all!"), but that reflects the delightful reality that we all "think different." Choose the techniques that best fit your needs and interests.

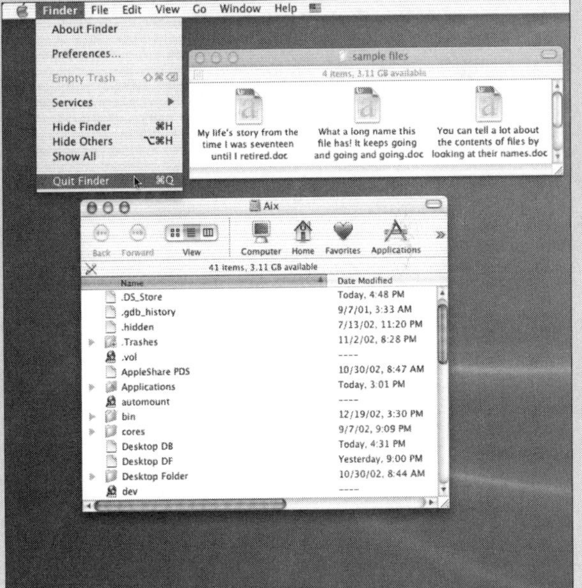

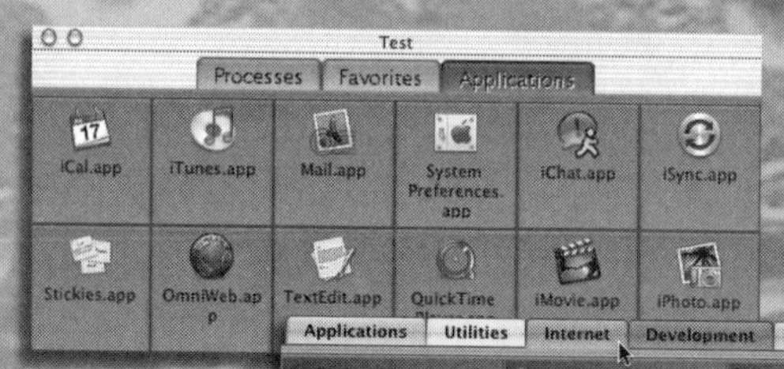

Desktop Pictures

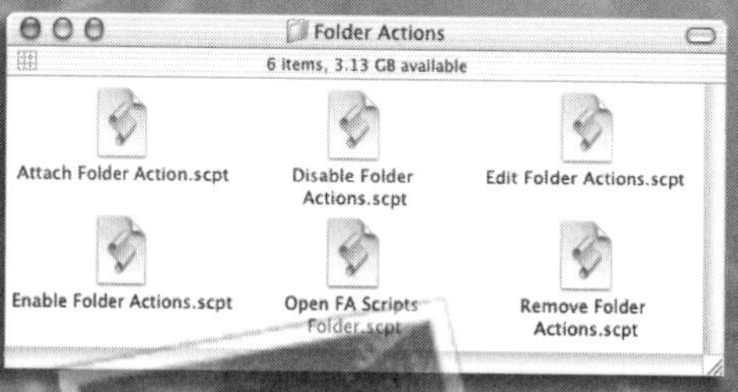

TECHNIQUE **10**

PUTTING MORE "TOOL" IN YOUR TOOLBARS

10.1

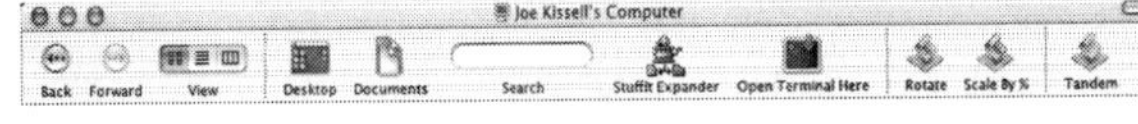

10.2

ABOUT THE FEATURE

Every Finder window contains a customizable area called the toolbar, which can give you quick access to navigation, searching, and file management tools. Toolbars are most effective when personalized to meet your needs.

All Finder windows have an area at the top known as the toolbar, as shown in **Figure 10.1**. Along with the Dock, this is one of the most striking changes from Mac OS 9's Finder appearance. And like the Dock, it is highly customizable, though its power is rarely exploited. In this technique, you see just how valuable toolbars can be.

You must first understand a couple of basics. First, every Finder window has the *same* toolbar — changes you make to one affect all of them. Second, you can selectively hide or show the toolbar for each window. To toggle toolbars on or off, you can either click the little pill-shaped button on the right side of the window's title bar or choose **Hide Toolbar** or **Show Toolbar** (as appropriate) from the **View** menu.

Toolbar buttons require only one click to use, just like icons in the Dock (and unlike the rest of the Finder). A single click on the Home button, for example, displays the contents of your home folder. You can also use drag-and-drop on toolbar buttons, so dragging a file onto the Home button on your toolbar moves it to your home folder. Likewise, dragging a file to an application icon on your toolbar opens the file in that application.

STEP 1: REMOVE TOOLS YOU NEVER USE

The first step in having a useful toolbar is to get rid of all icons you don't use. By default, Finder toolbars display, from left to right, Back and Forward buttons, a View selector, a divider; then buttons for your Computer, Home, Favorites, and Applications folders, respectively; and finally a Search box. (If your window is too narrow to display them all, click the chevron (») icon to display a pop-up menu with the remaining choices, as shown in **Figure 10.3**.) You can remove or rearrange all these elements — and, of course, you can easily restore them if you change your mind.

- Decide whether to eliminate the heart-shaped Favorites button. Because you have lots of places to keep aliases to favorite files and other easy ways to access them, this button might be superfluous. To remove it, hold down the ⌘ key and drag the button off the toolbar.
- Consider removing the View selector. Although you may change window views frequently, it's very easy to do by using menu commands on the **View** menu (or their keyboard equivalents). The extra space might come in handy; if you think so, you can ⌘+drag off the View selector as well.
- Pay attention to the buttons you use regularly. The **Computer**, **Home**, and **Applications** buttons are more a matter of personal work habits. By using the other techniques in this chapter and the next one, I've found that I rarely need to open any of those folders — and when I do, several other quick shortcuts can do the trick. However, your mileage may vary. If you don't use a given button at least a few times a week, consider removing it. You'll be glad for the extra space shortly.

TIP

Toolbars make the most sense with relatively wide windows because the icons don't shrink like those in the Dock do. You might find that Column View, which also works best with wide windows, is a good partner for your new toolbars.

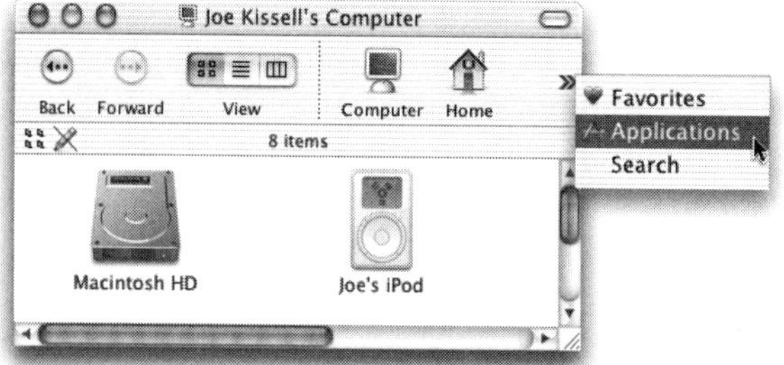

10.3

STEP 2: ADD TOOLS FROM APPLE'S COLLECTION

Now that you've cleared some space, fill it up with buttons that might be a bit more useful. Although you can add any icon on your computer to a toolbar, Apple supplies some special buttons that you might want to start with. To display them, right-click (or Control+click) on any part of the toolbar and choose **Customize Toolbar** from the contextual menu. The window changes (**Figure 10.4**) to reveal a wide variety of buttons from which you can choose.

TIP

Whatever else you do, I recommend leaving the Back and Forward buttons and the Search box. They come in handy in other techniques.

■ To add a button, simply drag it to the toolbar. You can arrange buttons in any order, and you can also drag to rearrange ones already there. The first item from this group you might consider is the Path control. Displaying your current folder's location within the file system has always been possible by ⌘+clicking the window title (**Figure 10.5**). This control does exactly the same thing, but without requiring you to use your other hand to hold down an extra key (**Figure 10.6**).

Beyond that, it's again a matter of which buttons, if any, appeal to your needs and style of working. I suggest, though, that you bypass the **Delete** button. As the name suggests, clicking this button deletes any selected files (by moving them to the Trash). However, doing this requires two clicks (select the file, then click the button). In a moment, I'll show you how you can add a Trash icon to your toolbar to delete files with a single click-and-drag.

■ When you're finished making changes, click **Done** to return your window to its normal state.

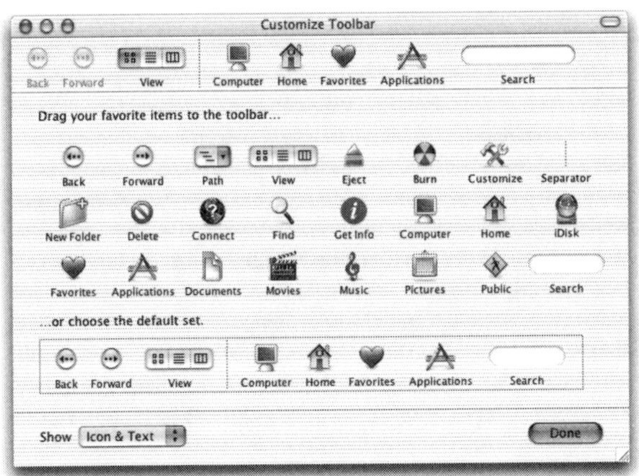

10.4

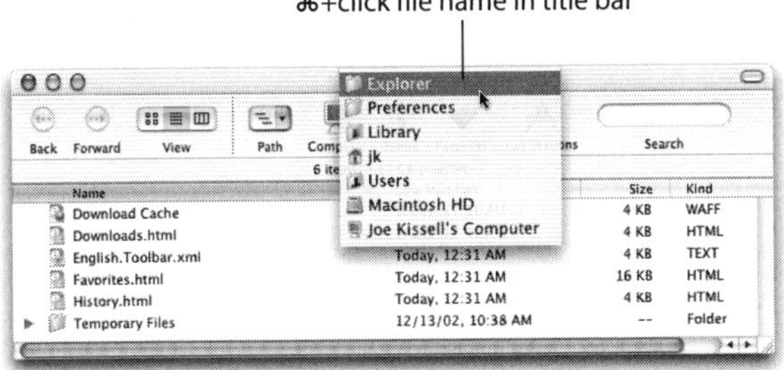

10.5

STEP 3: ADD YOUR OWN TOOLS

It's time to get creative and select icons of your own to add to the toolbar. These should be folders, files, or applications you want to use frequently. How do you decide which icons should go in the toolbar and which should go in the Dock? There's no magic formula (and no reason icons can't go both places). As a general rule, though, it makes the most sense for the icons in a Finder toolbar to be ones that open specific folders or act on files, whereas the Dock is a better place for applications (and folders or volumes you want to navigate quickly without opening any new windows). **Figure 10.7** shows a toolbar with the following useful icons added:

- ■ Desktop (displays the contents of your desktop folder)
- ■ Documents (displays the contents of your Documents folder)
- ■ StuffIt Expander (expands any file using drag-and-drop)

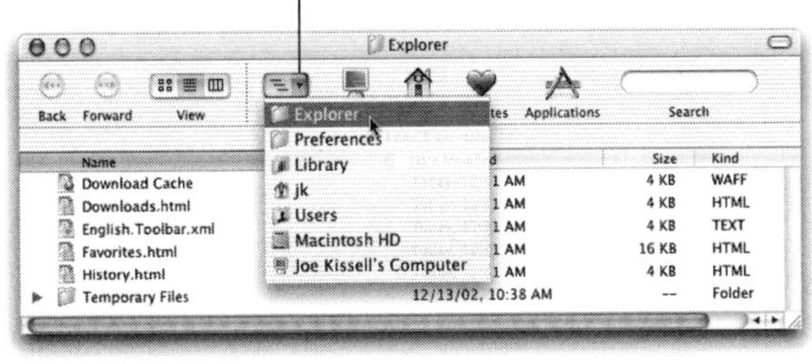

10.6

10.7

STEP 4: ADD THE TRASH TO YOUR TOOLBAR

If the **Delete** button that Apple provides as a built-in toolbar option doesn't quite cut it for you, put a Trash icon in your toolbar for conventional drag-and-drop file deletion. Here's how:

- Select any folder on your hard drive (or create a new one). Make an alias to this folder by pressing **⌘+L**. Name this new alias **Trash**.
- With the Trash alias selected, choose **Get Info** from the **File** menu. Click **Select New Original**.
- When the Open sheet appears, type `~/.Trash` and press **Return**. You'll notice that a folder called `.Trash` is highlighted, even though it's dimmed as being unavailable, as shown in **Figure 10.8**. Click **Choose** to reassign your new alias to the Trash. (Leave the Info window open for now.)
- You now have a folder alias pointing to the Trash, but it doesn't *look* like the Trash. To solve that, click the Trash icon in your Dock to open the Trash window. With no files selected, choose **Get Info** from the **File** menu to display the Trash info. Now click the icon in the Trash's Info window and press **⌘+C** to copy it. Switch to the Info window for your new alias, click the folder icon to select it, and press **⌘+V** to paste. Your alias should now look like the Trash (albeit with an arrow in the corner). You can close both Info windows.
- Last but not least, move it to a location where you won't accidentally delete it — perhaps your Documents folder. (If you miss having a Trash icon on your desktop, you can, of course, keep it there.)
- Now drag your new alias to the toolbar and you're done! **Figure 10.9** shows the final product. To use the toolbar Trash icon, drag files into it just as you would to the Dock's Trash. You'll notice that your toolbar Trash icon does not change to show that it has files in it, and even the real Trash icon in the Dock might not reflect the change until you click it. In addition, you cannot use this icon to eject removable media. But for deleting files quickly, you'll find that dragging them a short distance onto the toolbar rather than all the way to the Dock is generally quicker and easier.

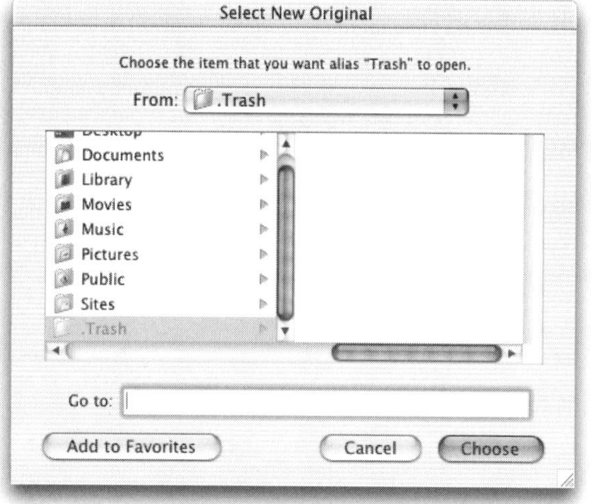

10.8

STEP 5: CHANGE THE DISPLAY MODE (OPTIONAL)

As you add icons to your toolbar, you may find it gets very crowded. You have three options for adjusting the display of your toolbar, and you can choose whichever one makes the most sense to you. The three options (Icon & Text Mode, Icon Only Mode, and Text Only Mode) are shown in **Figure 10.10**.

- If your Customize Toolbar sheet is open, you can change modes by choosing the one you want from the **Show** pop-up menu in the lower-left corner.

10.9

- If your Customize Toolbar sheet is closed, the quickest way to change modes is to right-click (or Control+click) on the toolbar and make your selection from the contextual menu that appears.

STEP 6: USE TOOLBAR SCRIPTS

AppleScript is Apple's easy-to-learn scripting language. Using tools such as Script Editor or the more powerful AppleScript Studio (included with the Developer Tools you installed in Technique 3), anyone can create powerful programs without having to study a complex, low-level language. AppleScript is ideal for manipulating files and folders in the Finder, and an AppleScript application can, like other applications, appear in your toolbar. Apple (and some third parties) have designed a number of AppleScripts, known as *toolbar scripts,* that are specially suited for use in toolbars. You are *not* going to learn AppleScript here. Instead, you find out where to find toolbar scripts other people have created and use them on your own toolbars.

- The first place to look is on Apple's Web site. Go to `www.apple.com/applescript/toolbar/`, where Apple has posted a large selection of scripts you can download, along with directions for using them.
- After you've downloaded a script and stored it somewhere safe (like your Documents folder), drag it onto a toolbar to install it. **Figure 10.11** shows a toolbar with a few of these scripts added.

10.10

- Some scripts are designed to function as a droplet (drag and drop a file onto it to process that file), and some are designed as applets (just click it and it will act on the entire contents of the window, or on selected files). Some can work either way. Read the instructions for each script to determine how it is intended to be used.
- One of my favorite toolbar scripts is Rotate Image(s), which changes the orientation of pictures from my digital camera right in the Finder — without opening Photoshop or even iPhoto. (This feature is especially effective in combination with Column View's Preview column.)
- Another favorite script comes not from Apple but from a developer named Marc Linyage. His Open Terminal Here toolbar script (available free at `www.entropy.ch/software/applescript/welcome.html`) is shown in **Figure 10.12**. One click, and a new Terminal window opens, with its working directory already changed to the current folder.
- To find more toolbar scripts, visit `www.versiontracker.com`. Click the Mac OS X tab and search for "toolbar script."

10.11

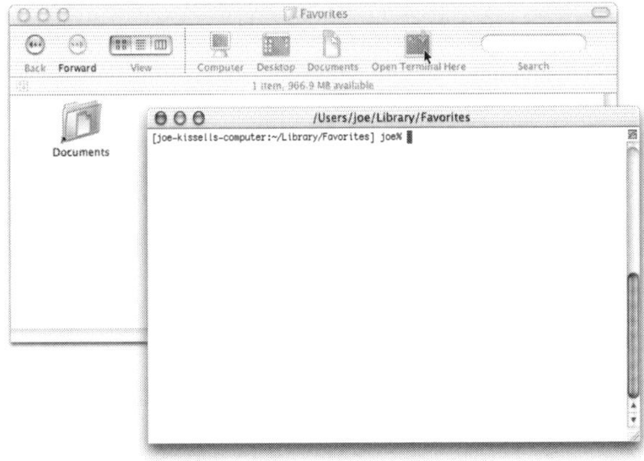

10.12

TECHNIQUE 11

ENHANCING THE LOOK AND FUNCTIONALITY OF YOUR WINDOWS

11.1

11.2

ABOUT THE FEATURE

Finder windows are both beautiful and functional with their array of Aqua controls and high-tech drop shadows. By taking a few extra steps, you can make them downright fun — and even more useful.

Mac OS X provides plenty of options for customizing your windows. Not only can customization make your Mac a lot more fun and interesting to look at, it gives you visual cues that help you locate particular windows and icons quickly.

Before you get to the technique, you should be aware of a sometimes confusing aspect of the Aqua interface: Windows and folders are two very different things. Using the words *window* and *folder* interchangeably is tempting (and I sometimes do). After all, every time you open a folder it shows up in its own window, right? Well, sort of — but in Mac OS X, you can have several windows open at the same time that display the contents of the same folder, and all of those windows can have different sizes, views, and other attributes. In addition, every time you press ⌘+N, you open a new window — but without opening any particular folder. So what are you really customizing here, folders or windows? And how can you tell which attributes will be saved when?

What you're actually customizing is the window attributes that are used by particular folders. If you open a folder, change the attributes of the window that appears, and then close the window, those attributes will be saved in that folder. The next time you open that folder, it displays in the same size, location, view, and so on as when you last saw it. If you have *just one window* open in the Finder, make changes to it, and close it, those settings will be used every time you open a new Finder window.

If you want to be sure the changes you make to a window affect only one folder, make sure it's not the *only* folder with an open window when you modify and close it. Conversely, if you really do want to change the attributes of all new windows, make sure the window you're modifying is the only one open at the time.

STEP 1: ADD A FOLDER BACKGROUND

Have you ever downloaded a piece of software, double-clicked the disk image, and seen something like **Figure 11.3**? It looks like a window, but not like any window on your computer. How did it get that way? Is this some black art that only Mac developers are privy to? Not at all. You, too, can customize the living daylights out of any window. Apart from the fact that it's a fun way to impress your Windows-using friends, customizing window backgrounds can be useful. If you have lots of windows open at once, picking out the one you're looking for is easy if it has a distinctive appearance. To customize a Finder window, do the following:

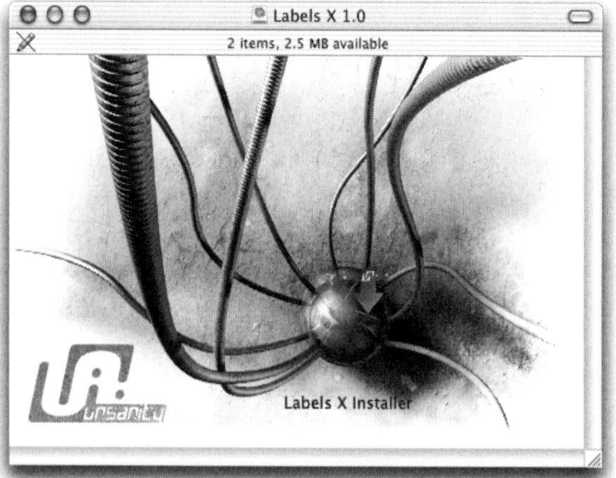

11.3

- First, prepare a graphic to be used for the background. This can be a photo from your iPhoto collection, a PDF file, a JPEG downloaded from the Web, or a drawing you created from scratch. There's just one catch: You need to make it the correct size for your window. When you place a graphic on your window background, it is not resized or scaled. A picture from your digital camera that's 1600 × 1200 pixels, for example, would show only a small corner when placed in a window. If you're starting with a large photo, use your favorite graphics program (GraphicConverter, Photoshop Elements, or whatever you have handy) to resize your image to dimensions that will fit comfortably in a modestly sized window — try 300 × 400 pixels as a first pass.
- Open the folder you want to customize. Be sure the window is in Icon View; background graphics can't be used in List View or Column View. The shortcut to activate Icon View is **⌘+1**.
- Press **⌘+J** (or choose **Show View Options** from the **View** menu) to display View Options. A floating window like the one in **Figure 11.4** appears.
- Make sure **This window only** is selected at the top if you don't want this picture to appear on the background of every single window. Click the **Picture** radio button at the very bottom of the window and then click **Select** and navigate to the graphic you prepared. After selecting the graphic, click **Select**. Your graphic will automagically be placed on the background of your window, as in **Figure 11.5**.

- Using the resize box in the lower-right corner of the window, resize the window so that the edges of the graphic are just covered.
- If your graphic is too large or too small, resize it in your graphics application and repeat the preceding procedure.
- If you don't have any appropriate pictures handy, you can still spruce up your windows by adding a solid color background. In the **View Options** window, click **Color** instead of **Picture** and use the color picker to select your favorite color.

STEP 2: USE CUSTOM ICONS

You can give any file or folder a unique, custom icon. As with window backgrounds, this can be more than decoration — it can help you easily pick out important folders in a window full of plain blue icons.

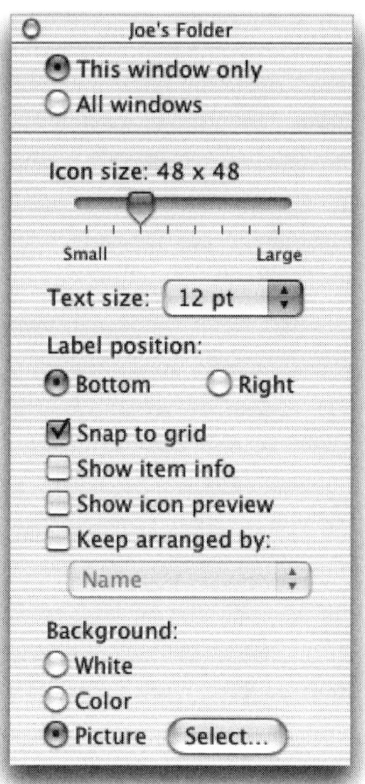

11.4

Custom icons are especially useful if you add multiple folder or volume icons to your Dock or toolbars.

Custom icons are easy to find. Sites such as `www.xicons.com` and `www.iconfactory.com` each have thousands of high-quality Mac OS X icons you can download for free.

- Download the packages you're interested in and unstuff them.
- Select a file that has an icon you want to use. Press ⌘+I (or choose **Get Info** from the File menu).
- Click the icon in the Info window to select it and press ⌘+C to copy it. Close the Info window.
- Now select the file or folder you want to use your new icon on. Once again, press ⌘+I to display the Info window. Select the icon and press ⌘+V to paste your new icon over it. This is illustrated in **Figure 11.6**.

11.5

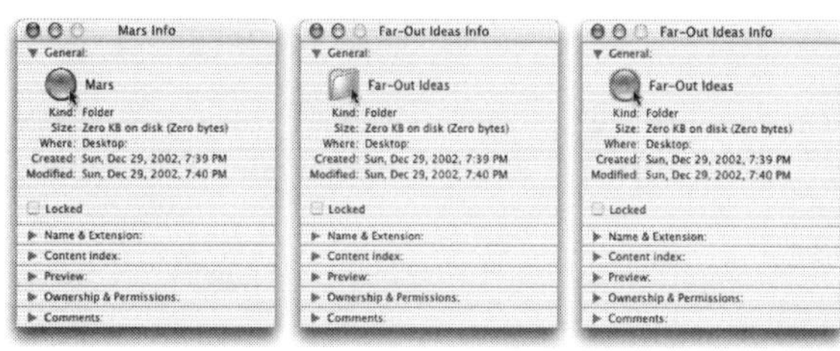

11.6

- If you ever want to remove your custom icon and revert to the default icon, just select the icon in the Info window and press **Delete**.

Although custom-designed icons often look best, you can use *any* graphic on your hard drive — including PDF files — as an icon. If you have a favorite photograph, drawing, or even a tax form you want to turn into an icon, it's easy.

- Open the file you want to use in Preview. (If it's a multi-page PDF, select the page you want to use in the Thumbnail view on the right.) Press **⌘+C** to copy the graphic.
- Select the icon in the Info window of the file or folder you want to customize and press **⌘+V** to paste.
- All your graphics files can also have instant custom icons. In any folder containing graphics files, choose **Show View Options** from the **View** menu. Click the **Show icon preview** checkbox, and each graphic icon in that folder turns into a miniature version of the entire image. See **Figure 11.7** for an example.

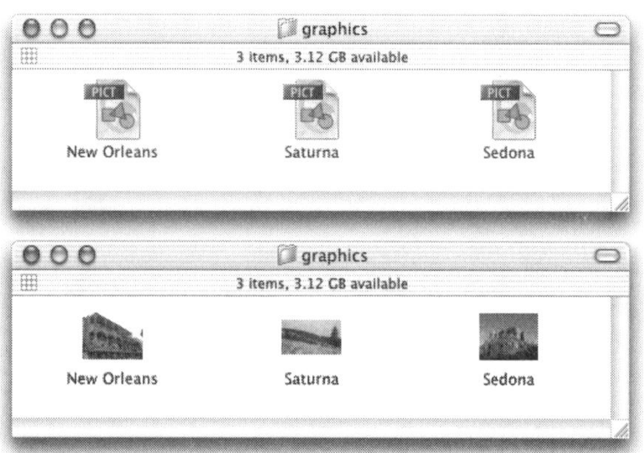

11.7

STEP 3: CUSTOMIZE ICON VIEW WINDOW LAYOUT

The View Options window has some additional controls for customizing your window display that I haven't mentioned yet. The options available vary depending on which view is active. First, you'll customize options for a window in Icon View (because that's what you've just been working with); then look at List View. Most of the layout options are self-explanatory, so I'll just mention them briefly.

- With the folder of your choice open and in Icon View, choose **Show View Options** from the **View** menu. Make sure the radio button next to **This window only** is selected at the top.
- Change the size of the icons in this window from mini to maxi (or anywhere in between) by moving the **Icon size** slider.
- Choose a larger or smaller font for filenames, if you want, from the **Text size** pop-up menu.
- If you prefer the filename to appear on the right, rather than underneath the icons, click the **Right** radio button beneath **Label position**. **Figure 11.8** shows a window with extra-large icons, a large font, and filename displayed on the right.
- Check **Snap to grid** to keep all your icons neatly aligned on an invisible grid.

TIP

You can use all the View customizations you've just tried on the desktop, too. Just click anywhere on your desktop, choose Show View Options from the View menu, and go to town.

■ If you check **Show item info**, an additional line of text will appear below the names of certain files, as shown in **Figure 11.9**. Folders, for example, will show the number of items they contain, graphics (of certain types) will show their dimensions in pixels, and audio files will display their length.

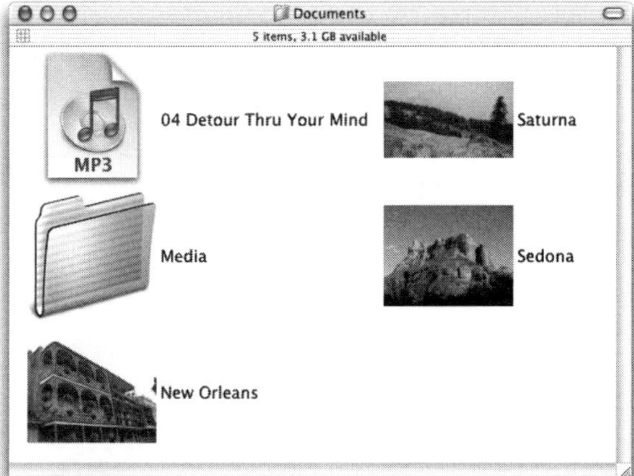

11.8

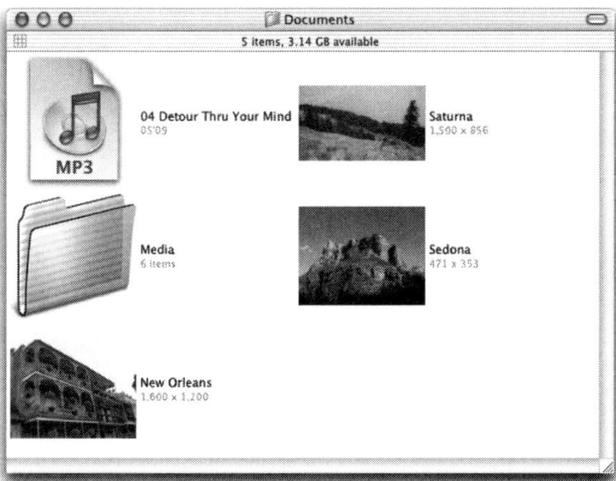

11.9

■ Finally, if you want your icons to organize themselves even when files are added or removed from the window, check **Keep arranged by** and choose **Name**, **Date Modified**, **Date Created**, **Size**, or **Kind**.

STEP 4: CUSTOMIZE LIST VIEW WINDOW LAYOUT

For windows in List View, you have some different options, as shown in **Figure 11.10**.

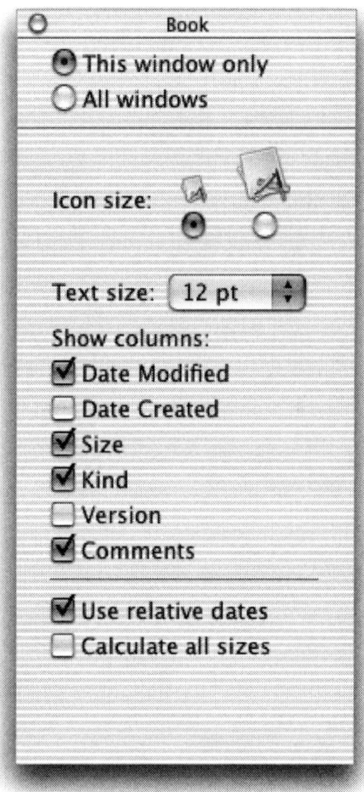

11.10

- Choose a larger size for List View icons, if you want, by clicking the radio button beneath the larger icon.
- You can choose which columns are shown for this window by checking the checkboxes next to the attributes you want to see. Of particular interest may be **Comments**. Displaying the Comments column in List View is the only way to see comments you've entered about files without opening the Info window.
- Every column header in List View is also a button that you can use to sort the window contents by that attribute. For example, click the **Date Modified** column header to sort files by date; click the **Name** header to sort by name. Clicking any header a second time reverses the sort order.
- You can also resize columns in List View to show more or less information. Position your pointer on the dividing line between two columns, and its shape will change to a vertical line with a pair of arrows. Click and drag left or right to change the column width.
- Finally, you can arrange columns. The only restriction is that the **Name** column must come first. If you would rather see the **Kind** column, for example, before the **Size**, you can easily do so. Click and hold the mouse button on a column heading, and when it changes to a "grabbing hand" shape, drag the column left or right to reposition it.

Figure 11.11 shows a window in List View with customized columns and icon size. For even more ways to customize your windows, see Technique 17, "Restoring 'Missing' Classic Features to Mac OS X."

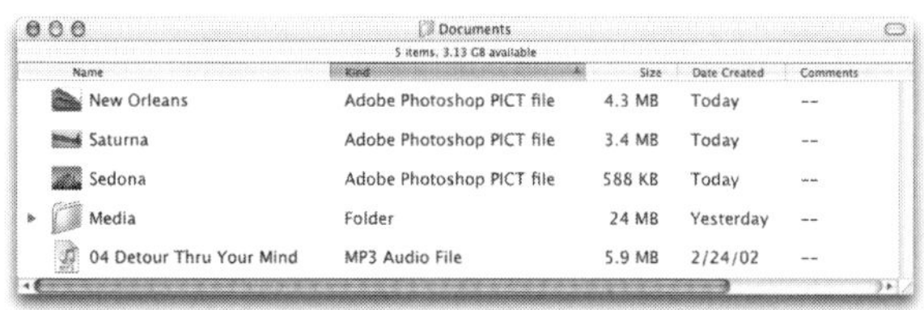

11.11

TECHNIQUE 12

AUTOMATING THE FINDER WITH SCRIPTS AND FOLDER ACTIONS

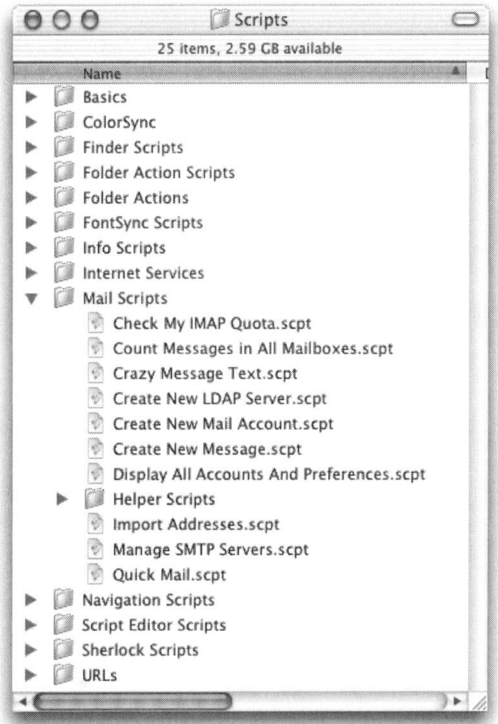

12.1

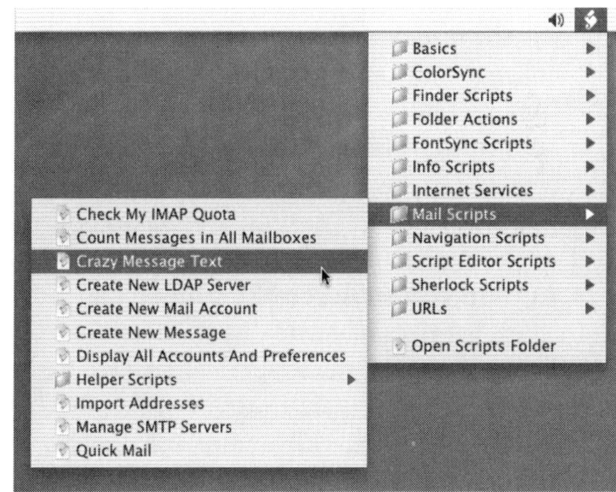

12.2

ABOUT THE FEATURE

AppleScript provides a convenient way to automate repetitive tasks without learning a lot of programming. Mac OS X includes two hidden features — the Script menu and folder actions — that make scripts even easier to use.

If you read Technique 10, "Putting More 'Tool' in Your Toolbars," you're already familiar with the idea of using AppleScript applications to add capabilities to your Finder windows. In this technique, you again use AppleScripts in the Finder, but in two different ways. First, you add a menu to the Finder toolbar to provide single-click access to your favorite scripts. Then you explore a super-cool (and little-used) Mac OS X feature called *folder actions.*

You can do everything in this technique without knowing any AppleScript at all. However, if you want to take these concepts further, you'll need to learn some AppleScript programming.

STEP 1: INSTALL SCRIPT MENU

Apple included a system-wide menu for AppleScripts in Mac OS X. However, probably thinking it would be confusing to beginning users, they left it deactivated by default. Before you do anything else, turn it on.

- Open the **AppleScript** folder inside your **Applications** folder. You'll see a folder icon named **ScriptMenu.menu**. Drag this icon to your menu bar (near your clock) and release the mouse button. The new scroll-shaped Script menu now appears on your menu bar, as shown in **Figure 12.3**.
- Click this menu to see a number of submenus filled with useful sample scripts supplied by Apple. Feel free to take some time to try out any that look interesting to you. A few fun (and somewhat useful) examples include the following:
  - **Current Date & Time** on the **Info Scripts** submenu opens a window showing the current date and time, with an optional button to copy this information to the clipboard.
  - **Current Temperature by Zipcode** on the **Internet Services** submenu displays a box for you to enter your current Zip code. After you've done so, the script checks a weather site on the Web, gets the current temperature, and displays it in another window.
  - **Crazy Message Text** on the **Mail Scripts** submenu (see **Figure 12.4**) asks you to enter some text, which it then uses to create a new Mail message in a wacky assortment of fonts, sizes, and colors. The result is shown in **Figure 12.5** (CP.2).

12.3

You will use a few other scripts in a moment.

Remember, AppleScripts are just mini-programs. An AppleScript may not have windows or controls of its own (though many do). Because AppleScripts are so varied, the best way to find out what a given script does is to try it out.

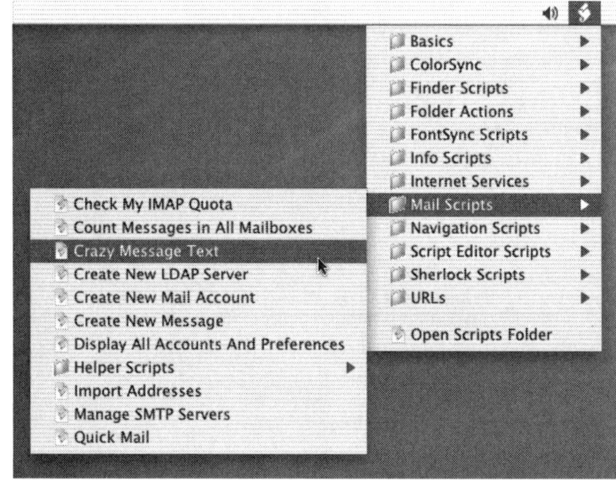

12.4

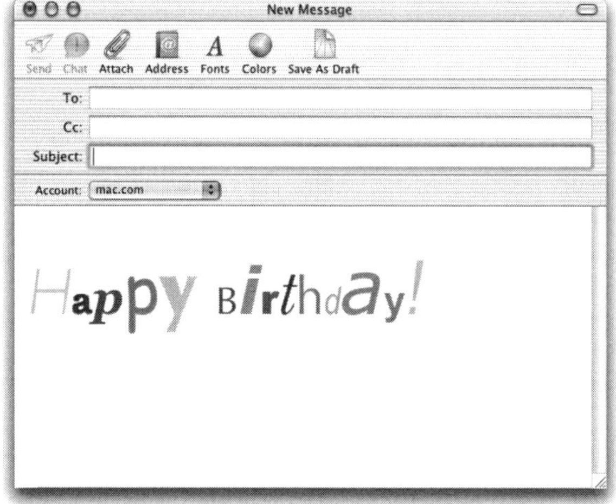

12.5

STEP 2: ADD NEW SCRIPTS

Although Apple's sample scripts are interesting, you can download hundreds of other scripts that will give you an astonishing array of features. (Note that the Scripts menu supports not only AppleScripts but also shell scripts and perl scripts.)

Here are a few sources for downloading new scripts:

- Apple's own AppleScript site at `www.apple.com/applescript/script_menu/` has a few additional scripts you can download.
- The sites `www.applescriptcentral.com` and `www.macscripter.net` both have large collections of AppleScripts and AppleScript-related information contributed by people from all over the world.
- Let's not forget our old standby, VersionTracker. Visit `www.versiontracker.com`, click the Mac OS X tab, and search for AppleScript for dozens of additional scripts.

After you have the new scripts, what do you do with them? You'll need to put them where the Script menu can find them.

- Move your new scripts to the **/Library/Scripts** folder. They should appear immediately on the **Script** menu. (To avoid making the menu too unwieldy, you might want to consider grouping your new scripts into folders, or placing them in an existing folder if appropriate.)

STEP 3: INSTALL FOLDER ACTIONS SCRIPTS

Now that you've activated the Script menu, you can explore an even more powerful way of using AppleScripts: *folder actions*. A folder action is a script that's "attached" to a folder so that it runs automatically when the folder changes in some way. Depending on what the script is designed to do, it can run when the folder window is opened, closed, or moved, or when items are added or removed from the folder — even if it's closed.

Just to give you a general idea of the possibilities, here are some examples of things you could do with folder actions.

- Run a series of Photoshop filters automatically on every file dropped into a certain folder.
- Convert audio, video, or graphics files to a different format or sort them into different folders depending on their attributes.
- Mail, upload, or compress files dropped on a folder without any further steps.
- Display an alert box when the content of a folder changes.
- Prevent a folder window from ever being moved or closed.

I should warn you right here that these possibilities, while intriguing, do come at a certain cost. Unless someone has already written exactly the script you need for your ideal folder action, you'll need to learn a bit of AppleScript to create your own (or at least modify someone else's script). AppleScript is not hard to learn, but it does take some time to understand and become proficient with it. The Web sites listed in **Step 1** point you to some great online and print resources for learning AppleScript.

That said, now you can get your feet wet. Although support for folder actions is built into Mac OS X, Apple suggests that you download an updated set of control scripts before beginning to work with them. Download and install these now.

- Enter **www.apple.com/applescript/folder_actions/FA_archive.sit** into your Web browser and press **Return**. The updated scripts download to your computer. Unstuff the archive (if it doesn't happen automatically). A folder containing six scripts appears, as shown in **Figure 12.6**.

■ Open the **/Library/Scripts** folder. It should look something like **Figure 12.7**. Open the **Folder Actions** folder and drag all four scripts inside it (*Attach Script to Folder.scpt, Remove Folder Actions.scpt, Disable Folder Actions.scpt, and Enable Folder Actions.scpt*) to the Trash. Now drag the six scripts from the **FA_archive** folder you just downloaded into the **Folder Actions** folder. You can close the Scripts window.

■ Click the **Script** menu and choose the **Folder Actions** submenu, where you can now see the six scripts you just installed. Choose **Enable Folder Actions.** An alert box appears to confirm that folder actions have been enabled.

STEP 4: ATTACH AND TRY OUT A FOLDER ACTION

Pick a folder, any folder. Attach one of Apple's sample folder action scripts to this folder and try it out, just to see how it's done.

■ Choose **Folder Actions** from the Script menu; then choose **Attach Folder Action** from the submenu. A dialog appears asking you to choose a Folder Action. (Initially, this list contains only the three sample scripts Apple provides, but you will see how to add your own shortly.) Select **add - new item alert** and click **OK**.

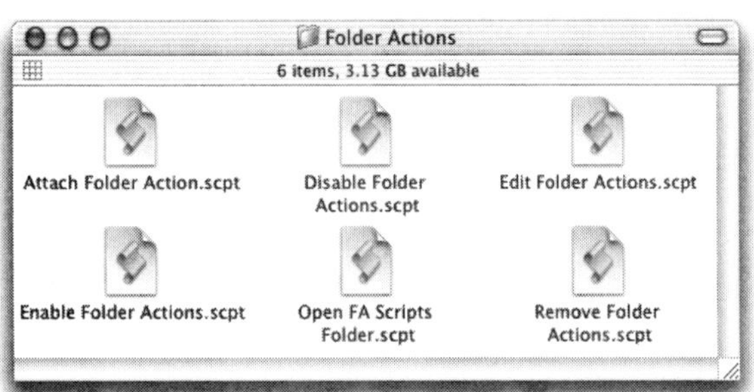

12.6

■ An Open dialog appears, asking you to choose a folder to attach the script to. Navigate to any folder you want to experiment on and click **Choose**. Another alert box appears to confirm that the folder action has been attached.

■ Now you're ready to try out your new folder action. Drag a file (again, any file will do) into the folder you just selected. The alert box shown in **Figure 12.8** appears. Click **Yes** to open the folder (if, for example, you want to return the file you just dragged in to its home) or **No** if you just want to dismiss the alert.

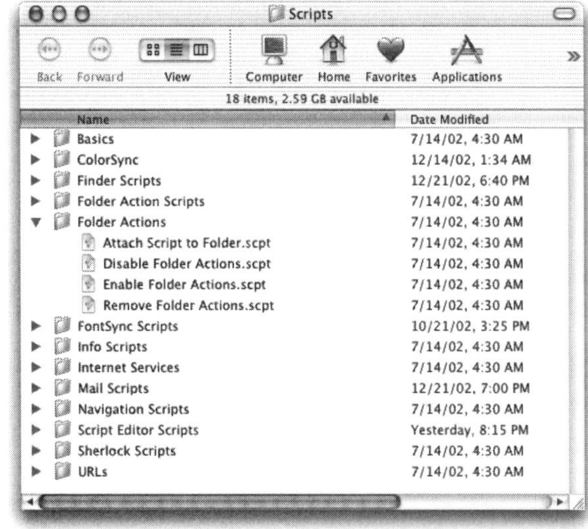

12.7

12.8

That's all there is to it. Attach a script and make changes to the folder — the script will run automatically. Feel free to try out the other sample scripts or just proceed to the next step.

STEP 5: CREATE YOUR OWN FOLDER ACTION

Now that you know how to attach and use a folder action, I will walk through the process of creating your own folder action script from scratch. This is *not* a course in AppleScript, so I'm not going to explain the ins and outs of the script you're about to use. For more details on writing folder action AppleScripts, visit `www.apple.com/applescript/folder_actions` or one of the other AppleScript sites mentioned earlier. This very simple script sorts files dropped onto its attached folder according to file extension.

- Open **Script Editor**. It's located in the **AppleScript** folder in your **Applications** folder.
- Enter the following code *exactly* as it appears here. (Note: Some long lines are split here to fit in this column, but should not be split when you type them. Wherever you see a line break followed by an indent, type the first line, then a space, then the text from the second line. Refer to **Figure 12.9** if you become confused.)

```
on adding folder items to this_folder
     after receiving added_items
tell application "Finder"
repeat with thisItem in added_items
set fileExt to name extension of
     (info for thisItem)
if (not (folder fileExt in this_folder
     exists)) then
make new folder in folder this_folder
     with properties {name:fileExt}
end if
move thisItem to folder fileExt in
     this_folder
end repeat
end tell
end adding folder items to
```

- When you're done, click the Check Syntax button on the toolbar, and your window should look like **Figure 12.9** (CP.3).
- Choose **Save** from the **File** menu. Enter **Simple Sort.scpt** for the name, make sure **Compiled Script** is selected in the **Format** menu, and save it in /Library/Scripts/Folder Action Scripts.
- Following the same procedure used in the last step, attach Simple Sort.scpt (which will now appear in the Attach Folder Action list) to the folder of your choice.

12.9

■ This script will sort all files dropped onto its attached folder by extension. If you have a file ending in a .sit extension, for example, the script will create a folder named "sit" within the attached folder and move your file there. This works whether or not the extension is visible in the Finder. To try it out, drop one or more files onto the folder with the attached script. Then open the folder to confirm that they have been sorted correctly. **Figure 12.10** shows an example of what the results might look like.

This is a very simple, quick-and-dirty example script, not one you would likely use every day. However, you can probably see how it could be enhanced to deal with many different situations. If you were to attach an improved version of this script to your Web browser's download folder, for example, you could automatically ensure that all files you download are sorted into useful subfolders.

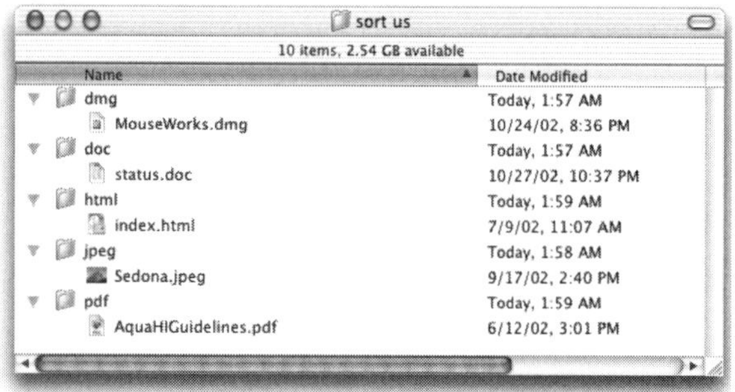

12.10

STEP 6: ADD FOLDER BADGES

One last detail. In Mac OS 9, attaching a Folder Action script to a folder automatically added an AppleScript *badge* to the folder's icon, to remind you that it was no longer an ordinary folder. Automatic badges are still missing from Mac OS X, but Apple provides a manual way to badge your folder icons so you'll know which ones have attached scripts.

■ Enter this URL in your browser: **www.apple.com/applescript/folder_actions/FAFolder.icns.sit**. If necessary, unstuff the archive, giving you a file named FAFolder.icns.

■ Select **FAFolder.icns** and choose **Get Info** from the **File** menu. Click the icon in the Info window to select it; then press **⌘+C** to copy it. Close the Info window.

■ Now select the folder you recently attached a script to. Again, choose **Get Info**. Now click the icon and press **⌘+V** to paste the badged icon over it. Close the window, and your folder will be badged, as shown in **Figure 12.11**. (If you later want to remove the badge, just select the icon in the Info window again and press **Delete**.)

12.11

TECHNIQUE 13

TAILORING THE DESKTOP TO YOUR PERSONALITY

13.1

13.2

ABOUT THE FEATURE

The desktop — the background area of your screen where your hard drive icon appears — can do more than collect files you haven't bothered to file any place else. It can also express your personality, entertain, or even relax you.

I try very hard to keep my desktop neat and organized — ideally showing only the icons of my hard drive and other mounted volumes. Yet despite my best efforts, it often ends up being a storage place for files I've downloaded or created but haven't taken the time to sort properly yet. They end up staying there for a long time, because I usually have a dozen or more windows open at once and they completely obscure the desktop — I barely know it's there.

Perhaps you're neater than I am and keep everything in its place. Or perhaps your monitor is so large that there's plenty of room for the desktop to show through, even with lots of windows open. If so, you're going to love this technique for customizing your desktop in some very cool ways. And if you do keep your screen cluttered like I do, this technique might impress you so much that you change your ways.

STEP 1: USE DESKTOP PICTURES

This technique starts slowly and works up to the good stuff. You may have noticed that Apple provides a selection of images you can use to replace the default swirly blue pattern. If you haven't experimented with the other available pictures, that's a good place to begin. To replace your desktop pattern, do the following:

- Open System Preferences and click the **Desktop** icon. The window shown in **Figure 13.3** appears. Under the words **Current Desktop Picture** is a miniature version of your current desktop pattern.
- The pop-up **Collections** menu lists several sets of images. When you choose a new collection, thumbnails of the pictures in that set appear in the list below. Scroll through each one of the lists to see the sample pictures. To try out one on your desktop, simply click it once and it will immediately appear in the background. (Notice that some of the images are wider than others — these are intended for wide-format displays like the Cinema Display, wide-screen iMac G4, or PowerBook G4.)
- To cycle through all the pictures in a certain collection automatically, click **Change picture** and choose how frequently you want the pictures to change. Check **Random order** to mix things up a bit.

After a while, you're bound to get tired of ladybugs, dewdrops, and swirly blue patterns. It's time to replace Apple's pictures with ones of your own.

- If you store your digital photos in your Pictures folder, choose **Pictures Folder** from the **Collections** menu to display thumbnails of your own photos. More likely, your photos are organized in subfolders within the iPhoto Library within your Pictures folder. To choose a folder of photos there (or anywhere else), click **Choose folder**, and navigate to where your photos are stored, as shown in **Figure 13.4**.
- As before, you can set a single image or create a slide show of your family vacation by adjusting the **Change picture** settings.

13.3

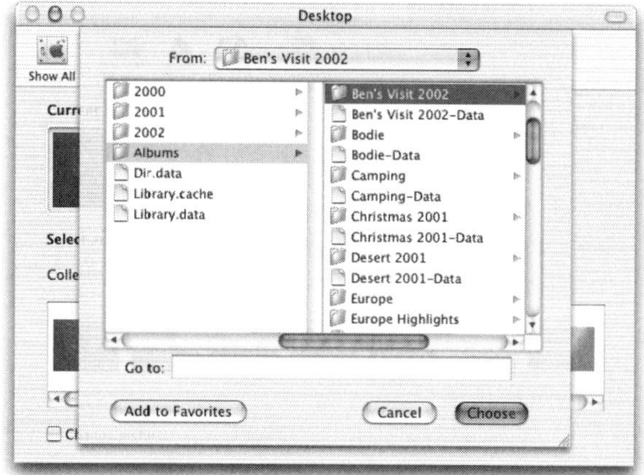

13.4

If you can see enough of your desktop to appreciate it, having pictures of your friends, family, or last weekend's car show cycling on your desktop can be very cool. But you can do better still!

STEP 2: USE A DESKTOP SCREEN SAVER

After the novelty of a desktop slide show has worn off, it's time to move up to the heavy-duty stuff: desktop animations.

You've probably noticed that Mac OS X includes a built-in screen saver. The Screen Effects pane of System Preferences allows you to choose and configure screen saver settings. Screen savers, of course, are animated — either subtly, like the gently panning, zooming, and crossfading Beach or Forest, or not-so-subtly, like the psychedelic Flurry setting. You can also, of course, use the same Pictures folder (or another folder of your own graphics) for a dynamic, animated super-slide-show presentation.

One of the coolest hacks to circulate around the Internet has been a very simple one-line command to display your selected screen saver as your desktop pattern — animation and all!

Open your Terminal application. Type the following all on one line, with no spaces after the / characters (and paying careful attention to the capitalization). Then press Return.

```
/System/Library/Frameworks/
ScreenSaver.framework/Resources/
ScreenSaverEngine.app/Contents/
MacOS/ScreenSaverEngine -background &
```

You should now have your screen saver running on your desktop, much like that shown in **Figure 13.5**. Cool, eh?

- Unless you have a *very* fast computer and a *very* expensive graphics card, you'll probably notice that running a screen saver on your desktop slows down the other programs on your computer considerably. To stop the screen saver desktop, go back to Terminal and enter the following and then press **Return**:

```
killall -m "ScreenSaver"
```

- If you don't want to have to type all that every time you turn on or off your desktop screen saver, you could set up aliases to those two commands as described in Technique 3. If you *really* don't like messing around in Terminal and have a spare $12, you can download xBack from Gideon Softworks (`www.gideonsoftworks.com/xback.html`), which adds a friendly icon to your menu bar that allows you to turn desktop screen savers on and off and configure them with ease.

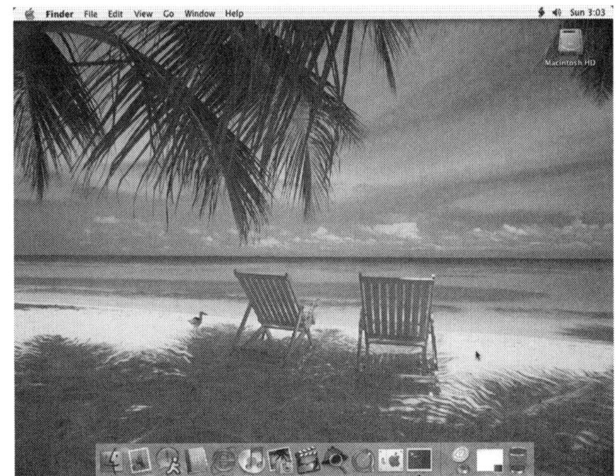

13.5

STEP 3: USE AN EVEN COOLER DESKTOP SCREEN SAVER

But wait, there's more! (Is there an echo in here?) Although desktop screen savers look cool no matter which module you're using, one screen saver is hands-down the most impressive, gotta-have toy. It's called SereneScreen, and it turns your screen into an incredibly realistic virtual aquarium, complete with bubbles and sound effects (if you want them). The wide variety of tropical fish are rendered on-the-fly, and with a high-end graphics card, the effect is absolutely stunning (see **Figure 13.6.**) Is that not groovy?

■ You can download a free demo version of SereneScreen from `www.serenescreen.com`; the full version costs $21.95. Although the demo works fine as a regular screen saver, it does *not* work as a desktop background. The full licensed version does, however, and it's well worth the money just to see the expressions on your coworkers' faces when they notice fish swimming behind your hard drive icons!

13.6

GETTING MORE FROM AQUA WITH HIDDEN PREFERENCES

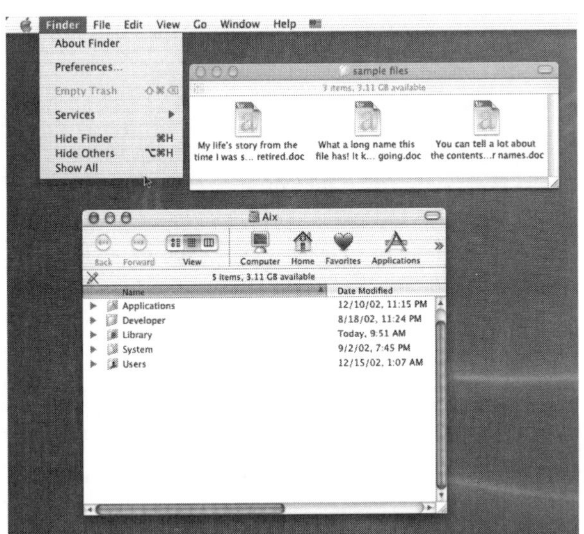

14.1

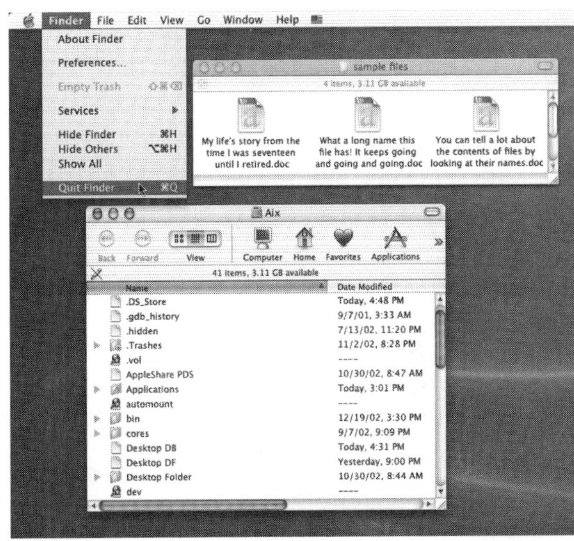

14.2

ABOUT THE FEATURE

The Finder — as well as the Dock and other programs — include hidden settings that enable interesting new features. With a little exploration, you can tap into this extra power.

I'm going to let you in on the worst-kept secret in Mac OS X. You can customize a large number of features far beyond the options in Preferences dialogs — all without any special tools or programming knowledge — if you just know where to look (and you will momentarily). Mac OS X makes exploring and tweaking the Finder and other applications much easier than they ever were in the Mac OS 9 days. It also allows you to discover some features that were always present but not visible in the user interface.

In this technique, you'll learn about two key ways of customizing the hidden features of Mac OS X. I'll take you through the whole process with the Finder to show you how it's done manually and then show you a free graphical app called TinkerTool that can do many of these things for you with just a few clicks. If there's an easy way, why even mention the hard way? Simple: You're learning techniques here. TinkerTool does a great job of modifying the Finder and the Dock, but you can apply the manual method you learn here to other applications as well.

But, first, I must again warn you: Messing with your system has the potential to, well, mess up your system. I urge you to back up all your work before trying any of this. Better yet, if you can experiment on a special installation of Mac OS X (on a separate drive or partition from your main system — or even on a different computer) you'll have a safety net in case something goes wrong. That warning duly rendered, you can dig in.

STEP 1: EDIT PROPERTY LISTS (THE HARD WAY)

If the thought of fiddling with hidden parts of your operating system that Apple clearly intended to be invisible fills you with dread, you can skip this step and move on to Step 2. If you're curious about the way things work, though, you may find this step interesting.

A *property list* is another name for a preference file. In the old days, each application stored its preferences in a different format, many of which could not be read or edited by any other application. Under Mac OS X, the property lists that store preferences for most applications are simple text files, formatted using a system called XML (for eXtensible Markup Language).

If you opened one of these files in a text editor like TextEdit, you would see something like **Figure 14.3**, which shows a small portion of the Finder's preference file. As you can see, it's not exactly poetry, but there are some plain English words in there, and with a bit of thought, you can probably see what some of the lines mean. Interestingly, this file gives you access to settings that don't appear in Finder Preferences (or anywhere else in the graphical user interface). They're built-in features, but the controls to modify them are hidden in this text file. Even more interestingly, if you want to experiment with these settings, you don't have to wade through XML in a text editor. You can use a much more attractive tool Apple supplies as part of the Developer Tools package called Property List Editor. The preceding file is shown in Property List Editor in **Figure 14.4**. If you were to make changes to this file, save it, and then relaunch the Finder, you would find that the changes took effect exactly as if you had changed them using the Finder Preferences dialog. To modify property lists, do the following:

> **NOTE**
>
> **There are other ways to make changes to your hidden preference files besides using Property List Editor. For example, if you know exactly what command to use, you can type a one-line command in Terminal that begins `write defaults com.apple.finder` (followed by some other parameters) to change the settings. I show you this way so that you can easily see where the settings are stored and how they're used.**

14.3

■ If you haven't already done so, run the installer on the Developer Tools CD that came with Mac OS X. (If you've already tried out Technique 3, you're good to go.) The **Property List Editor** application you'll be using is part of that installation.

■ Open **Property List Editor**. It's in the **Applications** folder inside the /**Developer** folder.

■ Choose **Open** from the **File** menu, type the following in the Go box (with no space after the / character), and click **Open**:

```
~/Library/Preferences/
com.apple.finder.plist
```

■ When the new window opens, click the disclosure triangle next to **Root**; you'll see something like **Figure 14.4**. This is the Finder's preference file. Some of the items in here might make no sense to you at all, but others will be fairly obvious.

The first thing you're going to do is add a **Quit** command to the Finder. It doesn't normally have one because it's supposed to be running all the time. But there are times you might want to be able to turn it off temporarily (like when you're playing with Finder settings).

■ Click any of the items under Root to enable the **New Sibling** button. Click **New Sibling**, and in the new field that appears, enter **QuitMenuItem**. Click in the **Class** column to display a pop-up menu of field classes; choose **Boolean**, which simply means this is a "yes/no" (or on/off) value. Then click in the **Value** column to display another pop-up menu of available values; choose **Yes** from this menu, as in **Figure 14.5**.

■ Save the file by choosing **Save** from the **File** menu. (You can leave the file open.)

■ Choose **Force Quit** from the Apple menu (or press **⌘+Option+Esc**). When the Force Quit window appears, select **Finder** and click **Relaunch**. (Don't worry, this is perfectly safe.) Your Finder quits and restarts in the background.

■ When all your icons reappear, click the Finder icon in the Dock to bring it to the front. Click on the Finder's **File** menu, and behold! It now has a **Quit** command. You will use this command shortly.

Congratulations! You just performed your first Finder hack. Read on to make a few more easy changes.

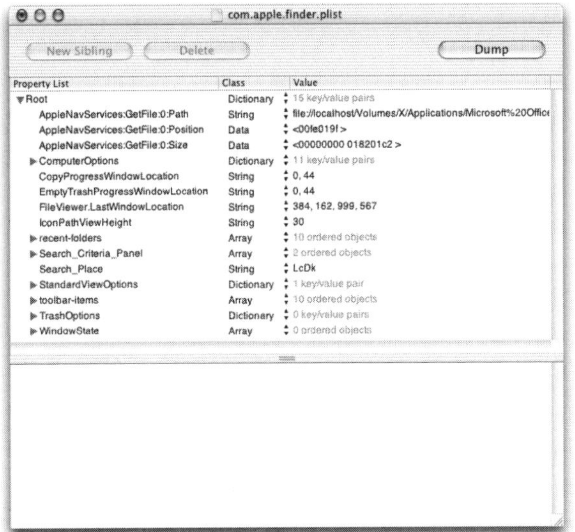

14.4

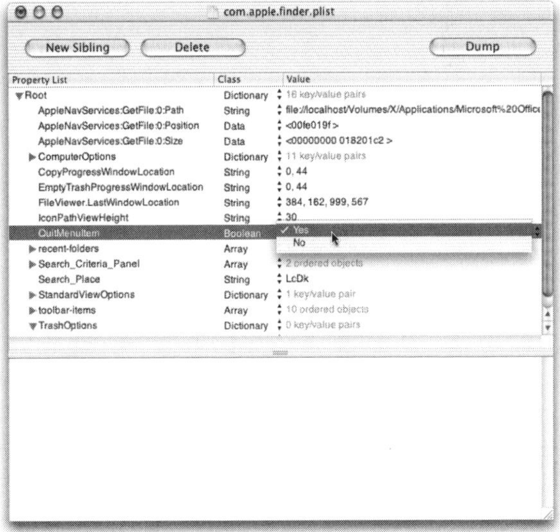

14.5

■ Back in Property List Editor, repeat the New Sibling procedure by adding an item called **AppleShowAllFiles.** Once again, this is a Boolean on/off switch. Entering **Yes** for the Value makes the Finder display all files, even ones that are invisible, like the hidden files that make up the UNIX layer of Mac OS X. (See **Figure 14.6.**)

■ Add a sibling called **MaximumLabelLines.** This time the Class is a number. This number is the maximum number of lines that will be used to display file and folder names when you're in Icon View. If you have some really long filenames, two lines might not be enough to display them, resulting in part of the name being cut off. Enter **1, 2,** or **3** in the Value column. (Although you can enter any number you want, the Finder will never display more than three lines.) **Figure 14.7** shows a folder containing some long filenames before and after applying this change.

■ The last change you'll make is to turn off Zoom Rectangles. As you may have noticed, opening an application causes an animation effect that looks a bit like a rectangle springing out of the spot where you clicked to fill the screen. If you find this animation annoying, you can use a hidden preference to turn it off. Enter a new sibling called **ZoomRects.** Make it a Boolean item with a Value of **No.**

> **WARNING**
>
> **Being able to see hidden files in the Finder can be educational — and occasionally useful — but if you accidentally delete some of these files, you can cause serious damage to your system. This is one setting I recommend turning on only when you need it and then turning it off again.**

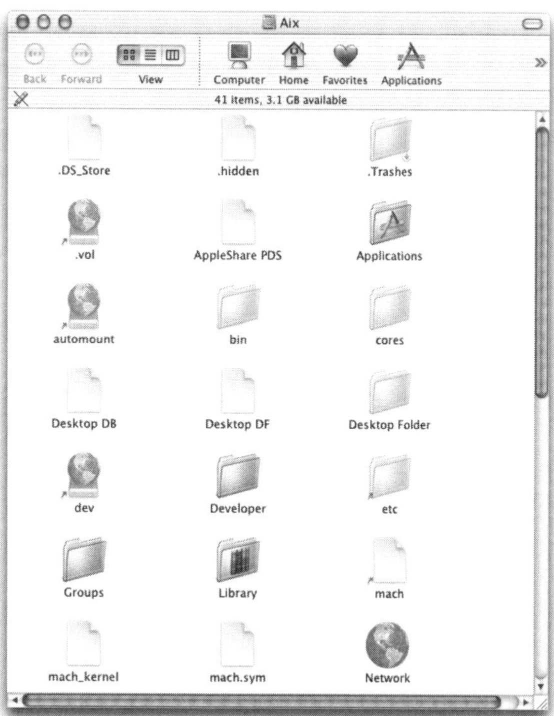

14.6

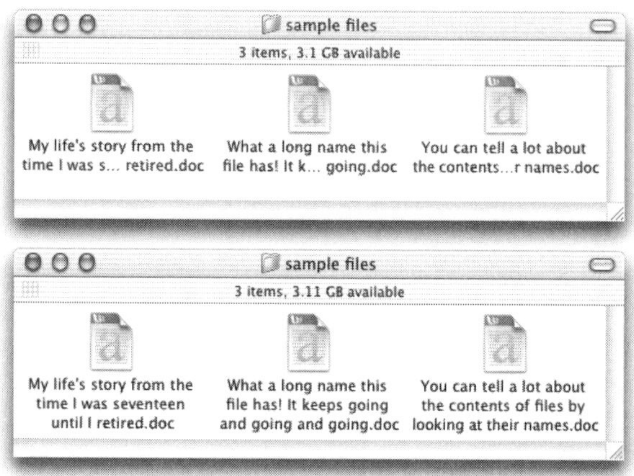

14.7

- As before, save the file. You're finished in Property List Editor, so you can also quit the application now.
- Now switch to the Finder. Before your changes can take effect, you'll need to quit it and restart it. Conveniently, your Finder now has a **Quit** menu command on the **File** menu. Choose it now. This time, the Finder may not restart on its own. If not, click the Finder icon in the Dock to relaunch it.

Enjoy your new Finder features! If you ever want to return to your defaults, follow the procedures in this step again and replace your new values with the old ones.

Using this same technique, you can examine and modify other preference files. The Dock, for instance, has some interesting hidden preferences (found in com.apple.dock.plist), which you modify by other means in Technique 15. Before modifying any other preference files, make a backup copy — just so you can restore the file to its previous state if you accidentally make a change that has unexpected results.

STEP 2: USE TINKERTOOL (THE EASY WAY)

If you want to save yourself a few steps, a freeware application called TinkerTool can make these and many other hidden Finder changes for you using a convenient, friendly graphical interface. TinkerTool can do a great many things, but I talk about just a few here. To use TinkerTool, do the following:

- Go to `www.bresink.de/osx/TinkerTool2.html` and download TinkerTool.
- Double-click and run the installer.
- When installation has finished, System Preferences opens automatically. Click the TinkerTool icon (at the bottom under **Other**), and you'll see the TinkerTool pane, as shown in **Figure 14.8**.
- The Finder tab includes controls to change the same settings you modified earlier. Check the appropriate checkboxes to enable or disable zoom rectangles, the display of hidden files, and the Finder's **Quit** menu command. To change the number of lines used to display filenames, make a selection from the **Icon View** pop-up menu. Another option is listed here that we didn't edit before: **Disable arrows**. Click this checkbox to hide the display of arrows in Column View to indicate which items (folders and volumes) will display their contents in another column when clicked.
- When you're finished making changes, click **Relaunch Finder** to activate them.

TinkerTool's other tabs allow you to modify additional hidden preferences, including Dock position, scroll bar arrow placement, system font settings, and the language used for Startup and Login screens. If you ever want to restore your preferences to their original, uncustomized state, the Reset tab allows you to do that with one click.

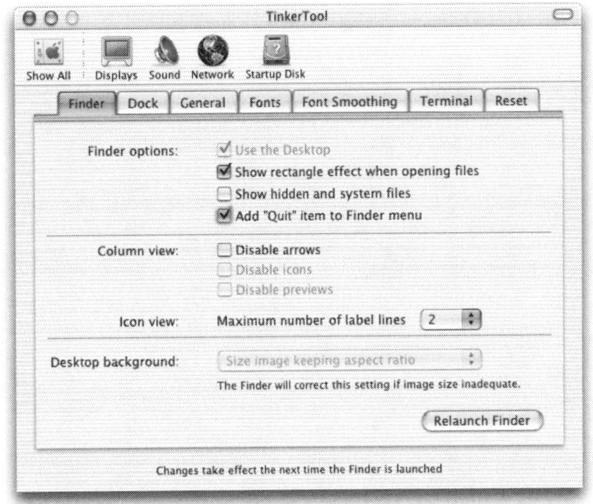

14.8

TECHNIQUE 15

DOCTORING YOUR DOCK

15.1

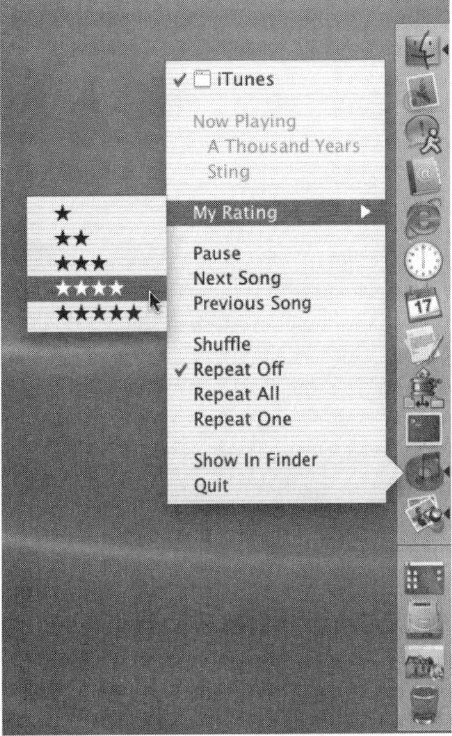

15.2

ABOUT THE FEATURE

The Dock is one of the most distinctive features of Mac OS X's user interface. Equal parts file launcher, application switcher, status indicator, and eye candy, the Dock wears many hats, but can also do much more than meets the eye.

In Mac OS 9, lots of interface elements were used for opening files, displaying status, or executing commands. Some examples were the Apple menu, the Application menu, the Control Strip, and the Launcher utility. In Mac OS X, Apple has attempted to bring the best features of all these widgets into one place: the Dock.

Most people who see the Dock for the first time think, "Wow, that's cool! Look at those large, beautiful icons! Watch that snazzy "genie" minimizing effect! And ooh, see the way those icons grow and shrink as I move the mouse over them!" After a while, though, it's easy to become frustrated with the Dock. You might find, for example, that it gets in your way as you try to do your work or that it doesn't have all the functionality you were hoping for. Fear not, for in this technique, you learn how to customize the

Dock to within an inch of its life, replacing annoyance with utility — and having a bit of fun in the process. To make this process even more interesting, you do all of this without opening System Preferences even once!

STEP 1: REMOVE ICONS YOU DON'T USE

Before you do anything else to the Dock, or even decide how large or on what part of the screen it will be, you should decide what goes in it. Out of the box, as shown in **Figure 15.3**, your Dock contains icons for the Finder and Trash (which can never be removed), System Preferences, and a handful of important applications such as Mail, Internet Explorer, and iTunes. However, you can freely remove any icons you don't use regularly — knowing that you can add them back later if you change your mind. The first step to having a useful Dock is to weed out icons you don't use often.

- The first icon you can remove is the one next to the Trash — it looks like an @ symbol on a spring. Clicking this icon simply takes you to the Mac OS X page on Apple's Web site. Because there are lots of other ways to get there, there's no need to keep this icon. Click and drag it off the Dock, and a little "poof" animation will confirm its deletion.
- Next, consider removing the QuickTime Player icon (the blue Q). Although you might use QuickTime Player frequently, if you're like most people, you'll rarely, if ever, need to open it manually. Instead, you'll probably double-click movies and other media files you've downloaded, opening the QuickTime Player automatically. So drag off the blue Q as well.

15.3

- System Preferences is another application you may use frequently, but opening System Preferences with a single click is always easy — it's on your Apple menu. You don't need to have it in your Dock as well.
- A couple of the icons are used to open iApps that require special hardware. If you use them frequently, having them in the Dock can be handy, but if not, consider removing them. If you don't have a digital camcorder, you probably don't use iMovie (the clapboard icon) very often, so you can remove that icon. Likewise, the iPhoto icon (the camera in front of a photograph) is primarily useful to those with digital cameras, and if you don't have one, you probably won't be using iPhoto very often. Remember, if you get new toys later and want to add these applications back into your Dock, doing so is a piece of cake.

I'll let you decide about the rest of the icons. As a general rule, if you don't use a particular application at least once a week, it's probably not a good use of space in your Dock. If you use it several times a day, you'll be very glad to have it there.

STEP 2: ADD USEFUL ICONS TO YOUR DOCK

The next step is to add to your Dock icons for applications and other files you need very frequent access to — that is, more frequent than the icons you just removed! In addition, you add some special icons that may not be obvious, but which can save you lots of extra clicking.

- To add an item to the Dock, just locate the file or folder you want and drag its icon into your Dock. All applications must go on the left side of the vertical line; everything else (like files, folders, and URLs) goes on the right side. Apart from that limitation, you can put your new icons anywhere you want; the other icons will scoot out of the way as you add new ones. You can also rearrange icons at any time by clicking and dragging them to another spot in the Dock. Try this now with any random file, and if it's not one you want to keep in the Dock, you can drag it right off again.

■ Consider the applications you use frequently. Perhaps you use Microsoft Office and work in Word, Excel, and Entourage all day long. Or perhaps you're a designer constantly switching among Photoshop, Illustrator, and InDesign. Whatever your work style, decide on the applications you use the most. Look through your Applications folder (and any other folders within the Applications folder) and add your most frequently used apps — but no more than five or six — to the Dock now.

■ Next think about individual folders that you access frequently, like your home folder, your Documents folder, or perhaps a document you're working on over a long period of time. Drag these to your Dock as well (remembering that they need to go on the right side of the vertical divider). Again, don't overdo it — too much clutter defeats the purpose of the Dock, which is simplicity. **Figure 15.4** shows a Dock customized with a new set of applications and folders.

■ Now for some less-than-obvious goodies. First, you can actually drag your hard drive icon into the Dock (**Figure 15.5**). As you will see in a moment, by doing this, you can get one-click access to most of your files with a handy pop-up menu. If you find yourself constantly clicking to open and close windows, this can be a great timesaver. As with other non-application icons, your hard drive will go on the right side.

■ Finally, my favorite: Put your desktop in the Dock, as shown in **Figure 15.6**. Although it may not look like it, your desktop is actually a special folder, and you can display all the files on your desktop in a regular window. You can also add this folder to the Dock, allowing you to see and open files on your desktop, even when you have so many other windows open that you can't see the desktop at all! To do this, open your home folder (the folder in the Users folder with your user name), find the **Desktop** icon, and drag it into the Dock — on the right side, of course.

STEP 3: ORIENT AND SIZE THE DOCK

When you first install Mac OS X, the Dock appears full-size at the bottom of your screen. If you have a Cinema Display (lucky you!) or multiple monitors, this might be fine. But for the average user with a single monitor at 1024 × 768 pixels, it's a terrible use of screen real estate. Because your monitor is wider than it is tall, you need to make the most of the vertical space you have available, and having the Dock use up so much of it leaves you with very little room for your own stuff. Luckily, this is easy to change.

■ The easiest way to change the size of your Dock is to move your pointer to the thin vertical line that separates your applications from everything

15.4

15.5

15.6

else. As you can see in **Figure 15.7**, the pointer shape changes to a bar with arrows above and below. Now you can simply click and drag up or down to change the size of your Dock. It's possible to make it very tiny indeed, if that is your preference.

- Your Dock does not need to go at the bottom of the screen — you may prefer to have it on the left or right edge instead, where space is at less of a premium. To orient your Dock vertically on the side of the screen, move your pointer to the vertical line again so that it changes to the double-arrowed bar. Now hold down the Shift key, then click and drag up and to the right to position it on the right, or drag up and to the left to position it on the left.

By default, your Dock will be centered on the edge of the screen where you've positioned it. But it's also possible to make it stick to one corner — for example, the lower-right corner — so that it will grow out to the left (if it's on the bottom) or toward the top (if it's on the right). This feature can make finding icons like the Trash easier, because they'll always be in the same position on the screen no matter how many other items you add to the Dock.

- To make your Dock stick to the right or bottom corner, open a Terminal window and type (all on one line, with a space between "dock" and "pinning")

```
defaults write com.apple.dock
     pinning end
```

- To make your Dock stick to the left or top corner, open a Terminal window and type (all on one line)

```
defaults write com.apple.dock
     pinning start
```

You need to quit and restart the Dock in order to see your changes. You can do this either by logging out and logging back in or by typing

```
killall "Dock"
```

If you want to undo your change to the Dock pinning location at some point, type (all on one line)

```
defaults write com.apple.dock
     pinning middle
```

Figure 15.8 shows a Dock on the right side of the screen, pinned to the bottom corner. One of the

> **TIP**
>
> **If you hold down the Option key while resizing your Dock, it will snap to certain fixed sizes at which the icons look best (corresponding to icon dimensions of 16×16, 32×32, 48×48, 64×64, and 128×128 pixels). For reference, the next-to-smallest fixed size (32×32) is the size all icons were in Mac OS 9. Don't they seem small now?**

15.7

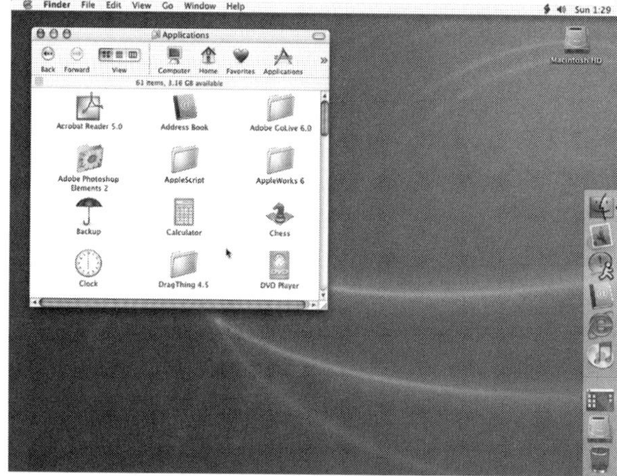

15.8

advantages of keeping your Dock in the lower-right corner is that your Trash will always stay put in the same corner of the screen where it always used to be.

STEP 4: RIGHT-CLICK DOCK ICONS

Most people use the Dock only for opening and switching applications. But its capabilities go way beyond that. Every item in your Dock is also a pop-up menu, with contents that vary depending on what type of item it is, and — if it's an application — whether it's running.

Ordinarily, the pop-up menus only display if you click and hold the mouse button on an icon for about a second. But you can avoid that delay with a right-click.

- For instantaneous access to Dock menus, right-click the icon with your multi-button mouse (or Control+click if you're using a one-button mouse).

Here are some examples of what you'll see on the menus:

- All running applications show a list of their open windows. So if you have Word running in the background with ten windows open, you can jump directly to the window you want by right-clicking Word's Dock icon and choosing that window name from the pop-up menu.

NOTE

There are other ways to edit the hidden Dock preferences that control how it's displayed. One way is to use Property List Editor to modify the com.apple.Dock.plist file, just like you did in Technique 14 for the Finder. Another way is to use the freeware TinkerTool application (also discussed in Technique 14) to edit these settings in a graphical interface.

- The commands **Show in Finder** and **Quit** also appear on applications' pop-up menus. Choose **Show in Finder** to open the window containing the application's icon, or **Quit** to quit the application without first switching to it. (If an application isn't responding, you can press the Option key while clicking the icon to change **Quit** to **Force Quit**; this method is quicker than pressing **⌘+Option+Escape** and choosing the application from a list.)
- Most applications show additional commands in their pop-up menus. Mail, for example, as shown in **Figure 15.9**, enables you to Get New Mail or Compose New Message without switching to the application first. Meanwhile, iTunes shows you the name of the current artist and song along with numerous other controls. Some applications have dozens of options available. Experiment with the ones you use to see what commands are available.

TIP

By using modifier keys (like ⌘ and Option) while clicking Dock icons, you can selectively show and hide applications, display the application icon in the Finder, and other neat tricks. These and other Dock shortcuts are listed in Appendix A.

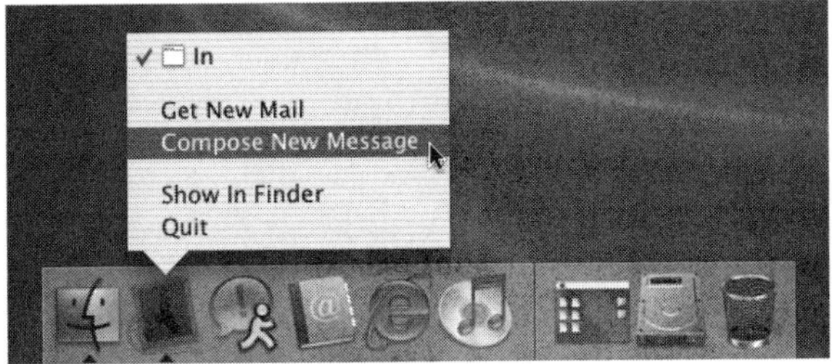

15.9

- If you have a volume (like your hard drive) or a folder (like your desktop folder or home folder) in the Dock, right-clicking or Control+clicking displays a hierarchical menu of all the files and folders inside it. This means that with a single click, you can open nearly any file, even if it's buried several levels deep. One caveat, however: Pop-up Dock menus only go five levels deep.

STEP 5: USE MAGNIFICATION AND HIDING

If you place a lot of icons on your Dock, it shrinks in order to accommodate them all. Even if you took a more conservative approach and have only a few Dock icons, you may want to keep your Dock small to save precious screen space. If the icons get too small, though, it can be difficult to tell what they are (not to mention difficult to click them accurately). Dock magnification can solve this problem.

- To turn on magnification, choose **Dock** from the Apple menu and choose **Icon Magnification** from the submenu. As your pointer enters the Dock, the nearest icon will grow to full size, and the ones on either side will scale partway up. See **Figure 15.10** for an example. When you move the pointer away from the Dock, they all return to normal size. (Be aware that if you have your Dock anchored to a corner, magnification will cause some icons to disappear off the edge of the screen momentarily.)
- To turn off magnification, once again choose **Icon Magnification** from the **Dock** submenu.

If even very small icons take up too much space for your taste or are too distracting, you can hide the Dock altogether. Even when it's hidden, it's still running, though, and will reappear instantly when your mouse approaches the edge of the screen where it's positioned.

- To turn on Hiding, choose **Dock** from the Apple menu and choose **Automatically Hide the Dock** from the submenu (or press **⌘+Option+D**). To turn off Hiding, repeat this step.

15.10

STEP 6: CUSTOMIZE APPEARANCE AND BEHAVIOR

If you have the hang of using the Dock and are still hungry for more, a number of downloadable programs can take you even further.

- Try out TinkerTool, the free preference pane mentioned in Technique 14; it can perform several Dock modifications for you quickly and safely with a friendly graphical interface — including the stick-to-a-corner trick used earlier. You can find it at `www.bresink.de/osx/TinkerTool2.html`.
- To customize your Dock further, try the shareware program TransparentDock, available from `www.freerangemac.com/pages/software.html` for a mere $8. In addition to the Dock-related features of TinkerTool, TransparentDock allows you to change the color and transparency level of the background, border, and even the application arrows on your Dock.

  And that's just the beginning. You can replace the Poof effect with your own animation, display hidden files in pop-up menus, or — my very favorite feature — eliminate the five-levels-deep feature for hierarchical menus.
- For the ultimate in Dock customization, look no further than Skin a Dock, a $10 shareware program available from `www.ittpoi.com/skinadock.html`. This amazing program allows you to change the overall appearance of your Dock in extreme ways, such as adding flames or grass around the icons or placing each icon in its own bubble. **Figure 15.11** shows two examples.

15.11

TECHNIQUE **16**

MOVING BEYOND THE DOCK WITH FILE LAUNCHERS

16.1

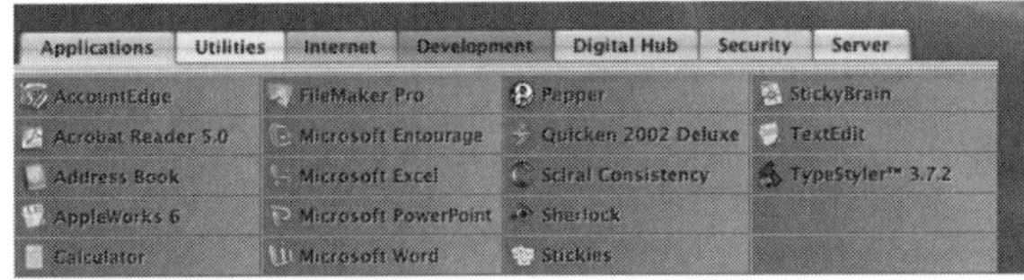

16.2

ABOUT THE FEATURE

File launchers are small utilities that make finding and opening your favorite applications, utilities, files, and URLs easy. The Dock can do all of this, too, but a number of third-party alternatives do it better.

If you've read Technique 15, you may be feeling pretty excited about all the things your newly customized Dock can do for you. Now I'm going to turn the tables on you and propose something shocking: You might want to stop using the Dock almost entirely and replace it with something else! Even though the Dock is pretty to look at and can be customized extensively, it remains limited in some important ways. Power users often choose to skip the Dock and use a third-party file launcher utility instead.

What exactly is a file launcher? There's no set answer to this question, but in general, a file launcher is a utility with the following features:

- Opens files, folders, applications, and URLs with one click.
- Allows you to drag and drop files onto its icons to open them.
- Shows you which applications are currently running (a *process viewer*).
- Enables you to group items into categories

The Dock has all these features except the last one, but that's pretty crucial. Although you can, in theory, drag hundreds of items into the Dock, beyond a certain number of items the utility and charm of the Dock drop off rapidly. The Dock's icons become small and difficult to pick out, and even with the magnification feature, using it can be awkward. (On an average-sized monitor, a Dock with more than 25 or 30 icons starts getting pretty crowded.) As this technique shows you, third-party file launchers pick up where the Dock leaves off, allowing you to organize dozens or even hundreds of items for quick and easy access.

Although you can hide the Dock and remove everything except the Finder and the Trash, you can't completely turn it off — at least, not without some serious hacking that might be more harmful than helpful.

STEP 1: CHOOSE A LAUNCHER

Because you're going to be using your file launcher many times a day, choosing one that closely meets your needs pays off. Your first step is to choose a launcher from among the many that are available. Fortunately, you can download and try out any or all of them for free. As you're evaluating file launchers, here are some questions to consider:

- Does it use screen space effectively? A launcher that covers too much of your screen will get in the way of your work. Some launchers always float above your other windows; some appear or disappear when your pointer moves in and out of a certain part of the screen; some behave more like regular windows; and so on. The best launchers allow you to choose the sort of window shape, position, and behavior that suits your needs.
- How easy is it to customize? Although you can customize every launcher in one fashion or another, some make it very easy whereas others require a series of awkward steps.
- Does it offer keyboard shortcuts? This feature may or may not be important for you, but some launchers offer the option to assign keyboard shortcuts to individual items, for another way of opening them if using the keyboard is more convenient than clicking.
- What does it look like? Some launchers have highly customizable appearances (sometimes called *skins*) that can adapt to your personality; others have just one set look. Some offer Aqua-friendly drop shadows, transparency, and rounded edges; others have a more distinctive appearance. Your launcher will be a regular fixture on your screen, so choose one you'll enjoy looking at.

With these thoughts in mind, here is a sampling of the best-known (and arguably the best) third-party launchers you can find. (For more choices, visit `www.versiontracker.com` and search the Mac OS X area for "launcher.")

- Aladdin's DragStrip ($20, `www.aladdinsys.com/dragstrip`) has been around for many years and is now available in a fully Mac OS X–native form. This relatively conventional launcher arranges your shortcuts on a series of tabs within a floating window. DragStrip is shown in **Figure 16.3**. DragStrip is easy to use but relatively light on features and customizability. Unlike the other two launchers mentioned here, DragStrip doesn't allow you to display a hierarchical menu showing the contents of folders and volumes on its tabs.

■ Drop Drawers X ($20, `www.sigsoftware.com/dropdrawers/`) is an unusual and visually striking launcher that has many enthusiastic fans. Instead of windows or palettes, Drop Drawers X places tabs on any edge of your screen. Move your pointer to a tab to slide out a drawer (as in **Figure 16.4**). A drawer can contain not only applications but also just about any type of content, including text snippets, URLs, movies, aliases, and even a Trash icon. (Thus, it can also serve as a kind of pasteboard or scrapbook for various sorts of information.) A Process Drawer shows just currently running applications. Drop Drawers X has extensive customization options, but has a steeper learning curve than DragStrip or DragThing (mentioned next).

■ Last but not least is my favorite, DragThing ($25, `www.dragthing.com`). Like DragStrip, it can display shortcuts of all kinds as icons on floating palettes. Like Drop Drawers X, its multi-tabbed windows can be turned into pop-out drawers at the edges of your screen (as shown in **Figure 16.5**). And like the others, it contains an optional process viewer window. Where DragThing really shines is in the depth of its interface choices. Nearly any size, shape, color, texture, or configuration of launcher you can dream up can be created with DragThing. Although it has a vast number of customization options, I find it more intuitive and easier to use than the other two.

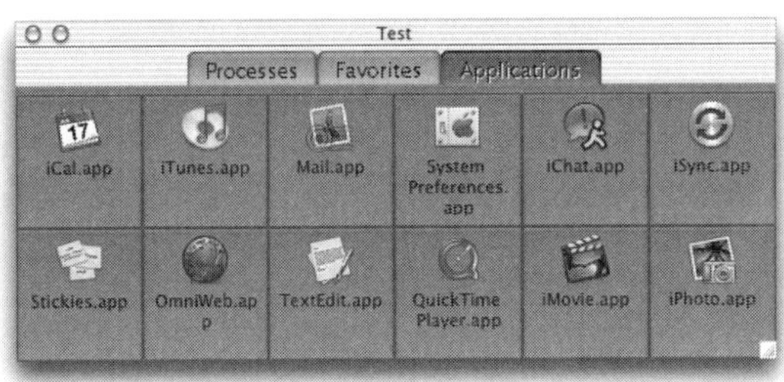

16.3

One minor caveat: Three of the Dock's features do not (yet) appear in any third-party launcher. First, it uses badges for certain icons to give you additional information. An example of this is the Mail icon in the Dock, which displays the number of unread

16.4

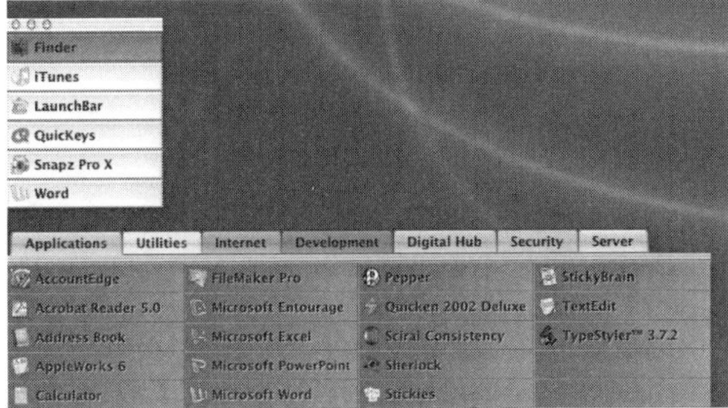

16.5

messages (see **Figure 16.6**) without requiring you to switch to the Mail application. Second, by right-clicking (or Control+clicking) the Dock icon of a running application, you can display a menu of open windows and other commands you can activate without having to switch to the application first. Finally, only the Dock (by way of its bouncing icons) lets you know when an application is in the process of launching. The good news is that because you can't entirely replace the Dock, it will still offer all these capabilities for your running applications. You can continue to use your Dock for what it's best at and use another launcher for everything else.

STEP 2: ORGANIZE YOUR LAUNCHER ITEMS

Now that you've chosen a launcher, what do you do with it? Well, it's time to load it up with your stuff. This is an art, not a science, so all I can offer are some general principles to consider:

- You'll invariably want to start by putting your most frequently used applications on your launcher. Applications generally go on a tab by themselves. If you have dozens of applications you use on a regular basis, consider splitting them into several tabs, such as Business Applications, Internet, Utilities, and Games (or whatever makes the most sense to you). An example is shown in **Figure 16.7**.
- Next, add the folders you access most often. This will work best with launchers (like Drop Drawers X and DragThing) that can display the contents of folders in a pop-up menu. Having a custom icon for your folder also helps — see Technique 11 for instructions.
- Think about the files you need to access on a regular basis. The files that you'll find most helpful to have in your launcher are those that you work on over long periods of time — a book or a term paper, for instance — or ones you have to update frequently, such as a schedule or form. You might also include instruction manuals or reference guides in PDF form that you regularly consult.
- Consider adding a few URLs. In many cases, your browser's bookmark menu is a more convenient place to store URLs, but a launcher can give you one-click access to some of your favorites even if your browser isn't already running.

16.6

> **TIP**
>
> **All the launchers described in this technique are based on the same metaphor as the Dock: an area of the screen dedicated to launching the items you have manually selected as being important. An entirely different — and much more powerful — paradigm is employed by the highly regarded LaunchBar utility. Although it serves the function of launching files, it does so in a way that does not require *any* space on the screen, relying on the keyboard rather than the mouse. Because it's more keyboard-oriented, LaunchBar is discussed in Technique 19, "Boosting Your Keyboard Efficiency."**

16.7

- As you add more items, be careful to limit the number of icons on any given tab. When a tab gets to ten or twelve icons, consider splitting its content into two tabs with more specific titles; for example, "Expense Reports" and "Budget Worksheets" instead of "Spreadsheets."
- Finally, do *not* try to put every icon you can think of in your launcher. If all you're doing is duplicating the contents of your Applications folder, for example, you're missing the point of a launcher — quick, easy access to the items you use most often. A launcher that's cluttered with too many items won't save you any time or effort. Concentrate on the items you use most frequently — or have to dig the most to find.

STEP 3: CUSTOMIZE YOUR LAUNCHER

After the hard work of organizing your applications and files, it's time to have some fun by customizing the appearance of your launcher. Choices like color, pattern, and fonts are purely a matter of personal taste and will depend on the capabilities in the launcher you've chosen. However, here are some practical considerations to keep in mind:

- All things being equal, a larger target is easier to hit than a smaller one. In choosing the size of your icons and views, think about how easy it will be to click the individual items without carefully positioning your pointer.
- Icons, as long as they're distinctive, can be recognized more quickly than text. If you have many identical folder icons, for example, that you can identify only by reading their labels, your eye will always have to read the labels to decide which is the right icon. On the other hand, the eye can easily detect an icon with a unique color or shape, making for faster recognition.
- In contrast to the last two items, text usually takes up less space than icons. If you have a great many items in your launcher and want to keep it from covering half your screen, smaller icons with accompanying text labels — perhaps to the side of the icons, where they use space more efficiently — might do the trick.

STEP 4: PARE DOWN YOUR DOCK

Now that you have a great launcher, what about your Dock? It will still always display the Finder, Trash, and icons for any open applications. But you can remove everything else from it, because all those other icons are already in your launcher. (It can feel sacrilegious or even scary to think about removing everything from your Dock, but just remember: They're only shortcuts. The original applications are still there, and you can add them back to your Dock later any time you want.) As a final touch, if you haven't done so already, move your Dock to an obscure area of the screen, make it smaller, and/or turn on Hiding to keep it out of your way. **Figure 16.8** shows a Dock with only the essentials (and running applications), pinned in the bottom-right corner of the screen using the tricks in Technique 15.

16.8

TECHNIQUE 17

RESTORING "MISSING" CLASSIC FEATURES TO MAC OS X

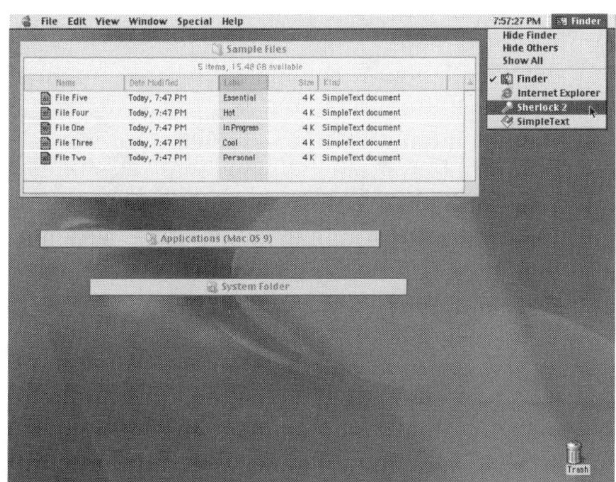

17.1

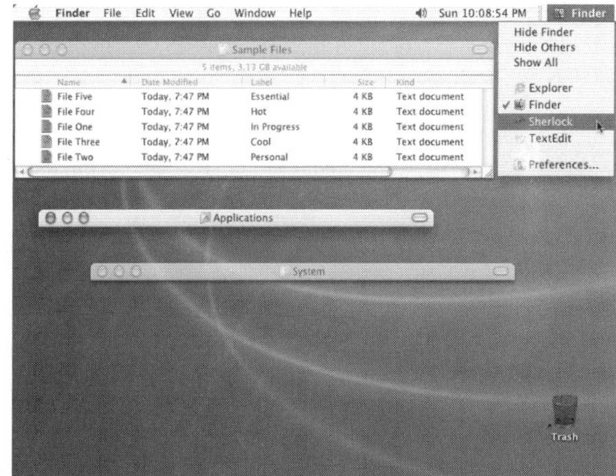

17.2

ABOUT THE FEATURE

Mac OS 9 is dead! Long live Mac OS 9! A number of useful interface features in the Classic Mac OS disappeared in Mac OS X. Clever programmers have found ways to bring some of them back.

No one will dispute that Mac OS X has made tremendous strides in the area of user interface. By comparison, the Platinum look of Mac OS 9 seems old-fashioned and passé. Yet, there's no escaping the fact that Mac OS 9 had some very handy interface features that, for reasons only Apple knows, have not found their way into Mac OS X.

Maybe you're a long-time Mac user who still hasn't gotten used to the new ways of Mac OS X and pines for the good old days. Or maybe you love every drop of Aqua, but still think a few things could be more convenient than they are. Whatever the case, in this technique, I show you how to restore several features to Mac OS X that were once present in Mac OS 9. In most cases, the Mac OS X versions of these features are even better than they were before.

Most of the steps in this technique involve the use of shareware programs. They're all quite inexpensive, though, and considering the tremendous effort these authors have put into making our lives a bit easier, I think every program mentioned here is well worth the requested fee. If you use these programs beyond the trial period, be sure to register the software and pay the shareware fee.

STEP 1: RESTORE THE APPLE MENU TO ITS FORMER GLORY

Mac OS X's Apple menu displays system-wide commands like System Preferences, Recent Applications and Documents, Restart, and Shut Down. In Mac OS 9, the Apple menu, apart from being more colorful, had a few additional tricks. For one thing, it was possible to add your own files and folders to the Apple menu. Folders displayed their contents in a handy pop-out submenu, providing a way to get one-click access to most of your files (much like you can do now in the Dock).

One of the folders that appeared in the Apple menu automatically was the Control Panels folder. Because each control panel had its own entry in this menu, you could access any one of them with a single click. (See **Figure 17.3.**) By contrast, although Mac OS X's Apple menu has a System Preferences command, it takes another click after the application opens to select the particular pane you want to use — not quite as convenient.

- To make your Apple menu customizable once again, download Unsanity's shareware FruitMenu ($10, `www.unsanity.com`). With FruitMenu installed (see **Figure 17.4**), you can add folders and files to your Apple menu much like you could in Mac OS 9. The hierarchical menus are even better, because they're unlimited in depth. (Mac OS 9 restricted you to five levels.) You can also add any of a large collection of special commands to your Apple menu, such as commands to arrange your windows or display your IP address. Best of all, instead of a single System Preferences command, you get a menu listing each pane, so you can jump to any pane with a single click.

STEP 2: ADD A CLASSIC-STYLE APPLICATION MENU

In Mac OS 9, the right side of the menu bar displayed the Application menu, which in those days meant a list of your running applications. With one click, you could not only switch applications, but also hide all the windows of the current application or hide everything *but* the current application. Although you can achieve similar functionality through a combination of the Dock and the Window menu, it's just not as easy as it once was.

- Download Frank Vercruesse's ASM ($12, `www.vercruesse.de/software`), which brings back the functionality of the old Application menu, as shown in **Figure 17.5**. It actually goes far beyond it, giving you the option

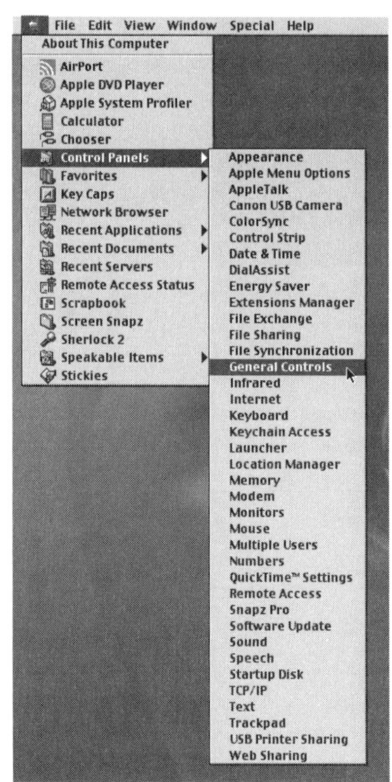

17.3

to display Dock menus in your ASM menu, change icon size, and many other options. If you've never broken the habit of zipping your pointer to the upper-right corner to hide your current application, ASM will be a breath of fresh air.

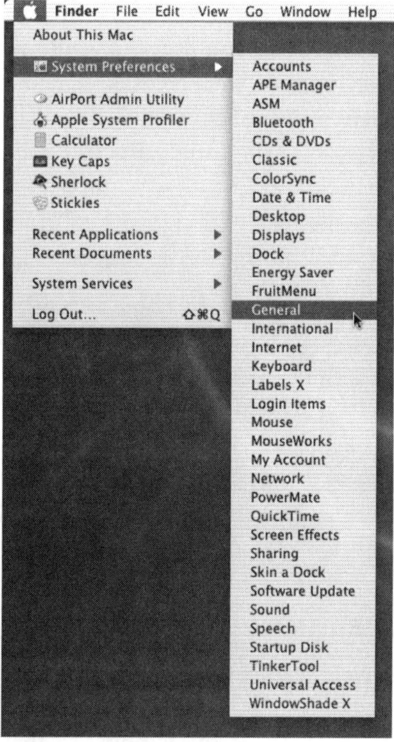

17.4

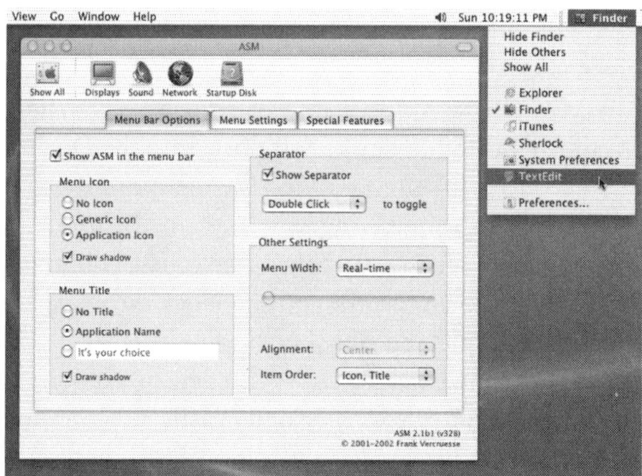

17.5

STEP 3: REPOSITION SCROLL BAR ARROWS

This very easy step requires no extra software, but removes a major annoyance for people accustomed to Mac OS 9. When you install Mac OS X, you'll notice that the Up and Down arrows on your scroll bars are together at the bottom. Every previous version of the Mac OS, as well as every version of Windows, put the Up arrow at the top and the Down arrow at the bottom — where, I think you'll agree, they make more sense. **Figure 17.6** illustrates the difference.

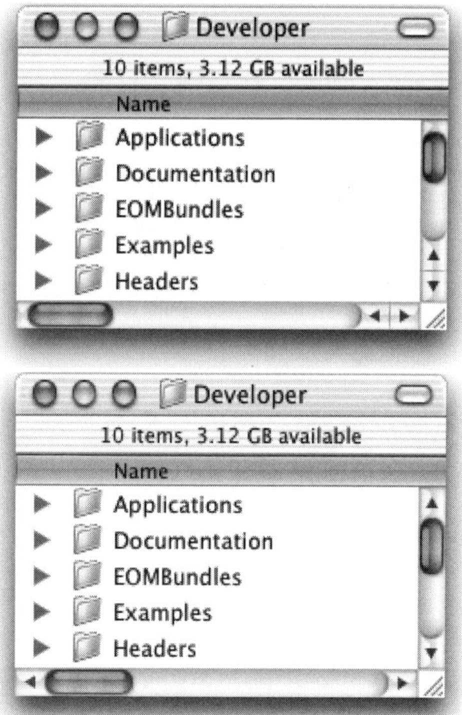

17.6

- To put your scroll arrows back where they belong, open System Preferences and click the **General** icon. In the middle section, you'll see **Place scroll arrows**; select the radio button next to **At top and bottom,** as shown in **Figure 17.7**.

STEP 4: MAKE FOLDERS OPEN IN THEIR OWN WINDOWS

By default, every time you double-click a folder icon inside a window, the contents of the new folder replace the previous contents of the window — without opening a new folder. This keeps your screen from becoming crowded with lots of extra windows, but it can be disorienting and confusing if you're used to opening a new window with every new folder.

- To make all folders open in windows of their own, choose **Preferences** from the Finder's **Finder** menu and check the box next to **Always open folders in a new window** (see **Figure 17.8**).

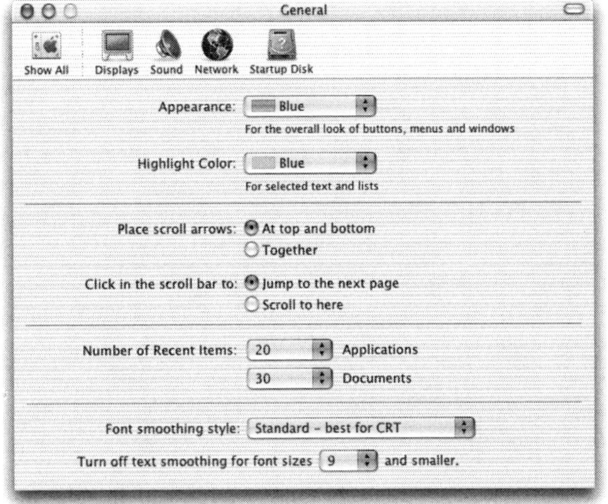

17.7

STEP 5: RESTORE FINDER LABELS

Although Mac OS X makes sorting files by criteria like name, date modified, and kind easy, Mac OS 9 offered an additional option called Labels. With a simple menu command, you could give any file or folder one of seven user-defined color and name combinations. When you applied a label, the file's color would change, and you could also use your label as a sorting criterion in List View — for example, displaying all the files you've designated as "Hot" at the top of the list, and "Boring" at the bottom.

- Go visit our friends at Unsanity (`www.unsanity.com`), who have brought back Labels in all their glory with their $10 Labels X, as shown in **Figure 17.9** (CP.6). As with Mac OS 9's Labels, Labels X changes icon color, has user-configurable colors and names, and adds an optional Label column to List View windows.

STEP 6: BRING BACK WINDOWSHADE

Mac OS 9 had a built-in feature called WindowShade. By double-clicking the title bar of any window, you could "roll up" the contents of the window so that only the title bar showed. This feature was very useful for times when lots of windows were open and you needed to reduce screen clutter without closing windows.

In Mac OS X, Apple wants you to use the yellow Minimize button to shrink windows into the Dock if you need to get them out of the way temporarily. The problem with minimizing windows to the Dock is that you can't see the window name unless you highlight the Dock icon. Although the Dock does display a thumbnail, picking out the window you want can be hard if your Dock icons are hidden or very small (or if your window contents aren't easily recognizable at postage-stamp size).

Luckily, Unsanity (`www.unsanity.com`) — the same folks who created FruitMenu and Labels X — have yet another $10 shareware program called WindowShade X that restores WindowShade functionality to Mac OS X.

- To bring back WindowShade functionality, download WindowShade X from the preceding URL, double-click its installer icon, and follow the on-screen instructions. **Figure 17.10** shows WindowShade X in action. In addition to rolling up windows, it can also make them transparent (to a user-selectable degree) among many other features. It's one of my very favorite Mac OS X interface enhancements. Check it out!

17.8

STEP 7: PUT THE TRASH BACK ON THE DESKTOP

Do you miss having a Trash icon on your desktop? Although a lot of third-party utilities you can download will put your Trash back on your desktop, you can also do it yourself very quickly and easily.

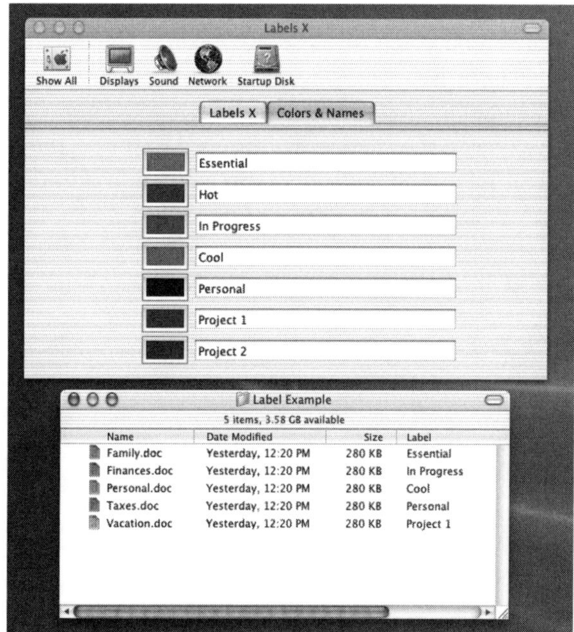

17.9

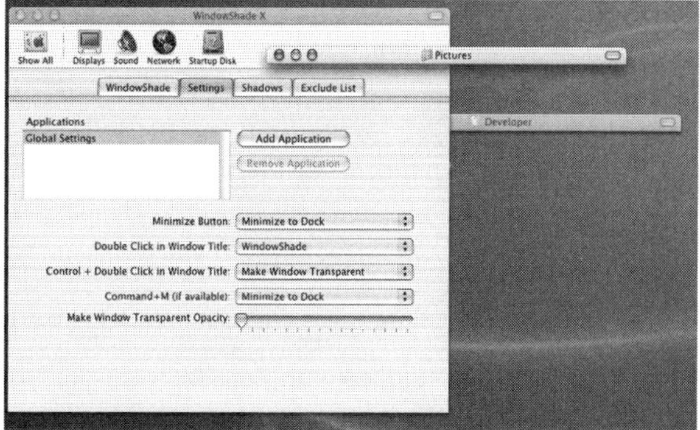

17.10

■ To put your own Trash icon on the desktop, flip back to Technique 10 and follow the directions in Step 4.

■ Instead of putting your new Trash icon on a toolbar, move it to the bottom-right corner of the screen — where nature intended it to be (see **Figure 17.11**).

■ To try out your new desktop Trash icon, drag a file onto it, then click the Trash icon in the Dock to confirm that the file was moved there. Remember that your fake Trash icon does not change to show that it has files in it, and even the real Trash icon in the dock might not reflect the change until you click it. In addition, you cannot use the fake Trash icon to eject removable media. However, it's still not bad for five minutes and no money.

17.11

Technique 3:

A transparent Terminal window allows you to see instructions on a Web page in the background.

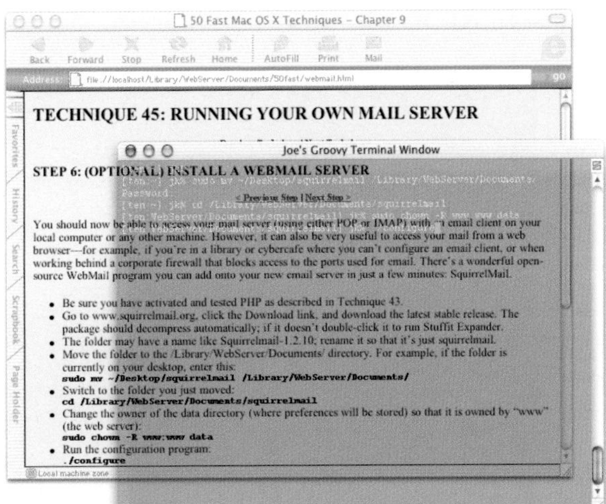

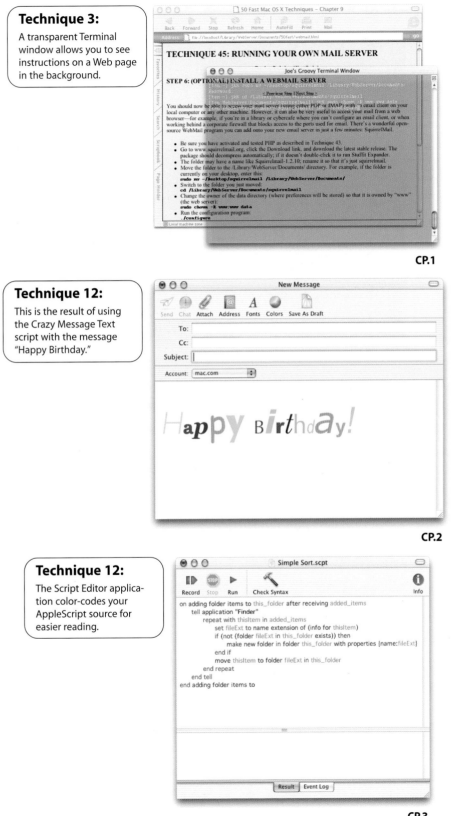

CP.1

Technique 12:

This is the result of using the Crazy Message Text script with the message "Happy Birthday."

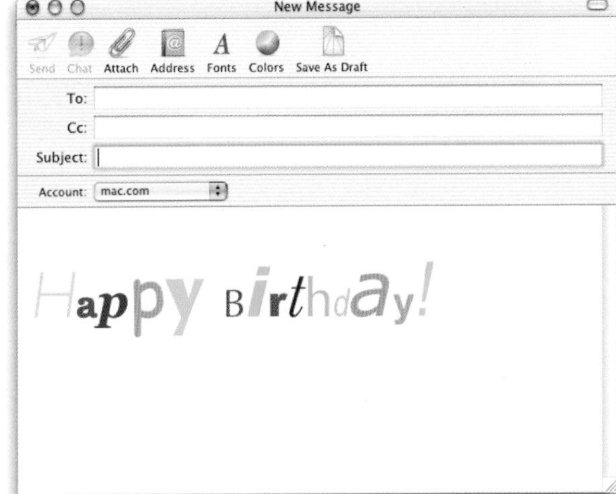

CP.2

Technique 12:

The Script Editor application color-codes your AppleScript source for easier reading.

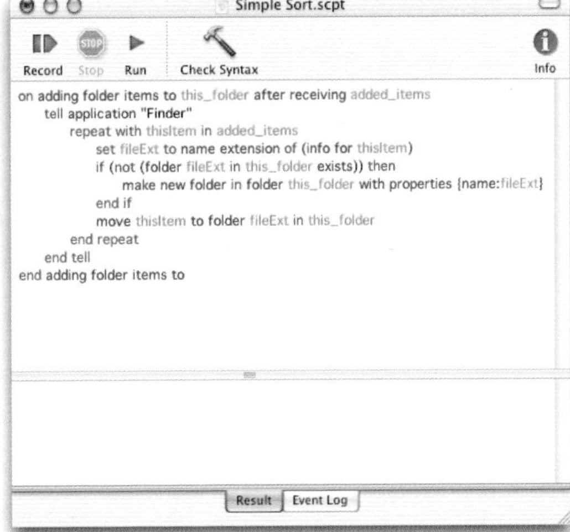

CP.3

Technique 13:

Ordinary desktop backgrounds can be boring. You can make your background dynamic, as in this example featuring moving fish, shimmering water, and a stream of bubbles.

CP.4

CP.5

Technique 17:

Using Labels X, you can apply Mac OS 9-style color Finder labels to files and folders.

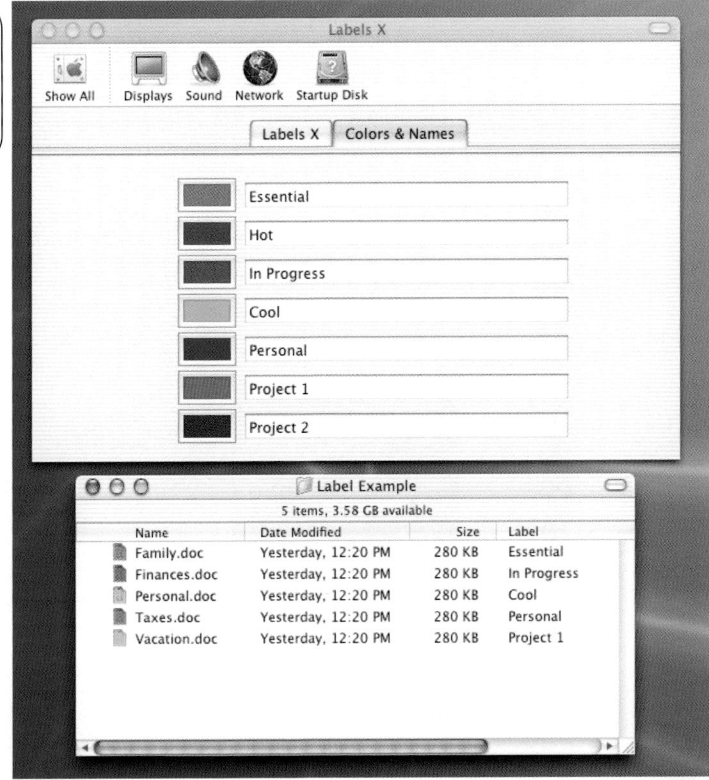

CP.6

Technique 26:

Mail can highlight the thread of a selected message in the color of your choice.

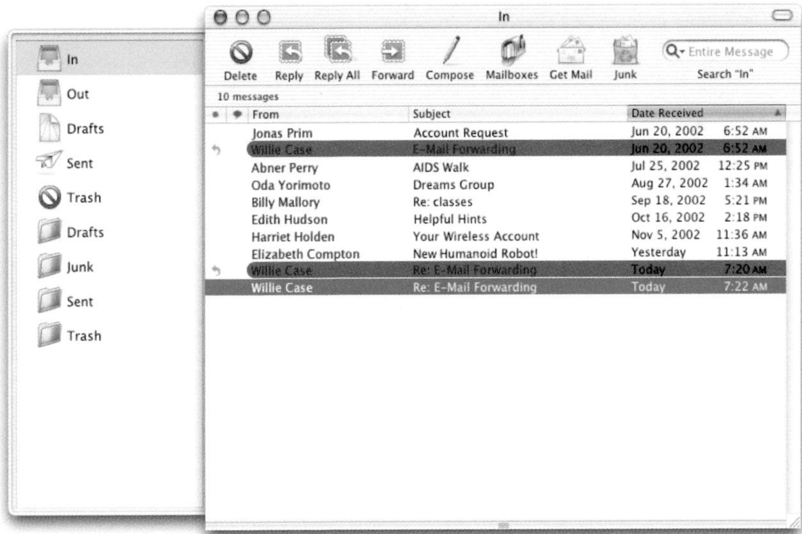

CP.7

Technique 31:

Using the free, open-source OpenOffice.org suite, you can open and edit Microsoft Office documents, including word-processing documents, presentations, and spreadsheets.

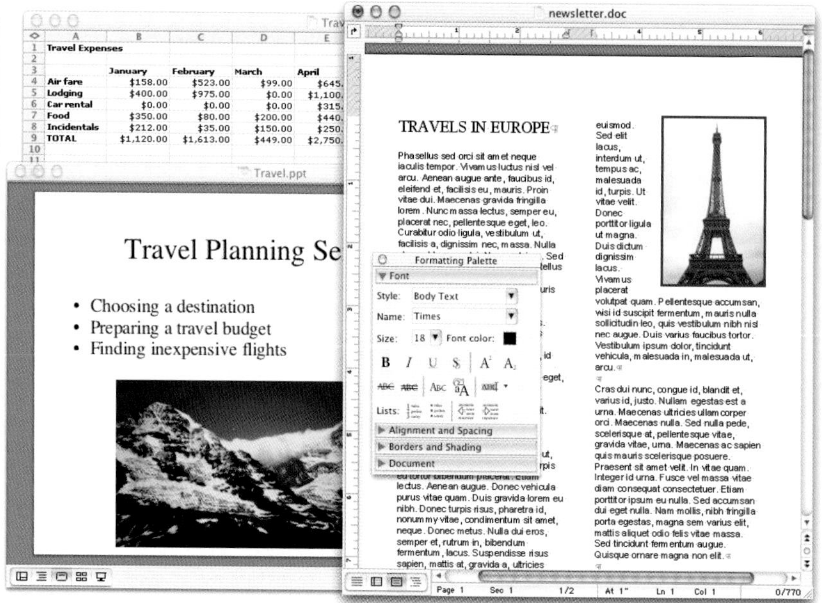

CP.8

CP.9

Technique 32:

Using VNC, you can view and control another computer's display remotely.

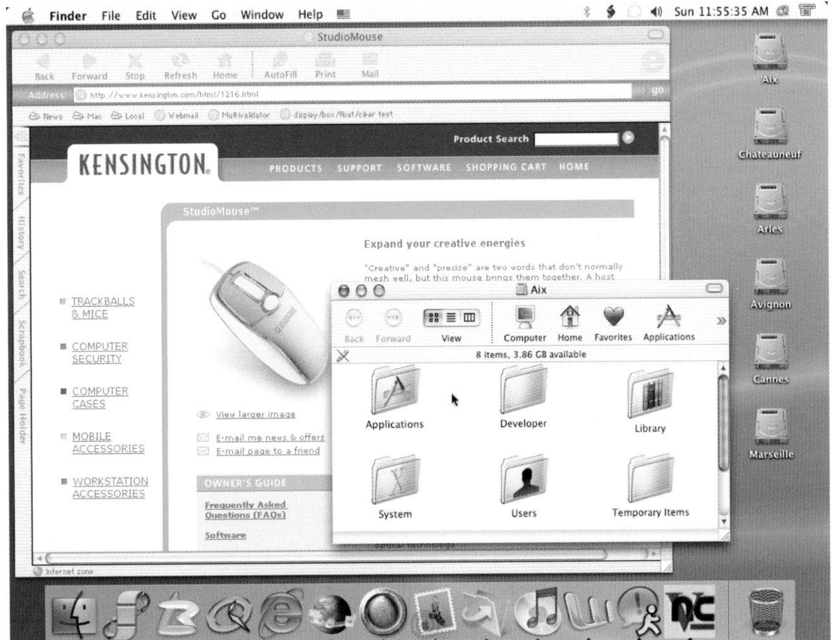

CP.10

CP.11

Technique 33:

Photoshop is a wonderful but expensive image-editing tool. You can get most of Photoshop's functionality for free using the GIMP.

CP.12

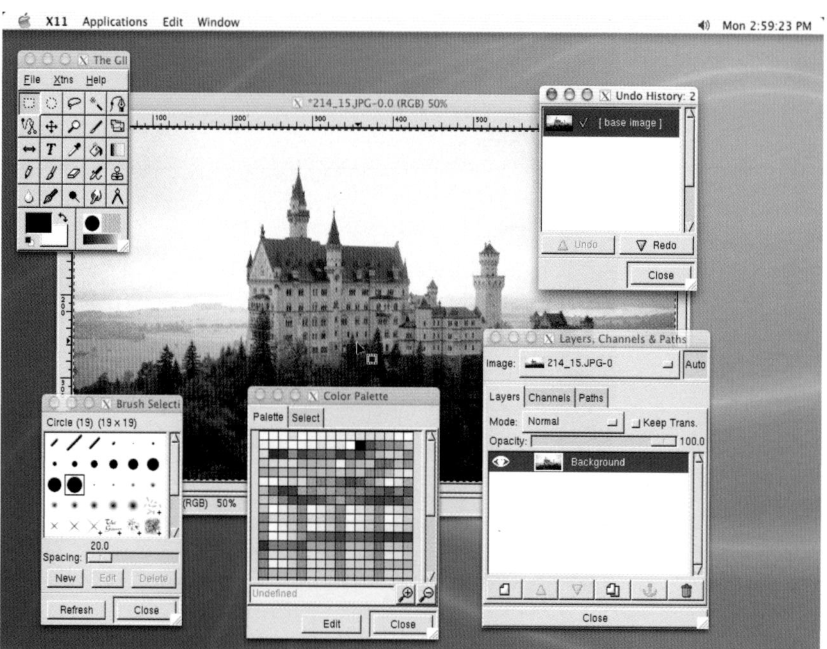

CP.13

Technique 36:

Using the Ken Burns effect in iMovie 3, you can turn still photos into moving images.

CP.14

Technique 37:

You can create a customized motion menu theme like this one in iDVD, complete with moving background and button images.

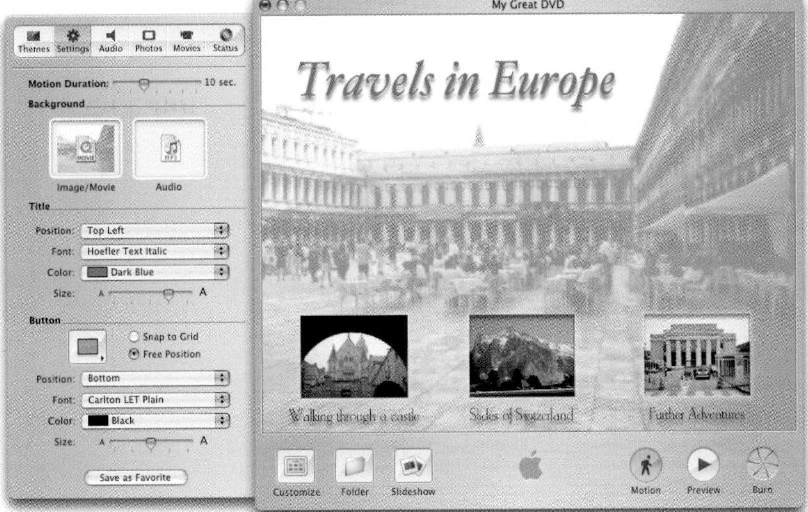

CP.15

Technique 47:

Applying performance-enhancing techniques can ease the strain on your CPU and RAM (as shown by these on-screen indicators) and give your Mac more breathing room.

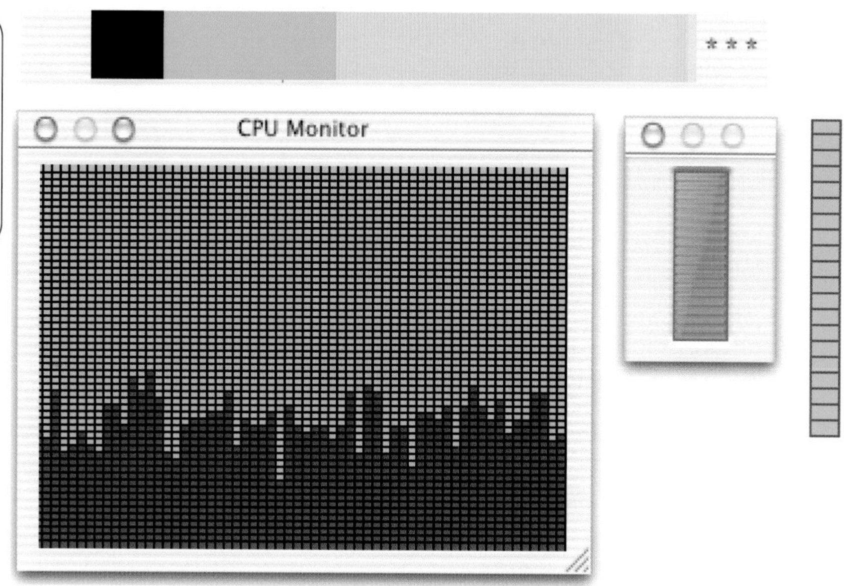

CP.16

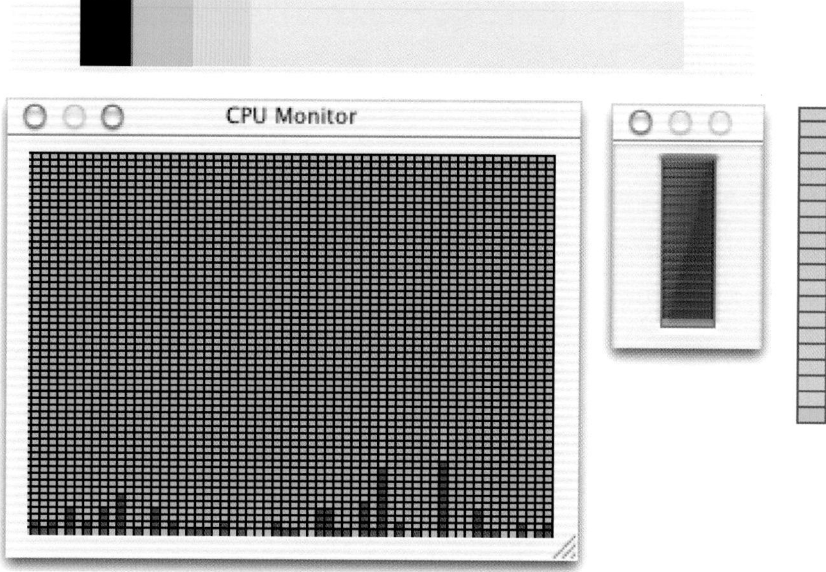

CP.17

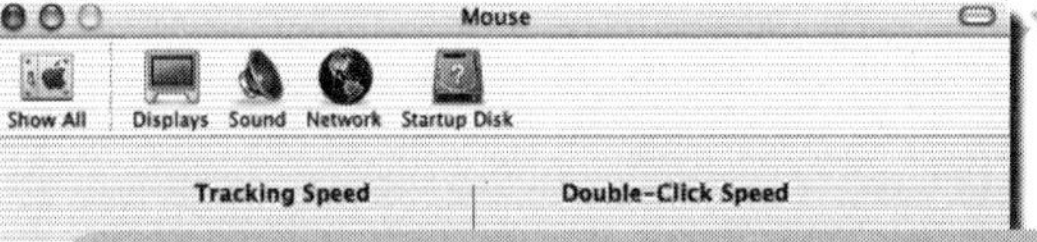

CHAPTER 4

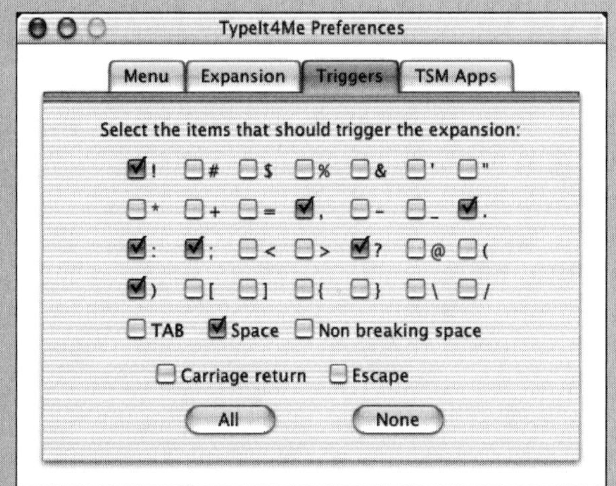

INPUT AND CONTROL TECHNIQUES

Your computer may have a beautiful flat-panel display, a powerful sound system, and plenty of processing power, but it won't do anything useful for you until you tell it what you want it to do — in other words, give it some input. Keyboards and mice are the input devices we're all familiar with, but there are other ways of getting data into your computer as well, including speaking into a microphone and writing on a graphics tablet. You probably spend several hours a day providing input to your computer in one way or another. In this chapter, I help you use that time more effectively by showing you great techniques for using all the most common input devices.

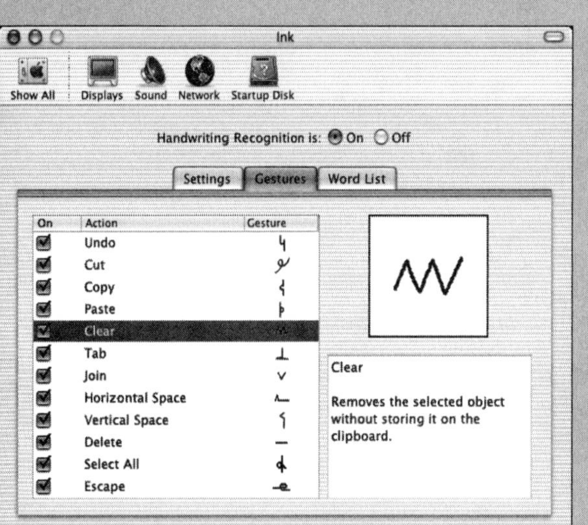

The first technique discusses the humble mouse (and its cousins, the trackball and trackpad), showing you how to minimize clicks and wrist movement. Then you take a look at the keyboard, whose capabilities extend far beyond typing. Turning to speech recognition, you see how to make your computer jump through hoops at the sound of your voice. Graphic artists and others with a graphics tablet learn how to get even more value from it with Mac OS X's Inkwell handwriting recognition. You round out the chapter by learning how to use Apple's Universal Access features — extending your reach beyond that of ordinary input methods.

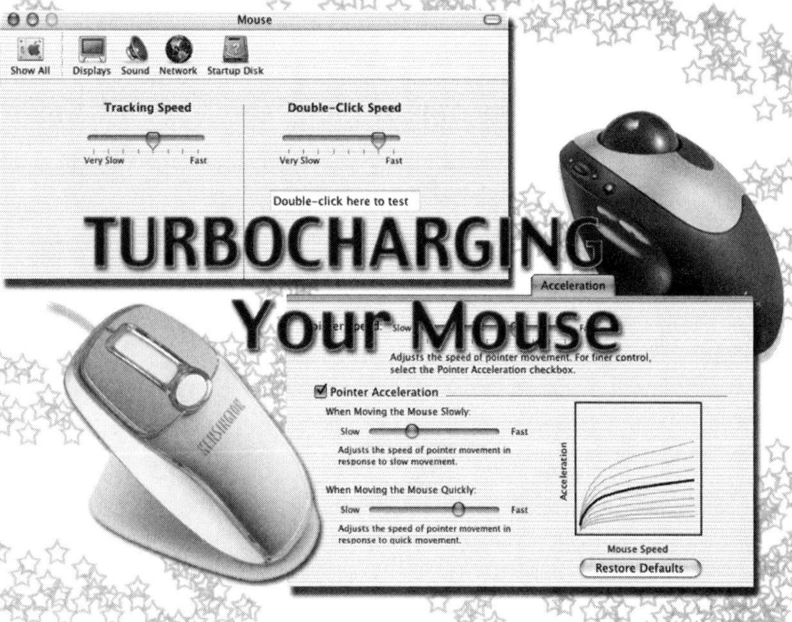

KEYBOARD Efficiency

Key Caps

Shortcuts

Type	Shortcut	Everywhere
	Change to columns	⌥^ C
	E-mail Morgen	⌘⇧^ M
	Hide Other Applications	⌘^ H
	Mount PowerBook Drive	⌘⌥^ P
	Paste Special	⌘⌥ V
	Shut Down	⌘^ Q
	Switch to Next Application	⌘ space
	Type Short Date	⌘⌥ D
	www.apple.com	^ F12
	Zoom	⌘⇧ Z

Non breaking space

TAB

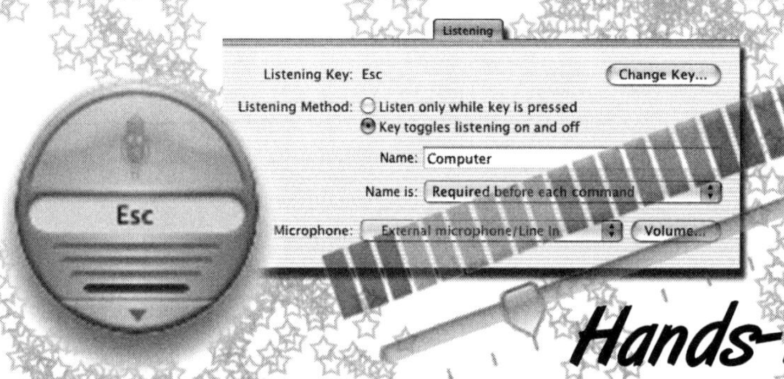

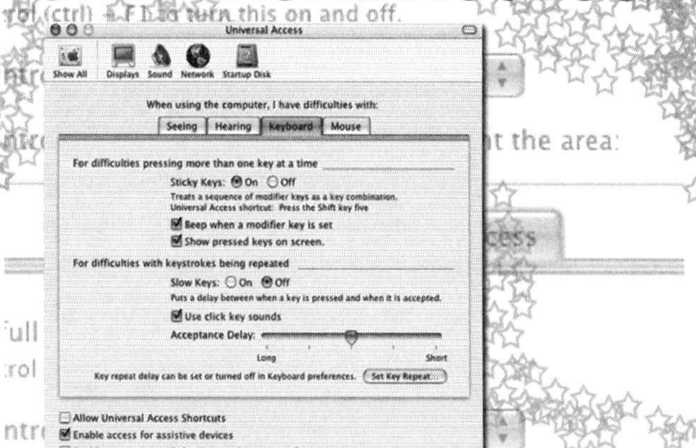

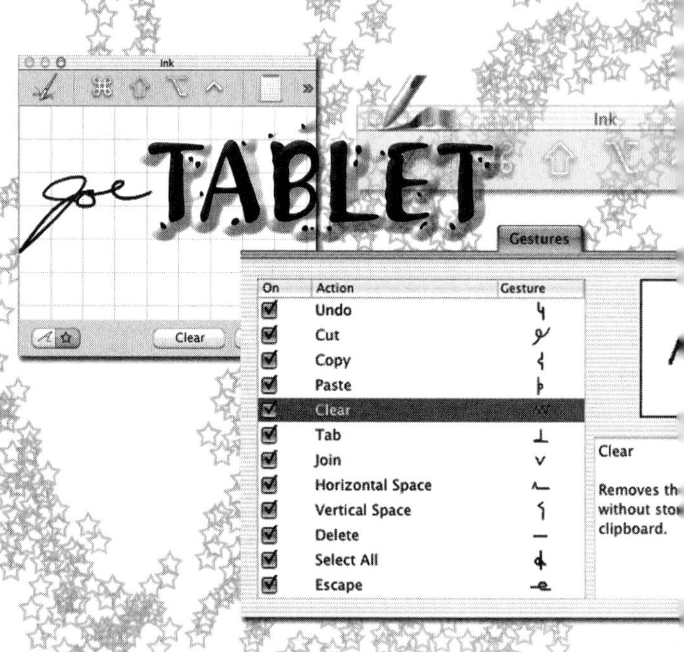

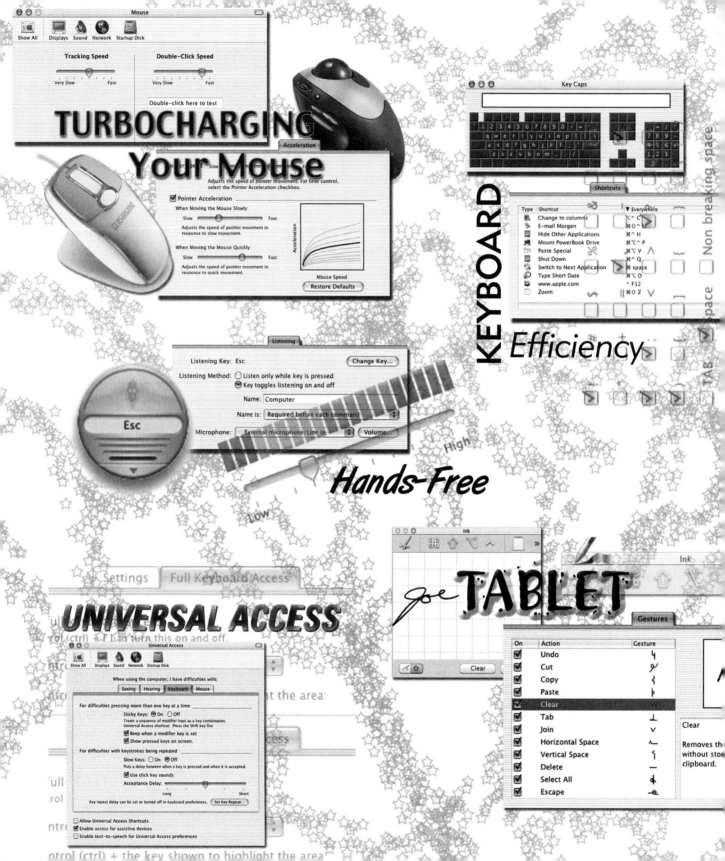

TURBOCHARGING YOUR MOUSE

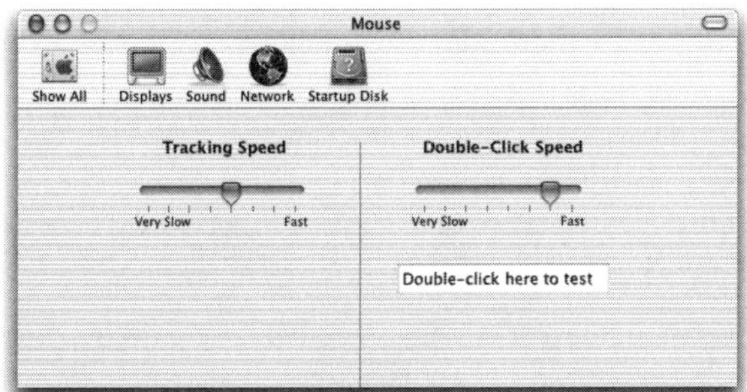

18.1

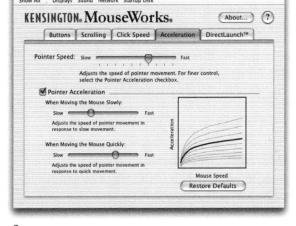

18.2

ABOUT THE FEATURE

A mouse (or other pointing device) is essential for interacting with Mac OS X's graphical user interface. This simple tool is also extremely powerful and customizable.

The mouse is such an integral part of the Mac experience that many people think of it as an extension of their hand. Yet, important as the mouse is, it's also underused — and often misused. In this technique, you focus on making your mouse use as efficient as possible.

I spent several years developing mouse driver software for Kensington, a major manufacturer of Mac mice and trackballs. Because of this, I have some strong convictions about the way input devices should be used. (I also, of course, have a bias toward the Kensington brand.) There are two cardinal principles of mouse efficiency. First, less movement is better than more movement. The farther and more often you need to move your mouse, the longer it will take you to accomplish tasks. The second principle is that fewer clicks are better than more clicks. The cumulative effect of all those extra clicks over the course of a day or week can be a significant decline in your productivity. In addition, because repetitive stress injuries have been associated with excessive mouse use, keeping your mouse movements down to a minimum can't hurt.

STEP 1: SELECT AN INPUT DEVICE

Although the Apple Pro Mouse is a thing of beauty and a wonder of industrial design, it is also, sadly, among the least efficient pointing devices you can own. One of the best things you can do to increase your productivity is replace it immediately.

Look for an input device that has the two essential attributes missing from Apple's mice: two (or more) buttons and a scroll wheel. These features enable you to make the most of some exciting features built into Mac OS X.

- Decide whether you prefer a mouse or a trackball. There is no right answer; it's a matter of taste and habit. Trackballs (like the Logitech Cordless Optical Trackman shown in **Figure 18.3**) take up less desk space because the base does not move. They also tend to require less wrist movement, which might help to reduce the risk of repetitive stress injuries. Mice come in a wider variety of shapes and sizes, and may, in some cases, provide a finer level of precision in controlling your pointer. The best way to choose an input device is to try 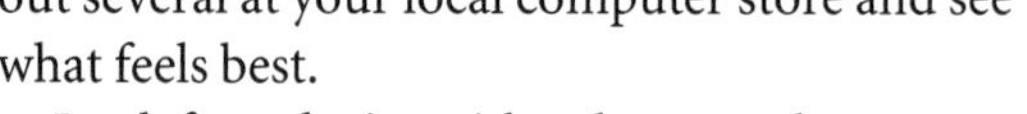
out several at your local computer store and see what feels best.
- Look for a device with at least two buttons, preferably three or four. Pay attention to how the buttons are positioned. Make sure the extra buttons are easy to reach with your fingers in a normal, relaxed position — but not so easy to reach that you press them accidentally while picking up the mouse.
- Choose an input device that has a scroll wheel (or a reasonable facsimile thereof). Some trackballs, like Kensington's TurboRing, use a movable ring around the ball in place of a wheel, and some mice, like the StudioMouse (shown in **Figure 18.4**), use a flat scroll sensor, similar to a trackpad.

STEP 2: FINE-TUNE YOUR POINTER ACCELERATION

Out of the box, your Mac is set to use a pretty slow mouse tracking speed. The effect is that in order to move your pointer all the way across the screen, you

18.3

18.4

may have to pick up and reposition your mouse two or three times. You can improve this movement dramatically.

NOTE

If you're using a PowerBook or iBook and have an external pointing device attached, your Mouse control panel will also contain a Trackpad tab. This tab has a separate Tracking Speed control for your trackpad, which you may want to respond differently than your external mouse, as well as other controls to customize the behavior of your trackpad.

- To adjust the tracking speed of an Apple mouse, click the **System Preferences** icon in your Dock and click the **Mouse** button (located in the Hardware section). Drag the **Tracking Speed** slider to adjust your pointer acceleration as shown in **Figure 18.5.**
- If you're using a third-party mouse driver, it may have its own controls to adjust acceleration. Kensington MouseWorks (shown in **Figure 18.6**) offers separate acceleration adjustments for slow and fast mouse movement.

STEP 3: MAXIMIZE CONTEXTUAL MENUS

By holding down the Control key and clicking your mouse button, you can display a pop-up *contextual*

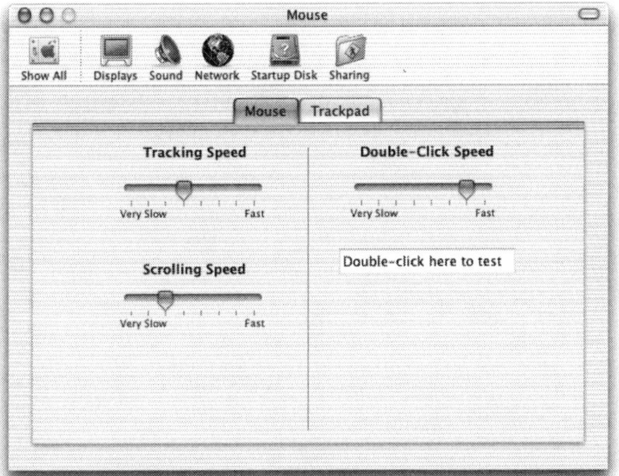

18.5

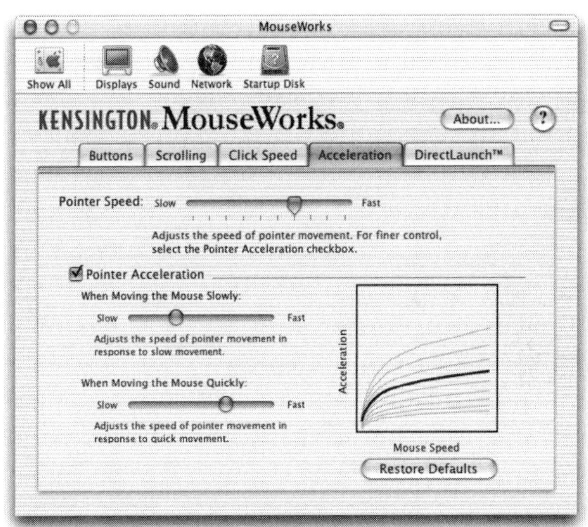

18.6

menu of commands that are relevant to your pointer location (such as an icon or text selection). **Figure 18.7** shows the contextual menu for a file in the Finder, while **Figure 18.8** shows the commands available for a selected word in Word v. X.

Using a contextual menu reduces both mouse movement and clicks. Unfortunately, this benefit is offset by the fact that you need to use both hands to display them, and what you save in clicks you make up for in extra keystrokes. This is where the extra buttons on your multi-button input device come in.

- Use your right mouse button instead of Control+clicking. When you plug in any multi-button USB mouse, Mac OS X automatically uses button 2 (usually the right button) to display contextual menus. If you're not accustomed to using contextual menus at all, try right-clicking every time you have an icon, text block, or other object selected. (If you're left handed, use a third-party mouse utility to make the right button Click and the left button Control+click.)

- Expand your contextual menus. Although the contextual menus built into Mac OS X are powerful, you can add even more useful commands by installing third-party utilities or plug-ins. In general, all you need to do is run the utility's installer (or simply open the application once if it doesn't include an installer) and then log out and log back in to see the new commands on your contextual menus. **Figure 18.9** shows the contextual menu of a Finder file as it appears before and after installing several such utilities.

One program that puts contextual menus to especially good use is StuffIt Deluxe, the legendary file compression utility from Aladdin (`www.stuffit.com`). The StuffIt contextual menu is shown in **Figure 18.10**. Examples from the shareware world include Launch Items X (`www.naratt.com/LaunchItems.html`), a package of highly customizable plug-ins that speed navigation; XRay (`www.brockerhoff.net/xray/`), a utility for viewing and modifying file attributes; and Zingg! (`www.brockerhoff.net/zingg/`), a free utility that enhances Mac OS X's ability to display

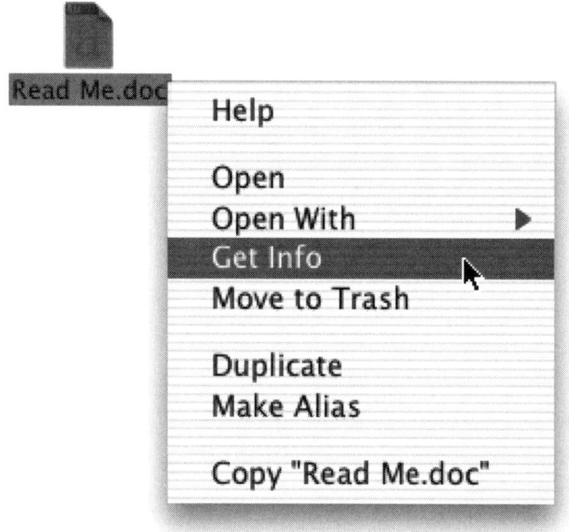

18.7

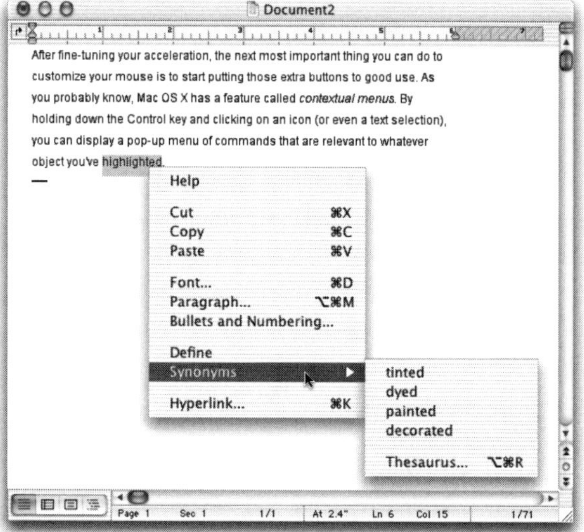

18.8

which applications are available to open a file. To find other contextual menu plug-ins, visit `www.versiontracker.com` and type **contextual menu** in the Search box.

STEP 4: USE A SCROLL WHEEL

Scroll wheels provide an excellent way to decrease the amount of movement your hand makes. Ordinarily, if you want to scroll up or down in a window, you need to move the pointer to the scroll bar and click the up or down arrow (or move the scroller up or down). This distracts you momentarily from the contents of your window, and also requires a lot of repetitive mouse movement.

Scroll wheels bypass all that by controlling window scrolling directly. Roll the wheel forward one click, and your window scrolls up a notch. Roll backward to scroll down; roll more quickly to scroll more quickly. You only need to move the wheel — the mouse itself doesn't move at all, and you can keep your eye on your document or Web page. Some more tips for using a scroll wheel include the following:

- If you're not accustomed to using a scroll wheel, force yourself to do all your scrolling with a wheel for a day. It will feel a little strange at first, but most people who try this out for a day get so hooked they can never go back to using a wheel-less mouse.
- Adjust your scroll wheel speed. If you want to scroll a bit more or less with each click of the

TIP

Even though contextual menus are a time saver, too many of them can actually slow you down. Contextual menus take longer to draw when there are a lot of plug-ins to process, and longer menus make finding the command you're looking for harder. For maximum value from contextual menus, limit yourself to two or three plug-ins you find especially useful.

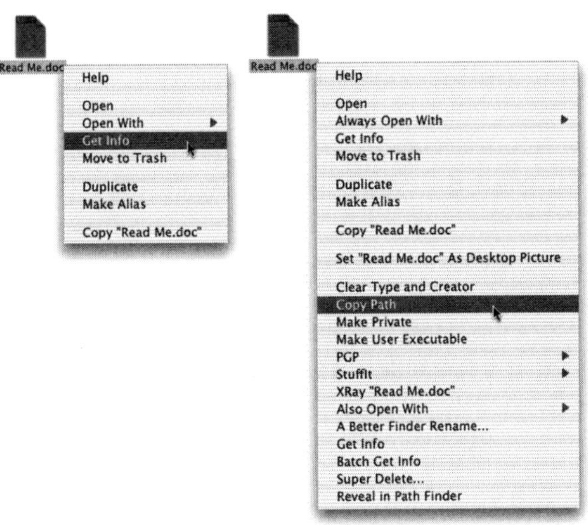

18.9

18.10

wheel, go to the Mouse pane of System Preferences (shown earlier in **Figure 18.5**) and adjust the **Scrolling Speed** slider. You can also adjust scroll wheel speed in most third-party mouse software packages.

- Use a wheel to scroll horizontally. If you're viewing a window that has a horizontal scroll bar, you can use your scroll wheel to scroll horizontally by pressing the Shift key while rolling the scroll wheel.

STEP 5: SET UP DRIVER OPTIONS

Almost every mouse manufacturer includes software to configure and extend the functionality of its input devices. These control panels are normally accessed using the System Preferences application. As an alternative, the shareware utility USB Overdrive (`www.usboverdrive.com`), shown in **Figure 18.11**, can give any input device advanced capabilities.

- If your mouse has more than two buttons, set one to Double-Click. Use your double-click button to open a file or folder, launch an application, minimize a window, or select a word in a text editor.
- Set additional buttons to perform tasks such as Drag (also known as Click Lock), which holds down your mouse button even though you've released it physically, or keyboard shortcuts like ⌘+C for **Copy** or ⌘+Z for **Undo**. Look through your mouse software's settings to choose actions that are useful to you.

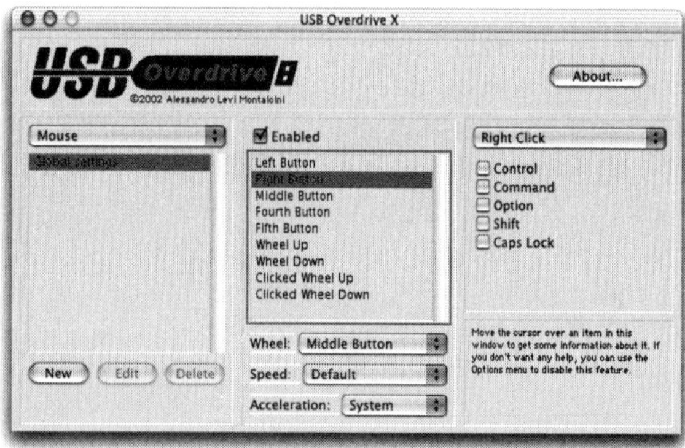

18.11

STEP 6: USE SPRING-LOADED FOLDERS AND WINDOWS

In keeping with the principle of "fewer clicks are better," you can erase extra clicks when moving or copying files by using spring-loaded folders and windows.

- Turn on spring-loaded folders. In the Finder, choose **Preferences...** from the **Finder** menu. The Finder Preferences window appears, as shown in **Figure 18.12**. Make sure the checkbox next to **Spring-loaded folders and windows** is checked. Adjust the **Delay** slider to taste. A fairly short delay makes the spring effect more useful.
- To use spring-loaded folders, drag a file onto a folder or volume icon and pause briefly with the mouse button still held down. The window will open, and as long as you continue holding the mouse button, you can move as many levels deep as you want. When you release the mouse button, the file moves to that folder, and all the intermediate windows automatically close.
- By using modifier keys while dragging, you can choose whether the file should be copied or moved. If the origin and destination of your file are on the same volume, dragging and dropping with contextual menus will move the file by default. To make a copy of the file, hold the Option key as you drag. If the origin and destination are on different volumes, the default drag-and-drop behavior is copying. To move the file instead, hold the ⌘ key as you drag. How can you

tell whether you're copying or moving? When copying, your pointer will always display a green + sign, as shown in **Figure 18.13**.

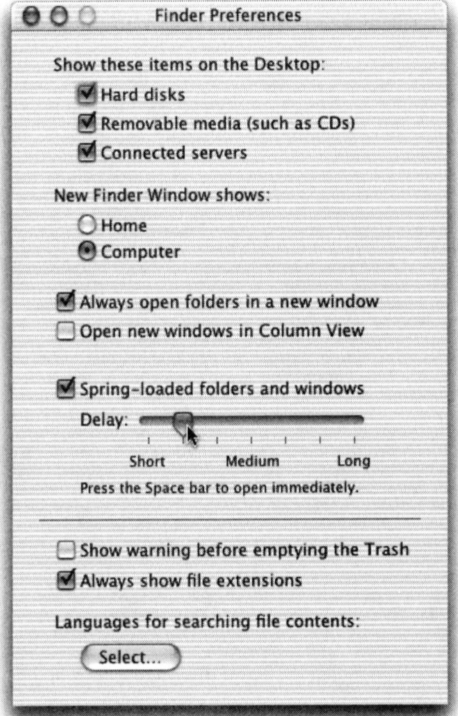

18.12

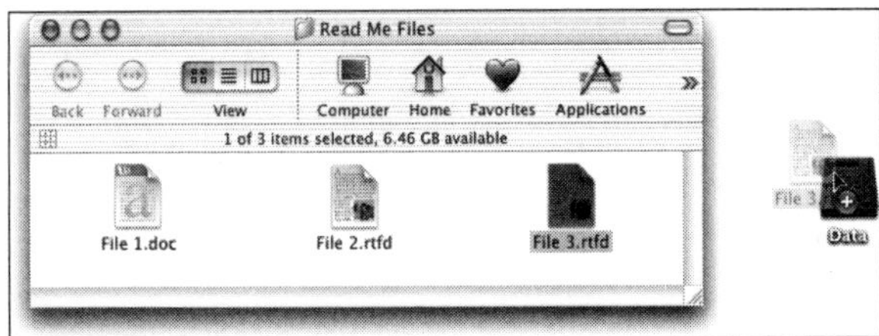

18.13

Spring-loaded windows are a variation on the default drag-and-drop behavior. If you drag a file into a window that is partially off-screen, it will spring completely onto the screen after a brief pause and then spring back to its original location when you release the mouse button.

STEP 7: EXTEND YOUR MOUSE'S REACH

Just as spring-loaded folders make moving or copying files easier, you should be able to locate and open nearly any file on your hard drive with a single click.

- Drag your hard drive icon to the Dock, as shown in **Figure 18.14**. You'll then get one-click access to most of the files and folders on your hard drive. The only limitation is that you can only navigate folders to a depth of five levels.
- To overcome the five-levels-deep limitation, try the excellent FruitMenu, a shareware program from Unsanity (`www.unsanity.com`). It allows you to customize both your Apple menu and contextual menus extensively, and it includes a hierarchical menu that can display the entire contents of your hard drive.

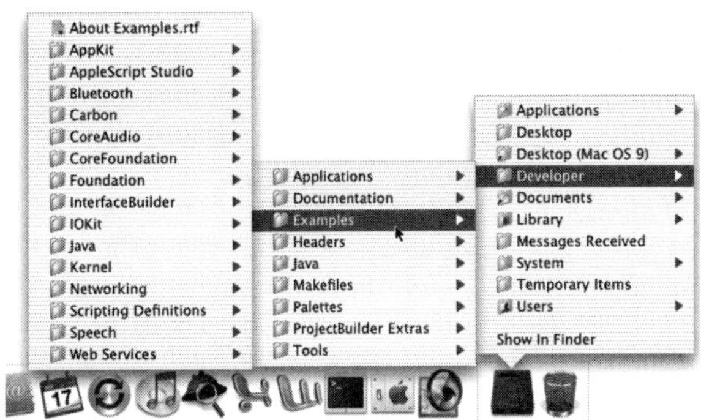

18.14

TECHNIQUE 19

BOOSTING YOUR KEYBOARD EFFICIENCY

19.1

19.2

ABOUT THE FEATURE

Along with the mouse, your keyboard provides the primary means of getting information into your computer. Proper keyboard skills, along with some third-party utilities, can increase your productivity tremendously.

Your computer screen is covered with graphical elements like icons, buttons, and menus — controls that ordinarily you activate using your mouse. The fact that you can find all the commands you need by clicking your mouse makes your computer easy to use. However, that ease of use comes at the cost of decreased efficiency. If your work involves a lot of typing (as opposed to, say, drawing), moving your hand back and forth between the keyboard and mouse — and moving your eyes back and forth between the text you're writing and on-screen controls — can slow you down more than you might imagine.

The cardinal rule for people who do a lot of programming, writing, or other typing is: Keep your hands on the keyboard as much as possible. If you read Technique 18, you know all about getting the most from every click of your mouse. In this technique, you do the same thing with your keyboard. You won't leave your mouse entirely behind, of course, but you'll work more effectively by using the keyboard as much as possible.

It goes without saying — but I'll say it anyway — that if you want to get the most out of your computing experience in general (and your keyboard in particular), you need to know how to touch type. If you use the hunt-and-peck method of typing, this technique will not benefit you at all, because it will be just as fast to use your mouse for most activities. If you haven't yet learned to type without looking at the keyboard, a program like Ten Thumbs Typing Tutor (available from `www.runrev.com`) can help you get up to speed quickly and painlessly.

STEP 1: LEARN KEYBOARD SHORTCUTS

If I could offer just one piece of advice to new users of Mac OS X, it would be this: Learn to use keyboard shortcuts. Almost everything you need to do *can* be done with a mouse, but in most cases, using the keyboard is faster and easier. This is particularly true if you're in the process of typing something and need to do something common like turn on boldface, undo your last action, or paste the contents of the Clipboard. Moving your hand off the keyboard onto the mouse, moving the pointer up to the menu bar, finding the right menu, choosing the command, and then moving your hand back to the keyboard is much more tedious than simply pressing two keys. If you do this dozens of times each day, you can easily see how much time and effort you can save by using keyboard shortcuts.

Mac OS X has a *lot* of keyboard shortcuts, and individual applications have many more. Listing all of them would take a long time, and you would never remember them all anyway. So concentrate on a dozen of the most important and common ones here, and refer to Appendix A for a more complete list.

■ Your assignment: Starting now, *never* use a mouse to perform the commands in **Table 19-1**. Force yourself to do them with the keyboard. After you get in the habit of using these shortcuts, you'll never want to go back.

Of course, lots of common keyboard shortcuts are not listed in this table. But if you can learn these, you'll dramatically increase your keyboard power. After you've mastered these shortcuts, you can learn even more by consulting Appendix A. An easy way to learn keyboard shortcuts, regardless of what application you're using, is simply to look at the menus. Most menu commands that have keyboard equivalents list those shortcuts right on the menu, as shown in **Figure 19.3**.

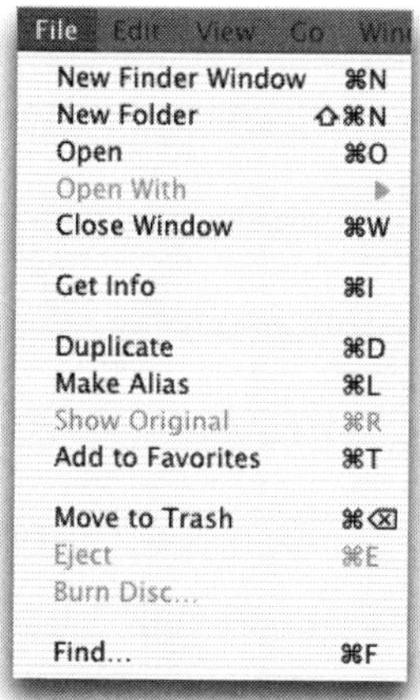

19.3

Table 19-1

Basic Keyboard Shortcuts

TO DO THIS	PRESS THESE KEYS	HOW TO REMEMBER IT	WORKS HERE
Undo your last action	**⌘+Z**	Z is the *last* letter in the alphabet; use this to undo your *last* command.	Almost everywhere.
Cut (delete) the current selection and put it on the Clipboard	**⌘+X**	Draw an X through something to cross it out.	Almost everywhere, but *not* used to delete files in the Finder.
Copy the current selection to the Clipboard	**⌘+C**	C for Copy.	Almost everywhere for text selections; in the Finder you can even copy files this way.
Paste the contents of the Clipboard at your insertion point	**⌘+V**	V is next to C on the keyboard; you usually paste right after you copy.	Almost everywhere.
Turn **boldface** on or off	**⌘+B**	B for Bold.	Most text-editing applications, including Mail.
Select all (text or icons, depending on the context)	**⌘+A**	A for All.	Almost everywhere.
Find (text or files, depending on the context)	**⌘+F**	F for Find.	The Finder and most applications.
Click the **default** (highlighted) button in a dialog — usually **OK**	**Return**	Return me to my main window.	Almost everywhere.
Save changes to the current document	**⌘+S**	S for Save.	Almost all document-based applications.
Close the current window	**⌘+W**	W for the Window you want to close	Almost everywhere.
Quit (exit) the current application	**⌘+Q**	Q for Quit.	Every application except the Finder.
Move the selected files to the **Trash**	**⌘+delete**	You're *commanding* the computer to *delete* files.	The Finder (for files and folders); iTunes; a few other applications.

STEP 2: USE YOUR APPLICATIONS' KEYSTROKE-SAVING FEATURES

Besides offering shortcuts like key combinations for Bold and Italic, some applications have extra features that can reduce the amount of typing you need to do in the first place. The available options depend on which applications you use most frequently. Here are examples for Web browsers and Microsoft Word:

- If you're tired of filling out forms in Web browsers every time you buy something, sign up for an account, or fill out a survey, your browser has tools that can help you out.

  Internet Explorer's AutoFill feature stores your name, address, phone numbers, and e-mail address. After you've filled this information in once, you can fill in any Web form instantly. To fill out your AutoFill Profile, choose **Preferences...** from Internet Explorer's **Explorer** menu and select **AutoFill Profile** from the list of categories. (See **Figure 19.4** for an example.) Fill out the form and click **OK**. The next time you're on a Web page with a form, simply press ⌘+' to fill in your data. (OmniWeb, Netscape, Mozilla, and Opera have very similar features.)

In addition to AutoFill, Internet Explorer allows you to enter your own custom list of words, names, and phrases that you type frequently. When you type the first few letters of one of these into a form, Explorer helpfully fills in the rest for you. To set up your list, choose **Forms AutoComplete** from the category list in Explorer's Preferences dialog. Click **Add...** to add new entries, make sure **Enabled** is selected and click **OK** when you're done. (iCab and Opera offer similar functionality.)

> **NOTE**
>
> **For even more time-saving browser tips, see Technique 29, "Web Browsing Secrets of the Rich and Famous."**

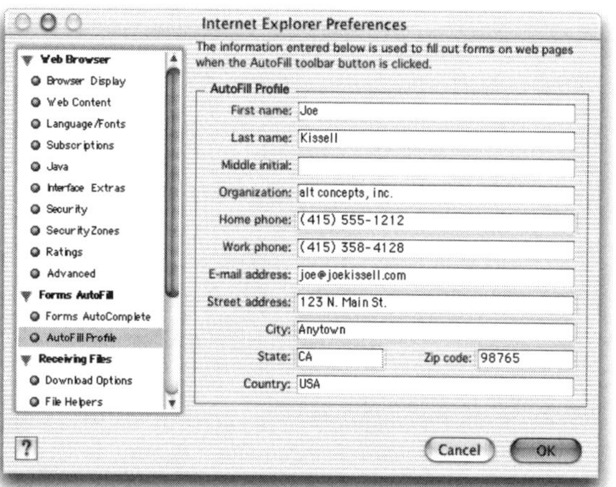

19.4

■ If you use Microsoft Word, you have a great feature called AutoText at your disposal. Similar to Internet Explorer's AutoComplete, AutoText lets you define a list of frequently typed words or phrases (and includes quite a few predefined entries to get you started). As you type, Word recognizes when you've typed the first few letters of an AutoText entry and offers to fill in the rest for you.

To set up AutoText entries, choose **AutoCorrect...** from the **Tools** menu in Microsoft Word and click the **AutoText** tab, as shown in **Figure 19.5**. Type a new word or phrase in the field labeled **Enter AutoText entries here** and click **Add....** Repeat for as many entries as you want and click **OK**.

To use AutoText, simply type the first few letters of one of your entries. A yellow box appears with a matching entry. To have Word enter the rest of the entry for you, press **Return**. If you don't want to use Word's suggestion, just ignore it and keep typing.

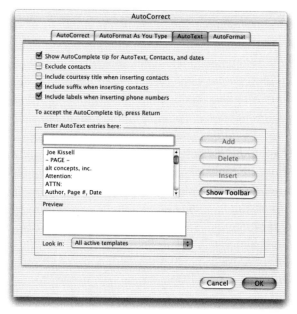

19.5

STEP 3: TYPE FASTER WITH TYPEIT4ME

Word's AutoText feature is terrific, but it only works in Word. Wouldn't it be nice if you could do the same thing in *any* application? A shareware program called TypeIt4Me (available from `www.typeit4me.com`) does this, and even goes a step further by eliminating the need to manually confirm each completion. I used TypeIt4Me extensively while writing this book. For example, instead of typing "Mac OS X" every time I used it, I simply typed **mx**, and when I pressed the space bar, TypeIt4Me automatically expanded it. This program can be wonderful for names, phrases, and other text you use frequently. You can also put all your most common misspellings in it to have them corrected automatically.

- Download TypeIt4Me from `www.typeit4me.com` and install it according to the directions provided.
- To activate TypeIt4Me, choose the "A" icon from your Input menu, as shown in **Figure 19.6**. Another menu bar icon appears next to it; this is TypeIt4Me's menu.
- As soon as you've typed a word or phrase you want TypeIt4Me to remember, select it and press **⌘+C** to copy it to the Clipboard. Then choose **Add an Entry...** from the TypeIt4Me menu, as shown in **Figure 19.7**. In the dialog that appears, enter the abbreviation you want to use for that entry. Be sure to choose something that you don't want to use on its own. For example, "us" would not be a good abbreviation for "United States of America," because you don't really want to end up with sentences like "Let's keep this between the two of United States of America."
- TypeIt4Me lets you customize *triggers* — the keys that indicate the program should expand what you just typed. Choose **Preferences...** from the TypeIt4Me menu and click the **Triggers** tab, as shown in **Figure 19.8**. Put a checkmark in the

19.6

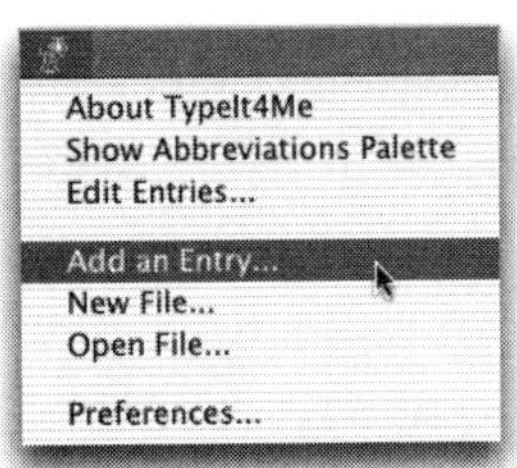

19.7

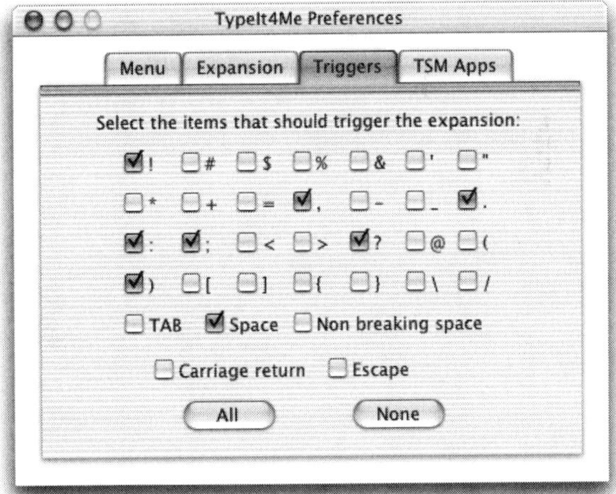

19.8

boxes next to all the punctuation you want to use as triggers. Deselect anything that you don't want to trigger expansion. For example, if I used "jwk" as an abbreviation for "Joseph William Kissell" but wanted to make sure it didn't expand if I put it in quotes, as I just did, I would uncheck the " box. To make sure it didn't expand when I typed my e-mail address, jwk@mac.com, I would uncheck the @ sign.

You're now good to go. As you type, TypeIt4Me automatically expands your abbreviations. The more abbreviations you add, the more useful it becomes. Be sure to consult TypeIt4Me's documentation for details on settings and features, and pay your shareware fee if you find it useful and continue to use it.

STEP 4: CREATE COMMAND SHORTCUTS WITH QUICKEYS

CE Software's QuicKeys (see **Figure 19.9**) is one of the legends of Mac software. It has been around for many years and has a huge base of loyal followers. In a nutshell, QuicKeys is an easy-to-use automation program. It can take a variety of tasks — such as mounting a server, selecting menu commands, opening files, and clicking buttons — and perform them with any key press you assign.

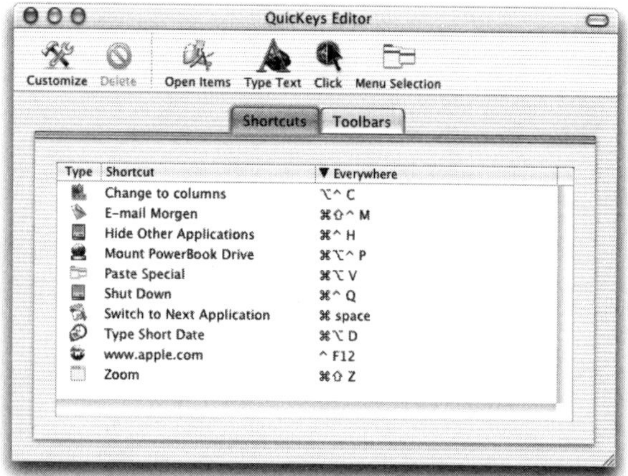

19.9

More importantly, it allows you to create shortcuts (also known as *macros*) that are sequences of several tasks. With a QuicKeys shortcut, a single key press can (for example) mount a server, copy a file, open that file in your favorite text editor, and print it.

QuicKeys is particularly useful for customizing the function keys (F1, F2, F3, and so on) at the top of your keyboard because they're often unused and offer a way to perform some common operations with just one keystroke. Because QuicKeys has more features than you can shake a stick at, I can't provide a detailed explanation of how to perform every task. I do, however, offer a few suggestions of shortcuts you might set up. Download a demo from `www.quickeys.com` to try these for yourself.

- Press **⌘+Shift+Z** to click the Zoom button on your window.
- Use **⌘+Control+Q** to save your current document and then quit the application.
- Press **F5** to print five copies of a document.
- Launch your Web browser and go to your favorite news site by pressing **F9**.

STEP 5: LAUNCH ANYTHING FROM THE KEYBOARD WITH LAUNCHBAR

Now for a quick thought experiment: Suppose you want to find a particular accent character using the Key Caps utility, but you're not sure exactly where it is on your hard drive. How many clicks will it take you to find and open it? Well, you might start by double-clicking your hard drive to open a new Finder window and then double-click your Applications folder to open it. After scrolling through the window and not finding Key Caps, you might next try opening your Utilities folder. Again, you would scroll through that window until you found Key Caps, and finally double-click to open it.

Instead of doing all that, how would you like to open Key Caps — without any preliminary setup and without knowing where it was — with exactly four keystrokes? LaunchBar (available from `www.launchbar.com`) is an amazingly clever utility that can do exactly this, and quite a bit more. I use it dozens of times every day because it eliminates the time and effort to find things, or even to set up shortcuts to them with the Dock, a file launcher, or a utility like QuicKeys. It just *knows* what you need and where to find it. It is so useful, in fact, that it's my very favorite utility of all time. See for yourself why it's so great:

- Download and install a free demo of LaunchBar from `www.launchbar.com`. LaunchBar adds a small icon to the edge of your menu bar, as shown in **Figure 19.10**.
- To begin using LaunchBar, you press a (customizable) key combination, such as **⌘+spacebar** or **⌘+Esc**. A small tab drops down from your menu bar (see **Figure 19.11**), listing the last item selected with LaunchBar. (If you want to open that item, just press **Return**.)
- Type the first letter in the name of the application you want to open. (If your application has more than one word, type the first letter of any of the words.) A list of matching applications drops down from the LaunchBar tab, as shown in **Figure 19.12**. More often than not, the application you want will already be highlighted. If it is, press **Return** to open it. If not, type the next letter in the name and the list will change to narrow your choices. Continue typing letters, if necessary, until you find the application you want — or use the arrow keys to scroll up or down the list.

As you use LaunchBar, it becomes smarter by learning which applications you use most often. It then intelligently rearranges its list of matching items accordingly. For example, LaunchBar knows that of all the applications beginning with "i," the one I use most often is iTunes, so that choice is always the first one selected when I type "i" after activating LaunchBar — even though it doesn't come first in alphabetical order. Likewise, it has figured out that I expect Microsoft Word to be selected when I type "w," even though the application name actually starts with "m" and other applications are on my machine that do begin with "w."

Although I've been talking about using LaunchBar for launching applications, it's equally good at launching documents and URLs, and can even create a new Mail message when you enter the shortcut for the recipient's e-mail address. In fact, this discussion just scratches the surface of LaunchBar's capabilities. Be sure to explore the demo version to find out more.

19.10

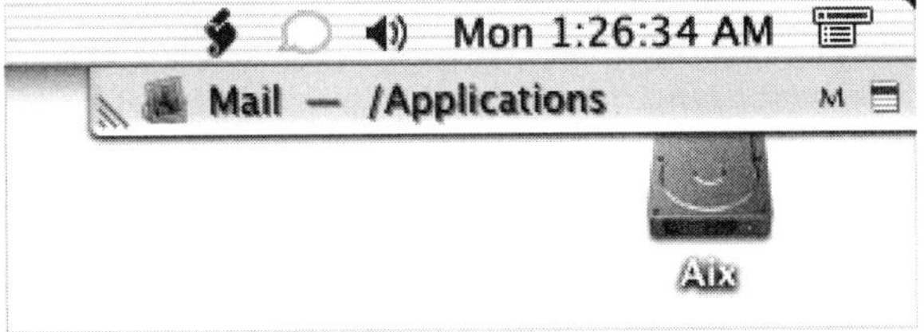

19.11

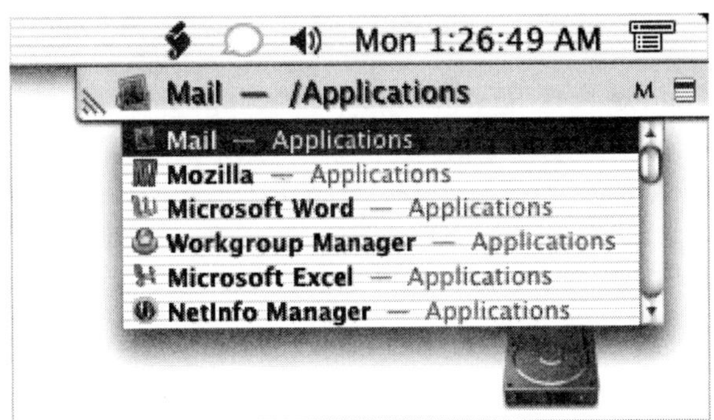

19.12

By the way (recalling the thought experiment at the beginning of this step), to open Key Caps with exactly four keystrokes, you use a shortcut to activate LaunchBar, such as **⌘+spacebar** (keystrokes 1 and 2); press **K** (keystroke 3), and Key Caps will most likely show up as the first highlighted item; then press **Return** (keystroke 4) to open it.

STEP 6: CONSIDER A NEW KEYBOARD (OPTIONAL)

All keyboards are not created equal. The keyboard that came with your Mac, although probably a very stylish match for your computer, may not be the best choice. Other keyboards from third-party manufacturers have features that can improve your comfort as well as offer additional shortcuts. Here are some factors to consider when shopping for a new keyboard:

- What do the keys feel like? For many people, this one concern overrides all others. It also means that evaluating keyboards without actually touching them in a store (or at a friend's house) is difficult. Keyboards vary in the amount of force needed to press the keys, the amount of springiness in the return, the feel when keys hit bottom (solid, mushy, or in between), and the sound the keys make, which can influence your perception of the feel. Judging the feel of a keyboard is highly subjective, but in general, you want a keyboard with a light enough touch to keep your fingers from becoming fatigued, and enough of a "bump," or *tactile feedback,* to indicate when a key has been pressed all the way without having to look.
- What is the shape of the keyboard? Several manufacturers sell keyboards that are split in the middle (see **Figure 19.13**) so that your wrists can remain at a neutral angle while you type. This arrangement can take some getting used to, but many people find it more comfortable than straight keyboards, and some evidence suggests it can reduce the likelihood of carpal tunnel syndrome.
- What bells and whistles does it have? Some keyboards have extra buttons to perform tasks like launching Web pages, controlling music playback in iTunes, or checking your e-mail. If you like the idea of dedicated buttons for tasks like that (rather than multi-key shortcuts you've set up yourself), consider one of these multimedia keyboards. Still other keyboards are wireless (great for a cluttered desk or typing with your feet propped up on a chair) or include extra USB ports.

Whichever keyboard you choose, keep in mind that your comfort is the primary consideration. You might want to inquire about a money-back guarantee before making your purchase, as it can sometimes take days or even weeks to evaluate the feel and features of a new keyboard.

19.13

TECHNIQUE 20

HANDS-FREE COMPUTING WITH SPEECH RECOGNITION

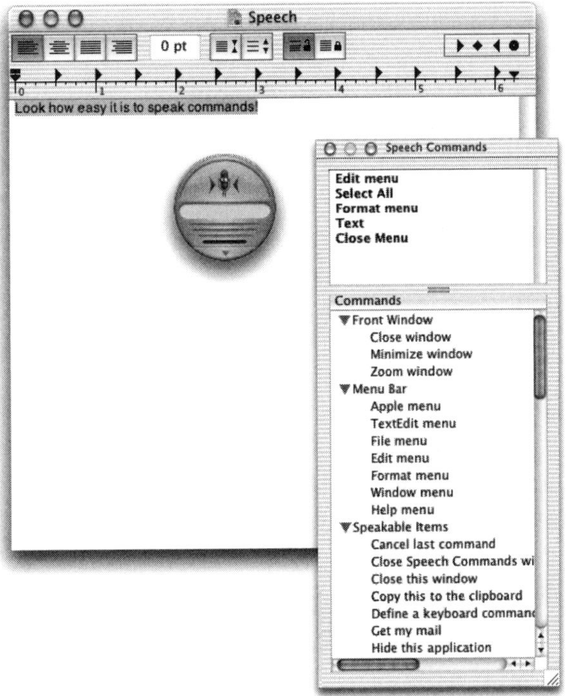

20.1

ABOUT THE FEATURE

Do you ever talk to your computer? Mac OS X's built-in speech recognition enables you to perform a surprising number of commands just by using your voice.

When the captain of the starship Enterprise wants the onboard computer to do something, he doesn't look for a keyboard or a mouse. He just speaks up and says: "Computer, calculate life support reserves," and a friendly voice replies out of nowhere: "Estimated survival duration is two more seasons before syndication." For more than 30 years, science fiction shows have drilled into us the expectation that someday we'll talk to computers as freely as we talk to each other and that they will actually understand us without the need for typing, mousing, or any other unnatural input methods. We're not quite there yet, but even a basic installation of Mac OS X has some pretty impressive speech recognition capabilities that can give you a small taste of the future.

Talking to your computer can be, well, kind of embarrassing. You're sure to get some funny looks from your family and coworkers. It can also be aggravating when the computer fails to recognize what you're saying, which unfortunately happens fairly often. Is it worth the effort? Can it be truly useful? It depends on your needs and the environment in which you use your computer, but here are some ways you might put speech recognition to good use:

- To avoid repetitive stress injuries. If you find that you experience wrist pain due to excessive keyboard or mouse use, speech recognition can help by reducing your dependence on your hands to operate the computer.
- To focus on your work. If you've read other techniques in this chapter, you know that switching back and forth between your keyboard and mouse, trackball, or graphics tablet is a recipe for inefficiency. Keep focused on your work by speaking commands that would ordinarily require switching to another input device.
- To do more things at once. Your computer can do useful tasks for you while you're busy cooking, cleaning, or reading. There's nothing like telling your computer to back up the hard drive while your hands are covered with pastry flour.
- To impress your geeky friends. OK, this is the *real* reason you want to use speech recognition. When it works correctly, it looks incredibly cool, and after all, isn't that one of the reasons you bought your Mac in the first place?

You need to fully understand two things about speech recognition before diving in. First, making speech recognition truly useful takes some preparation and setup — unlike many Mac OS X features, it's not enough simply to flip a switch. Second, it takes some getting used to. In the first half hour you play with speech recognition, you may find it frustrating that it doesn't work the way you expect. Stick with it. Learning to use speech recognition effectively is just like learning to type: You may not be fast or accurate at first, but you'll improve tremendously with practice.

STEP 1: CHOOSE A MICROPHONE

This first step is the most important one, and yet it's one most people ignore. Nothing impacts the effectiveness of speech recognition more than using the right kind of microphone. Conversely, using the wrong kind of microphone can yield such poor results that you'll conclude speech recognition doesn't really work at all. A good microphone doesn't have to be expensive; it just has to have the right design.

Your main goal in choosing a microphone is to ensure that it can pick up the sound of your voice very well, while rejecting other sounds. If your microphone is picking up nearby conversations, doors closing, music, and so on, this will seriously degrade Mac OS X's effectiveness at recognizing speech. So you want to look for a *directional* microphone — one that is only sensitive to sounds coming from a certain direction. You also want a microphone that can be positioned so that the likelihood of stray sounds being right in front of it is small.

Some Macs, such as PowerBooks, iBooks, and G4 iMacs, have built-in microphones. Although they will sometimes provide adequate performance (and are fine to use if you just want to try out this technique quickly), they are not the best quality microphones in the world, and they're prone to pick up the noise from your computer's hard drive and fan, limiting their accuracy. Before choosing a microphone, consider the following:

- Check to see whether your computer has a microphone jack. If it does, look for a microphone with a ⅛-inch plug (or an appropriate adapter). If not, look for a USB microphone. Be aware that USB microphones are more expensive and harder to find than standard microphones. As an alternative, the iMic adapter from Griffin Technology allows you to attach a conventional microphone to a USB port.

- Consider buying a headset microphone. This type of device fits on your head or ear and has an arm that brings the microphone close to your mouth. There are hundreds of different headset microphones, of varying designs and levels of quality. Some are wired (keeping you awkwardly tethered to your computer), while other, more expensive models are wireless, allowing more freedom of movement. Some headsets have just a microphone, whereas others include one or two earpieces for mono or stereo sound output. You can find my recommendations for the best headsets of each type — including prices and where to find them — on the book's Web site (`www.wiley.com/compbooks/kissell`).
- Consider using a desktop microphone stand (with a highly directional microphone) if you really can't stand the idea of wearing something on your head, but still need to get the microphone closer to your face. The only problem with fixed microphones is that they only work well if they are always pointing directly at your mouth. If you move forward or backward slightly or tilt your head to one side, you may have to reposition your microphone.
- Think about investing in an *array microphone* instead of a headset or desktop mic stand for the ultimate in convenience (and coolness). An array microphone is a small enclosure with several directional microphones and some high-tech digital signal processing circuitry. Unlike regular desktop mics, array microphones can follow your voice as you change position. They are also extremely effective at filtering out background noise. These capabilities come at a cost, of course — be prepared to spend upwards of $200 for a high-quality array microphone. As usual, check out the book's Web site for further information and recommendations.

STEP 2: CONFIGURE YOUR AUDIO INPUT

After you've selected and plugged in your microphone, you need to set up your Mac's audio system before beginning to use speech recognition.

- Open System Preferences and click the Speech button under "System." Click the **Speech Recognition** tab and then click the **Listening** mini-tab (**Figure 20.2**). At the bottom is the **Microphone** pop-up menu, which displays all audio inputs on your computer, as shown in **Figure 20.3**. (Your options will differ according to the hardware you have.) Choose the input source you want to use from this menu.

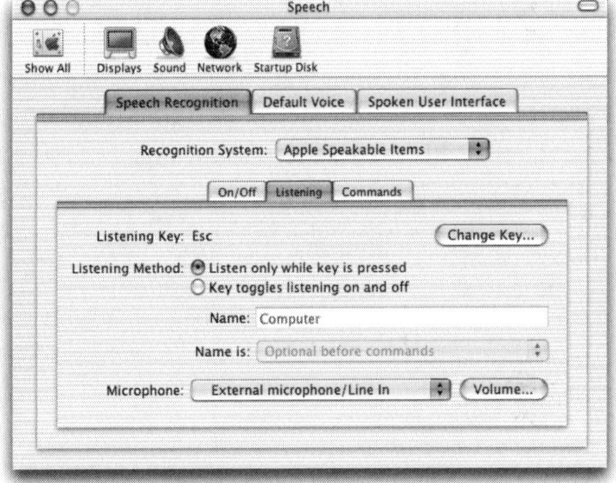

20.2

Name is: Optional before commands
Microphone
Built-in audio controller
✓ External microphone/Line In
Sound Input
Zoomed Video
Internal microphone
iMic USB audio system
iMic USB audio system
Vol

20.3

■ Next, click **Volume....** The Microphone Volume window appears, as shown in **Figure 20.4**. Use this window to adjust the volume (or input gain) of your microphone. To do so, position the microphone where you will have it for normal use and speak one of the commands listed (like "What Time Is It?"). Notice how the bars on the meter change as you speak. If the bars peak into the red area, move the slider to the left; if they stay in the blue area, move the slider to the right. Then, as you speak each command, make sure the text of the command blinks. If it doesn't, try moving the slider left or right a notch. When you've adjusted the volume so that all the commands are recognized, click **Done**.

STEP 3: ACTIVATE SPEAKABLE ITEMS

After your input is configured, you need to tell Mac OS X to begin listening for spoken commands. To activate Speakable Items, do the following:

■ Click the **On/Off** mini-tab, and where it says **Apple Speakable Items is**, click **On**. (If you want to be sure speech recognition is on automatically every time you log in, check **Start Speakable Items at log in**.)

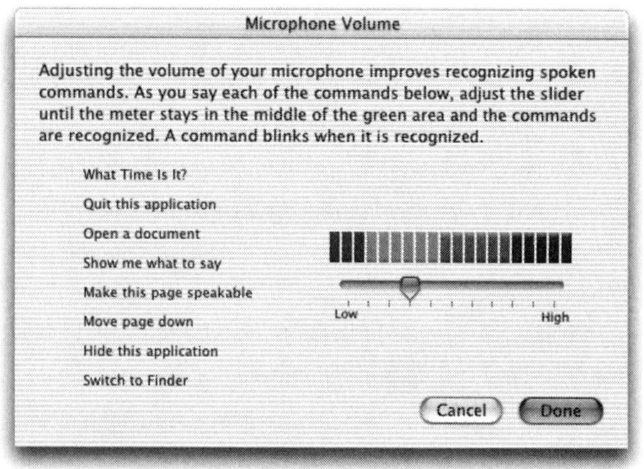

20.4

■ The Speech Feedback window appears, as shown in **Figure 20.5**. Initially, the window will show "Esc," which means "press **Esc** to give me commands." Hold down the **Esc** key and try a command or two, such as "What time is it?" or "Empty the Trash." You should hear a little "whit" sound when the computer recognizes your commands, followed by feedback in a synthesized voice.

■ To see what commands are available, hold down **Esc** and say "Open Speech Commands window." A floating window appears (shown expanded in **Figure 20.6**). The list is quite long, and it will grow or shrink depending on which application is in the foreground and what commands are applicable to the current window.

■ The best way to get used to using Speakable Items (and learn which commands work where) is to try out as many of the commands as possible. Try switching applications, opening and closing windows, choosing menu commands, and checking your mail.

STEP 4: CUSTOMIZE SPEAKABLE ITEMS

Now that you have your feet wet, you may want to make Speakable Items a bit easier to use.

■ For starters, holding down **Esc** every time you want to give a command can quickly become tiresome. To change this, go to the Speech pane in

20.5

System Preferences, click the **Speech Recognition** tab, and then go to the **Listening** mini-tab (as shown in **Figure 20.7**). Select the radio button next to **Key toggles listening on and off**. Now, after you've pressed **Esc** once, your computer will listen continuously until you press it again.

At this point, your computer is still expecting a "trigger" to tell it when you're giving it a command (rather than talking on the phone or to a coworker, for example), but now that trigger is a spoken word — "computer" by default. By preceding each command with the trigger word, your Mac can tell when you're trying to speak to it. The commands need to sound like "Computer, minimize this window" or "Computer, open Sherlock."

■ The trigger word doesn't have to be "computer" — replace it with anything you like. If you want to call your computer Cindy, just type **Cindy** into the **Name** field, and say "Cindy, tell me a joke" (or whatever else you want your computer to do). The Speech Feedback window displays the name you've chosen, as a reminder that it needs to hear that word to activate commands.

■ If you don't want to precede every single command with the computer's name, choose an option other than **Required before each command** from the **Name is** pop-up menu, shown in **Figure 20.8**. You can opt to have the computer stay in recognition mode for 15 or 30 seconds after each command — useful if you expect to give several commands in a row.

■ To make your computer listen absolutely all the time with no intervention at all, choose **Optional**

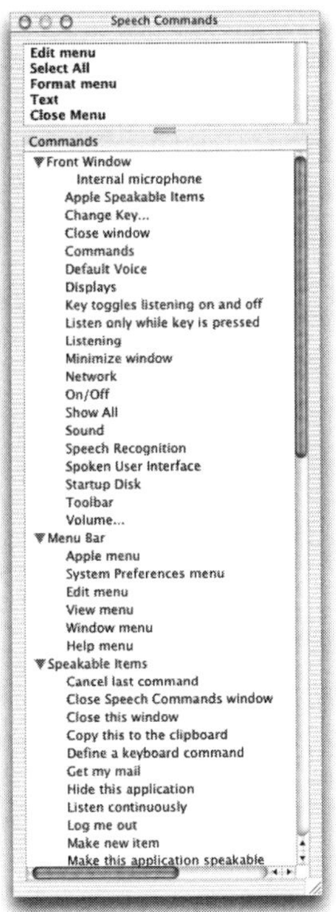

20.6

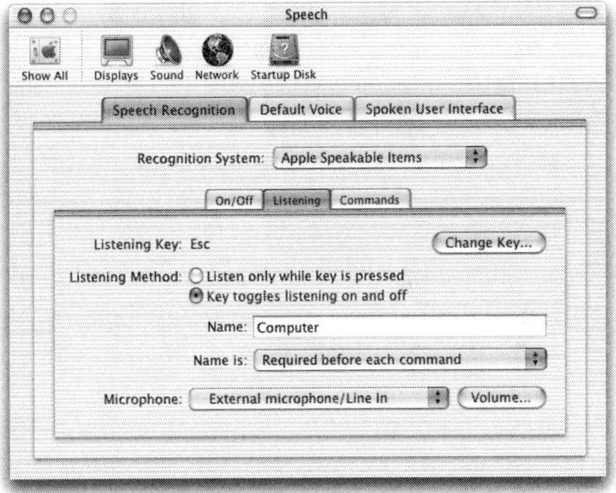

20.7

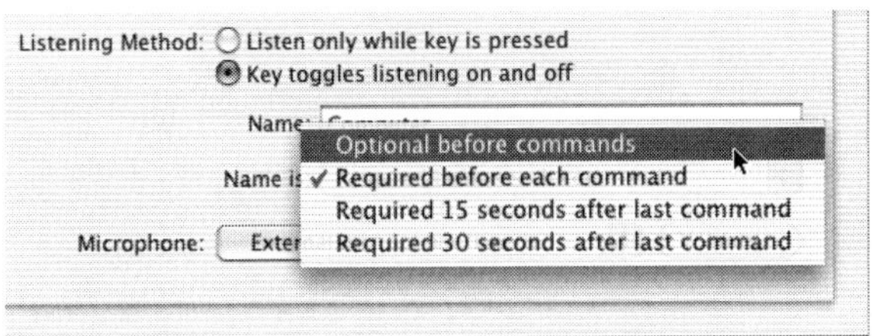

20.8

before commands from the **Name is** pop-up menu. (A checkmark appears next to **Optional before commands** on the menu to confirm that it is selected.) Your Mac will then try to interpret everything it hears as a command. If you need to temporarily stop your computer from listening, say, "Turn on push to talk." You then need to press **Esc** again to give commands. To turn push to talk off again, hold down **Esc** and say, "Listen continuously."

You can make speech recognition significantly more flexible — at a cost of slightly reduced accuracy — by turning on some additional options that are disabled by default (and disabling one that's enabled).

- Go to the **Universal Access** pane of System Preferences. Make sure **Enable access for assistive devices** at the bottom is checked, as shown in **Figure 20.9**. (Without enabling this feature, some of the modified Speech settings won't work.) Then return to the **Speech Preferences** pane, click the **Commands** mini-tab (see **Figure 20.10**), and modify the following settings:
  - Turn on **Front Window commands** to list all the buttons, tabs, and other controls in the frontmost window as speakable items.
  - Check **Menu Bar commands** so you can speak the name of any menu — in any application — to display its contents. This option in combination with the preceding one allows you to control almost every aspect of an application's interface with your voice.
  - As explained at the bottom of the tab, unchecking **Require exact wording of Speakable Item command names** enables speech recognition to recognize minor variations in wording for the built-in commands.
  - If you like to experiment, you can add your own commands to Speakable Items. When you click **Open Speakable Items Folder** on the **On/Off** mini-tab in Speech Preferences, you see where all the commands live — they're simply files in ~/Library/Speech/Speakable Items. If

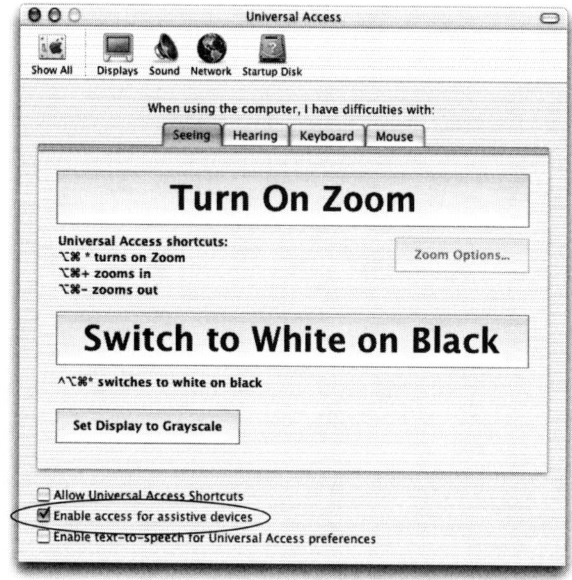

20.9

you drag the alias of a file, folder, or application into this window, it immediately becomes a speakable item, and you can speak its name to open it. If you want to get even fancier, any activity that can be automated with AppleScript can be made into a Speakable Item. Add your own compiled AppleScripts to this folder (or one of the application-specific subfolders) to extend Speakable Items even further.

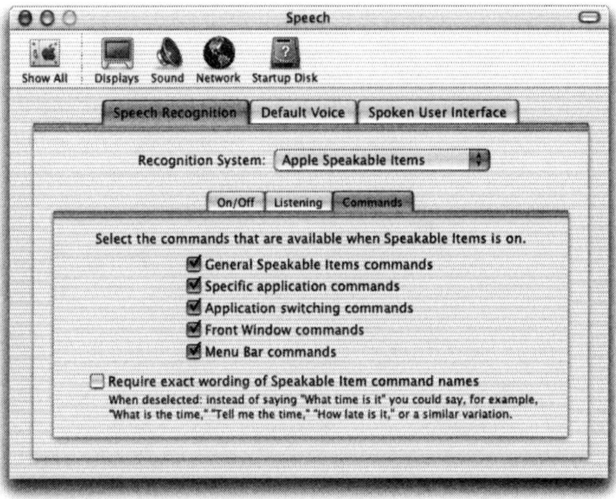

20.10

STEP 5: ADD DICTATION SOFTWARE (OPTIONAL)

When you've gotten used to performing commands and shortcuts with your voice, you may begin to wish you could *type* with your voice, too. As a matter of fact you can, using either of the two available dictation programs available for Mac OS X: IBM's ViaVoice (`www.ibm.com/software/speech/mac/osx/`) or iListen from MacSpeech (`www.macspeech.com`). With either of these software packages installed, you can speak to your computer in a normal, continuous fashion and have your words typed on the screen. You can also use voice commands to go back and correct mistakes or simply make changes to your document.

The current crop of dictation software is not bad — but it still doesn't approach 100 percent accuracy. You'll find that the software works more smoothly in some applications than in others. And you should also be aware that dictation software is much more sensitive than Apple's Speech Recognition to the quality and type of microphone being used. Those caveats aside, dictation software can be indispensable for those who cannot type, and for everyone else it can be a valuable tool if you like to think out loud — or just think it's cool to have your computer take a memo.

TECHNIQUE 21

USING A TABLET FOR HANDWRITING RECOGNITION AND MORE

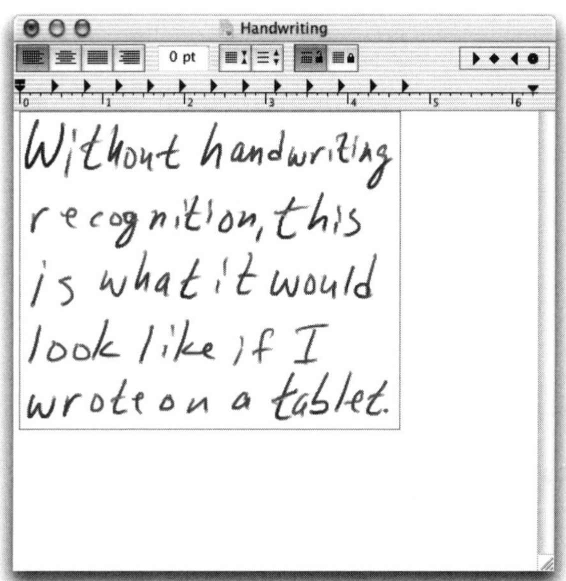

21.1

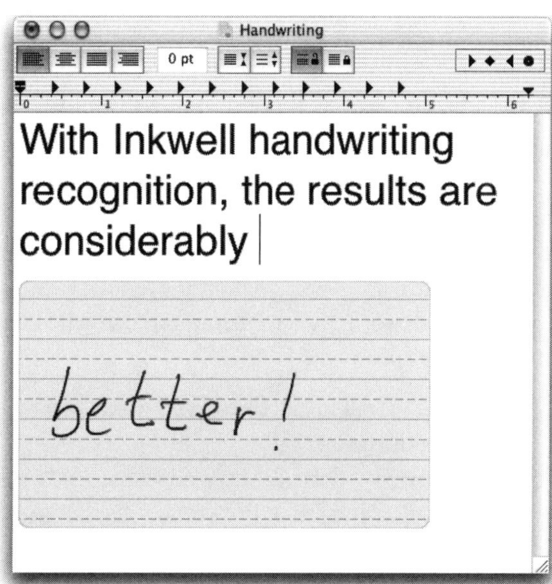

21.2

ABOUT THE FEATURE

Graphics tablets allow you to draw or paint using a pen-like stylus rather than a mouse. Mac OS X's Inkwell feature takes written input a step further by converting handwritten words into fully editable text.

The Mac has no shortage of input methods. Some tasks can best be accomplished with a keyboard, some with a mouse or trackball, and some with your voice. But for drawing, painting, and retouching tasks, nothing beats a graphics tablet and stylus. Tablets have been around for many years, constantly evolving and adding new features. At the same time, they have become quite affordable — you no longer need to be a professional graphic artist to justify owning a tablet.

Although drawing is the main function of graphics tablets, Mac OS X version 10.2 added an entirely new and exciting capability: handwriting recognition. Apple's Inkwell technology, which is based on software developed for the Newton PDA, allows any application — even Terminal! — to accept handwritten input just as if it were typed.

Although Inkwell is included with Mac OS X, a graphics tablet is not. Before you can proceed with this technique, you need to pick up a compatible tablet. By “compatible,” I mean one that has drivers for Mac OS X. Wacom (`www.wacom.com`) is the best-known supplier of graphics tablets, with choices starting under $100 and full support for Mac OS X.

STEP 1: INSTALL TABLET AND DRIVERS

After you plug your tablet into a USB port, you need to make sure you have the latest drivers installed — they’re not included with Mac OS X. Even if your tablet included a CD-ROM, I recommend checking the manufacturer’s Web site for the latest version, because the driver may have been updated since the CD-ROM was produced.

- Download and install the drivers according to the instructions supplied.
- After you install the driver, a new icon — Ink — appears in System Preferences, as shown in **Figure 21.3**.

21.3

STEP 2: USE BASIC HANDWRITING RECOGNITION

After installing your tablet and software, turn on handwriting recognition and try some basic input.

- Click the Ink icon in System Preferences to display Inkwell’s preference pane. Click the **On** button to turn on handwriting recognition. A floating palette called InkBar (**Figure 21.4**) appears, to remind you that Inkwell is active.
- Open an application that can accept text input, such as TextEdit or Mail, and open a new window. Using your stylus, begin writing anywhere on the tablet. A transparent yellow window appears, as shown in **Figure 21.5**, displaying what you write. When you stop writing, the window disappears,

21.4

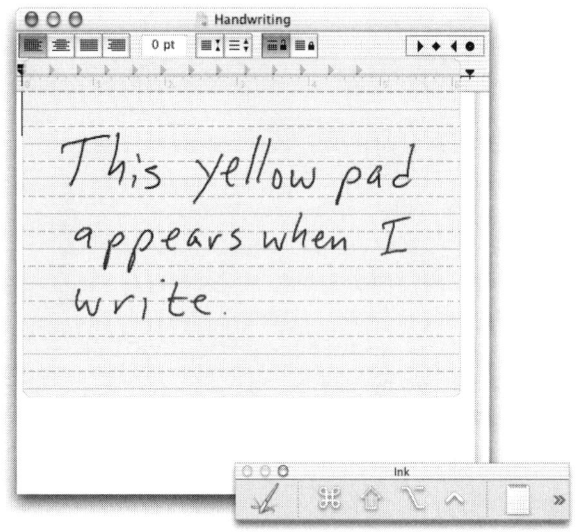

21.5

and your text appears at your insertion point. (Note: Inkwell recognizes only printed letters, not cursive.) For best results, write in a straight line (using the rules on the yellow window as a guide), use capital and lowercase letters, and try to keep your letters consistent in height.

- If you want to use your stylus as a mouse (to choose menu commands, move windows, and so on), tap the Pen button on the InkBar. It turns into a Pointer (**Figure 21.6**) to indicate that handwriting recognition is now off. Tap the Pointer button to turn handwriting recognition back on. (Your stylus may also have a button that toggles handwriting recognition on and off.)
- To use keyboard shortcuts with the stylus, tap one or more of the modifier icons on the InkBar (representing ⌘, **Shift**, **Option**, and **Control** from left to right) and write the character you want to use. For example, to Select All, tap the ⌘ icon, then write the letter *A*.
- Tap the notepad icon on the right of the InkBar to make the palette expand to display a writing area called InkPad, as in **Figure 21.7**. You can use this as a scratch pad for handwriting — unlike the transparent yellow "legal pad" windows, InkPad won't disappear or forget its contents as soon as you lift the pen. In addition, you can tap the Sketch (star) button in the bottom-left corner to put InkPad into drawing mode. In drawing mode, handwriting recognition is turned off, allowing you to sketch freely. Tap the **Send** button to insert your text (or graphic, if you're in drawing mode) at the insertion point. See **Figure 21.8** for an example.
- To close the InkPad window and return to normal writing, tap the notepad button again.

21.6

21.7

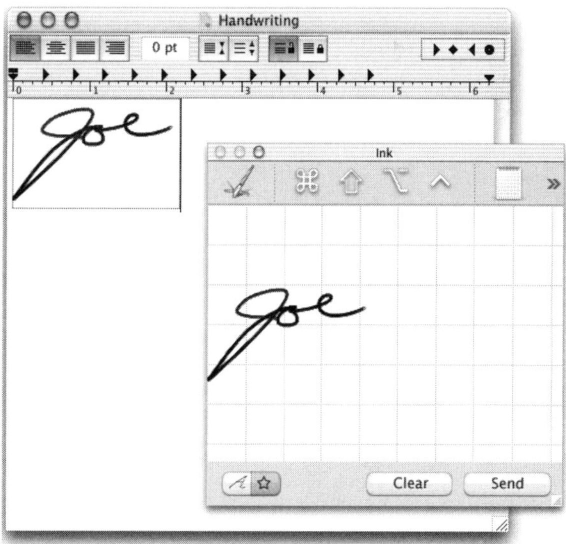

21.8

STEP 3: USE GESTURES FOR EDITING AND CONTROL

As you begin using handwriting recognition, you'll quickly find that you need to make corrections, backspace, delete words, and so on. Inkwell makes it possible to do all this without reaching for the mouse by including a set of *gestures* — special characters that are interpreted as commands when you write them.

- To display the available gestures, tap the chevron (») icon on the right side of the InkBar and choose **Open Ink Preferences**. Then click the **Gestures** tab, shown in **Figure 21.9**.
- To see how to draw a given gesture, select it in the list. An animation will draw the gesture for you in the preview window on the right. In most cases, direction matters: Although the gesture for Delete is a horizontal line, you must draw it from right to left. Drawing the same line from left to right inserts a hyphen.

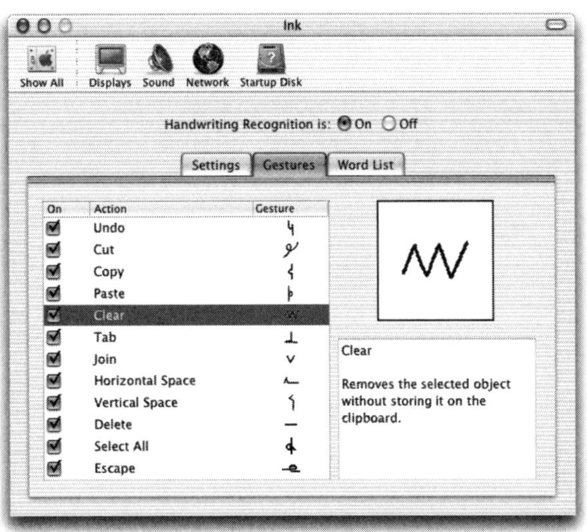

21.9

- You can use gestures in any document window that accepts Ink input. Use the stylus to position the insertion point (or make a selection) and draw a gesture to execute that command.
- Although you can't add your own gestures, you can disable any gesture you don't want to use by unchecking its **On** checkbox.

STEP 4: FINE-TUNE INKWELL OPTIONS

You can adjust many of Inkwell's characteristics to suit your needs. Here are some of the most useful settings:

- In the Ink Preferences pane of System Preferences, on the Settings tab, the **My handwriting style is** slider determines how Inkwell decides when to insert spaces. Move the slider to the right (more widely spaced) if you find that Inkwell often inserts extra spaces where you don't intend them. Move it to the left (more closely spaced) if it doesn't insert spaces often enough.
- Click the **Options...** button in the Ink Preferences pane to display additional settings for Ink (see **Figure 21.10**):
  - Move the top slider to adjust how long Inkwell waits after you stop writing before recognizing your handwriting. In general, a longer delay is easier for beginners because it minimizes cases of incomplete words being processed prematurely; expert users will prefer a shorter delay.
  - When you move the stylus, Inkwell waits a moment before "inking" — drawing on the screen — to be sure you really are writing and not tapping (using your stylus as a mouse). You can increase or decrease the distance you must cover before inking begins by moving the middle slider.

- You can use your stylus as a mouse to select text, click buttons, and so on even without turning handwriting recognition off. To do this, touch the stylus to the tablet but don't move it for a moment. (A click sound will confirm that your stylus has switched to mouse mode.) To adjust how long this delay is, move the bottom slider.
- Under "Other Options," check **Recognize Western European characters** to enable Inkwell to understand accented letters like ü, ø, and è.

■ Inkwell uses an internal dictionary to recognize words. To increase its accuracy with unusual words or names, click the **Word List** tab in Ink Preferences (see **Figure 21.11**) and click **Add...** to put your words on its list. (In practice, though, I have not been able to notice a difference. When I tried writing nonsense words like sgrzoni and wrhleid, Inkwell recognized them perfectly, even though they weren't on the Word List.)

■ You may not want the entire screen to be used for handwriting recognition. To use only the InkPad area for writing, go to the **Settings** tab in Ink Preferences and choose **Only in InkPad** from the **Allow me to write** pop-up menu.

STEP 5: ADJUST TABLET SETTINGS

Your tablet software most likely included configuration software to adjust settings beyond those available in Ink Preferences. To make handwriting recognition and pointer control more effective, check to make sure those settings have been optimized. In this example, you see the configuration options for Wacom tablets.

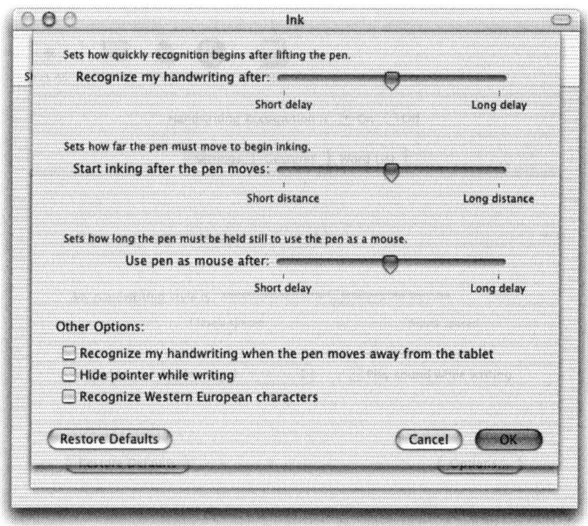

21.10

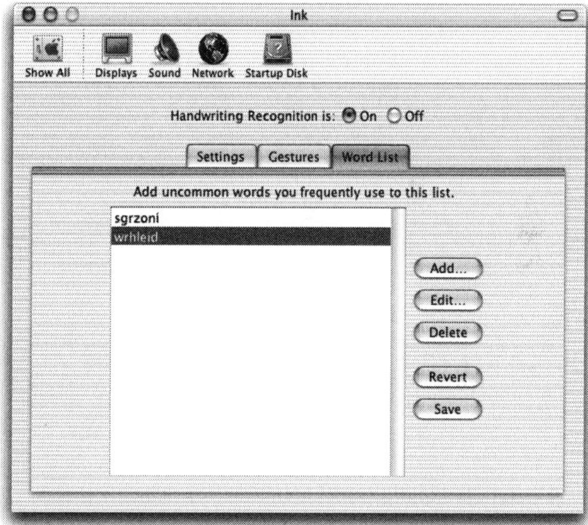

21.11

- Open the Wacom Tablet application, installed in the Wacom folder inside Applications. Tap the **Tip Feel** tab, shown in **Figure 21.12**.
- To adjust the pressure sensitivity of the stylus tip, move the **Tip Pressure Feel** slider.
- Use the pop-up menus on the **Tool Buttons** tab to change what the buttons and eraser on the stylus do. For example, you can set a button to double-click, Control+click (for contextual menus), hold down a modifier key, or pop up a custom menu.

For other settings, consult the documentation included with your tablet driver.

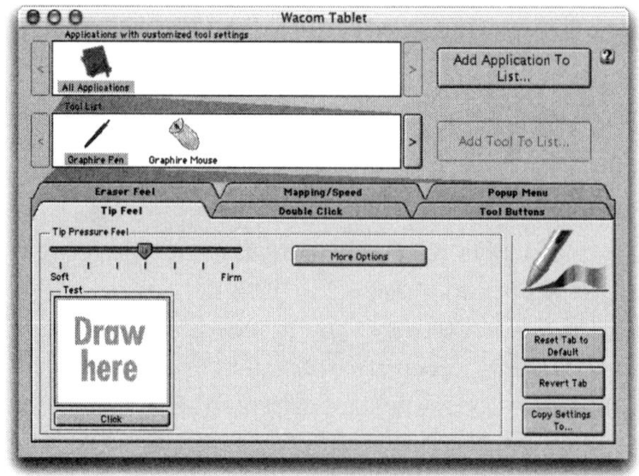

21.12

TECHNIQUE **22**

EXTENDING YOUR REACH WITH UNIVERSAL ACCESS

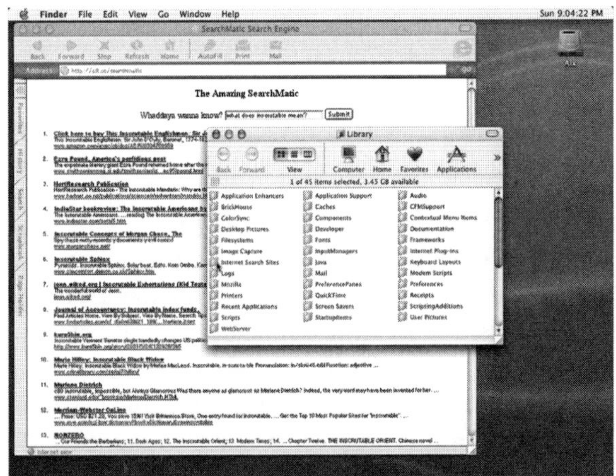

22.1

22.2

ABOUT THE FEATURE

Mac OS X includes extensive accessibility features, which make computer use easier for users with certain physical limitations. These features can enhance everyone's computer use by extending their access to controls and capabilities that are normally out of reach.

Millions of people find the display, mouse, or keyboard to be problematic ways of interacting with their computers. The tiny characters on high-resolution displays can be unreadable by those with impaired vision. Users with limited hand mobility or coordination may not be able to point with a mouse. Also, people without full use of both hands may find typing or performing keyboard commands difficult. To address the needs of such users, Apple has added a number of accessibility features to Mac OS X. These features are collectively known as *Universal Access.*

Even if you have no difficulties with standard input and output devices, Universal Access can be highly useful. For example, the features that allow you to perform mouse tasks using the keyboard (or vice versa) can be a lifesaver if your mouse or keyboard is broken. In addition, other utilities, including Apple's own Speech Recognition (as discussed in Technique 20), make use of the Universal Access features to perform their magic. In this technique, you activate and use all the major features of Universal Access.

STEP 1: NAVIGATE MENUS AND DIALOGS WITH THE KEYBOARD

You can control nearly every menu and button using the keyboard, even if you don't know the keyboard shortcut for a particular command. Apple calls this feature Full Keyboard Access.

- Turn on Full Keyboard Access by pressing **Control+F1**. Unfortunately, there is no visual indication that Full Keyboard Access is on.
- To navigate a menu, press **Control+F2**. The Apple menu appears. To choose a different menu, press the left or right arrow keys. Use the up or down arrow keys to choose a menu command. When the one you want is highlighted, press **Return**. If a menu item includes a submenu, press the right arrow to display the submenu or the left arrow to return to choices on the main menu. You can also move left and right between menus using the arrow keys without first moving to the top of a menu. To close a menu without choosing a command, press **Esc**.
- In a similar way, you can access controls in the Dock and other parts of the screen:
  - Press **Control+F3** to move focus to the Dock. As with menus, use the left and right arrows to move between Dock items and the space bar to activate them. (You can even use the up and down arrows to choose commands on Dock menus!)
  - Press **Control+F4** to switch to the next active window on the screen — regardless of the application to which it belongs.
  - Press **Control+F5** to move focus to the current window's toolbar. As usual, navigate between buttons using the arrow keys and use the space bar to make your choices.
  - If your current application has a floating palette (such as a Font or Color selector), press **Control+F6** to move focus to that window.
- In a dialog, you can navigate text boxes and lists using either the **Tab** key or the arrow keys. To access other controls, such as radio buttons, checkboxes, sliders, and pop-up menus, press **Control+F7**. At this point, you should notice a very subtle change on your screen: One of the controls (the Full Keyboard Access tab in this case) will have a blue "halo" around it, as shown in the before-and-after example in **Figure 22.3**. This

> **NOTE**
>
> **On a PowerBook or iBook, you may have set your function keys to control brightness and volume when used by themselves. If this is the case, you must hold down the Fn key while pressing the Control+function key combinations described here. Very important: You must press Control first, then Fn, and then the function key. If you hold down Fn first and then press Control and a function key, the command will not work.**

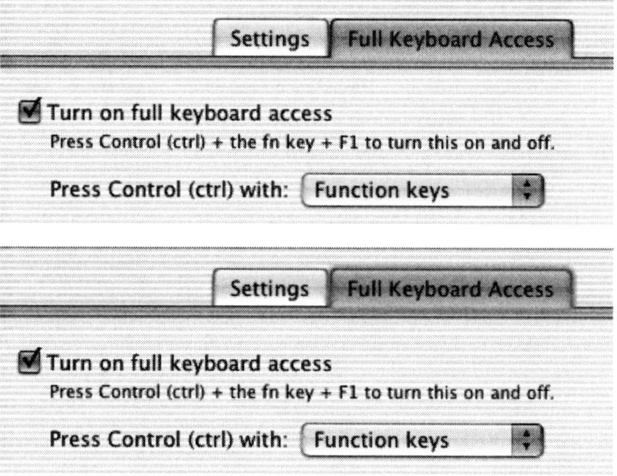

22.3

control is said to have *focus*. Press **Tab** to move focus to the next control, or press **Shift+Tab** to move backward. To check or uncheck a highlighted checkbox (or activate a highlighted icon), press the **space bar**. You can change the position of sliders or the selection on a pop-up menu by using the arrow keys. For radio buttons or tabs, only one control in a group will be highlighted; to move between controls, use the arrow keys.

If you don't like using **F1–F6**, you can choose your own shortcut keys for navigation. You can also avoid having to press **F7** every single time you want to access controls within a dialog.

- Open System Preferences and click the Keyboard icon under "Hardware." Then click the **Full Keyboard Access** tab. Make sure there's a checkmark next to **Turn on full keyboard access.** (There will be if you've already pressed **Control+F1** to turn it on.) Then choose **Letter keys** from the pop-up menu to use **Control** plus **m**, **d**, **w**, **t**, and **u** for the Menu bar, Dock, next active Window, Toolbar, and Utility window (floating palette), respectively. Or choose **Custom keys** to assign your own selections. All shortcuts, unfortunately, require use of the **Control** key.
- If you want to be able to access all controls in dialogs without explicitly turning on access every time, select the **Any control** radio button at the bottom of the window.

NOTE

Not all applications completely support Full Keyboard Access. For example, you can't control the numerous checkboxes and pop-up menus in Microsoft Word's Preferences dialog from the keyboard.

STEP 2: MOVE THE POINTER WITH THE KEYBOARD

At times even Full Keyboard Access won't give you the control you need. For example, you may be using an application like Word that doesn't support Universal Access. You may need to click and drag an icon or graphic without using the mouse. Or you may be faced with a broken mouse and need to do *everything* with the keyboard. For cases such as these, you can actually move and click your pointer with the keyboard. Your computer will behave just as if a mouse were being used.

- Open System Preferences (using keyboard navigation as discussed earlier, if necessary), click the Universal Access icon under System and then check **Allow Universal Access Shortcuts** at the bottom of the window as shown in **Figure 22.4.** This option allows keyboard commands to be used to turn on and off certain Universal Access features. Quit System Preferences after checking this box.

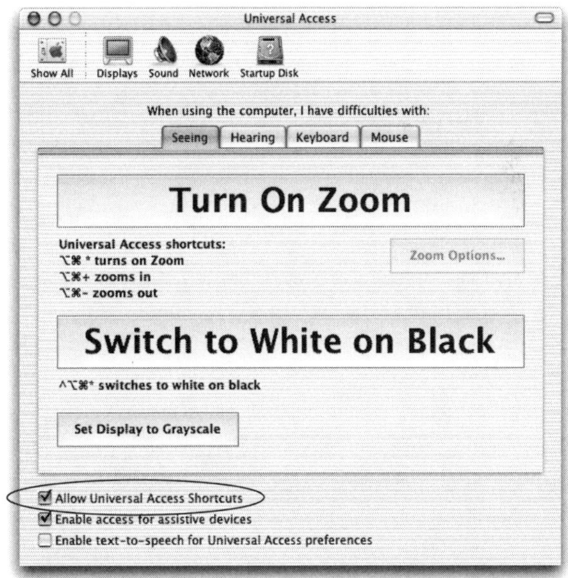

22.4

- Press the **Option** key five times in a row. The **Mouse Keys** feature will now be active, as confirmed by a distinctive sound.
- Press and hold the keys on your numeric keypad to move the pointer. The **4**, **6**, **8**, and **2** keys move the pointer left, right, up, and down, respectively; **1**, **3**, **7**, and **9** move the pointer diagonally. Press **5** to click the mouse. (On a PowerBook or iBook, you need to either activate **NumLock** or hold down the **Fn** key while using the virtual numeric keypad embedded in your standard keyboard.)
- You must hold down the keypad keys for a moment before pointer movement begins. To reduce this delay, open System Preferences and click the Universal Access icon. Click the **Mouse** tab. (See **Figure 22.5**.) Move the **Initial Delay** slider to the left for a smaller delay and right for a larger delay. (Remember, you can use the keyboard controls covered in Step 1 to adjust this slider.)
- To adjust the speed at which your pointer moves while under keyboard control, change the **Maximum Speed** slider.

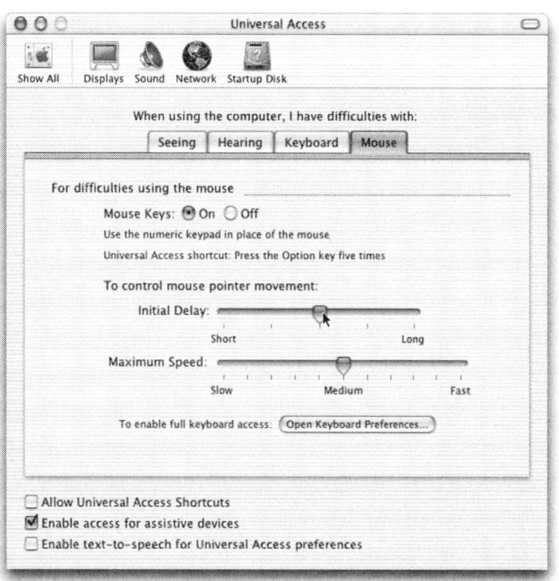

22.5

- To turn off **Mouse Keys**, press the **Option** key five times in a row again. Another sound plays to confirm the feature is off.

STEP 3: USE STICKY AND SLOW KEYS

So far, you've been using the keyboard to substitute for mouse actions. But most keyboard shortcuts require a certain amount of dexterity, such as pressing two or more keys at once. If you find this task difficult, you may benefit from *Sticky Keys* or *Slow Keys*, features designed to make the keyboard easier to use.

Sticky Keys allows you to activate multi-key commands one key at a time. For example, the shortcut **⌘+Option+Esc** (for Force Quit) requires three keys to be held down at once, but with Sticky Keys turned on, you can accomplish the same thing by pressing and releasing each key in sequence — first ⌘, then **Option**, and then **Esc**.

- To turn on Sticky Keys, press the **Shift** key five times in a row. (This requires that you've previously checked **Allow Universal Access Shortcuts** in Universal Access Preferences, as in the last step.) A sound plays to confirm that the feature is on, and while it's on, you will see an on-screen indicator every time you press a modifier key (⌘, **Option**, **Control**, or **Shift**), as illustrated in **Figure 22.6**.
- After Sticky Keys is on, press one or more modifier keys and then press the appropriate

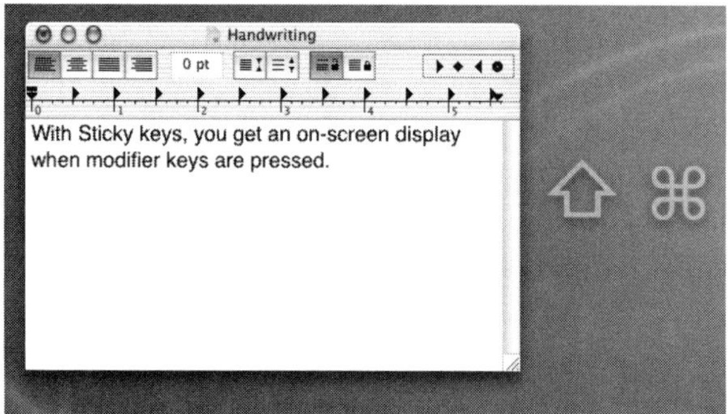

22.6

alphanumeric or function key to complete the keyboard shortcut. If you get partway through a key combination and change your mind, press **Esc** to cancel it.

■ To turn off Sticky Keys, press the **Shift** key five times again. A sound plays to confirm that the feature is off.

■ To modify Sticky Keys options, open System Preferences and click the Universal Access icon; then click the **Keyboard** tab, shown in **Figure 22.7**. When the **Beep when a modifier key is set** checkbox is checked, you'll get auditory feedback when a sticky modifier key is in use. Uncheck the box to turn off the beep. Similarly, if you don't want to see the on-screen modifier key display, uncheck **Show pressed keys on screen**.

Slow Keys prevents keys from being recognized if you press them too quickly. This can eliminate problems from runaway repeating keys, as well as reduce the effects of accidental key presses.

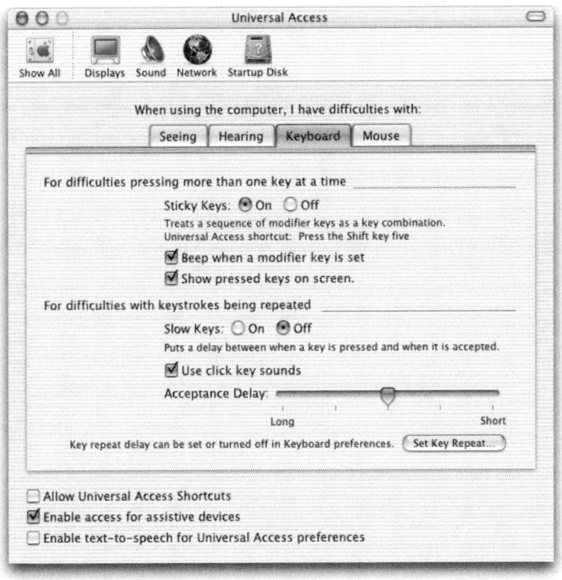

22.7

■ To turn on Slow Keys, click the **On** button next to **Slow Keys** on the **Keyboard** tab of Universal Access Preferences.

■ Move the slider to adjust how long a key must be held down before it is recognized. The same delay is used to determine how long it must continue to be held down before it begins to repeat.

STEP 4: ZOOM YOUR DISPLAY

Whether your eyesight is poor or your screen resolution is too high (or both), at times you will want to magnify a portion of your screen. The Zoom feature in Universal Access does just that — in any application.

■ If you haven't already checked **Allow Universal Access Shortcuts** in Universal Access Preferences, do so now.

■ Press **⌘+Option+*** to turn on Zoom. There is no visual indication that Zoom is active, but you can find out easily enough.

■ To zoom in to the portion of your screen where your pointer is located, press **⌘+Option++** (that's the ⌘ key, the Option key, and the plus key). You can press this key combination multiple times; each time it zooms in a bit more. **Figure 22.8**

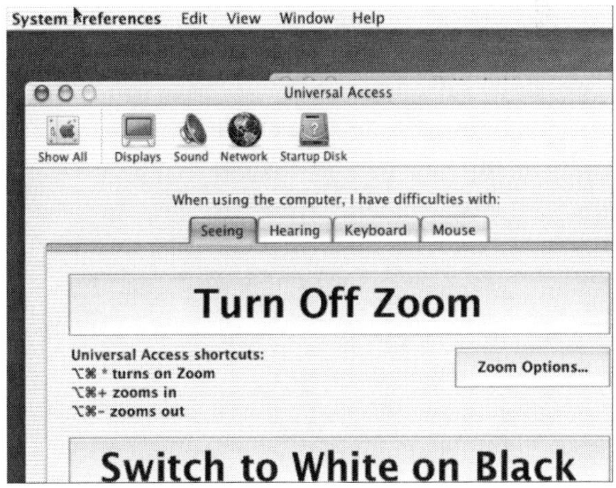

22.8

shows a screen zoomed in several increments. While you're zoomed in, your magnified display will move around as the pointer moves, allowing you to see portions of the display that are off the screen.

- To zoom out, press ⌘+**Option**+- (that's the ⌘ key, the Option key, and the hyphen key). Again, press multiple times to zoom out repeatedly.
- Your screen image will automatically be smoothed as it increases in size — which normally makes for better readability. To turn off smoothing while you zoom, magnifying the raw pixels, press ⌘+**Option**+\.

STEP 5: LISTEN TO YOUR COMPUTER

Mac OS X includes a text-to-speech capability that can read anything on your screen.

- Initially, the text-to-speech function is turned on for the Universal Access preference pane. If you don't want to hear everything you point at, uncheck **Enable text-to-speech for Universal Access preferences**.
- To use text-to-speech elsewhere, go to the Speech pane in System Preferences (**Figure 22.9**) and click the **Spoken User Interface** tab. The top part of this tab deals exclusively with alert messages. To have your computer speak an attention phrase (for example, "Alert!" or "Pardon me!"), check the box next to **Speak the phrase** and choose the phrase you want from the pop-up menu. If you want the computer to also read the text of the alert, check the box next to **Speak the alert text**. In addition, you can select which voice is used and how long the computer waits after displaying an alert to begin speaking it.
- Sometimes an application will need your attention when it's in the background. Even though it has displayed an alert, it's hidden behind other windows. Normally, an application's icon will bounce in the Dock to inform you that it requires your attention. To hear a spoken alert as well, check **Announce when an application requires your attention**.
- If you have difficulty reading the labels for controls in dialogs, check **Text under the mouse**. With this setting active, every time you move your

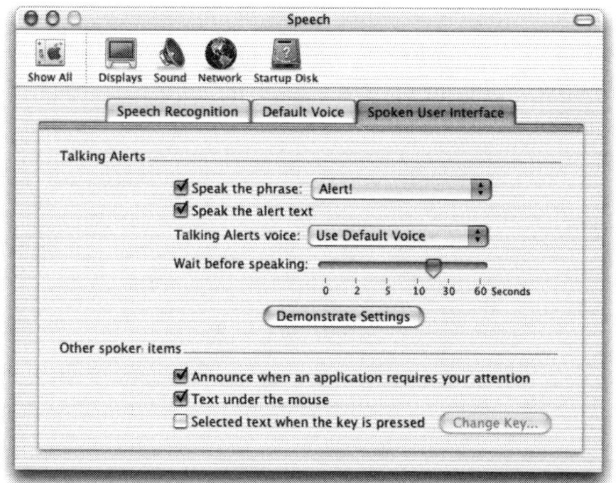

22.9

pointer over a control such as a menu title or a label in a dialog, your computer will read the label.

■ If you want to be able to listen to text in other sorts of windows — such as your word processor or Web browser — check **Selected text when the key is pressed** and choose a keystroke (such as **Control+S** or **F8**). After selecting a block of text, press your chosen keystroke, and the computerized voice will read it to you.

■ Mac OS X's default voice is called Victoria — a synthesized approximation of a 35-year-old female. Using the list on the **Default Voice** tab in the Speech Preferences dialog (see **Figure 22.10**), you can choose a different voice, or adjust the rate at which any voice is played.

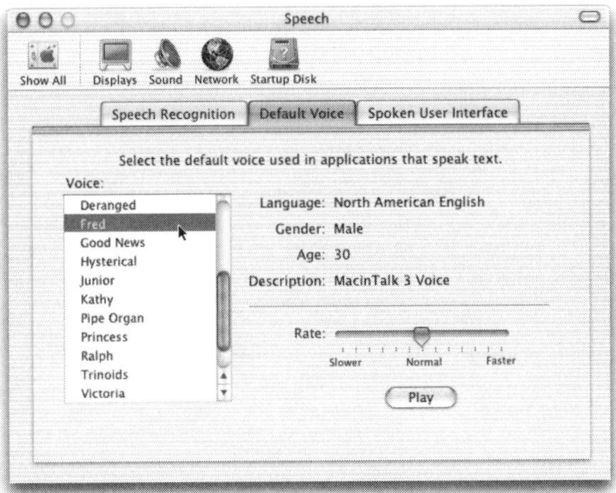

22.10

CHAPTER 5

NETWORKING & COMMUNICATION

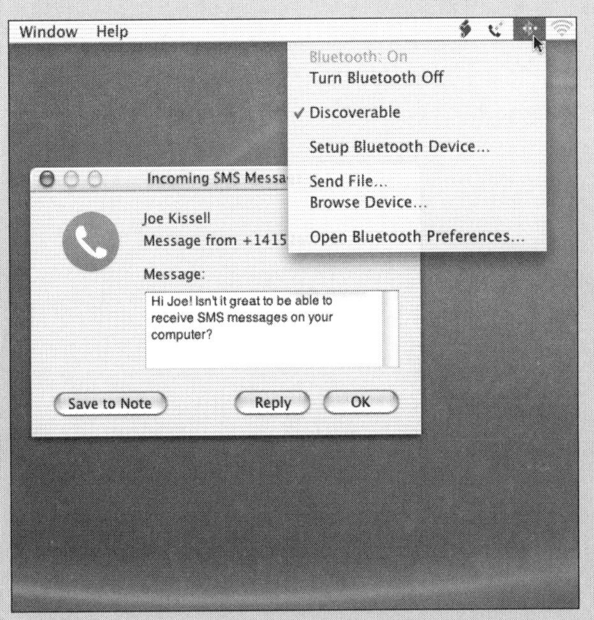

Most of the techniques in this book touch upon some aspect of networking or communication. Every time you send e-mail, update your software over the Internet, or browse the Web, your Mac is communicating with other computers. But a few common tasks involve a more direct form of networking. This chapter covers techniques that allow you to exchange data with other devices, while keeping your own computers secure in the process.

The discussion begins with Bluetooth, the exciting new wireless technology that lets your Mac communicate not only with other Macs, but also with a wide variety of other gadgets. Then you find out how easy it is to see and be seen by other computers, sharing files in both directions regardless of what operating system the other computers are running. The chapter ends with a look at the flip side of sharing: using a firewall to keep your data safe from those who shouldn't be sharing it.

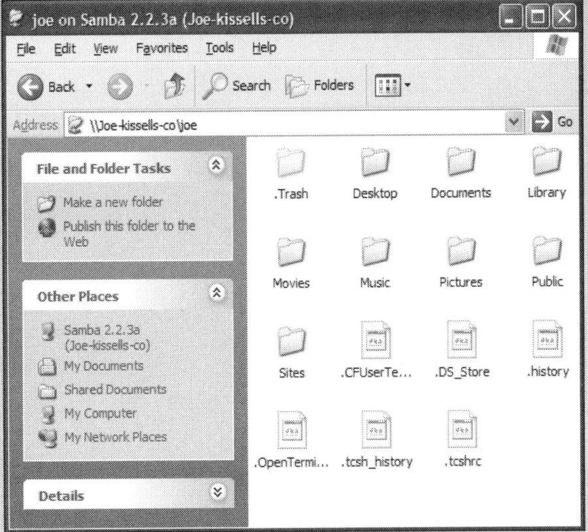

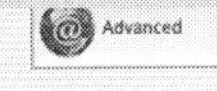

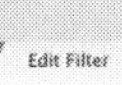

Cancel Save

Connect to Your Mac from a PC

Bluetooth

Use Public and Drop Box Folders

Set Up User Accounts

Built-In Firewall

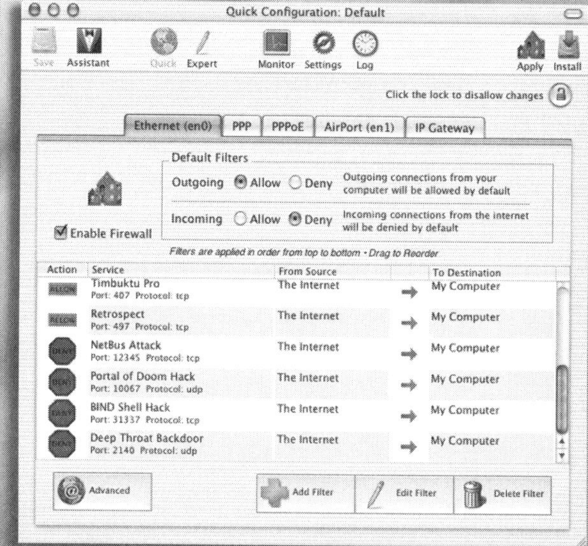

TECHNIQUE 23

COMMUNICATING WIRELESSLY WITH BLUETOOTH

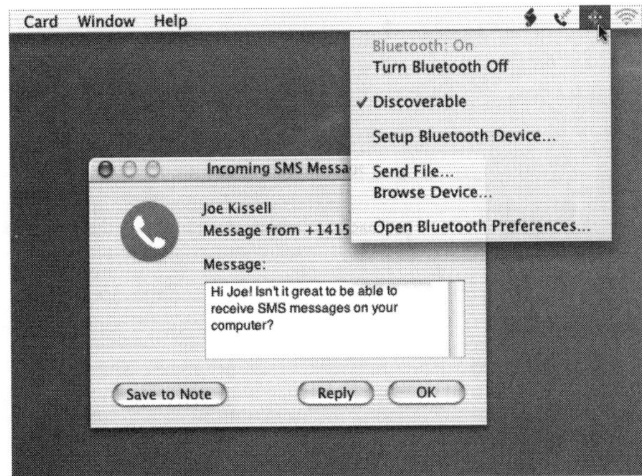

23.1

ABOUT THE FEATURE

Bluetooth is a wireless standard for low-speed, short-range communications. It's used by such devices as cell phones, PDAs, and printers — as well as computers.

Apple's AirPort cards and base stations brought fast, easy wireless networking to the Mac and helped to establish the immense popularity of the 802.11 wireless standard. Meanwhile, a very different kind of wireless technology was being developed, with the curious name of Bluetooth. Bluetooth has been around for years, but only recently has it built up momentum as the number of different products that use it has reached a critical mass. Now, it's as likely as not that your new cell phone, PDA, or wireless mouse uses Bluetooth to communicate with other products.

How is Bluetooth different from AirPort? Think of it in terms of the kind of cable it replaces. AirPort networking replaces your Ethernet network cable and is used to connect to the Internet or other networks. Bluetooth, on the other hand, is designed to replace the USB cables that would otherwise connect your peripherals. Unlike AirPort, Bluetooth is designed for very short distances (30 feet or less) and comparatively slow data transfer speeds. It also works even when there's no computer present. For example, you can transfer data from your cell phone directly to your PDA using Bluetooth.

Mac OS X currently allows you to use Bluetooth to communicate with cell phones, PDAs, and other Macs. In the future, Apple will likely expand the range of supported devices to include headsets (for speech recognition or voice recording), printers, and input devices such as mice and keyboards.

In order to use Bluetooth, you need a Bluetooth transceiver for your Mac and a second Bluetooth device of some kind. If your Mac doesn't have Bluetooth built in (and only a few new models did at the time this book was written), you can buy a tiny Bluetooth adapter (sometimes called a *dongle*) from the Apple Store or another retailer. Plug it into any USB port on your Mac, and you're ready to go. This technique focuses mainly on using Bluetooth with cell phones and other computers. Technique 40 covers synchronizing your Bluetooth-enabled Palm organizer using iSync.

STEP 1: SET UP BLUETOOTH PREFERENCES

Before you can use Bluetooth, you need to configure some basic preferences.

- Open System Preferences. After plugging in your Bluetooth adapter (if applicable), a new Bluetooth icon appears in the Hardware section of System Preferences. Click this icon to display the Bluetooth preference pane.
- Click the **Settings** tab, and you'll see something like **Figure 23.2**. Make sure the **Discoverable** checkbox is checked if you want other devices (computers, cell phones, and PDAs) to be able to find your computer. The term *discoverable* means your device will broadcast its name, so that other nearby devices can see it as being available. If your computer isn't discoverable, other Bluetooth devices won't know it's there. In general, you can't connect to a device that isn't discoverable, but an undiscoverable device can connect to other devices that are discoverable.
- The settings for **Authentication** and **Encryption** are up to you. In general, leaving these boxes unchecked results in faster and easier connections, whereas checking them results in greater security. *Authentication* means that each time a device tries to connect to your computer, you must enter the same password on both sides to confirm that you really do want the connection to happen. This procedure can prevent someone else from connecting to your computer without your permission. *Encryption* means the data being sent wirelessly between two devices is encoded so that it couldn't be read by someone nearby using equipment to snoop on the content of your transmissions.
- Check the box for **Support Non-Conforming Phones** only if you know your cell phone has difficulty connecting. Newer phones don't require this option.
- Check **Show Bluetooth status in the menu bar** to put a Bluetooth menu at the top of your screen. This menu, shown in **Figure 23.3**, gives you quick access to a number of Bluetooth-related settings.

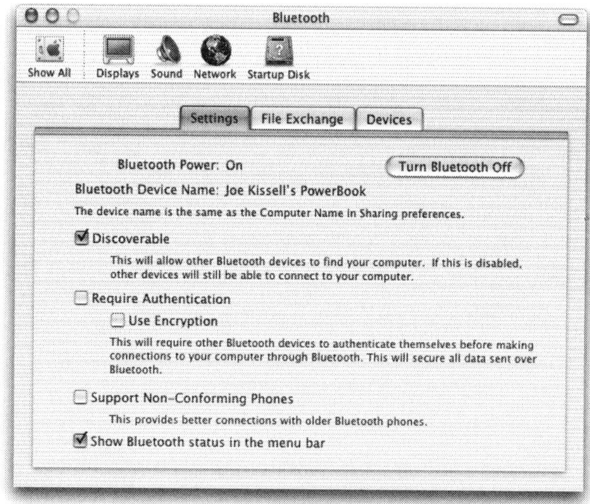

23.2

STEP 2: PAIR DEVICES

Before two Bluetooth devices can exchange data of any kind, they have to be *paired* — in other words, each device has to accept the other as a partner. Without pairing, there would be chaos — your computer could dial someone else's phone, another person's mouse could control your pointer, and so on. Pairing allows you to choose which devices your computer will recognize automatically when they're within range. To pair your chosen devices, follow these steps:

- On your Bluetooth cell phone, PDA, or another Bluetooth-equipped computer, make sure you've turned on Discoverability. Different devices do this in different ways. If the other device is a Mac with a Bluetooth adapter, you can make it discoverable by choosing **Discoverable** from the Bluetooth menu in the Finder. (Either option will work, but the second option is slightly more secure in that it automatically turns off discoverability after you have had time to pair the devices.) For any other device, consult the documentation that came with it.

23.3

- Go to the Bluetooth pane in System Preferences (if you're not already there) and click the **Devices** tab. Click **Pair New Device,** and a second window opens (**Figure 23.4**). Your computer searches for other Bluetooth devices that are both in range and discoverable. Select the device you want from the list and click **Pair**.
- If the other device requires authentication, an alert appears, as shown in **Figure 23.5**, asking you

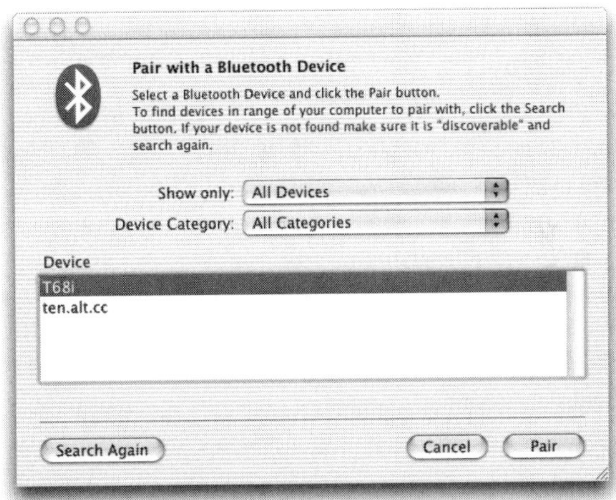

23.4

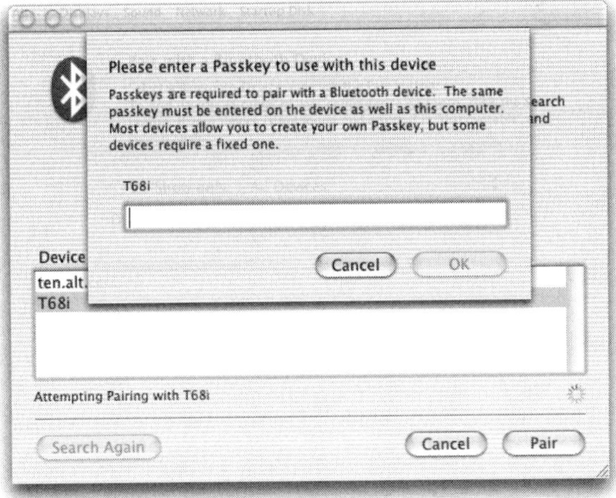

23.5

for a Passkey. Enter any sequence of four numbers here and click **OK**. A similar alert then appears on the second device. Enter the same Passkey that you just entered on your computer. If the Passkeys match, the device will be added to your list of Paired Devices. You may also see another dialog asking which services you want to be able to use with this device. For best results, select all possible options.

- Just as your Mac maintains a list of devices it has been paired with, so does your cell phone or PDA. When your Mac tries to connect with your other device, you may be given the option of adding your Mac to that device's paired list. This is a good idea because it eliminates the need to make your handheld device discoverable each time you use it for Internet access (discussed shortly).
- If you'll be using multiple Bluetooth devices, repeat this procedure for each one.

STEP 3: SHARE FILES WITH ANOTHER MAC

If you have two Macs nearby with Bluetooth capabilities, you can share files wirelessly without any special network setup:

- On the Mac that has the data you want to send, drop the file(s) or folder(s) onto the Bluetooth File Exchange icon, located in Applications/Utilities. (You can also open Bluetooth File Exchange by choosing **Send File...** from the Bluetooth menu.) A dialog appears, as shown in **Figure 23.6**, asking you to choose one or more recipients. Your paired devices that can accept files should already be listed here; if you don't see the device you want, make sure it's discoverable and click **Search** to locate it. After selecting one or more recipients, click **Send**.
- On the receiving computer, an alert appears (**Figure 23.7**), asking whether you want to Accept or Reject the file being sent. If you click **Accept**, the file will be copied to your Documents folder. When the copy is complete, another alert appears, asking whether you want to open the item just received.
- In addition to ordinary files, you can send Address Book entries. Click any name in Address Book and drag it onto the Bluetooth File Exchange icon to send it to the other computer as a .vcf file. If the recipient chooses **Open** when it arrives, it will automatically be added to his or her Address Book.
- (Optional) To decide beforehand what will happen to files you receive via Bluetooth, go to the Bluetooth pane in System Preferences and click the **File Exchange** tab, shown in **Figure 23.8**. Using the controls on this tab, you can choose

23.6

23.7

where you want received files to be stored and whether you want to see an alert asking what to do when someone attempts to send you files.

STEP 4: USE ADDRESS BOOK WITH YOUR PHONE

If you use Apple's Address Book application to manage your contacts — which I recommend — you can use it in conjunction with your Bluetooth cell phone to add some interesting features to both your computer and your phone. Note that these features only work when Address Book is open, though it can be running in the background.

> **TIP**
>
> **If you share files regularly using Bluetooth, consider dragging the Bluetooth File Exchange icon to your Dock, third-party file launcher, or Finder toolbar to make a shortcut for faster access.**

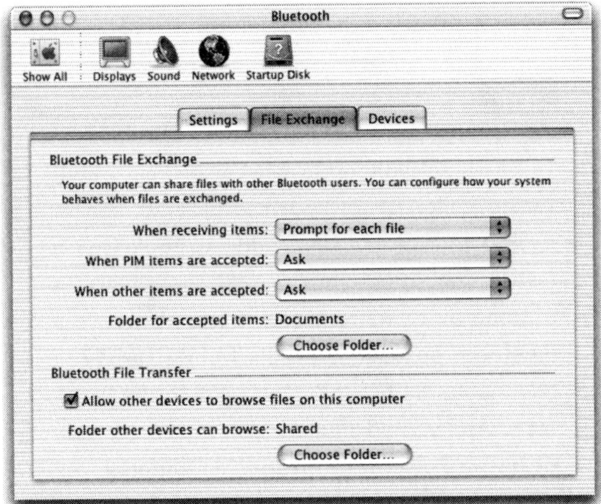

23.8

■ If you have already paired your phone with your computer, you'll notice a new button in Address Book: the Bluetooth button, shown in **Figure 23.9**. If the icon on the button is not already blue, click the button to search for your cell phone. After a moment, it will turn blue to indicate that it's ready to work with your phone.

■ You can now dial any number in your Address Book with your cell phone, even if the number isn't in the phone's memory. Select a contact, and click the *label* next to any of that person's phone numbers. A small menu pops up. (See **Figure 23.10**.) Choose **Dial** from this menu to dial that number, or, if the number belongs to an SMS-capable (SMS stands for Short Message Service) cell phone, choose **Send SMS** to compose an SMS text message.

■ If you receive a call on your cell phone and the caller is listed in your Address Book, your phone's Caller ID service will be used to look up the caller and display the name and number on your screen,

23.9

23.10

as shown in **Figure 23.11**. You can click a button to **Answer** the call, send back an **SMS Reply** (if the caller is using an SMS-capable cell phone), or simply send the call to your **Voice Mail**.

- If you receive an SMS text message on your cell phone, it pops up on your screen, as shown in **Figure 23.12**. You can reply using your computer by clicking **Reply** and typing in your message.

STEP 5: GIVE YOUR POWERBOOK WIRELESS INTERNET ACCESS

Here's the scenario. You're in the middle of nowhere (or, say, on a train) and you urgently need to send a file to a client, check on your server, or modify a bid on eBay. You have your PowerBook but there's no phone line (or wireless base station) in sight. Are you completely out of luck? Not at all, if your PowerBook has a Bluetooth transceiver and you have a Bluetooth-enabled cell phone in your pocket.

Instead of connecting your PowerBook to a phone line, you can use a Bluetooth connection to connect it to your phone, which in turn connects to the Internet. This is a bit cumbersome to set up, but very easy to use once you have — and though not especially speedy, this arrangement can give you basic Internet access in situations where no other solution is possible.

To do so, you need a cell phone with both Bluetooth and wireless Internet capabilities, as well as the appropriate service from your cell phone provider. Companies such as AT&T, Cingular, and T-Mobile all offer phones and service plans with the required features, but you may need to contact your provider to make sure your subscription has all the necessary functionality turned on.

- First, make sure you can connect to the Internet and browse the Web using your phone's built-in software. If your phone can't connect to the Internet by itself, you won't be able to get your computer to do so.

23.11

23.12

TIP

You may be wondering what's so great about seeing Caller ID on your computer screen or dialing your phone from Address Book. Isn't it just as easy to use your phone? These features become much more useful if you also have a Bluetooth headset (available from a variety of manufacturers for about $100). With the headset tucked behind your ear, you can sit at a café with your PowerBook on your lap and your cell phone in your pocket — and still make and receive voice calls wirelessly using the full power of your Address Book.

After pairing your phone to your computer (as in Step 2), you need to set up your computer to use your phone as a modem. This is similar to setting up any other dial-up account.

- Go to the Network pane in System Preferences. If this is the first time you've visited the Network pane since plugging in your Bluetooth adapter, you'll see an alert like that in **Figure 23.13**. Click **OK**. Then choose **USB Bluetooth Modem Adaptor** from the pop-up **Show** menu.
- Click the **Bluetooth Modem** tab. From the **Modem** pop-up menu, shown in **Figure 23.14**, choose your cell phone model — *not* your computer's built-in modem. If your cell phone is not listed, you may be able to use the settings for a similar model. For example, the Ericsson T39 settings also work with the T68 and T68i, which are not listed. If your phone model offers multiple speeds, try the slowest one first. If you get reliable connections with a slow speed, you can always try increasing it to a faster speed later. Be sure to uncheck **Wait for dial tone before dialing**, because your cell phone won't produce a dial tone. Before leaving this tab, make sure **Show modem status in menu bar** is checked — this option makes initiating the connection much easier.
- Click the **TCP/IP** tab and make sure the **Configure** pop-up menu is set to **PPP**. Then click the **PPP** tab. Fill in the information for your ISP here, including your **Account Name**, **Password**, and **Telephone Number**. If you're connecting to a conventional dial-up ISP, these fields should contain your usual dial-up settings. (Hint: if you get a "no carrier detected" error, try inserting a few commas after the telephone number; this increases the amount of time Mac OS X allows to detect a connection.) If you're using your cell phone carrier as your ISP (as in **Figure 23.15**),

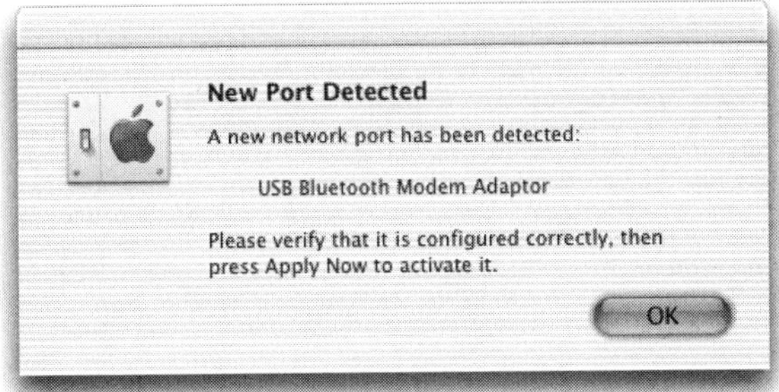

23.13

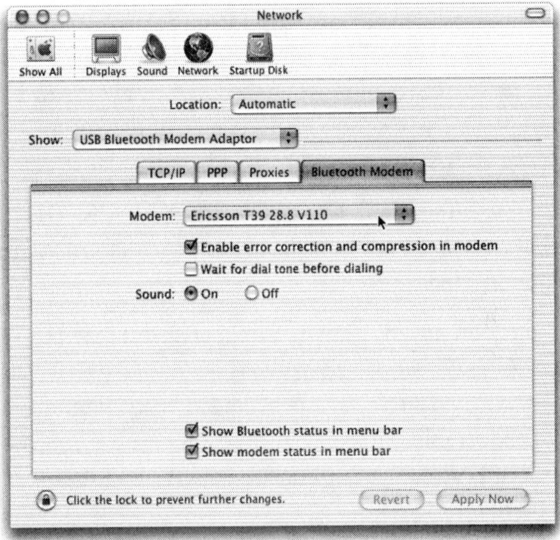

23.14

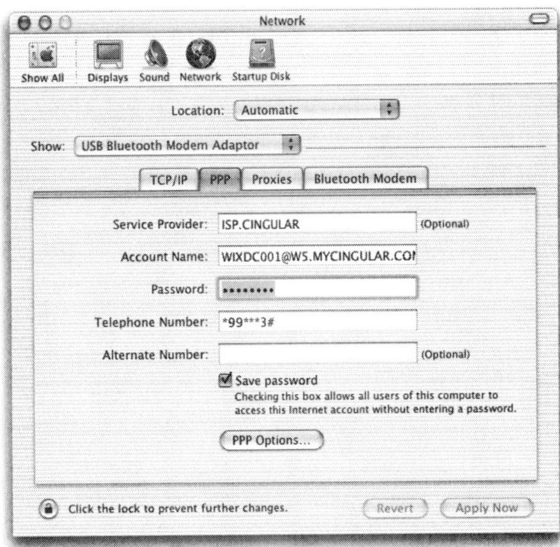

23.15

you will probably use the same account name and password as all other subscribers. Most importantly, the telephone number you enter may be a special code that varies based on the carrier and the model and configuration of your cell phone. A typical example is "*99***3#" (where 3 is replaced with the CID, or Context ID, of your phone — usually 1, 2, or 3). If you get stumped, contact your carrier's technical support department for assistance with these settings. Finally, check **Save password** to avoid being asked for your password each time you connect, and click **Apply Now** to save your settings.

That wasn't so bad, was it? OK, maybe it was — but you'll only need to do it once. Now for the fun part: get connected.

- If you haven't already added your Mac to your phone's list of paired devices (as discussed in Step 2), do so now. Also, make sure your phone is discoverable. This may be necessary even if you've already added your phone to your Mac's list of paired devices.
- Go to the Modem menu on your menu bar (see **Figure 23.16**) and make sure **USB Bluetooth Modem Adapter** is checked. Then choose **Connect** from the same menu. Your phone may ask you if you want to accept the connection. Answer **Yes.** Then, if required by your phone's settings, enter a password on the phone (any four-digit number, such as 0000, will do). An alert will appear on your computer's screen asking for a Passkey. Enter the same number in this alert that you just entered on your phone, and click **OK.** After a few seconds, your computer should be connected. You'll know it worked if you get no error message and a connection timer appears next to your Modem menu.

You can now send e-mail, browse the Web, or use any other Internet applications you may have — but be prepared to wait a while for information to download. If you get the error "Could not open the communication device" when you try to connect, check to make sure that your phone is Discoverable, and be sure you enter exactly the same numeric password on your phone and computer.

Remember that connections you make in this way will not be very fast. Depending on your carrier and the current network conditions at your location, you could get a data rate as low as 2400 bps or as high as 384 Kbps (the theoretical maximum of the new and rare 3G networks). Still, the convenience of a wireless network connection far from phone lines and AirPort base stations can make up for quite a bit of waiting.

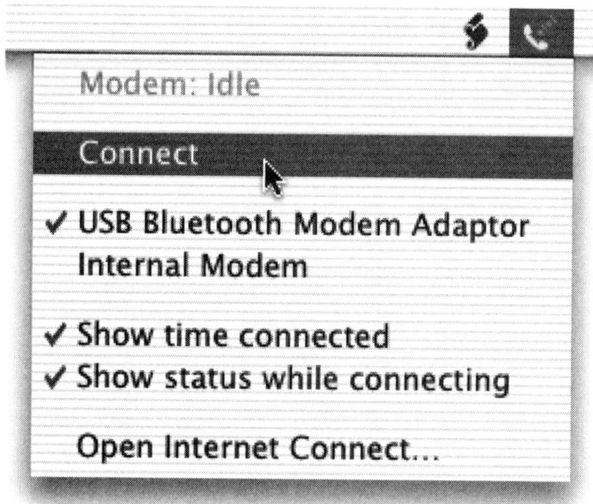

23.16

SHARING FILES WITH MAC AND WINDOWS COMPUTERS

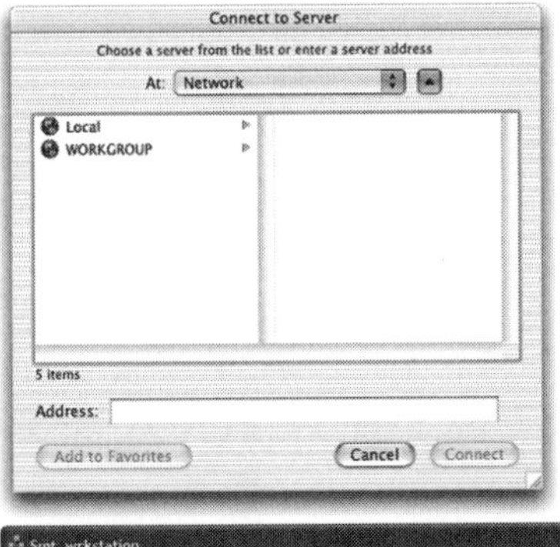

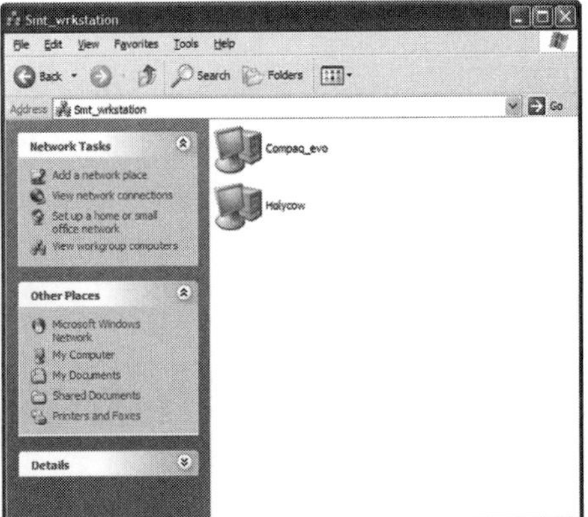

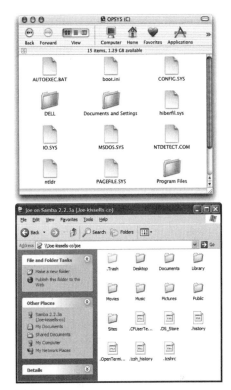

24.1

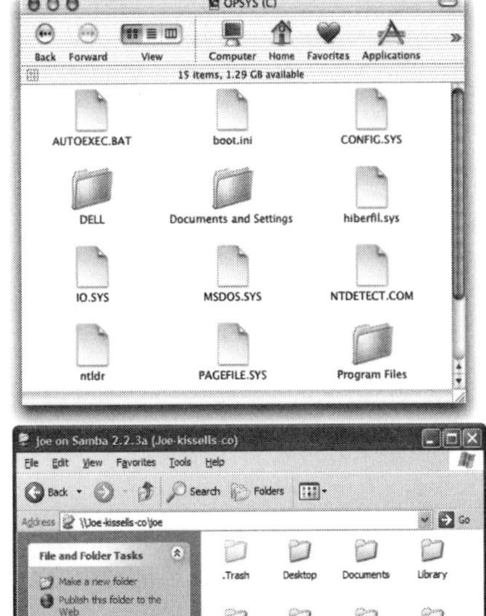

24.2

ABOUT THE FEATURE

Copying files from one computer to another is simple in theory, but can be tricky in practice — especially if the computers aren't both Macs. A few simple principles can make it easy to see files on other computers and make your files visible to them.

Networking — getting two or more computers to talk to each other — has always been extremely easy with Macs. At the same time, the networking world has become more complex, with an ever-increasing list of standards and technologies that must be accommodated. Also, Mac OS X, with its UNIX underpinnings, adds the complexities of ownership and permissions for every file and folder. Apple's marketing propaganda makes it *sound* like you can share all your files with a single click, but for many users, file sharing is an exercise in frustration.

This technique is all about sharing. It covers a simple, straightforward method for getting your Mac to talk to other machines and share information back and forth. What this technique does *not* cover is the minutiae of network administration. This is a fast technique — not a comprehensive one. So there will be no discussion about setting up groups, changing folder permissions, using NetInfo Manager, or all the other details of complex file sharing. But in the next few pages you learn the easy way to copy files from one machine to another quickly, in a variety of situations.

MAC-TO-MAC FILE TRANSFERS

If you want to copy files from one Mac to another (whether the other Mac is in the same room or in another country), you can use Personal File Sharing.

STEP 1: ADD NEW USERS

You can skip this step if you are not concerned about security — if there would be no harm in anyone in the world having access to the files you plan to share. In many cases that's true, and you can save a bit of time and aggravation by using Guest access as described later. But if you want to be sure that only the person or people you designate can see certain files, you'll need to start by setting up an account for them.

- Open System Preferences and click the **Accounts** icon (under "System"). The Accounts pane appears (see **Figure 24.3**).

TIP

If you want to share certain files with a group of people — but still keep them hidden from the rest of the world — simply create a generic account (with a Name such as "Joe's Friends" and a Short Name such as "friends") and then give everyone in the group the same password. Although this method is less secure than having individual accounts, it's also much less complicated to set up.

- Click **New User...** and enter the user's **Name** (normally the first and last name), a **Short Name** (a nickname, initials, or any other version of the user name that does not use spaces, punctuation, or capital letters), and a **New Password**, which you'll need to type a second time into the **Verify** field. You can ignore the other fields for now; click **Save** to create the user.
- Repeat this process for each new user you want to add.

STEP 2: USE THE PUBLIC AND DROP BOX FOLDERS

Now it's time to copy (or move) the files you want to share into a location where connected users will be able to see them.

- If you'll be connecting from the other Mac using your *own* user name and password (and mounting your own home folder), you don't need to do anything special. You'll have access to all your files, regardless of their location.
- In your home folder is a folder named Public (see **Figure 24.4**). This is the folder Guests (users

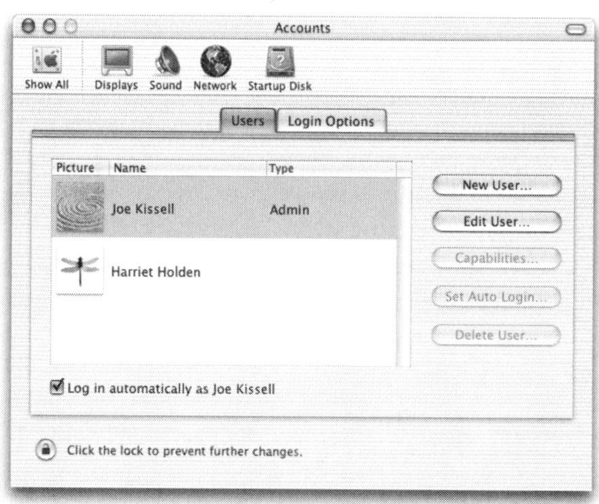

24.3

without their own user names or passwords) will see when they connect to your machine. To make a file available to anyone in the world who connects to your computer, copy it to this folder.

- To make a file available *only* to a particular user, open the **Users** folder at the top level of your hard drive and find the folder with that user's short name. Double-click it, and you'll see it contains another folder called Drop Box. Copy files for this user into the **Drop Box** folder.
- Your Public folder, too, contains a Drop Box folder. This is where other users who connect to your computer will put files they send to you.

STEP 3: TURN ON PERSONAL FILE SHARING

After putting files in their proper location, activate file sharing to make them visible to other computers.

- Open System Preferences and click the **Sharing** icon (under "Internet & Network"). The Sharing pane appears (see **Figure 24.5**).
- Check the **On** box next to **Personal File Sharing**. The message to the right will say "File

NOTE

In order for Personal File Sharing to work across the Internet, your Mac needs to have its own unique IP address. This doesn't have to be a *static* IP address, but it has to be one that isn't shared with other computers. (If your computer's IP address starts with 10, 127, 172.16 through 172.31, or 192.168, you can be sure it's not unique — though other addresses can also be shared.) If you connect to the Internet through a router or AirPort base station that's using NAT (network address translation), other computers outside your network won't be able to see you unless you've specially configured your router to direct all file-sharing requests to a particular computer (known as *port redirection*). See Technique 41, Step 7, for instructions on setting up port redirection with an AirPort base station.

24.4

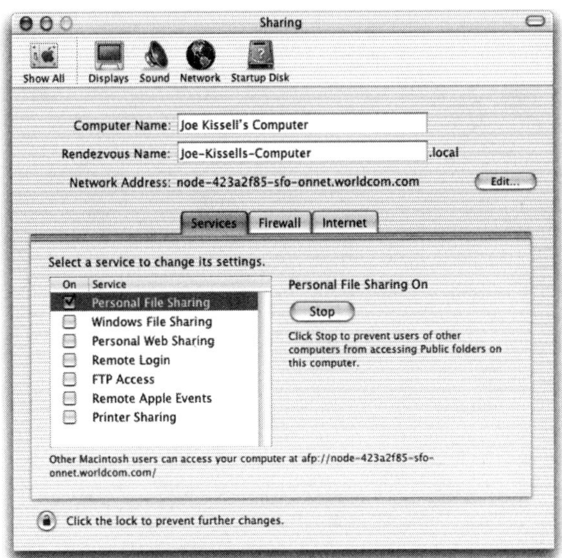

24.5

Sharing starting up" for a few moments and then change to "Personal File Sharing On." Your files are now shared, and you're ready to access them from another Mac.

- The text at the bottom of the window indicates the address at which your computer can be accessed. If you will be sharing files outside your local network, make a note of this address.
- To turn off Personal File Sharing at any time, return to the Sharing window and uncheck the **On** checkbox next to **Personal File Sharing**.

STEP 4: CONNECT FROM ANOTHER MAC

Now go to another Mac to make the connection and see the files you've shared.

- Assuming the other Mac is running Mac OS X, choose **Connect to Server** from the Finder's **Go** menu. The Connect to Server dialog appears (see **Figure 24.6**).

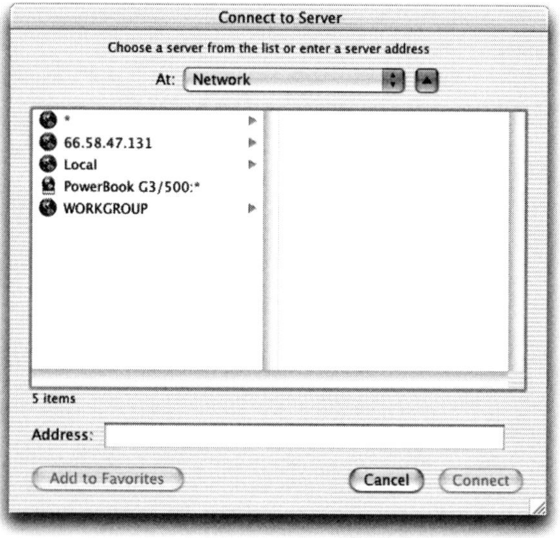

24.6

You can also see your files using Macs running Mac OS 8 or 9. To connect to your Mac OS X machine from a Mac running an older OS, open the Chooser (located in the Apple menu), select the **AppleShare** icon, click **Server IP Address**, and enter the address of the Mac OS X computer. Then click **Connect**.

Depending on your network setup, the left column may list several groups or categories of computers (as shown here), or individual computer names (including your own computer). If the Mac you're connecting to is on the local network and is running Mac OS X 10.2 or higher, the target machine's name should appear under the Local heading.

- When you've located the computer, select its name. If the computer doesn't show up in any of these lists — and it won't if it's not on your local network — you'll need to type its address (which you made a note of in the last step) into the **Address** field. Addresses for Macs using Personal File Sharing begin with afp:// (for Apple File Protocol), followed by the domain name (such as mycompany.com) or IP address (such as 123.45.67.89). After selecting or entering the name of the computer you want to connect to, click **Connect**.
- A dialog, shown in **Figure 24.7**, appears, asking for your user name and password (which you set up in Step 1). If you don't have an account, click the **Guest** radio button to get access only to the Public folder(s) and Drop Box(es) on the machine. If you do have an account, enter your short user name and password, and click **Connect**.
- One final dialog appears, as shown in **Figure 24.8**. This lists the *volumes* available on the computer you're connecting to. In this context, a volume can be either a shared hard drive or the home folder of any of the users with accounts on that machine. Select the volume you want to access and click **OK**.

■ An icon with the name of the newly mounted volume appears on your desktop. In addition, a new window called Volumes appears, listing all of your mounted volumes (including the one you just connected to). Double-click the icon for the volume you just selected to open it.

■ If you connected as Guest, you will only see the contents of that user's Public folder and the Drop Box icon belonging to that user. You can copy files from the Public folder onto your computer, but you cannot delete or modify files belonging to other users. To send files back to the other machine, you must drop them onto the Drop Box icon; you won't be able to add files to the Public folder.

■ If you connected with a user name and password and selected your own volume, you'll see not only the Public folder (and Drop Box) but also the entire home folder belonging to your user account (Documents, Pictures, Music, and so on). You can copy, move, or delete files freely within these folders. To send a file to the other machine that will be visible to all of its users, drag it to the Public folder. If you use your user name and password but mount a volume other than your own, you'll only have Guest-level access to it unless the owner has explicitly granted you rights to files on that volume.

24.7

NOTE

These directions assume that the computer that's sharing its files is running Mac OS X. You can also connect to computers running Mac OS 8 or 9. On a pre-Mac OS X computer using Personal File Sharing, open the File Sharing control panel and make sure Enable File Sharing clients to connect over TCP/IP is checked. If file sharing is turned on, you should be able to follow these same steps to mount its volumes from your Mac OS X machine.

MAC-WINDOWS FILE TRANSFERS

It used to be the case that sharing files with Windows users required special software, complex configuration, and a lot of luck. With Mac OS X version 10.2 and later, however, sharing files with Windows users is almost as easy as sharing them with Mac users.

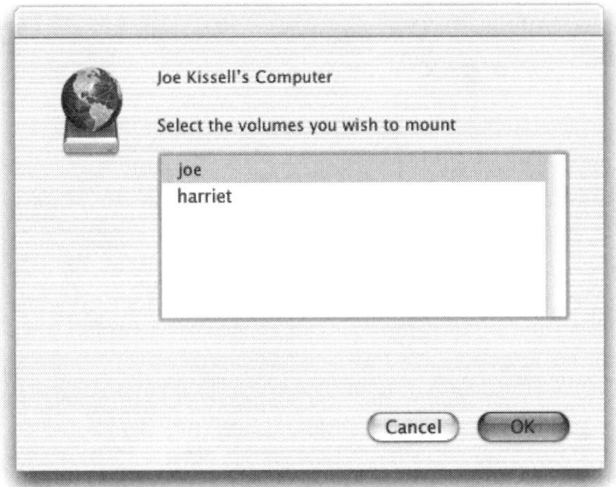

24.8

STEP 1: SET UP USER ACCOUNTS

Just as you did earlier when setting up file sharing from one Mac to another, you must give each Windows user who wants to connect to your Mac a user name and password.

- If you want to give access to a Windows user who doesn't already have an account on your Mac, open System Preferences and click the Accounts icon (under "System"). The Accounts pane appears. Click **New User** and enter the user's **Name** (normally the first and last name), a **Short Name** (a nickname, initials, or any other version of the user name that does not use spaces, punctuation, or capital letters), and a **New Password**, which you'll need to type a second time in the **Verify** field. At the bottom of this window (see **Figure 24.9**), check **Allow user to log in from Windows**. Click **Save** to create the user.

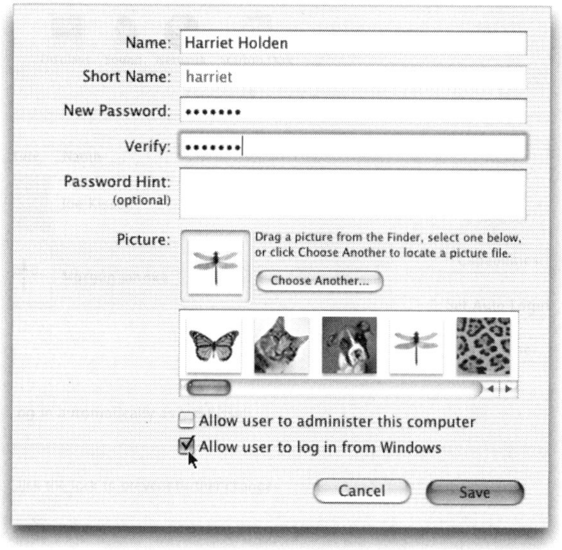

24.9

- If a user already has an account on your Mac, you just need to add the ability to connect from Windows. Select the user in the Accounts pane of System Preferences and click **Edit User**; then check **Allow user to log in from Windows**. You may be asked to reset the password; if so, you can simply reenter the same password you entered for that user originally.

STEP 2: MOVE FILES TO USER FOLDERS

When connecting to your Mac from a Windows computer, there's no concept of a Guest account — you can only get in if you have a user name and password. So the idea of Public and Drop Box folders works a bit differently.

- If you'll be connecting from the Windows machine using your *own* user name and password (and mounting your own home folder), you don't need to do anything special. You'll have access to all your files, regardless of their location.
- To make a file available to all Windows users who connect with a valid user name and password, copy it to the Public folder in your home folder.
- To make a file available to a particular user other than yourself, open the Users folder at the top level of your hard drive and find the folder with that user's short name. Double-click it, and you'll see it contains another folder called Drop Box. Copy files for this user into the Drop Box folder.

STEP 3: TURN ON WINDOWS FILE SHARING

As with Mac-to-Mac file sharing, after placing the files in the correct location, you must activate Windows file sharing so that Windows computers can see them.

- Open System Preferences and click the Sharing icon (under "Internet & Network"). The Sharing pane (see **Figure 24.10**) appears.
- Check the **On** box next to **Windows File Sharing.** Your files are now shared, and you're ready to access them from a Windows machine.
- The text at the bottom of the window indicates the address at which your computer can be accessed. If you will be sharing files outside your local network, make a note of this address.
- To turn off Windows File Sharing at any time, return to the Sharing window and uncheck the **On** box next to **Windows File Sharing.**

STEP 4: CONNECT TO YOUR MAC FROM A PC

Now go to a Windows machine on your network. (Note that the other machine *must* be on the same local network — Windows File Sharing does not work across the Internet the way Apple File Sharing does.)

- Open **My Network Places** (Windows XP or 2000) or **Network Neighborhood** (older versions of Windows) from the **Start** menu. (If My Network Places does not appear in the Start menu, you can open it by choosing **My Computer** from the Start menu and clicking the **My Network Places** link on the left.)
- If your Mac's icon appears (it may begin with the name Samba and a version number, with the actual computer name in parentheses), double-click it and then enter your user name and password. Your home folder will mount as a new volume. (Note that unlike with Apple File Sharing, you can't mount someone else's Public folder as a volume unless you know the person's user name and password.)
- If your Mac's icon does not appear — which will be the case as often as not on corporate networks — you'll have to dig for it a bit. First, click **View entire network** (or **View workgroup computers**) in the My Network Places (or Network Neighborhood) window. Then click **Microsoft Windows Network** to display a list of all available network machines, as shown in **Figure 24.11.** As in the Mac's Connect to Server dialog, they'll be organized into groups (sometimes called *domains, workgroups,* or *nodes*), so you may have

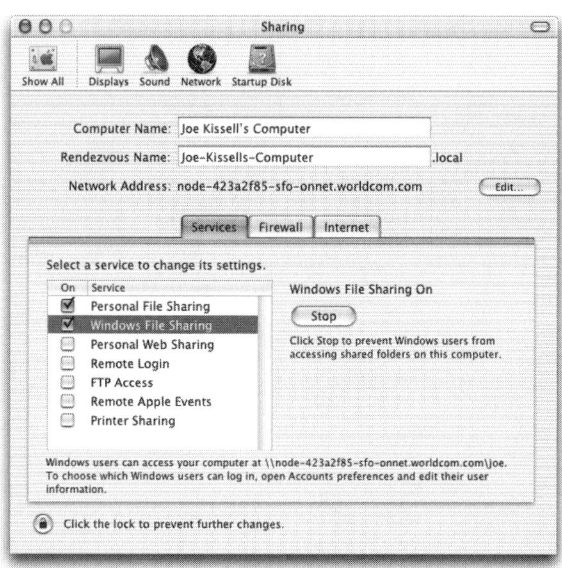

24.10

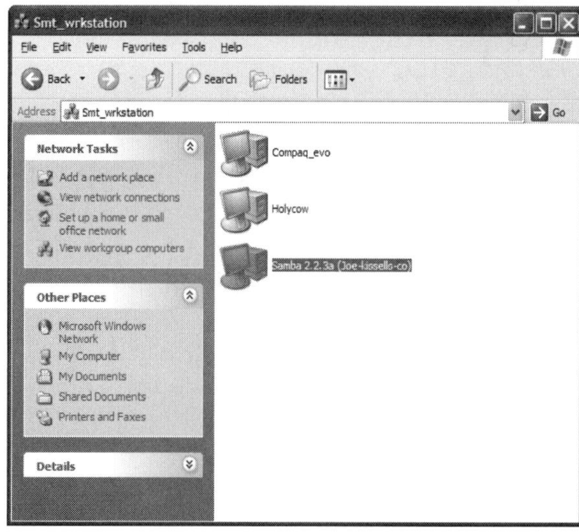

24.11

to double-click a workgroup icon before you'll see the computers in that group. There's no way to predict which group it will appear in without knowing about your individual network, but if you check each group in turn, you should eventually find your Mac listed. When you do, double-click it and log in as usual.

- If the Mac does not appear in any list, you may need to access it using its domain name or IP address, as you noted in Step 3. To do this, go to **My Network Places** and click the **Add a network place** link on the left. Using the Wizard that appears, select **Choose another network location** and enter a double backslash followed by the Mac's address, another backslash, and the name of the shared volume, for example, `\\192.168.0.70\joe` or `\\mycomputer.mydomain.com\myvolume`. Click **Next** to connect and enter your user name and password when prompted.

STEP 5: CONNECT TO A PC FROM YOUR MAC

If Windows users can see the files on your Mac, does it work the other way around, too? Absolutely. You can mount a Windows volume just as you would mount a Mac volume.

- Make sure you have an account (user name and password) on the Windows machine.
- At least one folder on the Windows machine must be shared and accessible to your user name. If this is not already the case, consult the Windows electronic Help for instructions.
- Back on your Mac, choose **Connect to Server** from the Finder's **Go** menu. The Connect to Server dialog appears. Any Windows machines on the network should be listed automatically — either individually or as part of a group. You may need to explore the various groups listed to find the machine you're looking for. When you do find it, double-click its name.
- A dialog (see **Figure 24.12**) appears, asking for your **Username**, **Password**, and **Workgroup/Domain**. If the **Workgroup/Domain** field isn't filled in already, you can probably leave it blank. (If that leads to an error message, contact your system administrator to find out what workgroup you should enter to connect to that PC.) Click **OK** to connect.
- Just as a Mac can have multiple volumes, so can a Windows machine. A dialog called **SMB Mount** appears, as shown in **Figure 24.13**. From the pop-up menu, choose the shared folder you want to mount and click **OK**. Your Windows shared folder will appear on your desktop as a mounted volume, and you can copy files in either direction just as you would with a Mac volume.

24.12

NOTE

You may have noticed another type of file sharing available on your Mac — FTP (file transfer protocol). In most cases, you won't need to use it; Personal File Sharing and Windows File Sharing are by far the most common means of sharing files, and FTP is not a very secure protocol. However, FTP might be useful in certain specific situations — for example, if you need to access files on your Mac from a Windows (or UNIX) machine that is *not* on your local network. To turn on FTP sharing, go to the Services tab in Sharing Preferences and click the On checkbox next to FTP Access. In order for others to access your files via FTP, they need an account (just as you set up for Mac-to-Mac file transfers). The remote user needs to know your Mac's address. (FTP addresses are ftp:// followed by an IP address or domain name.) Although Web browsers can connect to FTP servers, best results (and bidirectional transfers) can be obtained either by using an FTP client program, Windows Explorer (on a PC), or the Connect to Server command on Mac OS X.

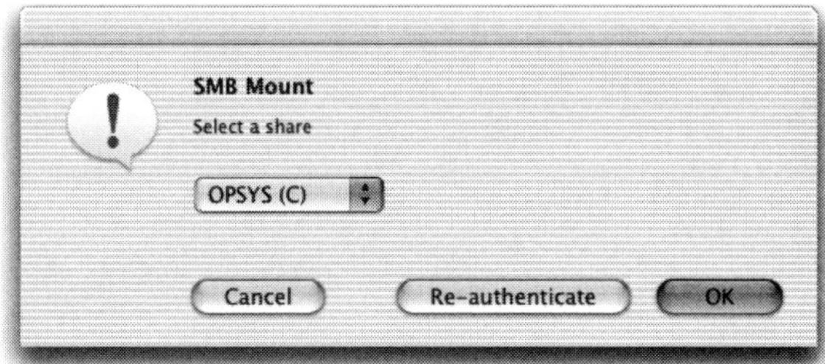

24.13

TECHNIQUE 25

KEEPING OUT THE RIFF-RAFF WITH A FIREWALL

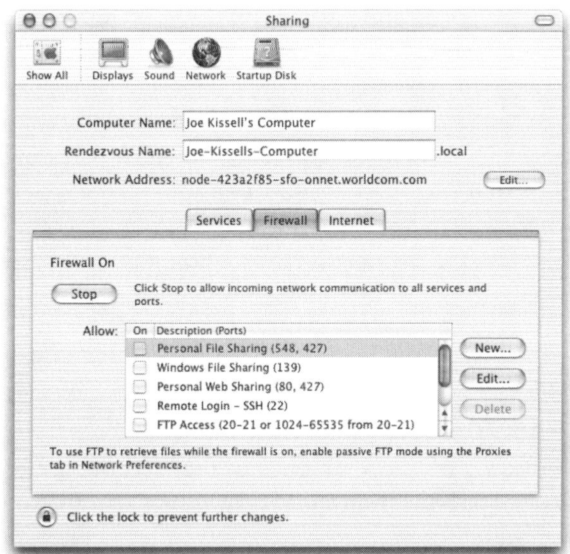

25.1

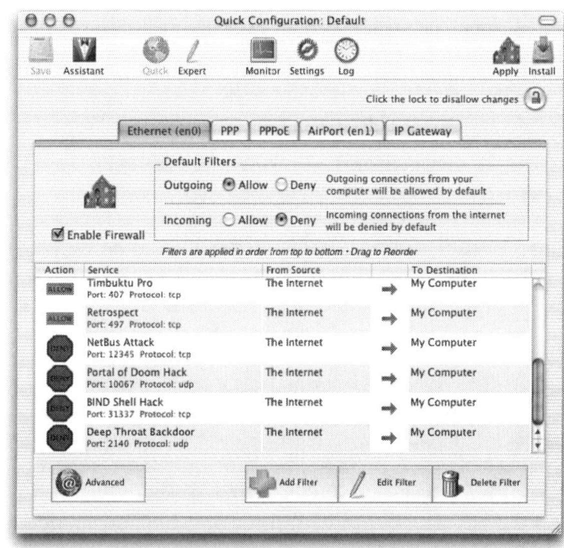

25.2

ABOUT THE FEATURE

A firewall is software that selectively blocks certain kinds of data from moving into or out of your computer. A properly configured firewall can keep your personal data from falling into the wrong hands and protect your Mac from outside attack.

There was a time, not so long ago, when only large companies and universities had continuous high-speed links to the Internet. Nowadays broadband Internet connections are the norm, and dial-up access is rapidly becoming obsolete. Running servers at home is becoming common, and many of us take for granted the ability to access our Macs anytime, from anywhere in the world. All this connectivity brings a lot of convenience, but with that convenience comes risk. If other computers can always see your computer, it's a potential target of someone wanting to steal information from you, damage your computer, or interrupt your network connection.

An essential tool for protecting your data is a *firewall* — a piece of software or hardware that selectively filters what kind of information can get into and out of your computer. Firewalls can be very complex, but for most users, Mac OS X's built-in firewall software — with the necessary configuration — can provide more than adequate protection. The problem is that most people never even bother to turn on their firewall because they don't understand how it works. This technique shows you everything you need to know for a basic configuration. You also see how a third-party utility called BrickHouse can give you more advanced protection by helping you to set up some of the hidden features of Apple's firewall.

STEP 1: UNDERSTAND WHAT YOU'RE DOING

This book is pretty light on theory, but firewalls deserve a bit of background. If you don't know what you're doing (and why) before you start, you could end up cutting off all access to your network. So here's a five-minute firewall primer.

Each type of service used on the Internet — such as HTTP and HTTPS for the Web or POP, IMAP, and SMTP for e-mail — has its own individually numbered *port*, which you can think of as a channel dedicated to one specific type of traffic. Your Web browser, for example, sends requests on port 80, because that is the channel used for HTTP. Even if mail is coming in at the same time on port 25, your Web browser won't know anything about it. This way, different types of information can be handled by the applications that understand them best.

Without a firewall, information can flow in and out of your computer freely on any of thousands of different ports — think of them as open doors and windows in your house. Ordinarily this is fine — you need to let some air in, let the dog out, invite neighbors over, and so on. But just as you probably wouldn't leave *all* your doors and windows unlocked *all* the time, it's not really wise to leave all your ports open. The reason is the same: Someone you don't know, and don't want inside, could use an open door (port) to vandalize, steal, or otherwise wreak havoc on your stuff. A firewall lets you specify which doors are open, to whom, and when.

The concept behind a firewall is quite simple. Pick a port and turn incoming or outgoing access on that port on or off. Do the same for the next port. Lather, rinse, repeat. You could, if you wanted, have all ports open by default and just turn off the ones you want to block. Because there are a great many ports, though, turning off every single one you want to block can be very tedious. If you forget one, you could leave a security hole that you'll later regret. For that reason, the easiest and safest way to set up a firewall is to start with *all* ports blocked, and only open up the ones that need to be open. That's what you do in the remainder of this technique.

STEP 2: TURN ON THE BUILT-IN FIREWALL

Activating Mac OS X's built-in firewall couldn't be easier. For basic protection, performing just this one step will suffice.

- Open System Preferences and click the **Sharing** icon (under "Internet & Network"). Click the **Firewall** tab, and you'll see something like **Figure 25.3**.
- Click **Start**. That's it! Your firewall is now actively blocking all ports except the ones you need for services your computer is providing.

The scrolling list displays the ports Apple's firewall can open automatically. The ones that are currently open will have a checkmark in the **On** column. You'll notice that you can't manually turn various ports on or off here. That's because Mac OS X assumes any services you're running on your computer — such as Personal File Sharing, Windows File Sharing, or Personal Web Sharing — will need to be visible to the outside world. If you turn off a service (using the checkboxes on the **Services** tab), the firewall will automatically block the associated port(s), and the relevant checkbox on the **Firewall** tab will disappear.

> **WARNING**
>
> **In general, the more services you provide, the less secure your computer, because there will be more open ports for malicious traffic to sneak through. So don't turn on any services "just because" — activate them only if you actually need them. You can make your open ports safer by using the security features associated with each feature. For example, file sharing can be made more secure by choosing good (hard-to-guess) passwords for the user accounts you've set up.**

STEP 3: UNBLOCK ADDITIONAL PORTS

After you've activated your firewall, you'll still be able to make *outgoing* requests on the blocked ports and receive replies back. Only incoming requests will be blocked. But you may be using software that needs to accept incoming requests on ports other than those listed. For example, if you need to use Timbuktu Pro or VNC to control your computer remotely, or Retrospect to back it up remotely, you must unblock the ports those programs use.

- To unblock a port, click the **New** button on the **Firewall** tab. A sheet appears with a pop-up menu containing some popular services you might want to unblock (see **Figure 25.4**). Choose a service from this list to enter its port number automatically and then click **OK** to close the sheet.
- If a port you want to unblock does not appear on this pop-up menu, you can add it manually. Choose **Other** from the pop-up menu, enter the

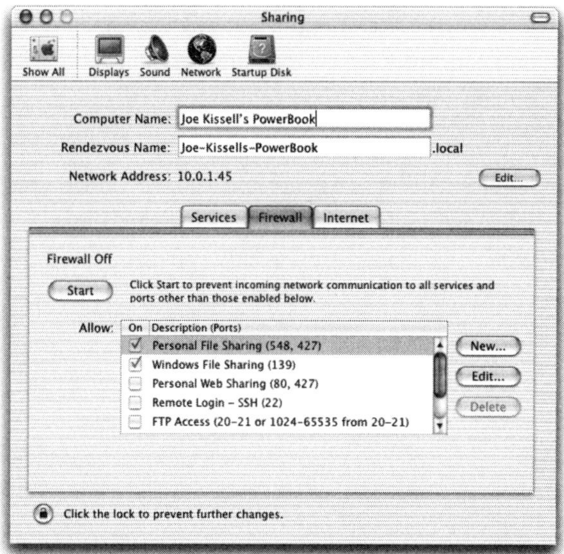

25.3

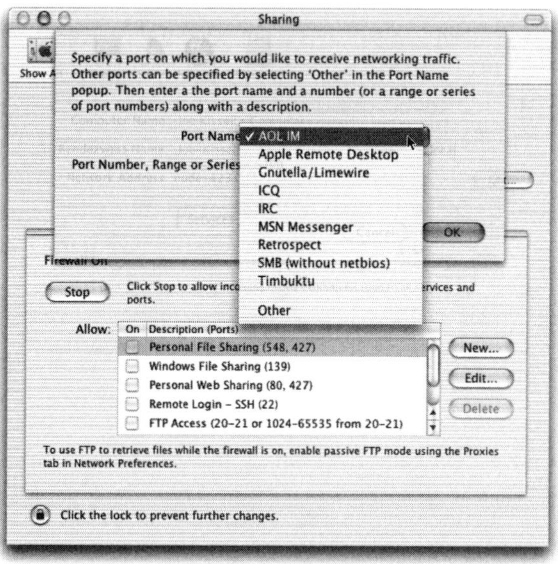

25.4

port number, and type a descriptive name for the new port. Then click **OK**.

In addition to ports for Timbuktu and Retrospect, you might want to unblock additional ports in the pop-up menu. AOL IM is used for iChat connections, and if you use other types of chat/instant messaging programs (such as ICQ, IRC, or MSN Messenger), you'll need to unblock them, too. If you share files using a peer-to-peer network, unblock Gnutella/ Limewire. (Obligatory reminder: Don't steal music.) If a network manager needs to control your machine using Apple Remote Desktop, unblock that port. Also, if Windows computers are having trouble accessing your computer even though you've turned on Windows File Sharing, you may need to unblock SMB (without netbios).

You might need to know about a few other common ports. Because these aren't listed in the pop-up menu of ports, you need to enter them manually using the **Other** command to unblock them.

- If you use iChat's Rendezvous feature to chat with users on your local network, unblock port 5298.
- To control your computer remotely using VNC (see Technique 32), you'll have to unblock port 5900.
- If you run a mail server on your computer (see Technique 45), you need to unblock ports 110, 143, and 25, for POP, IMAP, and SMTP, respectively.

STEP 4: ACCESS ADVANCED OPTIONS WITH BRICKHOUSE (OPTIONAL)

Apple's firewall allows you to selectively unblock any port. But you may want to do other, more advanced activities with a firewall. To wit:

- If your computer has multiple network connections — for example, an AirPort card, an Ethernet interface (or two), and a modem — you might want to have different firewall settings depending on which network interface is in use.
- You might want to block *outgoing* access on a certain port. For example, if you want to make sure nobody using your computer can download files with Limewire, you can block outgoing access on port 6346.
- You might want to restrict incoming access on a certain port to specific IP addresses. This would allow you, for example, to use your computer as an intranet Web server — giving access only to other computers within your network but not the general public.
- Conversely, you might want to block only certain computers from accessing (or being accessed by) various services on your computer.

As it turns out, Apple's firewall does offer all these capabilities and much more, but you can't get at them using System Preferences. If your firewall needs go beyond what Apple offers, your options are to use Terminal to modify the `ipfw` (IP Firewall) settings — not fun, even if you know what you're doing — or download a friendly graphical utility to make it much easier.

One such utility is called BrickHouse (available from `personalpages.tds.net/~brian_hill/`), shown in **Figure 25.5**. It provides a straightforward interface to advanced firewall settings. The documentation included with BrickHouse tells you everything you need to know to set up a very advanced firewall without ever using the command line.

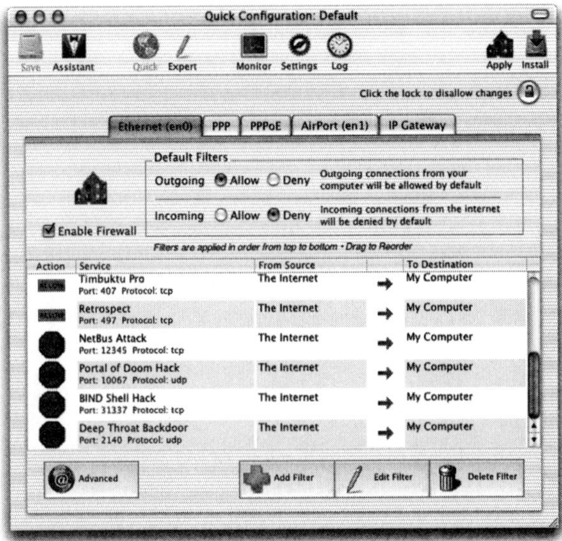

25.5

CHAPTER 6

E-MAIL & WEB TECHNIQUES

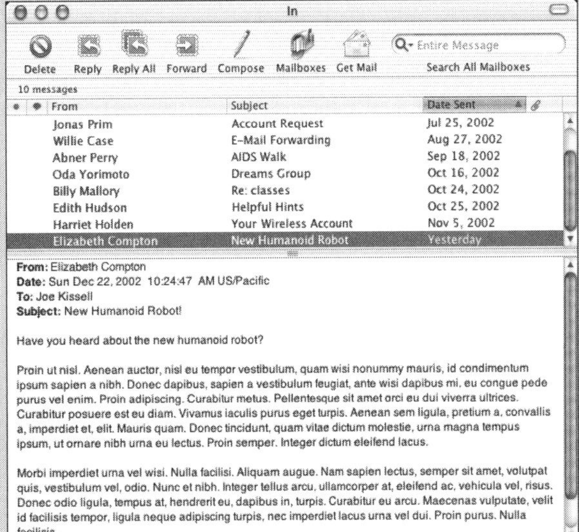

Every once in a while, I come across a survey asking me how many times a day I check my e-mail or how many hours I spend viewing Web sites each week. These questions always puzzle me, because e-mail and Web browsing have become, for many people, not separate activities but background tasks that go on all the time. My e-mail program is *always* open, always checking mail whether I look at it or not. And even when I'm not actively surfing, I'll pop into my always-open Web browser several times an hour — to look up a word, check the latest news, or verify a piece of information for the book I'm writing. Whatever else I do, e-mail and Web browsing are the two pillars of my computing experience.

If you take a similar approach to e-mail and the Web, you'll appreciate the techniques in this chapter. The first two techniques help you get the most out of your e-mail without letting it get to you. First, you look at ways to customize Mail to add functionality and make it easier to use. Then you zoom in on one of Mail's best features: Rules that can filter and sort all your mail for you with a minimum of effort. Turning your attention to the Web, you look at Sherlock 3, Apple's fantastic search utility for finding all sorts of Web-based content easily without using a Web browser. Finally, in a technique called "Web Browsing Secrets of the Rich and Famous," I take you beyond bookmarks and Forward/Back buttons and show you how to surf like a pro.

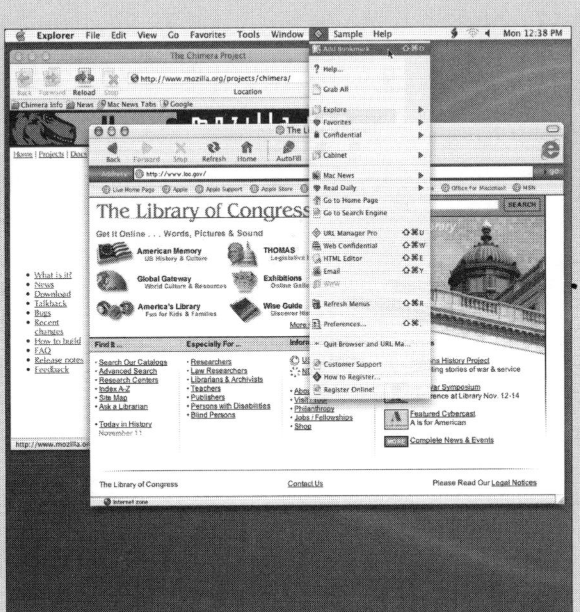

Secrets of the Rich & Famous
Mail
RULES
Sherlock 3
Signatures
Accounts
Fonts & Colors
Viewing
Composing
Signatures
Rules
Description
Personal
Business
Funny Quote
Add Signature
Edit
Duplicate
Remove
Select Signature: Personal
Show signature menu on compose window
In
Out
Drafts
Sent
Trash
Drafts
Junk
Sent
Trash
Delete
Reply
Reply All
Forward
Compose
Mailboxes
Get Mail
Junk
Archive Messages
Change SMTP Server
Create Mailing List
Create Rule
Export Messages
Remove Duplicate Messages
Send all Drafts
Web Features
Show All
Navigation
Appearance
Privacy
Web Features
Enable features that help interpret web pages.
Enable JavaScript
Enable Java
Enable Plugins
Popup Blocking
Enable popup bloc
The Library of Congress
Back
Forward
Stop
Refresh
Home
AutoFill
Print
Mail
Address http://www.loc.gov/
Live Home Page
Apple
Apple Support
Apple Store
.Mac
Mac OS X
The Library of Congress
Get It Online . . . Words, Pictures & Sound
American Memory
US History & Culture
THOMAS
Legislative Information
Global Gateway
World Culture & Resources
Exhibitions
Online Galleries
America's Library
Fun for Kids & Families
Wise Guide
Discover History & More
More Online Collections...
Filed Mail
Church
Friends
Junk
Lists
Money
Not at all Urgent
Sent
Rules
Description: Apple
If any of the following conditions are met:
Subject
Contains
Apple
Perform the following actions:
Transfer Message
to mailbox: In
Set Color
of background
Other...
Cancel
OK
Pictures
Channels
Internet
Pictures
Stocks
Flights
Dictionary
Translation
AppleCare
Picture Topic or Description
coliseum

TECHNIQUE **26**

CUSTOMIZING APPLE'S MAIL APPLICATION

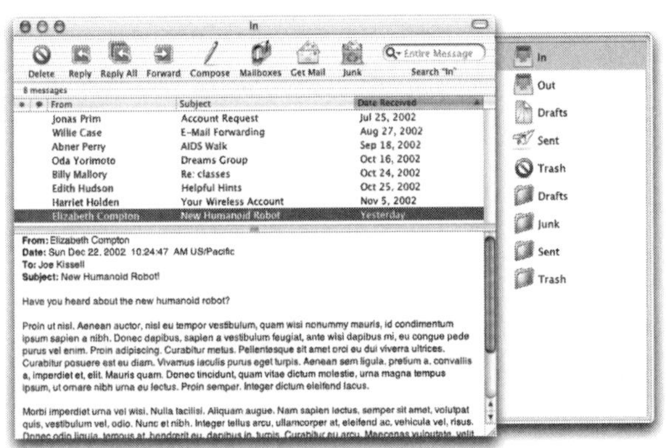

26.1

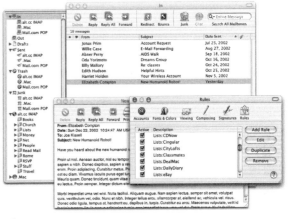

26.2

ABOUT THE FEATURE

Every copy of Mac OS X includes a fully featured e-mail application simply called Mail. You can personalize many aspects of this program to make it even easier and more convenient to use.

I'm very picky about the software I use for sending and receiving e-mail. I've tried every e-mail program I can get my hands on, looking for the one with the combination of features and layout that suits my particular needs and preferences best. Surprisingly, the one that comes closest for me — while by no means perfect — is the unassuming Mail application that's included as part of Mac OS X. Although early versions of this program were rather unimpressive, the version of Mail introduced with Mac OS X 10.2 is both powerful and flexible, with several unique features that make it especially appealing.

Some of the best parts of Mail, however, are not immediately obvious. Hidden behind its modest façade are some great features just waiting to be exposed. In this technique, you customize Mail to bring some of those features to the front and make it easier to use.

STEP 1: PUT THE MAILBOX LIST ON THE LEFT

It may seem like a small thing, but when I first started using Mail, it drove me crazy that the drawer containing the mailbox list was on the *right* side of the window. That seemed counterintuitive to me. It's also the opposite of every other e-mail program — not to mention other parts of Mac OS X. For example, in Column View, folders are displayed on the left, and their contents are displayed on the right. Because English users are accustomed to reading from left to right, having the container on the left seems most natural. Unfortunately, Apple didn't provide an obvious way of switching it to the left side. Here's the unobvious way:

- Choose **Hide Drawer** from the **View** menu (or press **⌘+Shift+M**). The drawer closes.
- Click the title bar of the window and drag it to the right so that it almost comes to the right edge of your screen.
- Now choose **Show Drawer** from the **View** menu (or press **⌘+Shift+M** again). The drawer opens on the left side (see **Figure 26.3**) because there's not enough room to display it on the right side. You can now move your window back to another part of the screen, and Mail will remember the drawer's location even when you quit and reopen the application.

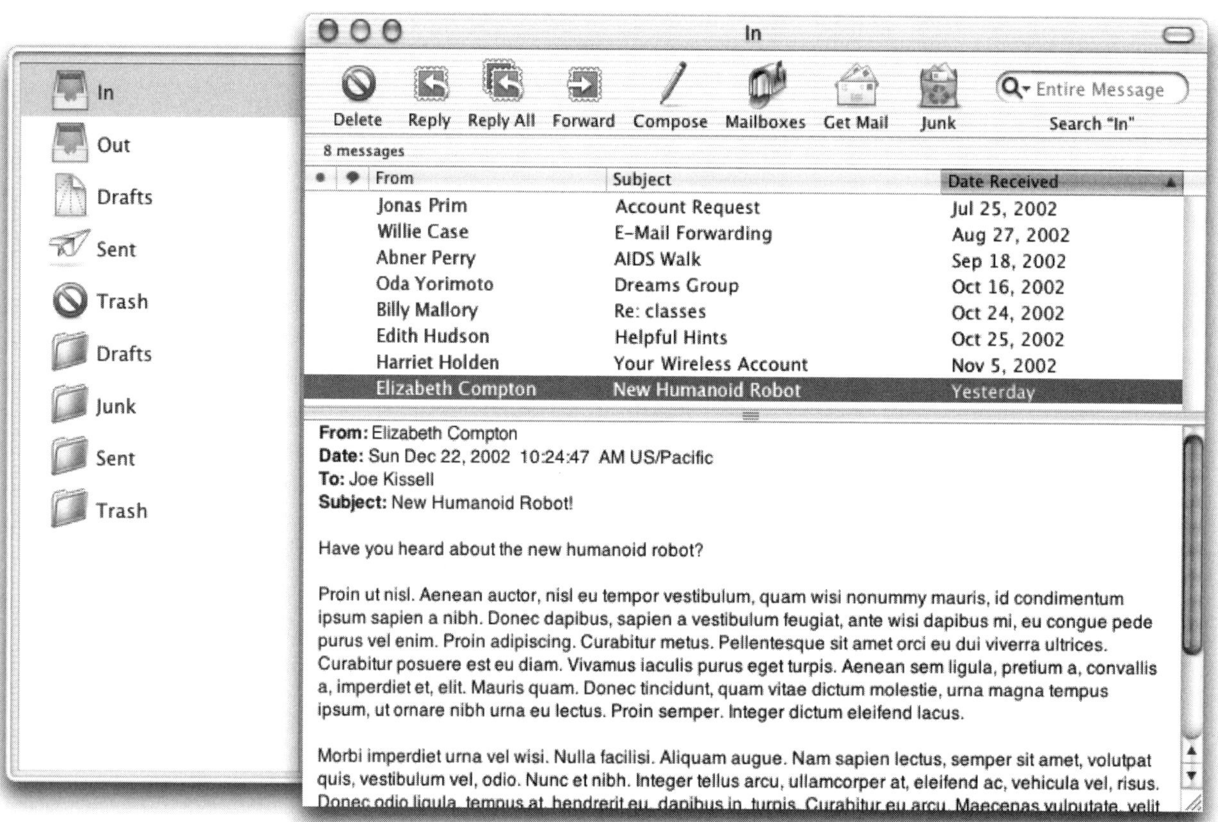

26.3

STEP 2: ADD ALL YOUR MAIL ACCOUNTS

Do you have more than one e-mail account? Many people have a home account, a work account, a just-for-junk mail account, and so on. Mail lets you access *all* your e-mail accounts in the same place at the same time.

- Choose **Preferences...** from the **Mail** menu. If the title bar doesn't say Accounts, as shown in **Figure 26.4**, click the **Accounts** button.
- Click **Add Account** and fill in the account information (see **Figure 26.5**) with the information provided by your ISP. Mail supports POP, IMAP, and .Mac accounts. Be sure you've chosen your account type using the pop-up menu at the top of the window.

NOTE

Mail cannot access Web-only e-mail accounts such as Hotmail or Excite Mail. These mail accounts are generally free, subsidized by the advertising you're forced to see when you log in to check your mail. Allowing access with an e-mail client like Mail would defeat the purpose by permitting you to bypass the ads. You may, however, be able to purchase POP access for an additional fee.

ABOUT POP AND IMAP

Although POP is the most commonly used account type, IMAP is rapidly gaining in popularity. With a POP account, mail is downloaded to your computer when you check it and then deleted from the server. With IMAP, your messages remain on the server — including, significantly, messages you've read and filed into folders. This can be extremely useful if you don't use just one computer for e-mail all the time. With IMAP, you can check your mail using your Mac at home, a Linux box at work, and a PC at a cybercafé halfway around the world — and always see exactly the same new, saved, and sent messages. It also makes moving from one e-mail program to another — or even one platform to another — much simpler, because you never have to export or import any mail messages.

Mail is designed to work especially well with IMAP accounts — in fact, Mac mail accounts actually use IMAP. Your existing ISP may offer both POP and IMAP access to your e-mail. Ask your ISP whether IMAP might be an option for you.

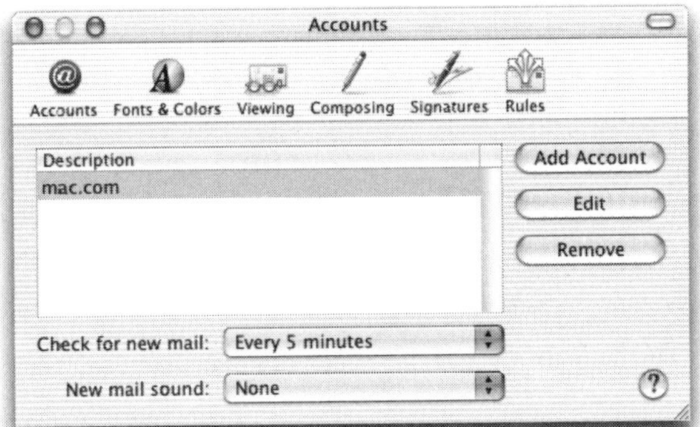

26.4

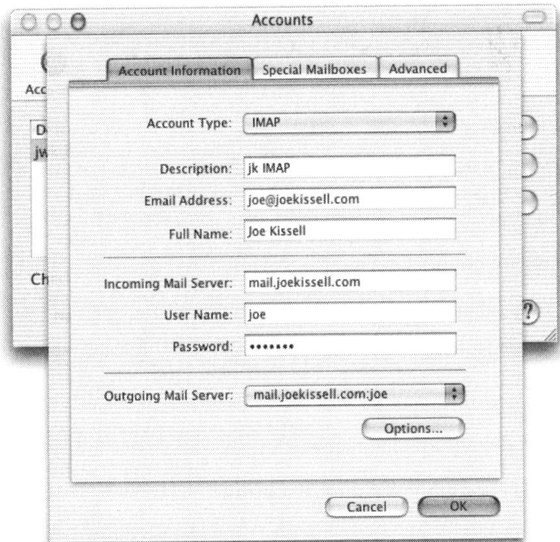

26.5

- Depending on the account type you've chosen, a variety of options will be available on the **Special Mailboxes** and **Advanced** tabs. Use these settings to specify how long to keep deleted mail in your Trash, whether to store copies of sent messages, and other options.
- Repeat this step for each e-mail account you want to add. **Figure 26.6** shows Mail with some additional accounts (and lots more mail folders). Because this list, including its subfolders, is quite long, I've reduced the icon size using the **Use Small Mailbox Icons** on the **View** menu. This allows me to see more mailbox folders at one time.

STEP 3: TWEAK MAIL PREFERENCES

Mail includes a great many preferences you can customize to suit your tastes. Here are some of the most useful ones:

- At the bottom of the Accounts pane in Mail Preferences are two pop-up menus, as shown in **Figure 26.7**. The first allows you to choose the frequency with which Mail checks for new mail. If you like instant gratification, set this for a small time period, such as **Every minute**. You can also choose a sound to be played when you have new mail — even if Mail is running in the background.
- Click **Fonts & Colors** in Mail Preferences to change the appearance of text in lists and messages. If you prefer to send messages as plain text (rather than with colors and styles), you may find it useful to check **Use fixed-width font for plain text messages**. This setting ensures that ASCII art and other spacing-sensitive content is displayed correctly.
- The **Viewing** pane has several controls worth considering. If **Show online buddy status** is checked, Mail will display a small indicator if the sender of a message is using iChat and currently

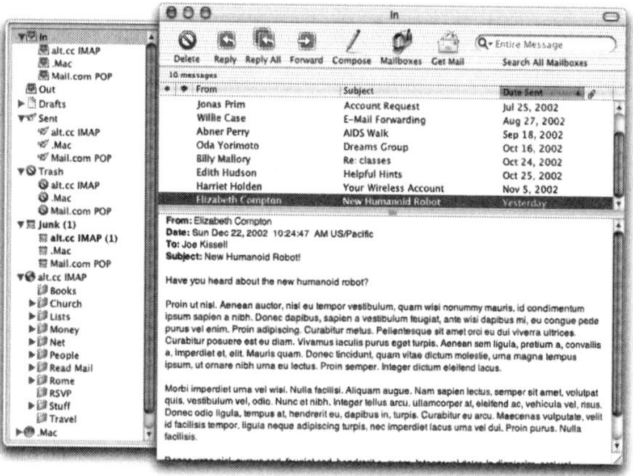

26.6

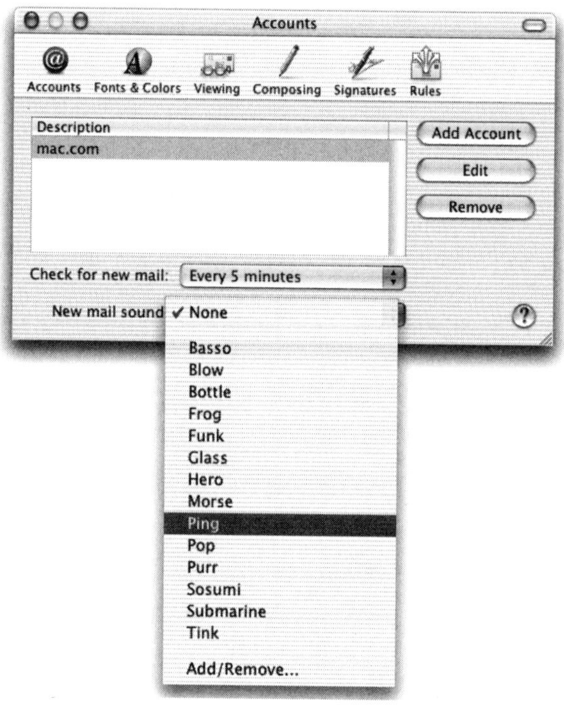

26.7

available. If you have a lot of messages in the same thread (replies to replies to replies), check **Highlight thread of selected message in color**. When you select any message, Mail will highlight all the other messages in the same thread so you can find them easily, as shown in **Figure 26.8** (CP.7). If you frequently get e-mail with embedded graphics you would rather not see, uncheck **Display images and embedded objects in HTML messages** to hide the graphics.

- The Composing pane has just one option I want to call your attention to: Format. By default, Mail sends messages in Rich Text format, which is another way of saying HTML. This allows you to include a variety of fonts, colors, and styles — as well as embedded graphics — in your messages. However, not all mail programs can display such messages properly. This is especially true of many cell phones, PDAs, and other handheld devices. Many people find colors and styles distracting in e-mail even when they do show up correctly. For maximum compatibility and minimum annoyance, I recommend choosing Plain Text.

- To add a signature, go to the Signatures pane of Mail Preferences (see **Figure 26.9**), click **Add Signature** and type or paste your desired text or graphics into the field that appears. You can access all the commands on the Format menu to add colors, styles, and so on. You're not restricted to just one signature: You can have as many as you want,

NOTE

An e-mail signature is simply a block of text that appears at the bottom of each message you send. Some people use signatures as a way to reduce typing. Instead of entering "Warmest regards, H. Winfield Tutte, Really Important Person Emeritus," you can just have an automatic signature with the same text placed at the bottom of each message. Other people like to include their address or phone number, a scanned signature, a favorite quote, or ASCII art.

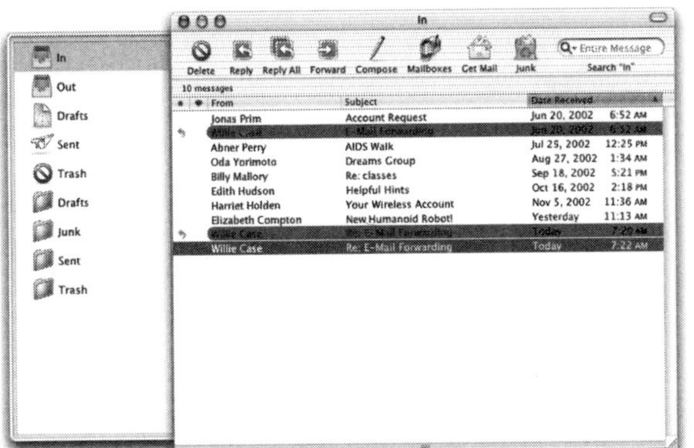

26.8

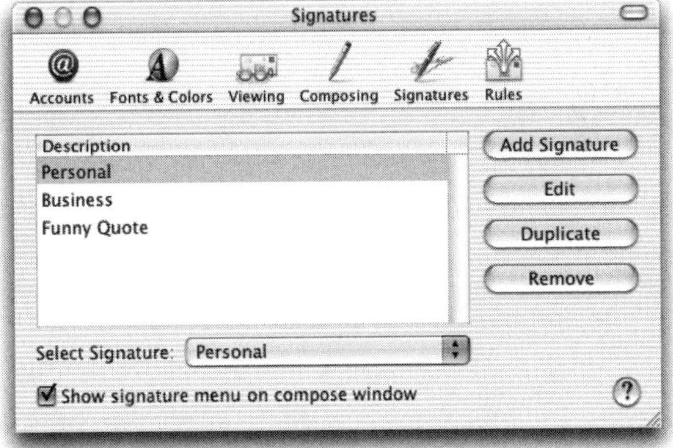

26.9

selected sequentially or randomly according to the **Select Signature** menu. If you check **Show signature menu on compose** window, you'll be able to choose the appropriate signature for each message you send, as shown in **Figure 26.10**, at the time you compose it.

STEP 4: HIDE THE PREVIEW PANE

The bottom part of the main Mail window, where your mail message is displayed, is called the Preview pane. The main value of the Preview pane is that it allows you to read messages without having to open them in a separate window. The downside is that, because it takes up so much room, you can't see as many subjects in the message list. Also, if the message you're reading is long, you may have to do a lot of scrolling to read it all. If you prefer to see more messages at a time — and more of each individual message when you're reading it — you can hide the Preview pane.

- To hide the Preview pane, double-click the bar that divides the message list from the Preview pane. (See **Figure 26.11**.) To view the contents of a message, double-click it to open it in a new window.
- To display the Preview pane again, double-click the divider bar, which has now moved to the very bottom of the window.

STEP 5: CUSTOMIZE THE TOOLBARS

Mail has three different toolbars: one for the main Viewer window, one for new messages, and one for messages you've received. You can customize all three of these to meet your needs.

- To customize any toolbar, right-click (or **Control+click**) the toolbar and choose **Customize Toolbar...** from the contextual menu. A sheet with available icons (**Figure 26.12**) will drop down, just as in the Finder. Click and drag icons onto the toolbar to add them; drag icons off the toolbar to

> **NOTE**
>
> **Unlike Finder toolbars, the toolbars in Mail don't allow you to drag in icons of your own, such as AppleScripts. You must select icons from the ones provided.**

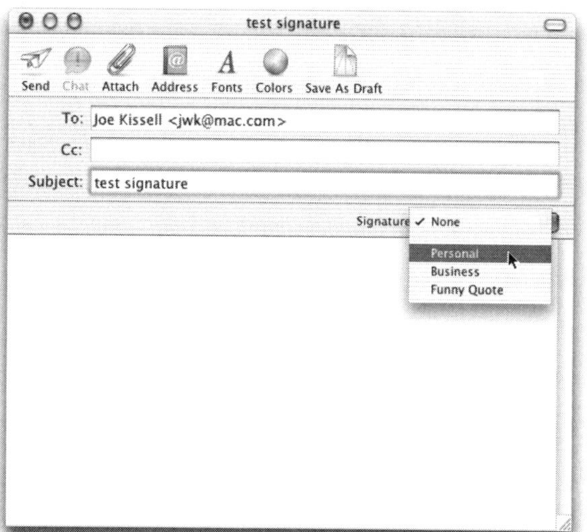

26.10

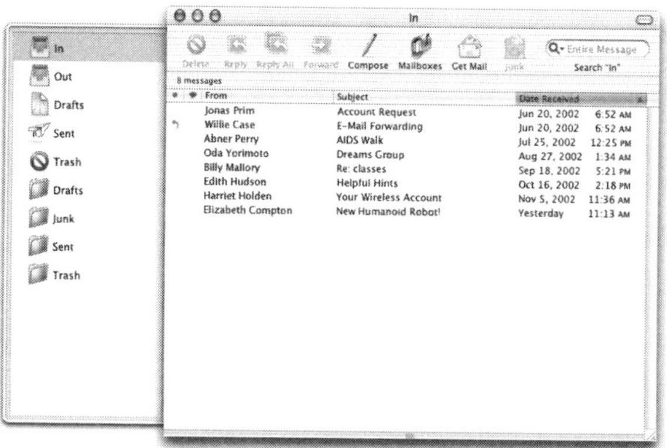

26.11

remove them. You can also rearrange icons just by dragging them to a new location.

■ When you customize the toolbar for a New Message, that toolbar will be used in all new message windows. Similarly, a toolbar customized for received messages will be used for all Received Message windows.

STEP 6: USE MAIL SCRIPTS

Several other techniques have discussed using AppleScript to automate various aspects of Mac OS X. Mail, too, is fully scriptable, and you can enhance Mail's functionality tremendously by adding some clever scripts from Apple and third parties.

■ Mail scripts are easiest to use if you've turned on the Script menu. If you haven't done this already, open the AppleScript folder inside your Applications folder. You'll see a folder icon named ScriptMenu.menu. Drag this icon to your menu bar (near your clock) and release the mouse button. The new scroll-shaped Script menu now appears on your menu bar, as shown in **Figure 26.13.**

■ Click this new menu to see several submenus, one of which is called Mail Scripts. These are scripts Apple includes to add functions to Mail. The best way to learn what these scripts do is to try them. Here are some examples:

- ■ If you're an IMAP user, **Check My IMAP Quota** calculates how much space your stored messages are occupying on the IMAP server and presents its results in a new mail message.
- ■ **Count Messages in All Mailboxes** creates a new mail message with a tally of the numbers of messages in each mailbox in your accounts — including Sent Messages, Drafts, and Trash.
- ■ **Manage SMTP Servers** allows you to delete unused servers from the pop-up list that

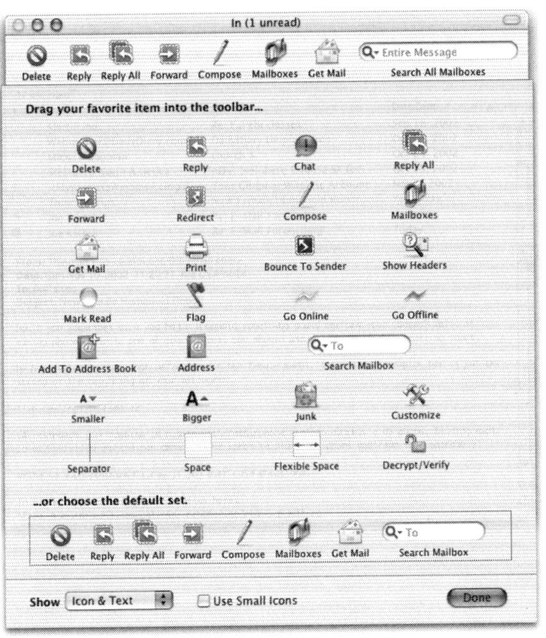

26.12

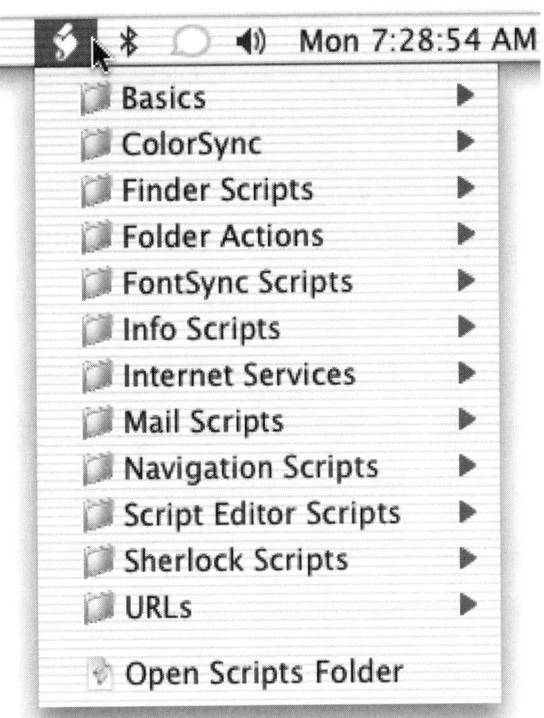

26.13

appears on the **Account Information** tab when adding a new account.

- Many more mail scripts are available from third parties. The best collection I've seen was written by Andreas Amann, and is available free on his Web site at `homepage.mac.com/aamann/Mail_Scripts.html`. After downloading this package, double-click the **Install Mail Scripts** icon. This adds an additional submenu to your Script menu, as shown in **Figure 26.14**. Among the new commands included are the following:
    - If you select several messages and choose **Create Mailing List**, the script will extract the e-mail addresses from the selected messages, add them to Address Book, and create a new Group containing all of them. You can then type that group name in the **To** field of a message to send mail to all those addresses at once.
    - To create a backup of some or all of your e-mail messages, select them and choose **Export Messages**. They'll be saved in standard .mbox format, which can also be opened by any text editor.
    - **Change SMTP Server** allows you to change the SMTP server used on the fly without manually making changes in your account preferences.

In the next technique, you look at yet another one of these mail scripts, which can assist in the creation of rules.

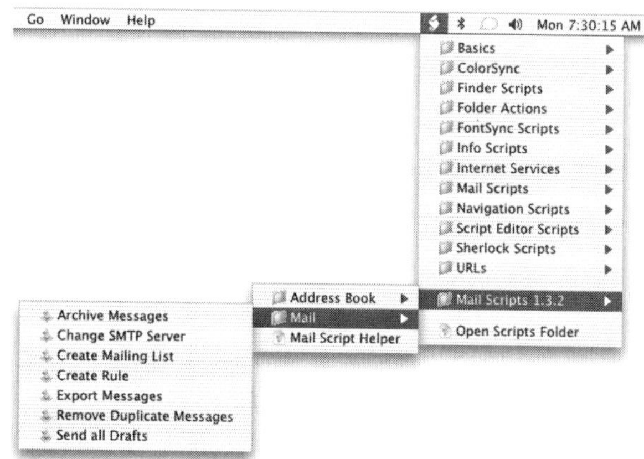

26.14

USING RULES TO KEEP YOUR IN BOX MANAGEABLE

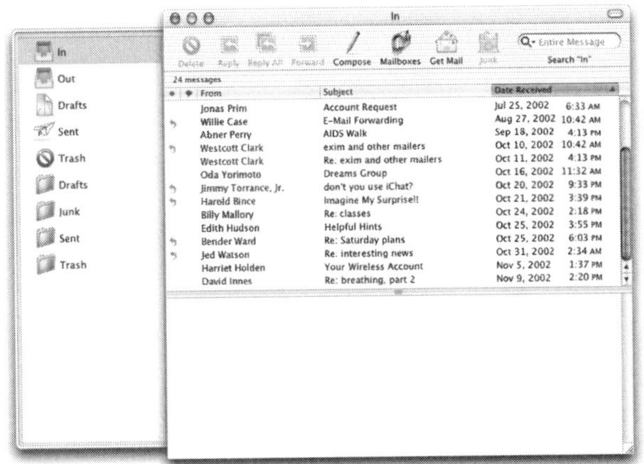

27.1

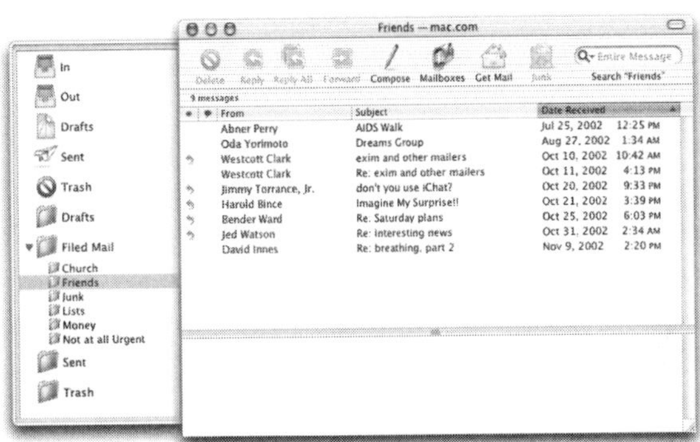

27.2

ABOUT THE FEATURE

Rules, also called *filters*, are simple instructions that tell Mail what to do with messages based on attributes you can specify. To sort, delete, or even reply to certain messages automatically, use a rule.

How many messages are in your In Box right now? For many people, the answer may be dozens, hundreds, or even — like some of my friends — thousands. Large numbers of unsorted messages make it hard to find what you're looking for and nearly impossible to tell what's important and what isn't.

I know what you're thinking: "There's just too much e-mail! There's no way I can read and respond to all my messages so mail just sits there waiting to be sorted." I, too, get a *lot* of e-mail — even if you don't count spam. Yet, I rarely see more than a half dozen or so messages sitting in my In Box. This doesn't mean I'm incredibly efficient, just waiting to read and reply to every message the instant it arrives. On the contrary, I can be quite lazy when it comes to answering mail. The key to my organization is allowing the computer to do all my sorting for me. Some messages are deleted before I even see them; some are put in a "Not At All Urgent" folder to read when I feel like it; and still others receive automatic replies or other processing without any manual intervention.

Although this sounds complicated and high-tech, it couldn't be simpler. Everything needed to do all this and more is built into Apple's Mail program and can be configured with just a few clicks. The key is a feature called *rules*. Rules (sometimes called filters) are simply descriptions of what to look for in messages, and what to do with messages that match the descriptions you've set up. In this technique, I show you everything you need to become a rules pro.

STEP 1: CREATE A BASIC RULE

Just to get the feel for creating rules, start with one that's simple but useful: It highlights all messages that come from anyone in your Address Book in a special color. That way, you'll be able to see at a glance which messages are from your friends — they'll stand out from the crowd.

- Choose **Preferences...** from the **Mail** menu and click the **Rules** icon. Your window should look something like **Figure 27.3**.
- Click **Add Rule**. The sheet that drops down (see **Figure 27.4**) is where all the action happens. Start by typing a descriptive name for your rule, such as **Mail from Friends.**
- Next, add a *condition* — some attribute of a message that Mail will look for. The condition pop-up menu initially says **From**; instead, choose **Sender is in my Address Book**.
- Finally, you have to tell Mail what to do when the condition is met. The second part of the window, "Perform the following actions," is where you do that. To keep this simple, choose **Set Color of Message** from the pop-up menu that says **Transfer Message**. The command then changes to simply **Set Color**. Next, decide whether you want to change the color of the background or the text in the message list. For now, choose **of background**. Then choose a color. All the choices in the **Color** pop-up menu are rather muted. If you don't like any of them, you can choose **Other...** and pick a brighter color using Apple's standard color picker. The final result should look something like **Figure 27.5**. Click **OK** to save your rule and close the Preferences window.

From now on, Mail will automatically apply this rule to all new incoming messages. But you don't have to wait until one of your friends sends you e-mail to try it out. You can also use rules on messages you've already received:

- To apply this rule, select all the messages in your In Box (or any other folder) and choose **Apply Rules To Selection** from the **Message** menu. Click any message to deselect the list, and you should see shaded backgrounds like those in **Figure 27.6** for messages that came from people in your Address Book.

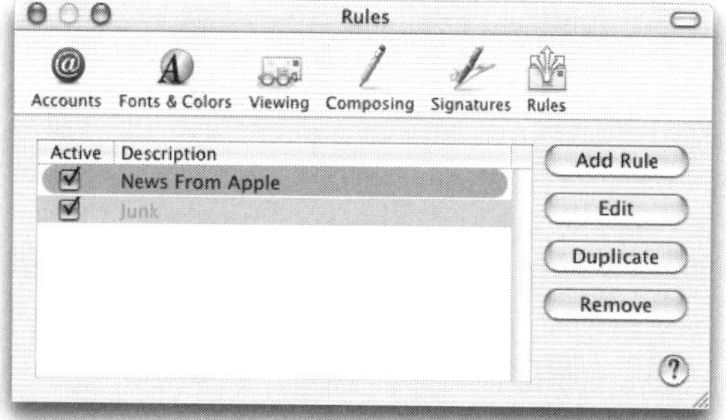

27.3

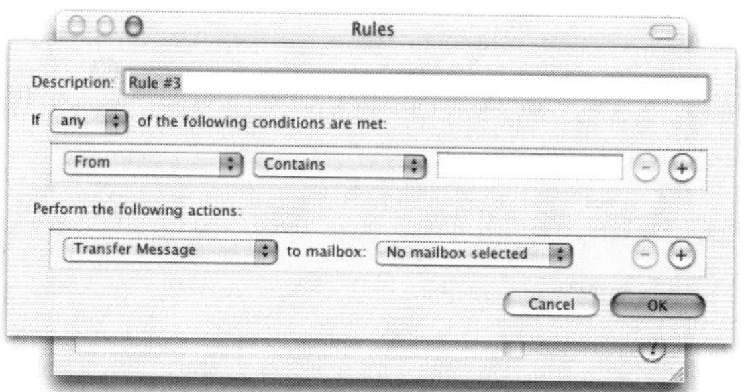

27.4

STEP 2: USE CONDITIONS

The "Mail from Friends" rule used a single, very simple condition — the presence of the sender's address in your Address Book. Mail offers a variety of conditions you can check for, such as the **To** or **From** address of the message, the **Subject**, **Message content** (text contained in the message), and so on.

Many of these conditions allow you to get very specific. For example, if a rule is looking for the word "Apple" in the subject of a message, you can decide what counts as a match — whether "Apple" is the *entire* subject (subject **Is equal to** Apple), is anywhere within the subject (subject **Contains** Apple), is at the beginning or end of the subject (subject **Begins with** or **Ends with** Apple), or is *not* in the subject (subject **Does not contain** Apple). **Figure 27.7** illustrates these options. In each case, if whatever you've specified as the condition turns out to be true, the action will be performed.

- To select a condition, first make a choice from the leftmost pop-up menu, shown in **Figure 27.8**. This indicates *where* Mail will look for a match. If a condition has additional options, make your next selection from the middle pop-up menu, which indicates *how* the match takes place. Finally, enter text (or an address) in the text field to tell the rule *what* to look for. Here are some sample conditions:
  - [To] [Does not contain] [jwk@mac.com]: This setting matches messages in which my e-mail address is not in the To field (meaning I was probably a Carbon Copy or Blind Carbon Copy recipient).
  - [Subject] [Begins with] [Ad]: This setting matches messages whose subjects begin with "Ad" (or "Adv" or "Advertisement"), as ads occasionally do.
  - [Message content] [Contains] [order has shipped]: This setting matches all messages whose text contains the phrase "order has shipped" — which is usually good news.

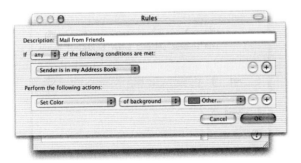

27.5

Jonas Prim	Account Request	Jul 25, 2002
Willie Case	E-Mail Forwarding	Aug 27, 2002
Abner Perry	AIDS Walk	Sep 18, 2002
Oda Yorimoto	Dreams Group	Oct 16, 2002
Billy Mallory	Re: classes	Oct 24, 2002
Edith Hudson	Helpful Hints	Oct 25, 2002

27.6

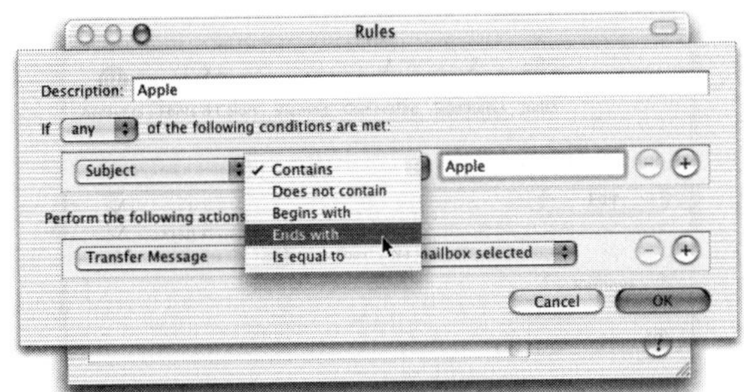

27.7

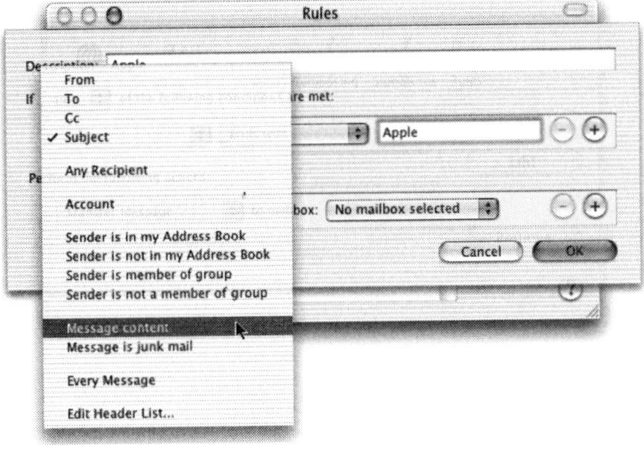

27.8

- [From] [Ends with] [@apple.com]: This setting matches all messages coming from *anyone* at Apple.

So how do you figure out what a condition should be? In general, you want the most specific condition that will produce a match. For example, suppose you subscribe to two different mailing lists from the same company — an "announcements" list that comes from the address announce@lists.company.com and an "upgrade" list that comes from the address upgrade@lists.company.com — and you want to perform some action on mail from both lists. Because the subject and content of these messages may vary, looking for a match in the **From** field makes the most sense. If your condition is very general, such as [From] [Contains] [company.com], it will match mail from both lists — but it will also match mail from sales@company.com, support@company.com, and so on. If your condition is too specific, such as [From] [Is equal to] [announce@lists.company.com], it will match just one list but not the other. In this example, making your condition [From] [Contains] [lists.company.com] will match all and only those e-mail messages that come from company.com's list server.

With that background, it's time to create rules to match messages from all mailing lists you subscribe to. For now, don't worry about the action part of the rule — you can fill that in later. Just create rules with conditions that match your mailing lists.

- Look at messages you've already received from the mailing lists. You'll be able to see exactly what their attributes are, and even copy and paste addresses into your rules.
- Look at both the **To** and **From** fields when creating your conditions. Some mailing lists use an individual's From address and a special group To address; others always have a special From address but an empty To field (because the recipients are blind carbon copied). If both the To and From fields seem to vary, see whether part of the subject is always the same.

STEP 3: ADD MULTIPLE CONDITIONS

Sometimes, no matter what you do, you can't come up with a single condition that will give you the results you want. Not to worry: A rule is not limited to looking for just one condition. You can have a dozen conditions if you like. For example, a rule could say, "If a message comes in from Jean *or* Jane, perform some action." On the other hand, it could say, "If a message comes in from Jane *and* it has the subject 'Good News!,' perform a different action."

- To add a condition, click the round + icon at the right of the condition area. A second condition row appears, as shown in **Figure 27.9**. Fill in the second condition just as you did the first.
- If you want a match to occur if *any* of your conditions are met, choose **Any** from the pop-up menu at the top of the window. This makes it an OR search, as in the first example at the beginning of this step.
- If you want a match to occur only if *all* your conditions are met, choose **All** from the pop-up menu at the top of the window. This makes it an AND search, as in the second example at the beginning of this step.

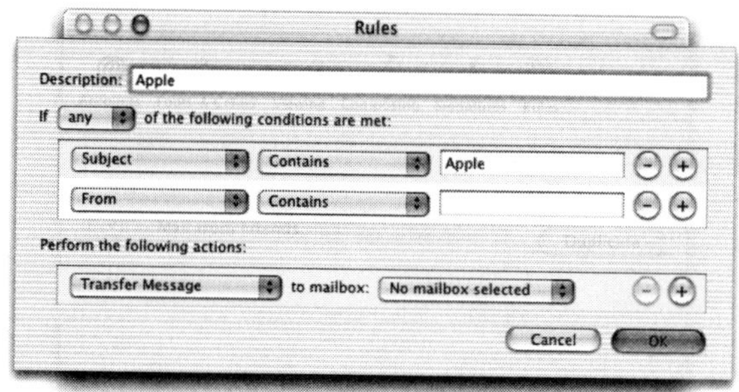

27.9

What if you want a match to occur if Condition 1 is met, but Condition 2 is *not* met? You can do this by making an AND (**All**) condition and changing the "how" pop-up menu in the middle for one of the conditions. I recently encountered just such a situation. I subscribe to a certain mailing list on which my name is occasionally mentioned. After manually deleting most of these messages, I eventually realized that I *only* wanted to read those messages that mentioned me (how vain!) — the rest I wanted to send straight to the Trash. So I set up my conditions like this:

If **all** of the following conditions are met

`[From] [Contains] [the list server's address]`

`[Message content] [Does not contain] [Joe Kissell]`

then, for the action, I chose **Delete Message**.

- Try setting up some rules with multiple conditions now. Again, don't worry about the actions yet; you get to that momentarily. For starters, if you have some conditions for matching mailing lists from the previous step, you might look for ways of combining them. This could be useful, for example, if you subscribe to several travel-related lists and want the same thing to happen to all of them.

STEP 4: USE ACTIONS

Now that you've learned how to match messages, it's time to do something with them. To select an action for a given rule, choose a command from the Actions pop-up menu at the bottom of the Rules window and fill in more details if needed. The two most frequently used actions are **Transfer Message** and **Delete Message**.

- To sort a message into a particular folder, choose **Transfer Message** and choose a mailbox from the pop-up mailbox menu, as shown in **Figure 27.10**. This requires, of course, that the mailbox you want to use has already been created. If not, go back to the Viewer window and choose **New Mailbox...** from the **Mailbox** menu. Select a name and location for your mailbox and click **OK**. You can now return to the Rules window and choose your new mailbox from the list.

TIP

You can create as many folders as you like — even putting folders inside other folders — but don't get carried away. Having too many folders can be just as bad as having too many messages. Concentrate on high-level categories such as Family, Friends, Lists, Money, Fun, or whatever best describes the mail you want to sort. When a folder starts accumulating too many messages, you can divide it into more specific subfolders.

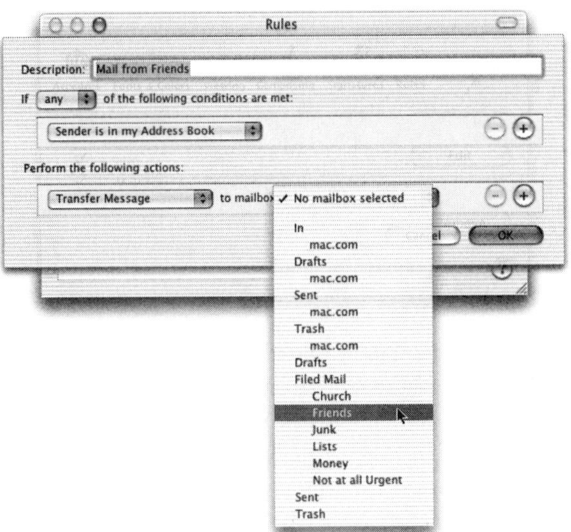

27.10

- To delete a message when your condition(s) have been matched, choose **Delete Message**.

You will now be able to add Actions to the rules you created in Steps 2 and 3. When you're finished, you should have all your mailing list messages automatically sorted into folders when they arrive.

After you get the hang of creating rules, you can do much more than sort mailing list messages. Try these actions:

- Use the action **Reply to Message** to send a canned response to all messages that meet your conditions. You can use this action for "Out of the office" or Vacation messages (assuming you'll leave Mail running on your Mac while you're gone), or to send out automated info when someone uses a special subject in a message to you. When you choose **Reply to Message**, you can click a button to open a window where you can type your reply.
- If you need to get a copy of messages that meet certain conditions at another mailing address — for example, your pager's e-mail address for especially urgent messages — use the **Forward Message** or **Redirect Message** actions. Forwarding and redirecting are similar, except that a forwarded message will list you, the person who forwarded it, as the sender, whereas redirecting a message will list the *original* sender in the From field. With either of these choices, you'll be asked to supply an e-mail address; when forwarding, you can also add text if you like.

NOTE

You can apply any rule — even a sorting or deletion rule — to mail already received. Just select one or more messages in your Viewer window and choose Apply Rules To Selection from the Message menu (or press ⌘+Option+L).

STEP 5: ADD MULTIPLE ACTIONS

Just as a rule can have multiple conditions, it can produce multiple actions. If you want to mark a message as read, change its background color, play a sound, *and* send an automated reply, you can do all of these actions with a single rule!

- To add a second action, click the + icon at the right of the action area. A second action row now appears, as shown in **Figure 27.11**. Fill in the second action just like the first, but keep in mind that any given action can only happen once per rule.
- Actions are performed in the order they're listed, so be careful when setting up multiple actions — especially if one of them is **Delete message**. If another action comes after that, it will fail, because the message will already be gone!

STEP 6: USE ORDERED RULES

So a rule can have multiple conditions *and* multiple actions. But wait, there's more! You can create as many different rules as you want, and they will all

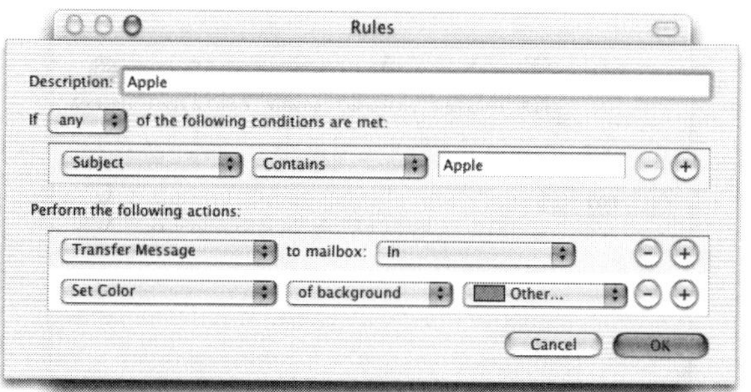

27.11

apply in order. This means that you can have the action of one rule depend on the action of an earlier one. An example is in order. Remember my "vanity" rule that deleted messages from a mailing list if they didn't mention my name? I added a second rule after that one that matched the same From address, and moved any messages from that list that were still there into my Lists folder. That way, the only messages the second rule had to worry about were the ones that hadn't been deleted by the first one.

Most of your rules will probably be independent of each other and can apply in any order. If you do need a pair of rules to apply in a certain order, though, you can reorder them.

- To change the order in which rules are applied, click the rule name in the Rules pane of Mail Preferences and drag it up or down, as shown in **Figure 27.12.**
- To turn off a rule temporarily without deleting it, uncheck the **Active** checkbox next to the rule's name.

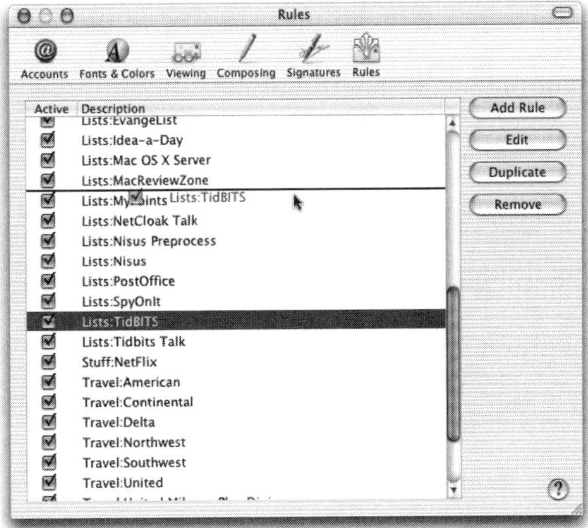

27.12

STEP 7: (BONUS) USE A MAIL SCRIPT TO CREATE RULES

As a reward for paying such careful attention to the intricacies of writing rules, I want to show you a shortcut that can do much of the dirty work for you. In the last technique, you installed the Script menu and a package of Mail Scripts. (See Step 6 of Technique 26 if you missed it.) One of these scripts, as it happens, can create basic rules for you automatically.

- Install the Script menu and Andreas Amman's Mail Scripts package if you haven't already.
- Select a message that you want to use as the basis for a new rule. Then choose **Create Rule** from the **Mail** submenu of the **Mail Scripts** menu, as shown in **Figure 27.13.**
- A dialog appears asking whether you want to use From, To, or Subject as a condition. Select the one you want and click **Continue.** A second dialog asks you to choose an action to perform. Again, make your selection and then click **Continue.** If the action requires more information (such as choosing a mailbox to transfer a message to), an additional dialog will appear.
- The new rule will be added to your Rules list automatically. You may need to edit it slightly, depending on your needs.

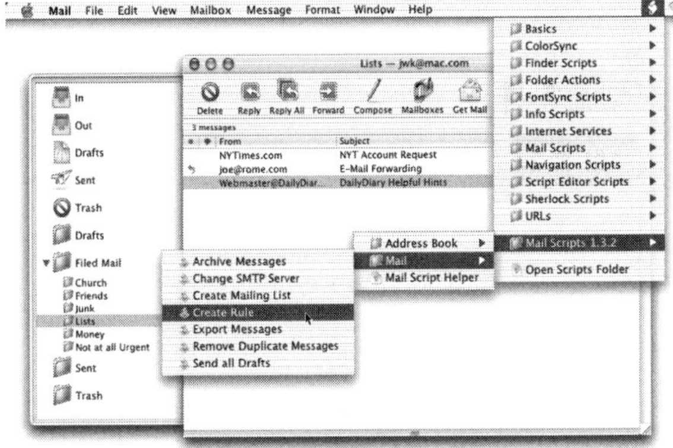

27.13

TAMING WEB SEARCHES WITH SHERLOCK 3

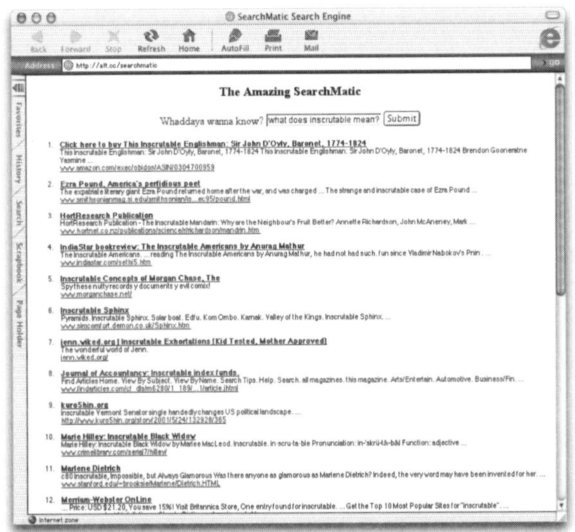

28.1

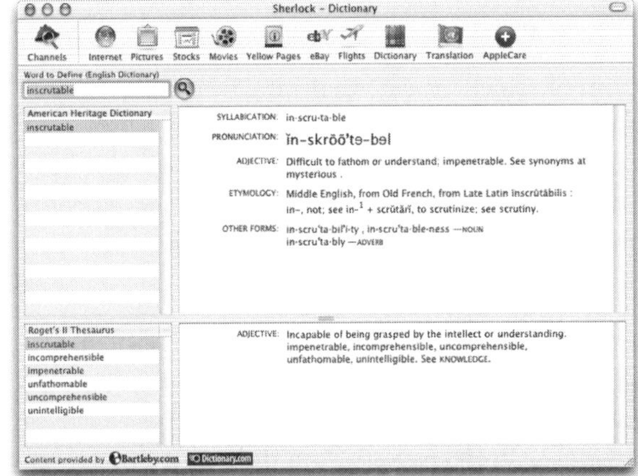

28.2

ABOUT THE FEATURE

Ordinary Web searches often force you to wade through hundreds of results to find the information you're looking for. Apple's Sherlock 3 gives you a better, faster way to search for particular kinds of information without even opening your browser.

If you've ever searched for information on the Web, you know that it can sometimes take a lot of clicking, waiting, and dodging ads to get to just the content you want. Even activities that should be very straightforward — like looking up the definition of a word, finding an address, or seeing what movies are playing tonight — can be enough of a hassle that you reach for the paper dictionary, phone book, or newspaper instead. You can be sure that your printed dictionary won't make you wait, click through advertisements, or remember URLs before it gives you your definition! Apple realized that online searching could — and should — be much easier, and its solution is a program called Sherlock 3, which is included with every copy of Mac OS X.

Unlike earlier versions of Sherlock, Sherlock 3 doesn't search your hard drive. It looks for information exclusively online. Without making you open a Web browser, sort through bookmarks, or switch from site to site, Sherlock 3 finds and presents just the information you want in a very easy-to-use interface. Apple supplies several categories of information called *channels* (Pictures, Stocks, Movies, Flights, and so on), and third parties can add additional channels. The next time you're tempted to open your browser to do a search, try it in Sherlock 3 instead. With this technique, you may never go back to your old way of searching.

STEP 1: ENTER YOUR PERSONAL INFORMATION

Some of Sherlock's most interesting features — such as finding movies in your neighborhood or giving you driving directions — depend on knowing a bit about you. Some of this information may have been entered automatically based on the information in your Address Book.

- Open Sherlock. You can use the Sherlock icon in the Dock, or double-click the icon in your Applications folder.
- Choose **Preferences...** from the Sherlock menu and click the **Locations** tab, as shown in **Figure 28.3**. Your e-mail address should already be filled in at the top; if it's not, enter it now.
- Click the word **home** in the **Locations** list. If your home address is not already entered on the right, enter it now. You can also make any needed corrections.

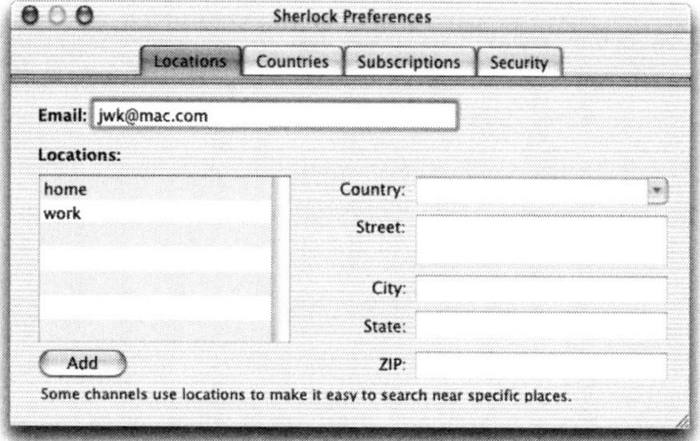

28.3

You can add as many additional locations as you like. For example, if you use your computer at work, while traveling, or at a local café, you can enter addresses for all of those places. You might also include addresses of family members or other locations you frequently travel to. The more locations you enter now, the easier it will be to use Sherlock later.

- To add a new location, click **Add**. A new location, called **Untitled**, will appear in the list. Double-click the word **Untitled** and enter a new name (such as "Work," "Summer Cottage," or "Mission Control"). Press **Return** when you're finished and enter the address information for that location in the fields on the right.
- When you've added all the locations you want to use, close the Preferences window.

STEP 2: SEARCH FOR "EASY" CONTENT

Most of Sherlock's built-in channels are so easy to use and self-explanatory that describing their operation in detail would be silly. (Sample: "To use the Dictionary channel, type a word and click the Search button. Results appear. You're done.") So instead of

NOTE

Although Sherlock 3 is a very powerful tool, it is not the only application to offer this type of searching — and perhaps not even the best. Watson, available from Karelia Software (`www.karelia.com/watson`), has more channels than Sherlock, including some very useful ones such as Amazon.com, Weather, TV Listings, and Recipes — and a very elegant interface. If you enjoy searching with Sherlock 3, you may find that Watson is well worth its modest price. Karelia provides a free demo version on its Web site. Check it out!

detailing every button and menu, I simply want to point out what some of the channels do, give you some hints on information you might search for with them, and suggest that you try them out yourself.

To switch channels, simply click one of the channel buttons on the toolbar. The rest of the window changes to reflect the options available.

- For general-purpose Web searches, you can't beat the **Internet** channel, as shown in **Figure 28.4**. It works just like any Web search engine, but with a twist: It simultaneously searches seven different databases and ranks all the results by relevance. Oh yeah — it does this without any annoying ads. Click an item in the results list to see a summary in the preview pane at the bottom of the screen, or double-click it to open the original page in your Web browser.
- Use the **Pictures** channel (see **Figure 28.5**) to search for images that match keywords you enter. Each time you click the green Search button, more pictures will be added to the list. To see a full-size version of an image, double-click it, which opens the Web page where the original image is located. You can then drag it to your desktop (or another window) to copy it. Tip: This is a great way to find graphics to send to your friends with iChat.
- Use the **Stocks** channel to look up any company's stock by name or ticker symbol. (While either name or ticker symbol will work, you might get better results with the ticker symbol, because, in some cases, a company's name may also be the ticker symbol for a *different* company, in which case the company with the matching ticker symbol will be displayed.) **Figure 28.6** shows an example. In addition to displaying current quotes, you'll see a chart of recent performance and news headlines relating to the company.

28.5

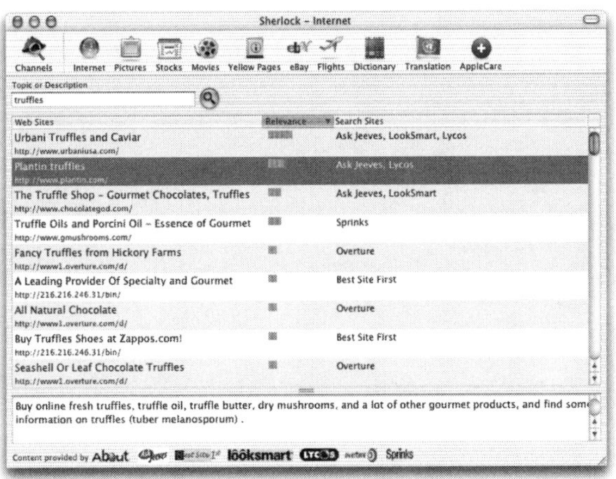

28.4

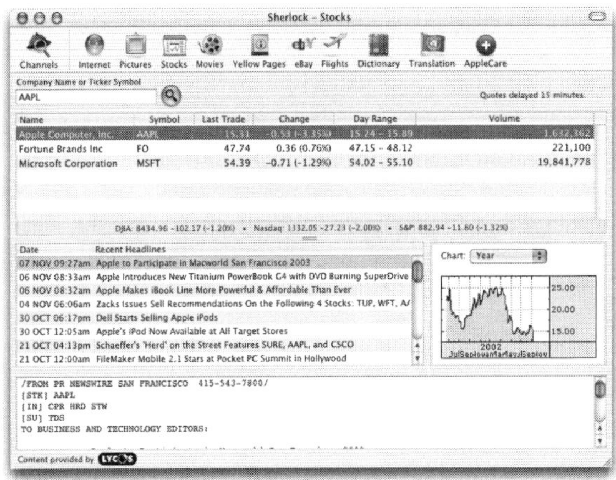

28.6

Click a headline to read the entire story in the bottom pane of the window.

- The **Dictionary** channel, shown in **Figure 28.7**, supplies not only definitions, but also pronunciation, etymology, and thesaurus entries. For writers, this is both handier and easier to use than paper dictionaries and thesauri, not to mention Microsoft Word's built-in dictionary.
- If you need a quick translation from one language into another, use the **Translation** channel, as in **Figure 28.8**. (This feature can be useful for foreign-language text found on Web pages, for example.) You can choose from 36 pairs of languages, including English to Greek, Chinese to English, French to German, and many more. However, don't rely too heavily on these translations, especially for highly idiomatic speech. Computers can provide a good rough draft, but can't replace human translators.
- For help with your Mac, the **AppleCare** channel, shown in **Figure 28.9**, is not only faster and easier to use than Apple's support Web site, it's actually faster and easier than Mac OS X's Help Center application. Strange but true.

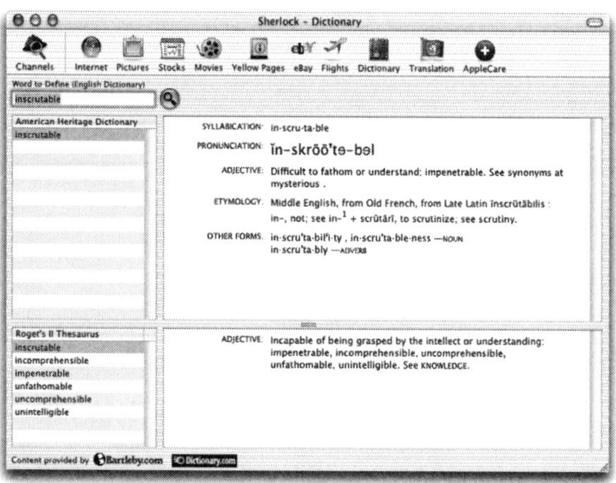

28.7

STEP 3: SEARCH FOR MOVIES

The **Movies** channel is my favorite, because it provides all and only the information I want, quickly and with virtually zero effort. In a nutshell, it displays showtimes, locations, summaries, and even QuickTime trailers, for movies playing at theaters near you.

- When you switch to the Movies channel (as in **Figure 28.10**), your home ZIP code should be filled in automatically. To search somewhere else, type a different ZIP code or city name.

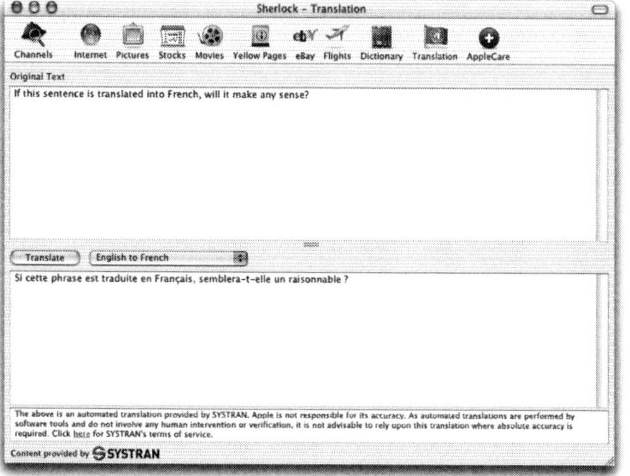

28.8

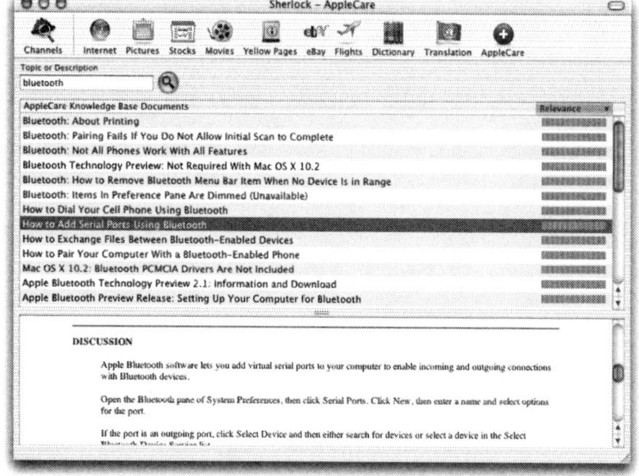

28.9

- By default, the **Showtime** pop-up menu lists today's date. To search for movies on a different day, make your choice from this menu.
- The Movies channel has two ways of organizing its results: by Movies or by Theaters. To switch views, click either the **Movies** button or the **Theaters** button at the top of the window.
- In Movies view, all available movies are listed in the first column. When you select a movie, the second column shows you which local theaters are showing it. Select a theater, and you'll see the showtimes in the third column. In Theaters view, you start by picking a theater in the first column and a movie in the second column.
- A synopsis, poster, and QuickTime trailer for the selected movie appears if available. You can find theater information (such as address and accessibility) at the bottom of the screen when you select a theater.
- If tickets are available for the selected show via MovieFone, a button will appear. Click this button to buy tickets. (Unfortunately, finding a theater for which the Buy Tickets button actually appears is relatively rare. After you've found the movie you want, you may need to go to `moviefone.com` or `fandango.com` — or even, perish the thought, the actual theater — to purchase tickets.)

STEP 4: SEARCH FOR BUSINESSES

Your local Yellow Pages provides information on businesses in your area. Sherlock's **Yellow Pages** channel provides information on businesses all over the United States — and not just the name, address, and phone number, but a map and even driving directions!

- To search for a business on the Yellow Pages channel (see **Figure 28.11**), enter a portion of the business name, along with its city and state, and click the **Search** button. As with the Pictures channel, if you don't find what you're looking for at first, you can click **Search** again for additional matches.
- When matches appear, click one to display a map and driving directions in the bottom part of the window. You can obtain driving directions from any of the locations you've set up in the Preferences (Step 1). Choose a different location from the pop-up **Driving Directions From** menu to recalculate the directions.
- Use the slider under the map to change the magnification. To slide the map up, down, left, or right, click the arrow buttons labeled **Pan**. The button in the middle of the Pan cluster re-centers your destination (marked with a star) in the window.

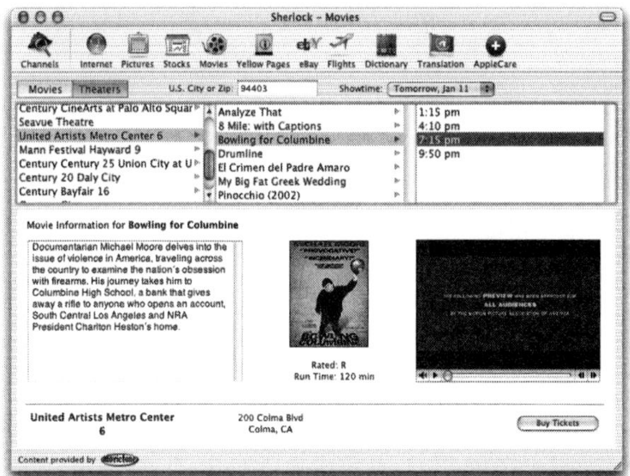

28.10

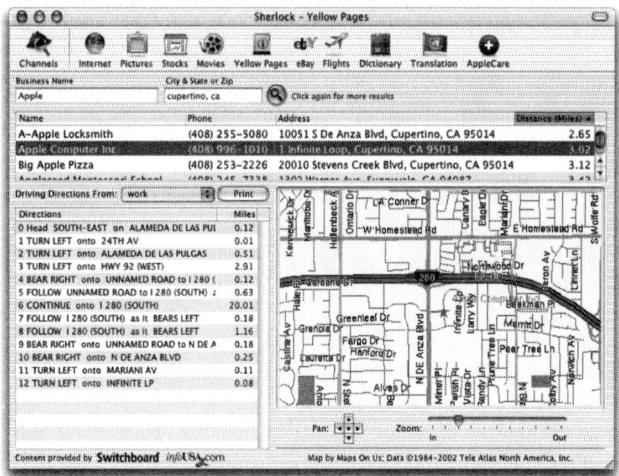

28.11

STEP 5: SEARCH FOR AUCTIONS

The **eBay** channel, shown in **Figure 28.12**, offers an easy way to search for and track auctions on eBay.

- To perform a basic search, enter an item description and click the Search button. To narrow your search to a particular category (such as Antiques) or region (such as San Francisco), use the **Category** or **Region** pop-up menus next to the Search button. You can also enter numbers in one or both of the **Priced between** fields to limit the search further by price. (The current high bids shown will be no lower than the number in the left field, and no higher than the number in the right field.)
- When found items appear in the results list, you can select one to see a picture (if available) and complete item information in the bottom portion of the window.
- You can sort your search (by title price, number of bids, or time to end) by clicking a column heading.
- To bid on an auction item, double-click it. Your browser will open and take you directly to the item's page on eBay.
- Click the **Track Auction** button at the bottom of the window to add this item to your Track list. This is just a bookmark list of your favorite auctions. To see the items on your Track list, click the **Track** button under the Search box.

STEP 6: SEARCH FOR FLIGHTS

I left this one for last because it's actually a bit of a disappointment: The **Flights** channel (see **Figure 28.13**) is probably not what you were expecting. It doesn't help you search for low airfares or plan your vacation. Its purpose, while useful, is a bit more mundane: It

28.12

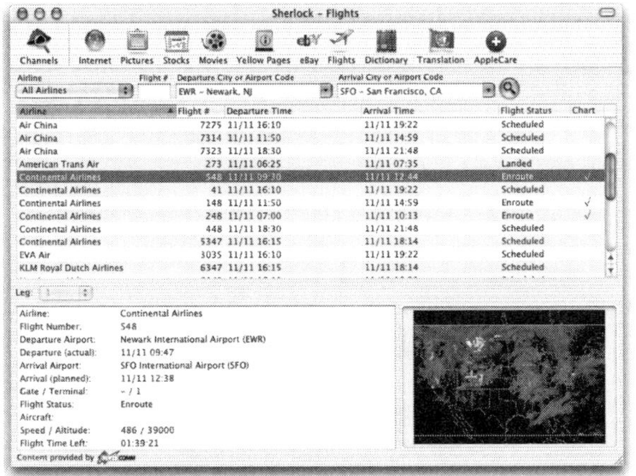

28.13

displays departure and arrival information for today's flights. If you want to see whether you need to rush off to the airport to pick up your boss or whether his flight's delayed in Chicago, the Flights channel is what you need.

- Start by selecting departure and arrival cities. You can either type a city name (or a three-letter airport code) or choose one from the drop-down lists. If you know the airline and/or the flight number, enter them as well, but the search will work with as little or as much information as you give it. Click the **Search** button.
- Matching flights will be displayed in the results list. Click a flight to display additional information at the bottom of the window, including the arrival gate, cruising altitude, and time remaining in the flight. Flights with a checkmark in the Chart column will display a mini map of the United States showing the flight path, with an airplane icon at the plane's current location.

TECHNIQUE **29**

WEB BROWSING SECRETS OF THE RICH AND FAMOUS

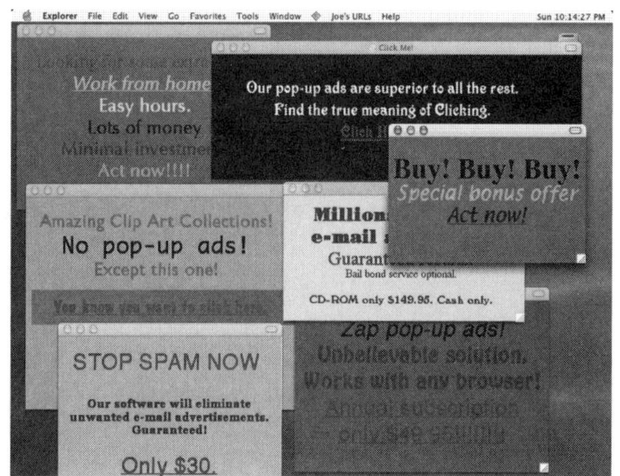

29.1

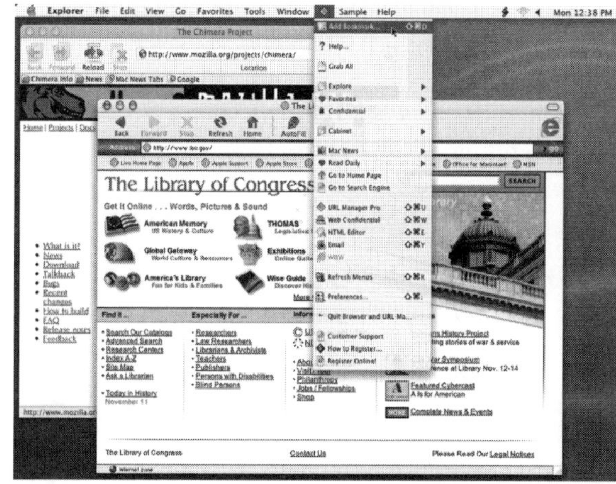

29.2

ABOUT THE FEATURE

As easy as browsing the Web is, getting lost in a sea of hyperlinks, pop-up windows, and forgotten URLs is easier. To keep your head above water, use the hidden capabilities of your browser and other Internet software.

Who needs a *technique* to browse the Web? You click links, go back, go forward, make bookmarks — all pretty simple stuff. Yet, have you ever visited a Web page that didn't display correctly? Have you ever experienced the annoying phenomenon known as pop-up (or pop-under) ads? Ever tried to get back to a page you *know* you were viewing earlier today, but can't recall its URL? Ever saved a bookmark and later realized you couldn't pick it out of the hundreds of others in your list? Annoyances such as these can make Web surfing anything but simple.

I have great news for you: You don't have to live with these annoyances anymore! By carefully choosing and customizing your browser, you can make all of your Web browsing much easier and more fun. With a few little-known tricks and shortcuts, you'll be surfing like a pro in just a few minutes.

STEP 1: USE THE RIGHT BROWSER FOR THE JOB

For years, Apple has included a copy of Microsoft Internet Explorer with Mac OS X, so many users got into the habit of using it and never gave a second's thought to using another browser. Then Apple began shipping its own Safari browser, which is much faster and sleeker than Internet Explorer, if lighter on features. Safari has become, for many Mac users, the new automatic browser choice. But these two programs are not the only browsers available for Mac OS X, and depending on your needs, they may not be the best. Each browser has its own strengths and weaknesses, and no single browser is perfect for every single Web site. Smart users have several browsers available, and switch among them as needed.

As long as you have an extra 100MB or so on your hard drive, I recommend downloading all (yes, *all*) of the browsers in Table 29-1. As you try each one out, you'll undoubtedly find one you feel especially comfortable with — that one will become your default browser. But keep the others on hand. When you encounter a page that doesn't display correctly (or at all) in one browser, try another. Finding a Web page that will not work in *any* of these browsers is extremely rare.

Table 29-1 lists each browser with some of its strengths and weaknesses. But remember: Browsers

TABLE 29-1

BROWSER COMPARISON

BROWSER	STRENGTHS	WEAKNESSES
Chimera (`www.mozilla.org/projects/chimera`)	Looks great — full Aqua look and feel, uncluttered interface, fast, and tabbed browsing for opening several Web pages at the same time in a single window.	Still in development — many features don't work yet.
iCab (`www.icab.de`)	Very small application size, fast, and easy to turn off pop-up ads.	Nearly nonexistent cascading style sheets (CSS) support.
Internet Explorer (`www.mactopia.com`)	Best compatibility, Scrapbook for saving pages, Forms AutoFill, and generally excellent CSS support.	Prone to crashing, can slow down under heavy loads, and difficult to block pop-up ads.
Mozilla (`www.mozilla.org`)	Approximately the same feature set as Netscape including tabbed browsing but without AIM.	Somewhat slow, very large, and somewhat nonstandard UI.
Netscape (`www.netscape.com`)	Lots of bells and whistles, tabbed browsing, and respectable CSS support.	Extremely nonstandard interface, large, bloated application, includes AIM, requires registration.
OmniWeb (`www.omnigroup.com`)	Supports services, highly customizable, and uses Keychain for user names and passwords.	Very weak CSS support and some JavaScript problems.
Opera (`www.opera.com`)	Fairly fast, supports all platforms, and relatively full feature set, including tabbed browsing.	Nonstandard UI and not as fast as claimed.
Safari (`www.apple.com/safari`)	Easily the fastest browser for Mac OS X; streamlined, brushed-metal interface; built-in Google Search; snapback feature; and easy bookmark management.	No form completion feature, limited configurability, and Flash performance is poor.

are constantly being updated, so the facts may have changed since this was written. Let your own experience be your guide. (**OmniWeb** is shown in **Figure 29.3**, **Safari** is shown in **Figure 29.4**, and Chimera is shown in **Figure 29.5**)

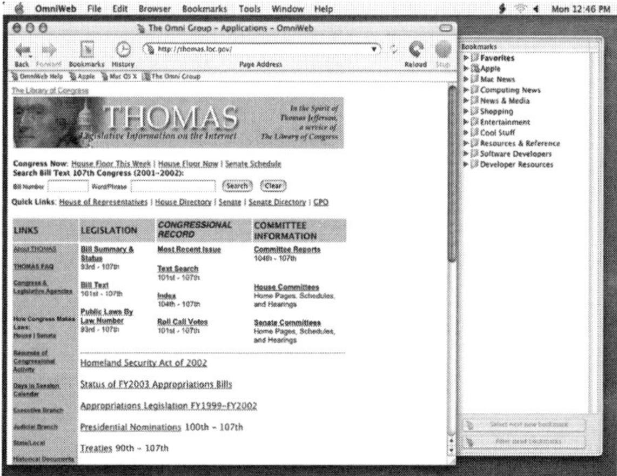

29.3

29.4

STEP 2: KEEP YOUR BOOKMARKS OUTSIDE YOUR BROWSER

If you're going to be switching browsers frequently, one problem you'll encounter is that the bookmarks you've saved previously in other browsers won't be available. New bookmarks you save will only appear for the current browser. A shareware program called URL Manager Pro offers the solution.

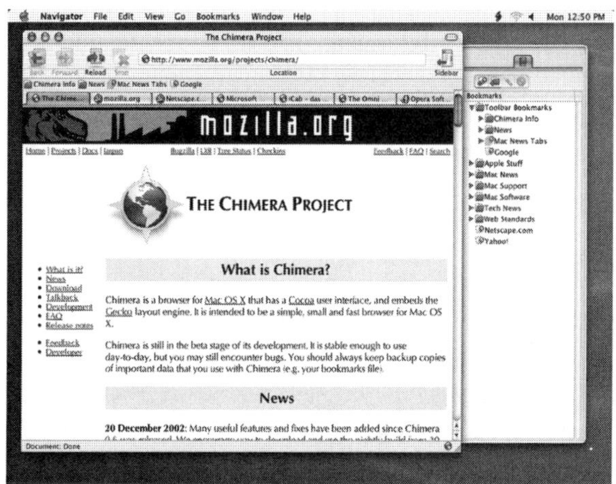

29.5

> **TIP**
>
> **After using a variety of different browsers, you may want to change your default browser — the program that will be used when another application needs to open a URL. To choose a new default browser, open System Preferences, click the Internet icon, and choose the Web tab. Choose a new default browser from the pop-up menu at the top of the tab. If your browser is not listed, choose Select... and navigate to the application on your hard drive. After changing your default browser, you'll need to log out and log back in for it to take effect.**

- Download URL Manager Pro from `www.url-manager.com` and install it according to the instructions included with it. To import bookmarks from your other browsers, choose your browser from the **Get from Browser** submenu of the **File** menu. URL Manager Pro then allows you to organize them (see **Figure 29.6**), and also display them in a system-wide menu that can be used in any browser (as shown in **Figure 29.7**).
- When you want to add a bookmark to the system-wide list, just press **⌘+Shift+D** (instead of **⌘+D**). URL Manager Pro will even ask you which folder you want to store your new URL in, so you can organize your bookmarks as you collect them.

STEP 3: DON'T TYPE ENTIRE URLS

All Mac browsers offer autocompletion for URLs. Instead of typing http://www.apple.com in the address bar, just type **apple**. Your browser will fill in the http://, www, and .com parts for you automatically. In addition, most browsers will remember URLs you've visited before, so typing just a portion of a long URL will be enough to trigger recall of the entire address.

29.6

STEP 4: MANAGE YOUR WINDOWS WHILE SURFING

As you're browsing Web pages, you'll sometimes come across links you want to follow without losing your place on your current page. When you click a link, the new page normally replaces the current page. But all Mac browsers offer a shortcut allowing you to open a link in a new window without replacing the current one.

- To open a link in a new window while browsing, hold down **⌘** while clicking the link. (Exception: In OmniWeb, hold down **⌘+Shift**.) The new window opens in front of the current one.
- Some browsers also allow you to open a new window *behind* the current one, so you can continue reading your current page, and come back to the linked pages later. To do this, hold down **⌘+Shift** while clicking the link. (Exception: In OmniWeb, hold down **⌘**.) Netscape and Mozilla do not offer a shortcut for opening links in windows behind the current one.

STEP 5: TURN OFF DEFAULT HOME PAGE LOADING

By default, every time you launch your browser or open a new window, that window will automatically display your home page (as specified in Internet Preferences or your browser's preferences). You may find this annoying, much like pop-up ads that appear even when you didn't ask to see them. In addition, the time it takes to load your home page can slow down your other Web browsing. Luckily, turning this off is easy. After you've done so, new windows will be blank, but you can still display your home page manually at any time by clicking the **Home** button. Here's how to turn off default home page loading in various browsers.

- **Chimera:** Choose **Preferences...** from the **Navigator** menu and click the **Navigation** icon. At the bottom next to "Load the home page when opening," uncheck **New windows**.
- **iCab:** Choose **Preferences...** from the **iCab** menu. In the category list on the left, select **Windows/Launch**. Then under "New Window opens," select **Empty window**. Also select the **Open empty window** radio button under "Browser" in the "At launch" section.
- **Internet Explorer:** Choose **Preferences...** from the **Explorer** menu. In the category list on the left, select **Browser Display**. Then under "Home Page," uncheck the box next to **Automatically go to this Home Page when opening a new window**.
- **Mozilla:** Choose **Preferences...** from the **Mozilla** menu. In the category list on the left, select **Navigator**. Then under "When Navigator starts up, display," select the **Blank page** radio button.
- **Netscape:** Exactly like Mozilla. Choose **Preferences...** from the **Netscape** menu. In the

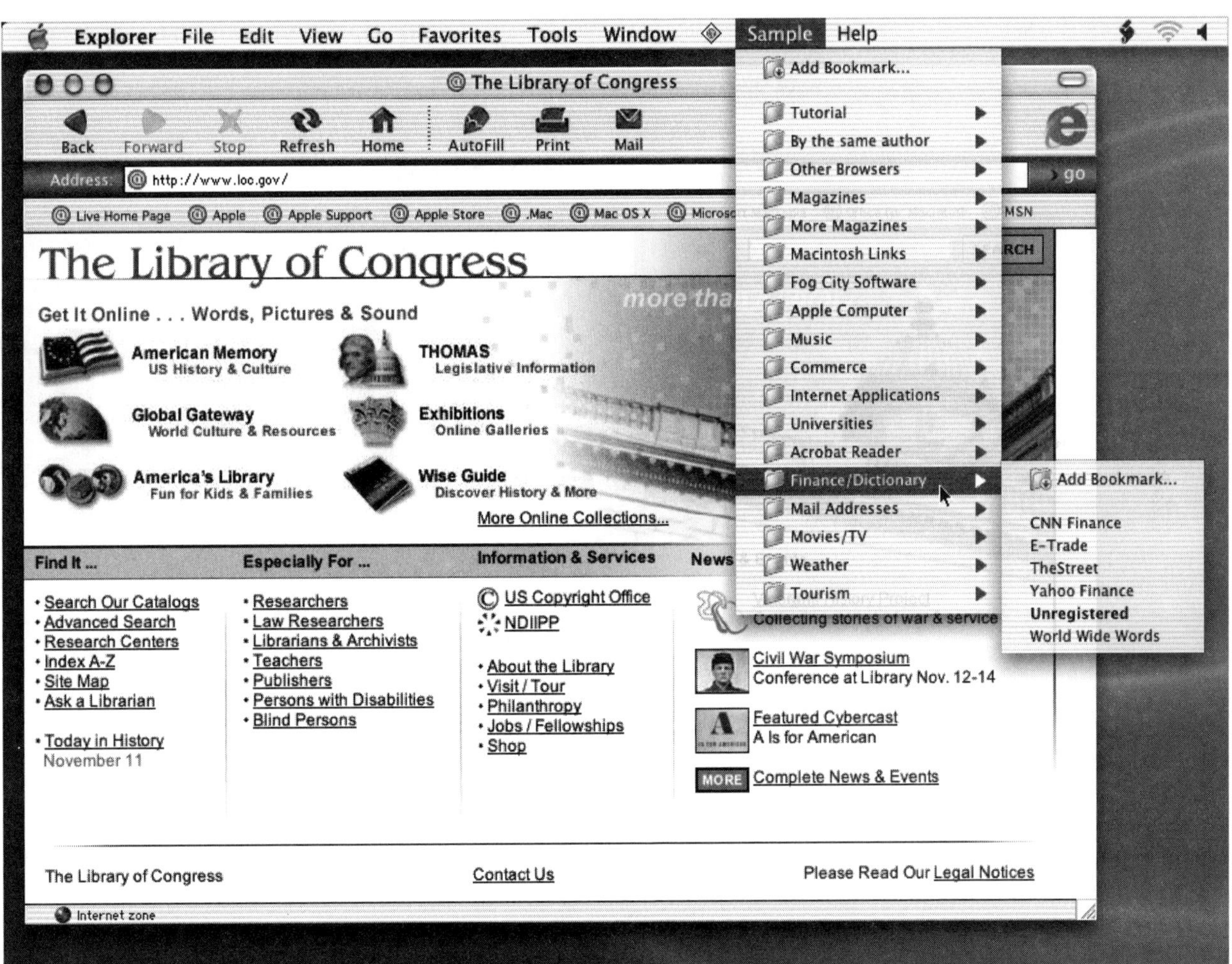

29.7

category list on the left, select **Navigator**. Then under "When Navigator starts up, display," select the **Blank page** radio button.

- **OmniWeb:** Choose **Preferences...** from the **OmniWeb** menu and click the **General** icon. Uncheck **Open start page when OmniWeb starts up** and **Open start page when OmniWeb's Dock icon is clicked**.
- **Opera:** Choose **Preferences...** from the **Opera** menu and select **Start and exit** at the bottom of the category list. Then select either **Show saved window setup** or **Start with no windows** under "Start."
- **Safari:** Choose **Preferences...** from the **Safari** menu and click the **General** button on the toolbar. Then go to the **New windows open with** pop-up menu and choose **Empty Page**.

STEP 6: ZAP POP-UP ADS

The most annoying thing about surfing the Web, by far, is the proliferation of windows that pop up above — or sometimes under — your main window when you enter or leave Web sites. Advertising everything from cameras to credit cards, magazine subscriptions to get-rich-quick schemes, pop-up ads can turn Web browsing into a real headache.

In order to understand how to get rid of pop-up ads, you need to understand how they work. Many Web pages include instructions in a programming language called *JavaScript* to do useful things such as dynamically change forms, display animations, and customize layouts for particular browsers. Not all Web designers use their power for good, however. JavaScript embedded in a Web page can cause your browser to open up another window — even if you didn't click a link or button to request it. Sometimes this cycle repeats, with each window you close triggering yet another one to open. The key to blocking pop-up windows, then, is to disable the JavaScript window commands when they weren't initiated by a mouse click. You usually don't want to turn off JavaScript altogether, because that can prevent perfectly legitimate sites from working properly.

Some browsers make it extremely easy to turn off pop-up ads; others make you work for it. Here's the scoop on each of the major browsers.

- **Chimera:** Choose **Preferences...** from the **Navigator** menu and click the **Web Features** icon. Put a checkmark in the box next to **Enable popup blocking**, as shown in **Figure 29.8**.
- **iCab:** Choose **Preferences...** from the **iCab** menu. In the category list on the left, scroll down to **InScript** and expand it if necessary. Under "InScript," select **Filter**. Then under "Scripts may..." uncheck the box next to **Open windows automatically**.
- **Mozilla:** Choose **Preferences...** from the **Mozilla** menu. In the category list on the left, scroll down to **Advanced** and expand it if necessary. Under "Advanced," select **Scripts & Plugins**. Then under "Allow scripts to," uncheck the box next to **open unrequested windows**. (While you're at it, disabling **Move or resize existing windows** and **Raise or lower windows** isn't a bad idea.)

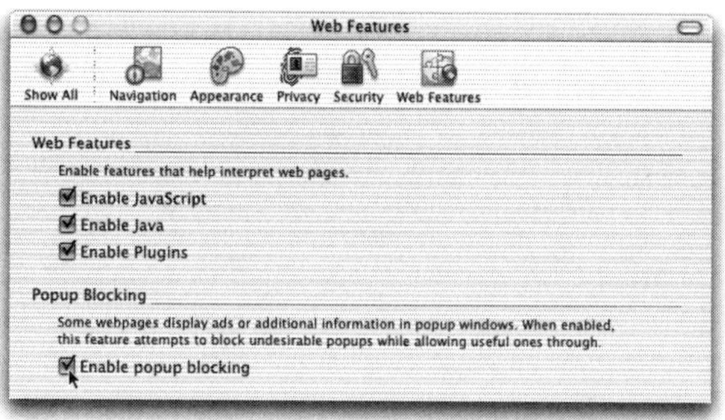

29.8

- **Netscape:** Choose **Preferences...** from the **Netscape** menu. In the category list on the left, scroll down to **Advanced** and expand it if necessary. Under "Advanced," select **Scripts & Plugins**. Then under "Allow Webpages to," uncheck the box next to **Open a link in a new window**. (As with Mozilla, you might want to disable **Move or resize existing windows** and **Raise or lower windows,** too.) Note that after unchecking **Open a link in a new window,** you must restart the application.
- **OmniWeb:** Choose **Preferences...** from the **OmniWeb** menu and click the **JavaScript** icon. Next to "Scripts are allowed to open new windows," select **only in response to a link being clicked**.
- **Opera:** Choose **Preferences...** from the **Opera** menu and select **Windows** at the bottom of the category list. Then uncheck the box next to **Accept pop-up windows**.
- **Safari:** Choose **Block Pop-Up Windows** from the **Safari** menu. Could it be any easier?

You may have noticed that **Internet Explorer** is missing from this list. Surprise: Internet Explorer doesn't have a simple switch for turning off pop-up ads. But with a bit more effort, you can still get the job done.

- Choose **Preferences...** from the **Explorer** menu. In the category list on the left, select **Security Zones** (under the Web Browser heading). In the **Zone** pop-up menu at the top of this window, make sure **Internet zone** is selected. Then, under "Set the security level for this zone," select the radio button next to **Custom (for expert users)**. This option enables the **Settings...** button. Click it. Scroll down to the bottom of this list, and you'll see two settings for **Scripting**. Using the pop-up menus, choose **Disable** for both Scripts and Scriptlets. (See **Figure 29.9**.) Then click **OK**.

So far what you've done is simply turned off JavaScript for all sites in the Internet zone, which simply means sites that haven't been designated for special treatment. Now you have to manually turn JavaScript back on for the sites where you do want it. You'll do this by adding those sites to a list of Trusted sites.

- When you get to a page where something isn't working — you click a link or button that is supposed to open a new window but it doesn't — you'll need to turn JavaScript on for that site by adding it to the Trusted list. First, select the page's URL and press **⌘+C** to copy it to the Clipboard. Then go back to the Security Zones panel of the Preferences dialog and choose **Trusted sites zone** from the **Zone** pop-up menu. Click the **Add sites...** button to display your list of trusted sites (which will be empty at first). Click **Add** and press **⌘+V** to paste in the URL of your current page. Then click **OK** repeatedly until you're back to your Web page. Click **Reload** to refresh the page, and JavaScript should be working again. You'll only have to do this once per site — Internet Explorer will remember your settings the next time you visit this page.

I can't sugar-coat this: The foregoing procedure is very awkward and does not make for a pleasant Web browsing experience. If blocking pop-up ads is high on your list of priorities, you might consider choosing one of the many browsers mentioned in this technique that allows you to accomplish this task with one or two clicks.

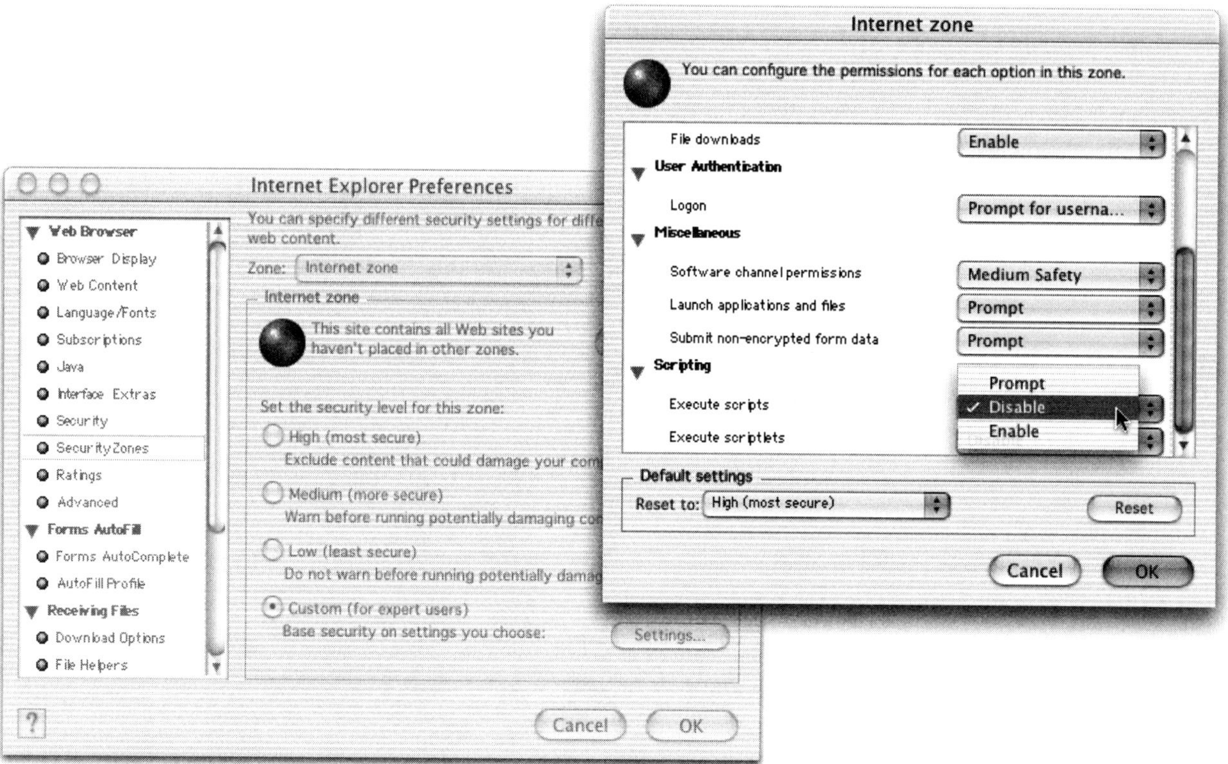
Internet zone
You can configure the permissions for each option in this zone.
File downloads
Enable
User Authentication
Logon
Prompt for userna...
Miscellaneous
Software channel permissions
Medium Safety
Launch applications and files
Prompt
Submit non-encrypted form data
Prompt
Scripting
Execute scripts
Execute scriptlets
Prompt
Disable
Enable
Default settings
Reset to:
High (most secure)
Reset
Cancel
OK
Internet Explorer Preferences
Web Browser
Browser Display
Web Content
Language/Fonts
Subscriptions
Java
Interface Extras
Security
Security Zones
Ratings
Advanced
Forms AutoFill
Forms AutoComplete
AutoFill Profile
Receiving Files
Download Options
File Helpers
web content.
Zone:
Internet zone
Internet zone
This site contains all Web sites you haven't placed in other zones.
Set the security level for this zone:
High (most secure)
Medium (more secure)
Low (least secure)
Custom (for expert users)
Base security on settings you choose:
Settings...
Cancel
OK

29.9

CHAPTER 7

COMPUTING MORE WITH LESS

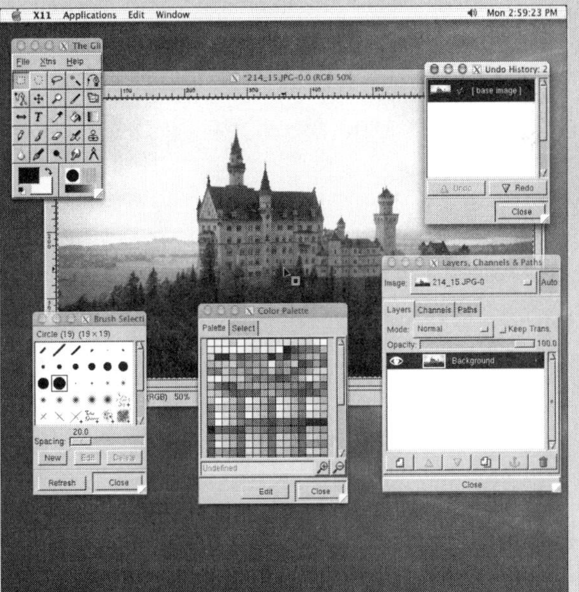

There's a frustrating imbalance between hardware and software prices. For $1,000, you can buy a brand new iBook — but then if you want to put Adobe Photoshop and Microsoft Office on your computer, those two packages alone will set you back another $1,000. Add on a few essential utilities, and you've spent much more than the cost of your hardware for the software you need to use it. When it comes to selecting a printer, you have a similar problem. You can buy a very inexpensive color inkjet printer — as long as you don't need PostScript printing or a network connection. Those two features can increase the cost of your printer by an order of magnitude.

Faced with this situation, many people do without software features they really need — or resort to copying software they haven't licensed legally. Fortunately, for Mac users there's a better way. Because Mac OS X is based on UNIX, getting UNIX software to run on your Mac is generally very easy. Thanks to the tireless efforts of thousands of programmers who contributed to the open source movement, you can obtain many high-quality, advanced UNIX applications for free.

Using the free software I discuss in this chapter, you can obtain nearly all the features of — and file compatibility with — major commercial software such as Photoshop, Word, and Excel. You can share your computer's screen with other computers much like you can with Timbuktu Pro. You can even magically impart PostScript printing to your inexpensive printer. UNIX software may be a bit harder to install, and may have an unfamiliar look and feel. But considering the price, you may well find the extra effort worthwhile.

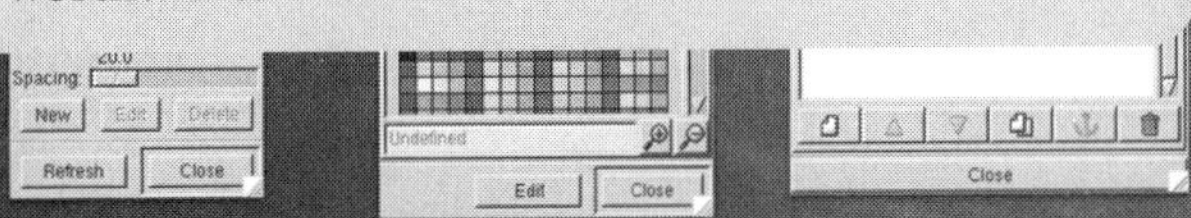

Gimp-Print

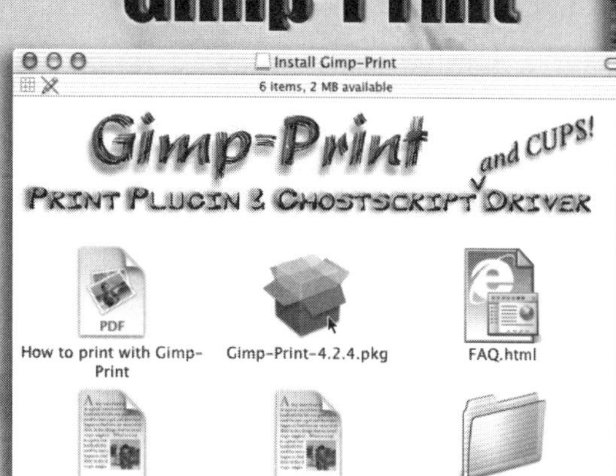

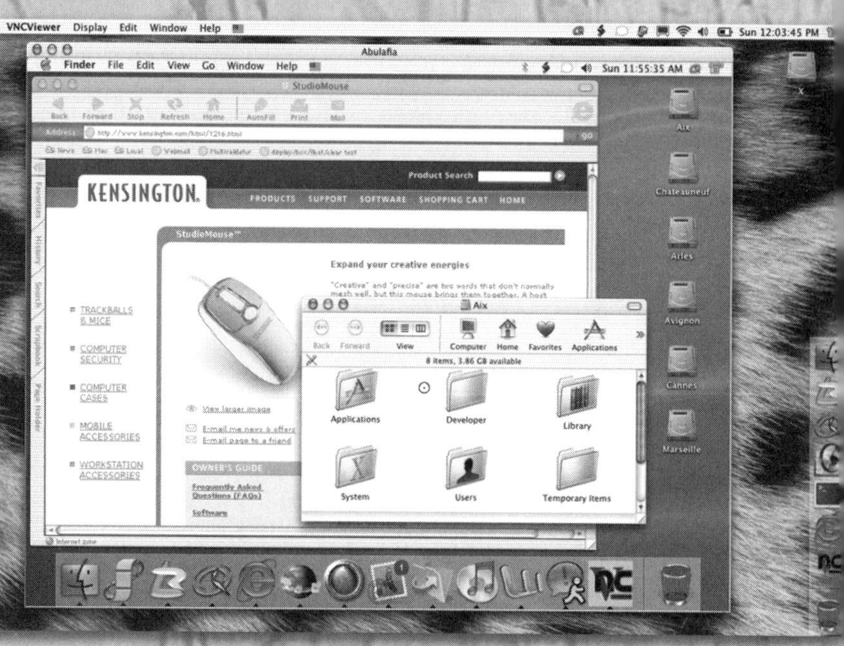

Virtual Network Computing

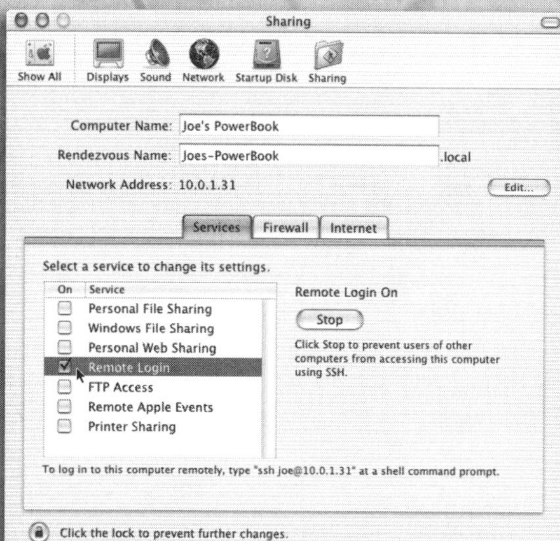

GIMP

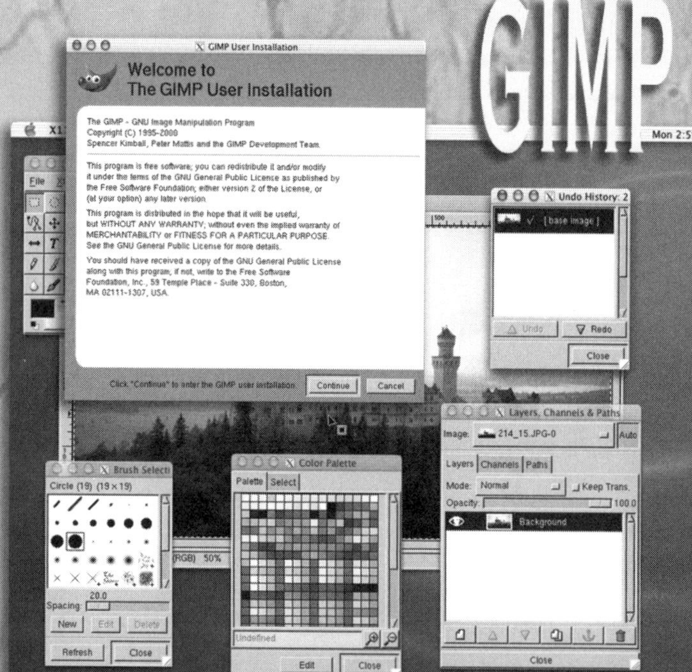

Remote-Controlling Your Computer

TECHNIQUE **30**

ENHANCING YOUR INKJET PRINTER

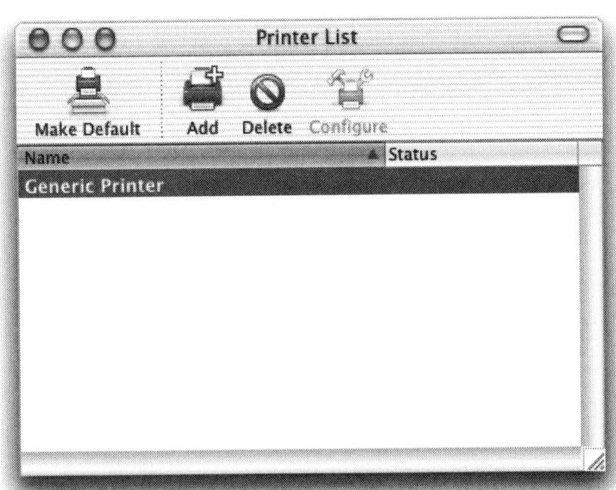

30.1

30.2

ABOUT THE FEATURE

With the help of some free software, even an inexpensive inkjet printer can have the capabilities of a networked, PostScript printer. The combination of Mac OS X's built-in CUPS (Common UNIX Printing System) support, free open-source printer software, and Printer Sharing makes it possible.

My original title for this technique was "Turning Your $99 Inkjet into a Networked PostScript Printer." Even though the title had to be shortened, the content remains the same. This is such a cool technique that it feels a bit like a magical spray paint that can turn your Yugo into an Acura. Using free software, you can add a PostScript interpreter — normally a high-end extra adding hundreds of dollars in cost — to almost any printer. In many cases, you can do this even if you have a printer that is not officially supported in Mac OS X. And thanks to the Printer Sharing feature added in Mac OS X version 10.2, you can access a single printer from any computer on your network, even if your printer just has a USB connection. Without Printer Sharing, you would need to spend still more money on a network printer or a print server.

The Jaguar release of Mac OS X introduced a new acronym to the Mac user's vocabulary: CUPS (for Common Unix Printing System). With

CUPS, your Mac can interact with printers the same way any other UNIX computer would. More importantly, some fantastic free software available on UNIX can now be used on your Mac as well. What are the practical benefits of CUPS? By following the steps in this technique, you'll get the following:

- Printer drivers for hundreds of models, including many without built-in support on Mac OS X.
- Higher-quality drivers for many existing printers, with access to more of your printer's features.
- The ability to print PostScript (including EPS files), even if your printer doesn't have a built-in PostScript interpreter.
- The ability to print from the GIMP, a free, high-end image editing application much like Photoshop. (See Technique 33 for details.)

In the final step, you learn how to share your printer with other users on your network.

STEP 1: INSTALL GIMP-PRINT AND ESP GHOSTSCRIPT

Gimp-Print is a collection of free, open-source printer drivers. More than 300 printers are currently supported, including most models from Canon, Epson, HP, and Lexmark, among others. The list includes everything from modest $99 inkjet printers through high-end color laser printers costing thousands of dollars, and the list is constantly growing. Chances are better than not that your printer will work with Gimp-Print. ESP Ghostscript, a separate package that's required by Gimp-Print, contains a PostScript interpreter — a program that converts PostScript data from an application or file into the individual dots used by your printer.

- Go to `gimp-print.sourceforge.net/MacOSX.php3` and download the Mac OS X version of Gimp-Print. The latest version at the time this book was written was 4.2.4, but there may be a more recent version by the time you read this.
- While you're there, also download the package ESP Ghostscript. You will need it in a moment.
- If you're using a USB printer, make sure it is plugged in and turned on. (This requirement does not apply if your printer is connected via Ethernet or AirPort.)
- Open the Gimp-Print disk image you just downloaded (see **Figure 30.3**) and double-click the Gimp-Print package icon. Follow the prompts to complete the installation.
- Next, open the ESP Ghostscript disk image, double-click the ESP Ghostscript package icon, and again follow the prompts to complete the installation.

STEP 2: CONFIGURE YOUR PRINTER

You may already have set up your printer using Print Center. In this step, you repeat the process to set it up to use a new printer driver. You can still use the old one at any time, simply by selecting it from the pop-up menu in any Print dialog.

- Open Print Center (in /Applications/Utilities).
- If your printer is connected via USB:

30.3

- Hold down the **Option** key and click the **Add** icon. A printer selection sheet appears.
- From the pop-up menu at the top of the window (see **Figure 30.4**), choose **Advanced**.
- Choose your printer from the pop-up **Device** menu, as shown in **Figure 30.5**.
- Choose your printer's manufacturer from the **Printer Model** pop-up menu. (If your manufacturer isn't on the list, choose **Generic**.) A list of models by that manufacturer then appears, as in **Figure 30.6**. Scroll until you find your model, select it, and then click **Add**.

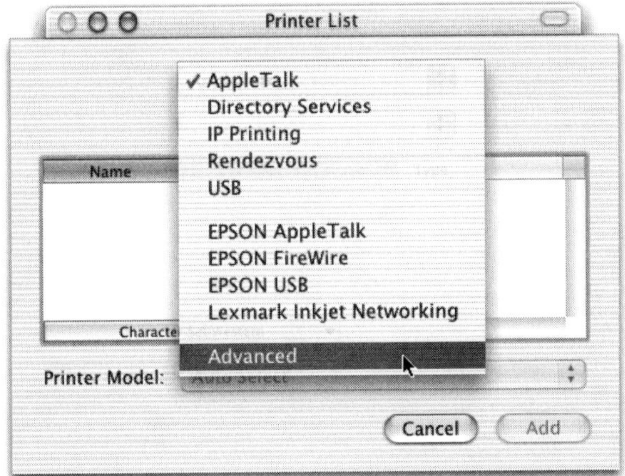

30.4

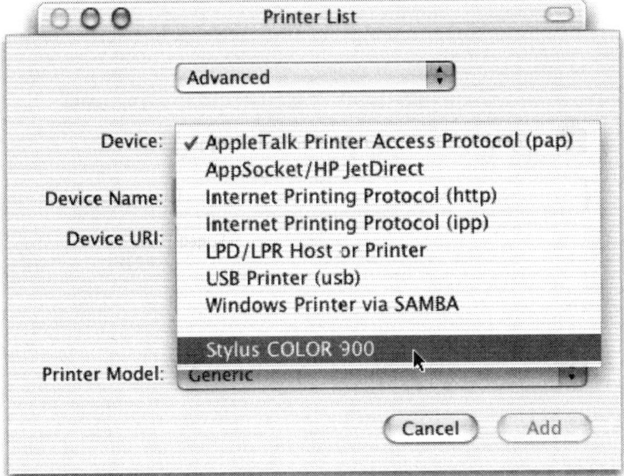

30.5

- (OPTIONAL) Type a new descriptive name for your printer into the **Device Name** field. Using a different name from the one used with the standard Apple driver can be helpful in case you later want to switch between the two drivers.

- If your computer and printer are connected using Ethernet (or AirPort):
  - Find out your printer's IP address. If you (or your network administrator) don't know what this address is, consult the documentation that came with your printer for instructions on determining the address. In some cases, you'll be able to display it on the printer's LCD screen; in others, you'll need to press a certain button to print out a Status page; in a few cases, you may need to run a desktop utility provided by the manufacturer to determine its IP address. If your system administrator has set up multiple print queues for your printer, you'll also need to know the name of the one you should use.

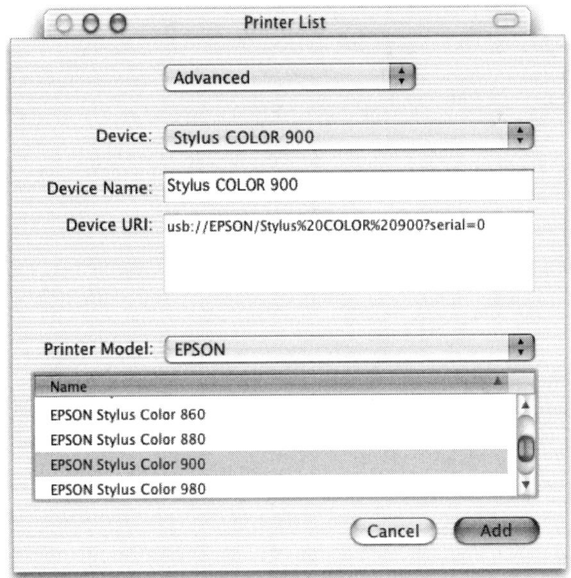

30.6

- Click the **Add** icon. A printer selection sheet appears.
- From the pop-up menu at the top of the window, choose **IP Printing**.
- Fill in your printer's IP address (see **Figure 30.7**). If you need to use a specific print queue, uncheck **Use default queue on server** and enter the name of the queue in the **Queue Name** box.
- Choose your printer's manufacturer from the **Printer Model** pop-up menu. (If your manufacturer isn't on the list, choose **Generic.**) A list of models by that manufacturer then appears. Scroll until you find your model, select it, and click **Add.**
- Your printer's IP address now appears in the printer list. If you want to give it a more descriptive name, select the IP address and press **⌘+I** to display Printer Info. Type a new name into the **Printer Name** box (along with its Location, if you like), as shown in **Figure 30.8**, and click **Apply Changes.**
- If you want to make your newly configured printer your default printer, select its name in the Printer List and click **Make Default**. The name should become bold.
- You can now close Print Center.

STEP 3: SET UP PRINT OPTIONS

You're now ready to try out your new printer driver. You'll have additional options and capabilities available, even though they may not be obvious at first.

- Open a document in any application (a simple TextEdit file or a short Web page might be good to experiment with).
- Choose **Print** from the **File** menu. The standard Print dialog appears. Make sure your newly configured printer is selected in the topmost pop-up menu.

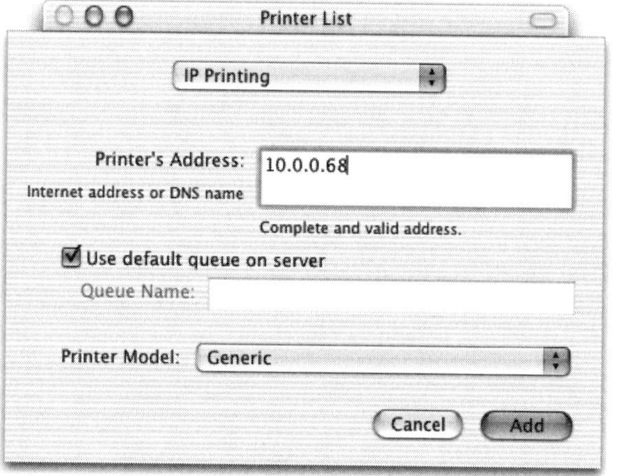

30.7

30.8

■ Go to the pop-up menu below the **Presets** menu and choose **Printer Features**, as shown in **Figure 30.9**. You will see different configuration options than those previously shown on the Print Settings pane. In many cases, the default settings will be just fine, but if you want to make any adjustments (say, to paper type or print quality), do so now. **Figure 30.10** shows an example before-and-after view: On the top is the Print Settings pane for an Epson Stylus Color 900 as it appears with standard drivers installed; on the bottom is the Printer Features pane with Gimp-Print installed. Note that more options are available than can fit on the screen at one time; to see additional options, choose **Expert settings 2** or **Expert settings 3** from the **Feature Sets** pop-up menu. If it appears that a setting you're used to is missing, it has most likely just moved to a different location or acquired a new name. In general, the Gimp-Print drivers offer a much wider range of configuration options than the ones Apple supplies.

■ Click **Print**. If everything has been set up correctly, your document should begin printing in a few moments.

STEP 4: TRY POSTSCRIPT PRINTING

Apple's built-in printer drivers do allow PostScript printing to inkjet printers — a welcome improvement over Mac OS 9, which required special software (or a printer with a PostScript interpreter built in).

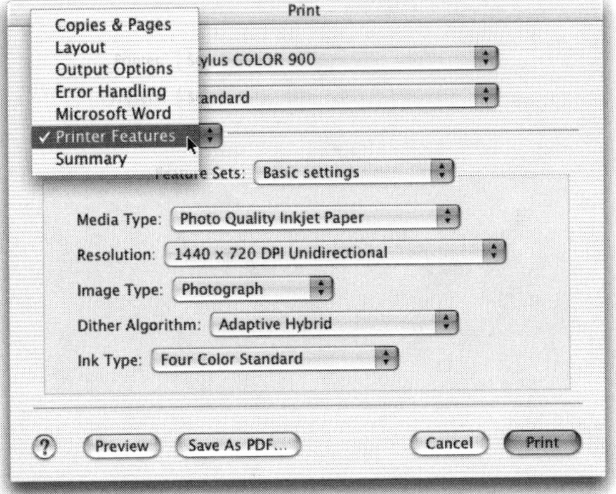

30.9

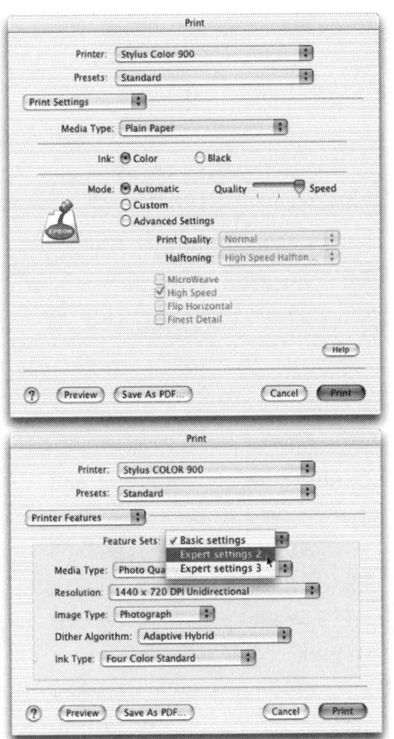

30.10

However, they don't provide any way of printing files that were saved in `.ps` (PostScript) format or EPS (Encapsulated PostScript) graphics. With Gimp-Print and ESP Ghostscript installed, you can now print these files directly.

- Open Print Center.
- In the Printer List, double-click the name of the printer you set up earlier. The Printer window opens.
- Locate a PostScript or EPS file. If you don't have one, or can't easily create one with a graphics program such as Illustrator or the GIMP, you can download some samples from the book's Web site (`www.wiley.com/compbooks/kissell`).
- Drag and drop the file into the lower portion of the Print window, as shown in **Figure 30.11**. The file will begin printing momentarily.

STEP 5: SET UP PRINTER SHARING

If you have a USB-connected printer that you want to share with other computers on your network, you can now do so with just a few mouse clicks.

> **NOTE**
>
> **Although the combination of Gimp-Print and ESP Ghostscript allows you to print PostScript and EPS files directly, some applications will still not produce high-quality PostScript output with embedded EPS images. Microsoft Word is a prominent example: When you import an EPS file, it will print at low resolution on inkjet printers regardless of which printer driver you use.**

- Open System Preferences and click the **Sharing** icon under Internet & Network.
- Click the **Services** tab and check the box next to **Printer Sharing,** as shown in **Figure 30.12**.

STEP 6: PRINT TO A SHARED PRINTER

If you think setting up a shared printer is easy, it gets even better when it comes time to print from another computer on your local network.

- On the other computer, choose **Print...** from any application's **File** menu.
- Click the pop-up **Printer** menu at the top of the Print dialog and choose the name of the shared printer, as in **Figure 30.13**. Click **Print**.

That's it! You don't need to add the printer to Print Center manually, and you don't need to install any special drivers on the remote computers. The computer that's sharing the printer handles all the processing and printer communication.

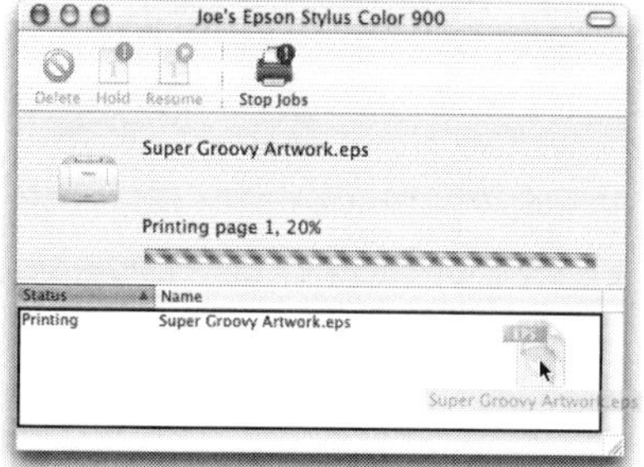

30.11

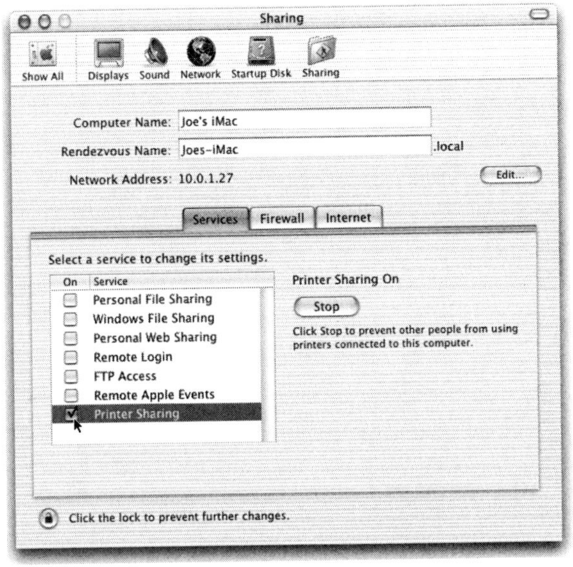

30.12

30.13

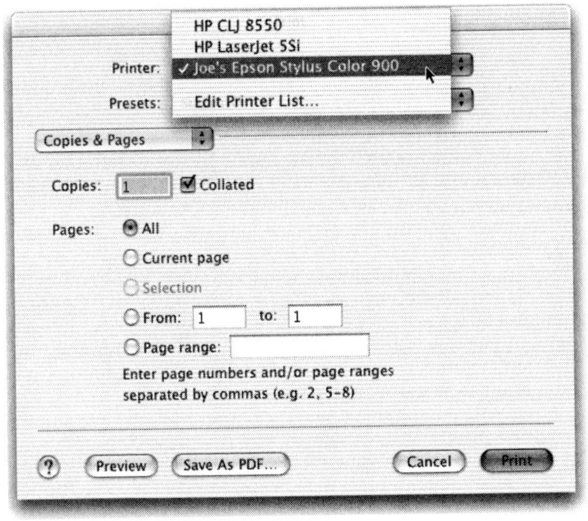

TECHNIQUE **31**

MICROSOFT-FREE COMPUTING WITH OPEN-SOURCE SOFTWARE

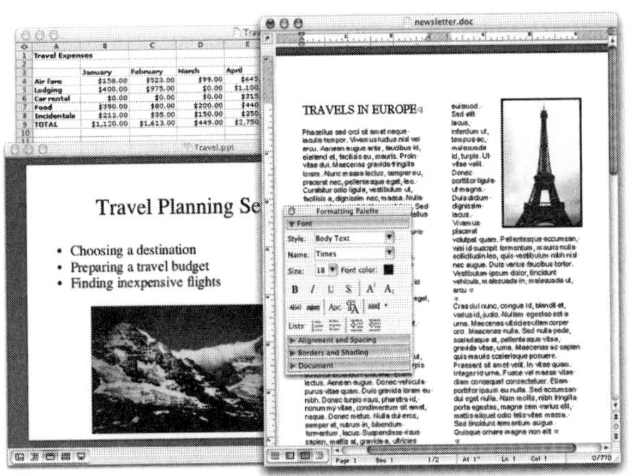

31.1

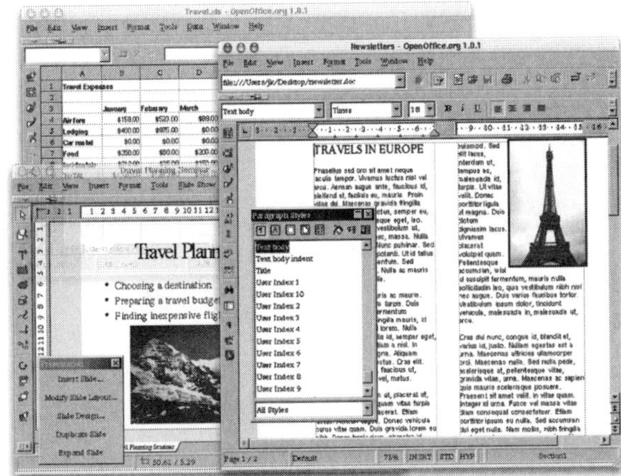

31.2

ABOUT THE FEATURE

Incredible but true: It's actually possible to run a Mac without any Microsoft software at all. Free, full-featured alternatives to programs such as Word, Excel, PowerPoint, and Internet Explorer can provide file compatibility while keeping your hard drive a Microsoft-free zone.

Over the years, I've owned and used many Microsoft products, some of which were extremely well designed and reliable. I also have a number of friends who work for Microsoft, all of whom are brilliant individuals of sterling character. Yet, there have been times when I wished I could rid my computer of every trace of Microsoft software. There are many reasons you might feel the same way. You might be put off by the high cost of Microsoft Office, be bothered by the difficulty of turning off pop-up ads in Internet Explorer, or just feel you would like an alternative — a chance to "Think Different." But in modern corporate life, almost everyone needs to be able to read and edit Word and Excel files, and that fact alone has made Office an almost mandatory purchase for many Mac users. As much as you might like to use something else, you're stuck. Or are you?

In terms of Web browsers, alternatives to Internet Explorer (such as Safari, Chimera, and OmniWeb) are pretty well known. It turns out that with just a bit of effort, you can also have, completely free, a set of applications that can provide virtually the same features as Word, Excel, and PowerPoint — including file format compatibility. Although you will have to get used to a somewhat un-Mac-like interface, you'll be able to get your work done without investing any more of your money in Microsoft.

The software you use in this technique is called OpenOffice.org. (That sounds like a domain name, and it is — it's the name of both the software and the code development project.) This open-source software is based on Sun's StarOffice office suite for UNIX, acquired from its German developers in 1999. Designed as a multi-platform alternative to Microsoft Office, OpenOffice.org is a mature, full-featured product. Although the Mac OS X implementation is, as you'll see, still a bit rough around the edges, it has all the features most users need — and is becoming more solid and polished all the time.

NOTE

Although I talk specifically about OpenOffice.org in this technique, you should also be aware of some other inexpensive alternatives to Microsoft Office. Perhaps the best known of these is ThinkFree Office (`www.thinkfree.com`), an office suite written in Java. It's relatively inexpensive and well supported, but not as full-featured as OpenOffice. Another inexpensive option is OpenOSX Office (`www.openosx.com`), which features Mac OS X installers for the open-source programs AbiWord (a word processor), Gnumeric (a spreadsheet) and other office programs. Although OpenOSX Office doesn't have the level of integration (or depth of features) of OpenOffice.org, it does offer easier installation and a somewhat prettier interface.

STEP 1: REPLACE YOUR WEB BROWSER

Yes, Apple includes Internet Explorer with Mac OS X. And, yes, it's actually a pretty good Web browser. But as I mentioned back in Technique 29 ("Web Browsing Secrets of the Rich and Famous"), lots of other choices are out there, and some of them give Internet Explorer a run for its money in terms of features. If you want to have an entirely Microsoft-free hard drive, you'll need to start by trashing Internet Explorer and replacing it with one or more alternatives. (Helpful suggestion: If Explorer is currently your only browser, don't forget to download the other browsers first, *then* delete Explorer. Downloading browsers from the command line can be challenging.)

- Because this chapter is about open-source software, you'll want to download either Mozilla (`www.mozilla.org`) or Chimera, shown in **Figure 31.3** (`www.mozilla.org/projects/chimera`). Both browsers are based on the same Gecko layout engine, and they share many features in common. Mozilla is much larger and more complex, but richer in features. Chimera is small, fast, and streamlined — without either the benefits or the drawbacks of Mozilla's vast feature set. Download one or both packages and install them in your Applications folder and add a shortcut to your Dock or other application launcher for easy access.
- Apple's own brand-new Safari browser is also based on open-source code — in this case, an HTML rendering engine called KHTML. You can download Safari from `www.apple.com/safari`.
- Other browsers you might consider are free (with a suggested donation in some cases), but not open-source. These include the highly regarded OmniWeb (`www.omnigroup.com`), iCab (`www.icab.de`), Opera (`www.opera.com`),

and, of course, Netscape (`www.netscape.com`).

No single browser can properly display every Web page. Disk space permitting, having several available is not a bad idea. Although you might have one particular favorite, being able to switch to a different browser is nice if you have difficulty viewing a certain Web page.

STEP 2: SAY HELLO TO X WINDOWS

OK, this isn't exactly a *step* in the sense of a procedure you need to perform, but before continuing, I want to give you just a little background on what you're going to be installing and using, because it's very different from the Mac applications you use on a daily basis.

Mac OS X programs all have a similar basic look and feel — the shapes of buttons, the behavior of scroll bars, the way you resize windows, and so on. The OS provides this visual interface, known as Aqua, and any application can make use of it. In the UNIX world, however, there is no single uniform graphical interface. There are a number of different methods of drawing and managing windows and their contents.

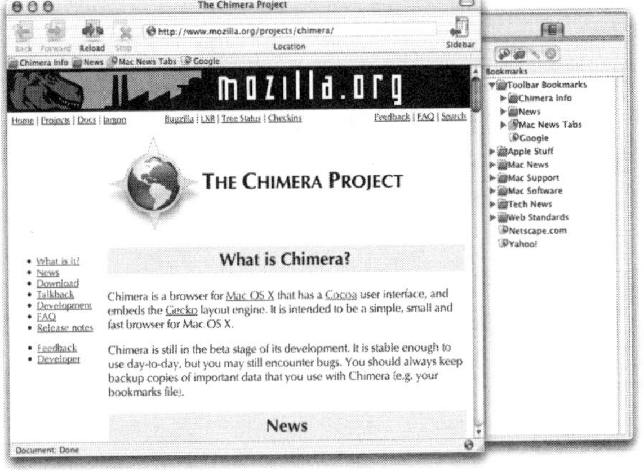

31.3

The most common one is a system known as X windows (also called X11 or just X for short — not to be confused with the X in Mac OS X!). X isn't a graphical UI per se — it's just a framework that allows windowed graphical interfaces to connect to the applications that provide the underlying functionality. X uses programs called *window managers* to impart a particular look and feel to the windows. The very same X program, running on two different UNIX computers with different window managers, could look quite different.

So what happens when you try to run an X-based UNIX program on Mac OS X? Usually nothing — it's looking for an X windowing system, and Aqua wasn't designed to work that way. You can, however, install X window software on your Mac to enable such programs to run in a full graphical environment. The software inside the windows may still look somewhat unfamiliar, but similar enough that you'll easily get the hang of it.

OpenOffice.org requires an X window system, so you must install one before doing anything else. Several different X window packages are available for the Mac. While this book was being written, Apple released its own X window software, simply called X11 for Mac OS X. This is the package I describe here, because it's the easiest to install and use and because it includes a window manager that imparts a familiar Aqua look and feel to the outsides of windows

NOTE

OpenOffice.org is hard at work on a new version of its software that will run as a native Mac OS X application without requiring X window software. Check the OpenOffice.org Web site for updates on their progress.

(though not their contents) without requiring any additional software.

When you run X window software (whether it's X11 or another package), all your X applications appear as windows within the master X environment. You will see only one application icon in the Dock, and although the X window manager will control the overall shape and behavior of the windows, the applications themselves may look very different from other Mac OS X applications.

STEP 3: INSTALL X11

Installing X11 is as easy as installing any other Mac OS X application.

- Go to `www.apple.com/macosx/x11/` and download X11 for Mac OS X.
- The installer may run automatically; if it does not, double-click the disk image (`.dmg`) file to mount it and then double-click the installer icon and follow the instructions to install the software.
- After you install the software, an X11 icon appears in your Applications folder. To launch X11, simply double-click this icon. X11 launches and opens a simple window, as shown in **Figure 31.4**. If you think this window looks a lot like Terminal, you're correct — it *is* a terminal program called xterm that runs your tcsh shell and allows you to interact with the UNIX layer of Mac OS X just like Terminal. The difference is that xterm is actually an X window application running within the X11 environment.

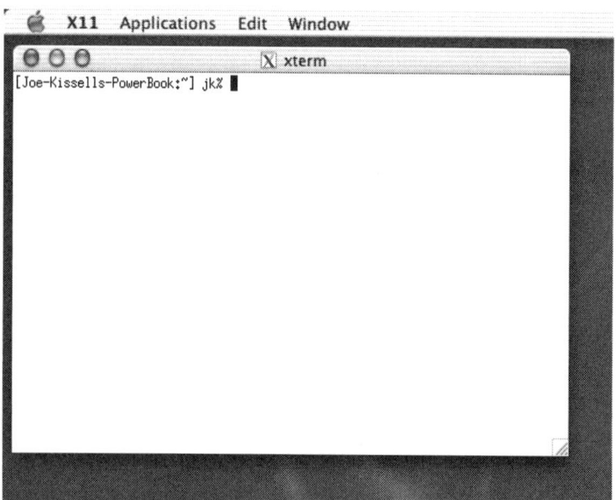

31.4

Of course, if all you wanted to do was run a terminal application, you would not need X11. But now that you have it installed, you can install and run any of a wide variety of X window applications. In the next step, you install the OpenOffice.org suite of office applications.

STEP 4: INSTALL OPENOFFICE.ORG

OpenOffice.org consists of four primary applications, all integrated into a single interface. The components are *Writer* (word processing), *Calc* (spreadsheets), *Impress* (presentations), and *Draw* (vector-based drawing). There's also an equation editor called *Math*. Each of these applications has a wealth of features, and covering them all in detail would take an entire book (or several). However, if you've used Microsoft Office, you'll find most of the menus, icons, and concepts very similar. The first step is to download and install it.

- Go to `www.openoffice.org` and download the latest Mac OS X version of OpenOffice.org.
- Make yourself a large cup of coffee, or perhaps go out for a leisurely lunch (depending on the speed of your Internet connection). The full OpenOffice.org installer is gigantic — more than 150MB. After it has decompressed, the disk image will be more than 400MB in size, so be sure you have enough hard drive space as well!
- When the download is finished, decompress the archive and double-click the disk image icon to mount it. Then double-click the installer icon and carefully follow the instructions. When you get to the Choose Subcomponents screen, make sure

you have all the checkboxes checked; this will ensure that the OpenOffice.org installer adds to your system any needed pieces not included in the X11 installer.

- At one or more points in the installation process, a separate installer may launch, asking you to enter your user name and password, and perhaps to answer some questions. Proceed through each installer in order (being sure to select the same volume for each one), and you will be returned to the main OpenOffice.org installer to complete the installation.

TIP

With OpenOffice.org and X11 being relatively new software, installation glitches sometimes occur. If a message appears asking "Where is your preferred X Window server?" scroll to the bottom of the list and select X11. If you see an error message or if the OpenOffice.org software does not open correctly, go to an X11 terminal window and enter the text that appeared in the final screen of the OpenOffice.org installer (as shown in Figure 31.5).

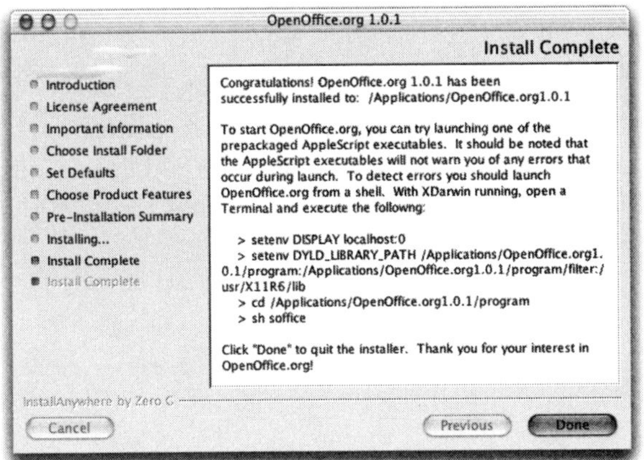

31.5

- When the installation is complete, you'll find a new folder called OpenOffice.org in your Applications folder. Open this folder and double-click the **Start OpenOffice.org** icon. After a few moments, X11 should launch and display an OpenOffice.org window, as shown in **Figure 31.6**.

STEP 5: LEARN THE BASICS OF X11 AND OPENOFFICE.ORG

Now it's time to explore. Keep in mind that you actually have two new programs in front of you: X11 (the application that provides a basic structure for window

NOTE

Although the current version of OpenOffice.org is an X application, the programmers who maintain the Mac version are working hard to give it a bona fide Aqua look and feel, with full support for all the interface features you've come to expect in Mac OS X. Future versions are expected to be much more Mac-like in their appearance, while retaining the same great functionality.

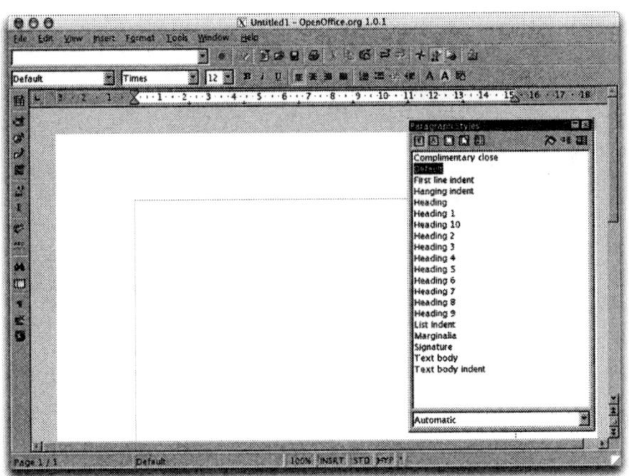

31.6

management along with the overall window shape and behavior) and OpenOffice.org itself (the application that runs inside the windows).

As is the case with all X applications, OpenOffice.org's menus appear within document windows, rather than on the main menu bar at the top of the screen. The main menu bar has commands that apply to the entire X11 environment (which can include other applications besides OpenOffice.org). You can resize, move, minimize, and close windows as you do in any Aqua application.

Here are some additional things to try:

- When OpenOffice.org initially opens, it displays an empty Text Document (including a paragraph style window). Try typing in this document, applying styles, changing the formatting, and saving the file — just as you would in Word. This exercise gives you a good taste of the layout and conventions of OpenOffice.org applications.

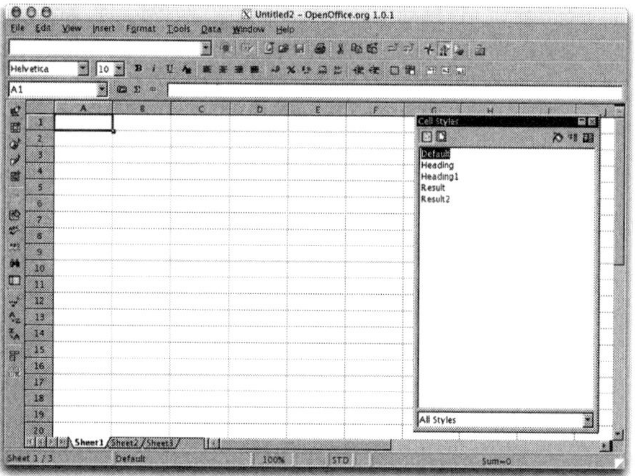

31.7

- To open a new spreadsheet, choose **Open** from the **File** menu and choose **Spreadsheet**. A new window opens, looking much like Excel. (See **Figure 31.7**.) Similarly, choose **Presentation** to create a PowerPoint-like presentation, or **Drawing** to create a new vector-based graphic.
- To learn about the features of OpenOffice.org, choose **Contents** from the **Help** menu in any OpenOffice.org window. The electronic help contains complete sections on the individual components such as Writer, Calc, Draw, and Impress.
- If you ever get completely stuck, just quit the entire X11 application, and double-click the **Start OpenOffice.org** icon again.

STEP 6: ADD COMMANDS TO X11'S APPLICATIONS MENU

As you experiment with OpenOffice.org in X11, you'll soon notice that you can't close your last document window without also quitting the entire OpenOffice.org application. After the application has gone, there are no icons to click, so how do you get it back? One way would be to open Start OpenOffice.org again in the Finder; another way would be to open a Terminal window in OpenOffice.org and enter the command to start the application. But because this is something you'll have to do frequently, you can make it much easier by adding commands for each OpenOffice.org component to the Applications menu in X11.

- Choose **Customize...** from the **Applications** menu in X11 (the main menu bar at the top of the screen, not the one inside an X window). The X11

Application Menu window (shown in **Figure 31.8**) appears.

■ Click **Add Item**. A new, highlighted row appears. Double-click the portion of the new row under the Name column and type the name of the first application you want to add — for example, `OOo Writer`. Then double-click the Command portion of the new row and enter `/Applications/OpenOffice.org*/program/swriter` to create a menu command that will launch Writer.

■ With the row you just added still selected, click **Duplicate**. Rename the new row to `OOo Calc` (or whatever you want to call the spreadsheet program) and change `swriter` in the Command column to `scalc`. Repeat this for OOo Draw (changing `swriter` to `sdraw`) and OOo Impress (substituting `simpress`). Your window should look like **Figure 31.9**. Click **Done**. You should now see your new commands in the **Applications** menu, as shown in **Figure 31.10**.

■ To launch any OpenOffice.org application by name, simply choose it from the **Applications** menu.

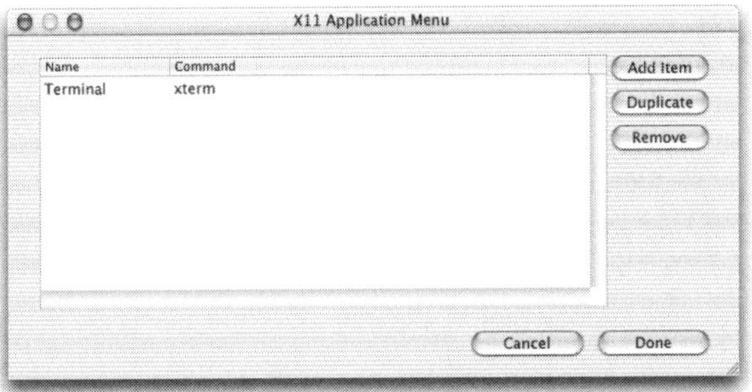

31.8

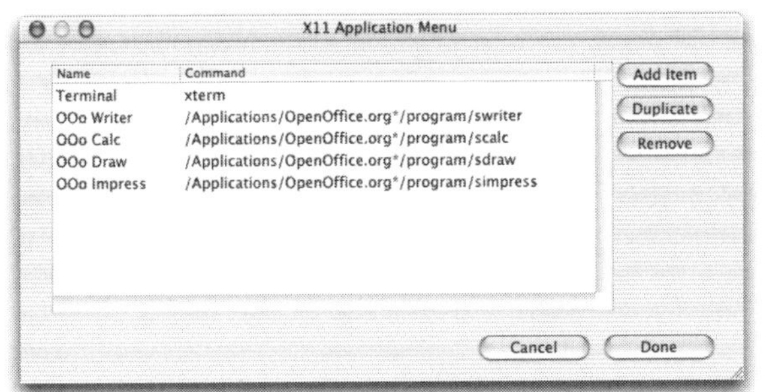

31.9

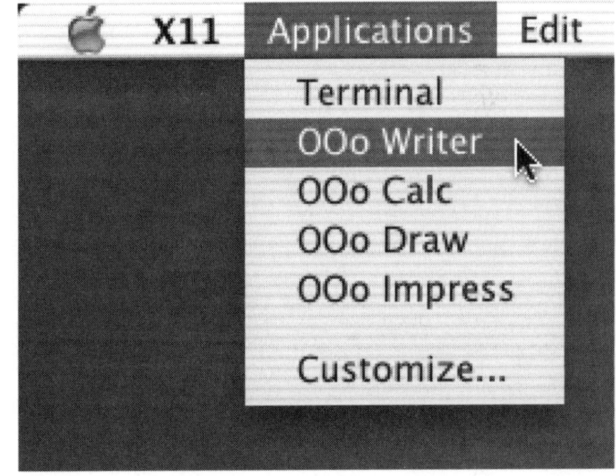

31.10

TECHNIQUE **32**

REMOTE-CONTROLLING YOUR COMPUTER

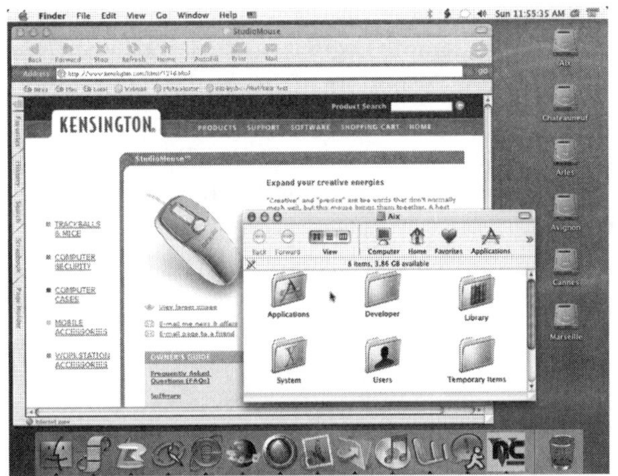

32.1

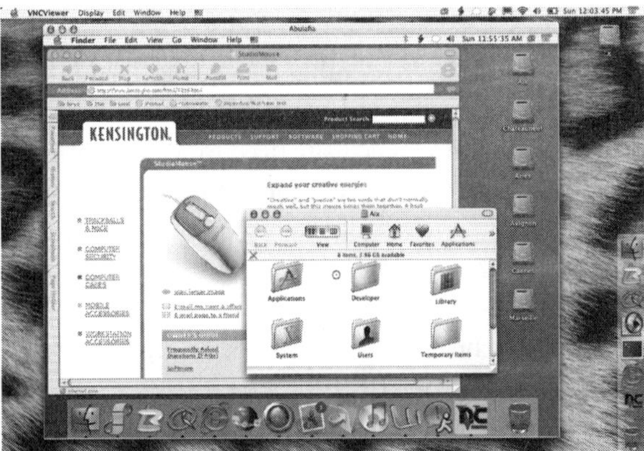

32.2

ABOUT THE FEATURE

One Mac can remote-control another using either a command-line interface with SSH (Secure Shell) or fully graphical screen sharing with VNC (Virtual Network Computer). You can even control your Mac from a PC!

At first glance, remote-controlling one computer with another might seem like a very geeky, "just-because-you-can" kind of thing to do. Unless you're some heavy-duty system administrator, why would you ever need to do that? Let me give you some examples.

- You work at home with your PowerBook over the weekend to finish the Big Project, but you need to edit a file using an application that's only installed on your desktop Mac at work.
- You're at work, but you urgently need to look up a transaction in Quicken — on your machine at home.
- You've just arrived in Rome for your month-long visit with your cousin. Then it hits you: You never printed out her address — it's in the Address Book on your computer at home!
- You're not a computer expert, but your son is. When something goes wrong, you can give him a call, but it sure would be nice if he could

actually see what's on your screen, take control of your pointer, and fix the problem.

- You have several computers at home, but they're in different rooms. You want to use the Mac in your den while working on your PowerBook in the back yard.

These are just a few of the many reasons you might want to add remote-control capabilities to your computer.

Depending on your needs, you might want command-line access to another Mac using Terminal (or a similar program on a Windows or UNIX machine). Or you might actually need to see the entire screen, move the pointer, and control everything on the other computer in a completely graphical environment. In this technique, I show you how to do both — and explain the benefits of each approach.

You may have heard of an excellent screen-sharing program called Timbuktu Pro, which does all this and more. Timbuktu is great, but it's not inexpensive. Also, it may be more than you need for simple, occasional access to another computer. In keeping with the theme of this chapter, I show you an open-source alternative to Timbuktu called VNC (for Virtual Network Computer).

STEP 1: SET UP YOUR COMPUTER FOR COMMAND-LINE ACCESS

If you want to be able to access your computer from another computer using a command-line interface, you can set it up very easily. Why would you want to do this? If your Mac is functioning as a server, you may want to start or stop a service, update files, or even restart your computer remotely. On a more mundane level, you may simply want to view a text file such as a shopping list when you're away from your computer. Tasks like this are ideally suited for command-line access, because it is very fast (even over a slow Internet connection) and can be used from almost any computer, often without installing any additional software.

Mac OS X contains a built-in command-line tool for remote access called SSH (for Secure Shell). Setting up SSH access to your computer requires just a few clicks.

- Open System Preferences and click the **Sharing** icon under "Internet & Network."
- Click the **Services** tab and check the box next to **Remote Login**, as shown in **Figure 32.3**.
- When **Remote Login** is selected, you'll see a message at the bottom of the window indicating the address you need to use to connect to your computer. Make a note of it. (It will normally be something like `ssh joe@10.0.1.28`, where *joe* is replaced with your user name and *10.0.1.28* is replaced with your computer's IP address or domain name.)
- You can now quit System Preferences.

STEP 2: CONTROL ANOTHER COMPUTER USING SSH

Now you can go to another computer and open a terminal session to the computer you set up in Step 1.

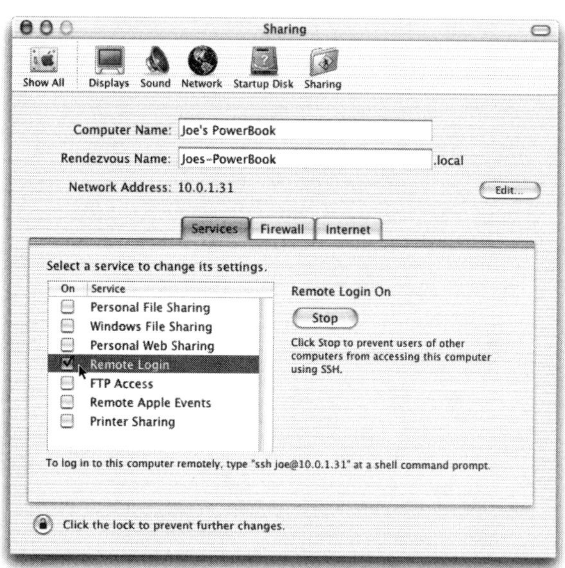

32.3

This requires using an SSH client, which is included as part of Mac OS X (and most UNIX and Linux systems). If the second computer is running Windows or a version of UNIX without an SSH client, you may have to download one (try `versiontracker.com`) before proceeding with this step.

- On a second computer, open Terminal (in /Applications/Utilities). If the other computer is not a Mac, you can use an Xterm window (on UNIX) or a standalone SSH client.
- Enter the text you wrote down from the previous step at the command prompt. For example:

```
ssh joe@10.0.1.28
```

- The first time you connect to a particular computer, you'll see a message like the one shown in **Figure 32.4**. This does not indicate a problem; type `yes` and press **Return**. You should then see a second message, which you can also safely ignore, that looks something like this:

```
Warning: Permanently added
  '10.0.1.28' (RSA) to the list of
  known hosts.
```

NOTE

In order to access your computer remotely, it must have a unique IP address. It doesn't necessarily have to be a *static* address, but it needs to be *unique*. This means that if your computer is connected to a router or firewall that uses NAT (Network Address Translation) to share one IP address among many computers, you probably won't be able to access it remotely unless the router is set up to use port redirection for port 22 (as described in Technique 41, Step 7) and the firewall has port 22 open (see Technique 25). You may, however, be able to access it from another computer on the same local network.

- Next you'll be asked to supply a password. Type the same password you use to log into your machine normally and press **Return**. Your prompt changes to display the IP address or domain name of the computer you've connected to as well as your user name. Your window will look something like that shown in **Figure 32.5**.

At this point, you can do anything on the remote computer that you could do if you were sitting in front of it using Terminal. For example, you can do the following:

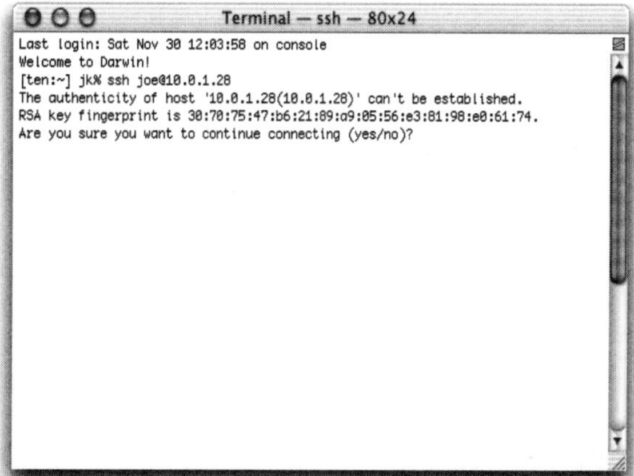

32.4

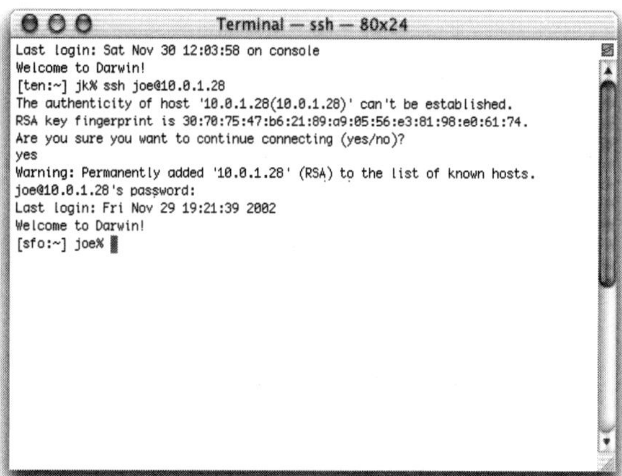

32.5

- Copy, move, rename, or delete files.
- View and edit text files with an editor like pico.
- Display running processes using `top`, and quit processes that are unresponsive using `kill`.
- Change application preferences, Web server configuration, and other settings.
- Run any command-line program installed on the remote Mac, including developer tools or other utilities you've downloaded.

When you're finished with your remote session, be sure to type **exit** and press **Return** to log out.

STEP 3: INSTALL A VNC SERVER

Remote terminal sessions can be useful for many small tasks and require very little bandwidth. Sometimes, however, you actually need to see what's on another computer's screen and interact with it as though you were sitting in front of it. For this, you'll need a screen-sharing program. VNC (for Virtual Network Computing) is a free package originally developed by AT&T that provides screen sharing across platforms. With VNC, you can control your Mac from a Windows machine, a Windows computer from a UNIX workstation, and so on.

WARNING

VNC is not a secure system — the data you send is not encrypted, so it could theoretically be intercepted and viewed by a third party. Although the real-world danger is probably very low, don't use VNC haphazardly. If you are concerned about security, you can encrypt your VNC datastream using an IPSec or SSH tunnel. Space constraints prevent me from describing that procedure in detail here. Normally, it requires some work on the command line, but the freeware GUI applications Vapor (for SSH tunneling) or VaporSec (for IPSec tunneling) from `afp548.com/Software` might be just what you need. Use one of these tools to create a tunnel for port 5900.

VNC consists of two components: a client and a server. The server is the part that runs on the Mac you want to control; it makes the screen available to other computers. The client is the part you run on the remote computer; it lets you see other computers' screens. Because VNC is open source, you may find several different versions of both the client and the server that will work on Mac OS X. You can freely mix and match VNC clients and servers, even if they're not from the same source.

- For the purposes of this exercise, use OSXvnc as the server. Go to `sourceforge.net/projects/osxvnc` to download it. It's a very small package that consists of a single file.
- After the download has completed, move the OSXvnc file to your Applications folder and double-click it. A window appears like the one shown in **Figure 32.6**.
- In most cases, the only thing you'll need to fill in is a password of your choice. Remember to choose something that's hard to guess; with this password anyone can gain full control of your computer. If you want to be sure VNC runs automatically when you start your computer, check the box next to **Start Server On Launch**.
- Click the **Start server** button at the bottom of the window. You can now hide OSXvnc if you like — but quitting the application will cut off sharing services.
- Make a note of your computer's IP address or domain name. If you don't know what it is, check the Network pane of System Preferences. You'll need this information to connect to your computer remotely. As with SSH, you can't connect to your computer from outside a local network unless it has a unique IP address; a router or firewall that uses NAT to share IP addresses will normally block access to your machine.

Your computer is now available to be shared. The next step is to install the client software on *another* computer and then use it to remote-control the first one.

STEP 4: INSTALL A VNC CLIENT

The VNC server application you downloaded in the last step is just a server — you can't use it to display another computer's screen. For that, you'll need a VNC client program. You have quite a few choices — all free and all having the same basic functionality. Some examples include the following:

- VNCDimension (`www.mdimension.com`)
- VNCThing (`www.webthing.net`)
- VNCViewer (`homepage.mac.com/kedoin/VNC/`)

Of these three, I have a slight preference for the last one, VNCViewer, so that's the one I use as an example here. The others are similar enough that you can easily figure out how to use them.

- Download the binary version of VNCViewer from the earlier URL, unstuff it, open the disk image, and move the application to your Applications folder (or another location of your choice).

STEP 5: REMOTE-CONTROL ANOTHER COMPUTER WITH VNC

With your VNC client installed, you are now ready to view and control the other computer's screen.

- Double-click the **VNCViewer** icon to launch the viewer.
- Choose **Open...** from the **Display** menu. You'll see a window like the one in **Figure 32.7**. In the **Hostname** field, fill in the domain name or IP address of the computer running the VNC server you installed in the last step.

32.6

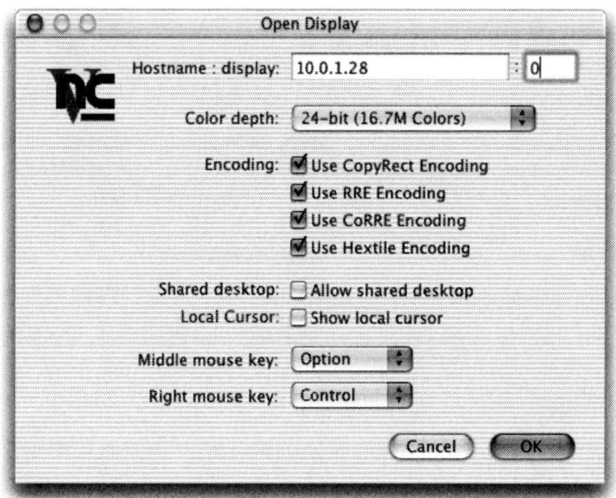

32.7

- The number in the field to the right of the colon (which may initially be 1) should be set to the same value as the **Display number** in OSXvnc on the server computer. This is normally 0, so change this number if necessary. You can leave the other options as they are for now.
- Click **OK** to connect to the other computer. When the password prompt appears, enter the password you set up on the server and click **OK** again. Your computer's screen should appear in a separate window, as shown in **Figure 32.8**.
- When your pointer is inside the VNCViewer window, it will appear as a small dot or circle (or both). As you move this pointer on your local

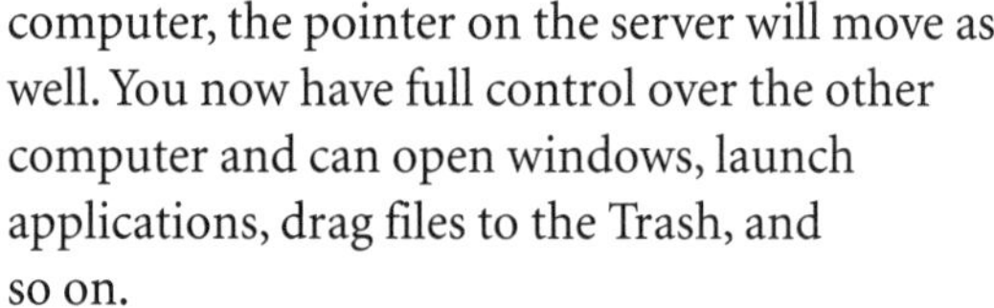

computer, the pointer on the server will move as well. You now have full control over the other computer and can open windows, launch applications, drag files to the Trash, and so on.

Depending on the speed of your network connection (on both ends), the size of your screen, and various other factors, you may find the VNC screen to be a bit sluggish in responding. One way to improve the speed is to change the bit depth in the connection window, as shown in **Figure 32.9**. Choosing a smaller number of colors to transmit will make the display less attractive, but doing so will make it much more

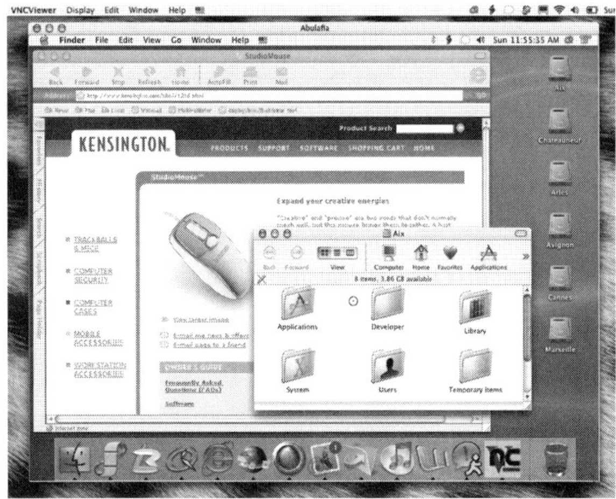

32.8

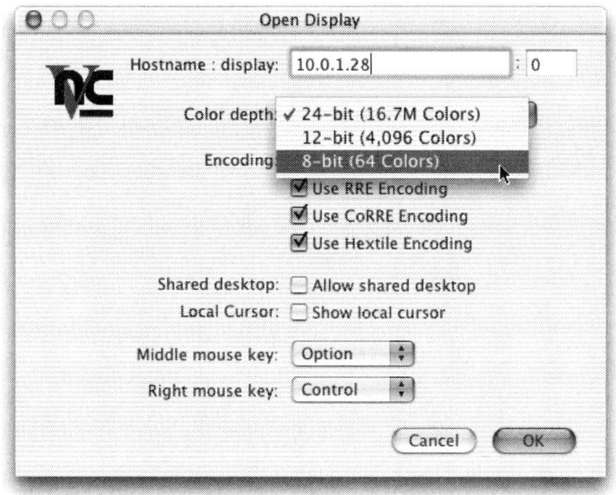

32.9

responsive because the smaller amount of data can be transferred more quickly.

VNC does, alas, have a few limitations you should be aware of. First, there's no mechanism for copying information from one computer to the other. For example, if you've copied something onto the Clipboard on your local Mac, there's no way you can paste what you copied in a window on the remote machine. Similarly, you can't copy files from one machine to another using VNC; that would require setting up file sharing and/or FTP access separately. You also can't dial into your own computer using a modem; it must have a persistent Internet connection — the faster, the better. If you need to get past these limitations, you might want to consider the commercial product Timbuktu Pro (`www.netopia.com`), which provides all these capabilities and more, in addition to the type of screen sharing offered by VNC.

Finally, keep in mind that VNC is not a Mac-only product. If you visit the main VNC Web site at `www.uk.research.att.com/vnc/`, you can also find servers and clients for Windows and UNIX. This means you can access your Mac from a friend's computer, a library, or an Internet café when you're away from home, simply by downloading a small viewer application. It also means you can install VNC servers on other computers you may use frequently, enabling you to control a Windows or UNIX machine (or several) from your Mac.

TECHNIQUE

ADVANCED IMAGE EDITING ON THE CHEAP WITH THE GIMP

33.1

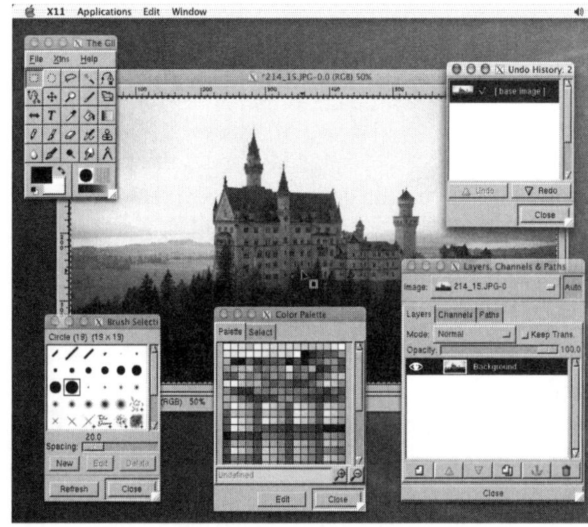

33.2

ABOUT THE FEATURE

A robust and full-featured image editor called the GIMP (for GNU Image Manipulation Program) provides advanced image editing, retouching, painting, and file conversion capabilities for the cost of familiarizing yourself with a UNIX-based graphical interface.

Photoshop is a fantastic image-editing program used by the vast majority of the world's graphic artists on both Mac and Windows platforms. While legendary for its power and flexibility, Photoshop is also a very expensive program, putting it out of reach for many users. (A much less expensive version, Photoshop Elements, has become quite popular for basic image editing, but lacks some of the high-end features of the full version.)

If your image editing needs surpass your software budget, you may find just the solution you need in yet another piece of free, open-source software called the GIMP. This odd-sounding acronym stands for GNU Image Manipulation Program, and it's the most widely used graphics software in the UNIX world. Thanks to Mac OS X's UNIX core, it's available to you, too.

Before you jump in and install it, I should make it clear that although the GIMP has many of the same capabilities as Photoshop, the interface is *very* different. Not only does it not look like Photoshop, it also doesn't look like ordinary Mac OS X programs. Like OpenOffice.org, the GIMP relies on X windows software for its look and feel, rather than Mac OS X's Aqua interface. But if you can get past the unfamiliar appearance, you'll find a powerful tool at your disposal.

STEP 1: INSTALL X11

If you have already installed OpenOffice.org as described in Technique 31, you can skip this step — you already have this software installed. If not, you'll first need X11, a program that allows X windows programs to run under Mac OS X.

- Go to `www.apple.com/macosx/x11/` and download X11 for Mac OS X.
- The installer may run automatically; if it does not, double-click the disk image (`.dmg`) file to mount it and then double-click the installer icon and follow the instructions to install the software.
- After you install the software, an X11 icon appears in your Applications folder. To launch X11, simply double-click this icon. X11 launches and opens a simple window, as shown in **Figure 33.3**. This window is very similar to Terminal — it provides a basic command-line interface to your computer.

STEP 2: INSTALL THE GIMP

After installing the X11 software, the next step is installing the GIMP.

- Go to `www.osxgnu.org/software/Xwin/Applications/gimp` to download the latest Mac installer for the GIMP. (Note: This installer is very large — over 120MB.) While you're there, I also recommend picking up the GIMP HTML manual.
- When the downloads have completed, double-click the **gimp** package to run the installer. Follow the prompts to complete the installation.
- If you plan to print from the GIMP, you'll also need to download and install Gimp-Print and ESP Ghostscript as described in Technique 30.

STEP 3: LAUNCH THE GIMP

You can open the GIMP from the X11 command line, but by adding a command to the X11 Applications menu, you can make launching the application much easier.

- Double-click the X11 icon to launch it if it's not already running.
- To launch the GIMP from the command line, open a terminal window (if one is not already visible within X11) by choosing **Terminal** from

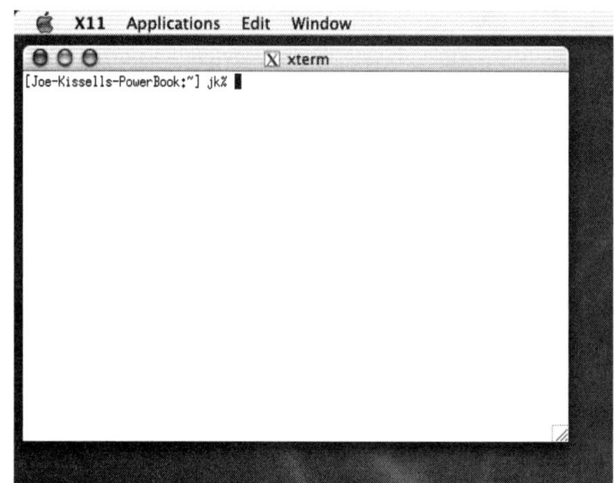

33.3

the **Applications** menu. Then type the following (all on one line, with a space after `shm`):

```
/usr/X11R6/bin/gimp --no-shm
--no-xshm
```

Press **Return**.

■ To add a **GIMP** command to the **Applications** menu so you don't need to remember the command-line instruction, choose **Customize...** from the **Applications** menu in X11. The X11 Application Menu window appears. Click **Add Item**. A new, highlighted row appears. Double-click the portion of the new row under the Name column and type `GIMP`. Then double-click the Command portion of the new row and enter the following (all on one line, with a space after `shm`):

```
/usr/X11R6/bin/gimp --no-shm
--no-xshm
```

This creates a menu command that will launch the GIMP. At this point, your window should look something like **Figure 33.4**. Now you can launch the GIMP simply by choosing **GIMP** from the **Applications** menu.

■ The first time you launch the GIMP, you'll see a dialog like the one shown in **Figure 33.5**. Click **Continue**, then follow the prompts to finish the installation, which includes creating the necessary directories to contain the support files.

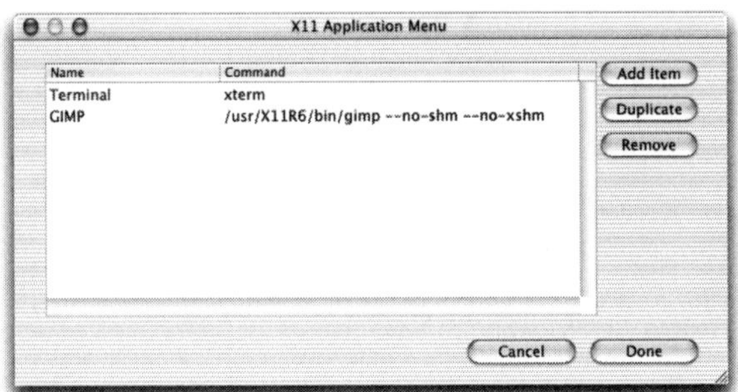

33.4

■ After this initial setup, you should see several GIMP windows, as shown in **Figure 33.6**.

STEP 4: LEARN GIMP BASICS

For complete instructions on using the GIMP, consult the HTML documentation you downloaded in Step 2. If you've used Photoshop or Photoshop Elements,

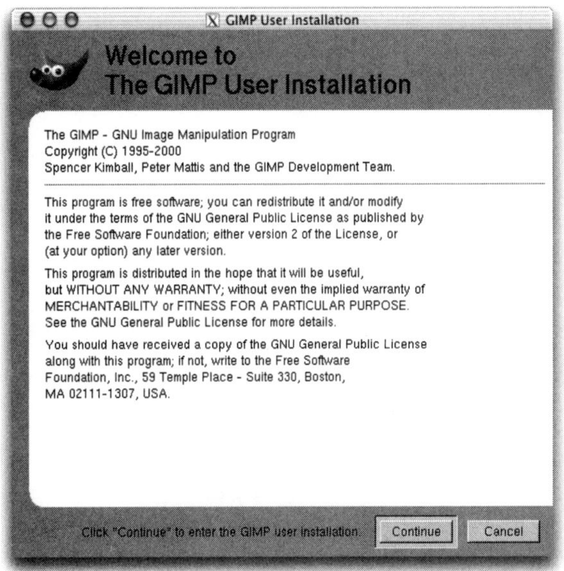

33.5

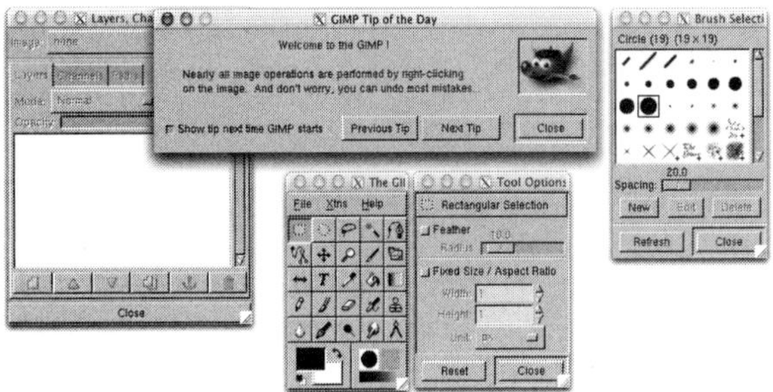

33.6

much of what you see in the GIMP will already be familiar. Here are some of the highlights of the interface to get you started.

- The GIMP's main window is the tool palette (**Figure 33.7**), which also contains the main menu bar. Using commands on the **File** menu, you can **Open** an existing graphic or create a **New** one from scratch. Try opening or creating an image now.
- Most of the tools on the palette (the Lasso, Magic Wand, Pencil, Paintbrush, and so on) work just like their Photoshop counterparts. One exception: The tool palette is not an "always-on-top" floating window, so you'll need to click the palette to make it active and click a second time to select a tool.
- While working in an image window, you may be wondering where all the commands are that are normally found on the menu bar. To access all the GIMP's menus, right-click anywhere in an image (or Option+click if you have a one-button mouse). A very complete pop-up menu appears (see **Figure 33.8**) featuring submenus for selection, filters, view options, image modes, and more. You can access the same menu by clicking the arrow in the upper-left corner of the document window, just below the close button.
- By default, the palettes visible are the main tool palette, Tool Options, Brush Selection, and Layers, Channels & Paths. To see other palette options (or to reopen any of the default palettes you've closed), use the **Dialogs** submenu of the right-click pop-up menu, as shown in **Figure 33.9**.
- To save a file in a different format, right-click and choose **Save As...** from the **File** menu. Use the

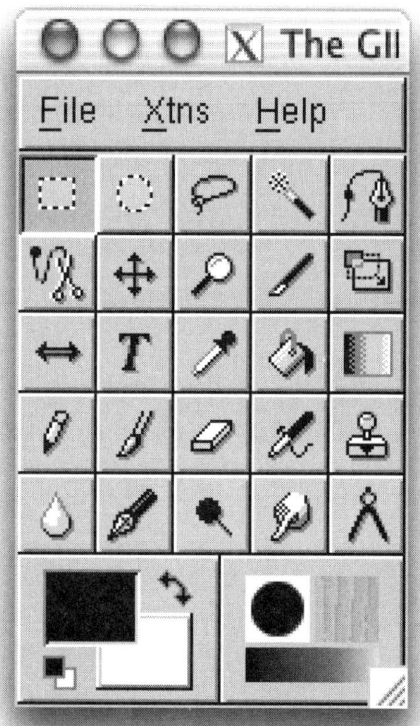

33.7

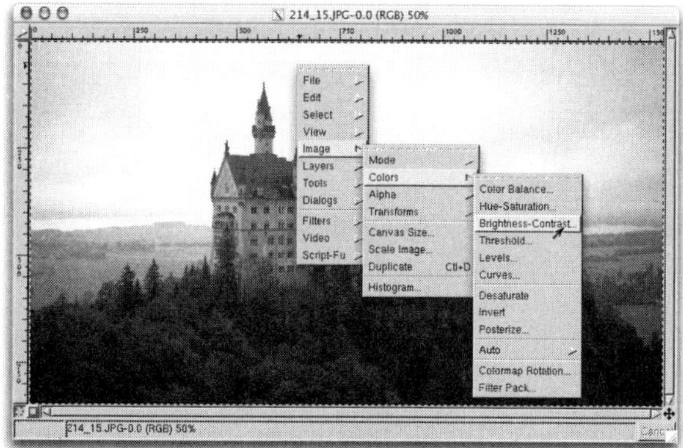

33.8

directory list on the left to navigate to the location where you want your file to be saved and type a filename in the Selection window at the bottom. To choose a file format, make a selection from the **Determine File Type** pop-up menu. After clicking **OK**, you'll be presented with additional options, such as compression or bit depth, as appropriate to the file format you've chosen.

■ To print an image from the GIMP, you will need to have installed Gimp-Print and ESP Ghostscript (and set up your printer in Print Center) as described in Technique 30. Right-click and choose **Print...** from the **File** menu. Make sure your printer is showing in the **Printer** pop-up menu at the top. Click **Setup** and scroll through the list until you find your printer model. Select it and click **OK**. (If you don't do this, you could end up sending raw PostScript code to your inkjet printer, which would result in page after page of garbage characters.) Click **Save Settings** to store your printer model in the GIMP's preferences and then adjust the other attributes to your liking and click **Print**.

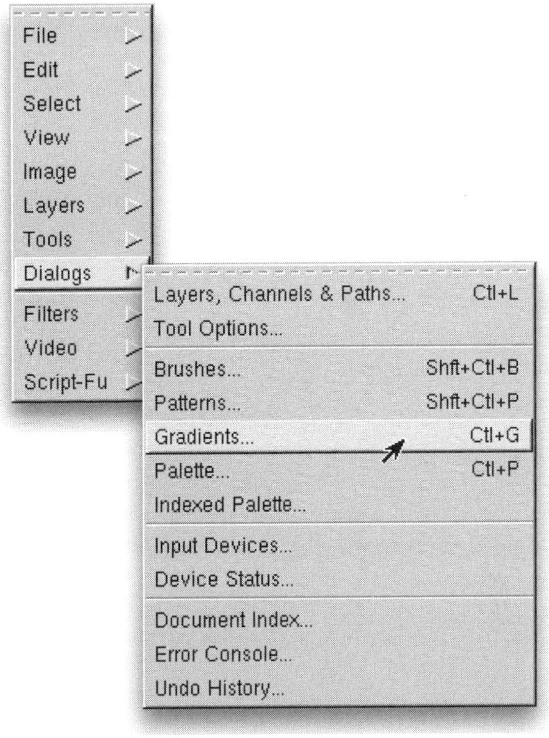

33.9

NOTE

The GIMP can read graphics in almost any format, including Photoshop (`.psd`) files. It can also save graphics in almost any format — *except* Photoshop. If you have a complex graphic in the GIMP that you want to edit later in Photoshop without losing layers or alpha channels, consider saving it in TIFF format.

CHAPTER 8

iAPPS: THE DIGITAL HUB AND BEYOND

Apple wants you to think of your Mac as being a *digital hub* — the center of a lifestyle that includes devices such as music players, digital cameras and camcorders, PDAs, and cell phones. All these devices can connect to your Mac, and the idea is that they become more powerful and useful when they work together rather than as independent gadgets. What makes the digital hub possible is the extraordinary software Apple supplies — their collection of iApplications. The first iApp was iMovie, which provided digital editing for camcorder footage. Then came iTunes, the much-heralded application for organizing your music collection, burning CDs, and synchronizing your iPod. iDVD made it easy to create your own DVD for use in nearly any home player. Finally, iPhoto added organization, viewing, and Web publication for photos from digital cameras. These four applications (collectively known as iLife) give you powerful yet easy-to-use tools for working with a wide range of digital media. The latest versions of these applications are now tightly integrated with each other, so that content from one application (say, your iTunes music library) is automatically available in other iLife applications (for example, selecting background music for an iPhoto slide show, an iMovie soundtrack, or an iDVD motion menu theme).

In addition to digital media, Apple wants your Mac to serve as the hub for data such as schedules (stored in iCal) and contact information (stored in Address Book, which is curiously missing an "i"). To keep all this data synchronized with portable devices such as PDAs, cell phones, and iPods, Apple provides iSync. Also, when you want to use Instant Messaging for a live conversation with a friend, naturally you'll use iChat. The list of iApps is constantly growing, but they all share a common theme: keeping you, your data, and your digital devices connected.

In this chapter, I present a number of techniques for using iApps. Because the range of features these applications provide is immense, I've had to choose just one or two tasks for each one that I think are particularly interesting. This will give you a good taste of what these applications can do, and give you some ideas for further experimentation on your own.

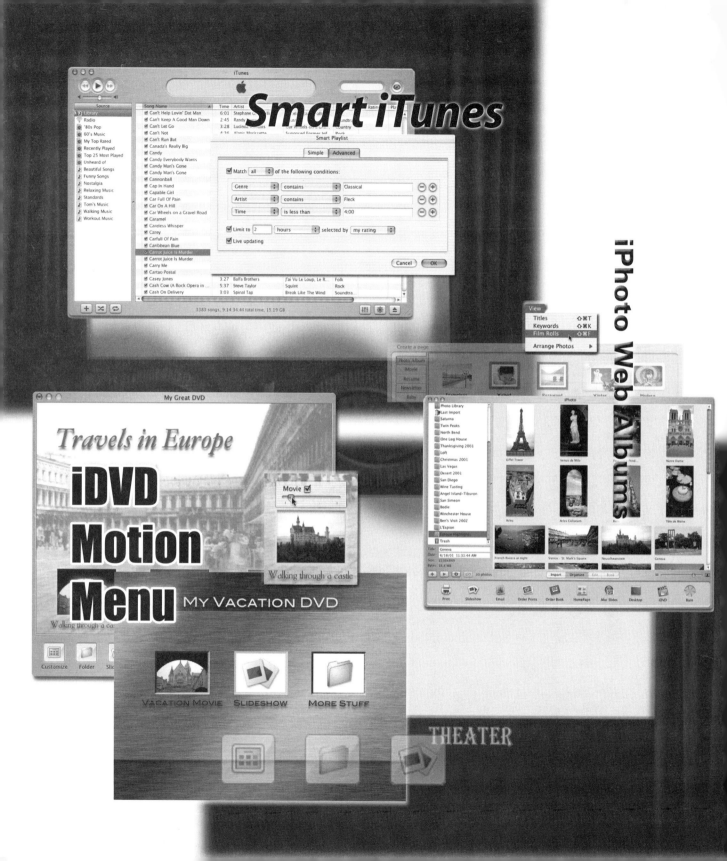

Smart iTunes
iPhoto Web Albums
iDVD Motion Menu
Smart Playlist
Simple
Advanced
Match all of the following conditions:
Genre
contains
Classical
Artist
contains
Fleck
Time
is less than
4:00
Limit to 2 hours selected by my rating
Live updating
Cancel
OK
My Great DVD
Travels in Europe
Movie
Walking through a castle
Customize
Folder
View
Titles
Keywords
Film Rolls
Arrange Photos
MY VACATION DVD
VACATION MOVIE
SLIDESHOW
MORE STUFF
THEATER

TECHNIQUE **34**

MAKING SMART iTUNES PLAYLISTS EVEN SMARTER

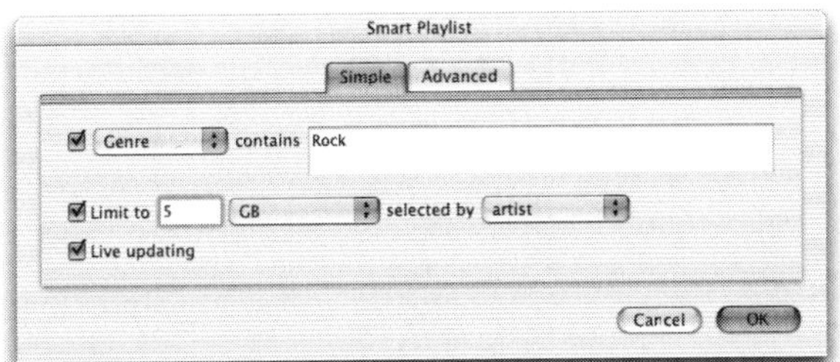

34.1

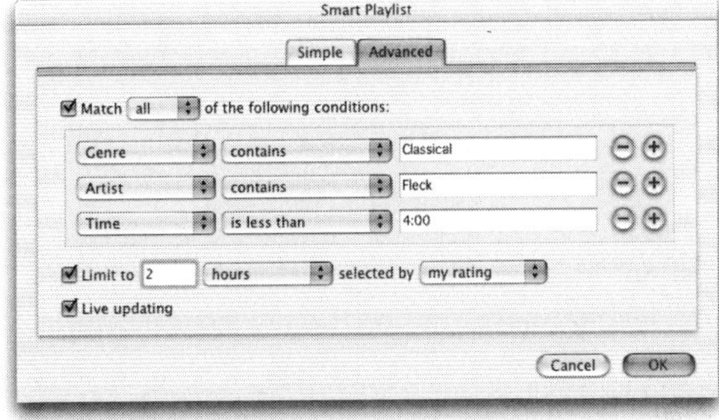

34.2

ABOUT THE FEATURE

Smart Playlists are lists of songs iTunes creates for you based on criteria you specify. Using Smart Playlists, you can organize a large music collection easily.

From the beginning, iTunes has allowed you to organize your music collection into *playlists* — user-defined groups of songs. If you have hundreds or thousands of songs in your collection, a playlist makes it easy to listen to a particular set, such as dance remixes, female vocalists, songs for a rainy day, holiday tunes, or any other grouping you might like. There's just one problem: Manually arranging huge numbers of songs into playlists can be very tedious and time-consuming.

Among the new features that appeared in iTunes 3 was a fantastic gem known as Smart Playlists. Similar to the rules used in Mail to sort your messages, Smart Playlists ask you to provide certain criteria, and then automatically create a list of matching songs. For example, you can have iTunes make a playlist of songs from the '80s, soundtrack music, classical pieces over ten minutes in length, your top-rated jazz tracks, and so on — all without your having to select individual songs manually.

A few sample Smart Playlists were included with iTunes 3, but these just scratch the surface of what this extremely cool feature can do. In this technique, you learn everything you need to get started and then make your Smart Playlists even smarter.

STEP 1: EDIT YOUR SONG INFO

When you insert an audio CD, iTunes automatically connects to an online database to determine the album's title, name of the artist, individual track names, genre, year of publication, and so on. If you then import the music as MP3 files, all this information is stored in the Tag portion of the song file. Smart Playlists makes use of the tags to determine how to categorize songs.

The only problem is that the information provided by the online database is often incomplete or inaccurate. For example, most albums don't automatically show their year of release. If you're trying to find all music from the '70s but your songs don't have dates listed in their tags, your playlist won't work. In addition, the Genre field, being somewhat subjective, is often something different from what you might expect. The divisions between labels such as Pop, Pop/Rock, Rock, Alternative, and so on are often blurry. Again, this becomes important when making a Smart Playlist: If your B-52's albums are classified as Dance, you won't hear "Love Shack" as part of your Pop music of the '80s list.

Filling in this information, especially if you have a lot of music already in iTunes, can take a long time. (It's much easier to fill in, say, the year of an album while you're actually importing it and have the CD case in your hand.) However, the more information you can add about the songs, the smarter your playlists will be. Beginning with your favorite songs, artists, or albums, edit their Tag information.

- To edit information for an entire album (such as the artist's name, the genre, or the year of publication), select all the album's songs in the iTunes song list and press ⌘+I. A window titled **Multiple Song Information** (see **Figure 34.3**) appears. The changes you make in this window affect all the selected songs. To make a change, check the box next to one or more tags, fill in the new info, and click **OK**. (Fields that are unchecked will not be changed.)
- To edit information for just one track, select the song name in the iTunes song list and press ⌘+I to display the Info window. Click the **Tags** tab (shown in **Figure 34.4**) to display the editable tag

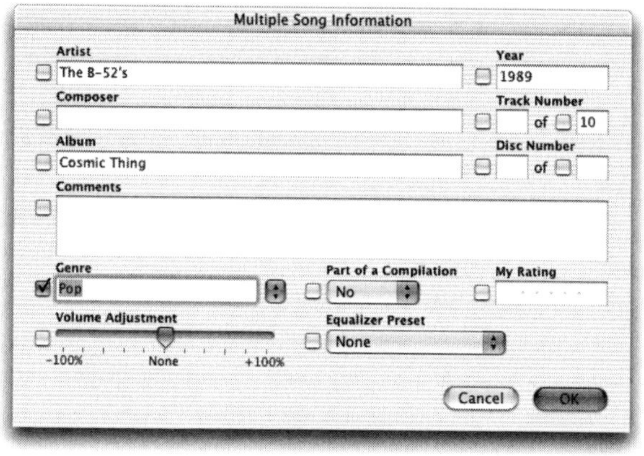

34.3

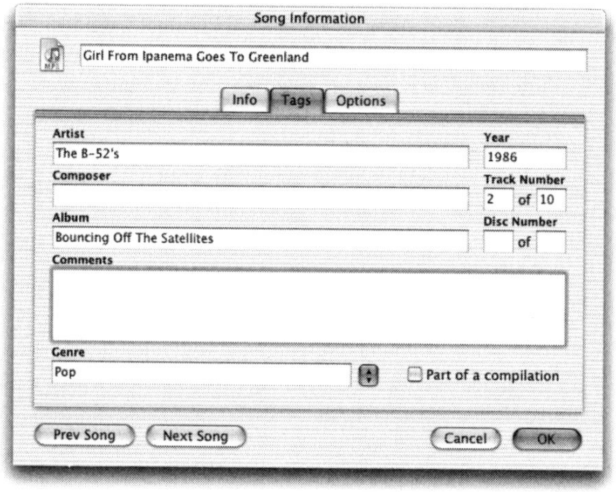

34.4

fields. Make any desired changes to the fields and click **OK** (if that's the only song you need to edit), or **Next Song** or **Prev Song** if you want to make changes to adjacent tracks.

As you fill in the tag information for your songs, keep these tips in mind:

- Be consistent with the Genre settings. It doesn't matter whether you consider Enya's music New Age, Meditative, or World — as long as you classify all songs or albums of the same type using the same Genre.
- Use Year to indicate when a song was first released. If you have the Beatles' "1" compilation album, it may list its year of publication as 2000. But what you probably care about is that "Can't Buy Me Love" came out in 1964. Smart Playlists work better if you use the year of a song's original appearance, rather than the year the CD was published.
- The Artist might be different from the Composer. If you know both, fill them both in. This allows you to create a Smart Playlist of all Bach pieces, whether performed by Walter (or Wendy) Carlos, the London Symphony Orchestra, or Poland's Marimba Duo. It also helps you to identify cover songs written by your favorite pop artists.
- You don't have to edit information for all your songs at once. Smart Playlists are smart enough to add or remove songs dynamically as information changes. So you can always edit more songs later, and your playlists will automatically pick up the changes.

STEP 2: RATE YOUR SONGS

Another new feature in iTunes 3 was My Ratings. On a scale of one to five stars (which can mean anything you want), you can rate how much you like each song. Smart Playlists can also use these ratings as one of their criteria — for example, you can list only high-rated songs or, conversely, filter out low-rated songs.

- The easiest way to rate a song is to select its name in the song list and click one of the dots in the My Rating column (see **Figure 34.5**). Click the first dot to assign a one-star rating, the third star to assign a three-star rating, and so on. You can change your rating at any time just by clicking in a different location. (To take away *all* the stars, click the leftmost star and then drag your pointer slightly to the left, as though you were dragging the star out of the list.)
- If iTunes is playing in the background, you can rate the song you're listening to without switching windows. Simply right-click (or **Control**+click) the iTunes icon in the Dock, select the **My Rating** menu, and then choose a star rating from the submenu.
- To give a group of songs the same rating, select all the songs in the song list and press **⌘+I** to display **Multiple Song Info**. Check the **My Rating** checkbox, select your rating, and then click **OK**.

Although you can use any criteria you like to determine how many stars a song gets, I'll make just one suggestion: If you really *dislike* a song (but still want to keep it in your iTunes collection for some reason),

34.5

consider giving it a one-star rating instead of no stars. This method helps you to distinguish songs with a bad rating from songs you haven't rated at all yet.

STEP 3: CREATE A SIMPLE SMART PLAYLIST

Smart Playlists come in two flavors: Simple and Advanced. Start by creating a Simple Smart Playlist to get a feel for how it's done.

- To create a new Smart Playlist, choose **New Smart Playlist...** from the **File** menu (or press **⌘+Option+N**). The Smart Playlist info window appears with the **Simple** tab selected, as shown in **Figure 34.6**.
- To select songs by **Artist**, **Composer**, or **Genre**, select one of those criteria from the first pop-up menu, make sure the checkbox next to the menu is checked, and enter all or part of the name you want to match in the text field. You can see an example in **Figure 34.7**: "Artist contains Peter" would match artists such as "Peter Gabriel," "Peter, Paul, and Mary," and "Oscar Peterson."
- To select a limited number of songs, or keep your playlist down to a set duration or size, click the **Limit to** checkbox, choose **minutes, hours, MB, GB,** or **songs** from the pop-up menu, and type the appropriate value in the text box. For example, you can make sure that your playlist includes no more than 25 songs, no more than 5GB (to fill up a low-end iPod), or that it lasts no more than three hours (for a party mix). When iTunes restricts the length of a playlist, you can decide how it chooses which songs to omit by making a choice from the **selected by** pop-up menu. The default choice is **random**. You can also choose **artist** (to sort songs in the playlist by artist name), **last played** or **most played** (to sort songs according to how recently or how often you've played them), or **song name** (to sort songs by their titles).
- You can use the Artist/Composer/Genre criterion and the Limit criterion separately or in combination. For example, choosing Genre without checking the **Limit to** checkbox selects all the songs in that genre, regardless of how many or

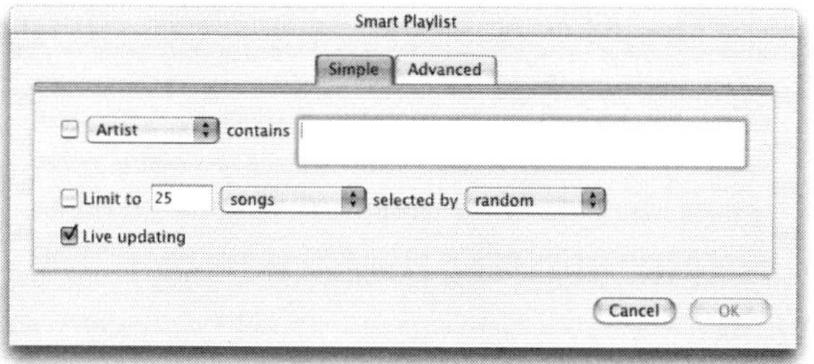

34.6

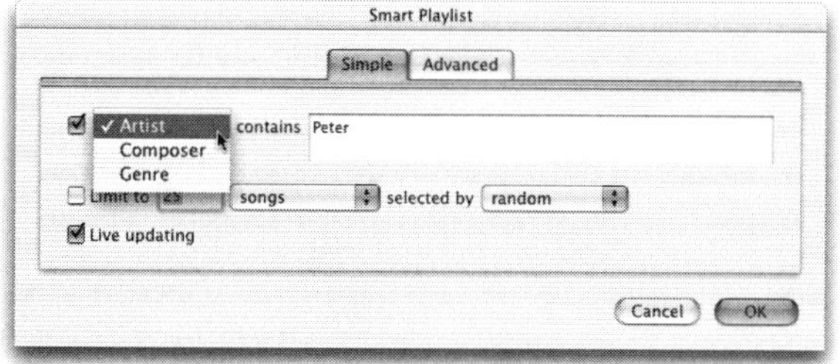

34.7

how long they are. Choosing **Limit to 15 minutes selected by random** creates a 15-minute-long playlist of randomly selected songs. Checking both boxes could give you, for example, a 15-minute selection of Soundtrack music.

- The **Live updating** tells iTunes to make the Smart Playlist dynamic. This means that if you later add music to your collection that matches your Smart Playlist criteria (or change tags for existing songs), your playlist will automatically be updated to reflect the changes. You may occasionally want to create a one-shot playlist from your existing collection and make sure it won't change later on. To do so, uncheck **Live updating**.
- To save your changes and build your playlist, click **OK** and then type a name for the playlist. Your playlist will now appear in the **Source** list, and you can play it simply by selecting its name and clicking the **Play** button.
- If you want to go back and edit an existing Smart Playlist, select the playlist's name in the Source list and press **⌘+I** to display the Smart Playlist info window.

STEP 4: CREATE AN ADVANCED SMART PLAYLIST

In some cases, a Simple playlist won't meet your needs. For example, you may want to select songs by date, by length, or by a combination of conditions ("all Sting songs from the 1990s that are over 5 minutes in length"). For this, you'll need to create an Advanced Smart Playlist. Advanced lists are really just like Simple lists, except that you have more choices.

- As with Simple playlists, your Advanced playlist can match conditions you specify, limit your list to a certain length or size, or both. To choose conditions to match, check the **Match** checkbox. The first pop-up menu allows you to choose what type of information to look for. In addition to choices such as **Artist** and **Genre**, you can now select **Year**, **Time**, **My Rating**, and numerous other conditions, as shown in **Figure 34.8**.
- The second pop-up menu allows you to specify how a match is evaluated. Simple playlists gave you just one choice — "contains." In an Advanced playlist, you can choose other options like **does not contain**, **starts with**, **is less than**, or **is in the range**, depending on which type of information you're checking for. After making a choice from

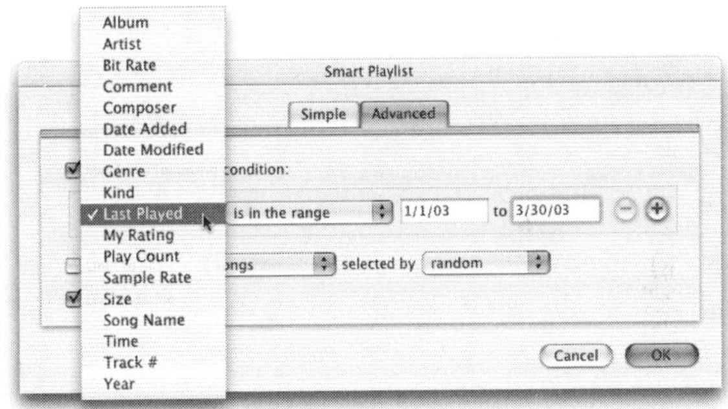

34.8

this menu, fill in the text field as appropriate. **Figure 34.9** shows an example.

- To add more conditions, click the + icon to the right of the first item. A new condition row will appear with the same options as the first one; fill this in the same way. When your playlist has multiple conditions, you can decide whether they must *all* be matched to select songs or whether *any* match will select a song by choosing **all** or **any** from the pop-up menu at the top. For example, if you want to select all Christmas songs, you might have a row that says "name contains Santa," a row that says "name contains Christmas," and a row that says "Genre contains Holiday"— with **any** selected, because a Christmas song might have one but not all of these attributes. On the other hand, if you want to select only Classical songs performed on banjo with a length of less than four minutes (**Figure 34.10**), you would choose **all**, with rows saying "Genre contains Classical," "Artist contains Fleck," and "Time is less than 4:00."
- The **Limit to** feature works just the same as it did for Simple playlists, with one exception. You now have additional sorting choices available in the **selected by** pop-up menu: **album, date added, genre**, and **my rating.**
- As before, make sure the **Live updating** checkbox is checked to keep your playlist dynamic. Click **OK** to save your playlist.

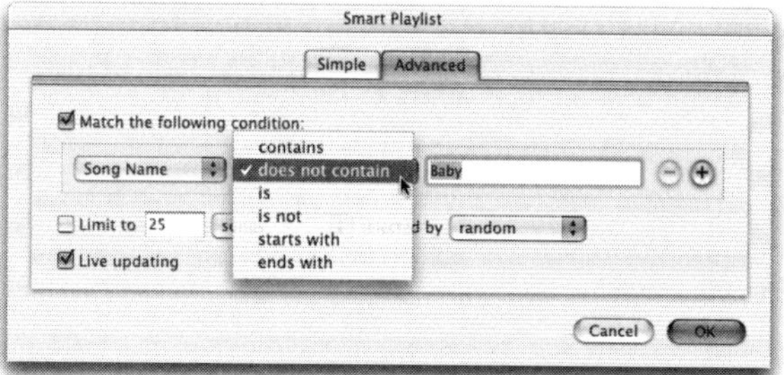

34.9

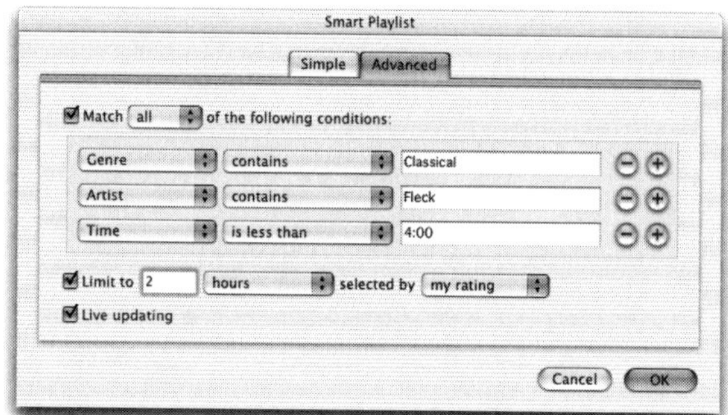

34.10

PUBLISHING iPHOTO ALBUMS ON THE WEB

```
Page1.html
<!DOCTYPE HTML PUBLIC "-//W3C//DTD HTML 4.01 Transitional//EN">
<html>
 <head>
  <meta http-equiv="Content-Type" content="text/html; charset=utf-8">
  <title>
  Europe Highlights
  </title>
 </head>
 <body bgcolor="#ffffff">
  <h2 align="center">
  Europe Highlights
  </h2>
  <a href="index.html">
  Page 1
  </a>
   | 
  Page 2
  <table cellspacing="2" width="100%" cellpadding="2">
   <tr>
    <td align="center" width="25%">
     <a href="Pages/Image20.html">
      <img src="Thumbnails/20.jpg" alt="204_4" width="132" height="240">
     </a>
     <br>204_4
    </td>
    <td align="center" width="25%">
     <a href="Pages/Image21.html">
      <img src="Thumbnails/21.jpg" alt="212_12" width="132" height="240">
     </a>
     <br>212_12
    </td>
    <td align="center" width="25%">
     <a href="Pages/Image22.html">
      <img src="Thumbnails/22.jpg" alt="005_5" width="132" height="240">
     </a>
     <br>005_5
    </td>
    <td align="center" width="25%">
     <a href="Pages/Image23.html">
      <img src="Thumbnails/23.jpg" alt="003_3" width="132" height="240">
     </a>
     <br>003_3
    </td>
   </tr>
   <tr>
```

35.1

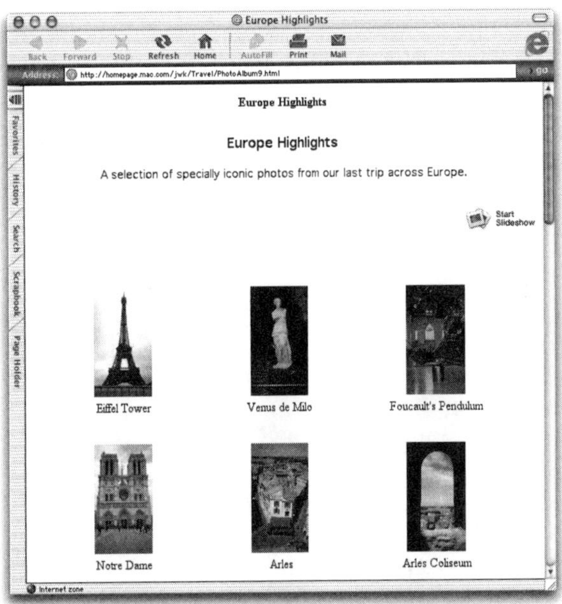

35.2

ABOUT THE FEATURE

iPhoto makes importing and organizing your digital photos easy. You can also publish your photo albums on the Web easily, even if you don't have a .Mac membership.

Creating a Web page full of photos used to be a very complicated process. First, you had to reduce all your pictures to the right size and save them as JPEGs. Then you probably would have created a second, smaller, or *thumbnail,* copy of each image. Next, you had to set up one or more HTML pages with tables displaying all of your thumbnails, each one linking to the original photo. If your collection spanned multiple pages, you could be facing hours of work and careful typing of confusing filenames. Lastly, of course, there was the matter of uploading all these files to a Web server — assuming you had one. Numerous utilities appeared on the scene with promises of simplifying this whole procedure (for a price). But the complications were enough to discourage many people from sharing their digital photos.

iPhoto changes all that. After plugging in your digital camera, you can have your photo album on the Web in just a few clicks. You don't need to know anything about HTML, FTP, or graphics editing — and you don't need any expensive software.

There is, however, a catch or two. One is that iPhoto is designed to work best if you have a .Mac account. If you're not willing to shell out the annual .Mac subscription fee, Web publishing becomes a little more involved. Also, although iPhoto creates Web pages very easily, you don't have a lot of control over how they look.

In this technique, you walk through the process of publishing photos on the Web from start to finish. Whether you're using .Mac, running your own Web server (see Technique 42), or using the services of another ISP, I'll show you how to get your photos online quickly and easily.

STEP 1: ORGANIZE YOUR PHOTOS INTO AN ALBUM

The first thing you need to do before publishing your photos on the Web is to decide which ones to display. Although you may have dozens or hundreds of pictures from your latest vacation, you don't necessarily want to put all of them on the Web. So you need to start by doing some sorting.

When you import photos from your digital camera, they're automatically added to your main photo collection, which you can view by clicking **Photo Library** in the album list. The most recent set of pictures you imported is listed in a special album called **Last Import**. Each batch of imported images is also assigned to a virtual Film Roll; to see images grouped by roll, choose **Film Rolls** from the **View** menu (see **Figure 35.3**). Displaying a particular batch of images such as Last Import or a Film Roll can be a good starting place for making an album.

- After opening iPhoto, make sure the **Organize** button at the bottom of the window is selected.
- To create a new album, choose **New Album** from the **File** menu (or click the + icon under the Album list). In the dialog that appears, enter a name for your album. (You can always change this later if you like.) Your new album now appears in the Album list on the left.
- In your main Photo Library (or a subset such as Last Import or a particular Film Roll), select the photos you want to publish and drag them to your newly created album. You can drag them in individually, or ⌘+click to select several and drag them in together.
- After you've added the photos you're interested in, select your album in the album list to display its pictures (see **Figure 35.4**). You can now rearrange pictures (by clicking and dragging them to a new location) or remove pictures from the album by selecting them and pressing **Delete**. (Deleting a picture from an album does not erase the picture from your main iPhoto collection.) Be aware that the order of pictures in your album will also be the order of pictures on your Web page.

35.3

As you organize your photos, keep a few tips in mind:

- The set of pictures you choose to publish on the Web might be a different one from an album you created for yourself. For example, you might have an album containing 100 pictures of your trip to Fiji, but only want to put a dozen of your favorites on a Web site. It's OK to make extra albums just to group pictures for Web publishing. When you create a new album, you're not making a copy of the picture, just making another pointer to it — much like an alias in the Finder. A given picture can appear in many different albums without wasting disk space.
- Although digital cameras make taking many different shots of the same scene easy, these shots can make for a boring Web page. Pick out just your best, favorite pictures to keep your viewers interested.
- Give some thought to the order in which you want your pictures to appear on your Web page. Vacation pictures often work best in chronological order, but you might also consider grouping them by geography, theme, or subject.

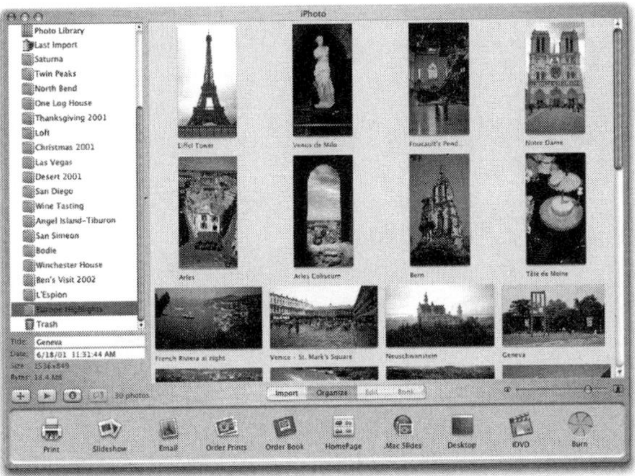

35.4

- You can put as many pictures as you like in an album, but there are limits to attention spans. An album with more than a few dozen pictures can sometimes be a turn-off. (Exception: There is no limit to the number of baby pictures a grandparent will want to see.)

STEP 2: ADD CAPTIONS

I can't overemphasize the value of good captions. You may clearly remember an event or trip, but without captions, your photos might have little meaning to your friends or family. (I'm speaking from experience here, having gotten puzzled feedback from friends looking at captionless albums I've published.) Because your photos will initially appear as thumbnails, a caption can also help your audience identify which ones they want to view in more detail.

- To add a caption to a photo, select the picture and type your caption into the **Title** field in the lower-left corner of the screen, as shown in **Figure 35.5**.
- It also helps to display captions beneath the images in the main window — just as they'll appear on your Web page. To do so, make sure

35.5

the **Titles** checkbox in the lower-right corner of the window is checked.

- For best results, keep your captions fairly short (one or two lines at most).

You're now ready to publish your album on the Web. What you do next depends on whether you have a .Mac account, a Web server running on your own computer (see Technique 42), or an account on another Web server. If you don't already have a Web site available, consult the book's Web site (`www.wiley.com/compbooks/kissell`) for some suggestions of hosting companies that will set one up for you.

If you have a .Mac account, move right on to the next section, "Publishing: .Mac." If not, skip to "Publishing: Other Web Servers."

PUBLISHING: .MAC

If you have a .Mac account, publishing your iPhoto album as a Web page takes just a few clicks. This feature alone can make a .Mac account well worth the annual fee.

STEP 3: UPLOAD YOUR PHOTOS TO A .MAC HOME PAGE

To publish an iPhoto album to your .Mac home page:

- If you haven't already done so at some point, enter your .Mac member name and password on the .Mac pane of Internet Preferences.
- Click the **HomePage** button at the bottom of the iPhoto window. A new window appears (see **Figure 35.6**) with a preview of your Web page. In this window, you can edit the name of your album, add a few sentences of explanatory text at the top, and even edit individual captions if you want. (This feature can be handy if your captions turned out to be too long to fit on the thumbnail page.)
- If you want your thumbnails to have a frame, click the icon at the bottom of the window corresponding to the shape you want. The leftmost icon will give you borderless thumbnails.

At the bottom of the window is a pop-up menu labeled **Publish to**. This displays your .Mac username, and — if you've set up multiple Web sites on your .Mac HomePage — the names of the additional sites. By way of explanation, your .Mac account allows you to have multiple Web sites. Each site, in turn, can have multiple albums. By default, all albums will be published to your main HomePage site. But you can separate your albums into multiple sites if you like. For example, your main site might be `homepage.mac.com/yourmembername`. If you add an album called Vacation, it might appear at `homepage.mac.com/yourmembername/PhotoAlbum1.html`. However, you could have two sites — Travel and Family, each with multiple albums. An album of your trip to Paris might appear at

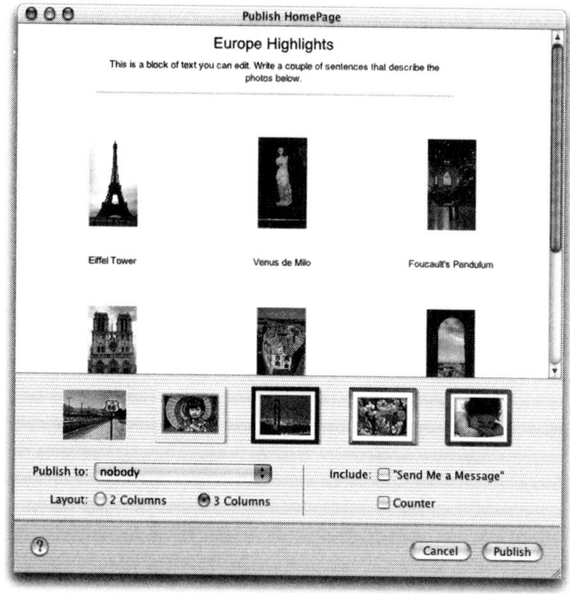

35.6

`homepage.mac.com/yourmembername/Travel/PhotoAlbum2.html`.

To add a new site to your .Mac HomePage:

- Go to `www.mac.com`, log into your account, and click the **HomePage** icon.
- On the right side of the window, click the arrow icon next to **Add another site,** as shown in **Figure 35.7**. The "Create a site" page appears.
- Enter a name for your new site and (if you want) a password and click **Create Site**. Your new site appears in the Sites window on the next page, as shown in **Figure 35.8**.

Each site that appears in this list will also appear in the **Publish to** pop-up menu at the bottom of iPhoto's Publish HomePage window.

- Choose the site you want to use from the **Publish to** menu and click **Publish**. Your pictures will be uploaded, and the next screen (shown in **Figure 35.9**) will show you the URL of your new Web page.

You're done! You can now go back and create additional albums if you want. If you're curious to know how to share your digital photos without a .Mac account, read on.

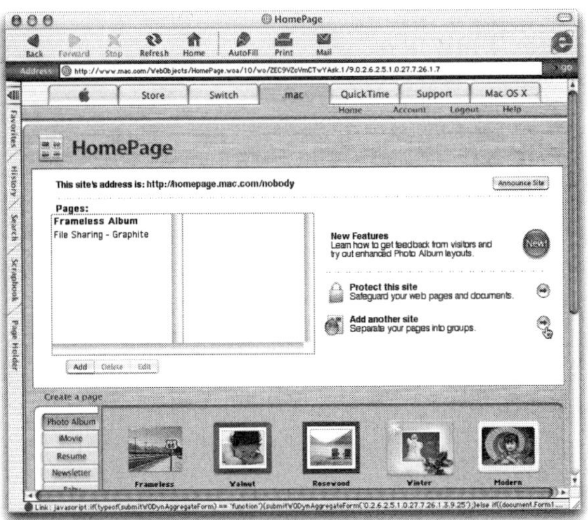

35.7

PUBLISHING: OTHER WEB SERVERS

Although publishing your photos to a .Mac HomePage is very easy, you can also publish them on any other Web server you may have access to — including Personal Web Sharing running on your very own computer. One advantage of using a different server is that you'll typically have much more space available for photos without paying a premium.

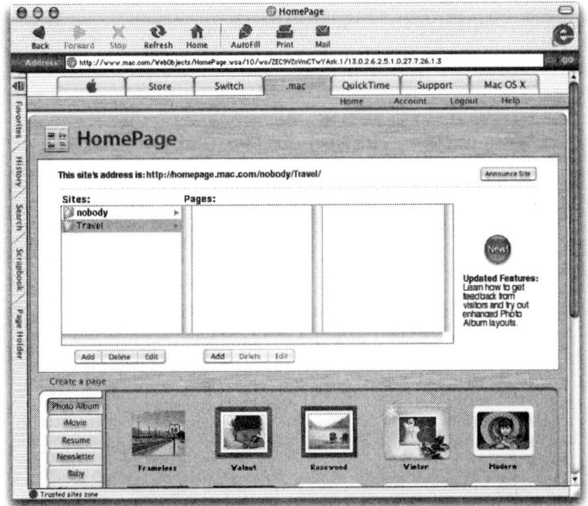

35.8

35.9

Another is that bypassing .Mac gives you more control over the look and feel of your Web pages.

STEP 3: SAVE YOUR PHOTOS AS A WEB ALBUM

To publish an iPhoto album to another Web server:

- Choose **Export...** from the File menu. The Export Photos window will appear; make sure the **Web Page** tab is selected (see **Figure 35.10**).

You define the overall appearance of your exported Web site in the Page section.

- Enter a name for your Web site. This title will appear in the title bar of the thumbnail pages, as well as on the page itself.
- Enter the number of **Columns** and **Rows** of thumbnails you want. (In general, three or four columns and six to ten rows make for a nicely proportioned Web page.) As you change the number of columns and rows, an indicator to the right will tell you the total number of pages that will be created. For example, if you have 33 pictures, at 10 rows of 3 columns, you'll have 2 Pages. You might consider adding just one more row to fit all the pictures on a single page.
- To choose a background color for your Web page (white is the default), click the square button next to **Color** and select a color using the standard color picker. If you would rather use a photo or other graphic as a background, click the **Image** radio button, then navigate to any graphic on your hard drive. The graphic you choose doesn't have to be part of your current album (or even included in iPhoto at all). It will be copied into your Web site for you.

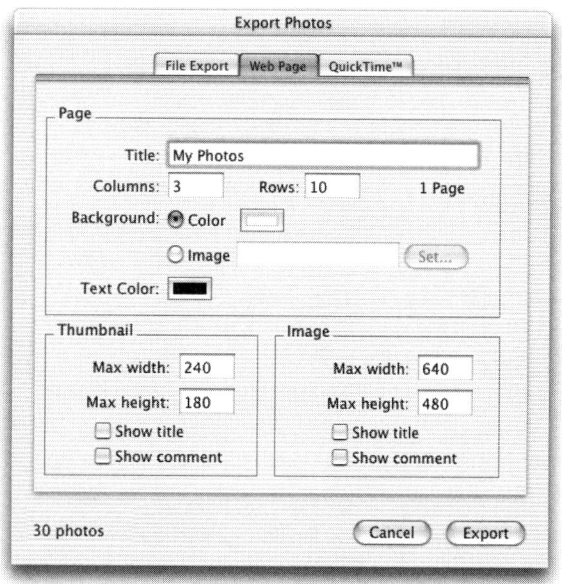

35.10

The Thumbnail section defines the size of the thumbnails (small previews of images) that will appear on your Web page(s). (You'll click the thumbnails to display the full-size images.)

- Enter a maximum dimension (in pixels) for the **Width** and **Height** of your thumbnails. If your thumbnails are too large, your site will take a long time to load; too small, and viewers won't be able to tell what they are. In most cases, the default measurements (240 × 180) are adequate.
- If you wish, check the boxes for **Show title**, **Show comment**, or both to display captions under the thumbnail images.

The Image section defines the attributes of the images that will be shown when a viewer clicks a thumbnail.

- Enter a maximum dimension (in pixels) for the **Width** and **Height** of your images. iPhoto will automatically scale your pictures to the correct size when they're exported. Although your digital camera might create much larger, higher-resolution images, these generally do not work well on Web pages because viewers may have to scroll to see the entire picture. Choosing dimensions that fit inside an average-sized Web page window without scrolling gives you the best results. If the default values (640 × 480) are too small, enter higher numbers, such as 800 × 600. (Remember: Even though your overall screen might have a higher resolution like 1024 × 768 pixels, the usable area of a Web browser window will be considerably smaller.)

■ If you wish, check the boxes for **Show title**, **Show comment**, or both to display captions under the full-size images.

■ When you've set all the options to your liking, click **Export**. Navigate to the location where you want your files to be saved and click the **New Folder** button and give the folder a name (such as Vacation). Then select your newly created folder in the list and click **OK**. iPhoto then generates the images, thumbnails, and HTML pages in the correct sizes, storing them in the new folder. (See **Figure 35.11** for an example.)

STEP 4: PUT YOUR ALBUM ON A WEB SERVER

Your Web album is now ready to go. If you want to preview it before putting it on a Web server, open the folder you just created and double-click the file **index.html**. Your album will open in your default Web browser.

If you're using Personal Web Sharing, you can publish your album simply by moving it to a new location on your hard drive. You have two choices:

■ To put your new album on the main level of your Web site, move the entire album folder (containing index.html and the folders of Pages, Images, and Thumbnails) into the folder /Library/WebServer/Documents. If your folder is named "vacation," other people could then view it by entering **http://*your-computer's-address*/vacation/** in their Web browser. (Don't forget the trailing slash at the end — it's important.)

■ To put your album within your personal area on your computer's Web site, move the entire album folder into ~/Sites. In this case, if your folder is named "vacation," other people would view it by pointing their browsers to **http://*your-computer's-address*/~*yourusername*/vacation/**.

If you use an outside ISP to host your Web site, you'll need to upload your new album folder to their server.

■ Most ISPs provide an FTP site where Web pages can be uploaded. The easiest way to do this is to choose **Go to Server...** from the Finder's **Go** menu. In the **Address** field, type the address of the FTP server provided by your ISP. It should begin with ftp:// — the entire address might be something like **ftp://ftp.my-isp.com/~myusername/**. Then click **Connect**. An Authentication window appears; enter the user name and password provided by your ISP. Your FTP site will then appear as a volume on your desktop.

■ Navigate to the desired location in the FTP volume and drag your album folder in to copy the files. Your album will be immediately available on your Web site; the exact URL will be your main Web site's URL followed by a slash and your album folder name.

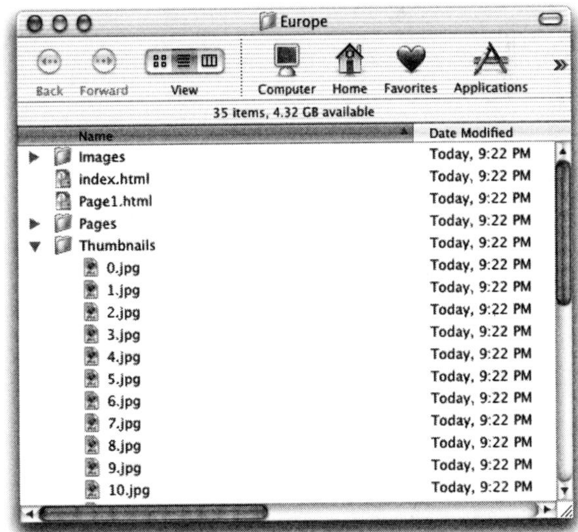

35.11

TECHNIQUE **36**

CREATING A VIDEO PHOTO ALBUM WITH iMOVIE

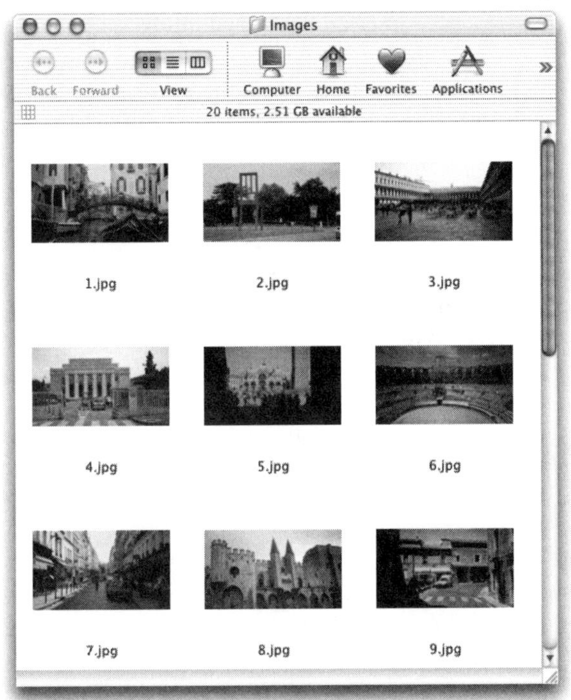

36.1

36.2

ABOUT THE FEATURE

Apple's entry-level video editing software, iMovie, is not just for camcorder owners. You can also create movies from still photos — complete with dissolves, soundtrack, titles, and special effects.

If you have a digital camcorder, you've probably discovered iMovie — an easy-to-use video editing application that lets you create professional quality movies from your home video footage. But you can also use all of iMovie's advanced tools — transitions, audio recording, titles, and special effects — with still images. More importantly, in iMovie 3 Apple has added a remarkable tool called the Ken Burns effect, which allows you to turn individual photos into moving images. A movie created from photos in this way can make a thoughtful gift or a compelling presentation. It's also a lot of fun! If you've been wondering what to do with those vacation photos or baby pictures, a video photo album might be just the thing.

Video photo albums go way beyond the simple slide shows you can create with iPhoto (or iDVD, for that matter). Instead of being restricted to a single time delay for all photos and a single background music track, you can freely mix and match transitions, sound effects, narration, and other embellishments with complete control over the final product. And you can easily package your finished movie on a DVD or as a downloadable QuickTime movie.

STEP 1: PREPARE YOUR PHOTOS

In this technique, I assume you're using iPhoto to organize your photos. (If you're not, you can import them into iPhoto simply by dragging a folder of pictures onto the iPhoto window.) Your first step is to organize your photos and get them into a format that will work well in iMovie.

- Create an album in iPhoto to hold the photos you'll use in your new movie. (If you need specific details on how to do that, refer to Technique 35.) Note that captions are not needed, and the order of your photos within the album does not matter.

You'll probably want to make sure your pictures are all in landscape format (wider than they are tall). Any photos in portrait format will appear with black bands on both sides in your movie. You may also want to give each picture an aspect ratio of 4:3 (four units of width to three units of height) so that it will match the shape of your TV screen when viewed at full size.

- To crop a photo so that it has a 4:3 aspect ratio, select the photo and click the **Edit** button below the photo window. This puts iPhoto into editing mode. You'll see a pop-up menu in the lower-left corner labeled **Constrain**. From this menu, choose **4 x 3 (Book,DVD)**. Then position the crosshair pointer at one edge of the photo and drag across it, as shown in **Figure 36.3,** to create a selection with a 4:3 aspect ratio. (If you don't get it right the first time, just click outside the selection and drag again to create a new selection.) If necessary, you can reposition the selected area simply by clicking it and dragging it up or down. When you're happy with the selected area, click the **Crop** button to crop your image to the selected size and shape.
- You can now quit iPhoto. (iDVD 3 added the capability to read iPhoto albums without having

36.3

to go through an additional step of exporting them.)

STEP 2: IMPORT AND ARRANGE PHOTOS

Now that your photos have been prepared, it's time to bring them into iMovie and arrange them to form the sequence you want in your movie. This used to be a multi-step process, but the tight integration between iMovie 3 and iPhoto 2 makes it much easier.

- Open iMovie. Choose **New Project...** from the **File** menu and give your movie a name.
- Click the **Photos** button on the toolbar. Thumbnails of your iPhoto library will appear in the window (see **Figure 36.4**). From the pop-up menu above the thumbnails, choose the album you want to use (as shown in **Figure 36.5**).

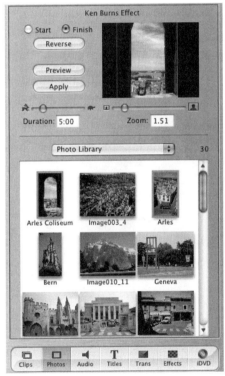

36.4

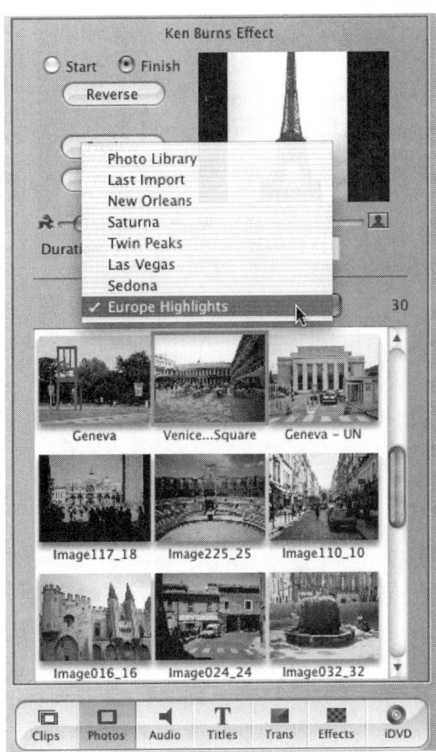

36.5

- Drag the thumbnails onto the clip viewer (the horizontal area at the bottom of the window) in the order in which you want them to appear (see **Figure 36.6**). You can rearrange them simply by clicking and dragging.

STEP 3: APPLY THE KEN BURNS EFFECT

iPhoto 2 added a very cool and powerful tool for creating video photo albums: the Ken Burns effect. This effect allows you to turn any still photograph into a moving image using a combination of panning and zooming. For example, you can start with the image zoomed in to show a face in the lower-left corner and then slowly zoom out to full size while panning across to the right. Using this effect — especially in combination with titles, music, and other visual effects — can add impact and interest to your photo album, taking it far beyond a mere slide show. To apply the Ken Burns Effect:

- Make sure the **Photos** button is selected on your iMovie toolbar. Select a photo (either from the thumbnail list or the clip viewer).
- Click the **Start** radio button at the top of the window to define how your image will be positioned when it initially appears (see **Figure 36.7**). Use the **Zoom** slider to change the starting magnification of the image, and drag the image preview to position the image on the screen.
- Click the **Finish** radio button to define how your image will be positioned at the end of the transition. Again, adjust the **Zoom** slider and drag the image to the desired location. You do not need to set up the intermediate points between Start and Finish; iPhoto will figure that out for you.
- By default, each photo displays for five seconds, during which time the image pans and zooms from your Start position to the End position. To change the effect duration for any photo, select it and enter a new value in the **Duration** box (or move the **Duration** slider to the left for a faster effect or to the right for a slower effect). Keep in

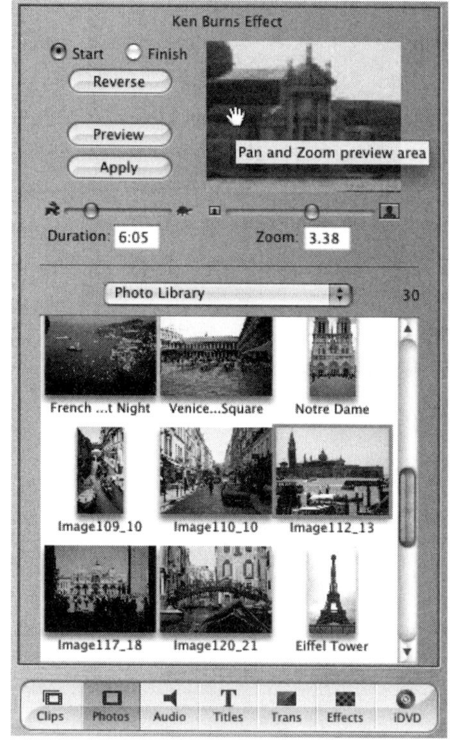

36.7

36.6

mind that the duration is listed in seconds, not minutes; to make a photo display for ten seconds, you enter "10:00," not "0:10."

■ If you want to see what your effect will look like using the thumbnail, click the **Preview** button.

■ When you have the effect set up the way you want it, click **Apply**. If the photo you selected was not already on the clip viewer, iMovie will add it for you as the last picture in the sequence. A red progress bar across the photo on the clip viewer indicates that iMovie is rendering your motion effect.

■ As you build your movie, you may want to preview longer sections of it to see how all the pieces fit together. To do so, select the item(s) in the clip viewer you want to see and click the Play button on the main viewer window.

STEP 4: ADD OTHER EFFECTS (OPTIONAL)

iMovie allows clips — or in this case, photos — to have other special effects, such as sepia tone, lens flare, fog, or soft focus. Use effects sparingly; too many can ruin the impact of an otherwise fine movie. But used judiciously — a black-and-white photo here, a little sharpening there — effects can add more appeal to your still photos.

■ Click the **Effects** button on the toolbar to display the available Effects (see **Figure 36.8**). To add an effect, first select a clip in the clip viewer, then click an effect in the list and adjust the parameters to your liking. To see how your effect looks on the full-size image, click the **Preview** button. When you're happy with the appearance, click **Apply** to apply the effect to the clip.

A given photo can include both the Ken Burns effect and other special effects, but the Ken Burns effect is always applied first. For example, if you use the Fairy Dust effect, it will always appear in the same position within the frame; it will not zoom or pan along with the rest of the image.

■ Repeat this step to add effects to multiple photos.

NOTE

iMovie 3 includes an extensive set of effects, transitions, and sound effects. To download more for free from Apple, visit `www.apple.com/imovie` **and follow the links for Video Plug-Ins in the "iMovie Downloads" section. You can also purchase effects and transitions from a number of third-party vendors. Check the book's Web site (**`www.wiley.com/compbooks/kissell`**) for some suggestions.**

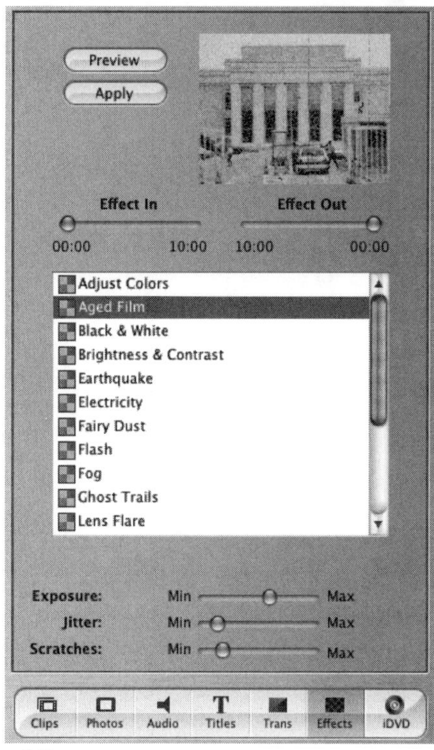

36.8

STEP 5: ADD TRANSITIONS

iMovie enables you to make your presentation even more interesting by putting transitions such as fades, wipes, and dissolves between your photos.

- Click the **Trans** button on the toolbar to display the available Transitions (see **Figure 36.9**). With a photo selected in the clip viewer, you can try out different transitions and adjust the speed (and, in some cases, the direction) of the transition. When you're satisfied with the result, add the transition to your movie by clicking it and dragging it to the clip viewer between two photos. (Suggestion: Keep transitions relatively short. With still photos, lengthy transitions can be distracting.)
- Repeat this to add transitions between additional pairs of photos. To remove a transition, select it in the clip viewer and press **Delete**.

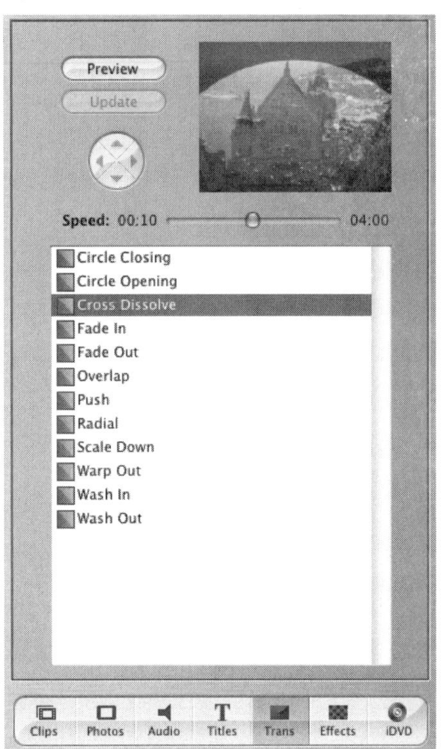

36.9

STEP 6: ADD TITLES

Your movie can include titles, ranging from a simple title at the beginning of the presentation to a caption on each photo or even a complete list of rolling credits.

- Click the **Titles** button on the toolbar to display the available Titles (see **Figure 36.10**).
- Select a title from the list to preview its appearance in the thumbnail image. Each title has a different range of options you can set, such as the text itself, the color, speed, direction, and so forth. Experiment to find the combination that looks best to you.
- To add a finished title to your movie, drag the title name onto the clip viewer at the location where you want it to begin, as shown in **Figure 36.11**.

STEP 7: ADD A SOUNDTRACK

An audio background can make your video photo album more interesting. Your soundtrack can include music, sound effects, your own narration, or any combination of these.

- Click the **Audio** button on the toolbar to display the audio controls. To add audio to your movie, you'll need to switch from clip viewer to the timeline view. Do so by clicking the clock icon.

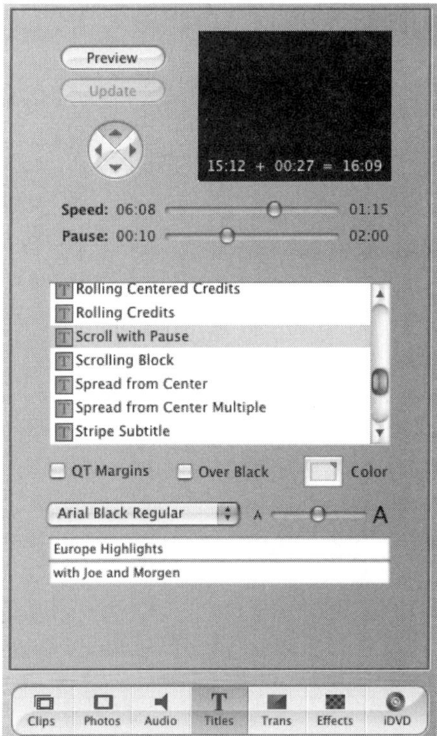

36.10

Figure 36.12 shows a movie's timeline and the Audio shelf.

■ Apple provides a large number of built-in sound effects, such as laughter, applause, and a film projector. To add a sound effect to your movie, drag the sound onto one of the audio tracks in the timeline at the point you want it to begin. If you want to find additional sound effects (as well as some free background music), visit `www.apple.com/imovie` and look for Audio Effects in the "iMovie Downloads" section.

■ To add your own narration to a movie, you need a microphone attached to your Mac. (For best results, use an external microphone so it doesn't pick up the sound of your computer's fan or hard drive.) Click the **Record** button (the round red button to the right of the Microphone level graph) to record your narration; click the **Record** button again when you're finished. Your narration appears as a colored box on one of the audio tracks in the timeline. You can move it to another location if you want, or add additional voice comments.

36.11

36.12

■ If you want to add a musical soundtrack, iMovie can use any MP3 file from your iTunes collection. Choose **iTunes Library** (or one of your iTunes playlists) from the pop-up menu at the top of the **Audio** shelf (as shown in **Figure 36.13**) to display the songs from your iTunes library. Scroll to the song you want to use, then drag it onto one of the audio tracks. (You can do the same thing for songs on an audio CD — without converting them to MP3 format first — by choosing **Audio CD** from the pop-up menu.) As with voice recordings, you can reposition the song to begin at any point. To use only a portion of a song, click the arrow at the left or right end of the purple song box on the timeline and drag it inward.

36.13

■ You can arrange any number of songs, voice recordings, and sound effects on either of the two available audio tracks. If you have multiple sounds being played at the same time, you may want to adjust their relative volume. To change the volume of an audio clip, check the **Edit volume** box at the bottom of the window. A horizontal line representing volume will appear on each of the audio tracks (as well as on the video track, for video clips with sound). To change the volume of any track, click on the line at the point where you want the volume to change and drag upward to increase the volume or downward to decrease it. **Figure 36.14** shows an example.

STEP 8: SAVE AND EXPORT YOUR MOVIE

After adding effects, transitions, titles, and audio, you'll want to preview your movie to see how the finished product looks — and perhaps make some last-minute changes. When you're satisfied with the finished product, you're ready to package it in a format other people can use.

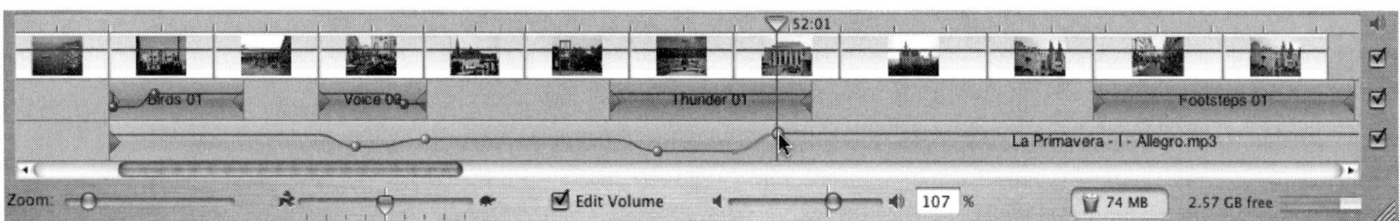

36.14

- First, choose **Save Project** from the **File** menu to save your movie project in iMovie format so you can go back and edit it later.
- If you're planning to put your movie on a DVD with iDVD, you don't need to do anything further; iMovie automatically saves files in such a way that iDVD can read them automatically.
- If you want to put your movie on a Web site or e-mail it to a friend, choose **Export Movie...** from the **File** menu. The Export Movie dialog appears, as shown in **Figure 36.15**. Then choose **To QuickTime** from the **Export** menu. Select a quality setting from the **Format** menu and click **Export**. Choose a filename and a location, and your movie will be saved in QuickTime format, ready for use.

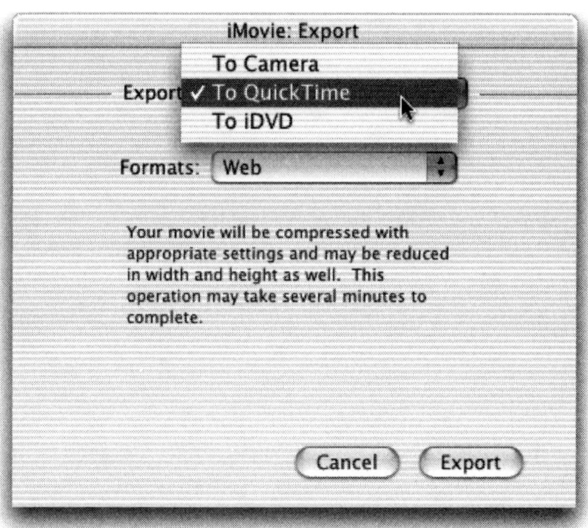

36.15

TECHNIQUE

DESIGNING A CUSTOM iDVD MOTION MENU THEME

37.1

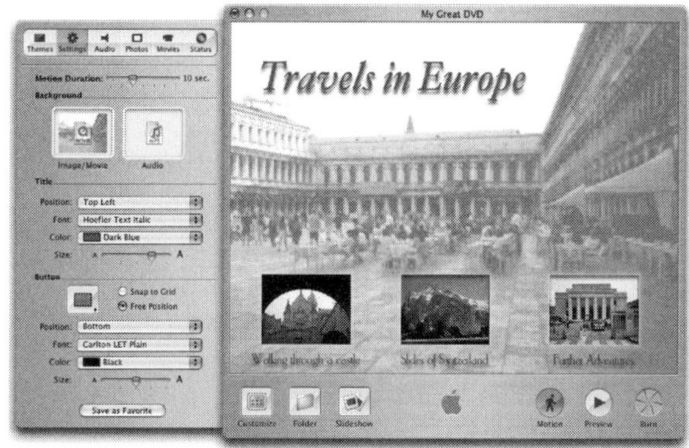

37.2

ABOUT THE FEATURE

A theme is a collection of graphics, video clips, and music that make up the background and buttons for DVDs you create. iDVD includes some outstanding prebuilt themes, but you can also design your own, for a uniquely customized DVD.

If you have a SuperDrive-equipped Mac, you can create DVDs that can be played on almost any standard set-top player. Your custom DVDs can contain movies you've created in iMovie, video photo albums (see Technique 36), or simple slide shows. All of these elements are tied together with a menu — the series of controls shown when you pop the DVD into your player. Like commercial DVDs, your custom DVDs can have highly dynamic menu screens, with moving images on the background and individual buttons, a musical accompaniment, and your choice of font and layout.

Apple provides an assortment of *themes* — some quite elaborate and flashy — to provide your DVD with its overall look and feel. But you can also create a completely new and unique theme. Although Apple does not provide the tools to give your custom theme the sophisticated features of, say, the Theater, Projector, or Picture In Picture themes, you can still create something novel and visually appealing. Whether you're looking for a unique feel for your home movies or a professional layout that emphasizes your corporate brand, a custom motion menu theme is just a few steps away.

STEP 1: PREPARE BACKGROUND MOVIE

The background movie will fill the entire screen; your buttons will float on top of it. It will play in a short loop (anywhere from 1 second to 30 seconds before repeating). In principle, you can use any movie, but for best results, you should prepare a special movie clip in iMovie just for this purpose. When selecting a clip to use, keep these things in mind:

- Part of your movie will be covered by buttons (which are playing their own mini-movies). So you'll get the best results with a movie clip that includes large background areas (sky, water, walls, and so on). If the entire clip consists of, say, faces, positioning the buttons without covering up an important part of the screen will be hard.
- Too much motion makes for a distracting background. Slow, gentle motions (such as ocean waves crashing on a beach, or a panoramic view of a landscape) work well.
- If your movie has lots of contrast, picking out the buttons and text labels from the movie can be hard. Scenes that have a consistent shade are better — and, in general, lighter colors produce better results than darker colors.

After you've chosen a movie to work with, you'll want to give it some special treatment in iMovie.

- Open (or create) the movie you want to use in iMovie. Your first job is to select a segment of the movie, no longer than 30 seconds in length (the maximum length of a loop in iDVD).
- Once you've trimmed your movie to a short segment, consider applying effects such as Black and White, Sepia Tone, or Soft Focus. All these effects can make the background less distracting and more professional looking. If your chosen clip is high in contrast, use the Brightness/Contrast effect to reduce the contrast (and, perhaps, increase the brightness).
- When you're finished with your movie, choose **Save Project** from the **File** menu. There's no need to export it as a separate file; movies saved in iMovie are automatically available from within iDVD 3.

STEP 2: PREPARE BUTTON MOVIES

Buttons in iDVD can do one of three things: play a movie, start a slide show, or open a folder containing yet another menu of choices. When you add a movie to iDVD, its button automatically plays a preview of the movie. However, even folders and slide shows can have moving buttons. If you want to add a movie preview to a button that's ordinarily static, once again you'll use iMovie.

- Using iMovie, open (or create) the movie you want to turn into a button. Because the button will be fairly small on the screen, select a movie clip without a lot of small details. You'll get good results if your clip features a single subject (such as a person's face or a well-known building) that fills most of the screen.
- Trim the movie to a relatively short segment — 30 seconds or less. If you use a longer movie, iDVD will still only play a short loop. Because the movies you add to buttons reduce the total amount of space available on the DVD, it doesn't hurt to keep it as short as you can.
- As with the background movie, save the project by choosing **Save Project** from the **File** menu. It will be available in iDVD without any further steps.

STEP 3: CUSTOMIZE YOUR DVD BACKGROUND

Prior to iDVD 3, the method for creating a full-motion background was a bit cumbersome: It required exporting a movie, locating it in the Finder, and dragging it into iDVD. Now the procedure is considerably easier.

- Open iDVD, choose **New Project...** from the **File** menu, and select a name and location for your DVD project.
- If the Customize drawer isn't visible, click the **Customize** button at the bottom of the window to display it. Click the **Movies** button, as shown in **Figure 37.3**.
- Drag the background movie file you created in Step 1 from the list up to the **Settings** button (see **Figure 37.4**), then — without releasing the mouse button — back down into the **Image/Movie** area in the Customize drawer, as shown in **Figure 37.5**. Your background movie will cover the background area, and if the **Motion** button is activated, it will also begin playing in the preview window. Initially, your movie will be set to play in a loop equal in length to the overall movie (if 30 seconds or less). To change the length of your movie segment, adjust the **Movie Duration** slider. (Note: The motion duration you choose using this slider applies to both the background movie and the individual button movies.) If you want to stop the background movie from playing while you work on the rest of your movie, click the **Motion** button to disable it.

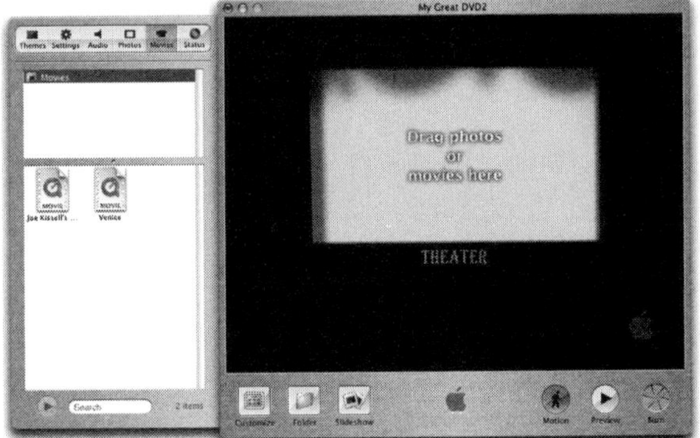

37.3

STEP 4: ADD BACKGROUND MUSIC

Along with a moving background, you can have music playing in a short loop while your DVD menu is displayed.

- In the Customize drawer, click the **Audio** button. iDVD will display the contents of your iTunes

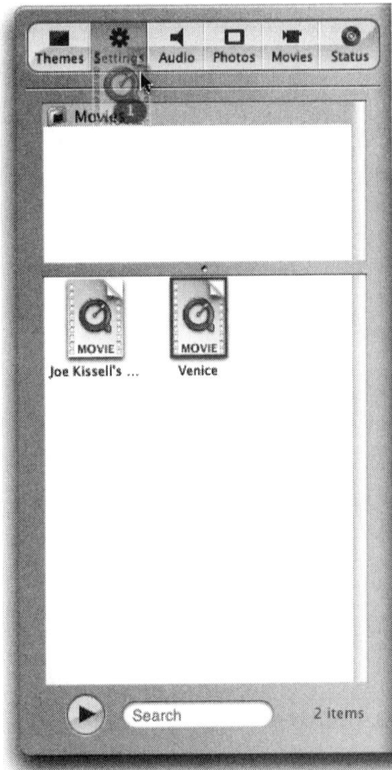

37.4

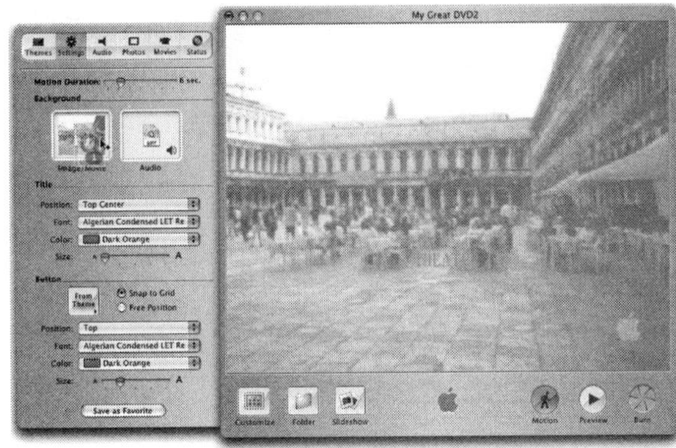

37.5

library, including your playlists. From this list, select an MP3 file to use as background music. For best results, choose an instrumental piece (or at least a song with a 30-second instrumental section). If you don't have any appropriate music, visit `www.freeplaymusic.com` for a wide selection of free music clips you can download.

- Drag the MP3 file from the Customize drawer directly onto the background of the DVD, as shown in **Figure 37.6**. To preview the audio (along with the movies), click the **Motion** button. The length of the audio loop will be the same as the length of the movie loops, as specified by the Movie Duration slider on the Settings pane.

STEP 5: ADD CONTENT TO YOUR DVD

Now that you have the preliminary work done, you can begin adding content to your DVD. If you've made other DVDs with iDVD, the procedure is basically the same, except for a few details. I won't go into all the specifics of iDVD operation here. If you need further instructions, choose **iDVD Help** from the **Help** menu.

37.6

- To add a movie, click the **Movies** button in the Customize drawer, select a movie, and drag it into the preview window. To add a slide show, click the **Photos** button to display your iPhoto library. Select a photo album and drag it into the preview window. To add a folder (which can contain other movies, slide shows, and folders), click the **Folder** button. **Figure 37.7** shows a DVD preview window with a movie, a slide show, and a folder. For more details on settings for slide shows and folders, consult the **iDVD Help**.
- Click and drag buttons to arrange them on the background. Click the title and captions on the preview window to fill in your own text. Using the controls on the Settings pane of the Customize drawer, adjust the fonts, colors, sizes, and alignment of your title and caption text. These controls are all self-explanatory, so I won't go into further detail here.

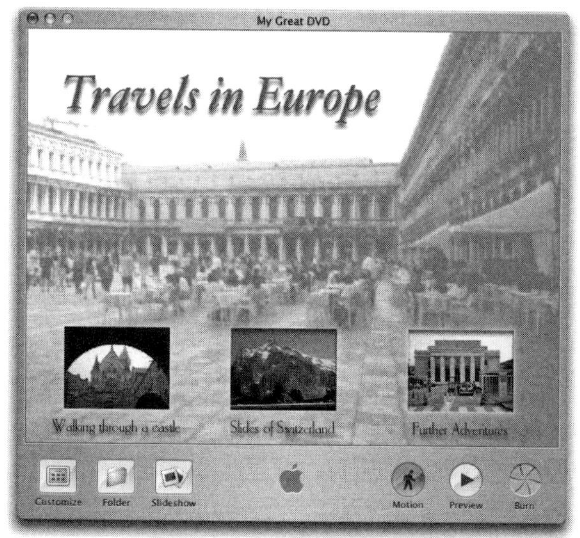

37.7

- To change the frame for your buttons, choose a different shape from the pop-up Frame menu in the Button section of the Settings pane. All buttons on your screen must have the same frame type.
- If your DVD contains movies, their buttons will automatically display a full-motion preview. When you select a movie button, a slider appears, as shown in **Figure 37.8.** You can move this slider to select a starting point for your movie. It will play from that point for the number of seconds specified on the Movie Duration slider and loop back to that starting point.
- To add the previews you created in Step 2 to folder and slide show buttons, just drag the movie files from the Movies pane in the Customize drawer onto the buttons in the preview window.

NOTE

You may be wondering whether you can also customize the frames for your buttons. Technically, it can be done — but it requires Photoshop, a bit of time, and a willingness to modify part of the iDVD application itself. In other words, it's not for the faint of heart — and it's a more complex procedure than I can cover in this technique. If you're really curious, visit the book's Web site (`www.wiley.com/compbooks/kissell`) for a link to online instructions.

STEP 6: BURN YOUR DVD

Before burning your DVD, be sure the Motion button is activated — your movies and background audio should be playing. If the motion is stopped when you burn your DVD, you'll get only still images on the final product.

- Click the **Burn** button and insert a blank DVD to save your creation.
- If you want to be able to edit your project later (or burn additional DVDs), be sure to choose **Save Project** from the **File** menu.

STEP 7: SAVE YOUR THEME AS A FAVORITE

All your customized settings — background movie and sound, fonts, colors, and sizes — can be saved to be reused for other DVD projects, just like the themes Apple provides. (Individual buttons, including movie previews, are not saved as part of a theme.)

37.8

■ With the Customize drawer open, click the **Settings** button.
■ Click the **Save in Favorites...** button at the bottom of the Customize drawer.
■ Enter a name for your theme and click **OK**.
■ If you click the **Themes** button and choose **Favorites** from the pop-up menu, you'll see your new theme there (see **Figure 37.9**). To apply this theme to any future iDVD project, select it from this list.

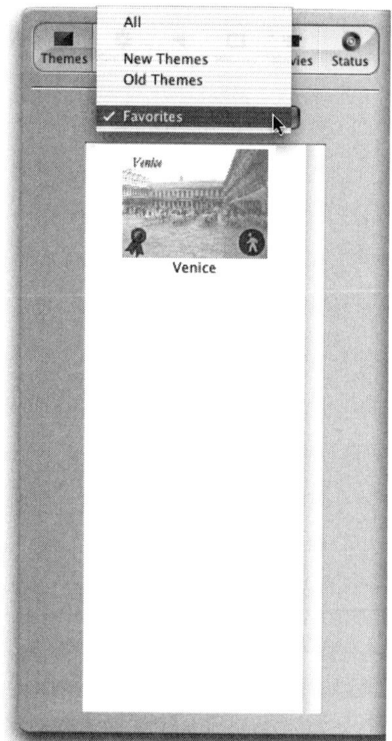

37.9

TECHNIQUE **38**

INTEGRATING iCHAT WITH MAIL AND ADDRESS BOOK

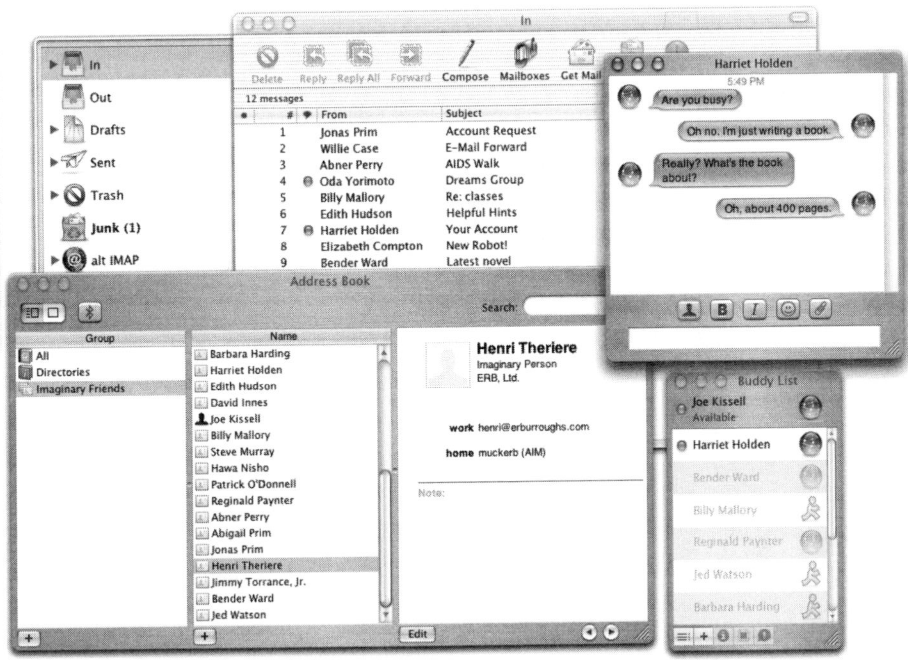

38.1

ABOUT THE FEATURE

By itself, iChat is a very cool instant messaging program. But the combination of iChat, Mail, and Address Book gives you a powerful integrated communication tool.

Apple's iChat instant messaging (IM) program allows you to communicate with your friends and workers with real-time text messages. But unlike other IM applications, iChat makes sending graphics, URLs, and fully styled text messages easy — all with Apple's trademark Aqua user interface.

Making iChat even more powerful is the way it can work together with Mail and Address Book. You can, for example, see whether the person who just sent you e-mail is logged in and if so, initiate an iChat session with just one click — or send an e-mail from within iChat. You can also create a Buddy List easily from entries in your Address Book, even if Address Book isn't open. Understanding how these three applications work together or how to move information from one program to another is not always easy. Never fear: This technique makes it all clear.

STEP 1: ADD IM ADDRESSES TO ADDRESS BOOK

The first step in getting iChat to work with Address Book is to make sure you have IM addresses listed for your contacts that have IM accounts. iChat supports several different kinds of IM addresses: Mac.com addresses, AOL Instant Messenger (AIM) screen names, and Netscape user names. You can enter any or all of these for a given contact.

- Open Address Book and select a contact. Click the **Edit** button to make the contact information editable.
- To add an IM address, look for a field with the letters AIM in light gray followed by "(AIM)." Click in this field and type the contact's AIM screen name or Netscape user name, as shown in **Figure 38.2**. (If the contact already has a Mac.com address listed as an e-mail address, you don't need to add it again.)
- If your contact has more than one AIM/ Netscape account, click the round + icon to the left of the first address and enter the additional user name in the next line.
- If you or one of your contacts needs an AIM screen name and doesn't already have one, have that person go to `aim.aol.com`, click the **New Users Click Here** button, and fill out the online form to set up a free account.

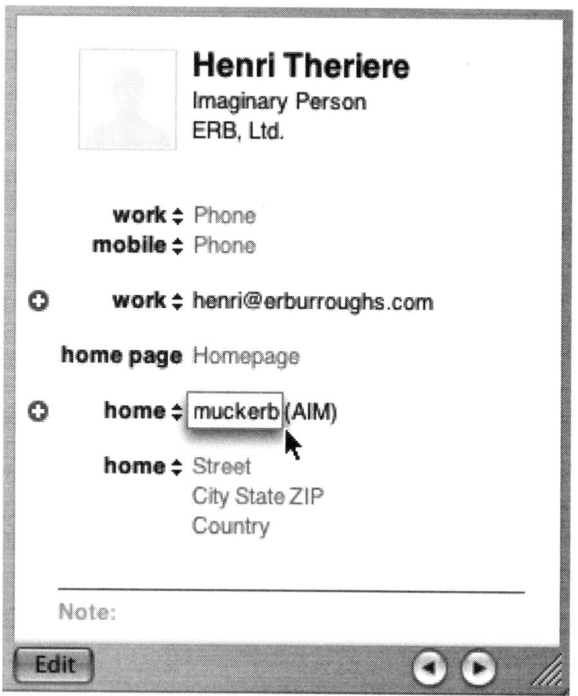

38.2

STEP 2: CREATE A BUDDY LIST WITH ADDRESS BOOK ENTRIES

After your contacts have IM addresses listed, adding them to your iChat Buddy List is easy. In fact, there are two easy ways to do it. Choose whichever one you prefer.

- If you have both Address Book and your iChat Buddy List open, select a contact name in Address Book (**⌘+click** to select multiple names) and drag the contact(s) to your Buddy List. This method only works if the contacts have a Mac.com or IM address listed; attempting to add any other kind of address produces an error message.

NOTE

Address Book can store other types of IM addresses, but they're not currently compatible with iChat. To enter a different type of address, choose Add Field from the Card menu, choose Instant Messaging, and then choose ICQ, Jabber, MSN, or Yahoo from the submenu. The appropriate field will be added to the card.

■ If you don't have Address Book open, you can access your entire contact list right from within iChat. Click the + button at the bottom of your Buddy List window. A sheet drops down displaying the contents of your Address Book (see **Figure 38.3**). Select a person's name (you can only select one at a time with this method) and click **Select Buddy**. If that person does not already have an IM address listed, a new sheet will appear prompting you to enter one.

STEP 3: START AN iCHAT SESSION IN MAIL

If you and one of your buddies are both logged in to iChat (or AIM), you can make use of some special features in Mail to make instant messaging even easier. You can see an indication that your buddy is online right in Mail, and you can even reply to the message using iChat.

■ First, be sure you're logged into iChat. To do this, choose **Available** from the iChat bubble menu as shown in **Figure 38.4**.

38.3

■ Next, check to see that Mail is configured correctly. Open Mail and look at the top of your main message list. You should see a column just to the left of From labeled with an iChat-like message bubble. This is your Buddy Availability indicator column. If you don't see this column, choose **Columns** from the **View** menu and choose **Buddy Availability** from the submenu.

■ When your mailbox contains a message from someone who's in your Buddy List — and also logged into iChat or AIM — that person's message will display a green dot in the Buddy Availability column, as shown in **Figure 38.5**. (The green dot will disappear if either you or your buddy log out of iChat/IM.)

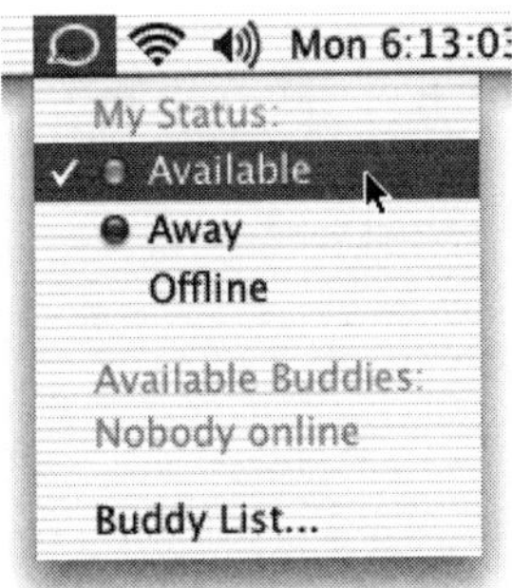

38.4

12 messages

●	#	💬	From	Subject
	1		Jonas Prim	Account Request
	2		Willie Case	E-Mail Forward
	3		Abner Perry	AIDS Walk
	4	●	Oda Yorimoto	Dreams Group
	5		Billy Mallory	Re: classes
	6		Edith Hudson	Helpful Hints
	7	●	Harriet Holden	Your Account
	8		Elizabeth Compton	New Robot!

38.5

- To start an iChat session with this buddy, select the message in Mail's message list and press **⌘+Option+I** (or choose **Reply With iChat** from the **Message** menu).

STEP 4: START AN iCHAT SESSION IN ADDRESS BOOK

Initiating an iChat session right from within Address Book is also easy.

- If you haven't already done so, change your iChat status to **Available.**
- Select a contact's name in Address Book. In his address card, click the label **home** (or **work,** as the case may be) next to the Mac.com or IM address and choose **iChat** from the pop-up menu, as shown in **Figure 38.6.** If the contact is online, a new iChat session will open; if not, an error message will appear.

STEP 5: PUT YOUR PHOTO IN iCHAT AND ADDRESS BOOK

Address Book can store photos of your contacts, and it shares these photos with iChat. If there are people on your Buddy List who include photos of themselves ("buddy icons"), those photos will also appear in Address Book. You can add a photo to your own Address Book record (or someone else's) using iChat, and this may be easier than using Address Book: iChat accepts photos via drag-and-drop or copy-and-paste, whereas Address Book can only read graphics files on disk. To add your photo to iChat and Address Book:

- Open iPhoto. Find a snapshot that includes your face. (Look carefully; there's probably one somewhere. If not, get a friend to snap a photo with your digital camera.)
- Select the photo and drag from the iPhoto window directly to the image area next to your name at the top of the iChat Buddy List. (You may need to reposition your windows so that you can see both iPhoto and your Buddy List at the same time.)
- A Buddy Icon window appears, as shown in **Figure 38.7,** allowing you to resize and/or reposition the image to fit in an iChat-sized square. Use the slider at the bottom of the window to shrink or enlarge the image and click

> **TIP**
>
> **You can also add a Chat icon to your Mail toolbar. To do this, right-click (or Control-click) the toolbar, choose Customize Toolbar... from the pop-up menu, drag the Chat icon onto the toolbar, and click Done. Click this new icon to start an iChat session with a buddy who's sent you a message.**

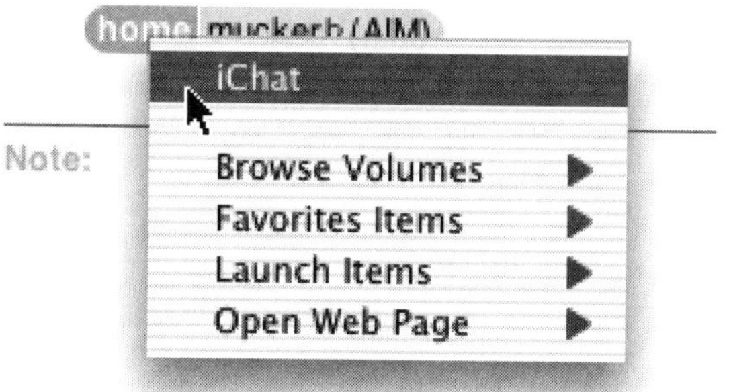

38.6

and drag to reposition it so that your face (with very little margin) shows in the square. After adjusting the picture, click **Done**.

Your picture now appears in iChat and in your Address Book card. You can follow the same procedure to add photos of any of your other contacts. If the contact does not already appear on your Buddy List, add the name to the Buddy List first. (You can delete it from the Buddy List afterward if you want, and the photo will remain in Address Book.)

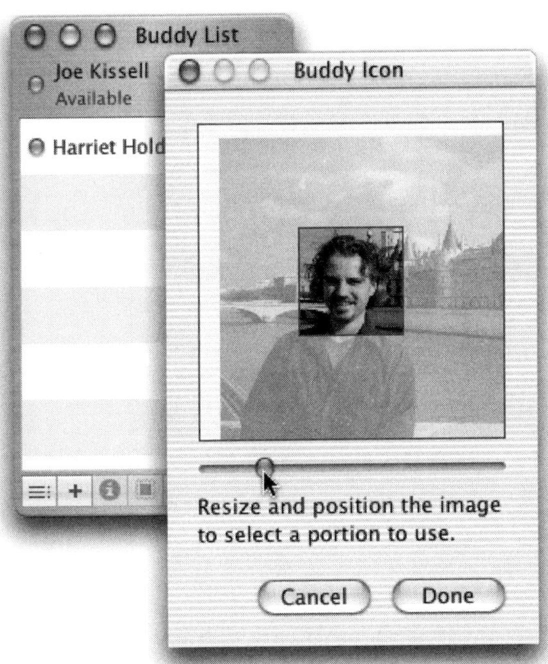

38.7

TECHNIQUE 39

USING iCAL TO MANAGE MEETING SCHEDULES

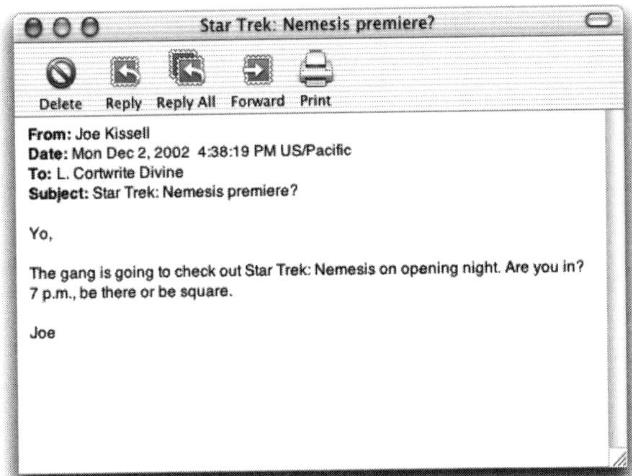

39.1

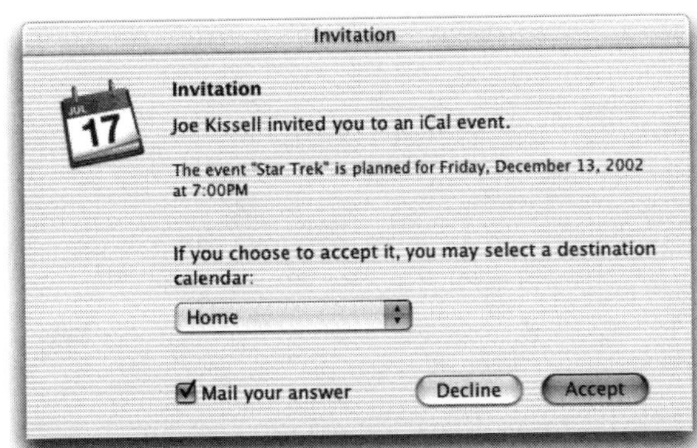

39.2

ABOUT THE FEATURE

Much more than an electronic calendar, iCal lets you share your calendar events with family and friends and subscribe to schedule information for all kinds of events. You can also use it to invite other people to meetings and track their responses.

My wife and I used to keep our family calendar on the refrigerator. This made it easy to see when we had outings and events scheduled — as long as we happened to be standing in the kitchen. More often than not, the times we had questions about each other's schedules were when we were out of the house. Now iCal has changed all that; in addition to a shared family calendar, we subscribe to each other's personal calendars (and synchronize this with our handhelds — see Technique 40), so we can always keep track of our individual and family events.

Although this system works superbly, it's often not practical (especially in a business setting) to share an entire calendar. If I want to schedule a meeting with several colleagues, I probably don't want to see every item on their schedules — or share every item on mine with them. What I really want to do is invite them to join me at a particular time and find out whether each person is available. In this technique, I show you how to use iCal as a tool for scheduling meetings. And remember, a meeting doesn't have to be work-related. It can be a movie, a party, a church gathering, or any event attended by multiple people.

But first, a big disclaimer: In the current version of iCal, meeting invitations (and responses) work *only* if both you and the other attendees are using iCal and Mail on Mac OS X. Other scheduling programs, such as Microsoft Outlook, Meeting Maker, or Now Up-to-Date, don't currently work with iCal. A future version of iCal may eliminate this limitation.

STEP 1: SET UP YOUR CARD IN ADDRESS BOOK

In order to send meeting requests and receive responses, you need to have your own contact info entered correctly in Address Book. If you've already done this, you can skip this step.

- Open Address Book. If there's a contact with your name, select it. Make sure your e-mail address is correct. Also look at the icon next to your name in the contact list. If it looks like the silhouette of a head and shoulders (as in **Figure 39.3**), you can move on to Step 2. If the icon looks just like all the others, choose **This Is My Card** from the **Card** menu to tell Address Book that this information applies to you.
- If there isn't already a contact with your name, add one now, being sure to fill in your correct e-mail address. With your contact record selected, choose **This Is My Card** from the **Card** menu.

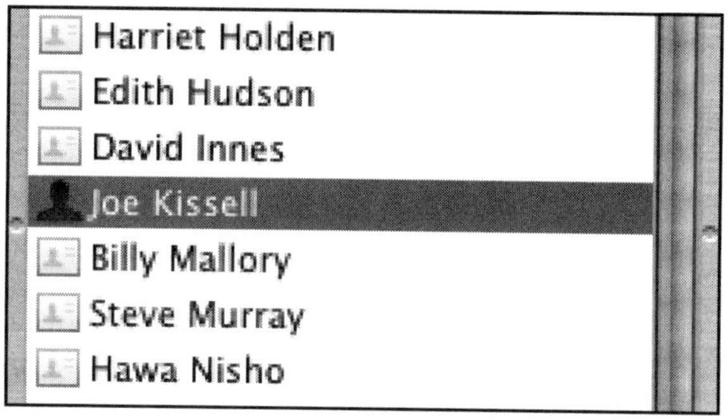

39.3

STEP 2: SET UP CONTACT INFO IN ADDRESS BOOK

You can only send meeting requests to contacts listed in your Address Book.

- To add a new contact, click the + icon below the **Name** column. To edit an existing contact, select the name and click **Edit**.
- Fill in as much information as you can in the Address Card, but at least include the person's name and an e-mail address.
- You can close Address Book when you're done; it does not need to be open when you schedule meetings.

STEP 3: CREATE A NEW EVENT IN iCAL

Now it's time to create an event in iCal. Do this as you would normally; just add an extra step at the end.

- First, select a calendar name. In Day or Week view, you can then click and drag on the calendar to specify the time range of the event. (In Month view, either choose **New Event** from the **File** menu or double-click the blank area on the date of the event.) If you are in Month view, the Event Info window appears automatically (see **Figure 39.4**); in Day or Week view, double-click the event after you've created it to display the Event Info window.
- Enter the date, starting and ending time, and a description of the event.
- To be reminded of the event with an alert, click the **Alarms** button (the one with the bell icon) at the top of the **Event Info** window and choose the message, e-mail, and/or sound you want to use, along with how far in advance you want the alert to appear. The alerts you choose here will also be used for your attendees (though they can modify

them later). If you want to be sure the other parties see (or hear) a reminder notice before the event, be sure to set up an alert now.

- If the meeting is a recurring event (something that happens once a week, for example), click the **Recurrence** button at the top of the window and specify how often the event happens.

STEP 4: INVITE ATTENDEES

After your event is set up, you need just a few more clicks to invite other people.

- Click the **People** button at the top of the **Event Info** window (shown in **Figure 39.5**). This area lists your invitees.
- To display your contact list without opening Address Book, click the **(other) People** button in the bottom-right corner of the main iCal window, or choose **Show People** from the **Window** menu. The People window (shown in **Figure 39.6**) appears.

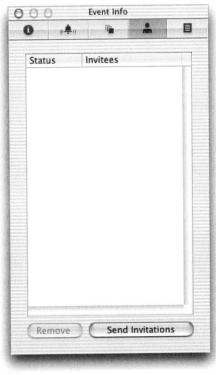

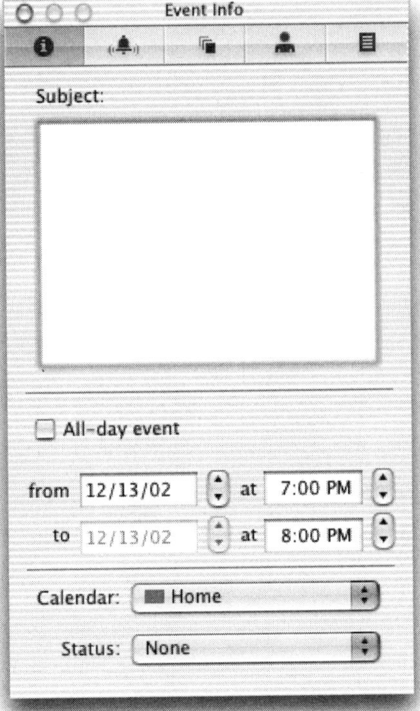

39.4

39.5

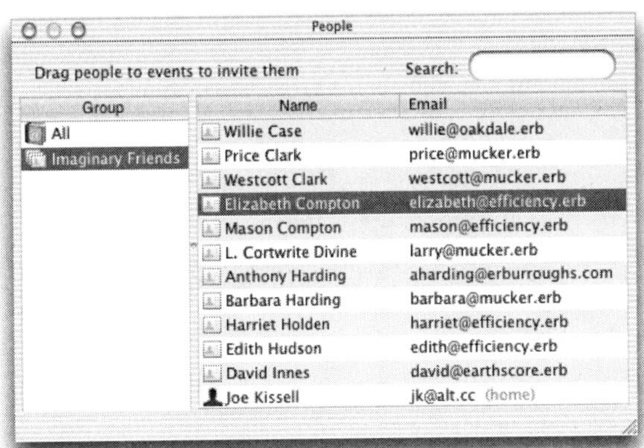

39.6

■ Select invitees from this list. To select multiple people, **⌘+click** their names in the list. When you've made your selections, click and drag the name(s) into the Event Info window, as shown in **Figure 39.7**.

■ Click the **Send Invitations** button. If Mail is not already running, it will open in the background now to send your invitations. The first time you do this, you'll see an AppleScript alert (see **Figure 39.8**). This safety feature is built into Mail to let you know another application is trying to use it to send mail behind the scenes. (You wouldn't want another program — including a virus — to send e-mail without your permission.) You can safely click **OK** to dismiss the alert and allow the mail to be sent. After you've given your permission, Mail will remember it until you quit; the next time you open Mail and try to send an invitation, the alert will appear again. So far, I have not found a way to avoid seeing that alert altogether; if I do, I'll put a note on the book's Web site (`www.wiley.com/compbooks/kissell`).

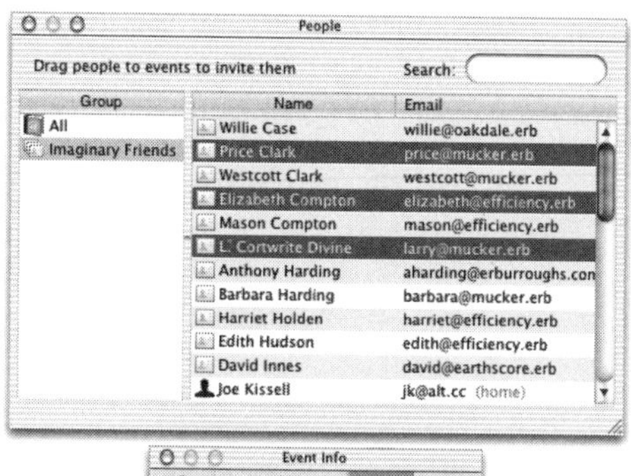

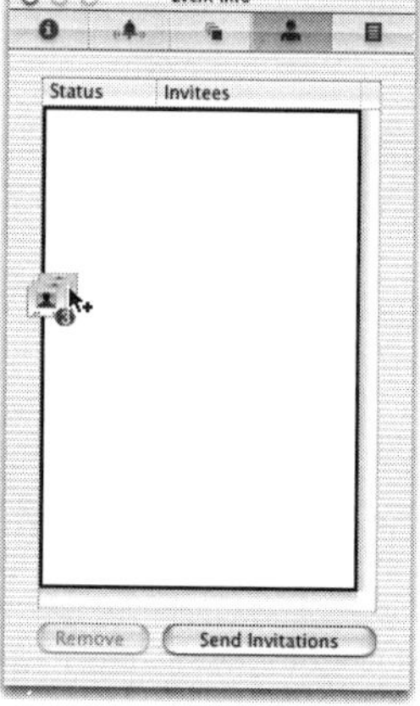

39.7

39.8

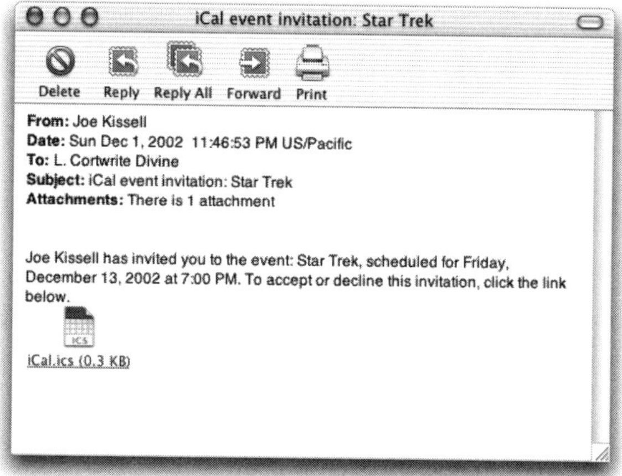

39.9

STEP 5: (FOR ATTENDEES) RESPOND TO INVITATIONS

If you're the person being invited to an event, you'll receive notice by e-mail, as shown in **Figure 39.9**.

- Click the **iCal.ics** icon in the e-mail message. iCal opens (if it's not already running), and a window like the one shown in **Figure 39.10** appears.
- To add this event to your calendar, choose a calendar from the pop-up menu at the bottom and click **Accept**. If you don't want to add the event, click **Decline**.
- If the **Mail your answer** checkbox is checked when you click **Accept** or **Decline**, iCal will open Mail to send your response to the person who invited you. (You can uncheck this box to add the event to your calendar without notifying its originator.) As before, Mail displays an AppleScript alert asking you to confirm that it's OK for another application to use it to send mail. Click **OK**.

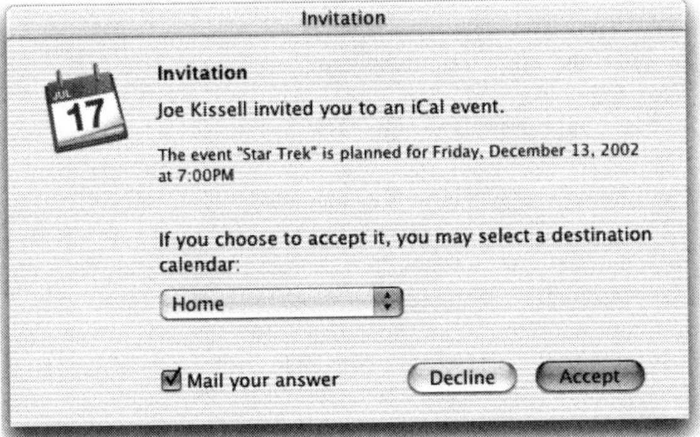

39.10

STEP 6: CHECK ON INVITATION STATUS

After an invitee responds to your invitation, you'll get an e-mail like the one shown in **Figure 39.11**.

- Click the **iCal.ics** icon in the e-mail message. iCal opens (if it's not already running), and a window like the one shown in **Figure 39.12** appears. Click **OK**.
- If you've invited several people to an event and you want to check on everyone's responses to date,

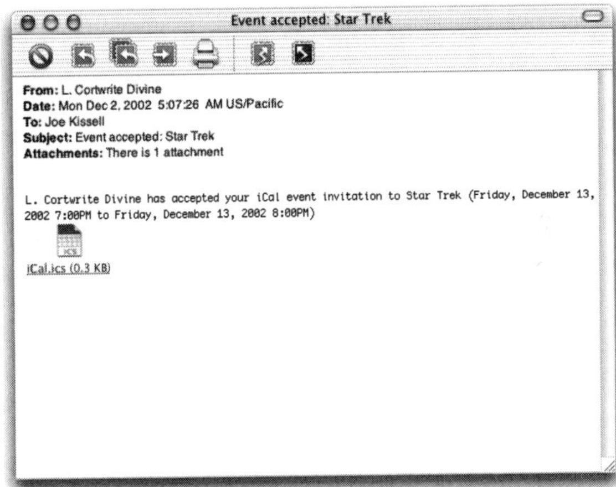

39.11

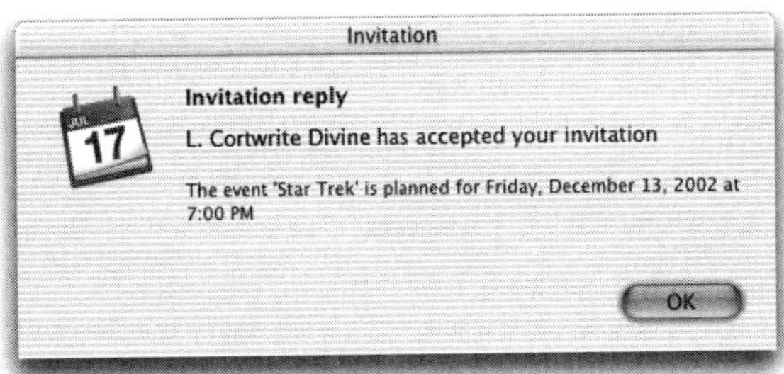

39.12

select the event in iCal and press ⌘+I to open the Event Info window. Click the **People** button at the top of the window to display the list of invitees, as shown in **Figure 39.13**. Next to each person's name will be **Accepted** or **Declined** if the person has responded to you, or **Pending** if no reply has been received yet.

That's all there is to it. Before ending this technique, however, I want you to be aware of a few iCal limitations. I hope these issues will be addressed in a future iCal update.

- If you decide to cancel an event and remove it from your calendar, invitees will not be informed automatically. You'll need to send them a message manually informing them of the change.
- If an invitee accepts your invitation and then later can't make it, you won't be notified automatically. There is a kludgy workaround: The invitee can delete the event from iCal, go back to your e-mail invitation, and click the iCal.ics icon again, this time clicking **Decline**.
- As I mentioned earlier, iCal requires invitees to be using both iCal and Mail; no other calendar or mail program will work. All meeting invitations do contain the name, date, and time of the event in plain text, however, so you can send invitations to other people with the caveat that they'll have a strange enclosure they won't know what to do with.
- There is currently no provision in iCal to schedule meeting rooms or other locations. To inform your invitees where an event will take place, be sure to enter that information in the Event Info window's Subject area.

39.13

TECHNIQUE **40**

KEEPING PDAS, CELL PHONES, AND iPODS IN SYNC WITH iSYNC

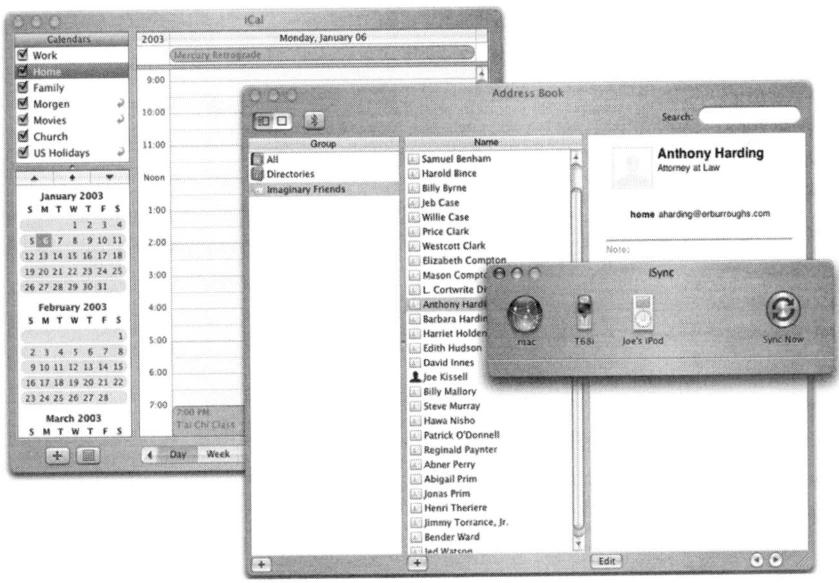

40.1

ABOUT THE FEATURE

iSync is Apple's new synchronization utility to keep contact, schedule, and to-do list data up-to-date on portable electronic devices — as well as other Macs. This ensures that data entered (or edited) on one device will be reflected on all the others.

For a long time, I've used three Macs on a daily basis: my home Mac, my work Mac, and my PowerBook. On each one of them, I need access to my contact and schedule information. I also own an iPod, a Palm organizer, and a cell phone, all of which have the capability of storing and displaying this data. Keeping all these devices updated with the same data used to be nearly impossible. I would make a change on my Palm but then couldn't get it synced to my iPod, or I would make a change on one computer that wasn't reflected on another — or on any of my portable devices.

With iSync, I no longer worry about whether or where I've modified data. With just a few clicks, I can make sure all my Macs and other digital devices have the same information. As wonderful as this is, how to set it all up wasn't entirely obvious — neither was how to deal with the glitches that occasionally arose. In this technique, I show you what I've learned about keeping personal data synchronized across all your digital devices.

STEP 1: INSTALL iSYNC

At some point in the future, iSync may be included as part of Mac OS X. Until then, you'll need to download and install it separately.

- At the risk of stating the obvious, you must have contact data entered in Address Book and/or calendar data entered in iCal to use iSync. If you haven't already added your information to these two applications, do so before proceeding.
- Go to `www.apple.com/isync` to download the iSync software. When the software has finished downloading, double-click the disk image icon to mount the disk image.
- Double-click the **iSync** package icon and follow the prompts to install iSync.
- The iSync application is stored in your Applications folder. For easy access, consider dragging it to the Dock to create a shortcut there.

If you have a Palm OS device, you'll also need to install the iSync conduit for Palm. Before doing this, you must already have HotSync 3.0 or higher and Palm Desktop 4.0 or higher for Mac OS X installed. Make sure you can sync your Palm device to your computer using HotSync before attempting to use it with iSync.

- To install the Palm conduit, double-click the **iSync_palm** package icon and follow the prompts to complete the installation.

NOTE

iSync works with Address Book and iCal, but does not currently support third-party applications such as Microsoft Entourage, Now Contact, or Now Up-to-Date.

STEP 2: SYNC YOUR DATA WITH .MAC (OPTIONAL)

iSync enables you to synchronize the address, to-do list, and calendar information on your computer with a copy on your .Mac account if you have one. There are two main reasons you would want to do this. First, it allows you to keep data on two or more Macs in sync. You can register each of your machines for access to your .Mac account and run iSync on each one. Any changes made to contact or schedule on one machine will then be available to the others. Even if you use only one Mac, though, there's a second reason you might want to sync it with your .Mac account: It effectively provides a backup copy of your data. In the event of a serious problem that destroys the data on your computer, you'll be able to restore your contacts and schedule items easily.

- Open iSync. Initially, the iSync window (shown in **Figure 40.2**) has just two icons: **.mac** and **Sync Now**.
- Click the **.mac** icon. The window expands as shown in **Figure 40.3**.
- Click **Register**. You'll be asked to supply a name for your computer. By default, your computer's name is specified in Sharing Preferences, but you can make it anything you want. Click **Continue**. iSync registers your computer and presents a display like the one in **Figure 40.4**. If you have already registered other Macs, they'll be listed at the bottom.
- The pop-up menu at the top labeled **For first sync** determines what happens the first time you

40.2

use iSync with this device. The default choice, **Merge data on computer and .Mac** is ideal for most users; it ensures that if any records are on your computer that aren't on your .Mac account, they're added — and vice versa. If you want to completely replace the data on the .Mac server with data from your computer, choose **Erase data on .Mac then sync**. Or, if you've already synchronized another device with .Mac and want to overwrite your current data with what's on the server, choose **Erase data on computer then sync**.

■ Click the **Sync Now** button. iSync connects to your .Mac account and synchronizes your computer.

■ To synchronize additional Macs, just repeat this step on each machine. After making changes to your Address Book or iCal on any machine, remember to run iSync again to upload the changes. Then run iSync the next time you use another registered machine to download the changes and apply them to your local copy.

STEP 3: ADD AND CONFIGURE HANDHELD DEVICES

Three types of handheld devices are currently compatible with iSync: iPods; Palm OS handhelds from Palm, Handspring, and Sony; and certain Bluetooth-enabled cell phones. (Synchronizing with a Bluetooth cell phone also requires your Mac to have Bluetooth support, either built-in or by way of an external adapter.) You can synchronize one, two, or all three

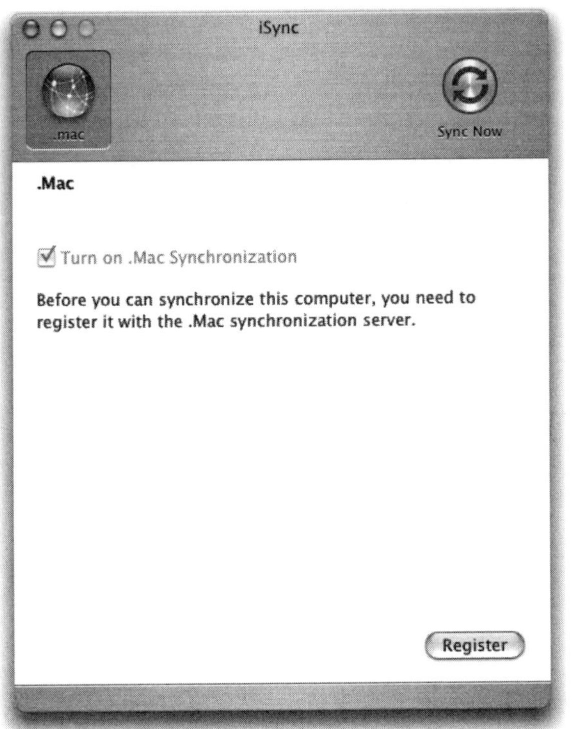

40.3

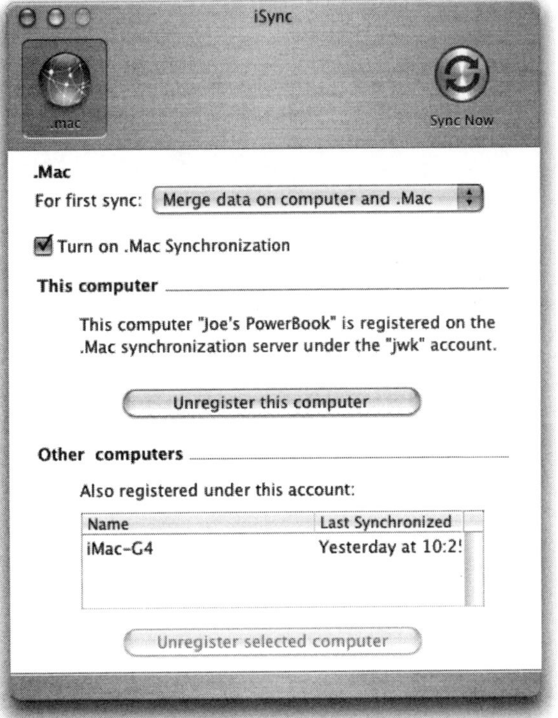

40.4

device types with your Mac. Each device must be added and configured before you can sync it.

To add an iPod, follow these directions:

- Make sure your iPod is connected to your computer. Choose **Add Device...** from the **Devices** menu. iSync scans for available devices and displays them in the Add Device window. Double-click the iPod icon to add it to iSync.
- The iSync window expands to display synchronization options as shown in **Figure 40.5**. The default options are generally what you want. To choose which contacts or calendars are synchronized, use the controls under **Contacts** and **Calendars** to make your selections.

To add a Bluetooth cell phone, you may need to do nothing — if you selected **Synchronize your Contacts and Calendar** when you paired your phone (see Technique 23), it will be added to iSync automatically. If you didn't select this option, follow these steps:

- Make sure your Bluetooth phone is in range and discoverable. (See Technique 23.) Open System Preferences, click the **Bluetooth** icon, and click the **Paired Devices** tab. If your phone is already listed, select it and click **Delete**.
- Click **New...**. Your phone should be listed in the window that appears. Select it and click **Pair**. Enter a passkey — which can be any sequence of numbers, such as 0000 — and click **OK**. Accept the pairing request on your phone and enter the same passkey.
- You will see a dialog like the one shown in **Figure 40.6** asking which services you want to use with your phone. You must select **Synchronize your Contacts and Calendar** for iSync to work correctly. (You may want to add the other services as well.) Click **OK**, and your phone will automatically be added to iSync.
- If you remove your phone from iSync for any reason, you can add it again by choosing **Add Device...** from the **Devices** menu.
- The iSync window expands to display synchronization options, as shown in **Figure 40.7**. In most cases, the default options work well. The **For first sync** pop-up menu works just like the one for

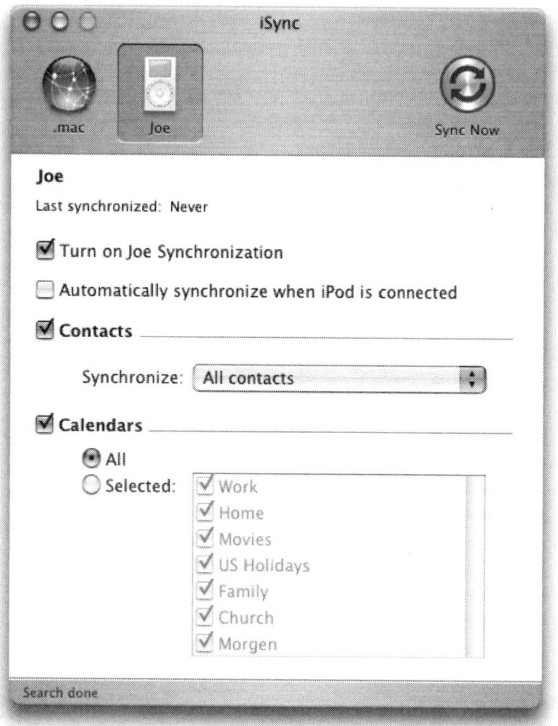

40.5

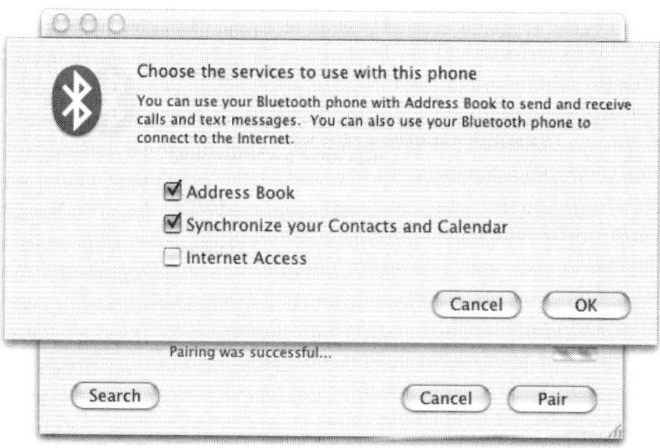

40.6

.Mac synchronization: You can choose to merge records on your computer and phone, overwrite your phone's data with what's on your computer, or overwrite your computer's data with what's on your phone. If you want to change which contacts or calendars are synchronized, use the controls in the **Contacts** and **Calendars** sections. To determine which iCal calendar is used for events you enter on your phone, choose a calendar from the **Put events created on phone into** pop-up menu. Because your phone's memory may not hold all the events in your iCal calendar, use the **Get events for the next** pop-up menu to add events for the next **week, 2 weeks, 4 weeks**, or **8 weeks**.

To add a Palm handheld, follow these directions:

- Open HotSync Manager (usually located in /Applications/Palm).
- Choose **Conduit Settings...** from the **HotSync** menu.
- You need to turn off the conduits that would ordinarily sync your Palm's contact and address data with Palm Desktop. To do this, double-click the **Address Book** conduit, select the **Do Nothing** radio button (see **Figure 40.8**), click the **Make Default** button and click **OK**. Do the same thing with the **Date Book** conduit and the **To Do List** conduit.
- Now double-click the **iSync Conduit**. Make sure the checkboxes for **Synchronize Contacts** and **Synchronize Calendars** are checked and click **OK**. You can now quit HotSync Manager.
- Your Palm device now appears in iSync. No further configuration is necessary.

NOTE

iSync synchronizes contact, address, and to-do list data from your Palm device to Address Book and iCal, but it does not synchronize Notes, because there is no analogous application built into Mac OS X. When you use iSync with a Palm device, your Notes will continue to be synchronized with Palm Desktop.

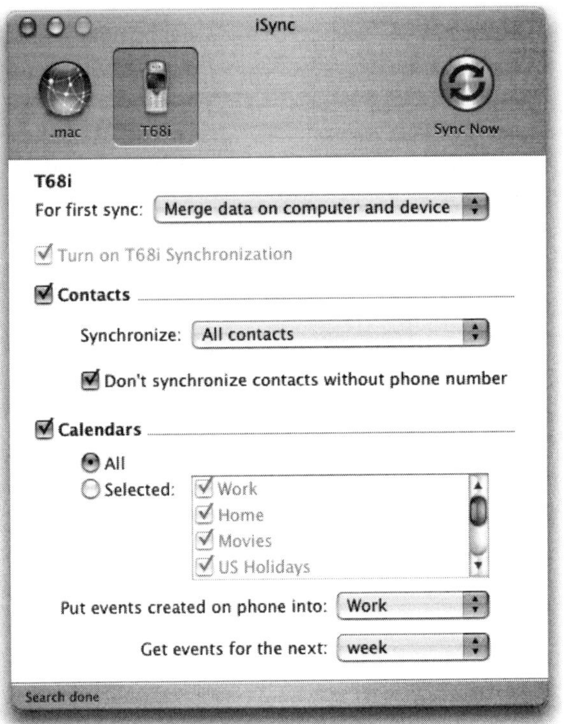

40.7

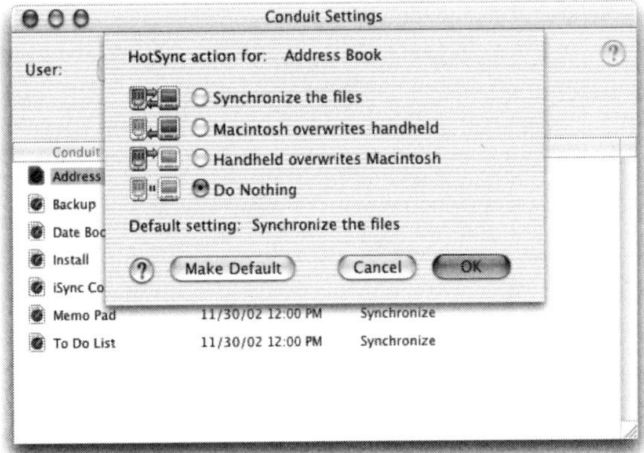

40.8

STEP 4: SYNC YOUR HANDHELD DEVICES

After you've set up your devices, using iSync is normally a matter of clicking one button, regardless of how many devices you have configured.

If you have an iPod, a Bluetooth phone, or both, do the following:

- Open iSync and click **Sync Now**. Your handheld devices (and .Mac account, if you've configured it) synchronize automatically.

If you have a Palm OS device, syncing is a two-step process:

- First, click the **Sync Now** button in iSync. An alert (see **Figure 40.9**) appears telling you to press the HotSync button on your device's cradle.
- Press the **HotSync** button now. The HotSync Progress window appears, just as it did before you installed iSync. When HotSync has finished its part of the process, the alert disappears and iSync finishes synchronizing with your device.

During an iSync session, if records are going to be added, deleted, or changed, iSync displays a warning like the one shown in **Figure 40.10**. You must agree to the changes by clicking **Proceed** for synchronization to continue. If you want to reduce or eliminate the appearance of this alert, choose **Preferences...** from the **iSync** menu (see **Figure 40.11**). To raise the threshold at which you're alerted of changes, choose **more than 1%**, **more than 5%**, or **more than 10%** from the pop-up menu. To turn off warnings altogether, uncheck the checkbox.

If a particular field is changed in a record on two different devices, a Conflict Resolver window (see **Figure 40.12**) appears. Select the version of the record you want to use on both devices (repeating, if necessary, for multiple conflicts) and click **Finish**. You can then choose whether to re-sync immediately to resolve the conflict, or wait until the next time you use iSync.

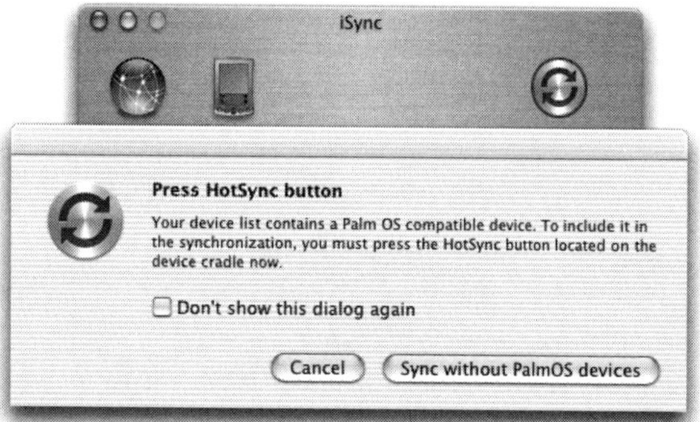

40.9

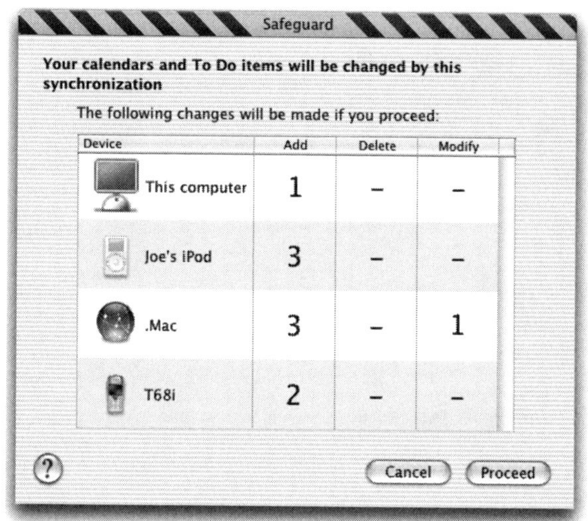

40.10

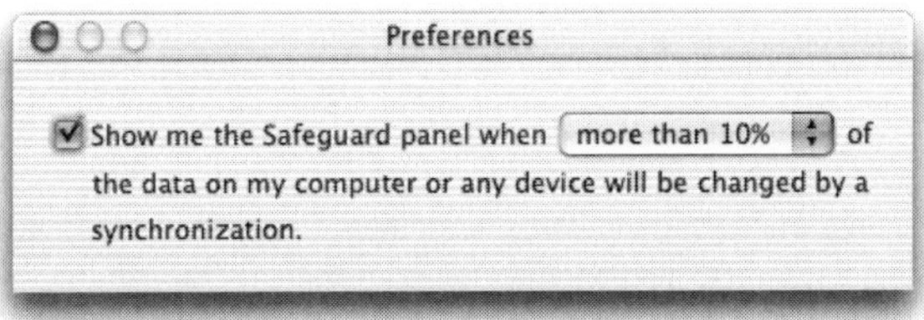

40.11

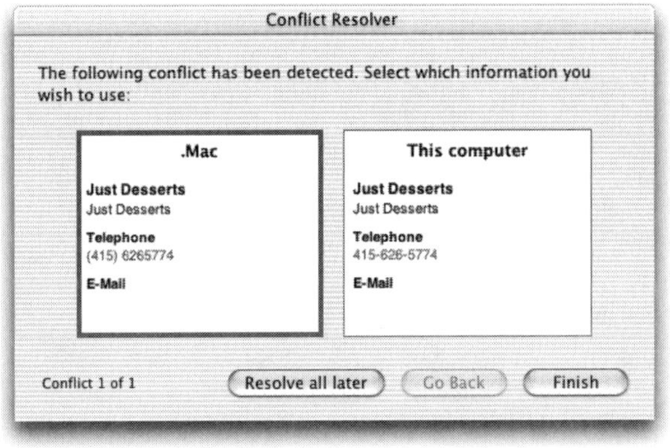

Conflict Resolver

The following conflict has been detected. Select which information you wish to use:

.Mac

Just Desserts
Just Desserts
Telephone
(415) 6265774
E-Mail

This computer

Just Desserts
Just Desserts
Telephone
415-626-5774
E-Mail

Conflict 1 of 1
Resolve all later
Go Back
Finish

40.12

CHAPTER 9

SERVER TECHNIQUES FOR NONGEEKS

Conventional wisdom says that only computer geeks would ever configure their own computers to run as servers. Servers, after all, are expensive, complicated high-tech things that only corporations have — aren't they? Not at all. Any time a computer is set up to respond to requests for information, it is operating as a server. If you've ever turned on Personal File Sharing to move a file from one Mac to another, you've already set up a server.

Of course, your Mac can do much more than share files. It can also function as a full-featured Web, mail, or database server (among other things). Using your own machine for these types of services — rather than relying on your ISP — can give you greater speed, flexibility, control, and convenience. And setting up your own server is actually quite easy, even if you're not wearing a propeller beanie.

I should mention that these techniques assume you have a full-time, high-speed Internet connection such as a DSL line or a cable modem — and that you are prepared to leave your computer on all the time. If your machine is functioning as a Web or mail server, other computers will not be able to reach it unless it is up and running with a live Internet connection.

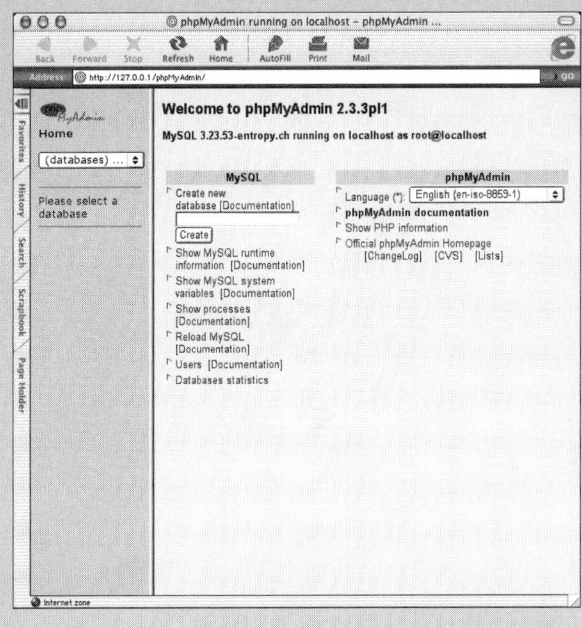

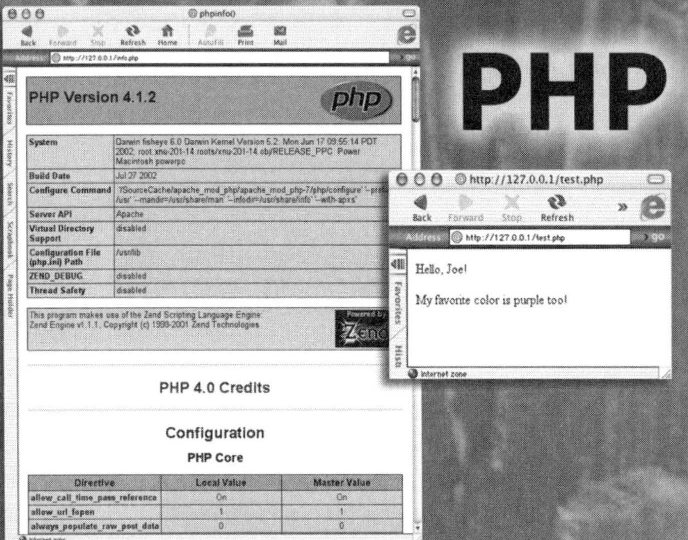

PHP Setup

DNS Records

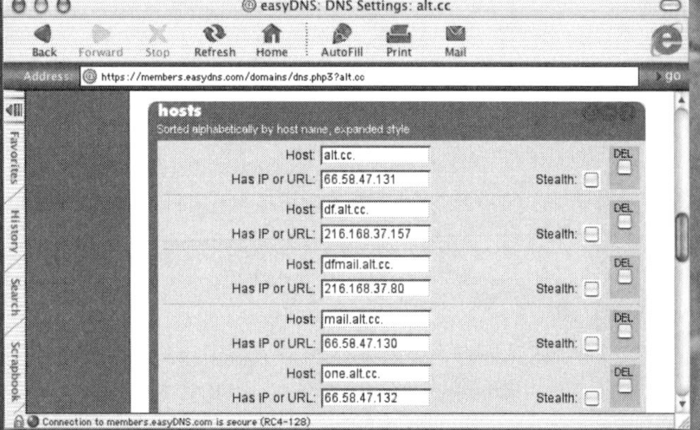

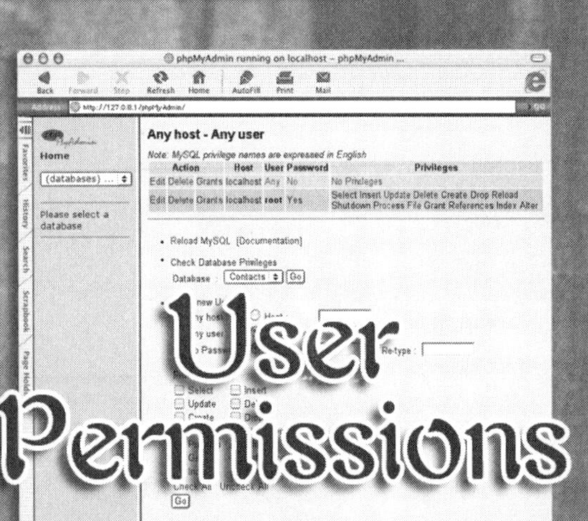

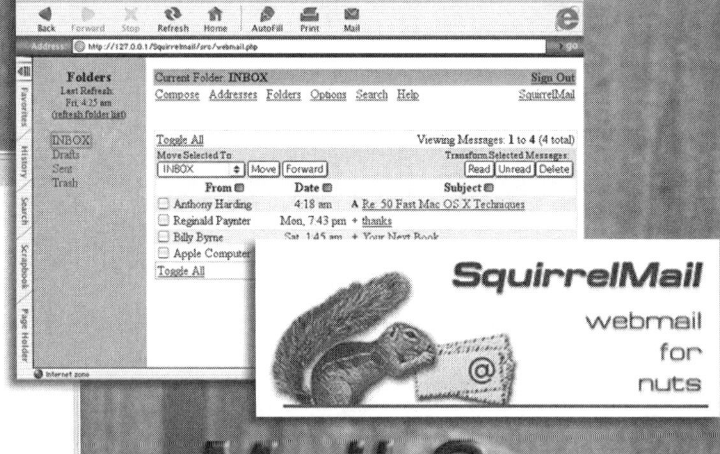

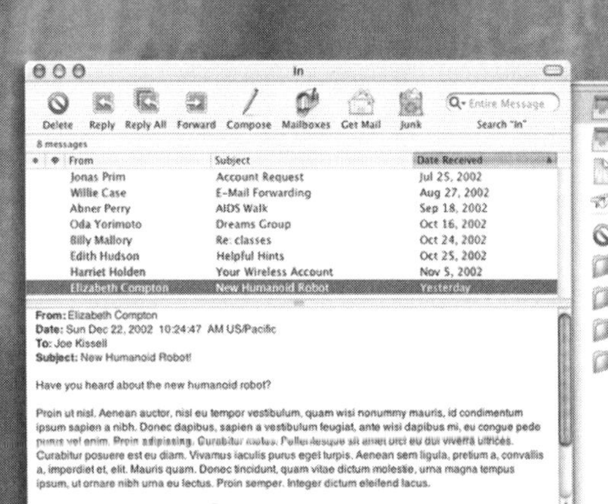

Mail Server

TECHNIQUE 41

GIVING YOUR MACHINE A DOMAIN NAME

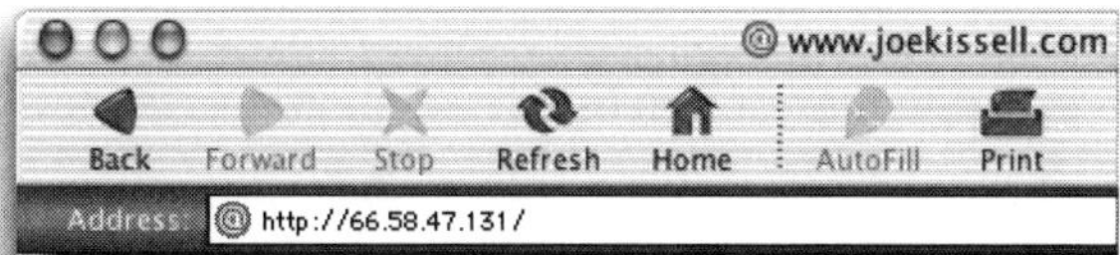

41.1

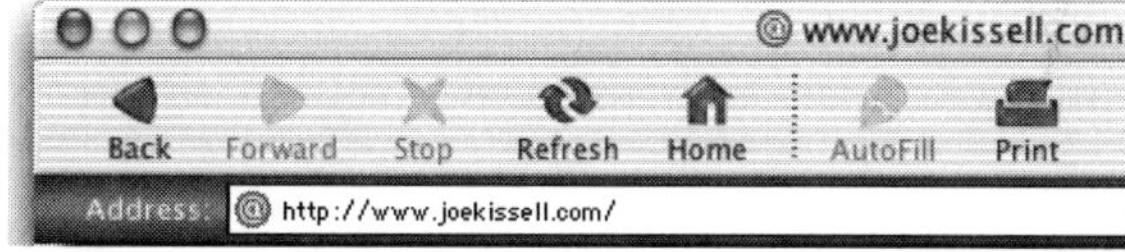

41.2

ABOUT THE FEATURE

Domain names like myname.com are not just for big companies. Your Mac can have its very own name, making it much easier for you to share files, control it remotely, or use it as a server.

In order for your Mac to access the Internet, it needs an IP (Internet Protocol) address, a number like 12.34.56.78 that uniquely identifies your computer. Sometimes your ISP or system administrator will supply a specific address, but more often than not, a special server on your network will dynamically assign an address for you each time you access the Internet. If you decide to use your computer as a server, other computers can connect to it by using its IP address. For example, if your IP address is 12.34.56.78 and you're running a Web server, another user would enter http://12.34.56.78 in a Web browser to access your site. If you're running an e-mail server, mail would be sent to yourname@12.34.56.78.

The two problems with numeric addresses are that they're hard to remember and they often change — your computer might have a different address tomorrow than it does today. If you're going to use your machine as a server — even if you'll be the only one to access it — you'll find it much handier if your computer has an easy-to-remember name (such as imac.joekissell.com) rather than just a number.

Giving your Mac a domain name is not hard, but it requires a small amount of money to pay for domain registration and DNS services. You'll also need an always-on Internet connection in order for the domain name to be of much practical use.

For this technique, I recommend reading through all the steps before beginning. You may find that performing these steps in a different order works better for your situation.

STEP 1: DETERMINE YOUR IP ADDRESS

Before you do anything else, you need to determine what type of IP address your computer has. IP addresses are either static (always the same) or dynamic (assigned each time you connect to the Internet).

- Open System Preferences and click the **Network** icon under Internet & Network.
- Choose your current Internet connection type (such as AirPort or Built-in Ethernet) from the **Show** pop-up menu.
- On the TCP/IP tab, look at the **Configure** pop-up menu. If it says **Manually** or **Using DHCP with manual IP address**, you have a *static* IP address. The address will be listed immediately below the pop-up menu, as shown in **Figure 41.3**; make a note of it.
- If the **Configure** menu says **Using DHCP** or **Using BootP**, you have a *dynamic* IP address. Your current IP address — which could change the next time you connect to the Internet — will be listed below the menu; make a note of it.

  If you connect to the Internet through a router, a firewall, or an AirPort base station, you may have an additional hurdle to deal with: NAT (Network Address Translation). NAT is a clever mechanism whereby multiple computers can share a single IP address. In a home networking setup, that address typically belongs to the router or base station, which in turn figures out which packets of information are destined for which computer on the local network. With NAT, your Mac might have a *private* IP address such as 10.0.1.22, but other computers would see the *public* (static or dynamic) address of your router. If you are using NAT, you'll need to know the router's public IP address, and also perform an extra step to make sure outside computers can see your Mac.
- Open your Web browser and go to **www.whatismyip.com**. At the top of the screen will be the IP address the Web server received your request from — either your own computer or an upstream router. Compare this number to the IP address you wrote down earlier in these steps. If it's the same, then you are *not* using NAT (and you can skip the last step in this technique). If it's different, you *are* using NAT, and the number you see in your Web browser is the address of your router. If that is the case, make a note of the router's IP address and be sure to follow the final step in this technique.

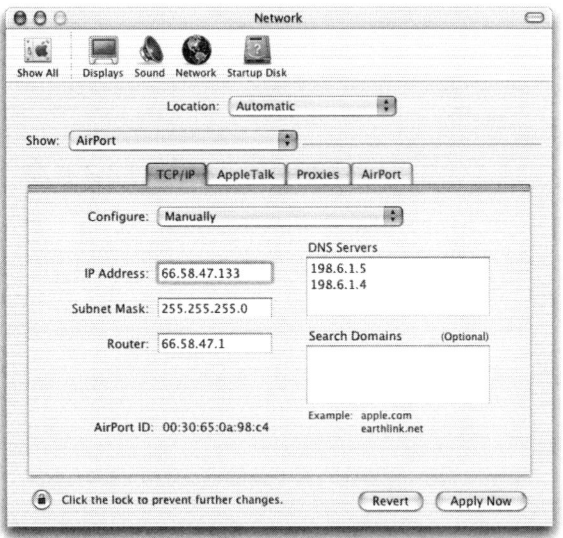

41.3

STEP 2: REGISTER A DOMAIN NAME

Now it's time to register your own domain name. If you've already done this at some point, you can skip this step. Companies called *registrars* assign domain names. In exchange for an annual fee (which can range from under $10 to thousands of dollars, depending on the registrar and the type of name you register), you can get exclusive rights to use a unique domain name, such as **yourname.com**. For example, I registered the domain name **joekissell.com**, which means I can use that name for my Mac — or give each of my Macs different names within the domain (such as **imac.joekissell.com**, **powerbook.joekissell.com**, and so on).

- Select a registrar. There are many; try a Google search for "domain registrar" for plenty of examples. I've personally used **easydns.com**, **verisign.com**, **directnic.com**, and **enic.cc** (which registers names in the .cc domain). Each registrar allows you to search for available names. Shopping around for the best prices, features, and service can pay off.
- When you've found an available name, complete the registrar's sign-up form to register and pay for the name.

STEP 3: CHOOSE NAME SERVERS

At some point in the registration process, you will be required to choose how the Domain Name Service (DNS) for your domain is handled. The choices vary widely from one registrar to another, but in general, you will need to select two or more name servers for your domain.

A name server is a computer that translates domain names into numeric addresses. To oversimplify a bit, when a computer tries to connect to, say, joekissell.com, it consults its local DNS server, which in turn sends an inquiry to one of the designated name servers for that domain. The name server replies with the IP address of joekissell.com, which is then forwarded to the computer that made the original request, allowing it to contact the server. (All of this usually happens transparently, in a fraction of a second.)

In order to make your own domain name point to your Mac, then, you have to tell your registrar which name servers to use and then (in Step 4) tell those name servers what your IP address is. Many registrars offer DNS service as part of their domain name registration package, which makes the whole process much more convenient.

If you have a static IP address, note the following:

- If your registrar provides DNS services, select the registrar's name servers.
- If your registrar does not provide DNS services, choose a separate DNS provider (see Step 4) and enter that provider's name server addresses.

If you have a dynamic IP address, you will need Dynamic DNS service. This allows you to give your computer a fixed domain name even if its IP address changes every time you connect to the Internet. Dynamic DNS works by using a small program on your computer to check for changes in its IP address. When a change occurs, the program connects to your DNS provider in the background and updates your name server records. Like magic, your domain name will point to your computer's new IP address. Note, however, that depending on your ISP and the DNS settings your domain uses, it can sometimes take anywhere from a few minutes to 48 hours for your computer's new IP address to propagate through the

NOTE

If for any reason you don't want to register a unique domain name, you can still use this technique. Several of the DNS providers listed in Step 4 allow you to set up your machine with names in their domains (such as joespowerbook.dyndns.org).

Internet. This can result in periods of time when your computer cannot be found from the outside, even if it is running properly.

- Find out if your registrar provides Dynamic DNS services. (Among those that do are **easydns.com** and **no-ip.com**.) If it does, select your registrar's name servers then move on to Step 4 to configure them.
- If your registrar does not provide Dynamic DNS service, select a Dynamic DNS provider in Step 4 and then come back and enter that provider's name server addresses.

STEP 4: (IF NECESSARY) CHOOSE A DNS PROVIDER

If your registrar does not provide DNS service — or if you have a dynamic IP address and your registrar doesn't provide Dynamic DNS service — you'll need to select a separate DNS provider, in addition to your registrar. But don't worry: DNS services are very inexpensive (in some cases, free) and quite easy to configure.

A DNS provider is simply an organization that maintains name servers. After signing up for an account with a DNS provider, you inform your registrar of its name server addresses. Then, you configure the name servers to point to your Mac.

Here are some suggested DNS providers. All of these offer — as an option — Dynamic DNS service. Their prices and services vary, but all offer similar fundamental capabilities.

> **NOTE**
>
> **Not all of these providers support NAT. If you use NAT on your network, choose either DynDNS or No-IP.com.**

- ZoneEdit, `www.zoneedit.com`
- EasyDNS, `www.easydns.com`
- DynDNS, `www.dyndns.org`
- DtDNS, `www.dtdns.com`
- No-IP.com, `www.no-ip.com`

When you sign up with one of these providers, they will provide you with the addresses of two or more name servers. Enter these in your domain name record on your registrar's Web site.

STEP 5: SET UP DNS RECORDS

This step may sound complicated, but it's actually very easy. In a nutshell, you need to enter your computer's domain name and its IP address in a form on a Web page. The specifics, however, can vary a bit.

Name servers store various kinds of records. For the purpose of this technique, your main concern is the most common type, called an "A" (or Host) record. It is a simple association between a name (such as www.mydomainname.com) and an address (such as 12.34.56.78).

- Using your DNS provider's Web interface (EasyDNS is shown in **Figure 41.4**), create a new "A" (or Host) record for your domain that points to your Mac's IP address. If you're using NAT, you must enter the public IP address your Mac is using for NAT — typically the IP address of your router (or AirPort base station) — *not* your Mac's individual IP address.

> **NOTE**
>
> **Another Dynamic DNS provider you might consider is DynIP.com. Its service is similar to the others listed here, but it provides its own proprietary client software. The Mac OS X version of its software was still in beta testing at the time this book was written.**

- If your computer has a static, public IP address, you can skip Step 6. If it has a dynamic address, just enter the current value and proceed to the next step.
- Repeat this procedure if you want to set up addresses for multiple computers (or multiple addresses for the same computer).
- If you plan to run your own mail server (see Technique 45), you will also need to set up an MX (Mail exchange) record to indicate which computer in your domain is functioning as the mail server — even if it's the same one you use for hosting your Web site.

STEP 6: (IF NECESSARY) CONFIGURE A DYNAMIC DNS CLIENT

If your computer has a dynamic IP address, then the DNS record you just set up might become inaccurate the next time you connect to the Internet. You *could* manually log into the DNS provider's Web site each time your IP address changes and manually update your DNS record. But there's a much easier way: Install software that watches your IP address for changes and, when necessary, automatically updates your DNS records.

> **NOTE**
>
> **Your computer can have many different domain names, by the way — joekissell.com, www.joekissell.com, and mail.joekissell.com could all point to the same computer.**

- Several dynamic DNS clients are available, but the one that works with the widest variety of DNS providers is Dynamic DNS Client, which you can download for free from `www.sentman.com/dyndns/`.
- After downloading and unstuffing Dynamic DNS Client, move the folder to your Applications folder. Then open System Preferences, go to the Login Items pane, and click **Add....** Navigate to the folder you just moved and select **DynDNS background carbon**.
- Log out and then log back in to activate the Dynamic DNS client.
- If you are using ZoneEdit or EasyDNS as your Dynamic DNS provider, be sure to download the extra **Plugin Updater for Carbon** from the same site. After Dynanic DNS is active, run the plugin installer and restart.
- Open the **Mac Dynamic DNS Client Carbon** application, as shown in **Figure 41.5**. Click **New** to open the Setup Assistant.

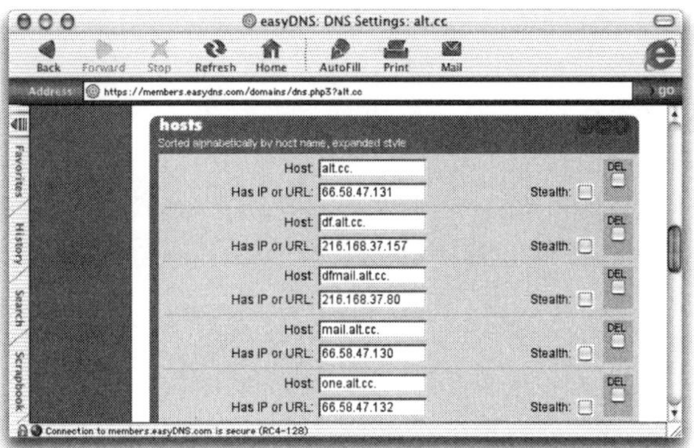

41.4

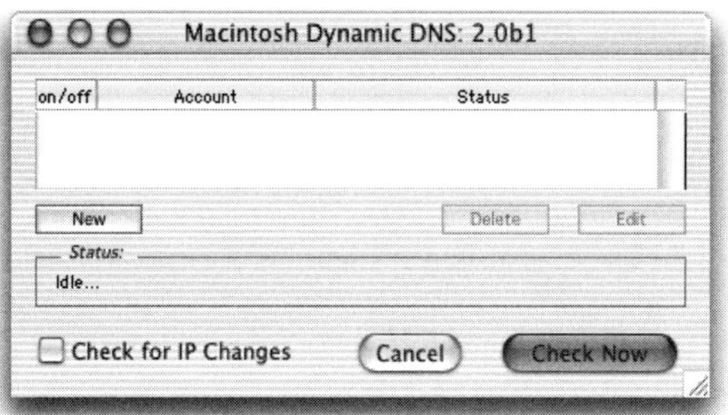

41.5

- Choose your Dynamic DNS provider from the Service pop-up menu (see **Figure 41.6**) and click the right arrow.
- Enter your domain name and the user name and password you selected for your Dynamic DNS provider and click the right arrow.
- On the next screen (as shown in **Figure 41.7**), choose **Use Local Address** unless you are using NAT as described earlier. (Remember, not all Dynamic DNS providers support NAT.) Click the right arrow.
- You can leave the Service Options screen blank for now. Click the right arrow. Then click **Save**.
- Back in the main window, check the box next to your newly added domain to turn it on and click **Check Now**. If everything has been configured correctly, your display should now list your IP address and the date and time.

If you don't use NAT, you're finished. Other computers can now reach your Mac by domain name. Of course, you'll still need to activate server software, such as a Web server (Technique 42), an e-mail server (Technique 45), or a VNC server (Technique 32). If you do use NAT, proceed to the final step.

STEP 7: (IF NECESSARY) SET UP PORT REDIRECTION

If you use NAT on your local network, your new domain name will now be pointing to the IP address of your router (or AirPort base station), rather than to your individual Mac. In order to use your Mac as a server, you need to tell your router to forward all requests for certain services (such as Web, file sharing, or e-mail) to your machine. This is called port

41.6

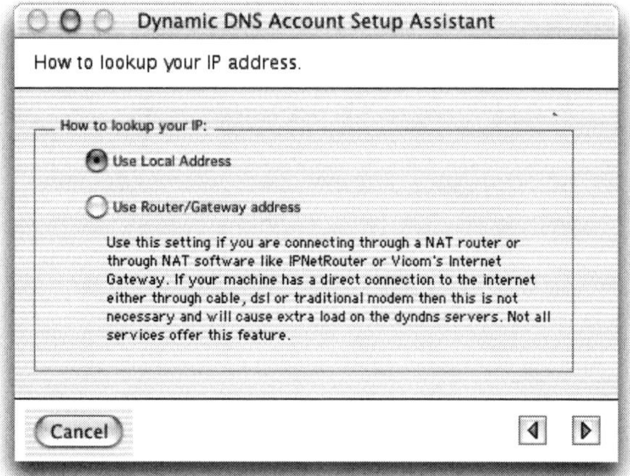

41.7

redirection (also known as port forwarding or port mapping).

Although port redirection gets around the limitations of NAT, there are a couple of catches. First, for any given public IP address (of which a home router will typically have just one), only one computer on your network can provide any particular service. For example, you can have only one Web server and one e-mail server per IP address (though those can be two separate machines). And second, you can only use port redirection if you have direct control of the router. If you're running servers on a home network with your own AirPort base station or cable/DSL router, modifying your router settings should be no problem. If your Mac is on a large corporate network that uses NAT, however, you might be out of luck — your local network administrator may not take kindly to the idea of reconfiguring the corporate router to direct Web (or e-mail) traffic to your Mac.

Every router has a different method for configuring port redirection. I'll show you how it's done for an AirPort base station; if you're using a different router, consult the instructions that came with it to determine how you need to configure it.

- Open the AirPort Admin application (in /Applications/Utilities) and select your base station. Click **Configure**.
- Click the **Port Mapping** tab (shown in **Figure 41.8**)
- Click **Add**, and the sheet shown in **Figure 41.9** appears.

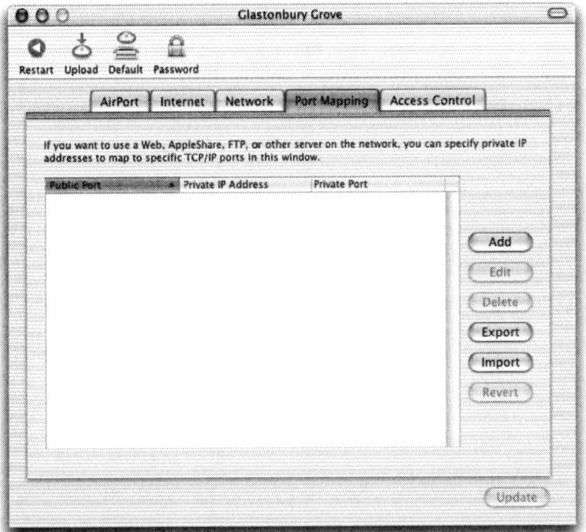

41.8

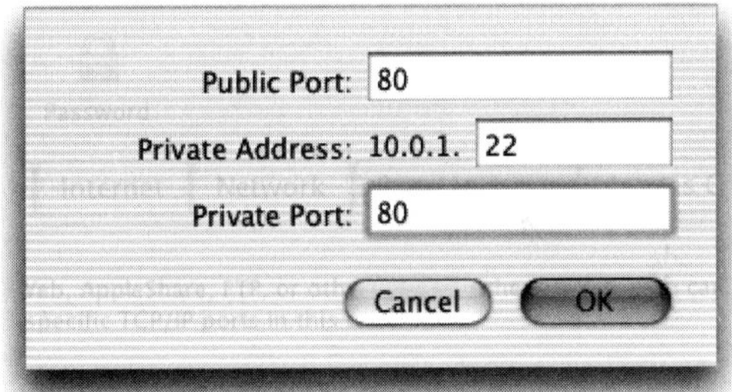

41.9

- To set up your machine to be a Web server, enter **80** for both the **Public Port** and **Private Port**, and enter your Mac's current IP address (as shown in Network Preferences) in the **Private Address** field. Click **OK**.
- Repeat this step for each service you want your Mac to provide, filling in the appropriate port numbers each time. If you're using your Mac as a mail server, enter **25** (for SMTP), **110** (for POP), and **143** (for IMAP). If you're using Personal File Sharing, enter **548**.
- When you're finished, your window may look something like **Figure 41.10**. Click **Update** to reprogram and restart your base station.

After your base station has reset, you can test your domain name.

- Start up Personal Web Sharing as described in Technique 42.
- Go to *another* computer (either on your local network or elsewhere), open a Web browser, and type the domain name you set up for your computer. You should see a basic Web page appear. (A peculiarity of port redirection is that a machine typically cannot contact itself using the public IP address or domain name, whereas it could if it had a unique IP address. To view your Web site on your own computer, enter **127.0.0.1** — or your computer's private IP address — in your browser's address window.)

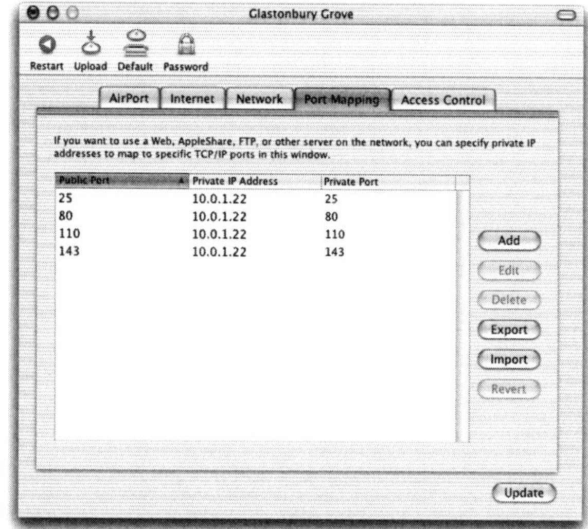

41.10

TECHNIQUE 42

TURNING YOUR COMPUTER INTO A WEB SERVER

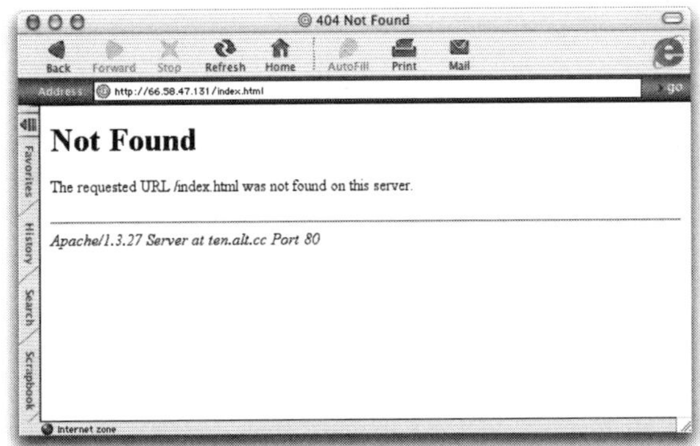

42.1

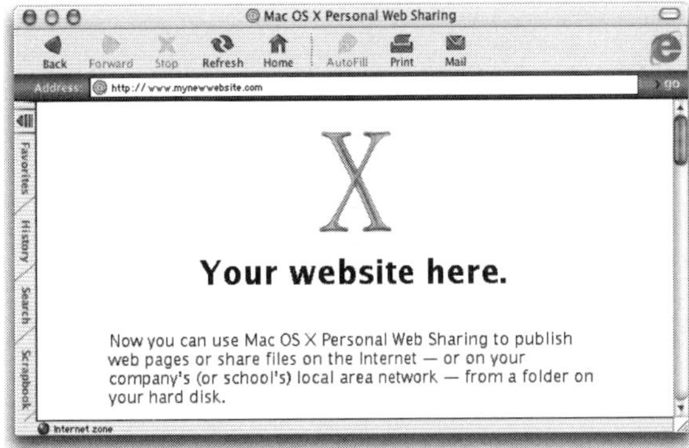

42.2

ABOUT THE FEATURE

With a high-speed Internet connection at your disposal, your computer can become a Web server, making publishing photos, databases, and other Web pages right from your home easy.

This technique is the easiest and fastest one in the book — it basically amounts to one mouse click. In fact, it's so simple it barely counts as a technique. But I felt it was important to talk about turning your computer into a Web server precisely *because* it's so easy.

Almost anyone can find a good use for a Web site, yet many people don't have one because of the perception that it's a complicated thing to set up. Many other people pay exorbitant fees to Internet service providers for Web hosting, even though they could accomplish the same thing — with much less effort — essentially for free.

There are also some people who can't imagine why they would ever want a Web site. Having one running on your own computer can be a surprising creativity booster. You may find yourself wanting to try things like the following:

- Maintaining a weblog (or *blog*) — a running commentary on some topic of interest to you
- Sharing photos and movies you've taken with family and friends
- Advertising your home-based business
- Publishing your own poetry, prose, or visual designs
- Raising awareness for a cause that's important to you
- Providing a discussion board for a group of coworkers

These are just a few of the many uses for a personal Web server. After you have the ability to publish files as easily as saving them, you may find a wide variety of additional applications.

Apple includes a powerful, advanced Web server called Apache with Mac OS X. Apache is the most popular UNIX Web server, used on many thousands of sites worldwide. When you activate the friendly-sounding Personal Web Sharing feature, you're actually starting up Apache. Although turning it on and off is easy, you can also dig into its more advanced features using Terminal, adding cgi scripts, databases, and other complex configuration options. PHP, discussed in the next technique, is just one example.

WARNING

Some ISPs use special filtering to prevent users from running their own Web servers. If your ISP is one of them, you may find that this technique does not work for you, even if you've performed all the steps correctly. There are some ways around this sort of filtering, but they're more complex than I can describe here. See the book's Web site (`www.wiley.com/compbooks/kissell`) for some pointers to resources that can help you deal with this situation. Much more importantly, a few ISPs actually forbid subscribers from running servers (even if you get around the filtering), and may cancel your account if you do so. Be sure to check your ISP's Terms of Service to see if you are permitted to run a server, and if not, consider shopping for a new provider.

STEP 1: PREPARE FOR THE CLICK

Before I get to the all-important mouse click that turns your computer into a Web server, you should take these preliminary measures:

- Use a high-speed, always-on Internet connection. Although running a Web server on a local network or even over a dial-up Internet connection is possible, you'll most likely want to make sure that any potential visitor to your Web site can access it at any time. For this, you need a permanent Internet connection, such as a DSL line or a cable modem.
- Get a domain name. This is optional, but highly recommended. If your computer does not have a domain name, you'll have to access it by IP address, something like http://12.34.56.78. Getting your own domain name is inexpensive and easy — just follow Technique 41.

STEP 2: TURN ON WEB SHARING

With those preliminaries out of the way, you can get your Web server running. To turn on Web Sharing:

- Open System Preferences and click the **Sharing** icon. Make sure the **Services** tab is selected.
- It's time for the click. Check the **On** box next to **Personal Web Sharing** (see **Figure 42.3**) You are now running your own Web server.
- If you ever want to turn off your Web server, just uncheck the **On** box.

STEP 3: TEST YOUR SERVER

Now verify that your server is working as it should:

- Open a Web browser and in the address box, enter **http://127.0.0.1** and press **Return**. (127.0.0.1 is a special address that always points to your own computer, no matter what its real IP address or domain name may be.) You should see the Apache setup page shown in **Figure 42.4**.

If you've set up a domain name for your computer, try entering that in your address box next. In most cases, you'll see the same results. (If you're using a dynamic DNS service and Network Address Translation, you may not be able to view your page from your own computer using its domain name.)

STEP 4: CUSTOMIZE YOUR WEB SITE

The Apache setup page you're viewing in your Web browser is located in /Library/WebServer/Documents. It's the one named index.html.en. You'll notice a number of index.html files, each with an additional two-character suffix. These suffixes indicate their language; Apache can automatically choose variations of a file, if present, for browsers running in other languages. To override all these choices, just include an index.html file with no extra suffix.

- Duplicate **index.html.en** and rename it **index.html**. (An alert appears asking whether you really want to change to the **.html** suffix; you do.) You can then use the modified page as the starting point for your site.

Many different programs can be used to edit HTML files. You might choose a friendly program with a graphical, drag-and-drop interface such as Adobe GoLive or Macromedia Dreamweaver, or a text-based program such as BBEdit. For basic editing, though, you already have an excellent tool on your system if you installed the Developer Tools package (as described in Technique 3). It's called Project Builder, and it's designed for editing any type of text file — especially those that contain source code (and HTML is just another programming language).

42.3

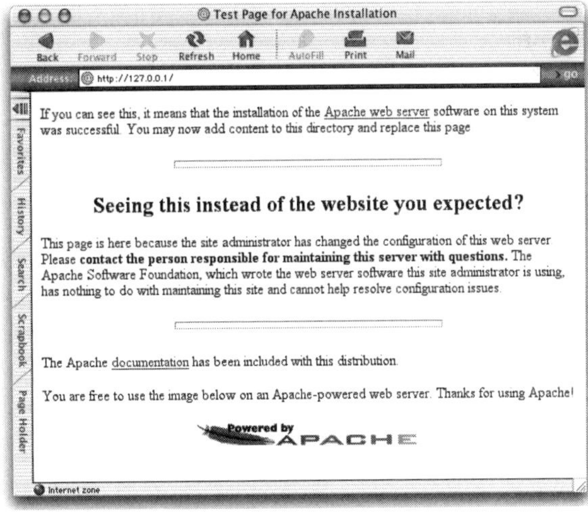

42.4

- Open the Developer folder on your hard drive and then open the Applications folder inside it. Locate the **Project Builder** icon. Drag the **index.html** file you just created onto Project Builder. A series of dialogs appear, asking you questions about the environment you want to set up; just choose the defaults for all of them. Your HTML document will appear in its own window, as shown in **Figure 42.5**.

If you're already familiar with HTML, you're now ready to edit to your heart's content. (Skip to Step 4 for some additional pointers.) If you've never seen HTML code in your life, it's not hard to learn. Here's a five-minute mini primer.

Most of the page is plain text, with formatting commands enclosed in pairs of angle brackets. For example, you'll see this line:

```
<h2 align="center">Seeing this instead
of the website you expected?</h2>
```

The `<h2 align="center">` tag means "use the second-level heading style for the text that follows,

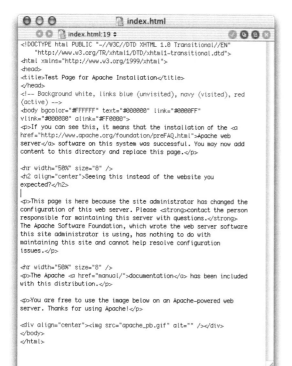

index.html
index.html:19

```
<!DOCTYPE html PUBLIC "-//W3C//DTD XHTML 1.0 Transitional//EN"
    "http://www.w3.org/TR/xhtml1/DTD/xhtml1-transitional.dtd">
<html xmlns="http://www.w3.org/1999/xhtml">
<head>
<title>Test Page for Apache Installation</title>
</head>
<!-- Background white, links blue (unvisited), navy (visited), red
(active) -->
<body bgcolor="#FFFFFF" text="#000000" link="#0000FF"
vlink="#000080" alink="#FF0000">
<p>If you can see this, it means that the installation of the <a
href="http://www.apache.org/foundation/preFAQ.html">Apache web
server</a> software on this system was successful. You may now add
content to this directory and replace this page.</p>

<hr width="50%" size="8" />
<h2 align="center">Seeing this instead of the website you
expected?</h2>

<p>This page is here because the site administrator has changed the
configuration of this web server. Please <strong>contact the person
responsible for maintaining this server with questions.</strong>
The Apache Software Foundation, which wrote the web server software
this site administrator is using, has nothing to do with
maintaining this site and cannot help resolve configuration
issues.</p>

<hr width="50%" size="8" />
<p>The Apache <a href="manual/">documentation</a> has been included
with this distribution.</p>

<p>You are free to use the image below on an Apache-powered web
server. Thanks for using Apache!</p>

<div align="center"><img src="apache_pb.gif" alt="" /></div>
</body>
</html>
```

42.5

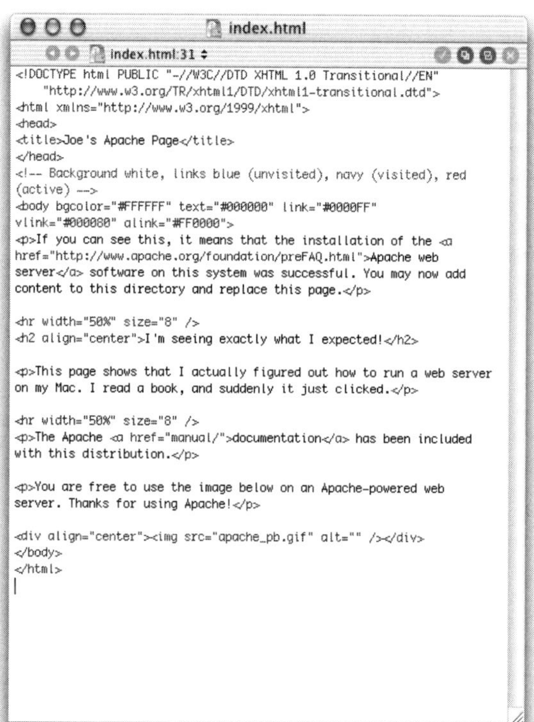

index.html
index.html:31

```
<!DOCTYPE html PUBLIC "-//W3C//DTD XHTML 1.0 Transitional//EN"
    "http://www.w3.org/TR/xhtml1/DTD/xhtml1-transitional.dtd">
<html xmlns="http://www.w3.org/1999/xhtml">
<head>
<title>Joe's Apache Page</title>
</head>
<!-- Background white, links blue (unvisited), navy (visited), red
(active) -->
<body bgcolor="#FFFFFF" text="#000000" link="#0000FF"
vlink="#000080" alink="#FF0000">
<p>If you can see this, it means that the installation of the <a
href="http://www.apache.org/foundation/preFAQ.html">Apache web
server</a> software on this system was successful. You may now add
content to this directory and replace this page.</p>

<hr width="50%" size="8" />
<h2 align="center">I'm seeing exactly what I expected!</h2>

<p>This page shows that I actually figured out how to run a web server
on my Mac. I read a book, and suddenly it just clicked.</p>

<hr width="50%" size="8" />
<p>The Apache <a href="manual/">documentation</a> has been included
with this distribution.</p>

<p>You are free to use the image below on an Apache-powered web
server. Thanks for using Apache!</p>

<div align="center"><img src="apache_pb.gif" alt="" /></div>
</body>
</html>
```

42.6

and center it on the page." At the end of the heading, a second tag </h2> turns off the h2 style.

- Try replacing some of the text with text of your own. Save the file and then go back to your Web browser and reload **http://127.0.0.1** to see the changes. (Don't worry about making mistakes, because you can always go back to the original **index.html.en** document and make another copy.) **Figure 42.6** shows the file with some changes in Project Builder, and **Figure 42.7** shows the same file as it appears in Internet Explorer.
- Paragraphs are marked with a <p> tag at the beginning and a </p> tag at the end; this tells your browser to put a little extra space above the paragraph.

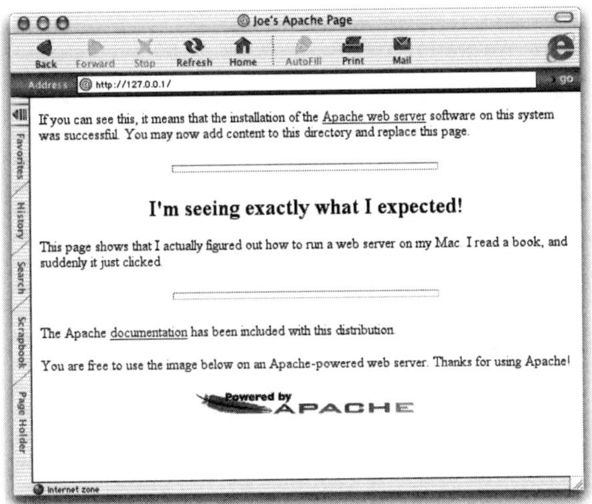

42.7

- To link to another file, place that file in the same folder (/Library/WebServer/Documents) and make sure it has a name that ends in **.html**. In your original file, insert the new file's name in an `a href` tag—for example:

```
<a href="newfile.html">Click this
link to go to the new file.</a>
```

- To link to an external URL, do exactly the same thing but place the URL where the file name would go:

```
<a href="http://www.apple.com">Click
this link to go to Apple's Web
site.</a>
```

- To include an image on your page, copy the image to the same folder as the HTML files, and include an `img` link that indicates the filename:

```
<img src="picture.jpeg">
```

STEP 5: ADD PERSONAL WEB SITES

Your machine is already set up to host not just one but several Web sites. Each user account (as specified on the Accounts tab in System Preferences) gets an individual Sites folder. If you open your home folder, you'll see your own Sites folder there. If you open this folder, you'll see another file named index.html — this is the Web page that goes with your user name. To access this page, add a tilde (~) character, your short user name, and a slash (/) after the URL in your Web browser — for example, http://127.0.0.1/~jk/.

The sample page shown at this location (see **Figure 42.8**) is supplied by Apple rather than Apache, and it contains more information on Personal Web Sharing and HTML.

- To add a new user site, simply define the new user name in Accounts Preferences. That user's site is immediately accessible at `http://your-domain-name/~new-user-name`. You can have any number of user sites active and available on your machine (in addition to the main site) at any one time.

STEP 6: LEARN MORE

Now that you have your own Web site up and running, you might want to learn more about HTML, Web design, and Apache to expand and enhance your Web pages. Thousands of books, Web sites, and other resources are available to teach you everything you might want to know. Consult your local library, bookstore, or this book's Web site (`www.wiley.com/compbooks/kissell`) for some specific recommendations.

42.8

USING PHP TO CREATE DYNAMIC WEB SITES

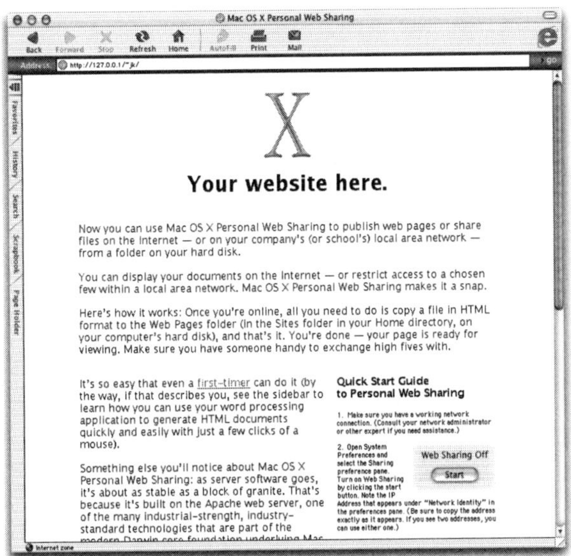

43.1

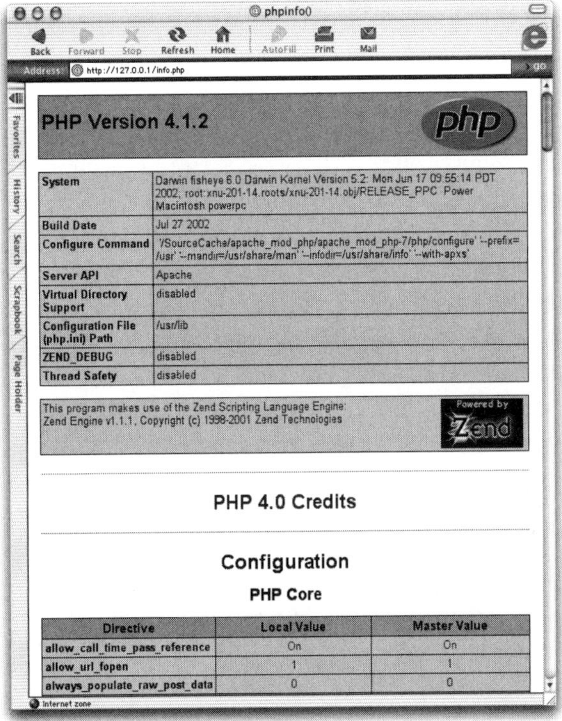

43.2

ABOUT THE FEATURE

By using PHP software with your personal Web server, you can create dynamic, interactive Web sites. The full PHP language is quite complex, but even beginners can achieve powerful results quickly by following a few basic pointers.

Throughout this book, I've pointed out tools and features built into Mac OS X that are hidden or turned off for one reason or another. In this technique, I show you yet another: a Web server add-on known as PHP, which can make ordinary Web sites come alive with all sorts of dynamic features. PHP has been used to add auctions, games, discussion boards, shopping carts, surveys, content management systems, counters, search engines, and guest books to Web sites — to list but a tiny sampling of its applications. It also makes a very nice way to display information from MySQL databases. (See Technique 44.)

PHP originally stood for Personal Home Page. It was a set of tools created by a programmer named Rasmus Lerdorf to help him collect information about visitors to his Web site. Eventually Rasmus made the software available to the public, where a large community of programmers expanded and enhanced its functionality. They also changed the meaning of PHP — it is now a recursive acronym that stands for PHP: Hypertext Preprocessor.

So what exactly is PHP and how do you use it? To oversimplify a bit, PHP is a scripting language designed to be embedded within HTML pages. When you create a Web page that includes PHP commands, it is processed by the PHP software on your computer before being delivered to users by Apache. Even if you don't know (or care to know) anything about programming, inserting some simple commands into your Web pages that will add dynamic features, communicate with databases, and much more is easy. After you get PHP up and running, you can also download thousands of prebuilt PHP packages that you can drop into your existing Web site to add new features with little or no effort on your part. And if you do care to learn a bit of programming, PHP is a great place to start.

STEP 1: ACTIVATE PHP

Although PHP is built into Mac OS X, it is turned off by default. Unlike the Apache Web server itself, which you can activate by clicking a checkbox in System Preferences, PHP requires a trip to Terminal to activate it.

■ Open Terminal. You'll need to edit your Web server's configuration file. To open the file in the pico text editor, enter

```
sudo pico /etc/httpd/httpd.conf
```

■ Press **Control+W** to enter Find mode, type **PHP** and press **Return**. As shown in **Figure 43.3**, you should see a line that reads:

```
#LoadModule php4_module
  libexec/httpd/libphp4.so
```

■ Uncomment this line by removing the # character at the beginning. It should now look like this:

```
LoadModule php4_module
  libexec/httpd/libphp4.so
```

■ Now scroll down just a bit further, to the end of the AddModule section, where you'll see this line:

```
#AddModule mod_php4.c
```

■ Again, delete the # character, leaving this:

```
AddModule mod_php4.c
```

■ Next, add a line that tells Apache to associate files ending in `.php` with the PHP engine. Press **Control+W** to enter Find mode, type **AddType application** and press **Return**. You should see this line:

```
AddType application/x-tar .tgz
```

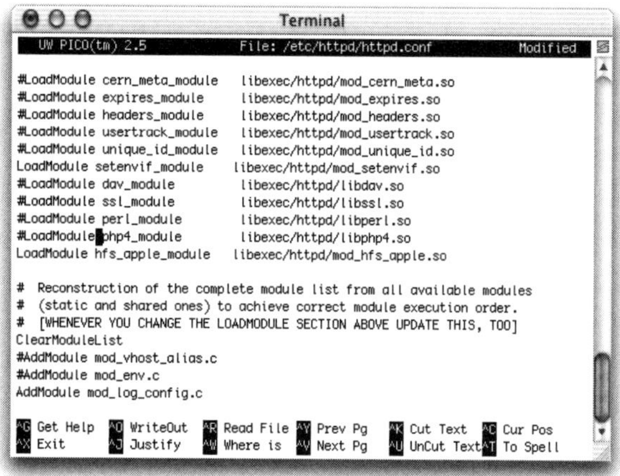

43.3

- Immediately following this line, add another:

```
AddType application/x-httpd-php .php
```

- Finally, tell Apache to look for files named index.php if no index.html file is found in a given directory. (This comes in handy for some PHP packages you'll download, such as SquirrelMail, which you install in Technique 45.) Press **Control+W** to enter Find mode, type **DirectoryIndex** and press **Return**. You should see this line:

```
DirectoryIndex index.html
```

- Add a space and `index.php` to the end of this line, which will then read:

```
DirectoryIndex index.html index.php
```

- Press **Control+X** to exit pico, answering **y** to save the buffer and pressing **Return** to confirm the filename.
- You must stop and restart Personal Web Sharing to activate your newly changed configuration file. Open System Preferences, go to the Sharing tab, and click **Services**. Uncheck **Personal Web Sharing** and then recheck it. Quit System Preferences.

STEP 2: TEST YOUR SETUP

Without actually learning PHP programming or installing extra software, you can easily confirm that PHP is installed and working. You'll need to create a *very tiny* HTML document. Although you can use BBEdit, Pepper, Adobe GoLive, or any other text editor to do so, doing it in Terminal is probably quickest.

- Open Terminal and create a new document in pico:

```
pico /Library/WebServer/Documents/
  info.php
```

- Enter just this one line:

```
<?php phpinfo() ?>
```

- Press **Control+X** to quit pico, followed by **y** to save the buffer. Press **Return** to confirm the filename.
- Open your Web browser and enter this address: `http://127.0.0.1/info.php`. This points to the Web server running on your own computer. If PHP is correctly configured, you should see an information screen like the one shown in **Figure 43.4**. Congratulations! PHP is now

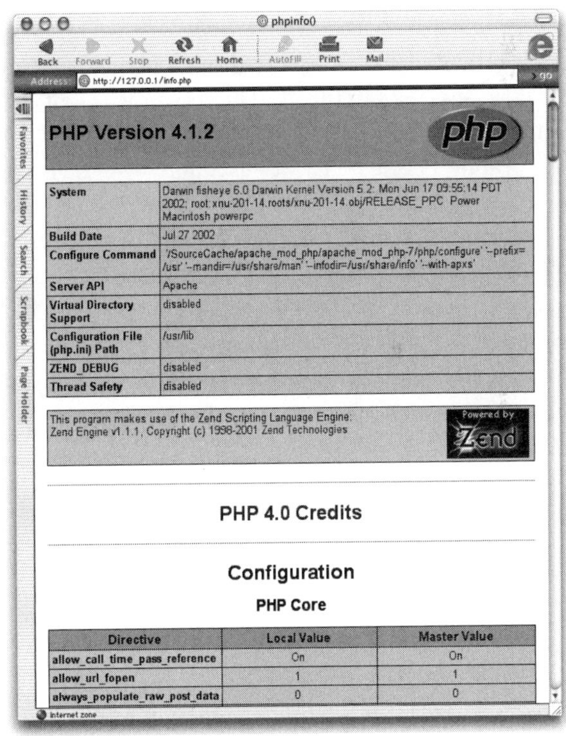

43.4

installed and functional. (If you do not see an information screen, double-check to see that you've followed Step 1 and Step 2 correctly — even a small misspelling can prevent proper behavior — and that Personal Web Sharing is turned on.)

STEP 3: DOWNLOAD A BETTER VERSION OF PHP (OPTIONAL)

The version of PHP Apple includes with Mac OS X does not have all the bells and whistles you might want for certain kinds of tasks. For example, on one of the Web sites I host, a user wanted to insert a PHP-based "goal thermometer" graphic to show how much money had been collected in a fundraising effort. The PHP code he found on the Web was supposed to work without any modification, but the graphics didn't show up, even though I had activated PHP as described in Step 1. The reason was that the default version of PHP didn't include support for the GD graphics library that was used to create the thermometer images.

Graphics support is just one of more than a dozen common features strangely missing from the default installation of PHP. If your needs extend beyond the basics, you can easily replace this installation with a new version that includes nearly every feature you might need.

- Go to Marc Linyage's excellent site at `www.entropy.ch/software/macosx/php` and follow the instructions there for downloading and installing a much more capable version of PHP.
- If you've already activated PHP by following Step 1, you can skip the steps under "Activating the PHP Module" on Marc's Web page. You will, however, need to turn Personal Web Sharing off and back on.
- Once again, point your Web browser to `http://127.0.0.1/info.php` to view the updated information on your PHP installation.

STEP 4: ADD DYNAMIC CONTENT

Now that PHP is up and running, it's time to learn some basics. A complete treatment of PHP would require its own book (see the final step for some suggestions), but here are a few pointers to get you started.

- PHP commands are embedded in HTML files. If you're comfortable working in HTML, PHP should be very easy for you to pick up. HTML files that include PHP commands are generally given names that end in `.php` rather than `.html`. This extension tells Apache that it needs to hand the files off to PHP for special processing before they're sent back to the computer that requested the page. (There are ways around this situation, but for simplicity's sake, I recommend that you start by using `.php` at the end of all your HTML files that contain PHP.)
- As you know, HTML tags are enclosed in angle brackets, like `<b>` for bold or `<p>` for a paragraph marker. PHP tags, too, are enclosed in angle brackets, but they include extra characters to distinguish them from ordinary HTML. PHP tags begin with `<?php` and end with `?>`. For example, a simple PHP command that prints "Hello world"

> **NOTE**
>
> **Even though this version of PHP *supports* numerous new features, that doesn't mean it includes all the software needed to use them all. For example, if you want to make use of its support for the GD graphics library or the MySQL database, you'll need to download and install those packages separately. Follow the links provided on the PHP download page for more details.**

on the screen would look like this: <?php echo "Hello world" ?>

■ You can put many lines of PHP commands inside a single set of <?php and ?> tags, but each command must end with a semicolon (;). You can leave the semicolon out if you have just one command between the tags.

Here are some sample PHP commands you can try, just to get started. Type these commands into a text file with a name that ends in .php — for example, **test.php**. To make it easy to see these commands in action, put your test.php file in /Library/WebServer/Documents, right where you created info.php earlier. Then, to access the file through your Web browser, enter http://127.0.0.1/test.php. Try the following simple commands.

■ To display which type of browser someone is using to access your Web page (and on which platform), enter

```
<?php echo $_SERVER["HTTP_USER_
  AGENT"] ?>
```

■ If you're using Internet Explorer under Mac OS X, the following shows up when you view that page from your browser:

```
Mozilla/4.0 (compatible; MSIE 5.22;
  Mac_PowerPC)
```

■ To display the current date and time in a Web page, enter

```
<?php print(date( "l, F d, Y h:i" ))
  ?>
```

■ When the Web page is viewed in a browser, it will display something like this:

```
Sunday, December 15, 2002 11:58
```

■ PHP gives you lots of extra capabilities for processing forms. To take a very simple example, you can collect data in a form and then use that information on a subsequent page. Create a document called **form.html** with the following contents:

```
<html>
<head></head>
<body>
<form action="test.php"
method="POST">
<p>Name: <input type="text"
name="name" /></p>
<p>Favorite color: <input
type="text" name="color" /></p>
<input type="submit">
</form>
</body>
</html>
```

■ Then modify your **test.php** file so that it looks like this:

```
<html>
<head></head>
<body>
<p>Hello, <?php echo $_POST["name"]
?>!</p>
<p>My favorite color is <?php echo
$_POST["color"] ?> too!</p>
</body>
</html>
```

■ Point your browser to the first file (shown in **Figure 43.5**), fill out the form, and look at the

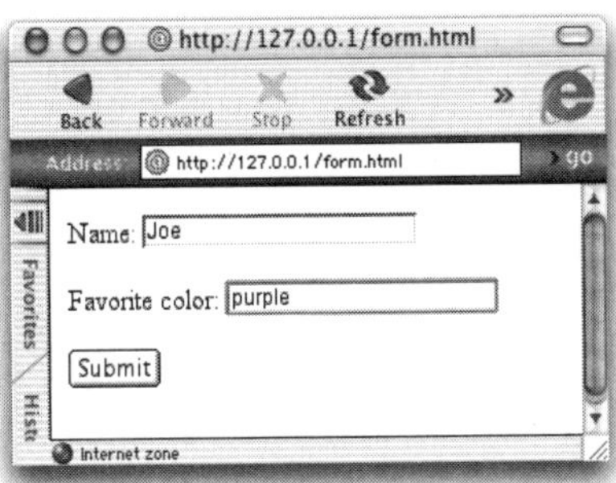

43.5

results (see **Figure 43.6**). You've just passed values from a form onto another page.

Usually, however, you want to do more than just display values from a form; you want to make decisions about what to do based on information the user has entered — for example, responding to inquiries or checking for errors. PHP provides a wealth of features for doing these sorts of activities. I'll demonstrate just two (variables and conditionals) in a simple example.

■ Make a few modifications to the form.html and action.php files you just created. Change **form.html** to read as follows:

```
<html>
<head></head>
<body>
<form action="test.php"
method="POST">
<p>Favorite color: <input
type="text" name="color" /></p>
<input type="submit">
</form>
</body>
</html>
```

■ Then modify **test.php** to look like this:

```
<html>
<head></head>
<body>
<?php
$clr = $_POST["color"];
if ($clr=="red" or $clr=="green" or
$clr=="blue") {
echo "$clr is a primary color.";
} else {
echo "$clr is not a primary color,
but it's still quite nice.";
}
?></body>
</html>
```

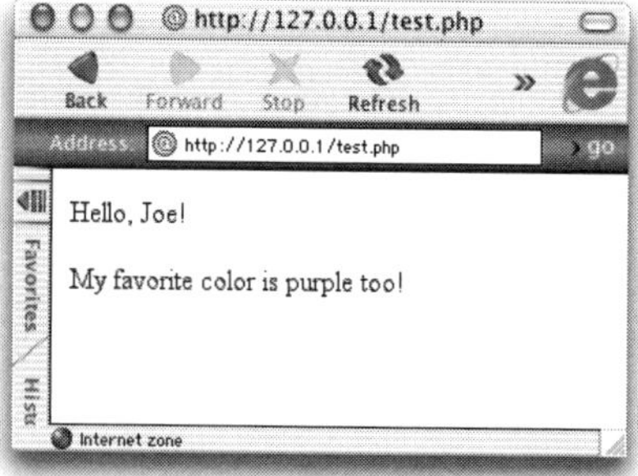

43.6

■ Point your browser to `http://127.0.0.1/form.html` and try submitting various colors. (Note that in this example, the color you enter is case sensitive; entering "blue" is not the same as entering "Blue.") If you enter "red," "green," or "blue," the response page will say that it is a primary color; any other value will produce an alternate message.

Here's what the new lines mean:

```
$clr = $_POST["color"];
```

This line creates a new variable, called `$clr`, which takes the value posted in the form's color field. In this example, you could have continued using the predefined superglobal variable `$_POST["color"]` throughout, but because this value is going to be referred to several times, using a simple variable is easier.

```
if ($clr=="red" or $clr=="green" or
$clr=="blue") {
echo "$clr is a primary color.";
}
```

Here you have a simple If/then statement. It says, if the value of `$clr` is either "red," "green," or "blue," do whatever appears between the following pair of braces `{ }`. In this case, the command within the braces just displays a message that includes the value of the variable. Notice that a double equal sign (==) is used for each item in the `If` statement. If a single equal sign (=) were used, it would actually modify the value of the variable, rather than just evaluate it.

```
else {
echo "$clr is not a primary color,
but it's still quite nice.";
}
```

If the first part of the `If` statement is not true, the command(s) between the braces following `else` will be executed. In this case, the command prints an alternate statement if you enter a color other than red, green, or blue.

STEP 5: USE PHP SOLUTIONS OTHERS HAVE WRITTEN

After you get a taste of PHP, the easiest way to add more advanced dynamic functionality to your Web site is to download PHP scripts other people have written — then, if you like, modify them to suit your needs. Because PHP is platform-neutral, you can run PHP pages on your Mac even if they were created on Windows or Linux machines.

Many Web sites contain sample PHP code. Here are two of my favorites:

- The PHPBuilder Source Code Snippet Library at `www.phpbuilder.com/snippet/`
- The HotScripts.com Scripts and Programs library at `www.hotscripts.com/PHP/Scripts_and_Programs/`

Both of these sites contain a vast number of scripts you can download and use as is — or tailor to your specific needs. They're organized by category (discussion boards, counters, multimedia, database, and so on) to help you find what you're looking for.

Another resource I'm quite fond of is Webmonkey.com. This Web developer's resource contains easy-to-follow instructions on a wide variety of topics, including PHP. They include not only sample code, but also a detailed explanation of why and how each piece of the code works. For example:

- Automatically add Next/Previous links to a series of numbered pages on your Web site: `hotwired.lycos.com/webmonkey/99/25/index2a.html`
- Build a Photo Gallery: `hotwired.lycos.com/webmonkey/01/27/index3a.html`
- Authenticate and track users: `hotwired.lycos.com/webmonkey/00/05/index2a.html`

Still more resources are listed on this book's Web site (`www.wiley.com/compbooks/kissell`), along with up-to-date links.

STEP 6: LEARN MORE PHP

If you're starting to think PHP is fun to use (and it is), you may want to go beyond the prepackaged solutions other people have written and build your own code from scratch. Hundreds, if not thousands, of resources — both electronic and print — can help you do this. Here are some suggestions to get you started.

For online instructions, try these:

- The official PHP documentation, which is extensive, lives at `www.php.net/manual`. Although the bulk of this online guide is rather dry, each page has comments, clarifications, and examples submitted by actual users, which makes it fabulously useful. Also, you can find a more user-friendly tutorial section at `www.php.net/manual/en/tutorial.php`.
- I mentioned Webmonkey earlier. Its PHP tutorial for beginners, which is a good place to start, is found at `hotwired.lycos.com/webmonkey/01/48/index2a.html`.
- O'Reilly's PHP DevCenter (`www.onlamp.com/php/`) has numerous articles on working with PHP.
- The HotScripts.com site (`www.hotscripts.com/PHP/Tips_and_Tutorials/`), also mentioned earlier, has an entire library of PHP

tutorials — hundreds — covering almost every imaginable topic.

If you would rather read about PHP on paper, you can choose from dozens of books, ranging from introductory tutorials to in-depth programming references. Here are a few random samples; for additional recommendations, consult this book's Web site (`www.wiley.com/compbooks/kissell`) or do a search on amazon.com for PHP.

- *Beginning PHP4* (Chris Lea et al., Wrox Press Inc.)
- *PHP Fast and Easy Web Development* (Julie C. Meloni; Premier Press)
- *Programming PHP* (Rasmus Lerdorf & Kevin Tatroe; O'Reilly Press)
- *PHP Cookbook* (David Sklar & Adam Trachtenberg; O'Reilly Press)
- *PHP for the World Wide Web Visual Quickstart Guide* (Larry Ullman; Peachpit Press)

CREATING AND SHARING DATABASES

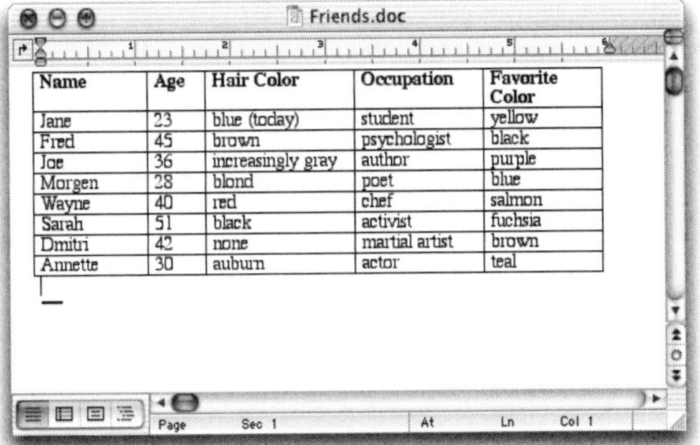

Name	Age	Hair Color	Occupation	Favorite Color
Jane	23	blue (today)	student	yellow
Fred	45	brown	psychologist	black
Joe	36	increasingly gray	author	purple
Morgen	28	blond	poet	blue
Wayne	40	red	chef	salmon
Sarah	51	black	activist	fuchsia
Dmitri	42	none	martial artist	brown
Annette	30	auburn	actor	teal

44.1

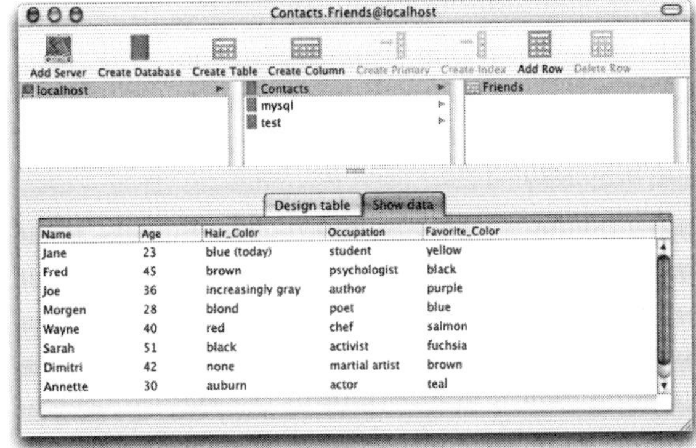

Name	Age	Hair_Color	Occupation	Favorite_Color
Jane	23	blue (today)	student	yellow
Fred	45	brown	psychologist	black
Joe	36	increasingly gray	author	purple
Morgen	28	blond	poet	blue
Wayne	40	red	chef	salmon
Sarah	51	black	activist	fuchsia
Dimitri	42	none	martial artist	brown
Annette	30	auburn	actor	teal

44.2

ABOUT THE FEATURE

MySQL is a free, powerful database you can use on your Mac to organize any sort of data — and even publish it on your Web site. Although it doesn't have the graphical tools of FileMaker Pro or AppleWorks, accessing and sharing your data using third-party clients or a Web interface is easy.

If you say the word "database" to a Mac user, most likely that person will think of FileMaker Pro or AppleWorks — easy-to-use graphical tools that enable you to organize your CD collection, names and addresses, or inventory data. Mention database to a PC or UNIX user, and you may get a different reaction — that user will probably think of Microsoft Access, acronyms such as SQL and ODBC, arcane command-line instructions, and high-end business applications. Databases, outside the Mac world, are often thought of as scary, complex things that only highly trained programmers and system administrators can really hope to understand.

In reality, a database is just a table (or several tables) — a type of container for holding structured information. Tables can be very simple or have hundreds of columns (fields) and thousands or millions of rows (records). Your database program determines the way you view, enter, and share that data.

Along with all the other benefits of Mac OS X's UNIX base, Mac users now have the ability to use a number of extremely sophisticated databases — all for free. You can use them to serve data to dozens or hundreds of other users, and even publish their contents on your Web page without ever paying a license fee. There is a small catch, however. The open-source databases you can install on Mac OS X, while very powerful, do not have the user-friendly interface of something like FileMaker Pro. You will have to "think different" and learn to deal with other sorts of interfaces — and in some cases, design your own.

The database I show you briefly in this technique is called MySQL, and it's one of the most popular open-source SQL (Structured Query Language) databases. SQL is a type of language used to send commands to a database and get information back, and if you install MySQL alone, you would have to learn a lot of weird command-line procedures to interact with it. Fortunately, it's possible to use MySQL without knowing the tiniest bit about the SQL language, thanks to a variety of front-end shells that do all the low-level communication for you. In fact, the beauty of SQL is that when you run a database on your computer, those who connect to it (yourself included) can use whatever client software suits them best — a shareware data browser, a custom Web interface, or a commercial database application.

STEP 1: DOWNLOAD AND INSTALL MYSQL

MySQL is an open-source database, which means anyone can download it, modify it, and compile the source code. However, several sources for versions of MySQL are already prepackaged for Mac OS X, complete with double-clickable installers — making it much easier to set them up. The version I recommend was put together by Marc Linyage.

- Point your Web browser to `www.entropy.ch/software/macosx/mysql/` and scroll down to the "Mac OS version 10.2" section (or a later version, if one is available). There you'll find a link to the latest build of MySQL; click to download it. If the archive does not uncompress automatically, double-click it to open it with StuffIt Expander.
- Double-click the package (`.pkg`) file to install it. Then return to Marc's Web page and follow the remaining instructions for setting up and activating MySQL, as there are some setup tasks that the installer itself cannot do. (You can also find instructions and a script there for removing MySQL, should you ever wish to do so.)
- For convenience, I recommend adding the /usr/local/bin directory to your PATH according to the directions listed.
- After setting up and activating MySQL, be sure to specify a password for the MySQL root user (which is different from the Mac OS X root user). To do this, go to a Terminal window and enter `/usr/local/bin/mysqladmin -u root password` followed by a space and the password you want to use and then press **Return.**
- In order to make MySQL start automatically when you turn on your computer, you must download a small startup package from the same page where you got MySQL, and copy it into /Library/StartupItems.

STEP 2: INSTALL PHPMYADMIN

Now your database program is running, but how do you enter or view data? There are many ways, but you can start with a program called phpMyAdmin. phpMyAdmin allows you to interact with your databases through a Web browser. It is simply a series of Web pages with embedded PHP commands (see Technique 43) that send SQL instructions to databases and display the results.

- If you haven't done so already, activate PHP following the instructions in Technique 43.

■ Go to `www.phpmyadmin.net` and download the latest version of phpMyAdmin. You'll notice there's a choice of `.php` files or `.php3` files. Choose `.php`.

■ After the download is finished, decompress the files, if necessary, using StuffIt Expander. You will see a folder on your desktop with a name like **phpMyAdmin-2.3.3pl1-php**. Rename this folder to simply **phpMyAdmin** for convenience.

■ Drag this folder into /Library/WebServer/Documents so that it will be accessible to your Web server.

■ Open a Terminal window. Switch to the directory you just installed by typing

```
cd /Library/WebServer/Documents/
  phpMyAdmin.
```

This software contains one configuration file you'll need to modify slightly. To do this:

■ Enter `pico config.inc.php` to open the configuration file in the pico text editor.

■ Use the down arrow to scroll down until you see this line:

```
$cfg['PmaAbsoluteUri'] = '';
```

■ You will need to enter your computer's IP address or domain name here along with the exact path needed to find the phpMyAdmin files. If your computer doesn't have a domain name (or if you'll only be accessing databases from this computer, you can use **localhost** in place of your domain name. The new line should look something like this:

```
$cfg['PmaAbsoluteUri'] =
  'http://localhost/phpMyAdmin/';
```

Use the down arrow key to scroll down a few more screens, until you find a line beginning with

```
$cfg['Servers'][$i]['password']
```

This line needs to contain the MySQL root password you set up in the last step. Enter that now between the two single quotes (''). Your file should now resemble **Figure 44.3** (with your password substituted for NewPassword).

■ Close and save the file. To do this, press **Control+X** to quit pico and then answer **y** when asked whether you want to save the buffer, and press **Return** to confirm the filename.

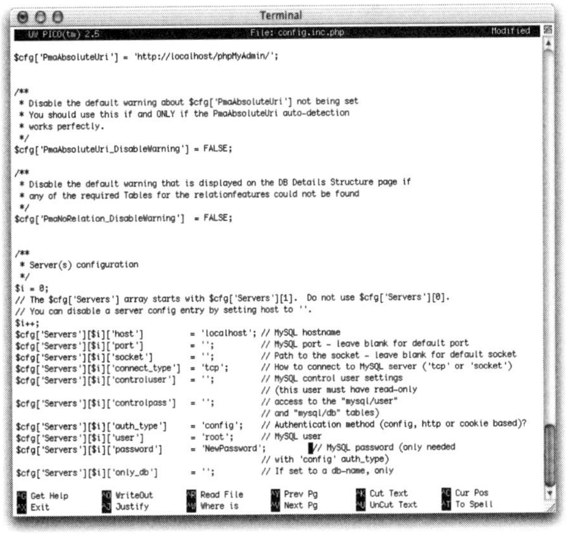

```
Terminal
UW PICO(tm) 2.5                 File: config.inc.php                 Modified

$cfg['PmaAbsoluteUri'] = 'http://localhost/phpMyAdmin/';


/**
 * Disable the default warning about $cfg['PmaAbsoluteUri'] not being set
 * You should use this if and ONLY if the PmaAbsoluteUri auto-detection
 * works perfectly.
 */
$cfg['PmaAbsoluteUri_DisableWarning'] = FALSE;

/**
 * Disable the default warning that is displayed on the DB Details Structure page if
 * any of the required Tables for the relationfeatures could not be found
 */
$cfg['PmaNoRelation_DisableWarning']  = FALSE;



/**
 * Server(s) configuration
 */
$i = 0;
// The $cfg['Servers'] array starts with $cfg['Servers'][1].  Do not use $cfg['Servers'][0].
// You can disable a server config entry by setting host to ''.
$i++;
$cfg['Servers'][$i]['host']          = 'localhost'; // MySQL hostname
$cfg['Servers'][$i]['port']          = '';          // MySQL port - leave blank for default port
$cfg['Servers'][$i]['socket']        = '';          // Path to the socket - leave blank for default socket
$cfg['Servers'][$i]['connect_type']  = 'tcp';       // How to connect to MySQL server ('tcp' or 'socket')
$cfg['Servers'][$i]['controluser']   = '';          // MySQL control user settings
                                                    // (this user must have read-only
$cfg['Servers'][$i]['controlpass']   = '';          // access to the "mysql/user"
                                                    // and "mysql/db" tables)
$cfg['Servers'][$i]['auth_type']     = 'config';    // Authentication method (config, http or cookie based)?
$cfg['Servers'][$i]['user']          = 'root';      // MySQL user
$cfg['Servers'][$i]['password']      = 'NewPassword';      // MySQL password (only needed
                                                    // with 'config' auth_type)
$cfg['Servers'][$i]['only_db']       = '';          // If set to a db-name, only

^G Get Help   ^O WriteOut   ^R Read File   ^Y Prev Pg   ^K Cut Text     ^C Cur Pos
^X Exit       ^J Justify    ^W Where is    ^V Next Pg   ^U UnCut Text   ^T To Spell
```

44.3

WARNING

Technically, the /Library/WebServer/Documents folder is not a very safe place to keep phpMyAdmin, because the general public can access that location (as long as they know, or suspect, that it's there) and get unrestricted access to your databases. You can make it safe, however, by setting up a *secure realm* that will require a user name and password for access. This is a fairly straightforward procedure, but more than I can cover here. Check out the book's Web site (`www.wiley.com/compbooks/kissell`) for more details.

- To use phpMyAdmin, just go to your browser and enter `http://127.0.0.1/phpMyAdmin` in the address bar. The phpMyAdmin main page (see **Figure 44.4**) appears.

STEP 3: SET UP USER PERMISSIONS

Before doing anything else — even creating a database — it's a good idea to set up user permissions. You already set up a root user, but that user account, like your Mac OS X root account, should not be used for day-to-day access.

- Click the **Users** link. The user configuration page (see **Figure 44.5**) appears.
- Type a new name into the **User name** field. Enter a password for the new user in the **Password** field, and again in the **Re-type** field.
- Check the boxes next to the privileges you want the user to have. In general, only the root user should have **Grant** permission (to create and modify user permissions), **Drop** permission (to delete databases), and **Shutdown** permission (to stop the server), but you can choose whichever permissions seem appropriate. (Click the **Documentation** link for more details on what the different types of permissions mean.)
- Click **Go** to add the new user.
- Repeat this step for each new user you want to add. When you're finished adding users, click the **Reload MySQL** link.

STEP 4: USE YOURSQL TO SET UP DATABASES

The phpMyAdmin program you just used to set up users can also be used to create and edit databases. (If you want to learn more, click the **Documentation** link for complete details.) However, only you — the root user — should use phpMyAdmin, because it allows unrestricted access to all your databases. A number of simpler, standalone programs can provide basic access to databases without all the bells and whistles of phpMyAdmin. I'll show you one such program here: YourSQL.

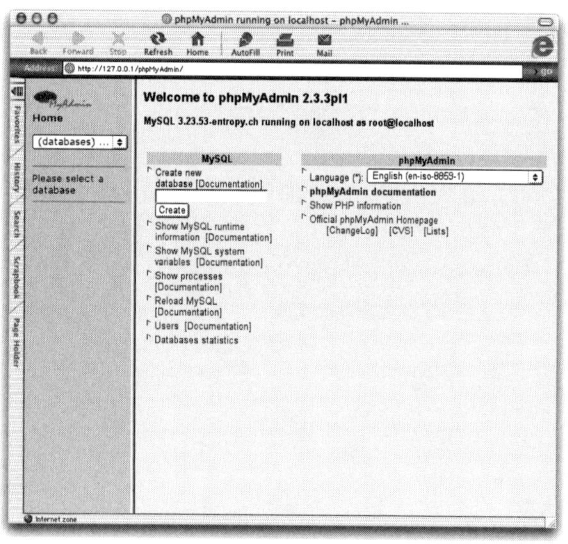

44.4

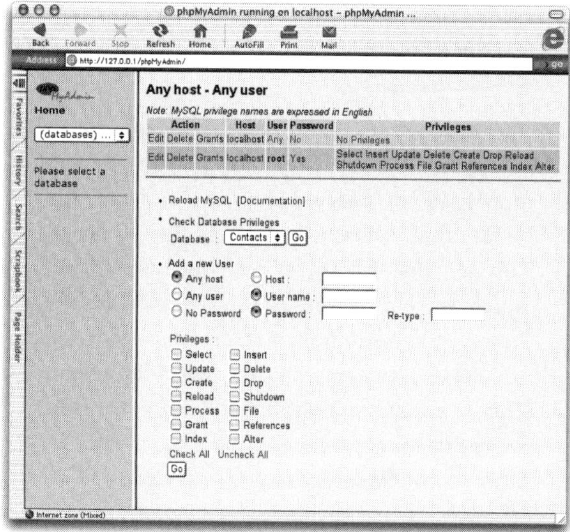

44.5

■ Download the free, open-source YourSQL package from www.mludi.net/YourSQL/. After unstuffing it, drag the YourSQL application to your Applications folder and then double-click it to open it. (See **Figure 44.6**.)

■ Click **Add Server** to set up a connection to your MySQL server. In the Logon window (**Figure 44.7**), enter the server's domain name or IP address (you can use **localhost** if you're running YourSQL on the same computer you installed MySQL on), and the User ID and Password for one of the users you set up in the last step. Click **Logon**.

■ Your server will appear in the leftmost column of the browser window. Select it to display the databases it is currently hosting. (Two default databases, **mysql** and **test**, appear. You can ignore these.)

■ To create a new database, click **Create Database** and enter a name. Your new database will appear in the list.

■ Each database can contain many separate tables (think of them as mini-databases), but for now you can just use one. Click **Create Table** and choose a name for your table. It then appears in the rightmost column of the browser window (as in **Figure 44.8**).

■ Next, add columns (that is, fields) to your database. A default column, initially named **new_column**, will already be filled in for you. To edit a column name or other attribute, double-click it in the list. (You can also right-click or **Control**-click

44.6

44.7

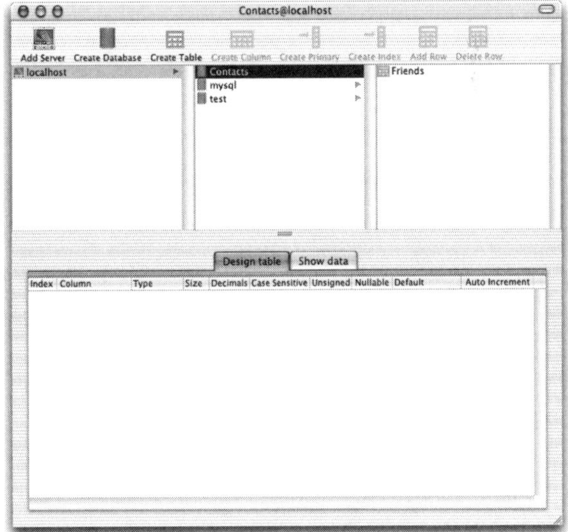

44.8

any item in the list to display a contextual menu of available column types and other options, as shown in **Figure 44.9**.) To add new columns, click **Create Column**. For experimental purposes, try adding just three columns to your database, such as **name**, **address**, and **phone**.

You'll notice that there are a number of other options for each column. In addition to choosing from a variety of data types (such as integer, floating-point number, and *blob* — binary large object), you can make auto-incrementing ID columns, index certain columns to facilitate searching, specify whether a column is case-sensitive, and so on. Consult the documentation in the **Help** menu — or even the phpMyAdmin documentation — for more information on what these options are and how they work.

After you have the basic structure of your database set up, it's time to add some actual data.

- Click **Add Row**. The bottom portion of the display switches to the **Show data** tab (**Figure 44.10**), displaying the columns you set up a moment ago. Click in a cell to edit its contents and then press **Tab** to move to the next cell. Click **Add Row** again and repeat for all the records you want to enter. See **Figure 44.11** for an idea of what your final display will look like.

STEP 5: SHARE YOUR DATA

In other techniques, I've shown you how to share files with Mac and Windows computers, how to share Web pages, and even how to set up e-mail accounts for other people. None of these things is hard to do. But when it comes to sharing databases with other users, you're in for a surprise. To activate database sharing, you have to do . . . *nothing*. That's right — your database was already shared, automatically, as soon as you turned it on. Any other users on the Internet — as long as they have a valid user name and password for your server (as set in Step 3) — can access your data right now.

To see your data (or edit it, if editing permissions are enabled), all another user needs to do is download one of the many SQL clients like YourSQL, and enter the IP address or domain name of your computer and his user name and password. SQL client software is available for every imaginable computer platform, so

44.9

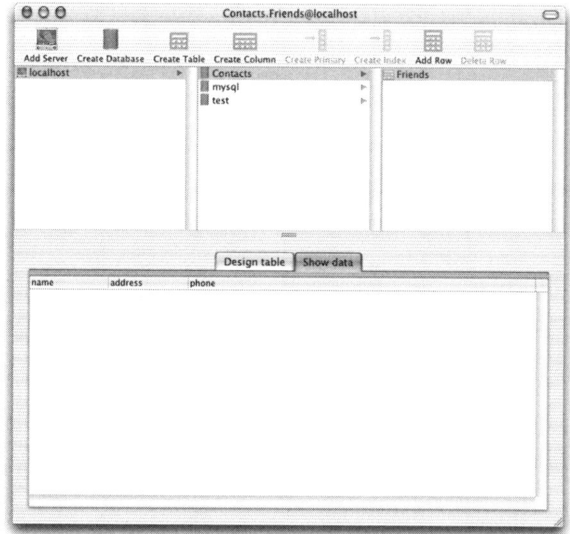

44.10

even someone using Windows or Linux can easily see and add to your database if you give him permission.

Of course, having data in a simple tabular form is not always the most useful way of presenting it — especially when it comes to binary objects such as graphics and sounds. Because you have already activated PHP (to use phpMyAdmin), you can use special PHP commands to display information from your databases on a Web page — including forms to search, enter, and edit data if that's what you want to do. Because it's on a Web page you create, you can arrange the layout, fonts, colors, and other visual elements exactly the way you want them.

I've set up a number of data-driven Web sites myself using PHP and MySQL, and it's a lot of fun. Unfortunately, there are far too many options to cover here. For an excellent basic introduction to MySQL and PHP that includes a sample Web page that talks to a MySQL database, visit `www.timestretch.com/site/web_dev_mysql_php/`. As usual, you can find further recommendations of learning resources on this book's Web site (`www.wiley.com/compbooks/kissell`).

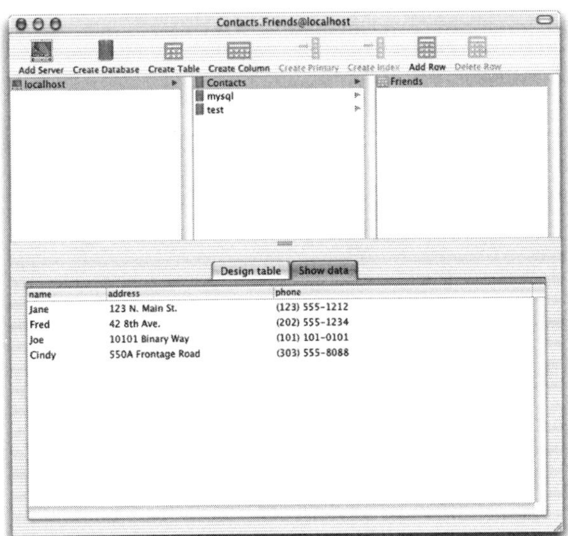

44.11

TECHNIQUE **45**

RUNNING YOUR OWN MAIL SERVER

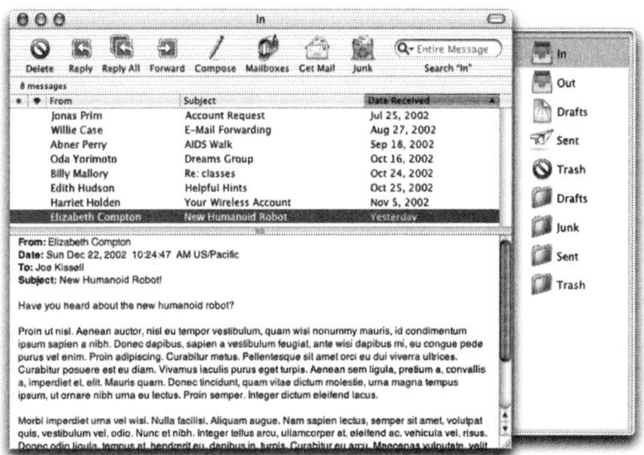

45.1

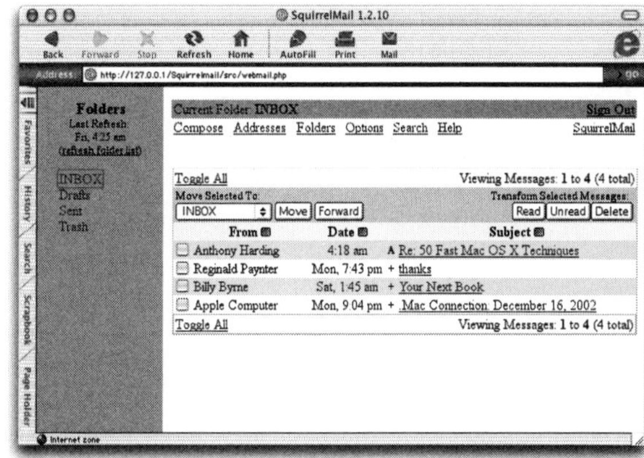

45.2

ABOUT THE FEATURE

If your ISP doesn't have all the functionality you want for your e-mail, you can run your very own mail server at home, complete with multiple accounts, POP/IMAP/SMTP access, and even WebMail.

Your Internet Service Provider (ISP) most likely provides you with a generic (POP) e-mail account. For many people, this is perfectly adequate. But there are a number of reasons you might want to consider bypassing your ISP and running your own mail server. For example, you may want to use IMAP to keep all your mail stored on a server, while many ISPs offer only POP access. You may want the flexibility to send or receive larger e-mail attachments than your ISP allows. Or you may want to set up numerous e-mail accounts for your friends and family without paying extra. In all of these cases, your very own mail server might be the solution.

Although it's convenient to talk about a mail server as though it's a single piece of software, it's actually several different programs working together. First, you'll need a program that sends mail from your computer to other computers (and receives incoming mail). This is known as a Mail Transfer Agent (MTA), and it uses a protocol called SMTP (Simple Mail Transport

Protocol). Next, there's the program that distributes mail to client software such as Mail, Eudora, or Entourage and allows you to download, organize, and delete messages. This is known as a Mail Delivery Agent (MDA). MDAs typically use either or both of two protocols: POP3 (for Post Office Protocol, version 3) or IMAP4 (for Internet Mail Access Protocol, version 4). You may also have add-on programs that provide access to your mail through a Web browser (WebMail) or perform spam filtering, virus checking, or other processing.

For each of these components of a mail server, there are numerous choices. In deciding which collection to recommend here, my primary consideration was ease of setup — after all, this is supposed to be a *fast* technique. You'll begin by setting up *sendmail* as an MTA. (Sendmail is known for being difficult to configure, but it's included with Mac OS X and the basic setup you'll be using is quite straightforward.) Next, you'll use the University of Washington's (UW) free *imapd* program as an MDA to provide both POP and IMAP access. Finally, I'll show you how to set up SquirrelMail, which provides Web-based e-mail access when you can't use a conventional mail client.

WARNING

Some ISPs use special filtering to prevent users from running their own mail servers. If your ISP is one of them, you may find that this technique does not work for you, even if you've performed all the steps correctly. There are some ways around this sort of filtering, but they're more complex than I can describe here. See the book's Web site for some pointers to resources that can help you deal with this situation. Much more importantly, a few ISPs actually forbid subscribers from running servers (even if you get around the filtering), and may cancel your account if you do so. Be sure to check your ISP's Terms of Service to see if you are permitted to run a server, and if not, consider shopping for a new provider.

If your mail needs become more complex, you might want to consider replacing some of the components here with other programs. For example, in place of sendmail you can use Exim, Postfix, or qmail; instead of UW IMAP you might choose Cyrus IMAP or Courier IMAP; and you could replace SquirrelMail with IMP, among others. Each one of these programs has its pros and cons; see the book's Web site (`www.wiley.com/compbooks/kissell`) for links to the other software, Web resources for working with them, and further suggestions.

STEP 1: PERFORM PRELIMINARY SETUP

Before getting down to business, you should check on a few preliminary items.

- Make sure your machine has a domain name, and that an MX record for your domain points to your machine. (See Technique 41.) Technically, your computer could function as a mail server without a domain name, but it would mean all mail would have to be sent to the computer's IP address (for example: **yourname@12.34.56.78**). Also, if you're using port forwarding as described in Technique 41, make sure ports 25, 110, 143, and 80 are directed to your computer.
- If your computer has a dynamic IP address, be aware that you may experience periods of bounced (or even lost) e-mail when the IP address changes. If you need to run a mail server from a machine with a dynamic IP, I suggest using a DNS provider (such as easyDNS or ZoneEdit) that offers backup mail service, which takes over automatically whenever your mail server is offline.
- Install Developer Tools. (See Technique 3.) Several of the tasks you perform here require programs installed as part of the Developer Tools package.

STEP 2: CONFIGURE SENDMAIL

The first program you'll set up is called sendmail. It's an SMTP server, which means it's responsible for sending outgoing mail to other computers and receiving incoming mail. Sendmail is included as part of Mac OS X, but it's not turned on or configured for use.

■ First, tell Mac OS X to turn on sendmail automatically when you start your computer. To do this, open Terminal and enter

```
sudo pico /etc/hostconfig
```

■ This opens a file called hostconfig in the pico text editor. You'll need to make two edits to this file. First, find the line (near the top) that reads

```
HOSTNAME=-AUTOMATIC-
```

and replace the word AUTOMATIC with your computer's domain name. (See Technique 41.)

For example, if your domain is wonderwidgets.com, this line should read as follows:

```
HOSTNAME=-wonderwidgets.com-
```

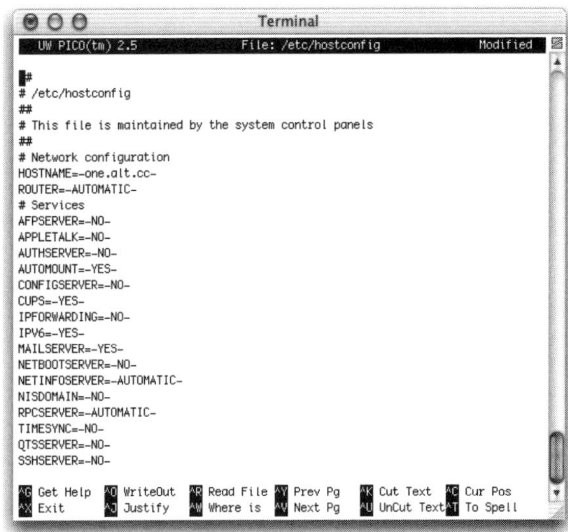

45.3

■ Next, look for a line that says

```
MAILSERVER=-NO-
```

and replace the NO with a YES, as shown here:

```
MAILSERVER=-YES-
```

Your hostconfig file will now look something like **Figure 45.3**. To save the file, press **Control+X**, answer **y** when asked whether you want to save the buffer, and confirm the filename.

■ Next, you need to make a few modifications to sendmail's configuration. The safest way to do this is to start with a generic configuration file that Apple supplies, modify it to suit your needs, and then compile it so that sendmail can read it. This is all quite a bit easier than it sounds. Here's what you'll need to enter in Terminal (all on one line, with no spaces after the / characters):

```
sudo cp /usr/share/sendmail/conf/
  cf/generic-darwin.mc /etc/mail/
  config.mc
```

This code makes a copy of the default configuration file, names it config.mc, and places it in the /etc/mail directory where it's easy to find. Next, edit this file:

```
sudo pico /etc/mail/config.mc
```

■ You'll be making just a few edits to this file. First, look for a line that says

NOTE

Before editing a file like hostconfig, you might want to make a backup copy just so you can go back to the way it was originally in case you make a mistake. To make a copy of hostconfig, enter this in a Terminal window: `cp /etc/hostconfig /etc/hostconfig.old`.

```
define('PROCMAIL_MAILER_PATH',`/usr/
  bin/procmail')
```

■ Position the cursor just below this line and add a new line that reads

```
define(`confDONT_BLAME_SENDMAIL',
  `GroupWritableDirPathSafe')
```

■ Note that the grave accent character (`) is used in two places in place of an opening single quote ('). After you've edited the file, press **Control+X** to exit, answering **y** to save the buffer and pressing **Return** to confirm the filename. Then use the following commands to compile it and put it where sendmail can find it, making a copy of the old file for safekeeping. As usual, type each command on a single line, even though the lines break here in this column.

```
m4 /usr/share/sendmail/conf/m4/cf.m4
  /etc/mail/config.mc >
  /tmp/sendmail.cf
mv /etc/mail/sendmail.cf
  /etc/mail/sendmail.cf.old
mv /tmp/sendmail.cf /etc/mail/
```

■ In order to make sure your system knows to look for this file when sendmail starts, enter these two commands (taking care to put a space on each side of the period (.) that appears by itself in both commands):

```
sudo niutil -create .
  /locations/sendmail
sudo niutil -createprop .
  /locations/sendmail sendmail.cf
  /etc/mail/sendmail.cf
```

■ Also, one folder needs to have special permissions in order to work with sendmail. To take care of that, enter

```
sudo chmod 1777 /var/mail
```

■ Because your Mac will be set up to send outgoing mail, you should be careful to control which computers are allowed to use it in that way. A mail server that's set up so that anyone in the world can use it to send outgoing mail is called an *open relay*. Even though that may sound convenient, spammers frequently use open relays to send massive quantities of junk mail without getting caught, because they can't easily be traced if they weren't required to log in to send mail. For this reason, it is prudent to restrict access for sending outgoing mail to only those computers you trust. Trusted computers could include machines on your local network or company domain, or computers owned by friends and family. To set the list of which computers can use your mail server for sending outgoing mail, enter

```
sudo pico /etc/mail/access
```

Type the domain name or IP address of each computer you want to grant access to on a line by itself, followed by a space and the word **RELAY**. You can enter individual IP addresses or use wild cards such as * to specify a range. When you enter domain names, any computer whose name ends in the domain you list will be permitted to relay mail. **Figure 45.4** illustrates some of the possibilities. When you're finished, exit pico and save your changes.

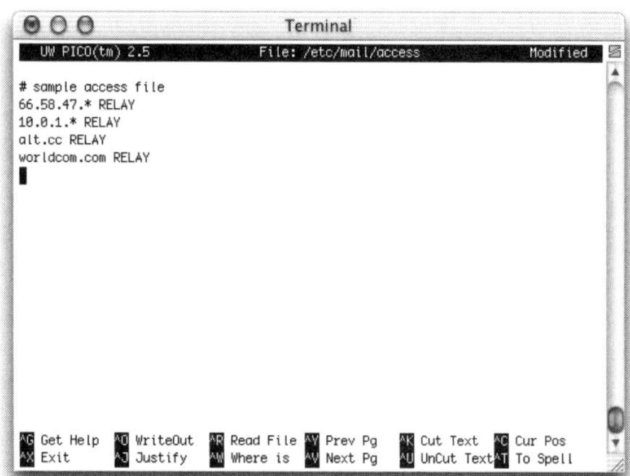

45.4

■ After creating the access file, you need to convert it into a special database format that sendmail needs. First, enter `cd /etc/mail` to switch to the mail directory and then enter

```
makemap hash access.db < access
```

Assign the necessary permissions to the `access` and `access.db` files by entering the following command:

```
sudo chmod 644 access access.db
```

■ Last but not least, you need to modify a file that lists the host names your computer will recognize when mail is sent to it. Normally, this includes your computer's domain name, but if you want to be able to receive mail by IP address (such as **user@12.34.56.78**) as well — or if your computer has multiple domain names — you'll need to add those, too. To edit this file, enter

```
sudo pico /etc/mail/local-host-names
```

Enter each name on a line by itself. At minimum, you should enter your computer's domain name and its IP address (or the IP address of your router or AirPort base station, if you use NAT (Network Address Translation — see Technique 41)). Your final file might look something like **Figure 45.5**

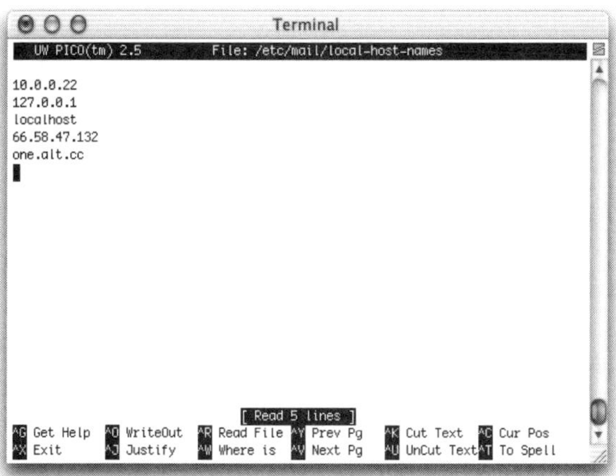

45.5

(but with your own IP addresses and domain names). As with the `access` and `access.db` files, enter `sudo chmod 644 local-host-names` to assign the correct permissions to this file.

■ When you're finished, restart your computer to activate sendmail.

STEP 3: INSTALL A POP/IMAP SERVER

While sendmail does the work of communicating with outside servers to send and receive files, you need additional software to view and organize your e-mail. The program that communicates with your client software (such as Mail or Eudora) is a POP or IMAP server. We'll install both now, so that you can access your mail using whichever protocol best suits your needs.

■ Go to `ftp://ftp.cac.washington.edu/imap/` and download the latest IMAP server source distribution. At the time this was written, the filename was imap-2002a.tar.Z, but there may be a newer version by the time you read

WARNING

The configuration you're installing here is relatively easy to set up and easy to use, but there is a downside: it's not terribly secure. I'll be the first to admit I take extra precautions on my own server — such as requiring SMTP authentication for outgoing mail and SSL for IMAP — to reduce the chance my server will be "borrowed" by spammers and to keep my e-mail safe from prying eyes. Unfortunately, there's just not space here to discuss the ins and outs of these extra security measures. See the book's Web site (`www.wiley.com/compbooks/kissell`) for some pointers to resources that can help you make your mail server more secure.

this. (See the book's Web site for an up-to-date link.)

■ After the file has downloaded, StuffIt Expander will probably decompress it for you automatically. If not, double-click the file to decompress it. It will create a folder with a name like **imap-2002a**.

■ Open Terminal and change to this directory — that is, type `cd` followed by a space and the path to the new folder, such as `~/Desktop/imap-2002a`. Then enter

```
pico src/osdep/unix/env_unix.c
```

■ Press **Control+W** to enter Find mode, type `mailsubdir` and press **Return**. You should see this line:

```
static char *mailsubdir = NIL;  /*
  mail subdirectory name */
```

■ Change this line to read

```
static char *mailsubdir =
  "Library/Mail/MyAccount";/* mail
  subdirectory name */
```

■ Press **Control+X** to exit pico; answer **y** to save the buffer and press **Return** to confirm the filename.

■ To compile the source code so it will run on your computer, enter

```
make osx SSLTYPE=none
```

You may see a warning that you are trying to create a version without SSL security. Answer **y** to dismiss this warning. (The SSL version of the server is indeed more secure, but also more complicated to configure — more so than there's space to describe here.) A series of messages will appear on your screen as the software compiles. When it's finished, move the IMAP and POP servers to their proper locations, as follows (with a space before /usr in the two places it occurs):

```
sudo mkdir -p /usr/local/libexec
sudo cp imapd/imapd
  /usr/local/libexec/
sudo cp ipopd/ipop3d
  /usr/local/libexec/
```

■ Just as you edited a file to make sure sendmail runs at startup, you must also tell Mac OS X to use the IMAP server (imapd) and the POP server (ipopd) at startup.

```
sudo pico /etc/inetd.conf
```

Look for this line:

```
##pop3  stream  tcp  nowait  root
  /usr/libexec/tcpd
  /usr/local/libexec/popper
```

■ First, uncomment it by removing the two pound characters (##) at the beginning; then replace `popper` with `ipop3d`. The line should now look like this:

```
pop3  stream  tcp  nowait  root
  /usr/libexec/tcpd
  /usr/local/libexec/ipop3d
```

Then uncomment (remove the ## from) the line

```
##imap4  stream  tcp  nowait  root
  /usr/libexec/tcpd
  /usr/local/libexec/imapd
```

which will then look like this:

```
imap4  stream  tcp  nowait  root
  /usr/libexec/tcpd
  /usr/local/libexec/imapd
```

■ Press **Control+X** to exit pico; answer **y** to save the buffer and press **Return** to confirm the filename.

■ Now restart your computer again to activate the POP and IMAP servers.

STEP 4: CONFIGURE USER ACCOUNTS

By default, you will automatically be set up with a mail account; your e-mail address will be your short user name followed by the @ sign and your machine's domain name. For example, if the user name you use to log into Mac OS X is **bob** and your computer's domain name is **somedomain.com**, your e-mail address would be **bob@somedomain.com**, and you can use your ordinary password to log into this account.

To give yourself (or others) additional e-mail addresses, simply create new user accounts for them on your computer.

- Open System Preferences. Click the **Accounts** icon.
- On the Users tab, click **New User...** and enter the user's full first and last name, a Short Name (which will be the first part of the e-mail address), and a password (see **Figure 45.6**). Click **OK**.
- Repeat this for each user account you want to set up.

45.6

STEP 5: CONFIGURE MAIL

Now you'll want to set up Mail to access the mail in your new account. This is very similar to the way you may have done it in the past.

- Open Mail and choose **Preferences...** from the **Mail** menu. Click **Accounts** and then click **New**.
- Choose **IMAP** or **POP** as the **Account Type** for mail. IMAP is a more modern, flexible protocol that allows you to keep your read and filed mail on the server so that you can access it from other computers as well. POP is more common, requiring you to download all mail messages to your local machine (which could be the same machine the mail server is running on). You can, if you want, set up *both* a POP account and an IMAP account to access the very same mailbox on the server.
- For **Email Address**, enter your short user name followed by an @ sign and the domain name of your computer.
- If you're setting up Mail on the same computer that's running your mail server, enter either **127.0.0.1** or **localhost** as the Incoming Mail Server. If you're setting up Mail on a different machine, enter your mail server's domain name here.
- For **User Name and Password**, just use your standard Mac OS X settings.
- For **Outgoing Mail Server**, click **Options...** and again enter **127.0.0.1** or **localhost** if you're setting up Mail on the mail server itself, or the computer's domain name if setting up Mail on another machine. Leave **Authentication** set to None. (Authentication is a good idea, but setting up your server to support it is beyond the scope of this technique.)
- Your configuration should now look something like **Figure 45.7**. Click **OK**. If everything is configured correctly, Mail should connect to your new

account without producing any error messages. You can now begin sending and receiving mail using your own computer as a mail server.

STEP 6: INSTALL A WEBMAIL SERVER (OPTIONAL)

You should now be able to access your mail server (using either POP or IMAP) with an e-mail client on your local computer or any other machine. However, accessing your mail from a Web browser can also be very useful — for example, if you're in a library or cybercafe where you can't configure an e-mail client, or when working behind a corporate firewall that blocks access to the ports used for e-mail. There's a wonderful open-source WebMail program you can add onto your new e-mail server in just a few minutes: SquirrelMail.

- Be sure you have activated and tested PHP as described in Technique 43.

45.7

- Go to `www.squirrelmail.org`, click the **Download** link, and download the latest *stable* release. The package should decompress automatically; if it doesn't, double-click it to run StuffIt Expander.
- The folder may have a name like Squirrelmail 1.2.10; rename it so that it's just **squirrelmail**.
- Move the folder to the /Library/WebServer/ Documents/ directory. For example, if the folder is currently on your desktop, enter this:

```
sudo mv ~/Desktop/squirrelmail
  /Library/WebServer/Documents/
```

- Switch to the folder you just moved:

```
cd /Library/WebServer/Documents/
  squirrelmail
```

- Change the owner of the data directory (where preferences will be stored) so that it is owned by www (the Web server):

```
$ chown -R www:www data
```

- Run the configuration program:

```
./configure
```

This program displays a menu of choices, as shown in **Figure 45.8**. You need to modify only a few settings.

- Enter **2** for **Server Settings** and then enter **1** for **Domain.** Type your computer's domain name (as set up in Technique 41).
- While on the Server Settings page, enter **10** for **Server** and then enter **uw** for the **University of Washington's IMAP Server.** Enter **r** to return to the main menu.
- Enter **3** for **Folder Defaults.** Choosing options **3**, **4**, and **5**, in turn, change the folder locations for INBOX.Trash, INBOX.Sent, and INBOX.Drafts to **Trash**, **Sent**, and **Drafts**, respectively. Enter **r** to return to the main menu.
- Enter **s** for **Save data** and then **q** for **Quit**.

That's all there is to it. Your Webmail program should now be ready to go. To try it out, open your Web browser and enter `http://127.0.0.1/squirrelmail`. You should see a screen like the one shown in **Figure 45.9**. Enter your user name (either the short or long version) and your password and click **Login**, and you'll have full Web-based access to all your e-mail. When you're away from your computer, substitute your computer's domain name for 127.0.0.1 — for example, `http://mydomain.com/squirrelmail`.

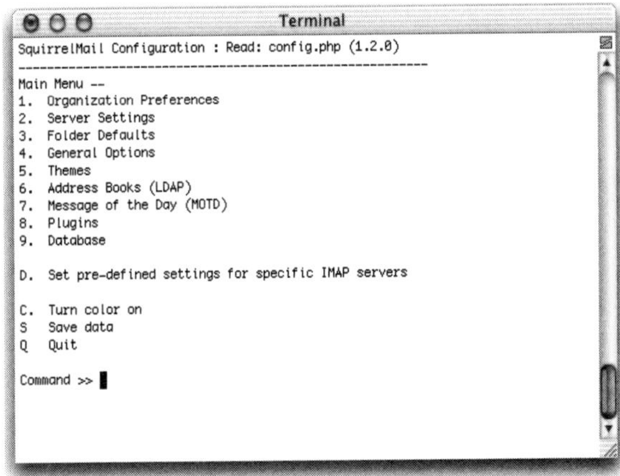

45.8

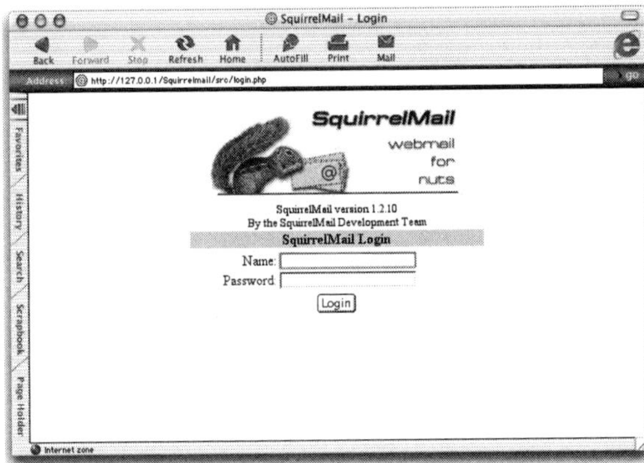

45.9

CHAPTER 10

MAINTENANCE AND AUTOMATION TECHNIQUES

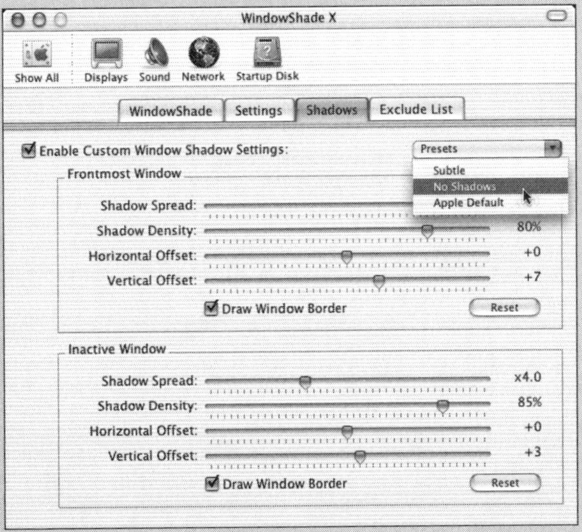

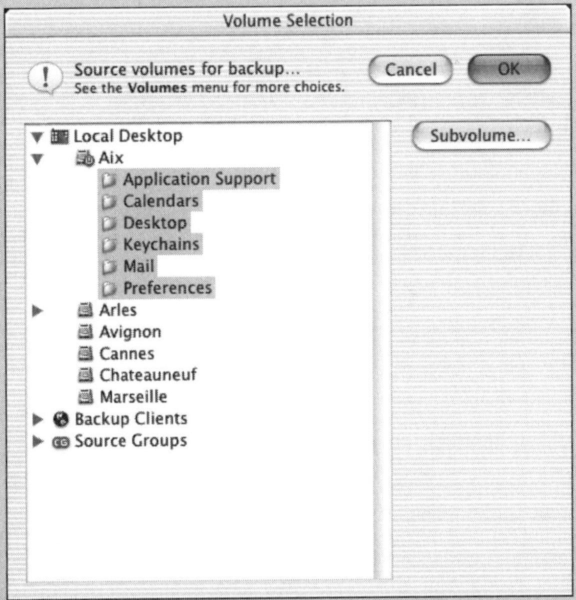

Mac OS X is a very stable and robust operating system. Compared with previous versions of the Mac OS, it is a paragon of reliability. However, no one has yet created a computer that works perfectly all the time. When problems inevitably occur, having some techniques at your disposal to deal with them helps. Taking preventive action can also keep your computer running more smoothly — and quickly.

The techniques in this final chapter deal with maintaining your computer — both to prevent problems and to solve them if they do occur. A crucial part of any maintenance routine is performing regular backups. Not all problems can be prevented or solved, but having a copy of your data (or two or three) in a safe place can dramatically reduce the impact of serious problems. As a result, two of these techniques are for creating backup copies of your data.

The final technique in this chapter, "Scheduling Activities to Happen Automatically," does have some potential maintenance applications — for example, you could schedule a file backup or disk utility to run while you sleep. But it has broader uses, as well. Your computer can help you maintain your sanity by performing repetitive or tedious tasks without requiring your direct involvement.

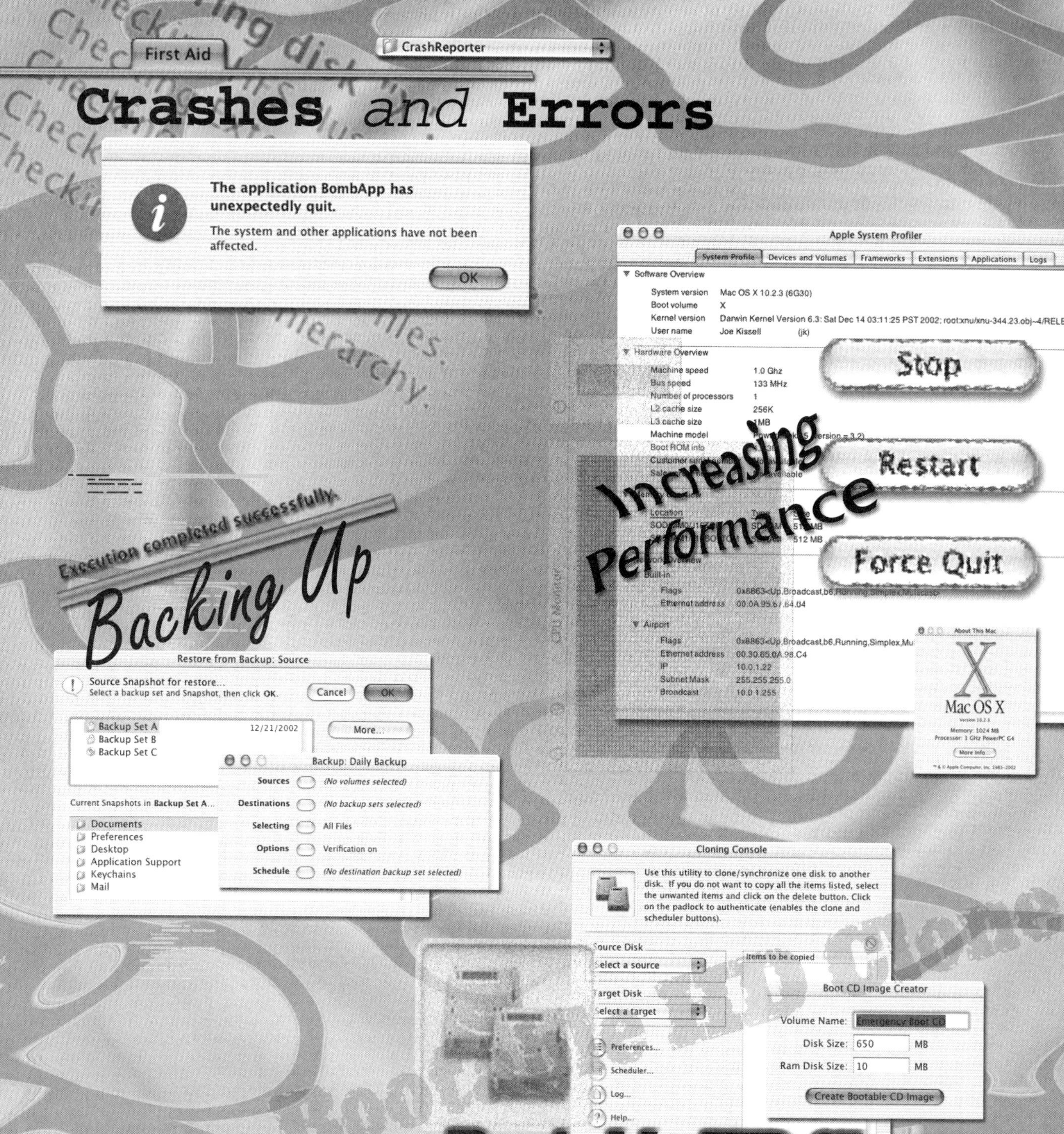
First Aid
CrashReporter
Crashes and Errors
The application BombApp has unexpectedly quit.
The system and other applications have not been affected.
OK
Apple System Profiler
Stop
Restart
Force Quit
Increasing Performance
Execution completed successfully.
Backing Up
Restore from Backup: Source
Backup: Daily Backup
About This Mac
Mac OS X
Cloning Console
Boot CD Image Creator
Create Bootable CD Image
Bootable HD Clone

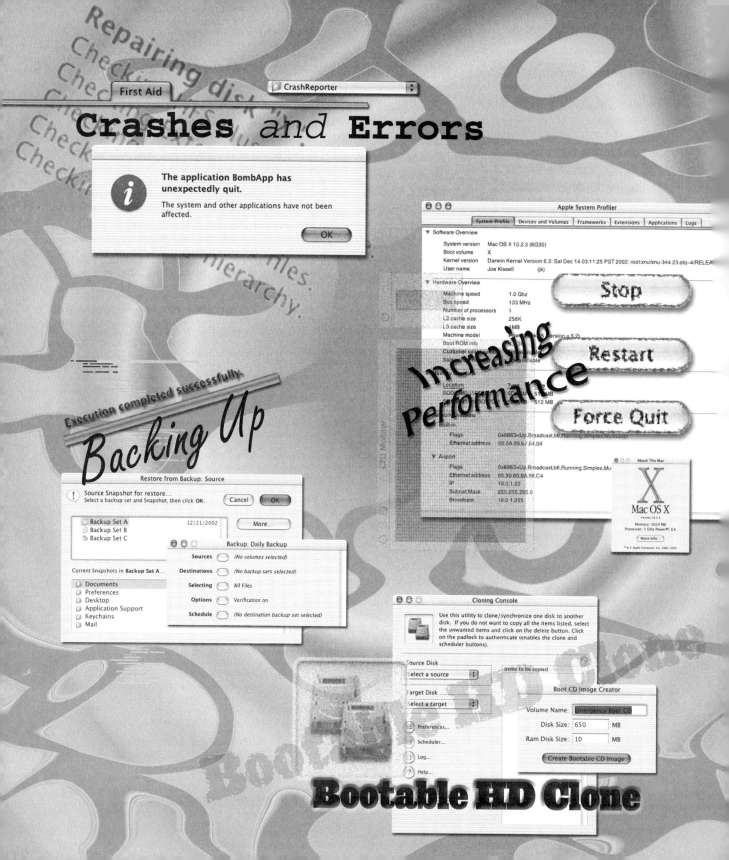

TECHNIQUE 46

RECOVERING FROM CRASHES AND ERRORS

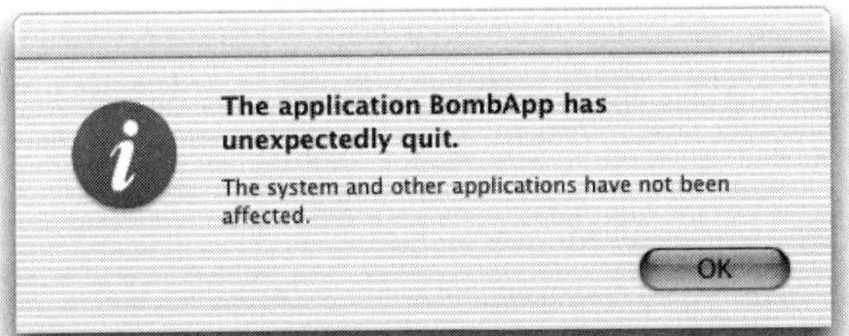

46.1

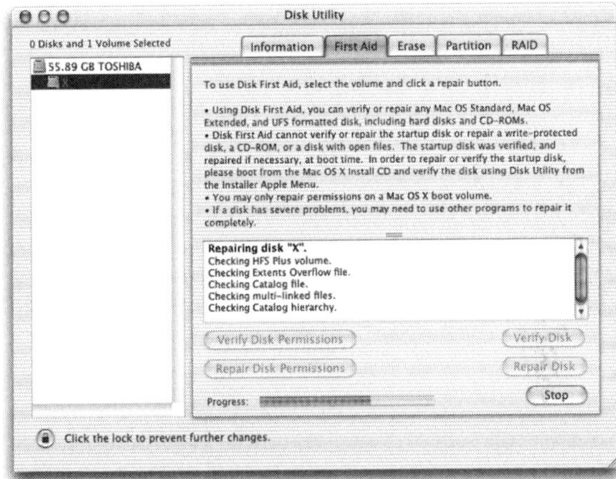

46.2

ABOUT THE FEATURE

Despite your best efforts, things will occasionally go wrong with your computer. Some basic steps will help you to get back in business and prevent future problems.

If you've kept up with Apple's marketing propaganda about Mac OS X, you know that it's fully buzzword-compliant. This advanced operating system includes important features like protected memory, preemptive multitasking, and journaling. You may not know what all these terms mean, but you probably have gotten the general idea that Mac OS X is supposed to be one of the most robust, crash-proof systems on the market. And so it is, especially compared with Mac OS 9. Crashes occur much less frequently, and when they do occur, they are usually not very severe — in most cases, simply restarting an application is all that is needed. The operating system itself rarely crashes completely.

And yet, no software is perfect. With determined effort (or just bad luck), you can get errors, crashes, and freezes to occur in Mac OS X. When they do, it's not always apparent how to return your machine to health — or how to prevent them from happening in the future. This technique helps you to recover from many kinds of errors. I can't pretend to give you a magic formula that will solve all problems, but I can at least point you in the right direction.

Crashes and freezes fall into two main categories: application crashes and system crashes. When an error occurs, it may not always be evident which sort of crash you're looking at. In general, however, application problems cause a single application to misbehave, while allowing you to use other applications that may be running at the same time. System crashes prevent you from doing *anything* with your computer. The technique for dealing with crashes is different depending on which sort of crash you're experiencing, so I discuss them separately. When in doubt, try the application instructions first and then move on to the system instructions.

APPLICATION CRASHES AND FREEZES

The most common type of crash involves an application that stops responding. You may see a colorful spinning beach ball cursor for a long time, or you may simply find that you can't activate, move, or type in any of the application's windows.

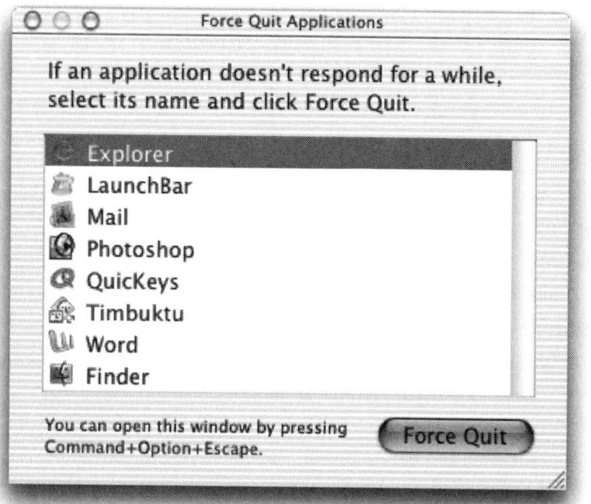

46.3

STEP 1: GET OUT OF A STUCK APPLICATION

If an application is stuck, try the following:

- Wait. (Really.) Sometimes applications just take an unexpectedly long time to respond, due to behind-the-scenes processing or delays introduced by other applications running in the background. Before taking any drastic measures, try waiting for five minutes or so to see whether the application comes back to life on its own.
- Force Quit. If an application doesn't respond even after several minutes, it may have crashed. To quit it, press **⌘+Option+Esc** (or choose **Force Quit** from the Apple menu). Select the application you want to quit from the list (see **Figure 46.3**) and click **Force Quit**. Sometimes an application will continue running for a while even after you've used Force Quit. If this happens, repeat the process and attempt to Force Quit it a second time. Applications nearly always quit on the second try.
- Sometimes, one stuck application can prevent other applications from responding. For example, you could find that iTunes and Internet Explorer are both unresponsive. Force quit these applications one at a time. In some cases, quitting one application causes another application to come back to life.
- If force quitting does not work, you probably have a system freeze. Follow the instructions later in the section "System Crashes and Freezes" to restart your computer.

STEP 2: CHECK THE CONSOLE AND LOGS

If an application crashes once, you can probably chalk it up to random chance and move on. But repeated crashes suggest a real problem that needs to be solved. Sometimes, determining the source of the problem is hard — it could have been a particular application, a third-party extension, or a glitch in Mac OS X itself. System logs maintained automatically by Mac OS X can help you pinpoint the culprit.

- Open the Console application in /Applications/Utilities. It displays a plain window (see **Figure 46.4**) listing the system messages generated by various applications since your Mac last started. Some of these messages are simply informative and don't necessarily indicate a problem (even if they contain the word "error"). But if you notice a series of errors related to an application that seems to be malfunctioning, the messages here can give you a clue as to what might be going wrong. You may also discover that an error points to a kernel extension or background application; I discuss these momentarily. Console messages, of course, were designed to be read by engineers. So in most cases, you'll want to contact the manufacturer of the software that produced the error messages, tell them what your console said, and ask what corrective action you can take.
- Choose **Open Log...** from Console's **File** menu. This displays the contents of the folder ~/Library/Logs/CrashReporter (see **Figure 46.5**). If an application crashes, information about what was happening inside the application and the operating system at the time of the crash is written to a log file. This can help determine what the problem was. Select a log file and click **Open** to view its contents. As with console messages, log files mostly contain a lot of numbers that look like gibberish to anyone who isn't a programmer. But you can at least tell which applications have crashed — and how many times — by glancing at the log files in this folder. When you've determined that a particular application is misbehaving regularly, you can contact the manufacturer with this log information for help in resolving the problem.

console.log

```
Mac OS X Version 10.2.3 (Build 6G30)
DOCK: CFMessagePortSendRequest returned -2
Dec 21 10:12:14 localhost WindowServer[172]: CGXDisableUpdate: Updates disabled by connection 0x6907 for over 1.000000
seconds

Dec 21 10:12:15 localhost WindowServer[172]: CGXDisableUpdate: Updates disabled by connection 0x6e03 for over 1.000000
seconds

2002-12-21 10:12:17.241 SystemUIServer[428] Loading 'MagicMenu'
2002-12-21 10:12:20.867 MagicMenuHotKeyDaemon[432] MagicMenuHotKeyDaemon Launched
ucontrol.config: 0 -> 1536
ucontrol.param1: 0 -> 0
ucontrol.param2: 0 -> 0
ucontrol.param3: 0 -> 0
ucontrol.param4: 0 -> 0
ucontrol.capslock: 0 -> 0
ucontrol.enter: 0 -> 0
ucontrol.scrollkey: 0 -> 8388608
ucontrol.scrollscale: 0 -> 10
aped[172]: Attach failed: 5, for PGPservice[486]
Dec 21 10:12:38 localhost last message repeated 2 times

Dec 21 10:12:46 localhost sendmail[396]: unable to qualify my own domain name (localhost) -- using short name

Dec 21 10:12:47 localhost sendmail[491]: My unqualified host name (localhost) unknown; sleeping for retry

2002-12-21 10:12:52.116 SystemUIServer[487] Loading 'MagicMenu'
Dec 21 10:12:53 localhost WindowServer[172]: CGXDisableUpdate: Updates disabled by connection 0x7607 for over 1.000000
```

46.4

STEP 3: UPDATE YOUR SOFTWARE

A common cause of conflicts, crashes, and freezes is outdated software. Making sure all your applications and utilities are up to date can increase your system's stability.

- Open System Preferences and click the **Software Update** icon. Click **Check Now** (see **Figure 46.6**) to check for updated versions of Mac OS X or any other Apple-supplied software. If new

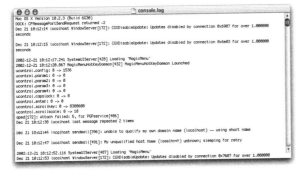

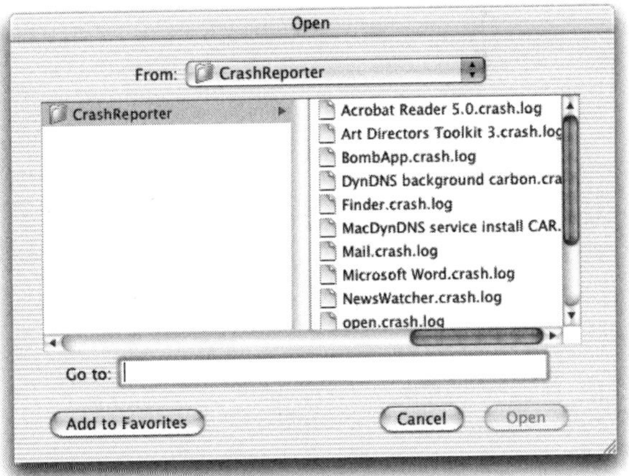

46.5

software is found, install it, restart (if prompted to do so) and then run Software Update again. Sometimes a newer update is dependent on an older one, and won't appear in the list until the older one is installed.

- Check the Web sites belonging to the publishers of software you have installed. This includes not only applications, but also shareware and freeware utilities and gadgets like the ones that have been mentioned frequently in this book. If there's a newer version than what you have installed, download it and update your copy.
- If you want to avoid the hassle of visiting lots of different Web sites looking for updates, try `www.versiontracker.com` or `www.macupdate.com`, both of which provide links to a wide variety of the latest updates.

If updated software does not solve your problem, contact the technical support department of the company that makes the malfunctioning software for assistance.

SYSTEM CRASHES AND FREEZES

Most crashes in Mac OS X are restricted to particular applications, and can be resolved without restarting your system. Occasionally, however, your entire computer will stop working. This can happen in several different ways. In one case, your pointer could freeze on the screen. In another, you could continue seeing the spinning beach ball pointer even after you force quit every application — including the Finder. Then there's the *kernel panic*, a type of low-level crash in which your entire screen dims and a box appears with a message in several languages saying you need to restart your computer. When a system crash occurs, here are some steps you can follow to recover.

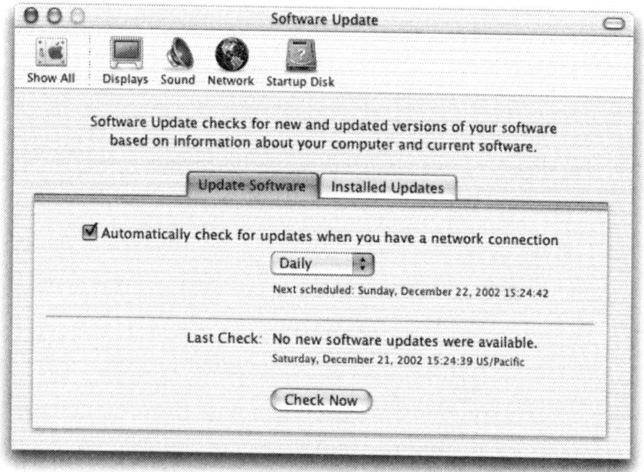

46.6

STEP 1: RESTART YOUR COMPUTER

The very act of restarting often solves whatever problem led to your crash in the first place. More often than not, when you restart after a crash, you can continue working as though nothing happened. However, because of the design of modern Macs, it's not always obvious *how* to restart if you're not able to access the Apple menu.

- If your keyboard has a power button, press **⌘+Control+power** to restart your computer immediately.
- If your keyboard doesn't have a power button but does have an eject key, you may be able to achieve the same result by pressing **⌘+Control+eject**.
- If your computer has a reset button (indicated by a small triangle icon), press that button to restart your computer.
- If none of the preceding ways of restarting works, press and hold your computer's main power button for about five seconds. This should cause your computer to shut down; you can then press the power button again to restart.

If your computer behaves normally after a restart, you don't need to continue with these steps. If, however, you experience repeated crashes, try the following.

STEP 2: WEED OUT LOGIN ITEMS

Many system crashes are caused by conflicts between the Mac OS and other software you have loaded. Often, the conflicting software is running in the background so you aren't even aware it's there. By turning off other software you don't need, you can reduce the chance of a conflict.

- Open System Preferences and go to the **Login Items** pane, as shown in **Figure 46.7**. You'll see a list of all the applications that open automatically when you log in. Look for the one you added most recently. (An application's installer may have placed it here automatically.) Select it, click **Remove**, and restart your computer.
- If the conflict goes away, you'll know you found the cause. If not, repeat this procedure for other Login Items. Note that some software (such as input device drivers or anti-virus applications) will not work correctly unless its corresponding login item has loaded.

STEP 3: REPAIR YOUR HARD DISK

When you repeatedly experience unexpected behavior on your computer — even after restarting several times and removing potentially conflicting software — it's time to run a disk repair utility. Apple includes a free one called Disk Utility with Mac OS X, and it can repair many types of disk problems.

- Restart your computer from a *different* volume from the one that needs to be repaired. A second copy of your system on another partition, or a bootable clone on an external hard drive (see Technique 49) would make a good choice for your alternate startup volume. Otherwise, use your Mac OS X installation CD. To start up from a different volume, go to the Startup Disk pane of System Preferences and choose the volume you want to use; then click **Restart.**
- After you've restarted from another volume, open Disk Utility (located in /Applications/ Utilities). If you've started from a CD, the Mac OS X installer may run automatically. At the first installer screen, choose **Open Disk Utility** from the **Installer** menu.
- Click the **First Aid** tab in Disk Utility. (See **Figure 46.8.**) In the list on the left, select the volume that is experiencing problems. Click **Repair Disk.** Disk Utility will check the integrity of your

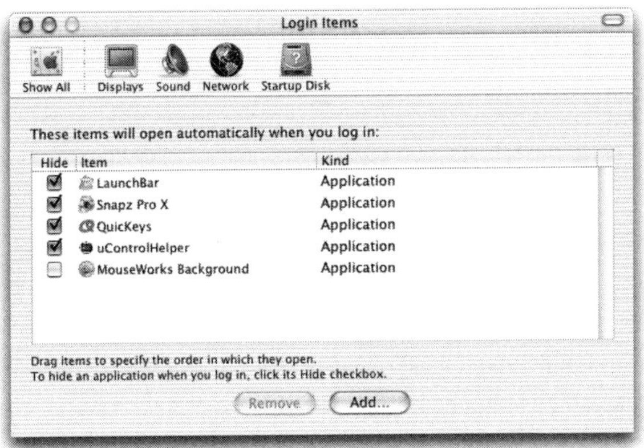

46.7

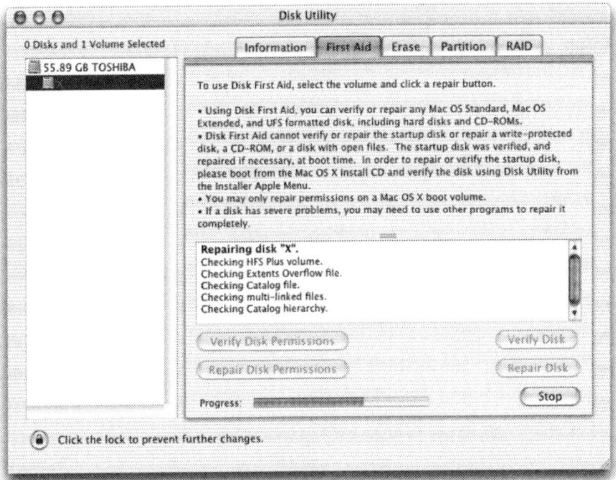

46.8

hard disk's file catalog and other attributes, and repair them if necessary.

- After the repair is complete, also click the **Repair Disk Permissions** button. Sometimes the ownership and permissions for system files can become altered, and this can prevent applications from operating properly. Clicking this button restores permissions for all your system files to their correct values.
- When the repairs are complete, quit Disk Utility and restart your computer from its normal startup volume.

If your hard disk has serious errors, Disk Utility may not be able to repair them (and it will usually display a message to this effect). If this happens, you'll need to purchase a heavier-duty third-party disk repair utility. The two best-known disk repair utilities for Mac OS X are Norton Utilities for Macintosh (`www.symantec.com`) and Drive 10 (`www.micromat.com`). Both utilities include a startup CD. After booting from this CD, run the utility to repair your hard disk. There are some cases in which one utility will be able to find and repair problems that the other can't. But if the repair utilities fail to fix your problem, this generally means you will need to reinstall Mac OS X. (See Step 6.)

STEP 4: ZAP YOUR PRAM

Every Mac has a special type of memory called Parameter RAM (PRAM) that stores certain system settings even when the computer is not running. PRAM includes information like the date and time, startup volume, audio level, and other very basic settings that your computer needs before the operating system has been loaded.

Sometimes, an inappropriate value in your PRAM can prevent proper operation of your system. Because PRAM is involved in many different aspects of your Mac's operation, it is difficult to say exactly which types of misbehavior it can cause. But because resetting (or *zapping*) it is easy, it's a useful tactic to employ when your computer is not working correctly and no other explanation seems to fit.

- To zap your PRAM, choose **Restart** from the Apple menu (or press your computer's reset button if it has one) and immediately hold down the ⌘, **Option**, **P**, and **R** keys. You will hear your computer's startup sound (unless the audio is muted). Continue holding them until you hear the startup sound a second time and then release them. Your computer should then restart normally.
- After your computer restarts, check your System Preferences. Some values, such as the Date & Time, may need to be reset.

STEP 5: LOOK FOR ROGUE KERNEL EXTENSIONS

If all the preceding steps fail to resolve your crashing problem, consider whether you may have a misbehaving kernel extension. Kernel extensions are different from what was called an *extension* in Mac OS 9, but can serve a similar purpose — adding functionality to your system at a very low level. The most common kernel extensions by far are device drivers. Drivers are software components that enable your computer to communicate with hardware you've attached. If you've added a third-party input device, scanner, PCI card, or other hardware, it probably included driver software in the form of a kernel extension. Some operating system enhancements also include kernel extensions.

Most kernel extensions are very well behaved — and, in fact, essential for proper operation of your hardware. Occasionally, though, you may install driver software for a new device you've purchased and find that it causes a conflict of some kind. For example, you may have an older version of the software that hasn't been updated for compatibility with the latest version of Mac OS X. If you suspect you have a software conflict but have ruled out login items, then checking for misbehaving kernel extensions is a good idea.

- Kernel extensions are stored in /System/Library/Extensions. Navigate to this folder in the Finder (see **Figure 46.9**), choose List View for the window, and click the Date Modified column to sort by date. The most recently modified kernel extensions appear at the top of the list and the oldest ones appear at the bottom. The vast majority of these extensions are supplied by Apple as part of Mac OS X — and most of these have similar modification dates. The newest ones and the oldest ones are the ones most likely to have been added by a third-party installer.
- Look through this list and see whether you can identify any kernel extensions you may have added recently as part of a software or hardware installation. In most cases, you can identify new items by name. If you notice a newly added extension that seems to be a likely source of conflicts, you can disable it temporarily to see whether the problem goes away.

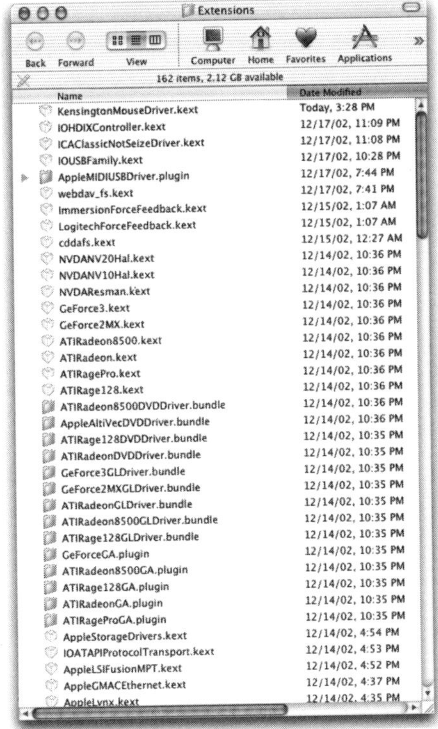

46.9

- To disable a suspicious extension, leave your Extensions folder open in the Finder and open Terminal.
- Type `sudo mv` followed by a space. Then switch back to the Finder window displaying your extensions and select the kernel extension you want to disable. Drag it into the Terminal window to insert its pathname onto the command line. Then type a space character followed by **~/Desktop/** and press **Return**. The entire line should look something like this:

```
sudo mv /System/Library/Extensions/
  some-driver-name.kext ~/Desktop
```

Enter your password when prompted. The extension will be moved to your desktop.

- Restart your computer. If the conflict goes away, you can be fairly certain the extension you moved was at fault. Contact the manufacturer of the product it came with to see whether an update is available. If the conflict is still there, repeat this process for any other suspicious extensions. To replace an extension you moved earlier (after you've determined it's not responsible for the crashes), reverse the preceding procedure. In Terminal, type `sudo mv` followed by a space. Select the kernel extension on your desktop and drag it into the Terminal window to insert its pathname onto the command line. Then type a space character followed by **/System/Library/**

WARNING

Do not disable any kernel extensions supplied by Apple, because doing so can prevent your computer from operating properly. If in doubt, don't touch it.

Extensions/ and press **Return**. The entire line should look something like this:

```
sudo mv /Users/your-name/Desktop/
  some-driver-name.kext /System/
  Library/Extensions/
```

■ Enter your password when prompted. The extension will be moved back into the Extensions folder. Restart your computer to reactivate the extension.

STEP 6: IF ALL ELSE FAILS, REINSTALL MAC OS X

In severe cases where every other repair attempt has failed, it is possible that some vital component of Mac OS X itself is damaged. If this happens, your only recourse is to reinstall the operating system. Although this sounds scary, it's actually not that bad. You can reinstall Mac OS X without erasing your hard drive or destroying the files you've created. You may have to reset some system preferences and reinstall system enhancements like preference panes, but in general it's relatively painless.

■ To reinstall Mac OS X, insert your Mac OS X installation CD and restart your computer. Hold down the **C** key as you restart to boot from the CD. Follow the prompts to install Mac OS X on the same volume where it was before.

■ If the version of Mac OS X on your installation CD is older than the version you had installed before, choose the **Archive and install** option. This creates a new system folder but saves the contents of your previous system so that you can manually replace any files you may need to restore your system to its previous state.

■ After installing and restarting, use **Software Update** to apply all the current updates to the Apple-supplied software.

■ Finally, if you performed the **Archive and install**, locate any needed preference files, fonts, or other files you need in your Previous System folder and drag them to the corresponding location in your new System folder.

TECHNIQUE 47

INCREASING YOUR COMPUTER'S PERFORMANCE

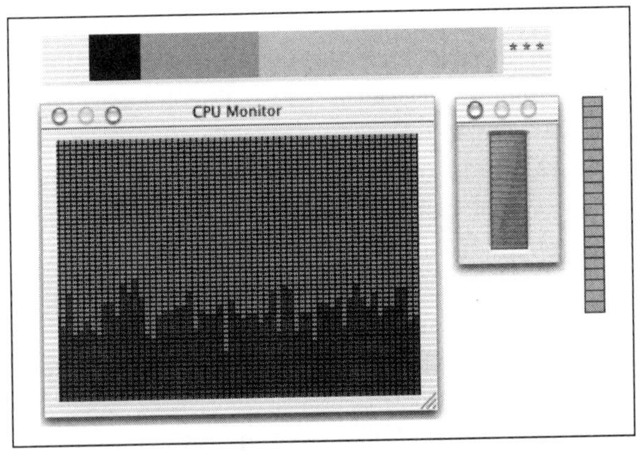

47.1

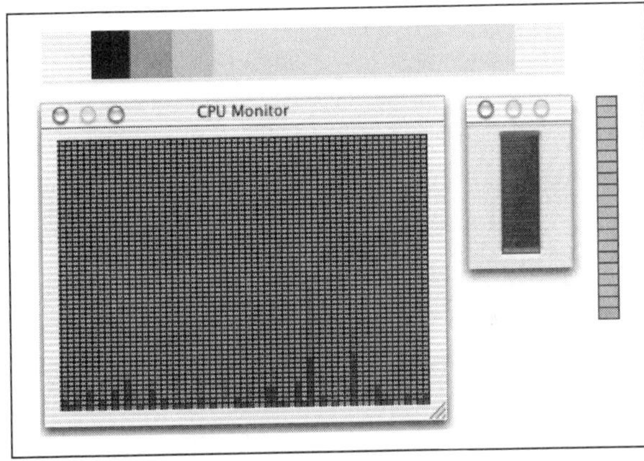

47.2

ABOUT THE FEATURE

Whether you have an older G3 iMac or the newest multiprocessor Power Mac, your computer can probably benefit from all the extra speed it can get. The simple steps shown in this technique can make your machine run faster and more efficiently.

I have never heard anyone complain about a computer being too fast. Even though Macs get faster with each new release, the demands users place on them increase at an even greater pace. Applications that perform complex graphics, audio, and video tasks keep even the speediest processors quite busy. Servers, calendars, e-mail programs, and other tools that may be running at any time all take their toll. Pretty soon, even the fastest new Mac can begin to feel sluggish.

Apple, of course, would like you to address this problem by buying next year's model. I wouldn't discourage you from doing that (I want next year's model, too!), but there are less expensive ways of getting extra performance from your computer. Here are some steps I've found helpful for increasing a Mac's performance.

STEP 1: ADD RAM

Mac OS X is very memory-hungry. Virtual memory is built into the system, so you can open lots of applications and files — even if you run out of physical memory — because your hard drive is used as a temporary storage place to supplement RAM. However, using virtual memory is much slower than using physical memory, because reading and writing data takes much longer with a hard drive than it does with silicon. The more virtual memory you use, the slower your computer's performance will become.

Most modern Macs can accommodate between 1 and 2GB of RAM. My advice is to add the maximum amount of RAM your machine will hold. Compared to the cost of your computer, the investment is small, but the performance increases are significant.

- To find out how much RAM is in your computer, choose **About this Mac** from the Apple menu. **Figure 47.3** shows the resulting window for a machine with 1GB (1024MB) of RAM.
- Most Macs have several internal slots that can accommodate DIMMs (Dual Inline Memory Modules). To see which slots are filled (and with how much RAM) and which are available, click **More Info...** to open the Apple System Profiler. Look under Memory Overview (shown in **Figure 47.4**) for a list of RAM modules in the various slots.
- To find the maximum RAM capacity of your computer — as well as instructions for adding additional RAM — consult the instruction booklet that came with your machine. This booklet also specifies which type of RAM module you should buy — there are a variety of shapes, speeds, and connector types.
- Be aware that in some cases, maxing out your computer's RAM will mean removing a smaller capacity module and replacing it with a larger one. For example, if your computer has two DIMM slots, each with a 256MB module, you'll have to remove both of them and replace them

47.3

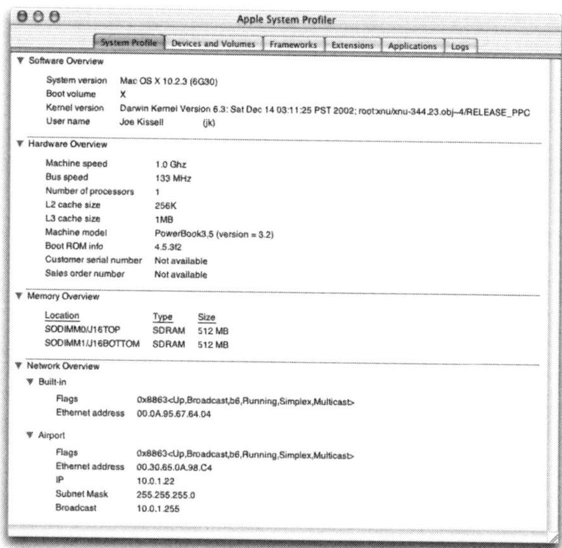

47.4

with 512MB modules to get the maximum possible RAM. The sacrifice is generally well worth it — and remember, you can always sell (or give away) your used RAM modules.

STEP 2: MOVE YOUR SWAP FILE TO ANOTHER VOLUME

This step is a bit strange, and somewhat controversial. Although I don't have performance test results to quantify the benefits, I have it on good authority (from an Apple engineer) that this procedure is the single best way — beyond adding RAM — to increase your Mac's performance. This is especially true if your Mac has a limited amount of RAM and you can't increase it for some reason.

When your computer uses virtual memory (as described in Step 1), it writes the information from your physical RAM onto the hard disk temporarily. The file that holds this data is called a *swap file*. The more you access virtual memory, the more often this file is read and written to. And the more it's changed, the more fragmented it can become. Your hard drive doesn't reserve an unlimited amount of space in one location for a particular file, so as the file grows, it may need to be split into pieces. The time it takes for your hard drive to find and reassemble all these pieces when it accesses virtual memory can make the process much slower.

NOTE

Some computers (such as the flat-panel iMac) have a second internal memory slot that is not user-accessible. To change the RAM in this slot, you'll need to take your Mac to an authorized dealer or service center. Often, however, the inaccessible slot is already configured with the largest DIMM possible before it leaves the factory.

The way to speed up the process is to put the swap file on a volume all by itself to make sure it never gets fragmented. To increase performance even further, put it at the center (or "beginning") of your hard drive, where the read/write head does not have to move as far to access it.

The first thing you'll need to do is prepare a volume to hold your swap file. By default, your swap file resides on your main startup volume. You can put it anywhere, but because it works best on a volume of its own, you should create a separate partition for the file. (A partition is simply a portion of your hard drive that is treated as a separate volume.) The very best results come from using a separate hard drive from the one where your system resides (a high-speed FireWire drive works especially well), but if that is not feasible, at least create a separate partition on your internal hard drive. Whether internal or external, you should plan to set aside between 500MB and 1GB of space for your swap file.

To create a new partition:

- Back up your important files, as described in Technique 48 — or better yet, make a bootable clone of your disk, as described in Technique 49, putting your files on an external hard drive or a DVD-R. Partitioning your hard drive erases *everything* on it.
- Start up your computer from the Mac OS X Installation CD (or the Software Install CD/DVD that came with your computer).
- When the installer runs, ignore the main window and choose **Open Disk Utility...** from the **Installer** menu. Disk Utility opens.
- Click the **Partition** tab, and select your hard drive from the list on the left. Choose the number of partitions (volumes) you want from the **Volume Scheme** pop-up menu. The topmost volume will be used for your swap file. Drag the bar beneath this partition to set it to the desired size — ideally, between 500MB and 1GB. Give the

volume a descriptive name. (See **Figure 47.5** for an example.)

■ Repeat this step for each of your remaining volumes. You can make as many or as few as you want, with whatever sizes and names are suitable for your needs. When you're finished, click **Partition**. Quit Disk Utility.

■ If you did not create a bootable clone of your hard drive, proceed with the (re-)installation of Mac OS X. Be sure *not* to install it on the partition you designated for your swap file! When you're finished, restart your computer.

■ If you *did* create a bootable clone of your hard drive, quit the Installer, restart, and hold down the Option key while your computer starts up. Select the volume containing the bootable clone and click the right arrow. After your computer finishes booting, use Carbon Copy Cloner (see Technique 49) to restore your backed-up files to one of your new partitions (again — anything except the one you designated for your swap file). Finally, restart from your newly restored main startup volume.

After you have a partition set aside for your swap file, the rest is easy.

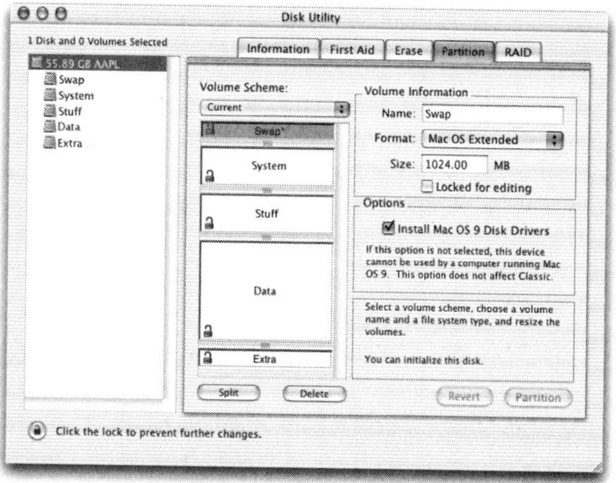

47.5

■ Download the free Swap Cop utility from `homepage.mac.com/jschrier/`.

■ Open Swap Cop, shown in **Figure 47.6**. Choose your designated swap file volume from the pop-up menu and then click **Change Swap Location**. Enter your administrator password when prompted, and click **Continue** when asked whether you're sure you want to move the swap disk. Click **OK** to dismiss the confirmation dialog and then quit Swap Cop and restart your computer.

■ After your computer has restarted, open Swap Cop again. It will automatically delete your old swap file. You can then quit Swap Cop.

STEP 3: TURN CLASSIC OFF (OR ON)

Although I said in the Preface that none of the techniques covers Classic, it does bear just a brief mention within the context of improving performance. The Classic environment can slow you down in either of two ways. If you use it frequently, the time spent waiting for it to start up can be very annoying. Conversely, if you use it rarely, the extra processing power it uses in the background when you're not actually running a Classic application can slow down the rest of your computer. In either case, checking on your Classic settings can help to speed up your Mac.

47.6

- If you do *not* use Classic often, be sure to turn it off when it's not in use. To stop the Classic environment, go to the **Classic** pane of System Preferences (see **Figure 47.7**) and click **Stop**. Also be sure **Start Classic when you log in** is unchecked.
- If you use Classic several times a day, the additional overhead from having it running all the time will be minor compared to the time you have to wait for it to start up. You might want to do just the opposite — make sure **Start Classic when you log in** is checked. That way your log in time is increased a bit, but you won't have to interrupt your work to wait for Classic to start when you open a Classic application.
- Regardless of how often you use Classic, consider turning off any extensions or control panels you don't absolutely need — this decreases Classic's startup time. To change which extensions are loaded, click the **Advanced** tab in Classic Preferences and choose **Open Extensions Manager** from the **Startup Options** pop-up menu. Click **Start**, and when Extensions Manager opens, uncheck any extensions that aren't needed by the applications you use.

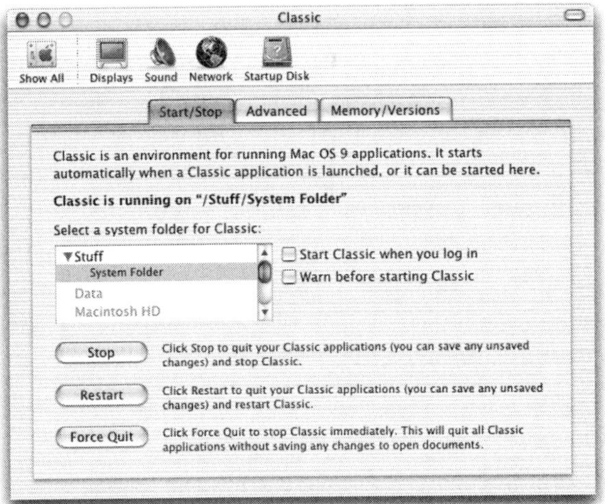

47.7

STEP 4: CUT BACK ON SYSTEM ENHANCEMENTS

As you use your Mac (and follow the techniques in this book), you're bound to accumulate all sorts of gadgets — extensions, plug-ins, and add-ons of all sorts that enhance your computer's functionality. After a point, however, the benefit gained from adding more and more utilities trails off as they begin to take a toll on your computer's resources. If you have lots of add-ons installed, consider paring back to just the most essential ones. Here are some prime examples:

- **Contextual Menu plug-ins.** If you have more than a few extra items in your Contextual Menus folders (to add additional commands to the menus that appear when you right-click or Control+click), it can take a very long time for the contextual menus to draw. If your menus draw slowly, they lose a lot of their value. Look through

NOTE

You can also make Classic sleep when no Classic applications are running. Adjust the slider on the Advanced tab in Classic preferences to set the sleep time. Although this reduces the processor time devoted to Classic when it's not in use, it does not turn it off entirely.

/Library/Contextual Menu Items and ~/Library/Contextual Menu Items for plug-ins you no longer need and move them to another folder (or to the Trash, if you're sure you won't want them again).

- **Login Items.** Having too many items open at login time can make starting your computer take a long time. In addition, many login items actually open background applications that run all the time, putting further strain on your processor. Open System Preferences, click the **Login Items** icon, and look for any items you may not need to open every time you log in (see **Figure 47.8**). Be careful, though: Some software will not work correctly if its Login Item entry is missing. Examples are input device drivers (like Kensington MouseWorks or Griffin PowerMate), QuicKeys, Virex, and some disk maintenance utilities.
- **Server tasks.** When you turn on Personal Web Sharing, Windows File Sharing, or any of the other options in the **Sharing** pane of System Preferences, you're starting up a background application that runs all the time. This even applies to the built-in firewall. Although none of these tasks uses a huge amount of processor time, you can gain a slight improvement by turning off any server options you don't use actively.
- **Animated Desktop Effects.** If you have set up your Desktop Picture to change frequently (like every five seconds), or if you've followed one of the techniques earlier in this book to display a slide show or animated screen saver on your desktop, you're probably slowing down your entire computer in exchange for this entertainment. If you can live without it and need a boost in speed, go to the **Desktop** pane of System Preferences and select a stationary desktop picture.
- **iTunes.** Playing a CD in the background as you work uses almost zero processing power, but if you're playing MP3 files, your computer has to expend a lot of effort decoding them. This can slow down other tasks you may be doing. If you're in need of some extra speed, try turning off iTunes, switching to a CD, or listening to music on your iPod, radio, or home stereo instead.

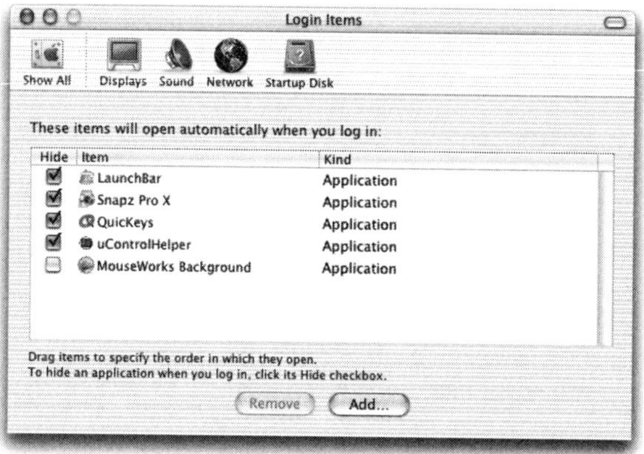

47.8

STEP 5: TURN OFF EXTRA GRAPHIC EFFECTS

The drop shadows, transparency, and special animation effects of Aqua are all beautiful to look at, but they also require a lot of processing power to create. Although most of this processing is done by your computer's graphics card rather than the main CPU, it can still slow your computer down by reducing the responsiveness of the display. If you're willing to trade some looks for a bit of a speed boost, consider turning off some of the special effects.

- To turn off the drop shadows that surround every window, download the shareware utility WindowShade X from `www.unsanity.com`.

After installing this software, log out and log back in to enable it. Then go to the WindowShade X pane in System Preferences and click the **Shadows** tab, as shown in **Figure 47.9**. Check the box next to **Enable Custom Window Shadow Settings** and choose **No Shadows** from the pop-up **Presets** menu.

- Your Dock makes use of several graphical effects that can slow it down somewhat. To adjust these, go to the **Dock** pane in System Preferences. For maximum responsiveness, turn off **Magnification** and **Animate opening applications** and choose the less-processor-intensive **Scale Effect** from the **Minimize using** pop-up menu.
- Having your display set to its maximum color depth (millions of colors) can in certain cases slow down the responsiveness of screen drawing. Go to the **Display** pane in System Preferences, click the **Display** tab, and choose **Thousands** from the **Colors** pop-up menu. If you don't do extensive work with photos or other graphics, you may find the difference in appearance almost unnoticeable, yet it can give your display a bit more zip.

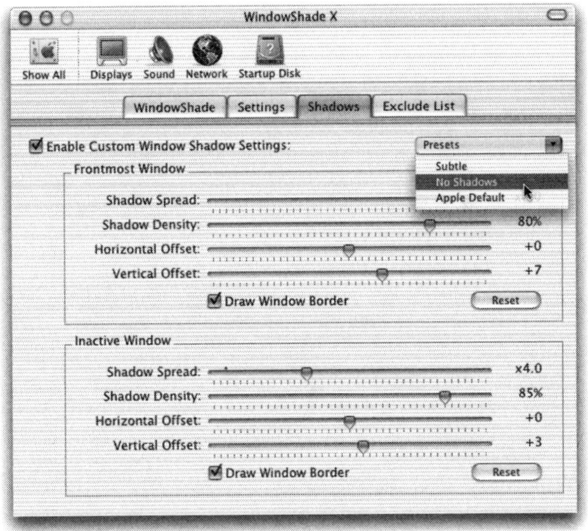

47.9

STEP 6: PERFORM JANITORIAL TASKS

Mac OS X, as you've heard repeatedly, has a core of UNIX. A standard part of the UNIX installation is a series of scripts that perform maintenance on the computer — for example, compressing old log files, updating the index that the **locate** command uses to find files, and removing unused temporary files to reclaim disk space. These maintenance tasks help your Mac to run more smoothly, and they are run automatically by **cron** (see Technique 50) in the middle of the night. (One script is run daily, another weekly, and a third monthly — though that timing is pretty arbitrary.)

This arrangement is fine if you leave your machine on all the time, but if you normally turn it off (or even put it to sleep) when it's not in use, these scripts never get a chance to run. However, running these scripts manually from the command line is easy.

- To run the daily maintenance script, open a Terminal window and enter `sudo periodic daily`.
- Type your administrator password when requested, and the script runs (normally completing in just a few seconds).
- Similarly, you can execute the weekly script by entering `sudo periodic weekly`, and you can activate the monthly script with `sudo periodic monthly`. The weekly and monthly scripts usually take longer to run than the daily script.

You can run any or all of these scripts as often as you like without causing any damage; once a week might be a reasonable interval.

TECHNIQUE **48**

BACKING UP (AND RESTORING) DATA PAINLESSLY

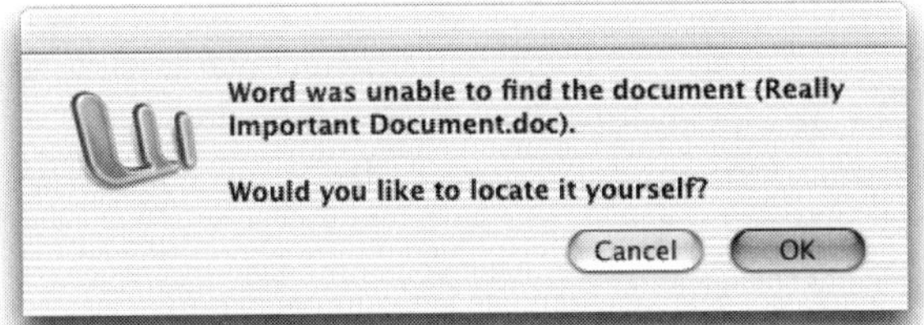

48.1

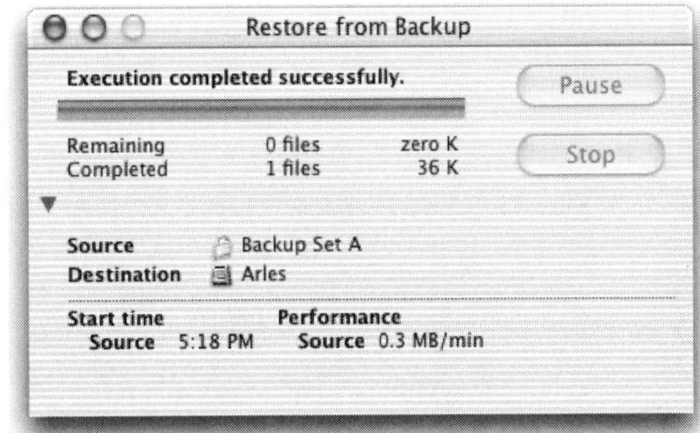

48.2

ABOUT THE FEATURE

Having a good backup strategy is the single most important step you can take to protect the investment of time and money you've put into your work. With the right approach, backups can be easy and nearly automatic.

There's a well-known maxim about backups: You can have convenience, security, or economy — or perhaps two of the three — but not all three at once. Everything comes at a cost. If you want a supremely convenient and secure system, you'll pay a lot for it; if you want to spend as little money as possible, you'll have to endure some inconvenience or a limited amount of security.

Having suffered some devastating data losses myself due to malfunctioning hardware (and, in some cases, user error), I've come to appreciate the value of a good backup plan. Even though you will incur a bit of expense and effort up-front, the savings of time and aggravation you'll realize when you need to recover a lost file will repay you many times over.

I've experimented with lots of backup programs, media, and methods. I've tried backing up with expensive commercial software like Retrospect Workgroup, various shareware programs, and Apple's own Backup application. I've backed up to DAT tape, CD-ROM, DVD-RW, Internet file servers, and hard drives. After years of trial and error, I've settled on a system that, for my needs, offers the best compromise among convenience, security, and economy — and that's what I describe here.

This may look like a lot of steps, but for the most part you only have to perform them once. Go through the bother of setting everything up, and it will operate automatically, behind the scenes, day after day. You'll barely remember it's there, except when it's time to swap hard drives or create an archive. If you do lose data and need to recover a file, you'll be very happy that you expended that initial effort.

STEP 1: UNDERSTAND THE SYSTEM

I've tried to steer clear of theory for most of this book, but for this particular technique you'll find it much easier to follow these steps if you understand the rationale behind this particular approach. The backup strategy I present has the following attributes:

- It backs up your important personal files, but not your system software or applications. Why? Backing up all that data takes a long time, and requires a huge amount of storage space, which can be expensive. Because reinstalling those items from their original CD-ROMs is relatively easy, I opt for speed and economy. However, I strongly urge you to follow Technique 49 ("Making a Bootable Clone of your Hard Drive") if you can, as this will greatly decrease the amount of time and effort required to restore your entire hard drive in the event of a major failure.
- It backs up certain kinds of media — MP3 files, photos, and movies — manually, to removable media, rather than as part of the automatic backup. The reason is that these files tend to change infrequently yet take a long time to back up (and occupy a lot of storage space). Your backups will go faster, and your backup media will go further, if these files are not part of your daily automatic backup.
- It backs up your data progressively. Terms like *incremental*, *differential*, *progressive*, and *archive* are often used to describe different kinds of backup techniques. Sometimes these terms are used interchangeably, while other times they mean very different things. Without getting bogged down in semantics, this technique starts by making a full copy of all the files you want to back up. Then, each night, it adds to the backup only those files that are new or different. But it still keeps the originals, as well as each changed version since that first backup. That way, if you need to go back to the version of a file that was current five days ago, you can.
- It uses multiple backup sets. When you perform a backup, the collection of files on the backup medium is known as a *backup set*. If you have only one backup set and the medium is damaged (or the data itself is corrupted for any reason), you'll be out of luck. For safety, it is always wise to alternate among multiple backup sets, so that if one is damaged, you have another way to recover your data.
- It uses a hard drive as the storage medium. Compared to other media, like CD-ROMs, DVD-RW, or tape drives, hard drives hold much more, are many times faster, and require little or no manual swapping. This convenience — and the fact that you won't have to buy new media on a regular basis — makes up for the higher initial cost. When your hard drive fills up, you can optionally archive its contents to CD or DVD for long-term storage.

STEP 2: BUY BACKUP SOFTWARE AND HARDWARE

Before you can have truly painless backups, you'll need to obtain some hardware and software. If you already have these items, you can skip to the next step. These things are not terribly expensive, but they're not free. Before you cringe and turn to the next technique, consider how much your data is worth. If you were to lose a day, a month, or a year of your work to a hard disk crash or a stolen computer, you would probably feel that the investment of a couple hundred dollars or so would have been a wise choice.

- The first thing you need is backup software. In order to perform the type of progressive backup that will provide you with the maximum ratio of safety to effort, you'll need a commercial backup utility. (With enough time and effort, you *could* build something comparable with free tools, but then this wouldn't be a *fast* technique.) There are several good choices at about the same price; my recommendation is Retrospect Express from Dantz (`www.dantz.com`), and I use it for the examples in this technique. See the book's Web site (`www.wiley.com/compbooks/kissell`) for recommendations on where to purchase Retrospect Express.
- Second, you need an external (FireWire, USB, or SCSI) hard drive. (Performing this technique using a partition on your built-in hard drive is certainly possible, but I don't recommend it. Even though you would be making an extra copy of your data, it wouldn't be safe from a hardware failure that took out your entire hard drive.) Nearly any type of external hard drive will do; it doesn't need to be especially fast or even very large. Shop around for bargains (and check the book's Web site for some tips). In general, look for a drive in the 10–30GB range. If the drive is too small, it will fill up quickly, requiring more frequent archiving. If it's too large, you increase the risk of data corruption as well as the amount of time spent archiving.
- Third, get *another* hard drive (or two) if you can. Am I kidding? Not at all. Experts recommend maintaining three rotating sets of backups, of which one is always kept in a different location. That way, if a disaster like fire, flood, or theft occurs and all your local backups are gone, you'll still be able to recover your data. Of course, even if you had just two hard drives, you could keep one off-site at any given time. A third one could be useful, though, for increased safety and convenience — or as a temporary location for a bootable clone.
- Finally — and optionally — if you don't already have a CD or DVD burner (such as a built-in SuperDrive or CD-RW/DVD-ROM combo drive), consider getting one. It is useful for archiving your digital media (such as MP3 files), to keep your normal backups streamlined. In addition, when your hard drives fill up, I recommend copying their contents onto CD or DVD for long-term storage. However, if you don't think you'll ever have a need to go back and see versions of files you created several months ago and don't care about long-term storage of your digital media files, you can skip this suggestion.

STEP 3: SET UP AUTOMATIC BACKUPS

After you've obtained a copy of Retrospect Express, install it according to the instructions provided. Make sure the hard drives you'll be using for your backups are mounted on the desktop. Then open Retrospect Express.

TIP

Whether you choose one, two, or three external hard drives, you might consider using your iPod as one of them — particularly if it's a larger capacity model and you don't have enough music to fill it up.

The first task you'll do is create a script that will automatically back up certain folders you designate, once per day.

- To create a script, click the **Automate** tab and then click the **Scripts** button. The Scripts window (see **Figure 48.3**) appears.
- Click **New...** to create a new script. A message may appear asking whether you want to use EasyScript to prepare your backup strategy. Answer **No**. A new window will appear asking which kind of script you want to create. Select **Backup** and click **OK**. Enter a name for your script (such as Daily Backup Script) and click **New**.
- The script window (see **Figure 48.4**) appears; this is where you set up all the attributes of the script.
- Click the **Sources** button. This is where you choose which folders (or *subvolumes*) you want to back up. In the Volume Selection window (shown in **Figure 48.5**), select your startup volume, then click **Subvolume....** Navigate to your home folder (/Users/*your-user-name*/) and select your Documents folder, which typically contains the majority of files you create and modify on a daily basis. Click **Define** to designate this folder as a subvolume that you will back up.
- Repeat this subvolume definition procedure for the following additional folders within your home folder. These should cover the majority of your important files, but if you have additional files elsewhere you want to back up, select those folders as well.

48.3

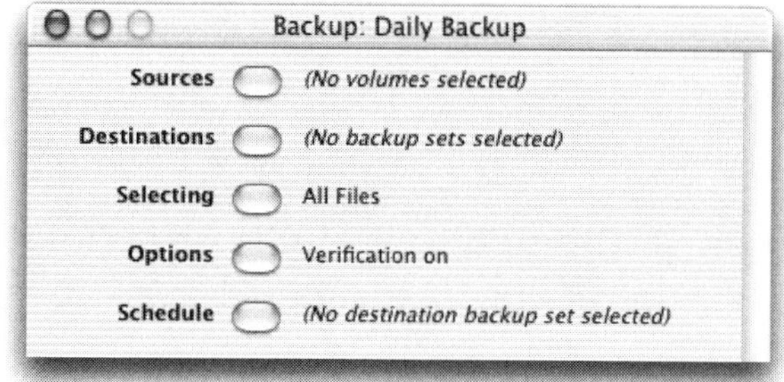

48.4

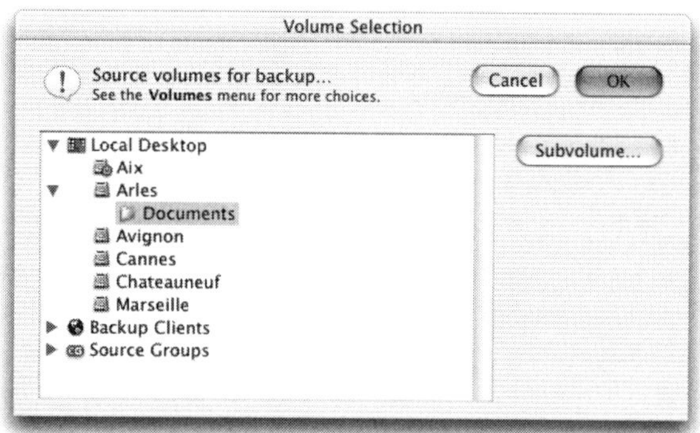

48.5

NOTE

Retrospect Express has a wide variety of options for backing up and restoring your files. Depending on your situation — the number and types of files you create, the type of backup media you have available, your budget, and so on — a different strategy may be better for you. Read the documentation included with Retrospect Express for details on other options and techniques.

- Library/Application Support (includes your Address Book and certain types of configuration files)
- Library/Calendars (contains your iCal calendar data)
- Library/Keychains (the keychains that hold your user names and passwords)
- Library/Mail (contains all your stored e-mail messages if you use Mail as your e-mail client)
- Library/Preferences (all the settings you've created for individual applications)
- Desktop (the files and folders on your desktop)

- When you're finished defining subvolumes, ⌘+click each of the folder icons you just defined (as in **Figure 48.6**) to select them and then click **OK**. Confirm that all your desired folders appear in the Sources list and then click **OK** again.

Now that you've selected the folders you want to back up, you need to select a destination for your backup set.

- Click the **Destinations** button. The Backup Set Selection window appears.
- Click **New...** to create a new backup set. For the **Backup set type**, choose **File** (as in **Figure 48.7**). If you want to encrypt your backups (recommended for security), click the **Secure...** button and enter your desired encryption type and password.
- Give your backup set a name (the default setting of "Backup Set A" is fine). Click **New...**, navigate to the hard drive you've chosen to use for your backups, and click **Save**. Click **OK**.
- Create a second Backup Set ("Backup Set B") with the same characteristics. If you have a second hard drive, choose that hard drive as its location. If not, save it to the same hard drive — but use a different partition if possible. If you have a third hard drive, repeat once again to create Backup Set C. When you're finished creating backup sets, click **OK** to return to the Script window.
- Click the **Options** button. Make sure the boxes next to both **Verification** and **Data compression** are checked. Then click **OK**.

Finally, tell Retrospect Express how often you want your backups to occur. If you're configuring two backup sets, I recommend having one set used each day for a week and then switching to the second set for each day of the following week (and continuing to swap between the two sets weekly). If you use three backup sets, you can make the schedules rotate every three weeks instead.

- Click the **Schedule** button. The Schedule window (shown in **Figure 48.8**) appears. Click **Add...** and choose **Day of week** for the kind of scheduler.

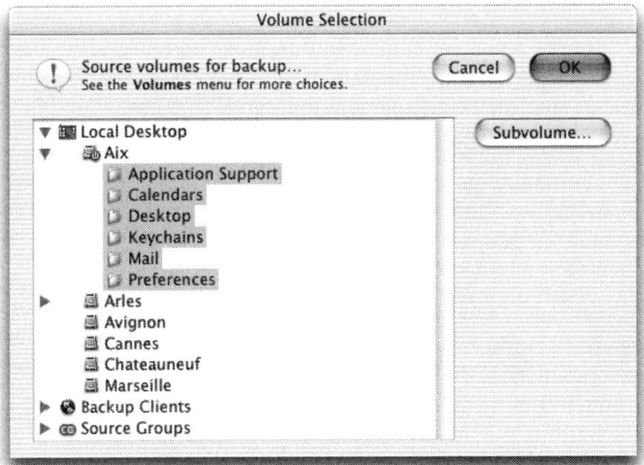

48.6

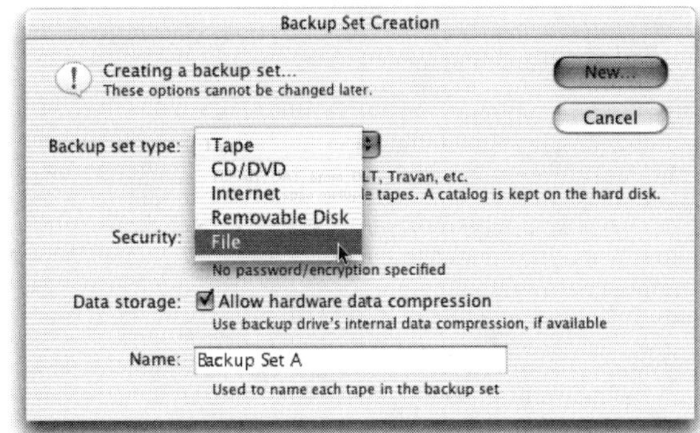

48.7

Click **OK**. Select the time of day you want the script to run. If you leave your computer on all the time, you might select a time in the middle of the night when you're not likely to be using it; if not, select a time you're sure your computer will be on. Select the days you want the script to run (I recommend every day), and make sure **2** is entered in the **Weeks** field — in other words, run the script on this day every other week. Chose **Normal Backup** from the **Action** pop-up menu and **Backup Set A** from the **To** pop-up menu. Click **OK**.

■ Repeat this step to create a second schedule similar to the first, but with two changes. For the **Start** date, select the date and use the up arrow to select the date one week from today. And choose **Backup Set B** from the **To** menu.

■ If you're using three backup sets, repeat one last time for the third set — and make sure the **Weeks** field for each of the three sets says **3** instead of **2**.

■ When you're finished, click **OK** to close the Schedule window and quit Retrospect Express. It reopens automatically when it's time to perform the backups.

As long as you leave your computer on and your hard drives connected, these two (or three) backup schedules will run automatically, every night, backing up your important files. You never even need to think about them unless your hard drive becomes full (Step 5) or you need to recover a lost file (Step 6). If you're using two hard drives, disconnect the first after it has completed its last daily backup for the week and take it to another location for safekeeping. At the end of the following week, bring it back so that it's ready to be used that night for the next backup, and take the first hard drive off-site.

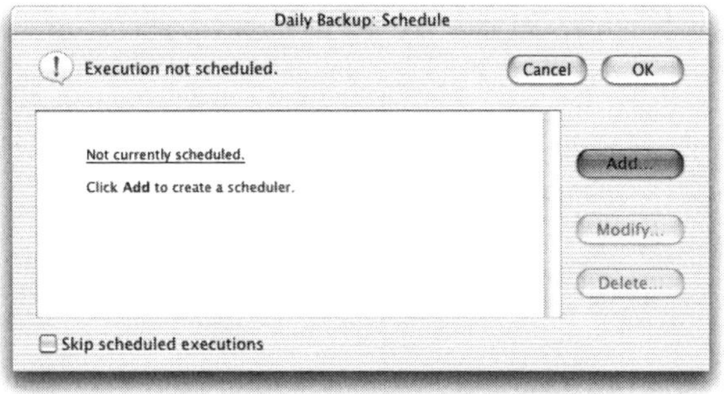

48.8

STEP 4: ARCHIVE DIGITAL MEDIA

You probably noticed that I left out your Music, Pictures, and Movies folders when creating the backup sets in the last step. That's because these folders can all grow to become absolutely huge, and including them as part of your daily backups would make them take a long time — and fill up your hard drives very quickly. Because the files in these folders typically don't change very often, you can make a separate backup set just for them — and instead of scheduling it to run automatically, just run it manually.

■ Follow the same procedure as in Step 3 to make a backup script for your digital media, with a few exceptions:

  ■ When selecting **Sources**, choose the Music, Pictures, and Movies folders as your subvolumes.

  ■ When selecting **Destination**, create a backup set of type **CD/DVD**. (This assumes, of course, that you have a CD or DVD burner attached, and enough blank discs to hold all of your media files.)

  ■ Don't create a schedule. You can run this script manually whenever you feel you've made enough changes to your media folders to warrant it. To run the script, click the **Immediate** tab in Retrospect Express. Click **Run**, select the script you want to perform, and click **OK**.

STEP 5: ARCHIVE BACKUPS (OPTIONAL)

There's no easy way to predict when your hard drive(s) will fill up. It depends on the number and type of files you create, the size of the hard drive, and the level of compression Retrospect Express is able to achieve. But even a small hard drive could easily take several months to fill. When it does fill — and if you're using multiple hard drives of the same size, they'll all get full at about the same time — you have three choices.

First, you can put the hard drive on a shelf to save its contents, and buy a new hard drive. That may be the simplest, but it's way too expensive for most of us. The second option is to erase the hard drives and start over. This allows you to recycle the media, but if you discover that you need a file that's more than a week old, you're out of luck: You already erased last week's backup. The third choice — and my recommendation — is to copy your backup sets onto CD or DVD for your archives and *then* erase the hard drives and begin again with fresh backup sets.

- Following the same general procedure as Step 3 or Step 4, create a new script using your backup hard drive(s) as the Source, and choosing **CD/DVD** as the backup set type under Destination.
- As before, do not create a schedule. You can perform this step manually whenever it's needed (every few months or so).
- After archiving your old backups, erase the hard drives manually. To do this, open Disk Utility, click the **Erase** tab, select the hard drive you want to erase in the list on the left, and click the **Erase** button.

NOTE

If you have iPhoto 2, you can use its built-in archiving feature to copy your digital photos to CD or DVD, and omit the Pictures folder from the Sources you select in this step.

- The next time your script runs, it will perform a full backup to that hard drive and add to it daily as it did before.
- Repeat this step as each hard drive fills.

STEP 6: RECOVER FILES

The only reason to go to all the bother and expense of keeping backups is to be able to restore files in case of data loss. Although you may be lucky enough never to have to do this, it's important to understand how it's done. In fact, it's an excellent idea to try this periodically even if you haven't experienced any losses, because recovering files will confirm that your backup sets, hard drives, and schedules are all functioning correctly. You don't want to wait until you've lost data to determine that a bad piece of hardware (or human error) has kept your backups from functioning.

- Open Retrospect Express.
- Click the **Immediate** tab and click **Restore**.
- Choose **Restore files from a backup** and click **OK**.
- In the Source window that appears (see **Figure 48.9**), select the Backup Set(s) where the files you want to recover are located. Each Backup Set contains multiple *snaphots* — one for each time the

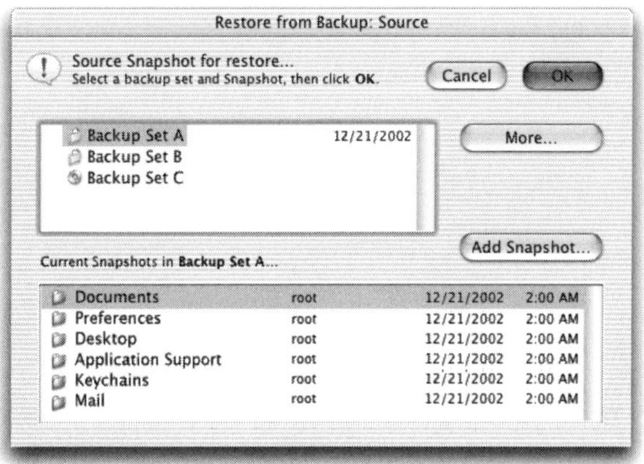

48.9

backup was performed. A snapshot is a list of all files current in your selected Source folders on the selected date. Select a snapshot and click **OK**.

■ Choose a destination — the volume the recovered files should be copied to. This should be different from the volume they're currently on. Click **OK**.

■ A **Restore from Backup** window appears. Click the **Files Chosen** button to display a list of all files in that snapshot. Select the ones you want to restore, as shown in **Figure 48.10**. To select multiple files, ⌘+click them (or Shift+click to select a contiguous range of files); to select all the files, press **⌘+A**. Click **Mark** to tell Retrospect Express to use the selected files. Close the file window when you're done.

■ Now click **Restore**. Retrospect copies the marked files from your chosen snapshot to the destination volume you selected.

■ If necessary, repeat this process for different versions of the same file(s) contained in other snapshots.

There are other ways to find and retrieve files within Retrospect Express backup sets. For more information, consult the documentation included with the application.

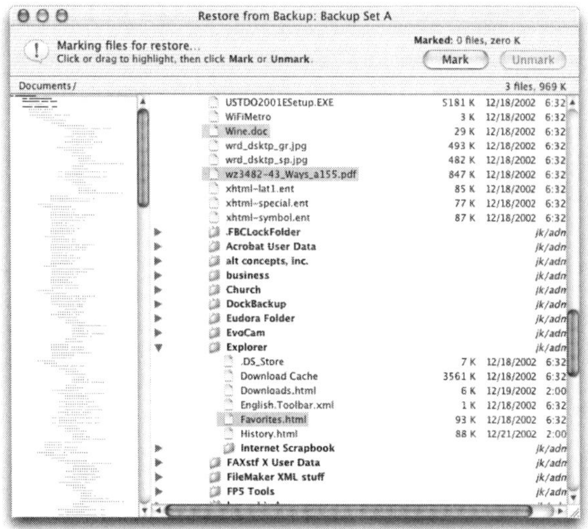

48.10

TECHNIQUE 49

MAKING A BOOTABLE CLONE OF YOUR HARD DRIVE

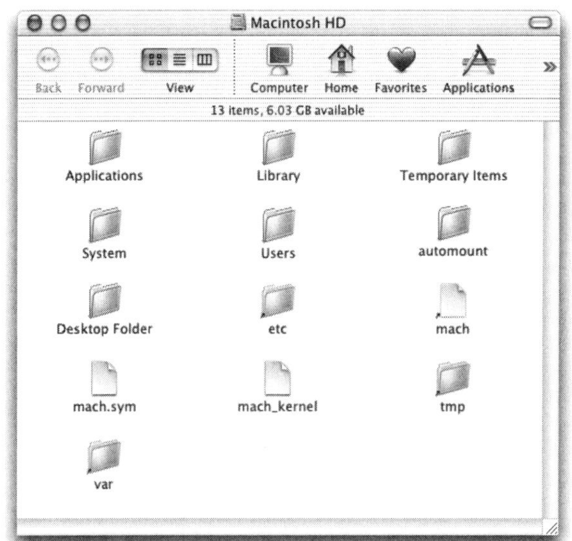

49.1

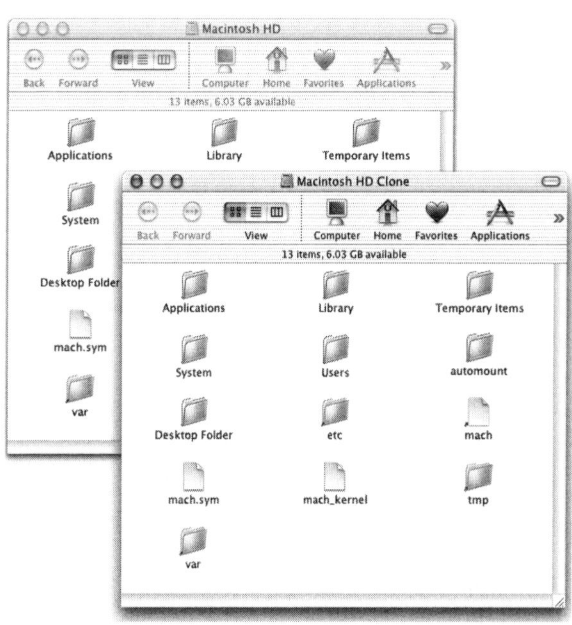

49.2

ABOUT THE FEATURE

Although backups help you restore lost data, there are times you may need an exact duplicate of your hard drive that can actually start up your computer. These bootable clones make testing, troubleshooting, and file recovery easier.

If you followed the instructions in Technique 48 for backing up your computer, your important files should now be safely copied to an external hard drive. Although this helps you to recover your work in the event of a serious problem, you won't be able to start your computer from the backup drive. In addition to regular backups, there are several reasons you might want an *exact* duplicate of your hard drive that can start (boot) your computer. This type of copy is known as a *bootable clone.*

Here are a few common reasons for making bootable clones:

- You want to repartition your computer's internal hard drive, then restore your entire system to one of the new volumes just as it was before — without having to install every application and file individually.

- You want to upgrade your system to a new version of Mac OS X, but *also* keep the old installation available intact in case of compatibility problems.
- You can't afford a few hours of down-time in the event of a serious crash, and need a backup method for running your computer — not just recovering files — at a moment's notice.
- You're writing a book that requires examples based on a clean installation of Mac OS X, but your internal hard drive is heavily customized and overloaded with third-party gadgets. You want to switch to a standard installation temporarily while making it possible to get back to your previous state.

Under Mac OS 9, making a volume bootable was easy: Just copy over your System Folder and open and close it to "bless" it. Unfortunately, due to the complexity of ownership, permissions, and invisible files on Mac OS X, simply copying your system files from one drive to another will not result in a volume you can boot from. Apple does include command-line utilities that, with careful use, will get the job done. But a third-party tool called Carbon Copy Cloner can make the job much easier.

STEP 1: PREPARE THE TARGET VOLUME

Before you can make a copy of an entire volume, you'll need another volume available that has enough free space. The target volume doesn't have to be as large as the source volume — it just has to be large enough to hold all the *files* on the source volume. So even though your hard drive might have a capacity of 60GB, if you've only filled up 2GB of that space, your target volume needs only 2GB of free space. That said, your target volume should be one of the following:

- An external hard disk (or a partition on an external hard disk). It gives you the fastest file copying performance.
- An iPod. Even a 5GB iPod — if not already full of music — can store an entire system. If you have not already done so, you must enable your iPod to function as a hard disk. With your iPod connected, open iTunes, select your iPod in the list on the left, and click the iPod options button in the lower-right portion of the window. Select **Enable FireWire disk use** (as shown in **Figure 49.3**) and click **OK**.
- A partition on your internal hard drive. If you make a bootable copy of your entire system on another hard drive partition, you can switch between the two volumes at startup time by holding down the **Option** key as you restart. (See Technique 47 for instructions on partitioning your hard drive.) Of course, if you're making a bootable clone in order to facilitate repartitioning your hard drive, this method won't work — repartitioning erases *everything* on your drive.
- A disk image. A disk image is a special file that behaves as a virtual volume. (Most Mac software

49.3

you download is packaged as a disk image.) You might choose a disk image if you want to be able in the future to restore your hard drive to its current state, but don't have a spare drive or partition that can serve as a bootable volume. Although you can't boot directly from a disk image, you can repeat the cloning process to copy files from a disk image back onto your hard drive, restoring it to its earlier state and keeping it bootable. You can also use a disk image to burn a CD or DVD so you can archive your system. If you do not already have a writable disk image of suitable size, you can have Carbon Copy Cloner create one for you during the copying process. You still need to have enough space on an existing volume to store the disk image file.

Some volumes *cannot* be used to create a bootable clone using this technique:

- A network volume. Your target volume must be attached to your computer physically — not by way of an Ethernet cable or AirPort connection.
- A CD or DVD. If you want to make a clone of your hard drive on a CD or DVD, you must first create a disk image as described earlier and then burn it. Unfortunately, Carbon Copy Cloner cannot use this procedure to make a *bootable* CD or DVD. (If you need to do this, skip ahead to Step 3.)

STEP 2: RUN CARBON COPY CLONER

Although creating a bootable clone using command-line tools in Terminal is possible, the best and easiest way to do it is to use a shareware utility from Mike Bombich called Carbon Copy Cloner.

- Go to `www.bombich.com` and download Carbon Copy Cloner.
- Drag the application folder to your hard drive to install it and double-click the installed Carbon Copy Cloner icon to open it. The application is shown in **Figure 49.4**.
- For best results, quit any open applications or server processes you may have running. Although Carbon Copy Cloner can work with open files, it may not correctly process any files that are added or changed while the copying is in progress, and other open applications may slow down the copying.

> **NOTE**
>
> **If you need to create a bootable clone directly to a network volume, a utility called PsyncX (sourceforge.net/projects/psyncx) can do it. It works similarly to Carbon Copy Cloner, but only copies entire volumes or folders — you can't choose an arbitrary subset of a volume to copy.**

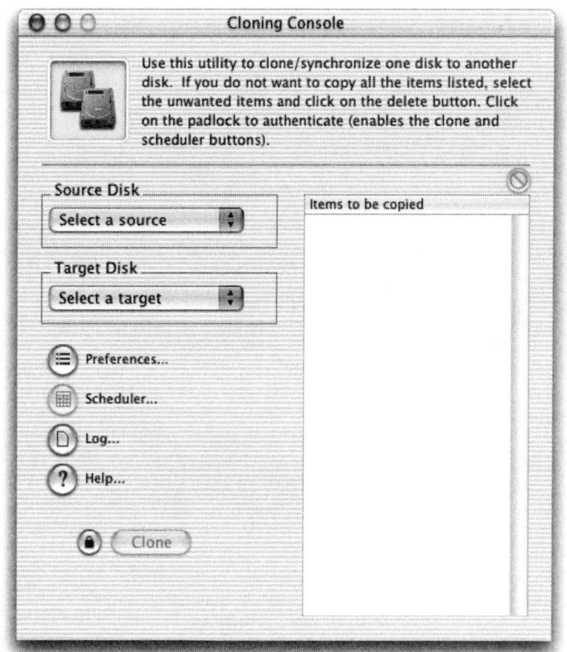

49.4

■ Select your Source Disk — the one you want to copy — from the first pop-up menu. The top level of files and folders will appear in the list on the right. Not all of these are necessary to create a bootable clone. If you want to reduce the size of your copy, you can skip files and folders you don't need. To omit a file or folder from the copy, select it and click the **Delete** button, as shown in **Figure 49.5**. If you want your copy to be bootable, however, be sure *not* to delete any of the following items: `bin`, `cores`, `Library`, `mach_kernel`, `private`, `sbin`, `System`, `usr`, and `.hidden`.

■ Select your Target Disk — where the copied files will be placed — from the second pop-up menu. If you want to place the files on a disk image (so that you can archive them to a CD or DVD), click **Preferences** and check the box next to **Create a disk image on target**. Note that you cannot use Carbon Copy Cloner to make a bootable CD or DVD (but see Step 3 later for an alternative).

■ Set other preferences to customize your copy. After clicking the **Preferences** button, you'll see a number of options (shown in **Figure 49.6**). In most cases, the defaults will work just fine. Be sure **Make bootable** is checked if you want to be able to start up from the cloned copy. If you're recopying a volume to a target that already has a bootable system and you want to overwrite the existing folders, check **Delete directories before overwriting**. (Consult the documentation that came with Carbon Copy Cloner for details on the other options.) Click **Save** to save your preferences.

■ Before you can create your copy, you must authenticate by clicking the Lock icon at the

49.5

49.6

bottom of the window and entering your administrator password.

■ Click **Clone** to begin the cloning process. Now get a cup of coffee — this could take a while. The amount of time depends on several factors, such as the number of files you're copying, the speed of your computer, and the type of hard drive you're using. Copies from one hard drive to another go faster than copies from one partition to another on the same hard drive. But copying an entire disk could in some cases take upwards of an hour.

When your clone is complete, you should be able to select it as a startup volume using the Startup Disk pane in System Preferences. Alternatively, if you press and hold **Option** while restarting, a screen will appear listing all the mounted volumes that have valid systems; select your new volume and click the right arrow to boot from it.

STEP 3: MAKE A BOOTABLE CD (OPTIONAL)

Although following Step 2 produces a bootable copy of your operating system on a hard drive or partition, it won't allow you to create a CD that can start up your computer. If you need to do this (and have a CD burner), the procedure is a bit different — and requires a second utility called BootCD.

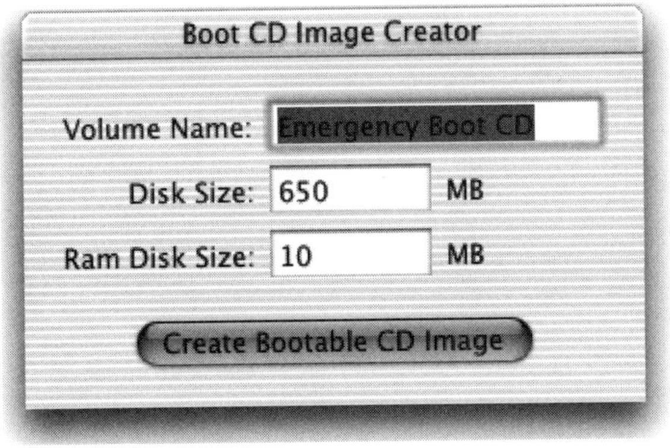

Boot CD Image Creator

Volume Name: Emergency Boot CD

Disk Size: 650 MB

Ram Disk Size: 10 MB

Create Bootable CD Image

49.7

■ Download BootCD from `www.charlessoft.com` and double-click the BootCD application to open it. (See **Figure 49.7**.)

■ Choose a name for your CD volume and a location to save the disk image and then click **Create Bootable CD Image**.

BootCD creates a new disk image that contains the basic components of your system — enough to start your machine, along with utilities like Disk Utility, Terminal, and Console. (This process can take a while; be patient.)

■ When it's finished, an alert appears, asking you to select applications to appear on your CD. Click **OK**, then optionally select one or more applications to include on your CD. Click **Cancel** to finish adding applications and then quit BootCD.

■ You should now have a new CD disk image. Because it's a CD and not a DVD, there will not be enough space remaining for the entire contents of your startup volume. However, if you do want to copy over a few files, you can double-click the image to mount it and then manually drag and drop the files you want to include. When you're finished, eject the mounted image.

■ Open Disk Copy (in /Applications/Utilities). Choose **Burn Image...** from the **File** menu. Navigate to the CD image you just created, select it, and click **Burn**. Insert a blank CD, click **Burn** again, and wait for the process to complete.

■ To start from your newly created CD, hold down the **C** key while restarting your computer. Be aware that booting from a BootCD-created CD can take a *very* long time — in some cases, 15 minutes or more. When the Login window eventually appears, enter `root` for the user name and `bootcd` for the password.

TECHNIQUE 50

SCHEDULING ACTIVITIES TO HAPPEN AUTOMATICALLY

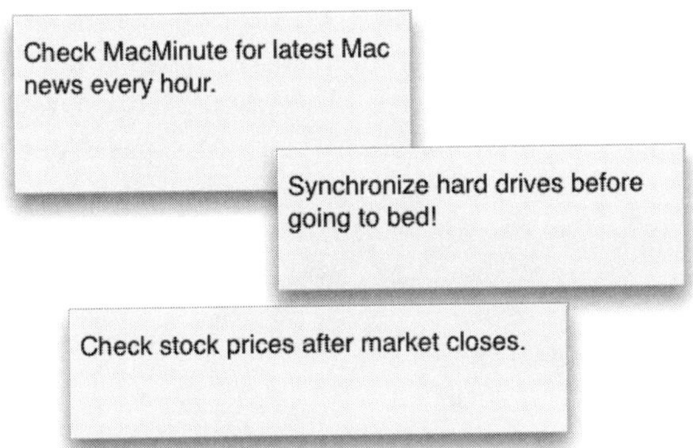

50.1

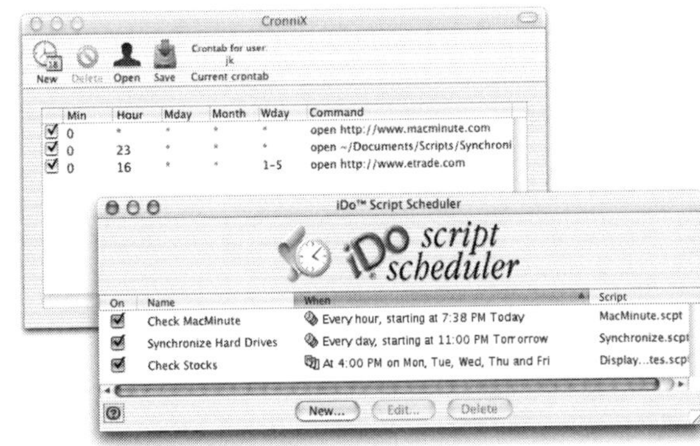

50.2

ABOUT THE FEATURE

Your Mac can work for you even when you're not around. With a few easy steps, you can configure your machine to run applications or scripts, back up files, or perform maintenance tasks at pre-set times.

Most of the activities you perform with your Mac require you to be actively involved: surfing the Web, writing a letter, creating a movie, retouching photos. But there are also lots of things your computer can do for you even when you're not sitting in front of it, moving the mouse and tapping on the keyboard. With a little planning, you can set up almost any type of activity to take place periodically, even if you're away from your machine — for example:

- Playing music from iTunes
- Starting large print jobs
- Running Photoshop filters
- Restarting your computer
- Downloading your mail
- Synchronizing files between volumes
- Encoding MP3 files

- Mounting or unmounting network volumes
- Displaying a message reminding you to take a break from typing

You could also create a schedule that combines several tasks. For example, a wake-up schedule could play an alarm clock sound and then download your mail, open a Web page with today's news, and put on some light music to help you get your day started. The possibilities are limitless.

There are many ways to schedule tasks in Mac OS X. I begin by showing you the manual way of doing it in Terminal — which is actually quite simple. Then I review a variety of graphical applications that can help you schedule tasks without using the command line.

STEP 1: SET UP THE TASK TO BE PERFORMED

The tasks you can perform with this technique are activated from the command line. For that reason, you'll need to begin by figuring out how to do what you want to do by typing a command in a Terminal window. Some of the activities you may want to perform require the preliminary setup work of creating (or downloading) an AppleScript. For best results, try typing these commands into Terminal manually first, to be sure they work. Then reuse them in the next step as part of a schedule.

- To open an application, enter `open` plus the complete pathname of the application (including the `.app` extension). If the application name includes a space, put the entire pathname in quotes — for example:
  - `open /Applications/Calculator.app`
  - `open "/Applications/Utilities/Disk Utility.app"`
- To open a file or folder, again use the `open` command followed by the complete pathname of the file or folder you want to open. If it's located within your home directory, you can use ~ as a shortcut. As before, use quotes to enclose any pathname that includes spaces — for example:
  - `open /Library/Documentation/Acknowledgements.rtf`
  - `open ~/Documents/spreadsheet.xls`
  - `open "~/Documents/My Expense Reports/Macworld Expo.xls"`
- To open a URL in your default browser (or other helper application), use the `open` command followed by a complete URL (that is, not just the domain name, like www.apple.com). You can use not only URLs that open Web pages, but also URLs that send e-mail, open FTP sites, or whatever else you want to do — for example:
  - `open http://www.alt.cc`
  - `open mailto:steve@mac.com`
  - `open ftp://username:password@ftp.site.com/folder1/folder2`

If you want to perform a more complex action, such as running Photoshop filters or downloading your e-mail, you will need to use a script (either an AppleScript or a shell script) to do it and then launch the script from the command line. Although I've mentioned scripts in several different techniques, there's not enough space here to go into any detail about how to write your own from scratch. However, you can download hundreds of scripts other people have written. One of them may well meet your needs — or be easily modifiable to do so. A great source for ready-to-run scripts is `www.MacScripter.net`. See the book's Web site (`www.wiley.com/compbooks/kissell`) for other recommendations on sources for prewritten scripts.

- If your AppleScript is saved as a compiled script but *not* as an application, you use the following command to run it:

```
osascript ScriptName.scpt
```

Be sure to include the .scpt extension on the end of the AppleScript. Note: If your compiled AppleScript requires user interaction (for example, displaying an alert dialog requesting additional information), it will not work with the `osascript` command. You must save it as an application in order to launch it from Terminal.

- If your AppleScript is saved as an application, you can open it just like any other application:

```
open /Path/to/Script/ScriptName
```

Note that in this instance, the script has no extension (like `.app` or `.scpt`).

STEP 2: SCHEDULE A RECURRING TASK

After you know how to perform a command manually using Terminal, you're ready to schedule it to occur automatically. The built-in UNIX program provided for scheduling tasks is called **cron**. It doesn't have the most intuitive interface, but after you get the hang of it, it's not bad at all. Although **cron** runs in the background looking for tasks to run, it is configured using a program called **crontab**, which simply stores scheduled tasks in tables.

- To begin, enter the following command so that crontab will use the more user-friendly **pico** (rather than the inscrutable **vi**) to edit your schedules:

```
setenv EDITOR pico
```

- To open a blank schedule for editing, enter

```
crontab -e
```

A new pico window opens, ready for you to type in your schedule items. This is where it gets just a bit tricky. Each task is represented by a series of numbers followed by the actual shell command (as described in Step 1). A sample task might look like this:

```
30 6 * * * open ~/Documents/Myfile.
  doc
```

Cron asks for five pieces of time/date information about each task. Each of these five items is specified in numeric form. You must enter one or more spaces or tabs after each item.

- The first slot holds the **minutes**. This is a number from 0 to 59 representing which minute of the hour a task takes place. So if you want a task to happen at 3:30, this number would be 30; if you want it to happen at 4:00, the number would be 0. You can also specify ranges or lists of minutes — for example 5,20 means the task will happen at 5 minutes and 20 minutes past the hour it's scheduled for.
- The second slot holds the **hour** (in 24-hour international format). This is a number from 0 to 23, where 0 represents midnight, 12 represents noon, 14 represents 2 p.m., and so on. Thus, a task scheduled for midnight would have its first two numbers both as 0; a task scheduled for 5:27 p.m. would have 27 as the first number and 17 as the second. Ranges and lists can be specified, as with minutes.
- The third slot holds the **day of month**, a number from 1 to 31. If you want a task to execute on the same date every month, enter that number here. If you don't want the task to be tied to any particular calendar date, enter an asterisk (*) in the third slot instead. You can also enter a range of dates. To have a task run on the 10th, 11th, and 12th of the month, enter 10-12 for the third item. To have it run only on the 2nd, 13th, and 29th, enter 2,13,29 (without spaces) for the third item.
- The fourth slot holds the **month**, a number from 1-12, where 1 is January and 12 is December. If you don't want to specify a month, use an asterisk (*) to mean that the task can take place during any month. You can specify a range or list of months: 1-3 is January-March, while 7,9 is July and September.
- The fifth and final slot holds the **weekday**. This is a number from 0-6, where 0 represents

Sunday, 2 is Tuesday, and so on. If you don't want the task to be tied to any particular day of the week, enter an asterisk (*). As with day and month, you can specify ranges: 1-5 means every weekday; 1,3,6 means Monday, Wednesday, and Saturday.

Because this form of notation is a bit unusual, some examples are in order. I'll include just the numbers (not the shell command itself) for simplicity.

- This task occurs every day at 6:30 a.m.:

```
30    6    *    *    *
```

- This task occurs weekday at midnight:

```
0    0    *    *    1-5
```

- This task occurs every February 14 at 5:15 p.m.:

```
15    17    14    2    *
```

- This task occurs every 15 minutes — all day, every day — during June, July, and August:

```
0,15,30,45    *    *    6-8    *
```

- This task occurs once a minute, every minute, every day:

```
0-59    *    *    *    *
```

- This task occurs at 2:10 a.m. every day in April:

```
10    2    *    4    *
```

Type a sample schedule item. Choose a time in the next couple minutes and a simple command. For example, if it's 3:30 in the afternoon, you might try this:

```
33 15 * * * open ~/Library/Preferences
```

Then press **Control+X** to exit. Press **y** to save your changes and press **Return** to confirm the filename. You've just created a scheduled task. In a few minutes, your Preferences folder should open automatically. You can remove this sample task at any time by entering `crontab -e` and deleting it from your crontab file.

Now fill in other schedule items to your taste. To display a list of all your scheduled tasks, enter `crontab -l`. **Figure 50.3** shows a sample crontab

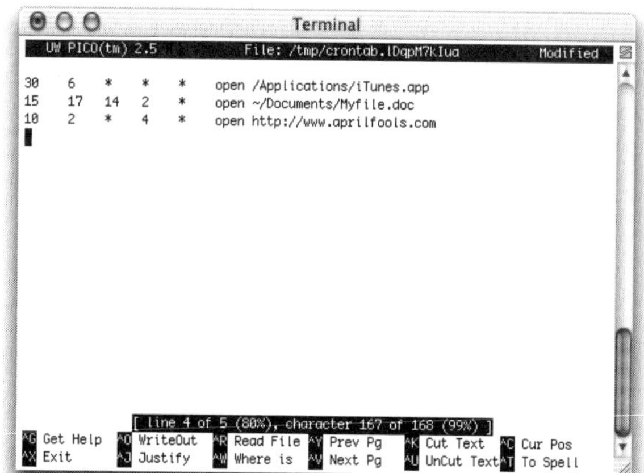

50.3

listing. As long as your computer is running when the task is scheduled, it should complete automatically. Note that scheduled tasks will not run if your computer is asleep.

STEP 3: USE A GRAPHICAL FRONT END TO CRON (OPTIONAL)

If editing convoluted text files in Terminal isn't your idea of a good time, you can also download a variety of graphical utilities that allow you to configure your crontab file in a more user-friendly way. I list a couple examples here:

- CronniX (from `www.koch-schmidt.de/cronnix/`) allows you to set up scheduled tasks following exactly the same structure as crontab itself — only with Aqua windows and lists (see **Figure 50.4**). You still have to enter all commands manually.
- piTime (from `pidog.com/piTime/`) has a slightly simpler and friendlier interface for opening files or applications (see **Figure 50.5**), and an Expert mode for performing other commands, like running scripts or opening URLs.

STEP 4: USE A NON-UNIX SCHEDULER (OPTIONAL)

The appeal of schedulers based on cron is that they're free and relatively simple to set up. But if you need to perform much more complex tasks, you might want to invest a small amount of money in a commercial application that will give you more flexibility. I list my two favorite examples:

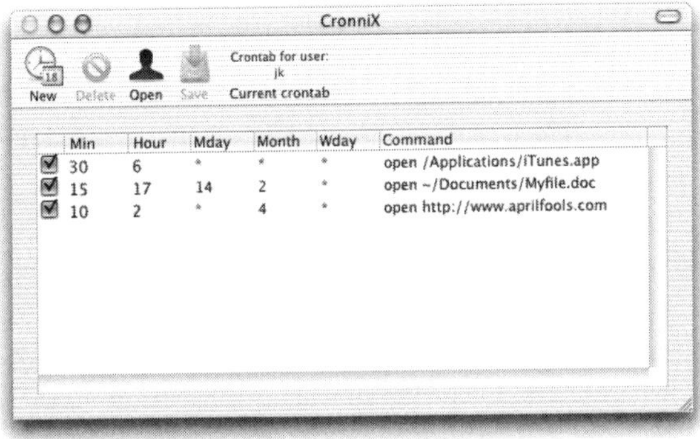

50.4

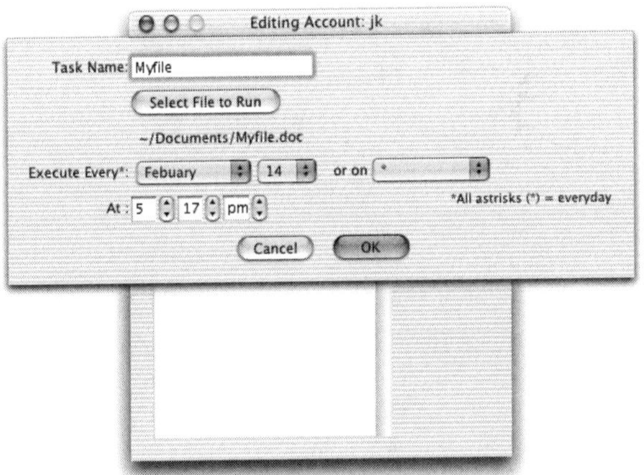

50.5

■ iDo Script Scheduler, from Sophisticated Circuits (`www.sophisticated.com`) is strictly for running AppleScripts, but it does this extremely well. You are not restricted to blindly launching a script; you can also specify any needed parameters. In addition to repeating schedules, you can choose a one-time schedule, and you can also set up scripts to be triggered by a hot key, or to run automatically when the system is idle. See **Figure 50.6** for a sample.

■ QuicKeys, from CE Software (`www.cesoft.com`) is the granddaddy of Mac automation programs. (See **Figure 50.7**.) In addition to launching files, applications, and URLs, you can use QuicKeys to select menu commands, click buttons in dialogs, mount and unmount servers, and dozens of other tasks — without requiring you to learn any programming languages or figure out a complicated user interface. QuicKeys macros can include many steps, and can be triggered on a schedule, by a hot key, or using a menu command.

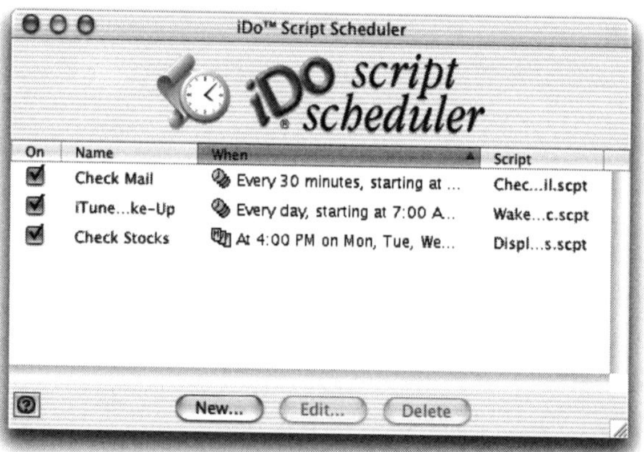

50.6

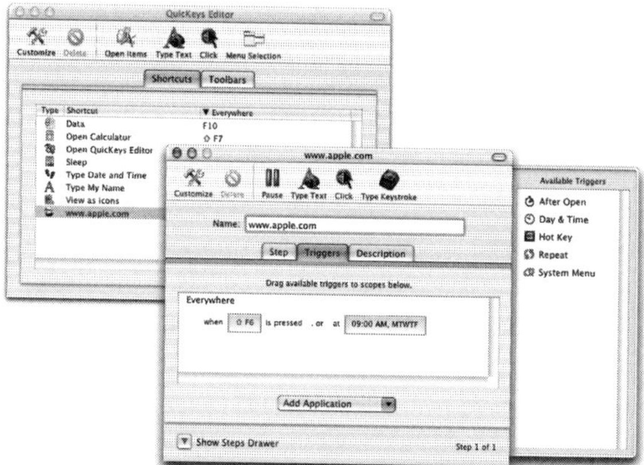

50.7

APPENDIX A
SHORTCUTS

Performing commands using the keyboard is almost always faster than using a mouse, but it's not always obvious how to do something from the keyboard. I've assembled a fairly complete list of keyboard shortcuts here for your reference. This list also includes some special shortcuts you can perform by using a combination of modifier keys and mouse clicks.

Rather than list the shortcut first then tell you what it does, I've listed the commands or actions on the left and the shortcut on the right. This should make it a bit easier to locate commands if you don't already know what the shortcut is.

STARTUP SHORTCUTS

When you turn on your computer (or restart it, if it's already running), you can use a variety of shortcuts to change the startup behavior. These can be especially useful if you have several drives or partitions with various operating systems installed.

STARTUP OPTION	HOLD THESE KEYS WHILE RESTARTING
Display all available startup volumes (newer Macs only)	Option
Safe boot (don't load third-party kernel extensions — similar to "Extensions Off")	Shift
Eject CD/DVD and start up from the internal hard drive	Mouse button
Start up from internal CD/DVD drive	C
Start up from an external drive (or the next SCSI device, if present)	⌘+Option+Shift+Delete
Start up from the first partition on your internal hard drive	D
Start up in FireWire Target Disk Mode (use your computer as a FireWire hard drive for another computer)	T
Start up from a network server (using NetBoot)	N
Start up in Mac OS X (if Mac OS 9 is on the same volume)	X
Clear your Parameter RAM ("zap the PRAM")	⌘+Option+P+R (hold until you hear a second startup sound)
Show Open Firmware	⌘+Option+O+F
Display Console messages during startup	⌘+V
Single-user mode	⌘+S

FINDER SHORTCUTS

The Finder has a wide variety of shortcuts available. I've grouped them into several categories for easier reading.

WINDOW NAVIGATION

You can use these shortcuts to move around in Finder windows without using the mouse.

ACTION	SHORTCUT
Open the selected folder	⌘+O or ⌘+down arrow
Open the selected folder while closing the current window	⌘+Option+down arrow
Open enclosing folder (move up a level)	⌘+up arrow
Open enclosing folder while closing current window	⌘+Option+up arrow
Select the desktop	⌘+ Shift+up arrow
Select the next icon in alphabetical order	Tab
Select the previous icon in alphabetical order	Shift+Tab
Display "hand" pointer to slide contents of the window in any direction	⌘+Option+click and drag
Display path to current folder	⌘+click the window title

The following shortcuts are applicable only in List View windows:

ACTION	SHORTCUT
Expand view of selected folder	Right arrow
Expand view of selected folder and all of its subfolders	Option+right arrow (or press Option while clicking the disclosure triangle)
Collapse view of selected folder	Left arrow
Collapse view of selected folder and all of its subfolders	Option+left arrow (or press **Option** while clicking the disclosure triangle)

MENU NAVIGATION

Most of these keyboard shortcuts are displayed on Finder menus, but I've included them here for your convenience.

COMMAND	SHORTCUT
Apple Menu	
Toggle display of the Dock	⌘+Option+D
Display Force Quit dialog	⌘+Option+Esc
Log Out	⌘+Shift+Q
Finder Menu	
Empty the Trash	⌘+Shift+Delete
Empty the Trash, including locked items, with no warnings	⌘+Option+Control+Delete or press Option while choosing Empty Trash
Hide the Finder	⌘+H
Hide all applications except the Finder	⌘+Option+H

COMMAND	SHORTCUT
File Menu	
Open a new window	⌘+N
Create a new empty folder	⌘+Shift+N
Open the selected file(s) or folder(s)	⌘+O
Close the current window	⌘+W
Close all Finder windows	⌘+Option+W or Option+click any window's Close button
Get Info on the selected object(s)	⌘+I
Get info on the selected objects in a floating Inspector Window	⌘+Option+I
Duplicate the selected object(s)	⌘+D
Make an alias of the selected icon(s)	⌘+L
Show Original file (for an alias)	⌘+R
Add selected object(s) to Favorites	⌘+T
Move the selected icons to the Trash	⌘+Delete
Eject a CD, DVD, or other removable media	⌘+E
Find files	⌘+F
Edit Menu	
Undo your last action	⌘+Z
Cut (delete) the current selection and put it on the Clipboard	⌘+X
Copy the current selection to the Clipboard	⌘+C
Paste the contents of the Clipboard at your insertion point	⌘+V
Select all (text or icons, depending on the context)	⌘+A
View Menu	
View current window as Icons	⌘+1
View current window as List	⌘+2
View current window as Columns	⌘+3
Toggle display of the current window's toolbar	⌘+B
Show View Options for the current window	⌘+J
Go Menu	
Go back to previous window contents	⌘+[
Go forward to later window contents	⌘+]
Open a new window showing the Computer	⌘+Shift+C
Open my home folder	⌘+Shift+H
Mount and open my iDisk	⌘+Shift+I
Open the Applications folder	⌘+Shift+A
Open the Favorites folder	⌘+Shift+F
Go to Folder...	⌘+Shift+G
Connect to Server...	⌘+K
Window Menu	
Minimize the current window to the Dock	⌘+M
Minimize all Finder windows	Option+click any window's Minimize button
Help Menu	
Display Help	⌘+?

MOUSE SHORTCUT

At the risk of stating the obvious, this is the most important shortcut for using a mouse in Mac OS X.

ACTION	SHORTCUT
Display a contextual menu for the selected object	Press Control while clicking the mouse button (or just click the right mouse button if your mouse has one)

DOCK SHORTCUTS

In addition to the shortcut **⌘+Option+D** to hide or show the Dock, several other shortcuts can be useful when working with Dock icons.

ACTION	SHORTCUT
Display a Dock menu for any item	Right-click (or Control+click) the item's Dock icon
Bring application to the front, hiding the current one	Option+click Dock icon
Bring application to the front, hiding all others	⌘+Option+click Dock icon
Show the original application for a Dock icon	⌘+click Dock icon
Prevent Dock from moving icons out of the way when you drag an item onto it	⌘+drag an item onto a Dock icon
Force an application in the Dock to open a file, even if it's of the "wrong" type	⌘+Option+drag a file onto a Dock icon

APPLICATION SHORTCUTS

Not all applications offer the same range of keyboard shortcuts. The ones listed next, however, can be found in the vast majority of applications.

COMMAND	SHORTCUT
Open a new document	⌘+N
Open an existing document	⌘+O
Close current window	⌘+W
Close all document windows	⌘+Option+W
Save changes to the current document	⌘+S
Quit (exit) the current application	⌘+Q
Print current document	⌘+P
Undo last command	⌘+Z
Undo next-to-last command	Depending on application, either press ⌘+Z again, or press ⌘+Option+Z. Not all applications support multiple Undos.
Redo last undone command	Depends on application. In some cases, you press ⌘+Z again to redo whatever you just undid. In others, press ⌘+Shift+Z or ⌘+Y.
Cut selected text or object	⌘+X

COMMAND	SHORTCUT
Copy selected text or object	⌘+C
Paste contents of the Clipboard	⌘+V
Select all text or objects	⌘+A
Turn boldface on or off	⌘+B
Turn italic on or off	⌘+I
Hide all windows of the current application	⌘+H
Hide windows of all other applications	⌘+Option+H

OTHER SHORTCUTS

The remaining shortcuts are applicable almost anywhere in your system, regardless of what application you're using.

GENERAL

The following shortcuts are for switching windows, applications, and keyboard layouts.

ACTION	SHORTCUT
Switch keyboard layouts if Input menu is visible (useful for TypeIt4Me)	⌘+spacebar
Switch to next open window in the current application	⌘+`
Switch to previous/next open application	⌘+Tab
Switch to any open application shown in the Dock	⌘+Tab (but continue holding ⌘ after releasing Tab; then press Tab again)
Switch applications (reverse order)	⌘+Shift+Tab

DIALOG BOXES

These options apply when a dialog is present (such as an error message or a "Save Changes?" alert).

ACTION	SHORTCUT
Click a button in a modal dialog	Press the first letter of the button's name
Click the default (highlighted) button in a dialog — usually OK	Return

POWER AND SLEEP

Use these shortcuts to restart, shut down, or put your computer to sleep using the keyboard.

ACTION	SHORTCUT
Display Sleep/Shut Down/Restart window	Power key (if you have one) or Control+Eject (Press the first letter of a button's name to click it.)
Force Restart	⌘+Control+Power key (if you have one) or ⌘+Control+Eject

ACTION	SHORTCUT
Force Shut Down	⌘+Control+Option+Power key (if you have one) or ⌘+Control+Option+Eject or simply press and hold the Power key for about five seconds
Sleep (only works on newer Macs)	⌘+Option+Power key (if you have one) or ⌘+Option+Eject

SCREEN SHOTS

Use these shortcuts to take a picture of your screen. It will be saved on the desktop in PDF format.

ACTION	SHORTCUT
Take a screen shot (full screen)	⌘+Shift+3
Take a screen shot (you select the area)	⌘+Shift+4
Take a screen shot (individual window or menu)	⌘+Shift+4; then press spacebar and click the mouse button after you see the camera icon

APPENDIX B
ESSENTIAL UNIX COMMANDS

The techniques in Chapter 1 covered some of the basics of UNIX — enough to familiarize you with Terminal, the general layout of the file system, and how to get around by using the command line. Although you can perform hundreds of other commands in a UNIX shell, you're likely to use only a handful on a regular basis. This appendix lists the commands I consider essential for the advanced Mac OS X user. If you're interested in learning even more, consult the book's Web site (`www.wiley.com/compbooks/kissell`) for recommendations of books and online resources.

The UNIX commands listed here are designed to be used in the Terminal application running the default tcsh shell. If you're using a different shell or a different command-line application, your mileage may vary.

UNIX BASICS

When interacting with a UNIX shell, you should be aware of some general principles. These are the very basics you should know before learning any of the specific commands.

ENTERING COMMANDS

To perform a command in UNIX, type the command name and press Return. Be aware that unlike the Aqua interface of Mac OS X, UNIX is case sensitive. So `Date` and `date` could be two separate commands, and if you type in a file or folder name without using the correct capitalization, you might simply get an error message.

Example: Type `date` and press **Return** to display today's date.

ARGUMENTS AND OPTIONS

Some commands require additional information, such as a filename or a particular setting. Anything typed on a line after a command to provide this extra information is known as an *argument.*

One type of argument is an *option* — which is to say, a particular version or form of a command. Options are usually preceded by a hyphen (-). Always type a space between the command and the option(s). If you want to include several options for the same command, you can usually string them together following the hyphen (with no spaces between the options).

Example: Enter `ls` to list the files in the current directory. Enter `ls -l` to list files in "long" format. Enter `ls -la` to list files in long format *and* include invisible files.

Another type of argument is a *filename.* To tell a command to operate on a particular file, type its name after the command (and the options, if any). Again, include a space before the filename.

Example: Enter `ls *.doc` to list files in the current directory ending in "`.doc`." Enter `ls -l *.doc` to display the same list, but in long format.

USING FILENAMES WITH SPACES

Mac filenames often include spaces. Because the space character is used to separate arguments from commands, the shell can get confused if you enter a filename that includes a space. There are two ways to solve this: (1) put the entire filename in quotes; or (2) type a backslash (\) before each space character.

Example: To delete a file named `Big Ideas`, you enter either `rm "Big Ideas"` or `rm Big\ Ideas`.

REPEATING PREVIOUS COMMANDS

The UNIX shell remembers the commands you've typed before. To reenter the last command you typed, press the up arrow key. You can press the up arrow multiple times to cycle through a long list of previous commands, or go forward in the list by pressing the down arrow. To enter a command you've displayed using the arrow keys, just press **Return**. You can also use the left and right arrow keys to edit a previous command (for example, replacing one argument with another). To cancel a command without pressing Delete repeatedly to backspace over it, just press **Control+C**.

GETTING HELP

UNIX has built-in help pages for many of its commands. To get more info on a particular command, use the `man` command (short for manual), followed by the name of the command.

Example: For help using the `cp` (copy) command, enter `man cp`.

While viewing a manual page, you can press the spacebar to move forward by a page, use the up or down arrow keys to scroll up or down a line at a time, or press `q` to quit. To find out more about the `man` program and the numerous options it offers, you can get help by entering `man man`.

ENDING A TERMINAL SESSION

When you're finished working in Terminal, always enter `exit` to end your session. The `exit` command can also be used to end SSH sessions, or to switch back to your regular user if you've used `su` to switch users.

NAVIGATION

Because the UNIX shell doesn't display lists of files or icons in windows the way the Finder does, you need to know a few things about getting from one place to another in the file system and determining what files are available for you to work with.

CHANGING DIRECTORIES

To change directories, enter `cd` followed by either an absolute or relative pathname.

Examples: To move to the Library directory inside the System directory at the top level of your hard drive, enter `cd /System/Library` (note the leading slash). To move to a directory named Preferences that's inside the directory you're currently viewing, simply enter `cd Preferences`. Type a space and two periods after the `cd` command (`cd ..`) to move up to the directory that encloses the one you're currently in.

To display your current pathname (location in the file system), enter `pwd`.

To move to your home directory, use the tilde (~) character: `cd ~`. You can also use the tilde as a shorthand in absolute pathnames: To switch to the Library directory in your home directory (regardless of your current location), enter `cd ~/Library`.

LISTING FILES

To display a list of files in the current directory, enter `ls` (for "list directory contents"). The `ls` command accepts several arguments, the most common of which are `-a` (for "all" — including invisible files) and `-l` (for "long" format which includes information such as owner, group, permission, and modification date). You can also use wildcards after `ls` to limit the list to files matching certain criteria.

Examples: To display all files in the current directory in long format, enter `ls -la` or `ls -al` or `ls -a -l`. To display only those files beginning with the letter *P*, enter `ls P*`.

LOCATING FILES

Just as the Finder's Find command can be used to locate files, the shell also has a `find` command. But it can be a bit complicated to use (enter `man find` and you'll see what I mean). An easier-to-use, if less flexible, find tool is called `locate`. Simply enter `locate` followed by a space and any portion of a filename (case-sensitive) to display all matching files on your hard drive.

Example: To find all files containing the name "Adobe" (but *not* "adobe" with a lowercase *a*), enter `locate Adobe`.

The `locate` program uses an index much like the Finder's search engine. This makes it fast, but the index is only updated about once a week, which means you may not be able to locate recently added files. To force the locate database to update, enter:

```
/usr/libexec/locate.updatedb
```

WORKING WITH FILES

Much of what you need to do in Terminal involves working with files in one way or another — viewing, editing, copying, moving, or deleting them, for example. This section covers common commands for working with files.

VIEWING TEXT FILES

To display (but not edit) the contents of a text file, you can use either of two commands: `more` or `less`. The `more` command is the original text viewer; as with `man`, you can page forward by pressing the spacebar. Press `q` to quit.

A similar effect is achieved using `less`. Like `more`, it displays text documents, using the spacebar to go forward and `q` to quit. Unlike `more`, you can also move backward through documents by pressing `b`; you can learn about a great many other options as well by typing `man less`. In other words: `less` is `more`.

EDITING TEXT FILES

If you want to edit a text file while in Terminal, the easiest way is to use the pico editor — type `pico` followed by a space and the name of the file you want to edit.

Examples: Edit the file `Proposal.txt` in the current directory by entering `pico Proposal.txt`. Edit your Apache configuration file by entering `pico /etc/httpd/httpd.conf`.

While in pico, you can use these shortcut key commands:

COMMAND	SHORTCUT KEY
Move forward one page	Control+V
Move backward a page	Control+Y
Delete the line the cursor is on	Control+K
Locate a word within the file	Control+W
Save a file (without quitting)	Control+O
Quit pico	Control+X

MOVING AND RENAMING FILES

To move a file from one location to another — or rename it in its current location — use the `mv` command. If you supply a second (relative or absolute) pathname as an argument, `mv` knows you're trying to move a file. If you just supply a new name, it knows you want to rename it.

Examples: To move the file `abc.txt` from its current location to your home directory, enter `mv abc.txt ~`. To rename the file `abc.txt` to `def.txt` (without moving it), enter `mv abc.txt def.txt`. To move the file `abc.txt` to your Desktop folder *and* rename it to `def.txt`, enter `mv abc.txt ~/Desktop/def.txt`.

The `mv` command doesn't know about the resource forks that are part of some Mac files (particularly applications designed for Mac OS 9). To make sure you're moving *complete* files, use the `MvMac` command, which works just like `mv` but is resource fork-savvy.

`MvMac` is installed as part of the Developer Tools installation. To use it, enter `/Developer/Tools/MvMac` followed by the filename(s)/pathname(s). If you want to be able to use it without typing its entire location, use pico to add this line to the end of your `~/.tcshrc` file:

```
set path = ($path /Developer/Tools)
```

This command adds the Developer Tools directory to the path your shell uses when executing commands. After making this change (and starting a new Terminal session), you can omit the "/Developer/Tools/" part of the command; just enter `MvMac` followed by the filename(s)/pathname(s).

COPYING FILES

The copy command, `cp`, works very similarly to `mv`. Enter `cp` followed by the name of the file you want to copy, then a space, then the location you want to copy it to.

Examples: To make a copy of the file `abc.txt` in the same directory but with the new name `def.txt`, enter `cp abc.txt def.txt`. To make a copy of the file `abc.txt` in the directory /Users/joe/Documents, enter `cp abc.txt /Users/joe/Documents` (or, if your user name is joe, you can simply type `cp abc.txt ~/Documents`). To make a copy of the file `abc.txt` in your home directory but with the new name `def.txt`, enter `cp abc.txt ~/def.txt`.

As with the `mv` command discussed earlier, `cp` doesn't know about resource forks. To copy files while keeping their resource forks intact, use `CpMac` instead. If you haven't entered the path to the Developer Tools to your .tcshrc file, the full command would be `/Developer/Tools/CpMac` followed by a space and the command arguments.

DELETING FILES

You can delete a file using the `rm` (for "remove") command. To delete a directory and all its contents, add the `-R` option. Remember that some Mac OS X files (such as applications) are actually *packages* — special folders that behave as though they were a single file. To delete such items you'll again need the `-R` option.

Examples: To delete the file `abc.txt`, enter `rm abc.txt`. To delete the directory named `Recipes`, enter `rm -R Recipes`. To delete the application `Clock.app`, enter `rm -R Clock.app`.

NOTE

As discussed in Technique 1 (Chapter 1), `rm -R` performs a *recursive delete*, which means it will delete not only the directory you entered but also all of its enclosed directories and files. A safer way to remove a directory is to use the `rmdir` command in place of `rm -R`, but if the directory is not empty, you will need to delete its contents manually before the directory can be deleted.

CREATING DIRECTORIES

To create a new folder in the Finder, you press ⌘+Shift+N. In Terminal, the analogous UNIX command is `mkdir` ("make directory"). To create a new directory, type `mkdir` followed by the name of the new directory.

Example: To create a new directory named `Recipes`, enter `mkdir Recipes`.

VIEWING AND EDITING FILE INFORMATION

In the Finder, if you want to get information about a file, you select it and press **⌘+I** to display the Info window. Some attributes, like file type and creator, aren't displayed in the Info window — to see those, you need a third-party utility like XRay. Another option is to use a Developer Tool called `GetFileInfo`. Like `MvMac` and `CpMac`, this tool is installed as part of the Developer Tools package, and it must be referenced by full pathname unless you add its path to your working environment (read the explanation of how to do this under the "Moving Files" section earlier).

Example: To get information about a spreadsheet file named `text.xls`, enter `/Developer/Tools/GetFileInfo test.xls`. The display will show something like the following:

```
file: "/Users/joe/Desktop/test.xls"
type: "XLS8"
creator: "XCEL"
attributes: avbstclinmed
created: 10/31/2002 10:29:37
modified: 10/31/2002 13:07:26
```

The attributes list tells you whether certain attributes are on (indicated by a capital letter) or off (indicated by a lowercase letter). For example, if the letter `A` is in uppercase, it means the file is an alias; if lowercase, it's not. A capital `L` means the file is locked; a lowercase `l` means it's not. For a complete list of attributes and their meanings, enter `man GetFileInfo`.

If you want to change a file's attributes, you can use the sister command `SetFile`. After typing `SetFile` and a space, enter `-a` (for attributes) followed by the attributes you want to change and then the filename.

Example: To change the file test.xls to be locked (attribute `L`) and invisible (attribute `V`), enter `/Developer/Tools/SetFile -a LV test.xls`.

To change the creator or type, use the arguments `-c` or `-t`, respectively.

Example: To change the file test.txt to have a creator of ttxt and a type of TEXT, enter `/Developer/Tools/SetFile --c ttxt -t TEXT test.txt`.

OWNERSHIP AND PERMISSIONS

Each file and folder in Mac OS X has attributes indicating its owner (the name of a particular user account) and group (a set of users with similar privileges). These attributes determine who is allowed what type of access to the file.

For owners, group members, and others (users who are not the owner or a member of the file's designated group), you can designate whether the file can be read, written, or (if it's a program, a script, or a folder containing them) executed.

Ordinarily, files and folders have the correct ownership and permissions automatically. If for any reason you need to change them manually, here's how you can do it.

LISTING OWNERSHIP AND PERMISSIONS

To display the owner, group, and permissions for files in the current directory, enter `ls -l`. A typical file listing will look something like the one shown in **Figure B.1**.

```
drwxr-xr-x  3 joe admin  102 Aug 14 14:57 Applications
drwxrw-rw- 23 joe admin  782 Nov 30 21:36 Stuff
-rw-r--r--  1 joe admin 1234 Nov 12 09:03 Documents
```

B.1

The first series of ten letters indicates permissions. The first one indicates whether the item is a directory (`d`) or just a file (`-`). Next are three sets of three letters: `rwx`, indicating whether a file has read permission (`r`), write permission (`w`), or execute permission (`x`). The first set of permissions is for the owner; the second set is for the group; and the third set is for others (everyone else). For any given slot in the ten-character series, a letter means that permission is ON; a hyphen (`-`) means it's OFF.

In the preceding example, the first item, `Applications`, and the second item, `Stuff`, are both directories (folders), as indicated by the initial `d`. The directory `Applications` has read, write, and execute permission for the owner (the first `rwx` set), and read and execute (but not write) permission for the group and others (`r-x`). The directory `Stuff`, on the other hand, has read and write (but not execute) access for the group and others — `rw-`. The file `Document` (which is not a directory because the `d` option is not set) has read and write (`rw-`) permission for the owner and read-only permission (`r--`) for both group and others.

In the middle of the line are two columns with names shown — the first displays the owner (in this case, the user named `joe` owns all three items), and the second displays the group (in this case, `admin` for all three). The last part of the line displays the file size in bytes, modification date, and time.

CHANGING OWNERSHIP

To change the owner or group of a file, use the `chown` command ("change owner"). In most cases, you can't change the ownership of a file you don't already own; if this is the case, precede the `chown` command with `sudo` to temporarily grant yourself root privileges.

The `chown` command can take one or two arguments (no hyphens required). If you enter just one name after `chown`, it's assumed to be the owner. To change both owner and group, enter the owner name, a colon, and the group name (without spaces). To change just the group name, enter a colon followed by the group name. Another way to change a file's group name without changing the owner is to use the `chgrp` ("change group") command followed by the group name and filename in that order.

Examples: To change the owner of a file named `Document` to cindy, enter `chown cindy Document`. To change the group of the same file to marketing without changing the owner, enter `chown :marketing Document` or `chgrp marketing Document`. To change the owner to root and the group to wheel, enter `sudo chown root:wheel Document`. (The `sudo` is needed because you're changing the owner to root.)

CHANGING PERMISSIONS

Permissions (also known as "access modes") determine what operations the file's owner, group, and others can perform. The command used to change permissions is `chmod` ("change mode"). As with `chown`, you can't normally change the permissions of files you don't own unless you precede the command with `sudo`.

You have several different ways of using the `chmod` command; I cover just the simplest one here. Follow `chmod` by one or more of the letters `u` (for user — that is, owner), `g` (for group), or `o` (for others), then a `+` or `-`, indicating whether you're adding or subtracting permissions, and then one or more of `r`, `w`, or `x` for read, write, or execute, respectively. Finally, type a space and the filename. Some examples can make this clearer.

Examples: Suppose you have a file `abc`, with permissions `-rw-rw-r--`. To grant the owner (user) execute permission, you enter `chmod u+x abc` (`u` for user, `+` for add permission, `x` for execute). The permissions string would become `-rwxrw-r--`. If you wanted to grant execute permission to the user, group, and others all at the same time, you could enter `chmod ugo+x abc` — making the string `-rwxrwxr-x`. To take away the group's write access, you enter `chmod g-w abc`, making the string `-rwxr-xr-x`. To grant others write access, enter `chmod o+w`, making the string `-rwxrwxrwx`.

If you want to instantly grant full privileges to everyone (`-rwxrwxrwx`), you enter `chmod ugo+rwx abc`. To give the file read-only access to the owner and no access to anyone else (`-r--------`), enter `chmod u-wx abc`, then enter `chmod go-rwx abc`.

ASSUMING ROOT AUTHORITY TEMPORARILY

Some UNIX commands (like changing the ownership or permissions of files you don't own, or modifying files owned by root) require root access. If you enter a command and get an error message like "Operation not permitted," it's probably because you entered it without root authority.

To temporarily assume root authority, type `sudo` (for "superuser do") and a space before a command. You'll be asked to supply your password. (Note that you must have an Administrator account to be able to use `sudo`.) After entering your password once, you can continue using `sudo` with other commands for up to five minutes without being prompted to reenter a password.

Example: If you type the command `rm abc` and get the error message "Operation not permitted," try `sudo rm abc`.

ASSUMING ROOT IDENTITY

If you need to perform a large number of commands as the root user and don't want to enter `sudo` before each one, you can actually log into the root account, giving you pretty much complete freedom to change or delete anything on your system. In order to do this, you need to have enabled the root account as described in Technique 2. You also need to use a great deal of care, because as root user you could easily cause irreparable damage to your system. Root access should only be used if you're sure you know what you're doing, and even then only when absolutely necessary.

The command to assume root identity is `su` (for "superuser" or "substitute user," depending on context). You can use the same command to log into another user's account (assuming you know the password). To log in as root user, enter `su` all by itself. To log in as another user, follow `su` by a space and the other user's short name, as in `su bob`.

After you've finished the activities that require root access, be sure to log out of the root account by entering `exit`.

WORKING WITH PROGRAMS

Running and quitting programs in a UNIX shell is a bit different than double-clicking icons in the Finder. Here are the basics.

RUNNING PROGRAMS

In general, you can run a UNIX command simply by typing its name and pressing Return. There are some exceptions, however. In a basic setup, the only commands available to execute in this way would be those located in the `/bin` or `/usr/bin` directories. (You can change to those directories now and enter `ls` to see what commands are available — there are quite a lot of them.)

If you download or create a new program that isn't located in one of those places, you need to either add the path to your environment (as discussed earlier under "Moving Files") or type the complete pathname to the file to execute it. If you happen to be in the directory where the executable is located, you can avoid typing the entire path and simply enter `./` before the program name — for example, `./MyNewScript`.

Some programs take a long time to run (or, in the case of server programs, are designed to run constantly). If you run a program and it doesn't quit, you'll no longer be able to do anything in your Terminal session. To run a program in the background, simply type a space and an ampersand (`&`) after the program name — for example, `./safe_mysqld &`.

VIEWING ACTIVE PROGRAMS

To get a list of all your currently running programs (including invisible background and server processes), enter `top`. `top` lists running programs along with information including how much of your CPU and RAM they're using, how long they've been running, and what their process ID (PID) is. Each program running at any given moment has a unique PID, which can be useful to know if you need to force it to quit. To quit `top`, simply press `q`.

If you don't want the real-time usage display of `top`, you can get a one-shot listing of all your current processes with PIDs and active time by using `ps` (process status). Using `ps` alone won't tell you much; you'll probably want to add the options `-a` (to display processes owned by other users, including the system) and `-x` (to display background processes that are running outside a terminal session). So the complete command would be `ps -ax`.

STOPPING ACTIVE PROGRAMS

If you're running a program that you want to interrupt before it's finished, the first thing you should try is pressing **Control+C**, which is analogous to ⌘+. or Esc in the Finder. Control+C simply aborts the current process.

In some cases, a process can get stuck in such a way that it no longer responds to Control+C. If this happens and you need to quit the process, use the `kill` command, which is analogous to the Force Quit command in Mac OS X. In order to kill a running process, you'll need to know its PID, which you can find by using either `top` or `ps -ax` as described earlier. Then use that PID as an argument for `kill`. For example, `kill 1386` will force-quit the program with PID 1386. On a rare occasion, even `kill` won't stop a program. To force a program to end in a way that it can't ignore even if it's severely misbehaving, add the `-9` argument: `kill -9 1386`.

Finding out the PID of a running program in order to kill it can be inconvenient. It's also possible to kill a program by name, using the `killall` command. Enter `killall` followed by the exact name of the application — and keep in mind that the `killall` command is case sensitive. So if an application called `Clock.app` won't quit, you could enter `killall Clock.app`, but `killall clock.app` wouldn't work because the case is incorrect. As with all other commands, you can't use `kill` or `killall` to stop a program you don't own. To assume root authority to stop such a program, enter `sudo kill` or `sudo killall` followed by the PID or name of the program.

ABOUT THE AUTHOR

Joe Kissell has worked in the Macintosh software industry for the past nine years. He previously managed software development for Nisus Software Inc. and Kensington Technology Group, and has written two other books on Mac software: *The Nisus Way* and *Cyberdog: Live Objects on the Internet* (with coauthor David McKee).

Following Apple's advice to Think Different, Joe founded alt concepts, inc., an Internet publishing company that chose not to squander capital on its corporate name. With the honorary title Curator of Interesting Things, he spends much of his time writing, speaking, consulting, and maintaining the "Interesting Thing of the Day" column on the company's Web site.

Interesting as is the pursuit of income, Joe also likes to do other things, such as studying t'ai chi and indulging in his hobbies of reading, cooking, traveling, and fiddling with synthesizers. Joe lives in San Francisco with his wife, Morgen Jahnke.

COLOPHON

This book was produced electronically in Indianapolis, Indiana. The screen shots were taken with SnapZ Pro X and manipulated with Adobe Photoshop 7. Design and layout were produced using QuarkXPress 4.11 and Adobe Photoshop 7 on Power Macintosh computers. The typeface families used are Chicago Laser, Minion, Myriad, Myriad Multiple Master, Prestige Elite, Symbol, Trajan, and Zapf Dingbats.

Acquisitions Editor: Michael Roney
Project Editor: Melba Hopper
Technical Editor: Pieter Paulson
Copy Editor: Paula Lowell
Editorial Manager: Rev Mengle
Vice President and Executive Group Publisher: Richard Swadley
Vice President and Publisher: Barry Pruett
Permissions Editor: Carmen Krikorian
Production Coordinator: Dale White
Cover Art: Joe Kissell
Quality Control Technicians: Laura Albert, Susan Moritz, Charles Spencer
Production: Beth Brooks, Sean Decker, LeAndra Johnson
Proofreading: Christine Pingleton
Indexing: Steve Rath

INDEX

A

B

C

D

E

F

Continued

G

H

I

Continued

Continued

T

Continued

U

V